MW01012903

Flavors of Malaysia

A Journey through Time, Tastes, and Traditions

The Hippocrene Cookbook Library

Afghan Food & Cookery
Alps, Cuisines of the
Aprovecho: A Mexican-American Border Cookbook
Argentina Cooks!, Exp. Ed.
Austrian Cuisine, Best of, Exp. Ed.
Belarusian Cookbook, The
Bolivian Kitchen, My Mother's
Brazil: A Culinary Journey
Cajun Cuisine, Stir the Pot: The History of
Cajun Women, Cooking with
Calabria, Cucina di
Caucasus Mountains, Cuisines of the
Chile, Tasting
China's Fujian Province, Cooking from
Colombian Cooking, Secrets of
Corsican Cuisine
Croatian Cooking, Best of, Exp. Ed.
Czech Cooking, Best of, Exp. Ed.
Danube, All Along The, Exp. Ed.
Egyptian Cooking
Egyptian Cuisine and Culture, Nile Style:
English Country Kitchen, The
Estonian Tastes and Traditions
Filipino Food, Fine
Finnish Cooking, Best of
Germany, Spoonfuls of
Greek Cooking, Regional
Haiti, Taste of
Havana Cookbook, Old (Bilingual)
Hungarian Cookbook, Exp. Ed.
India, Flavorful
International Dictionary of Gastronomy
Jewish-Iraqi Cuisine, Mama Nazima's
Kerala Kitchen
Laotian Cooking, Simple
Lebanese Cookbook, The
Ligurian Kitchen, A
Lithuanian Cooking, Art of
Malaysia, Flavors of
Middle Eastern Kitchen, The
Naples, My Love for
Nepal, Taste of
New Hampshire: from Farm to Kitchen
New Jersey Cookbook, Farms and Foods of the Garden State:
Ohio, Farms and Foods of
Persian Cooking, Art of
Pied Noir Cookbook: French Sephardic Cuisine
Piemontese, Cucina: Cooking from Italy's Piedmont
Polish Cooking, Best of, Exp. Ed.
Polish Heritage Cookery, Ill. Ed.
Polish Holiday Cookery
Polish Traditions, Old
Portuguese Encounters, Cuisines of
Punjab, Menus and Memories from
Romania, Taste of, Exp. Ed.
Russian Cooking, The Best of
Scottish-Irish Pub and Hearth Cookbook
Sephardic Israeli Cuisine
Sicilian Feasts
Slovenia, Flavors of
South Indian Cooking, Healthy
Trinidad and Tobago, Sweet Hands: Island Cooking from
Turkish Cuisine, Taste of
Tuscan Kitchen, Tastes from a
Ukrainian Cuisine, Best of, Exp. Ed.
Uzbek Cooking, Art of
Vietnamese Kitchen, A
Warsaw Cookbook, Old

Flavors of Malaysia

A Journey through Time, Tastes, and Traditions

Susheela Raghavan

Hippocrene Books, Inc.
New York

Food styling, interior, color, and jacket photographs by Susheela Raghavan and Geeta Uhl.

Book and jacket design by Wanda España / Wee Design Group.

For more information, address:
HIPPOCRENE BOOKS, INC.
171 Madison Avenue
New York, NY 10016
www.hippocrenebooks.com

Library of Congress Cataloging-in-Publication Data

Raghavan, Susheela.
Flavors of Malaysia : a journey through time, tastes, and traditions / Susheela Raghavan ; photographs by Susheela Raghavan.
p. cm.
ISBN-13: 978-0-7818-1249-8 (hardcover)
ISBN-10: 0-7818-1249-6 (hardcover)
1. Cookery, Malaysian. 2. Cookery--Malaysia. I. Title.

TX724.5.M4R345 2010
641.59595--dc22

2010009076

Printed in the United States of America.

DEDICATION

To my Grandparents, Periama and Thatha, whose adventurous spirits led them to Malaysia;

To Ma and Cha, who passed on to me their love of food, culture, and tradition, and who planted the seed of taste in me;

To my sisters and brothers and our husbands and wives, who shared with me the joy of family meals, hawkers' stalls, night markets and holiday feasts, and who have given me many memories of growing up in Malaysia;

To my daughter Geeta and all our children, the next generation, with hope that they continue to enjoy the enchanting flavors of Malaysia, and to carry on in their hearts some of the wonderful memories that I share in this book with my journey through time, tastes and traditions.

CONTENTS

ACKNOWLEDGMENTS

Malaysia is truly a multicultural place that history and time have woven together into "1 Malaysia"—a beautiful and colorful tapestry of diverse peoples. As voiced recently by Malaysian Prime Minister Dato' Sri Mohd Najib bin Tun Abdul Razak and his wife, Datin Seri Rosmah Mansor, the concept of "1 Malaysia" reflects a country with a rich and proud heritage that truly embraces all of its different cultures, their histories and traditions. Nowhere is "1 Malaysia" more proudly presented to the world than through its singular and wonderful cuisine. I hope my readers will also find my book a unique reading experience, not simply as a collection of recipes, but as a traveling companion along Malaysia's heritage trail.

For me, writing this cookbook has been truly personal . . . indeed a journey through time, tastes, and traditions. I've wished to create this book for more than twenty years. Finally after five years of research and writing, it has come to life. Accordingly, I wish to acknowledge first my parents' and grandparents' spirit in this long-awaited undertaking—remembering Ma and Periama (my grandmother) creating meals together, going to food stalls with Thatha (my grandfather), and sitting down at a meal to hear Cha's (my father) stories. Writing this cookbook brought back many memories of family get-togethers and outings, at home, coffee shops and food stalls. What motivated me most, however, was the inspiration from Ma during my many visits back to Malaysia. She was a perfectionist when it came to flavors and preparing foods, and was always there, patiently giving her support and helping me out with her recipes and other ingredient information. And I thank Cha for the sense of culinary adventure he gave me, always encouraging me to experience and appreciate all foods and cultures.

I thank my husband, Bob, and daughter, Geeta, for being there to taste my recipes and giving me their valuable input, not just with flavors, but also prodding me to think in terms of how to create these authentic preparations in a healthier and more practical fashion for today's busy cooks and savvy palates. Bob has been a tremendous help with the history and with the book's edits. Geeta has always motivated me to write this cookbook and I thank her for believing in me and especially encouraging me to style the foods and take the photos. She spent time editing the chapters, giving valuable recommendations, and taking many of the photos in Malaysia and my photo for the jacket cover.

I thank my sister Vas and sister-in-law Shanta for their delicious recipes and for being there whenever I needed support or had queries. I appreciate their patience whenever I asked them to test a recipe, in spite of their busy lives. I remember on many occasions taking notes in Shanta's porch kitchen while she cooked. Likewise, Vas has been helpful in passing on to me many of Ma's techniques and recipes. I also thank her for many of the title translations and assistance with food photos in Malaysia. I also thank my other family members—Prasnan (for taking me to try more hawker fare); Sathee (for driving me around to see old haunts); Rama (for providing me with her favorite recipes); Sree and his wife Diane (for giving me the cheesecake recipe); Suresh and his wife Mala (for tofu recipe ideas); Ravee (for his information on Malaysia's cultures); and all their families for their support. I wish to give a special note of thanks to my sister Prema, who passed away before this book came to fruition, and whose gentle spirit and memory served as an ongoing inspiration for me.

Tourism Malaysia, New York, has been a wonderful support for this book, especially Abdul Rahim Haron (Special Officer, Director General's Office, Malaysia) and Nurul Rahim Tmimi (Marketing Executive, New York). I first met Rahim while he was in the New York office. My good friend Nurul, always flashing her wide smile and projecting a great sense of humor, offered me a couple of her recipes, helped with translations of recipe names into correct Bahasa Malaysia, and gave answers to some of my queries. Also of support and were the other members of Tourism Malaysia, including Mohamad Taib Ibrahim (Deputy Director, International Marketing Division, Malaysia), Aliza Mansor (Senior Assistant Director, International Marketing Division, Malaysia), Norizah (Assistant Director, Shopping Malaysia Secretariat), and Salinda Sany (Deputy Director, Tourism Malaysia, New York). Tourism Malaysia also gave its kind permission to use several cultural photographs that appear in this book. Thanks also to Wan Latiff, Trade Commissioner (MATRADE), for including me, this book, and my Taste of Malacca spice blends in the Malaysia Kitchen for the World campaign.

Thanks to all at Hippocrene Books. My editor, Priti Chitnis Gress, and copyeditor and production manager, Barbara Keane-Pigeon, showed great professionalism throughout the process of editing the book and its recipes and photos. Particularly, thanks go to Priti for her patient support in moving this book through production and to its publication. I would especially like to acknowledge with great thanks George Blagowidow, my publisher, a warm and wonderful man who truly appreciates the world's cultures and food. He saw my passion for Malaysian cuisine and allowed me to create the style I wanted for this book. Thanks also to Wanda España for the beautiful book and jacket design.

I also thank all my Malaysian and American friends, too many to name, for their support and help, but especially Radha Chitty and Zubaidah Papush for their recipes, Patricia Nuzzo for her help with a few dessert recipes, and Karen Berman for her advice. Finally, I cannot forget to honor Malaysia's alleyways and roadsides, where warm, friendly food hawkers and street chefs create the humble specialties that have become iconic in Malaysia's food scene today.

FOREWORD

In this much anticipated and authoritative tome on Malaysian cookery, Susheela Raghavan takes us on a wondrous journey that covers time, tastes, and traditions. This book also explores Malaysian cuisine's origins—how other parts of Asia (India, China, Indonesia, Thailand), as well as the Middle East and Europe played a role in its development. With the combination of painstaking research, history, and Susheela's delightful family recipes and anecdotes, *Flavors of Malaysia* is much more than a cookbook and teaches us that food is a special gift to be revered.

Susheela Raghavan ensures that both novice cook and culinary historian alike will be able to prepare delicious recipes that transport them to Malaysia without ever having to leave home. Susheela's deep respect for tradition and authenticity are perfectly balanced by her sensible adaptations to the modern kitchen and pantry.

I have found Malaysian cooking to be my one-stop cuisine for tasting a little bit of all of Asia. When I first heard of Susheela's desire to pen a cookbook, I was beyond thrilled, I was ecstatic. I knew that her authentic recipes in combination with her thorough anthropologic research would guarantee a cookbook I could trust. Susheela's credible standing in the world of academics and foodies is even more enhanced by this amazing book. If you are a cook and fan of Malaysia, you need this book to gain comprehensive knowledge of the foods representing the many communities that constitute Malaysia. If you are a student of food, history, and people, this book makes Malaysia a familiar friend. And if you are afraid to cook Malaysian, let this book take you by the hand and introduce you to recipes you will share with pride.

In a world ever more global, if fusion cooking is to go beyond trendy, gratuitous additions of flavors that yield nothing special, Malaysian cooking is poised to be the face of the next generation of food. Over centuries, Malaysia has been a melting pot culture that brought diversity of great proportions together and kept it flourishing as a whole, even as the soul of each individual group was never lost or ignored. This phenomenon is now yours to savor, study, and share. As you cook, you will be exploring the cuisines of Indians, Indian Muslims (Mamaks), Malays, Chinese, Baba-Nonyas (Chinese and Malay heritage), Chittys (Indian and Malay heritage), Kristangs (Portuguese married to Malay or Nonya women), Eurasians (Portuguese, Dutch, English, and other Europeans married to locals), Arabs, Thais, and Indonesians. This cookbook introduces you to the fusion of Malaysian flavors that has taken place over generations and centuries. It is so old, that it seems new!

Malaysia may be the most intricately flavored melting pot of peoples and cultures that the world has. If China, India, Thailand, Arabia, Indonesia, Portugal, and the Netherlands are the ingredients in this pot, it is the spices and aromatics of these cultures that became the flavor of the broth. The religions and cultural beliefs of the people of each of these countries became the tempering spices, flavor enhancers, and finishing spices of the dish. As you turn the pages, and are led along this journey by Susheela Raghavan, you will discover how it is possible for people very different from one another to come together to find peace and magic in their union, and create something lasting. Malaysia is not a young country, and yet it is not that old, either. It is this juxtaposition of old and new, east and west, Hindu and Christian, Muslim and Buddhist that makes it dance. The food is never shy, never afraid to assert itself.

If you love grilled meats or chicken (*satay*), Susheela teaches you how to cook them with delicious success. If you like slow-simmered beef in a flavorful coconut sauce, you will never have to go to a restaurant to find it. If you are a world traveler and have enjoyed the noodles of Malaysia, prepared in a spicy coconut broth (*laksa lemak*), now you can make them yourself and be the star chef of your home and community. If you want to understand how spice blends from Southeast Asia developed as we know them today, in these pages you will find many a story about their uses, their journeys, and the politics and religions surrounding them. You will smell the scents and feel the textures of the marketplaces that enrich the cookery of Malaysia as you read along and discover the rich histories of streetside pantries that have for centuries been the muse to thousands of professional chefs, home cooks, and wanderers.

For those who revel in visual stimulation, the photos taken by Susheela Raghavan herself, lend a very personal touch to the book. By forgoing the services of a professional photographer, the heart and soul of the book remained in the hands of the author, which ensures that you read, cook, taste, and experience Malaysia as Susheela does. Get this book if you enjoy flavor. Get it if you want to vacation in Malaysia without ever leaving your home. Get it if you enjoy deeply delicious food. And certainly get this book if you are curious about a country that is as truly Asian as any can get. *Flavors of Malaysia* is a love affair between the author and the country and culture that formed her. Like all love affairs, it has its sweet and salty moments, its highs and lows and layers of discovery. As you turn the pages to new recipes, some never tasted or seen before outside of Malaysia, you are invited to the table of a large, lively, loving Malaysian family. Susheela's honest writing and generous sharing had me from page one. I knew I had surely missed intricacies on my first reading, and as I read again, I fell in love anew. To the many Asian cuisines it has embraced, Malaysia has given an identity that is at once unique yet always very familiar.

Susheela may have intended to document a recipe book for her family and friends, but what she has gifted to the world of food lovers and food history is the ultimate guide to Malaysian cookery and the culture, people, and history that shaped it. With these pages at your side, you will be cooking authentic Malaysian fare in no time. I know I will not need or want another Malaysian cookbook for a very long time. Unless, of course, Susheela decides to take us on another journey to explore the foods, history, culture, and people of her fantastic country.

Suvir Saran
Owner/Chef, Devi (NYC)
Author of *Indian Home Cooking* and *American Masala*

AUTHOR'S NOTE

I was born and raised in Malaysia during a time when we had a more intimate, tactile relationship with foods than we have today. I vividly recall watching my Grandma (Periama) grinding red chilies by hand for her fragrant *sambal tumis*, and my Ma hand-picking *kari* leaves from our garden for her aromatic crab curry. In our culture, it was common to serve meals on fresh banana leaves, and we ate using our right hand, without the barriers of utensils to separate us from the natural experience of eating. We also grew up without today's processed foods. If the ingredients were not in our garden, my Father (Cha) would take us to one of Malaysia's colorful "wet markets" where we would select our fish, poultry, and fresh produce.

Cha

Ma

Cha and Ma made eating an adventure, encouraging us to try cuisines of different cultures. So through home-cooked meals, hawkers, street foods, coffee shops, restaurants, and "open houses" (called "*rumah terbuka*"), when the different cultures celebrate their ethnic festivals, we came to appreciate and enjoy flavors from different ethnic and religious backgrounds. Because of Malaysia's long history of cultural integration, meals were always an opportunity to indulge in an endless array of culinary choices. On any given day, I would enjoy soup *mee* (noodles) from my school cafeteria; *rojak* (a spicy, mixed fruit salad) from a Mamak (Indian Muslim) hawker after school; *nasi lemak* (coconut milk-infused rice) from a Malay vendor for a Sunday brunch; *sago gula Melaka* (dessert made with sago, palm sugar, and coconut milk) from a Nonya tea shop; or fried rice from a Chinese *kopi kedai* (coffee shop).

For more than twenty years, I wanted to write this cookbook for my family and friends, to showcase Malaysia's cuisine to the world. This is not just a recipe collection, but a cultural and gastronomic journey through the centuries. I also wanted to honor Ma and Cha, and through the stories and anecdotes of our family, pass down to our children some memories of growing up in Malaysia. I hope that in the face of advancing Westernization, this book helps to preserve some of the culture and cooking of Malaysia.

Malaysian Culture and Cuisine

When I say I am from Malaysia, some Americans are surprised and respond, "But you don't look Malaysian." They immediately assume from my appearance that I am from India or Guyana. Some people think that all "Malaysians" are East Asian in appearance and culture. They do not realize that Malaysia and its cuisine have been enriched over the centuries through a melting pot culture of Indians, Indian Muslims (Mamaks), Malays, Chinese, Baba-Nonyas (Chinese and Malay heritage), Chittys (Indian and Malay heritage), Kristangs (Portuguese married to Malay or Nonya women), Eurasians (Portuguese, Dutch, English and other Europeans married to locals), Arabs, Thais, and Indonesians. To truly understand and appreciate Malaysian cuisine, you must be able to answer the question, "What does it mean to be Malaysian?"

Thus my effort begins with a historical account of the cultures of Malaysia, from ancient to modern. The stories, family anecdotes, and details in each chapter will also give you a better understanding and appreciation of this great, authentic "fused" yet multicultural cuisine.

Thatha (my grandfather) and Periama (my grandmother)

My Introduction to and Passion for Malaysian and Other Global Flavors

Over the years, as I traveled and lived around the world, I often found myself missing Malaysian flavors. Like most Malaysians, many of my culinary experiences have been personal, tied closely with friends and family. I wanted this cookbook to reflect my memories of growing up with a "soulful" understanding of the history and culture behind each recipe.

Cha, my Father, was born in Tellicherry (now Thalassery), on the Malabar coast of Kerala, South India. When he was ten years old, he came to live in Malaysia, studied in a Catholic school, the Anglo Chinese School in Klang, Malaysia, and eventually became an electrical engineer. A natural linguist, he was adept in English, Malay, the Indian languages Malayalam and Tamil, and some Chinese dialects. He also needed to learn Japanese during the Japanese occupation of Malaysia in World War II. Cha became the district engineer for the National Electrical Board and we moved from town to town throughout Malaysia every few years, till we settled in Petaling Jaya, near Kuala Lumpur. We saw a lot of the country and were exposed to different regional cuisines, including Kuantan (on the east coast), Muar and Segambat (in the south), and Kuala Lumpur, Petaling Jaya, and Klang (on the west coast). He would also take us on trips to explore neighboring towns during our school holidays or weekends.

Cha was a true food adventurer. He encouraged us to try new foods and regularly brought home some kind of food to snack on after dinner—curry puffs, *satay* (grilled meats), *nasi goreng* (fried rice), or *char kway teow* (stir-fried rice noodles). Food, drinks, and company were his life, and when it came to eating, he had no boundaries or religious restrictions. He was also a great food ambassador. Friends and family would listen with enchantment to his stories while savoring the delicacies he ordered. Cha passed away in 1999. Today, whenever I eat at places he took us, especially the Coliseum or an old Chinese coffee shop, memories of him flood back.

Ma was born in a suburb of Klang, on Batu Tiga rubber plantation where her father, whom we called Thatha, was the manager. Thatha, a pilot, was from Mahe, Kerala, a French enclave. Her mother, whom we called Periama, a Chettiar, came from Salem, near Coimbatore in Tamil Nadu. Thatha spoke French, English, and Malayalam, and Periama spoke Tamil. As children, we looked forward to their visits because Periama would indulge us with her vegetarian and Chettiar (or Chettinad) cooking—her famous fish curry, aromatic shrimp-fry, and spicy vegetable stir-fries—while we listened to stories of her youth and her adventurous and daring journey to Malaysia in her Tamil interspersed with broken English.

Ma went to Convent school in Klang, then to a teachers training college and became a teacher of English at the Methodist Girl's School in Klang. She left her career after her fourth child was born, but helped us tremendously with our homework. I have five brothers and three sisters, and am the third born. Ma was a creative cook and exposed us to new dishes every week. Fussy about the flavor and quality, she would spend hours in the kitchen peeling shallots, which she considered more flavorful than onions, and inspecting and washing each *sayur* leaf. Instead of buying ready-made powders she dried her own spices and sent them to the mill to be freshly ground. She would tailor specific spice blends for her chicken, meat, vegetable, and fish curries. All of her ingredients had to be fresh and impeccably clean. Ma took her time, like an artist with her canvas, tasting and perfecting each dish. I remember many a time waiting hungrily for our lunch! Ma would also ask each of us what we wanted for the next day's meal. Getting a consensus, she then created something different each day. We became "food snobs" at an early age, exposed to new flavors, dishes, and ingredients. Ma's gift for creating delicious dishes became renowned in the neighborhoods where we lived. She cooked for local functions and voluntary organizations, but most of all I remember her glued to the radio listening to cooking shows, or clipping recipes from newspapers. In her later years she was confined to a wheelchair because of osteoarthritis, but she would still supervise the cook in the kitchen. She kept her old notes and clippings, some worn-out and tattered, hoping one day I would get my cookbook done. On my visits back home, Ma showed me how to cook many of the dishes in this cookbook. She passed away in January of 2002. Each recipe in this cookbook is suffused with memories of her.

My family
(*I am second from the left in the top row*)

My Malaysian Family

My eldest brother, Prasnan, is married to my cooking mentor and an amazing chef, Shanta, who is adept at making any dish in the blink of an eye. They have two children, Previna and Shasti. Next is Raveendran, who migrated to the U.S. and now lives in Puerto Rico with his wife Georgina, while his boys, Johan and Iskandar, live with their families in France and Hawaii.

I am the third sibling and the oldest girl. After me comes my sister Vasantha (or Vas). She is married to Divakaran and they have four children—Vinod, Vijay, Priya, and Prita. Vas is another great chef in the family and has shared many of her delicious recipes with me. Next is my brother Satheesan, married to Catherine (or Kay). They have a daughter, Shobana. Then come my two sisters, Remani (Rama) and Premala (Prema). Rama lives in Macclesfield, England, and her boys, Daniel and Adam, grew up enjoying her Malaysian-style roasts, pies, and ribs. Prema, who passed away in 2004, was a lover of hawker foods and folk music. My youngest brothers are Sree and Suresh. Sree lives in New Jersey with his wife, Diane, an excellent baker, and their children, Kristopher and Cristina. Suresh, the youngest, lives in Malaysia with his wife Mala and their two children, Davee and Dhiran.

My American Family

Geeta, my daughter, grew up with Malaysian flavors at home, and on regular trips to Malaysia, she especially enjoys their delicious noodles and spicy vegetable stir-fries. During the traditional American holidays, Geeta savored her American favorites but with a Malaysian twist, such as roast chicken with curry flavor, spicy *sambal* pasta, spice-infused potatoes, or lamb with black pepper and preserved soybeans. Like me, Geeta continually seeks new flavors. Bob, my husband, also loves Malaysian foods, especially hawker

My family with grandparents (*I am on the far right*)

delights—*roti canai* (flaky flat bread), *satay*, and *mee goreng*. In Malaysia, the vendors are usually amazed when he asks for fiery bird peppers called *cili padi* with his dishes.

My Professional Interest in Food, Flavors, and Culture

After my schooling in Malaysia, I studied microbiology at Bombay (now Mumbai) University. There I was attracted to the unique and affordable street foods and treated myself once a week to spicy take-outs from the Chinese restaurants, as the food at the Women's Hostel on Marine Drive was unpalatable. Remember, I was a food snob by then, thanks to Ma! These Chinese dishes had an Indian twist, different from the Chinese food I ate growing up. Bombay's cosmopolitan offerings had flavors from all over India—including Mughlai, Goan, Keralan, Marathi, Gujarati, Bengali and Punjabi.

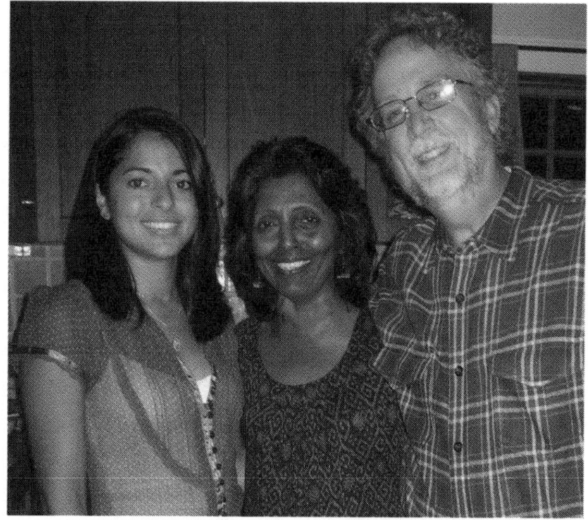

Geeta, myself, and Bob

Instead of going home during holidays, I went on cultural eating tours of India. I traveled with friends to Kashmir (delicious meatballs), Delhi (freshly baked aromatic *tandooris*), Amritsar (addictive rice puddings), Cochin (delicious coconut-based fish curries), Madras, now Chennai (great *thosais* and *sambars*), Goa (spicy steak with Portuguese wine), and even stopped at a Hyderabad truck stop where I had the best chicken *biryani*.

After a year of teaching in Malaysia, I went to Reading University in England to pursue a Masters in Food Science and Nutrition. What a change! Food was bland. I survived—thanks to a bottle of chile sauce from Ma! The following year I opted for a dorm that had a common kitchen and that saved my life. I splurged on a skillet and saucepan, and cooked pasta, eggs, and vegetables with simple Malaysian touches. After I graduated, I took a job in Belize, Central America, where I ran a community-based food processing plant, teaching women from rural areas to make preserves, sauces, baked goods, relishes, and pickles using local fruits and vegetables. There I enjoyed the local staples—rice and beans, fish *escabeche*, *recado* seasoned stewed chicken, and *tamales*—even though the cooking lacked the flavor impact I was used to.

I came to the U.S and pursued my PhD in Food Science. After two years, I left the program and began my career in the food industry, initially in research and later in product development. During this time, working with spices and flavors interested me most. This led me to work for spice and flavor companies, focusing on ethnic flavors and seasonings. Later I started my own food consulting business, and I taught Food Science at New York University for about seven years. I have written extensively about ethnic cuisines and cultures, and have organized and given numerous presentations and seminars on similar topics. In 2000, I authored my first book, *Handbook of Spices, Seasonings and Flavorings*, whose second edition was published in fall of 2006.

Creating This Cookbook

I regularly visit Malaysia to connect with family and friends, savor the foods, and of course, relax on the beautiful and tranquil beaches. During these trips, I learned a great deal watching Ma, Shanta, and Vas cook. I was amazed at Ma who, even at an older age, spent hours in the kitchen and never got bored with cooking and always having the best for us. None of us can match her patience for details.

I have often traveled to many regions of Malaysia to savor their foods, study their culture, take photos, and learn some cooking. I still continue to do so. No matter what, I always make time to sit and enjoy the local hawkers'specialties, while reminiscing about the past. Growing up, hawkers were our 'chefs' and street carts and stalls were our 'restaurants.' I would also visit the bustling wet markets (*pasar basah*) and night markets (*pasar malam*), a must-see for any visitor, to sample local foods and observe the culture.

With this book, the home cook or chef can easily create any Malaysian dish, from the well-known *satay* (grilled chicken or meat), *acar* (spicy pickled carrot and cucumber), and fragrant *nasi lemak* (coconut-infused rice), to the less familiar aromatic *laksa lemak* (noodles in spicy coconut broth), beef *rendang* (beef slow simmered in coconut milk), or a hot and spicy *sambal*. In my recipes, I have taken the edge off the heat, fishiness, and pungency, yet I retain their authentic delicious flavors while satisfying today's taste buds and health concerns. My recipes can also be used to add a Malaysian twist to your favorite Western foods. I have also simplified Malaysian cooking, whenever needed, by giving substitutions for difficult-to-find ingredients, and by modifying traditional cooking techniques. The busy cook will be able to capture the true essence of a recipe and still prepare it in less than an hour and some even within 30 minutes.

Taste of Malacca Spice Blends

When in Malaysia, I often spend a day in Malacca, where I enjoy wandering down the narrow and twisted streets and visiting the historic temples, mosques, and churches that reflect its polyethnic community. Malacca was a fabled kingdom in Southeast Asia during the fifteenth century. Its great wealth and fame grew from its fabulous bazaar where Chinese, Indian, Arab, Siamese, Javanese, and Malay traders converged to buy and sell the treasures of the East. The greatest treasures of Malacca could be detected in the very air itself—the scent of the exotic spices of Asia and the rest of the world.

My Taste of Malacca Spice Blends continues this culinary journey. I launched Taste of Malacca Spice Blends after more than twenty years of corporate research and product development, and culinary experience in the food, spice, and flavor industries. For a quicker and more convenient way to make the delicious recipes in this book, you can use my spice blends under the Taste of Malacca brand, available through www.tasteofmalacca.com. They adapt authentic Malaysian flavors for today's palates and busy lifestyles.

The Malaysian Spice Blends reflect Malaysia's diverse heritage—Malay, Indian, Chinese, Indian Muslim, and Eurasian—as well as Malacca's unique community—Baba-Nonyas, from Chinese and Malay ancestors; Kristangs, descendants of the Portuguese and Dutch settlers with locals; and Chittys, of Indian and Malay heritage.

Taste of Malacca Spice Blends not only taste great, but come with healthy and quick and easy-to-prepare recipes. They have only all-natural ingredients with no MSG, no preservatives, no yeast extracts or hydrolysates, no hydrolyzed plant protein (HPP) or hydrolyzed vegetable protein (HVP), no fillers, and no salt or sugar. They are also dairy free, gluten free, and Kosher.

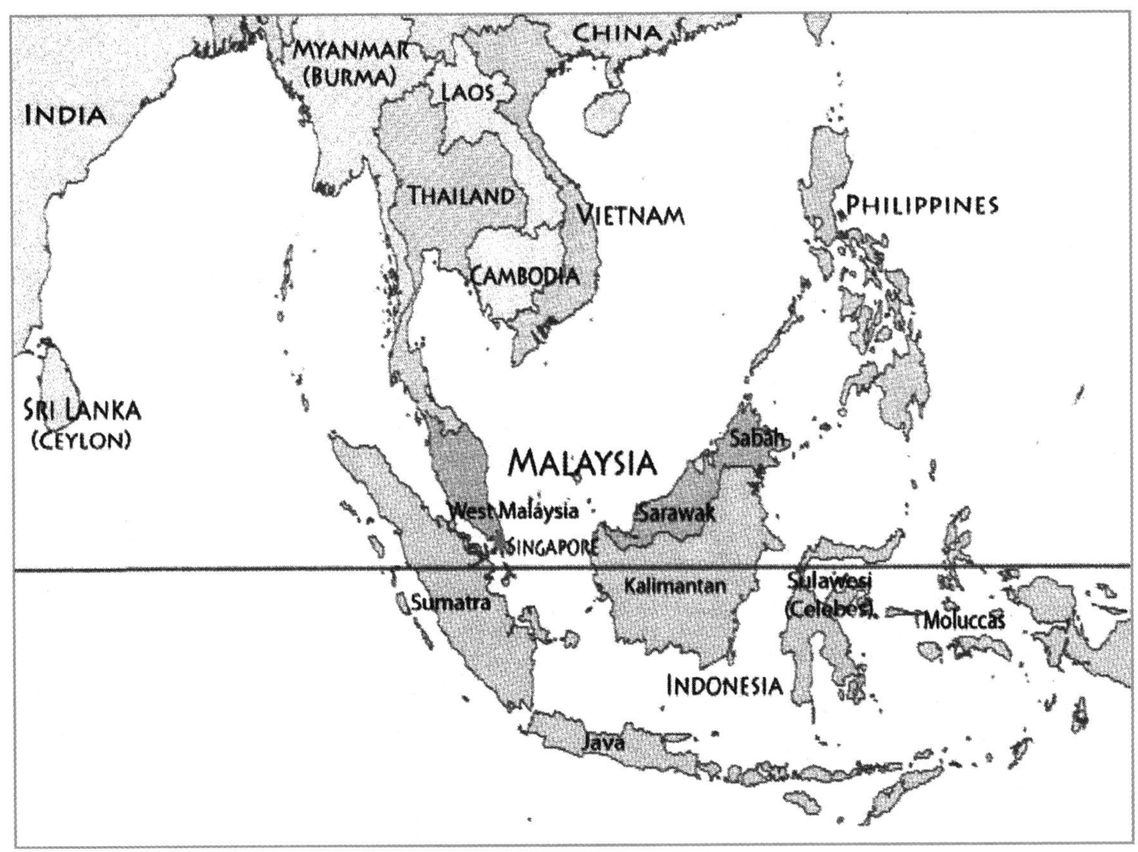
CHINA
MYANMAR
(BURMA)
LAOS
INDIA
THAILAND
VIETNAM
PHILIPPINES
CAMBODIA
SRI LANKA
(CEYLON)
Sabah
MALAYSIA
West Malaysia
Sarawak
SINGAPORE
Kalimantan
Sulawesi
(Celebes)
Sumatra
Moluccas
INDONESIA
Java

INTRODUCTION

Malaysian cuisine, an alluring collage of ethnic foods and cooking styles, offers an array of tastes, aromas, and textures. Malaysian food is assertively flavorful and occasionally fiery. It makes liberal use of many Asian ingredients we have come to love: lemongrass, ginger, coriander leaves (cilantro), chilies, coconut milk, star anise, tamarind, and curry powders. Malaysian food also offers new flavors for the adventurous home cook or chef to explore: *bunga kantan* (wild ginger flower), pandan leaf, *daun kesum* (laksa leaf, also referred to as Vietnamese coriander), galangal (a relative of ginger), *belacan* (fermented dried shrimp paste), and palm sugar (*gula Melaka*).

Malaysia has always been a cultural melting pot because of its location at the crossroads of the Asian spice trade routes. Merchants sailing both east and west on the shifting monsoon winds landed ashore on the slim Malayan Peninsula, which juts downward from the Asiatic continent and separates Indian Ocean ports from markets on the South China Sea. Over centuries, traders and conquerors from Hindu, Buddhist, Islamic, and Christian empires infused Malaysia with great cultural, linguistic, religious, and culinary influences. Malaysia's cuisine is a creation of this historical and cultural alchemy.

To afford the reader a true appreciation of Malaysian cuisine, this introductory chapter provides an overview of Malaysia's cultural history and peoples; and describes its foods and seasonings derived from this rich cultural heritage, its street foods, and finally, the regional variations and subtleties found in Malaysian cuisine.

The History of Malaysia and Its People

Malaysia is a relatively young country. Founded as the Federation of Malaya, it achieved independence (or *Merdeka*) from British rule in 1957. In 1963, when Singapore and the East Malaysian states of Sabah and Sarawak on the island of Borneo joined the Federation, it was renamed Malaysia. Singapore seceded in 1965, resulting in the Malaysia we know today.

Malaysia consists of thirteen states and three federal territories (Kuala Lumpur, Putrajaya, and Labuan). In Peninsular, or Western, Malaysia, nine of the states are sultanates (Perlis, Kedah, Perak, Selangor, Negeri Sembilan, Johor, Pahang, Terengganu, and Kelantan) and two states are headed by governors (Malacca and Penang). Sabah and Sarawak, the two remaining states, are four hundred miles across the South China Sea, where they share the island of Borneo with Indonesia's state of Kalimantan and the Sultanate of Brunei. Peninsular Malaysia's northern border meets Thailand, while the city-state of Singapore lies to its immediate south. The Indonesian Archipelago forms a crescent around Malaysia, sheltering its west coast and stretching to its south and east.

Early Malaysian History

Archeological finds show relics of early human activity in Sarawak's Niah Caves more than 35,000 years ago, among the oldest in the world. The first evidence of human settlement in Peninsular Malaysia is approximately 10,000 years old. While the history of humankind in Malaysia is lost in the mists of time, there are different theories regarding the first human migration to Malaysia, much of it based on anthropological studies of the aboriginal people of Malaysia, the Orang Asli ("Original People").

Some anthropologists believe the Orang Asli arrived in three waves of migration to Peninsular Malaysia. The oldest group is the nomadic Negritos, who arrived about 25,000 years ago, some say from the Andaman Islands, and inhabited the forest regions, mainly Kelantan and Perak. The next oldest group is the Senoi, who are largely jungle dwellers, living communally in longhouses in the mountains of Central Malaysia. Their language, Temiar, is related to those of the Mon of Burma and hill tribes of Vietnam and Cambodia.

The Proto-Malays (from the Greek *protos* meaning first) are the third group of Orang Asli immigrants. They arrived in Peninsular Malaysia about four thousand years ago from South China and settled mostly in Pahang, Johor, Negeri Sembilan, and Selangor. The Proto-Malays are much more diverse, unlike the Negritos and Senoi who are grouped by common languages and customs. They are animists, Christians or Muslims, and some have their own languages while others speak only Malay. The sea-going Proto-Malays are the Orang Laut, found mainly in coastal Malacca and Johor. Beginning around 300 B.C., another wave of immigrants known as Deutero-Malays (from the Greek *deuteros* meaning second) arrived from South China. These two groups (Proto- and Deutero-Malays) became part of the present-day Malay population.

In Eastern Malaysia, on the island of Borneo, there are numerous indigenous groups. In Sabah (formerly North Borneo), the major indigenous groups include the Kadazan-Dusuns, the Bajaus (a seafaring people), and the Muruts (literally the "hill people"). Sarawak is home to more than twenty-five ethnic groups, the major ones being the Ibans (or Sea Dayaks), Bidayuhs (or Land Dayaks), and the Melanaus.

Early Indian Influence: The First Malay Kingdoms

Trade with India had a profound and permanent effect on Malaysian culture and foods, starting in pre-Christian times and becoming substantial by the first centuries AD. For a thousand years thereafter, there were frequent movements of traders, adventurers, and Buddhist and Hindu priests from the south and east coasts of India. During these early years of trade, merchants relied on the monsoon winds, which changed directions seasonally. South Indian merchants would arrive at the Malay Isthmus and wait for months for a change in monsoon winds for their return trip home. During these long stopovers, Indian traders created families with local Malay women.

Commerce as well as intermarriage and cultural assimilation resulted in several Malay "Indianized" states. These new kingdoms were based on Hindu or Buddhist concepts of state, royalty, and court life, whose rulers were Indian or Indianized local chiefs. In Kedah, there is a large Buddhist-Hindu archeological site preserved at Lembah Bujang that emphasizes the great influence by the Pallava and the Chola kings of India from the fourth to the thirteenth centuries. Other Buddhist-Hindu kingdoms include Langkasuka in Kedah, the present-day Thai state of Pattani, and Pan-Pan (sometimes called Tan-Tan), a Hindu kingdom believed to have existed around the third to seventh century AD, somewhere in the East Coast Malaysian states of Kelantan or Terengganu. The greatest of these Indianized kingdoms was Srivijaya in Sumatra. While records of its beginning are scarce, Srivijaya was established around the fourth century AD and ruled most of Southeast Asia. At its height, the Srivijaya Kingdom held suzerainty over Sumatra, the Malayan peninsula, and parts of Borneo, Java, and other Indonesian islands. These Indianized kingdoms in Malaya utilized the Sanskrit language, Indian names for the months, and Indian systems of measurement.

In addition to introducing Buddhism and Hinduism to Malaysia, Indian traders ultimately helped introduce Islam as well. Tamil Muslims from the Malabar Coast ("Klings") and the Bengalis from the Coromandel Coast ("Chulias") of India, and smaller groups from Gujerat and Bombay came as traders and eventually settled in Kedah, Malacca, and Penang, bringing their Islamic beliefs with them. Over the centuries, many other waves of Muslim immigrants landed on Malayan shores, settled, and intermarried, including Muslim peoples from Java, Sumatra, Sulawesi (formerly Celebes), and other Indonesian islands, as well as Pakistan and the Middle East. Under the Malaysian constitution, all of those people who follow Islam, habitually speak Malay, and follow Malay customs (or *adat*) are considered part of the Malay population.

Even today, much of the non-Islamic content of Malay *adat* still clearly reflects their ancient Hindu origins, including those customs that mark major life events—birth, engagement, marriage, death—as well as law and court ceremonies. For example, the traditional Malay marriage ceremonial rites (*mandi lulur, majlis berinai,* or *bersanding*) are Hindu in origin. There are also striking similarities between Hindu and Malay ceremonies marking puberty, pregnancy, and even certain festivals. Hindu Indian art and literature based on the *Vedas* is reflected in the puppet shadow play of Kelantan, *wayang kulit,* which is based on the *Ramayana*, a Vedic epic. Morever, many words in the Malay language still reflect their Sanskrit origins, including *Bumiputra* ("sons of soil"), a Malaysian legal term broadly defining those of Malay origin.

The Sultanate of Malacca

According to the Malay literary masterpiece *Sejarah Melayu* (the *Malay Annals*), Parameswara, a refugee Hindu prince from the Srivijaya kingdom of Sumatra, founded the great city-state of Malacca around 1400 AD. Parameswara chose Malacca because of its potential as a port capable of competing with other established entrepôts. Large numbers of Indian Muslim traders from Gujarat, Tamil Nadu, and Bengal were prominent intermediaries in the spice trade between Asia and Europe, and traded frequently in Malacca. Along with their commerce, the Indian Muslim merchants introduced Islam to Malacca. Intermarriage also enhanced the spread of Islam. Parameswara married a princess from the Sumatran Sultanate of Samudra-Pasai (present-day Aceh) and converted to Islam, changing his name to Raja Iskandar Shah.

During the Sultanate of Malacca, the first formal diplomatic relations between Malaya and China were established. Parameswara visited China, seeking the Ming dynasty as a powerful ally against the Kingdom of Siam. Like the South Indian merchants, Chinese traders also stayed in Malacca and established families while awaiting a shift in monsoon winds. The writings of Chinese officials during this time speak of Bukit China, a community of primarily Fukien Chinese traders who had settled there. The Sultanate of Malacca was so successful that by the beginning of the sixteenth century the population of Malacca swelled tremendously with foreign traders.

The Portuguese Conquest of Malacca

The sixteenth century was Portugal's "Age of Discovery." At this time, Indian Muslim traders sold spices to Arab merchants in the Middle East, who in turn sold them to Europe through the city-state of Venice. Malacca was their primary collecting point for spices, including pepper, nutmeg, and clove, from around the islands of Malaya and Indonesia. The Portuguese adventurer Alfonso de Albuquerque declared his intention to seize the spice trade from Muslim hands. Initially, he conquered the port of Goa, India, in 1510, and in 1511 he seized Malacca. Albuquerque assumed control of the spice trade with his capture of Hormuz at the mouth of the Persian Gulf in 1515.

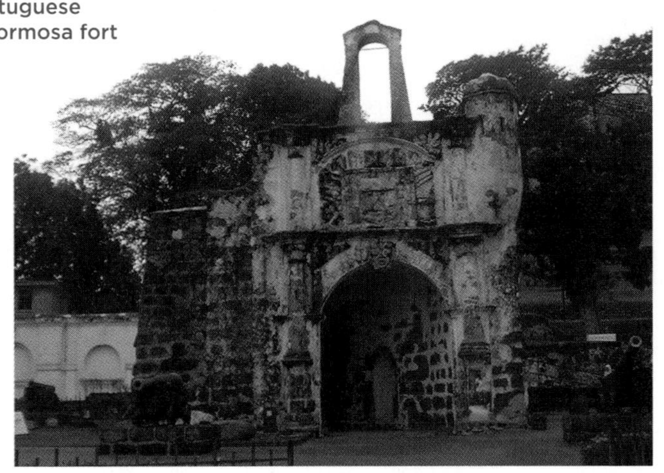

Portuguese A'Formosa fort

The Portuguese ruled Malacca for the next 130 years, which ultimately ended Malacca's reign as a mighty trading port. Unlike free-trading Malays, Portuguese monopolistic practices caused Asian spice traders to favor other ports in Southeast Asia. Portugual's conquest of Malacca also marked the beginning of European colonial efforts to dominate Malaya, with the Dutch and the British attempting, in succession, to impose colonial rule. The result was a series of European interventions in local Malayan politics, shifting allegiances and territories among the Malay Sultanates, a series of treaties between European and Asian powers, and mass migrations of Chinese and Indian workers to Malaya. All of these events left their political and cultural marks on present-day Malaysia.

The Dutch Conquest of Malacca

In the sixteenth century, along with the Portuguese, Dutch mercantile companies established a formidable presence in Southeast Asia, particularly in the pepper and spice trade. In the early seventeenth century, the Dutch East India Company established its headquarters in Java at Batavia, now known as Jakarta.

In January 1641, the Dutch East India Company and the Sultan of Johor succeeded in taking Malacca from the Portuguese. While the Portuguese mismanagement of its colony had greatly diminished Malacca as a significant trading port, the Dutch siege left the town in ruins. The Dutch rebuilt Malacca and ruled it without interruption for the next 150 years. They used Malacca largely as a military base to control the Straits of Malacca, and it never regained its status as a trading port, or its former wealth and glory. In 1795, when French Revolutionary armies captured the Netherlands, the Dutch gave Malacca to the British to avoid its capture by the French. In 1808, the British returned the city to the Dutch who then traded it back to the British for Bencoleen in Sumatra.

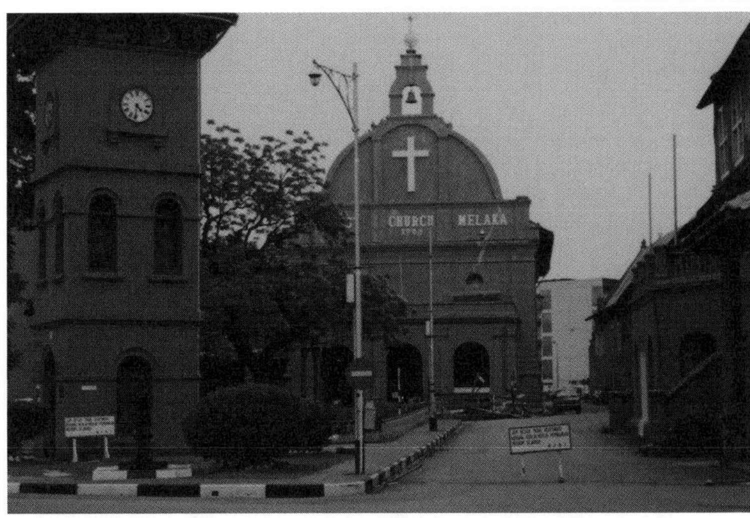

Malacca town center with Dutch Christ Church

Migrations of people throughout Southeast Asia during this time changed its face politically and culturally. The southern "leg" of Sulawesi (formerly Celebes) was populated mainly by three sea nomadic groups, the Makassar, Bajau, and Bugis (or "Buginese"), who plied the trade routes of Southeast Asia. The Bugis are ethnically Malay. In 1667 the Dutch invaded Sulawesi and defeated the Makassar Sultanate, which led to the migration of a number of defeated Makassar and Bugis allied princes, who conquered or infiltrated the Malayan Peninsula, the Malayan states of Borneo, the Riau Archipelago, and elsewhere in Southeast Asia. One such Bugis group became the rulers of Johor, in the south. The Bugis expanded their influence to a number of kingdoms on the Malayan Peninsula, in Perak and Kedah, and in Selangor's Klang and Linggi districts, where, unchallenged, they eventually became sultans themselves.

Dutch military activities also had a significant impact on the Minangkabau community of Sumatra. In 1667, the Dutch destroyed Aceh's control over the Straits of Malacca. Subsequently, Minangkabau traders moved from central Sumatra to the coasts and across the Straits of Malacca to join earlier Minangkabau settlers in Malaya. The Minangkabaus brought with them a matrilineal socio-cultural system by which property and authority descended through the female side. Later the Minangkabaus formed a confederation of nine small states, now the Malaysian state of Negeri Sembilan (or the "Nine Lands"). The Bugis and Minangkabau gradually adopted the Malay language and Malay titles, and intermarriages among Bugis, Minangkabau, and Malay royal families reinforced political alliances.

The British Enter Malaysia

In the middle of the eighteenth century, while official British interest in the Malayan Peninsula was minimal, private British traders conducted an increasing amount of commerce, and in 1786 established the port of Penang. British power expanded in 1800 when the Sultan of Kedah granted the British territorial control over the mainland coast across from Penang, named Province Wellesley. In 1824, the ruler of Riau-Johor gave up authority over Singapore to the British in exchange for a pension, and in 1826, the British combined Singapore, Malacca, Penang, and Province Wellesley into a single administrative unit called the Straits Settlements. In the Straits Settlements, Penang flourished as a regional trading port, while Singapore grew to become the dominant economic power in the region.

Peninsular Malaya Relations with Thailand

Historians believe that Thai-speaking peoples arrived in the northern Malayan Peninsula beginning in the seventh century and began slowly displacing Malay peoples. By the thirteenth century, the Malay kingdom of Ligor (now the Thai town of Nakhon Si Thammarat) had become first a vassal state and then part of the Thai kingdom of Ayudhya.

From Ligor, the Thai claimed sovereignty over the northern Malay Sultanates of Patani, Kelantan, Kedah, Perak, and Terengganu. Between the fourteenth and twentieth centuries, Thai control over the sultanates of northern Malaya varied considerably. Centuries of contact with the Thais resulted in a Malay culture in these sultanates that was distinct from the "classic" Malay culture of the Johor Sultanate, reflected in the dialect, cultural rituals, and foods of Northern Malaysia.

British, Thai, and Malayan Political Relations

In the nineteenth and early twentieth centuries, the northern Malayan sultanates began seeking assistance from the British to offset the perceived threat of Thai rulers to their existence. Rather than aiding the Malayan Sultanates, the British took steps that helped seal Thai control over them. The Thai-British treaty of 1909 set Malaysia's current international border with Thailand. The treaty, in which the Malayans did not participate, divided the northern Malayan sultanates into two parts. Britain gained control over portions of the Sultanates of Kedah, including Perlis, and the Sultanates of Perak, Kelantan, and Terengganu. These four states, along with Johor, later became the Unfederated Malay States. The Thais kept the remaining portions of Kedah, including Setul (now the Thai province of Satun), and the Sultanate of Patani, now the modern Thai provinces of Pattani, Narathiwat (Menara), Songkhla (Singgora), and Yala (Jala). The British originally requested control over the Sultanate of Patani as well, but the Thais refused. This left the Sultanate of Patani, a center of Islamic learning and one of the most historically significant Malayan kingdoms, under the control of the ethnically and culturally distinct Thais. (Even today, the population of these four Thai states remains a Malay-Muslim majority, and a Malay insurgency there continues to challenge Thai rule.)

British Malaya

Between 1909 and 1957, the British effectively controlled Malaya. The British aggressively developed the Malayan tin industry and plantation crops such as tea, rubber, and palm oil through vastly expanded immigration of foreign workers, particularly Indians for agriculture and Chinese for tin mining.

Indian Immigration under the British

With an equatorial climate, abundant rainfall, and a year-round growing season, the British viewed Malaya as an undeveloped estate waiting for exploitation. Accordingly, the British encouraged commercial agriculture as a primary enterprise in Malaya. Operating plantations required labor to perform arduous, repetitive tasks. In addition, roads needed to be constructed and railroad track laid through jungle, swamps, and highlands to deliver the agricultural products produced by the new plantations. Thus began a growing demand for low paid, unskilled labor in Malaya, particularly from the end of the nineteenth to the early twentieth century.

The British began importing labor from their colonies in Southern India and Ceylon (now Sri Lanka) for plantation work. They also sought skilled workers and educated Indians to staff commercial enterprises and government departments as clerks, administrators, and technicians. Doctors and teachers were recruited from India as well. The English-speaking immigrants from Kerala monopolized the clerical and other administrative positions in the British government. The Malayalees generally were able to speak Tamil, as well as Malayalam and English, and soon became prominent as overseers on European-owned rubber and oil palm plantations (including my grandfather, Thatha). A number of Indian merchants, bankers, financiers, and contractors, principally Chettiars and Marakkayar Muslims of South India, immigrated to Malaya where they prospered as well.

Chinese Immigration under the British

Overseas Chinese who settled in Malaya emigrated primarily from the southeast provinces of Guangdong (Kwangtung and Canton), Fukien (Fujian), and Guangxi (Kwangsi). The nineteenth-century expansion of plantations and tin mines increased the value of Chinese labor, which was becoming a staple article of commerce. The monsoon winds brought cargoes of Chinese to British ports, where workers were purchased, based on their skills and health. Kidnapping and indenture of Chinese workers continued up till the early twentieth century, when indentured labor was abolished.

Chinese immigration in the twentieth century increased dramatically up till the Japanese occupation during World War II, to the point where the Chinese outnumbered Malays in Malaya.

Malaysia Today: Its Cultures Foods and Flavors

Malaysia today continues to be a land of great cultural and ethnic diversity. Sociologists have classified over 180 identifiable ethnic groups in Malaysia. According to the most recent available (2008) population estimate, Malaysia comprises 53.3 percent Malay, 26 percent Chinese, 7.7 percent Indian, 1.2 percent Others (which includes Eurasians), and 11.8 percent Indigenous Peoples. *Bumiputras* (or *Bhumiputra*, from the Sanskrit word meaning "sons of soil") refers to Malays, Orang Asli, and some indigenous peoples from Sabah and Sarawak.

While the people of Malaysia come from different cultural backgrounds, we all share a common passion—food! The Malay language itself reflects our obsession with food. In addition to "*apa khabar*" ("how are you?"), I might greet a friend in Malaysia by saying, "*sudah makan*?" ("have you eaten?"). And what makes Malaysian curries, sambals, stir-fries, and noodles so unique and so full of flavor? It is the combination of a number of spices, fragrant roots, lemongrass, dried shrimp paste (*belacan*), coconut milk, preserved soybean paste (*taucheo*), *kasturi* lime, and tamarind juice. Let's look at some of the basic ingredients and seasonings that make Malaysian cuisine truly unique.

Common Malaysian Seasonings and Ingredients

The 'soul' of Malaysian cooking is the *rempah*, which refers to spices, both dry spices (including cumin, coriander, fennel, cinnamon, clove, and star anise) and wet spices (including turmeric root, galangal, chilies, lemongrass, *belacan*, tamarind, and ginger). *Rempah* is the base for curries, *sambals*, stir-fries, *laksas*, and stews. *Rempah* ingredients are finely or coarsely ground using a mortar and pestle (*batu lesong*), food processor, or blender. After the ingredients are pounded or pureed, they are continuously stirred in oil (a process called *tumising* that takes away the raw tastes of the ingredients) till the oil starts seeping out of the *rempah* paste and the paste develops a fragrant aroma. Then the other ingredients are added—chicken, shrimp, meats, fish, or vegetables. For *tumising*, cooks generally use plenty of oil. I use less oil in my recipes and thus less time *tumising*, but still end up with a delicious sauce.

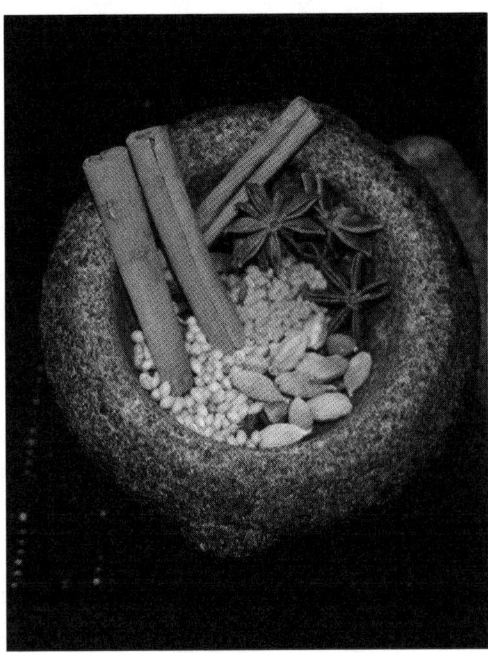

Spices in Ma's mortar and pestle

A year before Ma passed away, she finally parted with her treasured mortar and pestle. Today, I use it to pound my *rempah*. It is among my greatest treasures! And whenever I use it to prepare recipes in this cookbook, memories come flooding back of Ma and Periama (my Grandma) in our kitchen.

Periama's other favorite *rempah* grinder was the bigger *batu giling* (a rectangular and flat stone or granite-based block also known as *ammi kallu* or *metate*) that was kept atop a concrete pedestal outside the kitchen at the back of our house. On it she ground the dried red chilies that had been soaked in water to make our curries and *sambals*. Periama turned grinding chilies into an art. Using both her hands on the stone rolling pin (*metlapil*), Periama moved it to and fro, as she pushed in pieces of chilies toward the center, adding a little water at a time, and finely grinding them into a smooth paste. She then scraped the paste and placed it in a saucer and

I remember Periama (my grandmother) sitting on the kitchen floor, bent over the mortar, ready to work on the *rempah* ingredients. She did not raise her head up even for a moment, but concentrated on what she was doing. She began with the shallots, pounding them into a soft paste, and scraping them out. Next, she added garlic and ginger and pounded them for few minutes and then took them out. Then she added the soaked and drained dried whole red chilies, which took longer pounding. She used just enough water to get the paste moving and rotated the pestle to pound in a circular motion. The work required some exertion. She carefully took the end of her sarong and wiped her face, then continued pounding.

brought it into the kitchen to make her fish curry. As I worked with chilies later, I used to wonder how she never got a "burn"!

Curry—a Popular Malaysian Cooking Style

I cannot talk about the different ethnic cuisines of Malaysia without discussing curries, a cooking style common among all of Malaysia's ethnic groups. The word "curry" is really a British translation of the Tamil word *kari*, meaning sauce. In Malaysia, we have a curry that we all enjoy and which reflects its polyethnic make up. Malaysian curries usually have Indian and Malay origins, and are prepared from a blend of dry spices and/or wet spice pastes. A number of curries also reflect Chinese influence through the use of soy sauce, star anise, white pepper, ground fennel seeds, and *taucheo* (preserved soybean paste), while others have Portuguese influence with tomato paste, vinegar, sweet spices, and potatoes.

Malaysians use specific spices to complement chicken, beef, pork, lamb, seafood, or vegetables. For example, my Grandma told me that fenugreek is the special spice for fish dishes; coriander for chicken; cinnamon and clove for enhancing beef; star anise, a must for pork dishes; and turmeric for vegetable and lentil dishes. Turmeric is also used by Indians and Malays as a 'sterilizing' marinade for poultry.

In predominantly Malay regions of Malaysia, curries cooked with coconut milk are referred to as *gulais*. The backbone of traditional Malay curries is a wet paste of shallots, garlic, chilies, galangal, turmeric root, and lemongrass cooked with coconut milk and/or tamarind juice. Depending on the type of curry, dry spices such as coriander, cumin, cinnamon, clove, black pepper, and fennel seeds are added, as well as local herbs and flowers, including salam leaf, turmeric leaf, *laksa* leaf, and *bunga kantan* (wild ginger flower). *Rendang* is a slow-simmered coconut-and-spice-based Malay curry, made with beef (page 177), chicken (page 287), fish, or shrimp. *Sayur lodeh* (page 223) is another Malay curry made with mixed vegetables simmered in coconut milk and spices.

Indians generally use an array of dry spices with shallots, garlic, ginger, tamarind juice, and/or coconut milk to prepare their great variety of curries. Most Indian curries that I grew up with have South Indian and Sri Lankan origins. In Malaysia, they taste quite different from the original Indian styles, because they incorporate local flavorings.

Ma made Chinese, Malay, Nonya, and Eurasian-style curries in addition to her Indian curries. She listened fervently to radio cooking programs for new recipes to try. I especially enjoyed Ma's intensely flavored dry curries called *peratils* and *varuvals*. Our favorite curries were a simple chicken *varuval* dry-fried with spices in hot oil (page 167), a fragrant fish curry (page 198) that Cha enjoyed, egg curry that Periama taught her (page 172), and mutton *peratil*, goat meat cooked in a seasoned sauce (page 185). Ma's festive curries were vegetable *kurma* (page 283), Chettiar shrimp (page 291), and a chicken *kurma* (page 168) that guests savored during our open house at Deepavali celebrations.

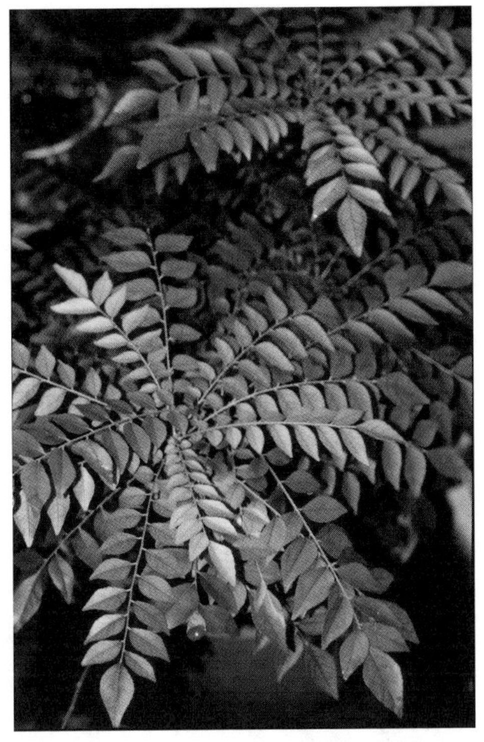

Ma's curry leaf plant

For Indian curries, Ma and Periama would dry roast whole spices and grind them to give a fresher aroma. They fried the whole or ground spices in hot oil for about 30 to 60 seconds before adding chicken, meats, fish, tofu, or vegetables. Ma generally prepared her curries in a metal wok, but sometimes used a clay pot, deep pot, or saucepan.

Eurasian curries can be fiery, vinegary, and/or sweet, depending on whether they have Portuguese, Dutch, or British influence. My British-Eurasian neighbor made her curries mild with tomatoes, black pepper, star anise, cinnamon, and Worcestershire sauce. Ma's good friend Mrs. Collar (of Portuguese ancestry) cooked hot and vinegary curries using vinegar, soy sauce, chilies, dried shrimp paste, and black peppercorns. Her fiery chicken curry *debal* (page 289) was our favorite.

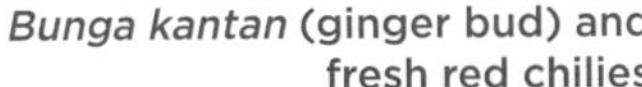

Bunga kantan (ginger bud) and fresh red chilies

The Kristangs of Malacca have combined Portuguese, Indian, and Malay spices and ingredients into unique curries (called *cari*). Kristangs generally add souring agents—vinegar, tamarind juice, lime juice, *belimbing*, unripe mango, papaya, or other sour fruits—along with coconut milk, shrimp paste, soy sauce, chilies, and wet or dry *rempahs*. They sometimes add pineapple for sweetness and candlenuts for thickening. Some traditional curries are *ayam vindaloo* (page 169), *cari seccu* (dry mutton curry), and a spicy salted fish curry.

The Nonyas of Penang and Malacca tend to enjoy curries with pork, beef, and seafood, flavored with Malay and Chinese ingredients, including *belacan*, chilies, lemongrass, tamarind, and coconut milk. Typical curries are *ikan* or *udang assam pedas* (hot and sour tamarind fish or shrimp curry, page 201), *sayur lemak* (similar to *sayur lodeh*, page 223), *kari Kapitan* (page 162), and chicken *kurma* (page 168). Many Nonya and Kristang curries tend to be similar in flavor, such as *kari Kapitan* and *assam pedas,* sometimes with each group claiming that a particular curry is their own. I have tried my best to attribute them to the appropriate creator based on my research.

Now let us examine the present-day ethnic groups, their foods, and flavors.

The Malays

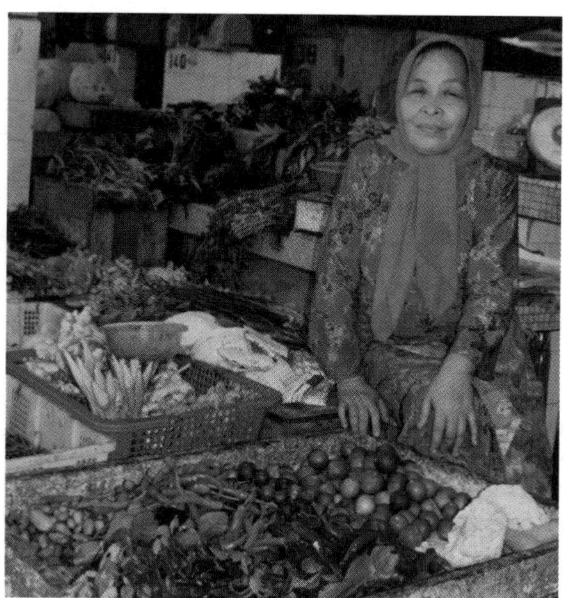

Malay market vendor, Petaling Jaya

The Malays migrated to present-day Malaysia from many places. Immigrant groups included the original Orang Asli; Pakistanis; Hindu and Muslim descendants from India; Bugis and Makassars from Sulawesi; Bataks and Minangkabaus from Sumatra; the Javanese from Java; the Boyenese from Bawean; and others from Thailand, the Middle East (Arabs and Turks), and southern China. All of these peoples assimilated and many intermarried. As the history of Malaysia illustrates, the Malayan Peninsula and Archipelago also experienced many conquests and cultural influences over time. It had "Indianized" Malay kingdoms, "Javanese" Malay kingdoms, and Malay kingdoms ruled from Southern Thailand, Sumatra, and the Riau Islands. Also, in the 1930s, a large percentage of Indonesian-Malays migrated from the neighboring Indonesian islands to swell the overall Malay population in Malaya. Today, all of those people of Malaysia who practice Islam, regularly speak Malay, and follow Malay customs (*adat*) form the Malay population.

For Malays, rice is the staple in a meal. Like the Indians, but unlike the Chinese, they do not bring out their meals in courses. Side dishes of chicken, meat, seafood, and vegetable curries, *acars* (spicy pickled vegetables), and spicy *sambals* (fiery pungent condiments) accompany the main course of rice. Indeed, the Malay word *nasi* is not only the name for cooked rice, but also the word for a meal. Malay flavors can be mild, fiery, sweet, sour, or pungent depending on several factors: the region they come from (for example, whether they live in close proximity with Thais or Indonesians); their cultural backgrounds (whether they are of Batak, Bugis, Minangkabau, Arab, or Indian Muslim origin); and the influence of Chinese, Nonya, or Indian cooking.

Some typical Malay ingredients are roots and rhizomes (turmeric, galangal, and ginger); fresh *cili padi* (fiery bird peppers) and *cili boh* (ground chile pastes); *kerisik* (toasted grated coconut) and *santan* (coconut milk); *gula Melaka* (sweet, sugary sap of the palm tree); lemongrass, pandan leaf, *ulam* (fresh herbs and greens that are beneficial for health); *limau kasturi* (calamansi limes) and *asam Jawa* (tamarind). Their favorite dry spices are coriander, cumin, turmeric, fennel, cinnamon, and clove. *Belacan* is a ubiquitous flavoring in Malay cuisine, added in sparing amounts (in paste or powder form). It is made from small shrimp-like crustaceans (called krill or *geragau*) that are fermented, cured with salt and sun-dried. *Belacan* does not taste "fishy" when cooked, but rather subtly enhances a dish.

The best-known Malay dish is *satay* (or *sate*, pages 65), grilled chicken or meat. The *satay* vendor reigns over food stalls in the evening. He fans the burning charcoals till they are glowing, and places a dozen or more sticks of tender chicken, mutton, or beef over them. Each *satay* vendor has a "secret recipe" for his marinade, which typically includes turmeric powder (*kunyit*), shallots, lemongrass (*serai*), coriander, and cumin. He serves you the *satay* along with a spicy peanut sauce (*kuah kacang*, page 66), a cooling side of cubed cucumbers and sliced onions, and *ketupat*, compressed white rice. In some regions of Malaysia, cooks prefer a short-cut stove-top version called *satay goreng* (fried *satay*, page 178).

Another Malay favorite is beef *rendang* (page 177), a rich, slow-simmered, dry-cooked beef cooked with coconut milk, chilies, galangal, and toasted grated coconut. Other popular Malay dishes include *ayam masak merah* (a tomato-and-chile-based chicken, page 284), *ikan assam rebus* (tamarind-based fish, page 205), *ayam percik* (grilled spicy chicken, page 166), *daging kerutuk* (dry beef curry, page 182), and *sambal tumis udang* (chile-tomato-based shrimp, page 204). Because Malays are Muslims, pork is *haram* (forbidden) and meats must be *halal* (slaughtered and prepared under Islamic religious principles). Their vegetables dishes—*sayur lodeh* (page 223), *pajeri* (page 232), and *kangkung belacan* (page 228)—are also enjoyed by all. Fragrant Malay rice dishes for festive and special occasions also incorporate Arab and Indian influences.

The most significant festival for Malays is Aidilfitri, popularly known as Hari Raya Puasa, which marks the end of the fasting period of Ramadan (Chapter 11). Delicious seasoned rice dishes—*nasi goreng* (fried rice, page 123), *nasi ulam* (herb rice, page 125), *nasi kuning* (yellow rice, page 118), *nasi kemuli* (spiced rice, page 120), *nasi minyak* (ghee rice, page 121), or *nasi bukhari* (aromatic festive rice, page 278)—are traditionally enjoyed on this special day.

The Chinese

Most Malaysian Chinese still trace their roots back to South China (classified by language dialects). Currently about 38 percent of the Chinese speak primarily the Hokkien dialect, 21 percent Hakka, 20 percent Cantonese, and 9 percent Teochow. Mandarin, Foochow, and Hainanese are other dialects. They brought the provincial cooking styles of Southern China and their traditional ingredients to Malaysia, including noodles, preserved soybean paste (*taucheo*), tofu, garlic, ginger, toasted sesame oil, and soy sauce. A typical Chinese meal centers on steamed white rice, accompanied by soup, many different styles of stir-fries, and steamed or braised seafood, poultry, meat, and vegetables. One of the greatest Chinese gifts to Malaysian cuisine is a large variety of noodle creations, enjoyed for breakfast, lunch, and dinner, as well as snacks. Noodles take on unique flavor dimensions with Malay, Indian Muslim, Indian, and Nonya cooking. Spices, chilies, *belacan*, *taucheo*, tomato sauce, and tamarind juice transform ordinary noodles into flavorful *kari mee* (page 149), *mee Bandung* (page 146), spicy *meehoon* (rice vermicelli, page 83) and braised *Hokkien mee* (page 144). Because noodles symbolize longevity for Chinese, many special noodle dishes have been created for festive occasions and birthdays.

Being influenced by the local ingredients and cultures in Malaysia, the Chinese immigrants to Malaysia also reinvented their own cuisines. Chinese food in Malaysia tends to be milder than Malay and Indian cooking, but many of their dishes have become spicier and more intense, using Malay *cili padi* (bird peppers), *belacan*-based condiments, Indian spices, and curry stocks. Many Chinese-style dishes are unique only to Malaysia, and cannot be found elsewhere. Chile pork (page 186), *daging kicap* (beef in soy sauce, page 181), *udang taucheo* (shrimp with preserved soybeans, page 200), braised spicy long beans (page 230), stir-fried bean sprouts (page 229), and *popiah* (fresh spring rolls) are some Chinese dishes we enjoyed growing up.

Traditional Chinese meals are a family affair. Most large restaurant tables feature a rotating "lazy Susan" so that everyone can easily share from a great variety of dishes and condiments. This "lazy Susan" has also been adopted by other ethnic cultures as well as in our home where it became part of our everyday meal table.

Yin and yang are two opposing natural forces that the Chinese believe should be kept in balance for one's well-being. And in Malaysia, the Chinese use ingredients and techniques to balance the yin and yang in order to stay healthy. If a person has too much yang, one experiences hyperactivity, overstimulation, and fever; and if there is too much yin in a person, weakness, tiredness, and chills result. Cantonese meals strive to balance the yang foods considered "hot" (chicken, red meats, eggs, garlic, dried ginger, sesame oil, wine, starchy foods, salt, mushrooms, mango, and durian) with "cooling" yin foods (greens, sweet spices, clear soups, cucumber, bean sprouts, cabbage, carrots, crab, duck, tofu, sugar, mangosteens, tangerines, lychees, and rambutans). Even cooking techniques play a role in preserving this balance. Roasting and deep-frying are yang, while steaming and simmering are yin. Stir-frying is the best for creating the yin-yang balance.

Cheng Hoon Teng, Chinese temple, Malacca

The Cantonese are one of the most urbanized groups of Chinese in Malaysia, with more than 80 percent living in cities and towns, such as Kuala Lumpur, Ipoh, Kuantan, Seremban, and Sandakan (in Sabah). They are the majority in the states of Negri Sembilan, Pahang, Perak, and parts of Sabah. Upscale restaurants in Malaysia frequently serve Cantonese-style foods that are steamed or stir-fried in light and slightly sweet sauces with a touch of oil. Cantonese cooking highlights the crisp textures, colors, freshness, and delicate, natural flavors of the ingredients. Cantonese are noted for their dim sums, dumplings, stir-fries, and mild noodle dishes. Meats are generally roasted, braised, stir-fried, or steamed with vegetables. Typical Cantonese specialties include sweet and sour chicken, shrimp, fish, or pork, bird's nest soup, dumplings, winter melon soup (page 82), *yee mee* (page 140), stir-fried *kailan* (Chinese broccoli, page 222), and stir-fried mixed vegetables (page 224).

Hokkien people are the descendants of the earliest Chinese settlers in Malaysia who came mainly from Fujian (also called Min) province in China. Hokkien is the largest Chinese dialect spoken among Chinese groups in Malaysia and is the most common Chinese dialect used in Johor, Malacca, Penang, Kedah, Perlis, Terengganu, Kelantan, and Sarawak. The Hokkiens are famous for their flavorful braised noodle and pork dishes. Many Hokkien recipes call for the liberal use of Fujian soy sauce, which some Malaysians claim is the richest and most flavorful soy sauce. Their noted contributions are braised *Hokkien mee* (page 144), *popiah basah* (fresh spring rolls, page 70, a Mamak take-off), and *oh chien* (oyster omelet flavored with chilies and garlic). One of the most popular Hokkien breakfast foods in Malaysia is *bakuteh* (pork rib soup, page 87), a pork and herbal broth prized for its medicinal value and enjoyed as a morning pick-me-up at coffee shops.

Teochew-speaking Chinese constitute the fifth largest Chinese dialect spoken among Chinese in Malaysia. Teochew ancestors came from the vicinity of Swatou or Shantou in Northern Guangdong and Southern Fujian provinces in China. Major concentrations of Teochew-speaking Chinese are found in Kedah and Perak states. Teochew dishes are pork, fish, and fish broth based. Fish ball soup, *sup mee* (page 83), or rice porridges (congee) are served with fried fish, pickled vegetables, and boiled eggs. Malaysia's signature Teochew creation is *char kway teow* (page 139), made with stir-fried fresh broad rice noodles. Originally an inexpensive sustenance for hard-working Teochew immigrants, it is now a quick everyday meal for all Malaysians. Another popular Teochew dish is *lok-lok* or steamboat (a Chinese version of the fondue).

The Hakka are a subgroup of the Han Chinese people whose ancestors migrated from northern and central China around the Yellow River between the fourth and eighteenth centuries to the provinces of Guangdong, Jiangxi, and Fujian in Southern China. Thus, they are called Hakka, Kechia, or Khek, which means "guest people" in Chinese. Although the Hakka dialect may contain elements from both Mandarin and Cantonese, it is a distinct language. Hakka-speaking Chinese are widely dispersed throughout Malaysia, usually in more rural areas. Hakka is the most populous dialect in Sabah and Sarawak, parts of Johor, Selangor (in Kuala Lumpur), and Pahang. Hakka dishes are simple—salt-baked chicken, beef ball soup, or their most noted breakfast dish (and our family's favorite Sunday brunch), *chee cheong fan*, steamed rolled rice noodles with tofu and vegetables stuffed with fish paste.

The Hainanese are the smallest Chinese dialect group in Malaysia. Their language is linguistically related to Fujianese and Teochew. The Hainanese came to Malaysia from the southern Chinese island of Hainan, located off the coast of Guangdong province. The Hainanese are generally urbanized, and mostly concentrated in the states of Selangor and Malacca. A well-known Hainanese dish in Malaysia is chicken rice served with a chile ginger dip (page 126).

There are a small number of Chinese Muslims who live in Penang and elsewhere in Malaysia who tend to form close, tight-knit communities, and who maintain a way of life that is distinct from other Muslim groups and the non-Muslim Chinese. Their food is *halal* and incorporates Malay and Chinese flavors.

The Indians

The vast majority of Indians in Malaysia trace their ancestry to South India. While most Indians in Malaysia speak both Malay and English, we tend to categorize them linguistically, including Tamils (from Tamil Nadu), Malayalees (from Kerala), and Telegus (from Andhra Pradesh). Tamils, Malayalees, and Telegus make up over 85 percent of the people of Indian origin in Malaysia. There is also a large community of Tamil-speaking immigrants from Sri Lanka (formerly Ceylon), who tend to identify themselves as "Ceylonese" or "Jaffnas," rather than Indian or Tamil. North Indians are a minority, largely comprised of Punjabis, with a small portion of Bengalis, Gujaratis, and Sindhis. For census purposes, people of Pakistani and Bangladeshi origin are counted as Indian. The

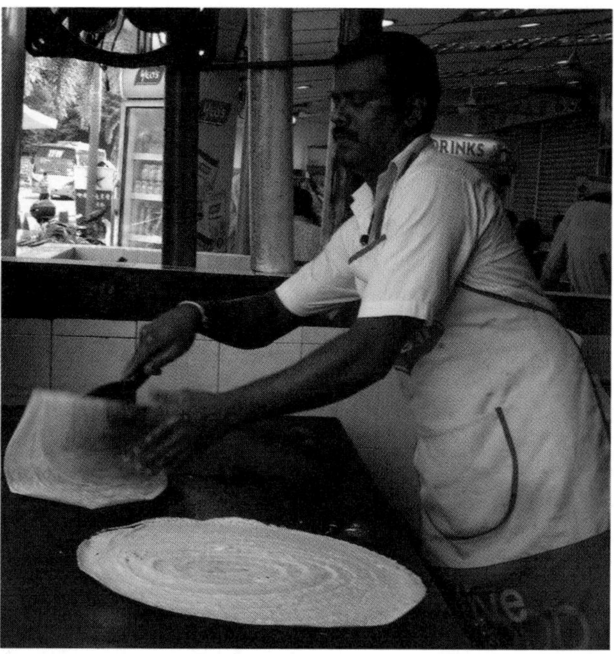

Indian *thosai* vendor at Batu Caves near Kuala Lumpur

South Indian Tamils and Telegus are concentrated mainly in Perak, Selangor, and Negri Sembilan. Malayalees live primarily in Perak, Kuala Lumpur (Selangor), Negri Sembilan, and Johore Bahru (in Johor). While most Malaysians of Indian origin are Hindus, there are also sizeable communities of Indian Christians and Muslims, and Sikhs, as well as a small number of Jains.

Malaysia's Indian-style dishes reflect the diversity of the Indian community, and many dishes borrow flavors from Malaysia's other ethnic groups, making them truly unique and not found anywhere else in the world. In Malaysia's South Indian cuisine, rice is the centerpiece of every meal. Eating South Indian-style in Malaysia is a special experience, particularly for Westerners. A mound of rice is placed in the middle of a fresh banana leaf and surrounded by accompaniments—fish curry (page 198), dhal, spicy dry curried okra (page 221), or cucumber *pachadi* (page 97). At the end of the meal, you signal that you are finished by folding the banana leaf in half, which makes for easy cleanup. An important warning about the folding technique: You fold the banana leaf toward you to signal to the host that you enjoyed the meal, while folding the leaf away from you means that you were not happy. In many vegetarian homes and restaurants, a *thali* with *katoris* (stainless steel plate for the rice and stainless steels cups for the side dishes) sometimes replace the banana leaf. One of my favorite vegetarian meals is Periama's *masala vadai* (spiced lentil cakes, page 61), *nasi limau* (lime rice, page 122), *thosai* (page 69), and *sambar* (page 88).

While the list of spices in South Indian cooking might surprise the uninitiated, they are the key to tasty Indian cuisine. Indeed, many say that spices are the heart and soul of Indian cooking, and this is particularly true of South Indian fare in Malaysia. For each "curry" or sauce recipe, the quantity and proportions of spices varies by region and also by the cook, each one using her special recipe or secret blend. My elder brother Prasnan's favorite dish was Ma's spicy fried fish (page 206), which she made with soy sauce, ginger juice, and her blend of chilies, coriander, cumin, fennel, fenugreek, and turmeric. For Prasnan, Ma would specially add extra chilies. Nowadays, many home cooks rely on commercially avail-

On my husband's first trip to Malaysia, I took him to a traditional "Banana Leaf" restaurant. After the meal was placed on a banana leaf, Bob turned and looked at me, eyes wide and quizzical, silently asking, "where are the knives, forks, and spoons?" I smiled, started to eat with my right hand, and quoted a famous saying: "Eating foods with cutlery is like making love through an interpreter."

able *masala* blends. In Malaysia, there are specific curry blends for preparing meats, seafood, and vegetable curries because certain spices go best with specific ingredients.

In Malaysia, there is a community of South Indians called Chettiars, who are a caste of bankers from Tamil Nadu. The Chettiars, also called Nagarathers, traded in Southeast Asia since early times and came to Malaysia in the nineteenth and twentieth centuries. In the U.S., their cooking style is called *Chettinand* cooking. My grandmother, Periama, was a Chettiar who came to Malaysia as a teenager and married my grandfather Thatha, a French-speaking Keralite. Some Chettiers are vegetarians, while others practice vegetarianism a few days a week. For most of her life, Periama was a strict vegetarian, and she would not use pots or pans that were used to cook meat. Later in life, she began to eat fish, and she made the best fish curry (page 198) I ever had. We also savored her fragrant shrimp and egg curries.

The Ceylonese (or Sri Lankan) Tamils are another important South Asian community. My sister-in-law Mala and her family are of Ceylonese ancestry. She has become a strict vegetarian and introduced me to many fiery Ceylonese-style dishes. On one of our visits to their home, she served as hors d'oeuvres a dry mushroom curry and a spicy tofu curry (page 233) smothered in a sauce made from tomato paste and dried red chilies. Both dishes had meaty tastes and textures. I also remember having delicious Ceylonese stir-fried Chinese mustard greens and cabbage, spicy chicken *varuval*, and fish curries at my friend Vasantha Kandiah's home. Their flavors were quite different from Ma's. Other famous Ceylonese contributions are both breakfast dishes—hoppers and *putu mayam* (stringhoppers or *iddiappam*). Hoppers are made with rice flour, coconut milk, and at times even with fermented palm toddy. They have a soft, spongy, well-risen center, and golden brown, crisp edges. Cha, my father, would bring hoppers as a treat for Sunday brunch, and we would eat them piping hot, topped with brown sugar, fish curry, or hot sambal. *Putu mayam* are circular pieces of extruded steamed vermicelli-like rice noodles, typically served with a coconut-milk-and-curry-based thick soup called *sothi* (page 77), or topped with grated coconut and brown sugar.

The flavors of Malaysian Indian dishes have evolved over time as they took ingredients from Malay and Chinese cooking. Ma's lamb *kurma* (page 282), black peppercorn chicken (page 170), spicy fried fish (page 206), spicy egg curry (page 172), mutton *peratil* (page 185), and stir-fried cabbage (page 226) all have unique Malaysian flavors.

While North Indians represent only a small percentage of the Malaysian Indian community, their cuisine has become popular. Many upscale North Indian restaurants have emerged through the years, and their breads and tandooris are now also prepared at Mamak cafes and some South Indian outlets. All Malaysians enjoy their breads, such as naan, *chapatti*, *puri*, and *parathas*. Garam masala ('hot' spice), yogurt, and nuts are added to their meat dishes, which are rich and fragrant but milder than South Indian dishes. Popular dishes are tandoori chicken, chicken *korma*, *tikka masala*, shrimp *masala*, chicken *makhani*, lamb *vindaloo*, *saag ghosht*, and chickpea, cauliflower, and potato curries.

Malaysian Communities of Mixed Heritage and Special Interest

Because of Malaysia's pluralistic society, it is only natural that the people of Malaysia blend culturally and intermarry. Many of these groups have had a substantial impact on the food and eating habits of Malaysia. They include the Straits Chinese or Chinese Peranakans, also referred to as Baba-Nonyas (Chinese-Malay); Kristangs (Cristangs) or Cristaos (Portuguese-Malay) and other Eurasians; the Chittys or Indian Peranakans (Indian-Malay); the Mamaks (Indian Muslim-Malay); the Sam-Sam (Thai-Malay); and the Chinese communities of Kelantan and Kuala Terengganu, referred to as Cina Kampung (Village Chinese) and Cina Bandar (Town Chinese).

The Straits Chinese or Chinese Peranakans—the Baba-Nonyas

The Straits Chinese or Peranakan Chinese, also known as Nonyas (or Nyonyas) for women and Baba for men, is a well-known mixed heritage community in Malacca. *Peranakan*, a Malay word derived from *anak* ("child"), literally means "to give birth to a child," but its most accepted meaning is "locally born." Chinese traders established the community during the Malacca Sultanate (1402-1511). At that time, an imperial edict by the Chinese emperor limited the ability of women to leave China, so many Chinese men married local Malay women and Malay influences were incorporated into the Peranakan way of life. During the same period, the Ming emperor of China sent one of his daughters to marry the Malacca ruler. She was accompanied by five hundred female attendants who married local men, and this further extended the Chinese Peranakan community. While the majority of the Straits Chinese live in Malacca, many also settled in Penang and Singapore, and smaller groups in Kedah, Kelantan, and Patani (in Thailand), while others assimilated into other cultures.

Most Chinese Peranakans practice the religions of their Chinese ancestors and are Taoists or Buddhists, while some are Christians. They converse in Malay and English. The Baba Malay language, a combination of Malay and the Hokkien Chinese dialect, was once widely spoken by the Straits Chinese community, but is near extinction today. The Chinese Peranakan's dress and cuisine have been greatly influenced by Malay culture. Babas traditionally dress in Chinese-style buttoned tunics and loose trousers and Mandarin gowns. Nonyas wear Malay-style embroidered blouses called *sulam* (*kebaya* in Malay), batik sarongs, and beaded slippers.

Nonyas in batik sarongs and *sulam*

A unique fusion of Chinese, Malay, and other local flavors, Nonya cuisine has become extremely popular. Nonya foods have a stronger dose of spices than traditional Chinese dishes. The Chinese wok and Indian claypot are the primary cooking utensils. Like Malay food, it uses abundant amounts of chilies, even the fiery *cili padi*, lemongrass, fragrant rhizomes, pandan leaf, tamarind juice, and dried shrimp paste called *belacan*. Nonyas also have their versions of a number of Malay and Indian Muslim dishes, such as *nasi lemak* (coconut-infused rice, page 117), *rojak* (spicy salad, page 94), *nasi kuning* (yellow rice, page 118), *ikan assam rebus* (spicy sour fish, page 205), *nasi ulam* (herb rice, page 125), and the aromatic *sambals*.

Unlike the Malays, Nonyas do not have a religious prohibition against pork. Nonyas follow the Chinese practice of cooking with all parts of the chicken, pig, and cow, including stomach, feet, skin, and liver, to make wonderful soups, stews, stir-fried vegetables, and braised and steamed meat dishes. The Nonyas also prepare unique curries combining Malay, Indian, and Chinese ingredients—spices, fragrant roots, coconut milk, *kasturi* limes or tamarind juice, soy sauce, and *taucheo*.

Nonya cuisine developed where the Chinese assimilated, specifically Malacca and Penang. Thus arose two flavor traditions, Malacca Nonya with Kristang and Indonesian influences (being in close proximity to Sumatra), and Penang Nonya, with Thai influences (being near Thailand). Malacca Nonya cuisine is sweet and mildly spicy, with coconut milk, candlenuts, *belacan*, and *taucheo*, while Penang Nonya cuisine features tangy and spicier notes using tamarind juice, lime leaves, fiery chilies, ginger flower (*bunga kantan*), and black shrimp paste (*hae ko*).

The fragrant spicy noodle broths called *laksas* are unique to Nonya cuisine. *Laksa* has traveled to other states and taken on the local flavors. The two favorite Nonya *laksas* are Penang *assam laksa* (page 153), which contains thick rice noodles served in a tangy fish broth flavored with herbs, and the Malacca *laksa lemak* (page 151), wheat noodles served in a rich coconut milk and herb broth.

The Nonyas are also famous for their desserts and cakes, a legacy from their Malay ancestors. *Gula Melaka* (palm sugar), coconut milk, and pandan leaf are dominant flavorings with glutinous rice, tapioca, and sago pearl-based cakes. My favorites are *sagu gula Melaka* (page 252) with chilled pearls of sago drenched in a rich, addictive sauce of coconut milk, pandan leaf, and *gula Melaka*; and *kueh dadar*, a pandan-flavored crepe with sweet coconut filling (page 250).

Nonya festivals reflect their Chinese ancestry and they celebrate a number of Chinese holidays, including Chinese New Year, *Cheng Beng* (homage to ancestors), and Mooncake Festival. Nonya foods, like the Chinese, symbolize long life, happiness, and prosperity. Pork *pong teh* (stewed pork, page 188), *nasi lemak* (coconut-infused rice, page 117), *ayam sioh* (tamarind coriander chicken, page 164), chicken curry (page 171), or *sambal belacan* (page 101) served during these festivals blend Chinese and Malay ingredients.

The Kristangs and Other Eurasian Communities

The Portuguese community or Gente Kristangs of Malacca trace their origins to the sixteenth century, when Portuguese colonists settled in Malacca and married local Malay or Nonya women. The current Portuguese settlement was built in the 1930s, about one kilometer south of the town, in a coastal area formerly known as Ujang Pasir. About two thousand persons of Portuguese descent now live there. Though they acquired many aspects of Malay culture, they remain staunch Catholics (their name *Kristang* or *Cristang* means "Christian"). In addition to Malay, they speak Papia Kristang or Cristao, an archaic form of Portuguese with Malay grammar. The term Kristang has come to mean not only their language, but also the Portuguese descendants themselves, their culture, and traditions. The Kristang settlement has food stalls that offer a unique Portuguese-Malay cuisine, as well as a cultural center that features Kristang dance, music, and cultural events.

Kristang celebration

Many of the dishes from Portugal and its colonies around the world were brought to Malacca and adapted to the local tastes. They are *debal* (devil's) curry (page 289), a Portuguese legacy; *vindaloo* (hot and tangy curry, page 169) from Goa; pork stew with kidney beans, based on the *feijoada* from Brazil; *mohlyu*, a seafood dish prepared in spicy coconut milk curry, from Kerala; and *arroz gordu*, a seasoned gumbo rice from Macau. The Portuguese who settled in Malacca easily adapted their cooking with local *rempah* (spices) and cooking techniques.

Kristang food is Portuguese cooking transformed with Malay, Indian, and Chinese ingredients. Like their European ancestors, they have stews, soups, grilled and baked items, potatoes, and bread, but these assimilated local flavors and became totally different from their motherland cuisine. The Kristangs developed many dishes with Chinese influence, including soups, stir-fries, rice porridges, noodles, tofu, and seasoned pan-fried meats. Since they live in close proximity to the Nonyas (and many intermarried with them), they have many similar dishes. For example, *ayam kari Kapitan* (Captain's chicken curry, page 162) is renowned as both a Nonya and Kristang dish. Others are *ikan chuan-chuan* (fish with preserved soybeans, chilies, and vinegar, page 212), *ambilar kacang* (tangy long beans curry), and *chapchye* (mixed vegetables with vermicelli or mung bean noodles).

Because the Kristangs are traditionally fishermen by trade, recipes are generally seafood-based. For example, the classic Portuguese baked fish (*pesca assa*, page 207) combines the traditional Portuguese love for baked fresh fish with a dash of local spices and ingredients. Other popular seafood preparations include spicy fish stews, fried fish, stuffed fish, and pickled fish, also known as *escabeche* in other parts of the world.

For Kristangs, white rice signifies blessings for the home and is served at most meals, either plain or flavored. One signature rice dish is sweet and savory tomato rice (*nasi tomato*, page 119), combining flavor elements from the Portuguese, Indians, and Chinese. The Portuguese brought the tomato to Malaysia, and it is used in many dishes to balance fiery chilies and savory spices. Pork *cari feng* (minced pork curry), chicken *vindaloo* (page 169), *daging kicap* (soy sauce beef), *daging semur* (stewed beef, page 180), and *satay daging goreng* (fried beef *satay*, page 178) are some popular Kristang dishes. Kristangs love the simple fiery condiments (*sambals* and pickles or *acars*, Chapter 3) made from *cincalok* or *belacan* (dried fermented paste of tiny shrimp or krill), salted fish, sour fruits (green mango or *belimbing*), Worcestershire sauce, vinegar, lime juice, chilies, *taucheo*, and soy sauce.

The Portuguese also brought with them their love of cakes, custards, and sweets, prepared with eggs, sugar, flour, tapioca or sago, pandan juice, and coconut milk. Some of the most popular desserts in Malaysia are Portuguese in origin. Pineapple tarts (*kueh tat*, page 254), pastry filled with crushed spiced pineapple, is their most important contribution. All Malaysians prepare them for their festive occasions. Another favorite is semolina cake, or *sugee* cake, made with almonds, vanilla, and lemon rind.

Kristangs are one group of Eurasians in Malaysia, but there are others as well, Europeans who intermarried with locals. Today, Eurasians are a small ethnic minority and many have emigrated overseas. Eurasians from the Dutch settlers in Malacca are difficult to identify as a group because they have moved to larger cities and towns and blended in with other communities. The Dutch in Malacca brought with them not only European cooking traditions but flavors found in their Sri Lankan and Indonesian colonies. Dutch Eurasian beef stew called *semur* or *smoore* (page 180) requires slow-cooking beef with vinegar, sweet soy sauce, potatoes, coriander, black peppercorns, and cinnamon, garnished with fried onion. Kristangs also have their own version of *semur*, prepared with Worcestershire sauce, vinegar, red wine, and sweet spices, and served at Christmas with bread and *sambal belacan*.

Most of my Eurasian neighbors were descendents of the Portuguese or English. Eurasians generally employ long-simmering stewing techniques with meat and fresh seafood, adding potatoes, yams, carrots, and breadcrumbs with some light seasoning. My neighbors cooked British pies, pot roasts, Salisbury steak, and lamb chops, but they also flavored them with soy sauce, oyster sauce, mushrooms, and sweet spices to create interesting new flavors, including stir-fried vegetables with preserved soybeans or rice vermicelli with curried meatballs served with soy-sauce-based chile dips.

Another English legacy is English afternoon tea, a daily ritual for Malaysians, whether at home, in hotel cafes, or restaurants. My favorite teatimes were at home when Ma served curry puffs (page 57), pineapple tarts (page 254), cakes, and sandwiches with cucumber, sardine, or *sambal* shrimp (page 204). A few years ago on a trip to Sandakan, Sabah, I had a wonderful "high tea" with scones and clotted cream, samosas, sandwiches, and pastries at a colonial English tea house set in a beautiful garden atop a hill nearby the home of the American writer Agnes Keith.

The Peranakan Indians—the Chittys

The Chittys of Malacca, also referred to as Peranakan Indians (not to be confused with the Chettiars, the South Indian moneylending caste), are a staunchly Hindu Indian community celebrating all the Hindu festivals, such as Deepavali, Thaipusam, and Pongal, with foods reflecting their mixed heritage. Otherwise they are completely Malay in socio-cultural terms, such as language (they speak Malay and English but have no knowledge of Tamil), dress, and cultural practices. In physical appearance Chittys are nearly identical to Malays. The generally accepted origin theory of the Chittys (which means "merchant" in Tamil) holds that they are descendants of traders from Tamil Nadu, Southern India, who were frequent visitors to Malacca during the Malacca Sultanate. They kept their Hindu faith, but eventually their children lost the language of their Indian ancestors and instead speak Malay, the language of their mothers. The Chittys assimilated into the Malay culture, yet have Indian names and practice their own Hindu traditions and rites. Chittys also place importance on paying respects to their ancestors and have some annual ancestral celebrations. A few of them also intermarried with the Nonyas.

Chitty Vinayagar temple, Malacca

On a recent visit to Malaysia, I stopped by their community, Kampung Tujah, located at

Jalan Gajah Berang in Malacca, where I also visited their temple and museum. The caretaker of the museum, Kathia Devi, was hospitable and friendly, dressed in a sarong and *kebaya panjang*. She explained to me their history and culture, and was excited for the world to learn about their diminishing community. Their temple, Sri Poyyatha Vinayagar Moorthi Temple, located on Jalan Tokong (Temple Street), is the oldest functioning Hindu temple in Malaysia. The Hindu community of Malacca built the simple pinkish colored temple in the 1780s to honor Lord Ganesha.

My friend Radha, a Chitty from Malacca, explained some of the important festivals celebrated by her community (Chapter 11). During Parchu, which follows the Chinese and Nonya tradition of paying homage to departed family members through elaborate ceremonies, special Indian- and Malay-inspired foods are served on banana leaves (a traditional Hindu style of eating). My two favorites are their *sambal ikan bilis* (an original Malay specialty, page 103) and *nasi kemuli* or *kembuli* (a Malay-style festive rice, page 120).

Chittys celebrate another festival called Sadangku, the fertility celebration of a girl's coming of age, also celebrated by Tamils (with similar name). Foods play a significant role in this ceremony, in which girls dress in Malay attire and get blessings from the community elders. The foods served have flavors from Malay and Indian cultures, and include ghee rice (page 121), lamb curry, chicken curry (page 171), *ikan lauk pindang* (fish boiled in tamarind juice), cabbage in coconut milk (page 290), and the essential *putu*, an Indian steamed rice flour dish served with brown sugar and grated coconut.

The Indian Muslims—the Mamaks

The Indian Muslims, or Mamaks as they are sometimes called, are an important community in Malaysia. Generally they are descendants of South Asian Muslims from India or Pakistan, who mostly settled in Penang, Kedah, Perlis, Selangor, Malacca, and Johor. Most are of Tamil descent, from the Malabar Coast and the Coromandel Coast, with smaller groups from Gujarat, Bengal, and Bombay. Like the Arab traders, many had a nomadic history of trading along the coasts of Indonesia and Malaysia, ultimately settling and marrying local Malays. These intermarriages usually occurred between an Indian man and a Malay woman. They arrived in Malaya as early as the tenth century from Samudera (now called Aceh) in Sumatra, and continued to immigrate through the twentieth century.

The Mamaks in Malaysia seem to partake of two ethnic worlds, including participation in the institutions and activities of both Indian and Malay communities, such as Malay and Indian chambers of commerce, as well as multi-ethnic Muslim organizations. They often keep close cultural ties to India and speak Tamil fluently. Many have assimi-

Mamak street vendor, Penang

lated into the Malay Muslim communities. Malays, who saw the Indian Muslims as different from the Hindu-Tamil population, coined the term "Mamak" ("maternal uncle" in Tamil). While some perceive the term Mamak as derogatory, it is generally agreed that the term is derived from a general usage for "uncle," and is translated as "my respected friend."

The Jawi Peranakans were an elite group of Indian Muslims in Malaysia who were separately identified in the British census statistics in the mid-nineteenth century. (*Jawi* is an Arabic word used to identify the Malay Archipelago, including Malaysia and Indonesia.) The Jawi Peranakans settled throughout Malaysia, primarily in Penang. These Jawi Peranakan chose their spouses carefully, seeking mates with wealth and status, particularly from prosperous families of Muslim communities and Malay royalty. Although Jawi Peranakan sought to adopt the Malay culture, they maintained a distinct identity. Today, however, most of them identify themselves as Malays. Their cuisine has dishes similar to the Indian Muslim and Malay communities of Malaysia.

Mamaks have become successful businesspersons (shipping, importing, and baking) and politicians. They specialize in the food business and own grocery stores, restaurants, and eateries all over Malaysia, and are also great "street chefs" who work from street stalls and *kedai kopi* (coffee shops). Today, trendy Mamak cafes in urban centers are thronged with people of all ages and ethnic groups. Malays enjoy Mamak food because it is "*halal*" or permissible under Islamic law.

Mamaks are versatile chefs who combine Malay, Chinese, and Indian ingredients and cooking styles to create many quintessential Malaysian dishes. A standard Mamak food stall's menu offers *teh tarik* (sweet milk-based frothy tea, page 262) and different varieties of *roti canai. Roti canai* (which is similar to the Indian bread called *paratha*) is their signature dish. This fluffy, crispy, and flaky layered bread is cooked on a flat-iron skillet with lots of oil or ghee. *Roti canai* is frequently served with dhal, fish or chicken curries, or *kurmas. Roti bom* is a buttery version, while *roti tisu* is a paper-thin version. Their most famous *roti* is *murtabak*, my father's favorite, which is layered *roti* filled with seasoned ground mutton, egg, and onions.

My favorite Mamak fare are the all-popular *mee goreng* (fried noodles sometimes called *Mamak mee*, page 136) and *mee rebus* (aromatic spicy noodles, page 142), also Ma's favorite take-out. *Mee goreng* is best eaten hot off the wok. When my brother Sathee taught English at the University of Malaya, he would treat us to meals at the University Club, where we ordered heaping servings of Indian *mee goreng*. The Club was reminiscent of the British Colonial era, with rattan tables and chairs set outdoors under a verandah, and madly spinning ceiling fans to chase away the tropical heat. We always requested side dishes of sliced *cili padi*, fresh, fiery-hot bird peppers served in soy sauce. My husband Bob would pile on the *cili padi* and eat the *mee goreng* till his face turned fire engine red! I honestly think this was an excuse for him to quaff down large quantities of ice-cold Malaysian beer, which he claimed he needed to put out the fire.

Mamak curries have Arab, Malay, and South Indian origins, resulting in unique tastes. For example, fish head curry and chicken *kurma* (page 168) use Indian spices and Malay flavorings as well. Mamak fragrant rice dishes include *nasi biryani* (page 280), *nasi minyak* (ghee rice, page 121), *nasi kuning* (yellow rice, page 118), *nasi bukhari* (festive rice, page 278), or *nasi tomato* (page 119). In Penang, Mamak foods abound because of the large Indian Muslim population. *Nasi kandar* is a Mamak meal similar to *nasi campur* ("mixed" rice) that is popular with lunch crowds. Cooked white rice is accompanied by an assortment of dishes, including mutton *peratil* (dry-curried goat or lamb meat, page 185), *nasi minyak* (ghee rice, page 121), *cili sotong* (chile squid, page 211), *dalcha* (meat-flavored dhal, page 285), and *rasam* (spicy sour tomato soup, page 76).

Ethnic Minorities on the Thai-Malaysian Border

Modern Malaysia reflects the historically close social relationship between Thais and Malaysians. Up till the British Colonial era and the ultimate consolidation of the Thai-Malaysian border in 1911 and 1949, the borders were relatively fluid. Malay sultans in Patani, Kelantan, Terengganu, and Kedah governed their people with a great degree of autonomy, and under the suzerainty of Siamese (Thai) kingdoms, which left social and economic commerce relatively unencumbered by the modern concepts of international borders. Ethnic Thais now make up 1 percent of the population of Kelantan. The village of Tumpat in Kelantan has over two hundred Thai Buddhist temples. The Thai dialect they speak, *Tak Bai*, is distinct from the national Thai language and strongly influenced by Malay.

The Sam-Sam (referring to the offspring of Thai Buddhists and Malay Muslims) live on both sides of the western Thai-Malaysian border, in Kedah and Perlis, and the Thai state of Satun. They adopted Islam and speak a Thai and Malay Creole. Today, despite the formalities of national borders, cross-border relations continue, resulting in a significant Thai influence on the culture and cuisine of Northern Malaysia, particularly in Kelantan, Kedah, Terengganu, Perlis, and Langkawi.

The original Thai-style restaurants that appeared during the early 1980s in my hometown, Petaling Jaya, served a milder Chinese-style cuisine. But in later years, Malays from Kelantan in the northeast and southern Thailand started *tom yam* stalls which spread throughout Malaysia. Spicy Thai-Kelantanese flavors characterize popular dishes, such as *sup tom yam* (hot and sour soup, page 80), chicken *padprik* (with fiery chilies and lime leaves), *nasi goreng kampung* (spicy fried rice, village-style), *nasi Pattaya* (chicken fried rice wrapped in an omelet), and *nasi lala* (oyster fried rice).

Cina Kampung (Village Chinese) in Northeast Malaysia

Scattered throughout the rural areas of Kelantan and Terengganu are small Chinese villages called *Cina Kampung*. The first Chinese settlers came to Terengganu and Kelantan during the fifteenth century A.D and some of them were the orthodox Muslims from the Yunnan province, who assimilated into the Malay culture. Others came from Fujian Province in China.

The Cina Kampung ancestors settled and farmed lands that were originally empty, but are now surrounded by Malay neighbors. In fact, a visitor to Cina Kampung could mistake the Chinese residents there for Malays, because their way of life is so similar. They speak Malay, occasionally interspersed with Thai and Hokkien words. They have maintained their Buddhist religion and rarely married outside their communities, but many of the Cina Kampung residents have taken Malay names. Thai and Malay flavorings such as lemongrass, Thai basil, Kaffir lime leaf, galangal, and *budu* (anchovy sauce) have influenced the cooking of Cina Kampung .

Malaysian Food and Flavors

When, Where, and How We Eat

A visitor to Malaysia will find delicious food everywhere and in every type of venue. Visit Malaysia's modern capital, Kuala Lumpur, and dine at a four-star restaurant, or munch on curry puffs at an Irish-style pub. Cross the causeway from Singapore to a bustling night market (*pasar malam*) in Johor Bahru and dine alfresco under the twinkling sky; or enjoy chile crab at a *makanan laut* (Chinese seafood restaurant) in Klang, my birthplace. In Penang, enjoy a late breakfast of *roti canai* and fish curry from a Mamak vendor after a walk around the historic town; or in Ipoh, have a hearty lunch of *char kway teow* from a Chinese coffee shop (*kedai kopi* or *kopitiam*). While eating places abound in Malaysia, if you ask any Malaysian for his or her favorite spot for food, they will surely identify their favorite hawker—a skilled chef who will serve you sumptuous cuisine on a banana leaf, in a bowl, on a plastic plate, or wrapped in paper to go.

Food Hawkers, Our Street Chefs

The ubiquitous food hawker is the greatest symbol of our shared passion for food and the cultural blending that has created Malaysia's wonderful cuisine. Malaysia is a hawkers' paradise. They are everywhere, selling prepared foods, fruits, snacks, and beverages from pushcarts and stalls, at roadside corners, street alleys, near offices or hotels, or in front of coffee shops. Hawkers are our culinary gems, and growing up, these kitchens-on-wheels were our "restaurants." For any visitor, a hawker's meal provides the essence of Malaysian cuisine.

When I was very young, mobile hawkers sold their goodies door-to-door. Some pushed carts while others traveled by bicycle. They carried their wares over their shoulders, on a pole with two baskets balanced on either side, or pushed in mobile carts. The hawkers came right to our front porch! The *satay* man carried a makeshift stove and grilled our *satay* just for us. When he finished, we handed him our plates to fill with succulent sticks of barbecued chicken, with sides of the *kuah kacang* (spicy peanut sauce, page 66), *ketupat* (a type of compressed white rice, page 281), and slices of cool cucumbers.

While some hawkers traveled around selling their wares, others set up in one particular spot every day, alongside shops, in alleyways, near temples, offices, or small hotels. They displayed their cooked dishes in aluminum trays covered with clear plastic for customers to view. Some would set out small wooden or plastic stools beside their cart, or you could just stand around the cart and enjoy your meal.

These mobile hawkers typically specialize in one particular kind of cuisine or dish. For example, on a busy street, a Malay woman in a *tudong* (headscarf) would display delicious colorful Malay *kuehs* (miniature cakes) on her cart in glass cases. On the corner, you could find an old Chinese man selling steamed chicken rice (*nasi ayam*, page 126), while an Indian hawker stood nearby, displaying containers of colorful, chilled beverages such as lemonade, rose syrup, or lychee juice.

Durian vendor, Kuantan

When you visit Malaysia, make sure you go to a "hawker center," which is an outdoor version of the "food courts" found in most shopping malls. When you order hawker-style Malaysian food you are not limited to any one ethnic cuisine. You can have Malay grilled meat (*satay*, page 65) followed with Nonya-style fried rice (*nasi goreng*, page 123), Chinese broccoli with *taucheo* sauce (page 222), and end it with a shaved ice dessert (*ais kacang* also called *air batu campur*, page 246).

Our family loved eating alfresco-style at the hawkers' center in "Old Town" in our hometown of Petaling Jaya ("P.J."). Today's diners may look for ambience, presentation, and style when eating out, but the food was always the main attraction for us. In the evening, you could eat in the warm glow of lightbulbs strung around the stalls and in the branches of the stately banyan trees that sheltered our wooden benches and chairs. Each of the Old Town stalls displayed a simple sign listing their specialties. Hawker food was always freshly prepared right in front of you, such as *char kway teow* (page 139) sizzling in a cast iron wok, or *roti canai* dough thrown in the air. On other occasions, we would sit at our table and each of the hawkers would come and ask us if we wanted to order from them. It was truly a culinary experience, sitting under the twinkling stars and eating freshly prepared foods. You could also order food to go, called *bungkus* in Malay or *ta pau* in Chinese.

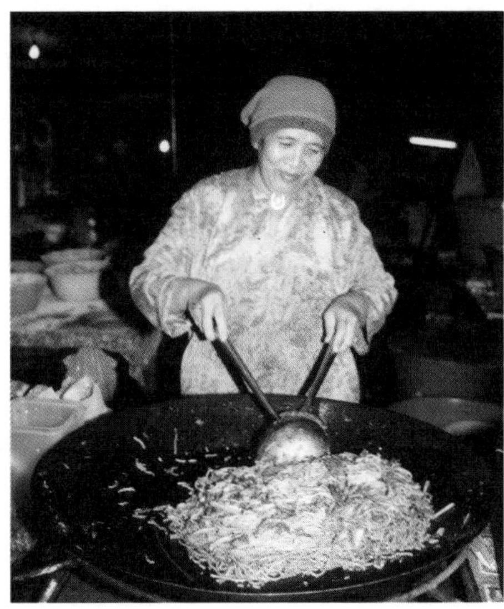

Malay hawker stir-frying noodles, Kota Bahru

Another dining option is found at *pasar malam*, open-air night markets that feature clothing, mats, kitchenware, CDs, toys, and other knick-knacks, as well as cooked food and beverages, fresh vegetables, fruits, meats, and chicken. This is where many locals shop. It is great to walk around and taste some of the local delicacies. Because each state has its specialty foods, I always make it a point to go to a *pasar malam* whenever I travel around Malaysia. These are fun places to sample authentically prepared local fare, and at the same time shop for inexpensive items for your kitchen or home.

While the days of hawkers coming to your doorstep are long gone, many still cart their goodies in tourist and work areas. Gas-fired grills are quickly replacing charcoal grills. In larger cities and their suburbs, many hawkers are confined to certain areas of the city or government-sponsored hawkers' centers. In addition, many office cafeterias and shopping malls have air-conditioned, modern food courts. With kitchens and preparation areas, these are more elaborate than the traditional hawkers' stalls, but still pay homage to this classic Malaysian way of dining.

Coffee Shops, Restoran, Mamak Cafés, and Nasi Campur Stalls

In addition to hawker stalls, we also loved coffee shops as kids. Known as *kedai kopi* or *kopi tiam* (as the Chinese Hokkiens call them), these shops were frequently small and crowded, but they had indoor seating. They generally occupied the ground floor of old shophouses. They were open throughout the day till late at night. Some had round marble tabletops and wooden chairs set beneath large overhead fans. In those days, many people went to coffee shops to socialize over a cup of thick black coffee with sugar (called *kopi-o*) or sweetened tea with condensed milk, and a snack. And many, like us, went there for a meal. Various coffee shops had their specialty items, including *dim sum*, *nasi goreng* (fried rice, page 123), *chee cheong fan* (steamed rice noodle rolls and stuffed vegetables in a broth), or *bakuteh* (pork rib soup, page 87).

There were also clubs and pubs where you can have a taste of the Western cuisine with local touches, prepared by Chinese and Indian chefs.

The legendary Coliseum Café, Kuala Lumpur's original dining spot for Western foods, was my father's (Cha) favorite haunt. Built in 1921, it was one of Malaysia's first modern restaurants and a popular watering hole for colonial planters, miners, and traders. Cha, for a change, enjoyed their chicken in gravy with peas, carrots, and corn; breaded pork chops; thinly sliced steak or lamb cooked with black pepper and soy sauce (page 181); and their toasted sandwiches. During my youth, we did our shopping in the same neighborhood and if we were lucky, Cha would take us for lunch or dinner at the Coliseum Café. Whenever I visit it, I am always transported to another era, "watching author Somerset Maugham at the bar, having his cold beer, and chatting with his fellow colonials."

While the Coliseum Café was one of Malaysia's first modern hotel-style restaurants, slowly restaurants (called *restoran* or *kedai makanan*) with larger indoor kitchens capable of serving more elaborate meals began to replace the hawker stalls and coffee shops. In large cities and around colleges, Mamak cafes have sprung up, replacing many of the old Chinese coffee shops. These are trendy air-conditioned places, open 24 hours a day, serving inexpensive snacks and meals. "Mamaking" (like pubbing or going to bars, except without alcohol) has become a way of life with students and young adults, who come to socialize or have a cup of coffee or *teh tarik* (page 262), Malaysia's cappuccino and snack on curry puffs, *roti canai*, or other snacks.

Nasi campur, *nasi kandar*, or *chap chai peng*

The Coliseum Café was divided into two sections. As you entered, to the left was the bar room, which traditionally served as a social club for Malaysian men after work. (Even today many private clubs, such as the Royal Selangor Club, still prohibit women from sitting at the bar with men). At the bar, their signature snack was crispy fried *ikan bilis* (baby anchovies), seasoned with chilies, onion, and lime. Besides the bar, the room offered tables with bamboo chairs for relaxing and enjoying a drink or a snack of curry puffs or sandwiches. The Coliseum's other room was for seated diners, mainly families and office workers, who came to enjoy Western-style food, a change from their regular meals. The Chinese chefs have infused western dishes with local flavor. The Coliseum also held *dansants* (tea dances) every Wednesday evening during its early days.

Today the Coliseum has replaced the swinging saloon-style door that I recall (to keep the modern air-conditioning in and the traffic fumes out), but its décor remains largely unchanged. Its antique furniture and worn table settings still beckon those with nostalgia for colonial times. It has become a favorite with the locals, who come for its seasoned steak sizzlers, baked crabmeat, and caramel custard pudding. Through the years, they have added *nasi goreng* (less spicy and without *belacan*), *char kway teow*, *mee goreng*, and other local Chinese favorites. Many of the dishes are still cooked over charcoal and firewood stoves.

restaurants ("mixed rice" outlets, serving cooked rice with accompanying meats, fish, or vegetables) are popular with office workers at lunchtime. Customers choose their dishes, which are then brought to their table with a big mound of cooked white rice, yellow-tinted rice (*nasi kuning*, page 118), or coconut-infused Malay-style rice (*nasi lemak*, page 117). Alternately, the food can be packed to go, priced according to weight. Seafood restaurants, called *makanan laut*, are found all over Malaysia. They specialize in Chinese-style dishes that feature shrimp, squid, fish, and crab, served with chile-based dips and toppings.

The Coliseum Café, Kuala Lumpur

The Typical Malaysian Meal Day

Breakfast in Malaysia is not the light or sweet affair of American breakfast foods, such as cereals and pastries. Rather, Malaysian breakfasts are savory. *Nasi lemak* (page 117) and *roti canai* served with dhal curry (page 231) or fish curry (page 198) are favorite breakfast meals. My husband Bob and daughter Geeta are both hooked on *roti canai,* while I enjoy *nasi lemak*. Bob, usually a late riser during holidays, never fails to slip out early in the morning for a quick trip to the local Mamak café, and if we are lucky, will bundle a few back to the house!

Ma's favorite breakfast—*thosai* (or *dosai*, page 69)—was served with *sambar* (page 88) and coconut chutney as a special Sunday treat for us when Periama (Grandma) was home. Another Chinese breakfast favorite growing up was *chee cheong fan* (steamed rice flour noodle rolls) topped with spicy, savory, and sweet sauces. And then some lucky Saturdays, we had *paus* (steamed Chinese buns) with roast pork (*char siew*) and sweet bean paste. Obtaining *paus* required a fifteen minute ride to the bus station terminal in Petaling Jaya. The Chinese hawker opened a couple of wooden baskets to get the *paus.* As he opened the baskets, steam gushed out into the crowded bus station. He placed the freshly steamed *paus* on plain plastic, wrapped them in newspaper, and tied them with string. We would have these with our coffee or tea for a late breakfast. The *paus* were soft and moist and the savory pork filling tasted divine. Ma enjoyed sweet *paus* as she did not eat pork.

Working Malaysians often spend a leisurely lunchtime enjoying their meal outside the home. *Nasi campur* or *nasi kandar*-style meals—cooked white and yellow rice served with several accompaniments—are served in restaurants or by hawkers. A steaming plate

In Malaysia there are many American 7-11 convenience stores. One morning, Bob had a hankering for a donut and stopped by one. The stores are set up just like their U.S. counterparts, down to the coffee machines and nearby donut case. Bob picked out a large pastry assuming it was filled with cream or jelly. As we drove off, he took a sip of his tea, followed by a large bite of his pastry. His eyes widened with surprise at the unexpected taste. He looked down at the pastry to find it was filled with tiny fish (*ikan bilis*) swimming in a spicy *sambal* sauce, not the confectionary he was expecting!

of noodles, including *mee goreng* (page 136) or *char kway teow* (page 139), or a bowl of *kari mee* (page 149) or *laksa lemak* (page 151) are common lunch items.

Malaysian teatime, which goes from late afternoon till 6 p.m., means piping hot *teh* (tea brewed with condensed milk) or *teh tarik* ("pulled tea" blended with condensed milk, page 262). Teatime also calls for a variety of Nonya or Malay cakes (*kuehs* or *kueh-kueh*, Chapter 10), made with glutinous rice, pandan juice, and palm sugar, Western-style cakes, cookies, savory snacks, and fresh cut fruits. A bowl of *rojak* (spicy fruit and vegetable salad with peanuts and tamarind sauce, page 94), *goreng pisang manis* (fried sweet banana fritters, page 67), curry puffs (page 57), and *samosas* (filled with vegetables, potatoes, or meat) are also served.

Dinners, usually centered on rice or noodles, can be festive affairs. Soups and appetizers may start the feasting. They are followed by entrees and side dishes that vary by ethnic preference, but often include fish of every possible type, chicken, meat (the choice depending on religious strictures), and a large array of greens and other vegetables. While many Western practices have arrived in Malaysia, eating dinner in front of the TV has still not quite caught on. Dinner is still a significant social event in Malaysia with family and friends gathered around the table, often sharing from communal plates or bowls that are spun around the center of the table on a lazy Susan. Despite our large and "on the go" family, we still sat down together for dinner.

Regional Cooking of Malaysia

In Malaysia, not only does each ethnic group have its signature dishes, but each state has its own cooking style and flavors based upon its unique history, geography, and cultural influences. The taste of chicken curry, grilled fish, *acar*, *mee goreng*, or beef *rendang* can vary from state to state. For example, in the northeastern states of Kelantan and Terengganu, where there is a strong Malay presence, chicken curry is cooked with coconut milk and fragrant roots; in Selangor state, where there is a strong Indian influence, the dish has a heavy dose of spices; and in Negeri Sembilan, which was settled by the Minangkabaus of Sumatra, the curry is fired up with bird peppers.

I will now take you on a journey through Malaysia and the states, cities, and towns that I grew up in. Their distinct foods and flavors evoke fond memories for me, and I sin-

cerely hope this culinary "tour" will inspire you to try your hand at some of the recipes that follow it.

The Cuisine of Northwestern Malaysia

The Northwest states of Malaysia include Perlis, Kedah, the island of Penang, and Perak.

Perlis

Perlis is the smallest state and is located at the northernmost part of Malaysia's west coast. Thailand is its neighbor to the north, and Kedah borders its southern and eastern regions. Perlis has beautiful stretches of green and gold *padi* fields (depending on the season), limestone hills, rustic villages, and sugarcane fields. It was originally part of the Kedah Sultanate and at times was subject to foreign rulers, including the Acehnese from Sumatra, Thais, and the British. It has had historical trade relations with India and the Middle East and with traders who traveled on the monsoon winds.

The majority of the population in Perlis is Malay and its cuisine reflects strong Malay flavors with Thai and Arab influences. Malay and Thai peoples live on both sides of Perlis's arbitrarily set border with Thailand, so hot, spicy, and sour Thai-style Malay flavors predominate. Lemongrass, Kaffir lime leaves, tamarind, fiery chilies, lime juice, and fish sauce that characterize Thai cooking are commonly used. Perlis claims to serve the best *sup tom yam* (page 80) in Malaysia. Coconut milk-based curries such as *gulai daging* or *ayam* (beef or chicken curry), *daging kurma* (beef kurma), and slow-simmered chicken *rendang* (page 287) and beef *rendang* (page 177) are popular.

Because of its proximity to the sea, Perlis has many seafood stalls and restaurants. Local favorites include deep-fried spicy *cili sotong* (chile squid, page 211), *gulai ketam* (crab curry), and grilled fish wrapped in banana leaf, called *ikan panggang*. The local *laksa* called *laksa utara* ("northern *laksa*") is made with flaked fish (generally eel) in a spicy broth with translucent rice noodles and topped with shredded cucumbers, torch ginger bud, onions, *belacan*, and herbs. Popular vegetable dishes in Perlis include stir-fried bean sprouts with cockles, *belacan*, and tamarind juice (reflecting Chinese, Indian, and Thai influences), fruit *rojak* (page 94), and *acar mangga hijau* (page 96, a spicy green mango salad similar to Thai *somtam*). There are a number of popular desserts in Perlis—*sagun* (made with toasted, desiccated coconut, sugar, and flour), *gomak* (steamed coconut and rice flour with coconut-flavored filling), and *ais kacang* (also called *air batu campur*, shaved ice topped with savory and sweet flavorings, page 246).

Kedah

Kedah is in the northwest corner of Peninsular Malaysia, neighboring Perlis, Perak, and Thailand with Pulau Langkawi, a popular beach resort, off its coast. This region attracted Indian, Chinese, Acehnese (from Sumatra), Thai, Burmese, Arab, and European traders and conquerors. Nowadays, Kedah cooking reflects its multiracial population of Malays, Chinese, Indians, Thais, and a strong Indian Muslim (Mamak) influence. Mamak stalls sell many of their specialties, *laksa Kedah*, *daging kicap* (beef in soy sauce, page 181), and Kedah-style *mee goreng* (stir-fried noodles, page 136).

Kedah is the rice bowl of Malaysia. If you drive through Kedah during the harvesting season you will see beautiful golden rice (*padi*) fields set against the green rolling hills. Rice is the staple food in Kedah, eaten with *gulais* (coconut milk-based curries) that have Indian and Malay flavors, including the spicy *udang assam pedas* (spicy shrimp, page 201). Many Kedah *gulais* are subtle and sweet, their heat balanced with sweet spices, sugar, and other ingredients, and thus less fiery than normal. Similar to Thai cooking, coconut milk, tamarind juice, spices, chilies, and sugar are added to give dishes light, tart, spicy, and sweet flavors. A favorite rice dish is *nasi ulam* (page 125), rice cooked with a variety of herbs and vegetables, and a must for Ramadan meals.

Istana Kenangan in Kedah

Pulut, glutinous rice, is a favorite snack prepared with mango, durian, jackfruit, and banana, or made into *ketupat* (compressed rice cakes). Cooks in Kedah transform noodles, introduced by Chinese immigrants and traders, into unique stir-fries, soups, and spicy broths. The well-known *laksa Kedah* has thick noodles in a spicy, tangy broth flavored with tamarind and mackerel flakes. Kedah also has a northern-style stir-fried rice vermicelli with Chinese and Thai flavorings, prepared with chile paste, *taucheo* (preserved soybean paste), fish sauce, vinegar, and soy sauce.

Kedah has a coastline and substantial rivers, so seafood features prominently in its dishes, including spicy grilled fish with tamarind dip, spicy stir-fried shrimp and squid, fish in coconut-infused curries, and barbecued fish. Seafood dishes are generally served with *ulam*, an assortment of fresh herbs and vegetables with fiery *sambal belacan* (page 101). *Kerabus*, or spicy salads (Chapter 3), are very popular. Malay desserts include *dodol* (caramel-like candies made with coconut milk and palm sugar), *bengkang* (sweet rice flour cakes), and *kueh karas*, a sweet crispy Kedah specialty.

Penang

Penang (or Pinang) includes Pulau Pinang ("island of betel nut tree"), called the "Pearl of the Orient," and the mainland port of Butterworth. The island of Penang is located off Malaysia's northwest coast. Penang's beaches, colonial buildings, English teahouses, Mamak shops, Thai, Burmese, Chinese, and Indian temples (the most famous one being the Kek Lok Si Temple, the largest Chinese Buddhist temple in Malaysia) nestled among the island's hills evoke an old-world atmosphere.

Penang's hawker cuisine is truly unique—Chinese, Indian, Nonya, Malay, and Mamak cooking styles combine with Thai and Arab influences. Signature hawker dishes that I enjoy when there are *char kway teow* (stir-fried rice noodles, page 139), *popiah* (savory spring rolls, page 70), *assam laksa* (noodles in tangy broth, page 153), *kari ayam Kapitan* (Captain's chicken curry, page 162), *inchee kaybin* (fried chicken), and *kicap ikan* (fish in soy sauce, page 199). *Kerabus* (salads, Chapter 3), seasoned with ginger flower (*bunga kantan*), bird peppers, palm sugar, and toasted grated coconut (*kerisik*), are hawker favorites.

In Penang, Chinese hawkers offer *oh chien* (oyster omelet), *lorbak* (pork sausage rolled in tofu skin), and *lok-lok* (meaning "dip dip"). *Lok-lok* is a Chinese fondue-style meal where customers place skewered seafood, vegetables, chicken, meats, and other foods in a pot of boiling stock at the center of the table. When cooked, they are dipped in a variety of sauces. Indian cuisine is widely available in Penang, especially South Indian and Indian Muslim (Mamak) dishes. One very popular Mamak meal is *nasi kandar*, rice accompanied with various curries, condiments, and fried items. Malay foods in Penang have Sumatran, Arab, Nonya, and Thai influences, some favorites being eggplant and pineapple *pajeri* (page 232), *ikan panggang* (grilled fish), *acar betik hijau* (green papaya salad, page 100), and *nasi minyak* (ghee rice, page 121).

The Chinese Peranakans (or Baba-Nonyas) of Penang are Chinese settlers (mostly Hokkiens) who married local Malay women. Though they dress and speak Malay, they practice Chinese rituals and ancestor worship, and have also adopted British ways and styles. Similar to the Malacca Chinese, their cooking is a combination of Chinese and Malay, with *belacan* (dried shrimp paste), chilies, fresh roots, and fragrant leaves. But unlike Malacca Nonya cooking, Penang Nonya dishes incorporate Thai influences and have more sour notes, from tamarind and fruits like unripe mango or *kasturi* limes. *Assam laksa* (noodles in a spicy sour broth served with a dollop of pungent shrimp paste, page 153) and *udang assam pedas* (a hot and sour tamarind-based shrimp curry, page 201) are notable creations. Like Malays, Nonyas enjoy seasoned rice—*nasi lemak* (coconut-infused rice, page 117), *nasi kuning* (yellow rice, page 118), or *nasi ulam* (herb rice, page 125).

Perak

Perak is the second largest state in Peninsular Malaysia. It borders Kedah and Thailand to the north, Kelantan and Pahang to the east, Selangor to the south, and the Straits of Malacca to the west. Pulau Pangkor is a small offshore island and a popular beach destination. Perak was part of the Hindu-Malay kingdom called Gangga Negara, founded by Merong Mahawangsa, king of Kedah (a descendant of Alexander the Great), which collapsed after an attack by King Rajendra Chola of Coromandel, South India, during the eleventh century. The Sumatran kingdom of Aceh dominated Perak for over a century, which led to significant contact with Indian and Middle Eastern traders.

Perak's rich tin mines attracted numerous Chinese immigrants, many of whom settled in Perak's capital city of Ipoh, which today is famous for its *char kway teow* (page 139). Outside Ipoh are many limestone caves that have built-in temples, a noted one being the Tokong or Sam Poh Temple, a Chinese Buddhist place of worship. Ipoh has many old-style coffee shops (*kopi tiam*) serving *kaya puff* (flaky pastries with sweet coconut egg jam filling) and *tong shui* (sweet tonic based desserts). *Tempoyak*, a preserved durian fruit prepared with chilies, is a favorite snack.

While all of the communities of Southern China are well represented in Perak, the most popular dishes are Cantonese, such as stir-fried bean sprouts (page 229), steamed chicken rubbed with salt and herbs, sweet and sour crab, and *dim sum*. Besides Cantonese recipes, there are other popular delicacies, including Hakka-style noodles with pork or chicken broth, and spicy sour *Ipoh laksa* with dried shrimp paste (*belacan*); and many Thai influenced dishes, such as pandan chicken, steamed fish with sweet chile sauce, and *tom yam* seafood soup. The curries here are tart and milder. Favorites include *assam sotong* (squid in tangy tamarind-based sauce), *ikan assam rebus* (fish in tamarind sauce, page 205), and *udang pindang* (shrimp in coconut milk). Perak offers many varieties of *rendang*, a spicy, slow-cooked coconut curry. One, called *rendang tok*, is served for festive occasions together with compressed rice called *nasi impit* (page 281).

After Cha's retirement from the National Electricity Board in Kuala Lumpur, he worked in Lumut, Perak, as an engineer for the Malayan Flour Mill for some years. It was during this period that we visited him on one of my trips home. I remember taking a ferry across to Pangkor Island, with its wooden houses on stilts, and watching the fishing boats of Lumut slowly working their way across the Straits of Malacca to Pangkor. At Pangkor, we feasted on *nasi lemak bungkus* (coconut rice wrapped in banana leaves) from a Malay hawker for a late breakfast. Then we enjoyed the cool and refreshing *ais kacang* (also called *air batu campur* or simply *ABC*, page 246), shaved ice with red beans, corn kernels, gelatin bits, and peanuts topped with condensed milk and rose syrup. I cherished the evenings when Cha came to see us and we sat on the open verandah of our beach cabana, watching the sunset and the sky turning into gorgeous colors while the locals were scurrying home along the beach. As we enjoyed this breathtaking scenery, we sipped on hot tea and feasted on *kueh dadar* (greenish pandan-flavored crepes with grated coconut filling, page 250) while watching my daughter, Geeta, play on the beach.

The Cuisine of Malaysia's Urban Hub—Selangor

Migrants from neighboring regions as well as conquerors from far-off lands came to make their fortune in the coastal state of Selangor, the "Gateway to Malaysia," and created the modern city of Kuala Lumpur. Selangor was originally one of the states settled by Minangkabaus who migrated from Sumatra, across the Straits of Malacca. Later, Buginese from Makassar, in present-day Sulawesi, came to the area, and in the eighteenth century established Selangor as an independent state, which they ruled. Today, the local Malay cuisine has Javanese, Sumatran, and Bugis origins. Indian food tends to reflect South Indian, Sri Lankan, and Indian Muslim influences, while Chinese cooking comes primarily from the Cantonese, Hokkien, Hainanese, and Hakka communities.

Klang (Kelang)

Ma grew up in Klang, which was then the seat of the Sultanate of Selangor. Her father, Thatha, an air force pilot, became the manager of a rubber plantation under the British. After her teacher's training in Klang, Ma met my father who was training to become an electrical engineer. He worked under the British and the Japanese during the occupation, and he learned to speak Japanese. I was born in Klang and attended kindergarten there. Thus, Klang holds special memories for me.

Klang was a busy port during the nineteenth century. The tin rush lured many Chinese to Selangor, and the port served as a point of entry for migrant settlers and as an export hub for the tin mining industry. Today, Klang is an old-world town with a sizeable Chinese and Indian community that is known for its seafood restaurants that serve stir-fried shrimp and crab in a variety of flavors—sweet and sour, black pepper, chile, and steamed. It is also known for its specialty herbal soup, *bakuteh* (page 87), a creation of the Hokkiens. There is a "little India" in Klang with cafes and stalls selling South Indian-inspired dishes and snacks, including the well-known banana leaf rice meal with accompaniments, aromatic *biryanis*, and *nasi campur* meals. Malay delicacies in Klang are *lontong* (compressed rice cubes) in a meat soup, *mee Bandung* (page 146), and *mee Jawa* (similar to *mee rebus*, page 142).

Petaling Jaya (PJ)

Petaling Jaya (or "PJ" as we call it), located in Selangor, was a planned city built by the British as a suburb of Kuala Lumpur for the many commuters and to solve a growing over-population problem. Originally PJ was a residential town, but through the years it grew into a booming international commercial hub as well. My teen and adult years were spent in PJ. For me it was a food haven, and I vividly remember all the hawker centers, vendors, and coffee shops we frequented for meals. PJ has all the Selangor specialties—*Hokkien mee* (page 144), *bakuteh* (page 87), *mee goreng* (page 136), *sup mee* (page 83), *satay* (page 65), *yee mee* (page 140), or *nasi ayam* (page 126). You can also find signature dishes from all over Malaysia in cosmopolitan PJ, including Johor's *mee rebus* (simmered noodles, page 142), Malacca's *laksa lemak* (noodles in spicy coconut broth, page 151), Kelantan's *sup tom yam* (page 80), Ipoh's *char kway teow* (stir-fried noodles, page 139), or Penang's *popiah* (fresh spring rolls, page 70). Western fast food chains, international restaurants, coffee bars, and Mamak cafes also cater to the young and busy adults.

Kuala Lumpur (KL)

Kuala Lumpur (or KL as locals call it), whose name means "muddy estuary," is located at the confluence of two rivers, the Sungai Lumpur and Sungai Klang. This area was first settled by Minangkabau immigrants, then by the Buginese who panned the streams for tin. Later, numerous Chinese immigrants settled here, mining for tin, and KL became a tin collecting center. In 1880 it superseded Klang as the state capital.

Today, KL is a cosmopolitan city in which skyscrapers, such as the twin Petronas Towers, share the skyline's Moorish-style architecture, including the National Mosque with its minarets and the Railway Station. Adding to KL's charm are the many colonial era buildings, such as the Tudor-style Royal Selangor Club and the Coliseum Café, which are

Kuala Lumpur post office

set alongside Hindu and Chinese temples and quaint Chinese shop houses and coffee shops.

My sisters and I went to school in KL and completed our last year of primary school at St. Theresa's Convent, a Catholic school. St. Theresa's was located on Brickfields Road, today called Jalan Tun Sambandan, where a large Indian community of Keralites, South Indian Tamils, Sri Lankan Tamils, and Indian Muslims reside. Here was Ma's favorite *mee rebus* (page 142) hawker, an Indian Muslim, located in front of our favorite movie theater, Lido cinema. Both are not there today. Brickfields Road is near the Bungsar (now called Bangsar) area, settled mostly by Sri Lankan Tamils, who worked on the railway. Today, it has become a bustling residential and commercial area and a trendy place to find gourmet food, with many restaurants serving local and international cuisine.

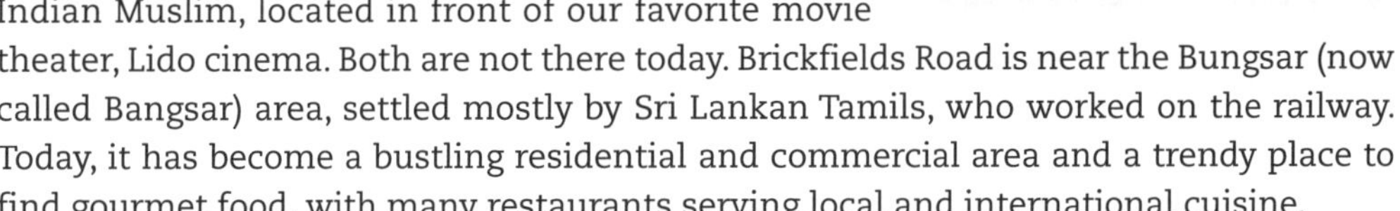

Bukit Nanas Convent, our secondary school, was tucked away on top of Pineapple Hill ("Bukit Nanas") in central KL. Down the hill from Bukit Nanas Convent School was Market Square, just east of the Klang River, which has become the commercial center for the whole town. You can find numerous hawker stalls scattered throughout Market Square. Most of them are located outdoors, but some are in the indoor shopping centers, such as Central Market. Central Market, built in 1936, was a large wet market where we often shopped for fresh ingredients. Now it has become a popular tourist center with trendy franchise outlets, handicrafts, food stalls, cafes, and smoky pubs. After shopping at Central Market nowadays, we usually dine on *nasi goreng* (fried rice, page 123), *murtabak* (egg-and-meat-layered flatbread), or pandan chicken at one of the Malay or Mamak stalls, Thai cafés, or pubs.

Chinese immigrants congregated around Market Square and south into Chinatown. To the north, across Java Street (now Jalan Tun Perak) the Malays took root, and nearby, the Indian Chettiars settled, and were joined in later years by Indian Muslim traders. Just east of the Market Square is Padang (now Merdeka) Square, which was the focal point for the British Administration, with the nearby Tudor-style Royal Selangor Club. North of Market Square is Jalan Masjid India, "little India Colony," which has many Indian and Indian Muslim clothing and accessory shops and outdoor food stalls serving snacks, sweets, and *nasi campur* for lunch.

After school, we took a fifteen-minute walk through rows of old shops housing the moneylenders (Chettiars), Indian sweet shops, and textile stores, to the bus stop on Foch Avenue (now Jalan Tun Tan Cheng Lock) in Chinatown. I remember lining up with my school friends and squeezing through the crowd (not an easy task when you are tiny!) to get onto the bus to go home. I was happy to get a seat, but many times stood all the way home, a thirty-minute bumpy ride to our home in Petaling Jaya. Nearby Foch Avenue, on Petaling Street, were dozens of stalls serving Chinese specialties. My friends and I sometimes enjoyed a lunch of *nasi ayam* (Hainanese chicken rice, page 126) or *wantan mee* after school or a weekend movie at the now-demolished Rex cinema. Also located here is the famous Hindu temple built in 1873, Sri Maha Mariamman Temple, where Ma sometimes took us. The Chinese Taoist temple, Sze Ya Temple, built in 1864 by its prominent founder, Kapitan Yap Ah Loy, is also located here.

The Cuisine of Southern Malaysia

The south of Malaysia includes Negeri Sembilan, Malacca, and Johor.

Negeri Sembilan

Negeri Sembilan is located on the southwest corner of Peninsular Malaysia. The dishes of Negeri Sembilan have strong influences from the Minangkabaus who brought Sumatran hot and spicy dishes cooked with the small-but-fiery bird peppers called *cili padi* and coconut milk. Negeri Sembilan is well known for its slow-simmered fiery and flavorful *rendangs*. Beef or chicken *rendang* (pages 177 and 287) is often served with *lemang*, seasoned glutinous rice placed in bamboo stems, lined with banana leaves, and cooked over a low fire. *Gulai kuning* (yellow coconut curry), *keladi assam pedas* (hot and sour sweet potatoes), and *acar timun nanas* (spicy cucumber pineapple salad, page 98) are local favorites.

Malay mosque

Port Dickson ("PD") in Negeri Sembilan is located on the Straits of Malacca about 37 miles from Kuala Lumpur. PD was a small fishing village named Arang, "charcoal" in Malay, so called because the village produced charcoal from a nearby carbon mine. During the 1880s, the British established Port Dickson to facilitate the transportation of ore from the tin mines of Negeri Sembilan. Over time, PD slowly declined in value as a port, and by the time we were growing up PD had become a sleepy beach town frequented on weekends by the expatriates and locals from nearby larger towns who were attracted to its ten miles of white sandy beaches, shaded by palm, coconut, and banyan trees. As children, PD was our weekend holiday resort because it was close to our home, but also because Cha (my father) loved to swim and enjoy the sea breeze.

On our way to Port Dickson we often stopped at Seremban, also in Negeri Sembilan, to enjoy the Minangkabau-influenced cuisine, or to pick up freshly cut fruits, drinks, or packets of *nasi lemak* (coconut-infused rice, page 117) with *ikan bilis sambal* (spicy baby anchovy sauce, page 103). One of the local drinks was *air jando pulang*, a beverage unique to Negeri Sembilan, made with the pulp and juice of young coconut and mixed with brown sugar.

Malacca (Melaka)

Malacca, today called Melaka, is located in the southern part of the southwestern coast of the Malaysian Peninsula, on the Straits of Malacca, facing the island of Sumatra. The state of Negeri Sembilan is to the north and Johor to the east. Malacca's cuisine is a melting pot of flavors contributed by early traders, conquerors, and immigrants.

Today, when you visit the historical district of Malacca you can wander down Jonkers Street (now called Jalan Hang Jebat), once a wealthy traders' street, and now a haven for antique collectors. The rich Peranakan heritage lives on in the original Chinese, Dutch, and British buildings that have now become shops, restaurants, and boutique hotels. Portuguese tiles adorn the interior courtyards of colonial-style restaurants, with Dutch red clay buildings bordering its bustling waterfront shophouses. At the end of Heeren and Jonker Streets is Harmony Street, now called Jalan Tokong (or Temple Street), renowned for its houses of worship, including Kampung Kling Mosque, built in 1748 for the Indian Muslim traders; Malaysia's oldest Hindu temple, Sri Poyattha Vinayagar Moorthi Temple, built in 1781 for the Chettiars and Peranakan Indians; and Cheng Hoon Temple built in 1646, the oldest Chinese temple in Malaysia.

Everywhere in Malacca, you will find Chinese seafood restaurants, Malay stalls, European pubs, Nonya hotel cafes, Kristang markets, and Chitty homes offering varied and delectable dishes for visitors. Nonya, Chitty, and Kristang cuisines have evolved from the communities that settled there. The most popular Nonya dishes are *laksa lemak* (savory noodles in coconut milk, page 151), pork or chicken *pong teh* (with preserved soybeans, page 188), chicken *kurma* (page 168), and *ayam sioh* or *itek sioh* (tamarind coriander chicken or duck, page 164). Chittys have skillfully combined their Indian and Malay heritage to create delicious *sambal ikan bilis* (anchovy sauce, page 103), *nasi kemuli* (a festive rice, page 120), *kobis rebus berlada* (cabbage in coconut milk, page 290), and *acar timun nanas* (pickled cucumber pineapple salad, page 98). Kristangs have spiked their Portuguese heritage foods with local flavorings, including *nasi tomato* (tomato rice, page 119), *daging semur* (spicy stewed beef, page 180), *pesce assa* (baked fish, page 207), chicken curry *debal* (page 289), or chicken *vindaloo* (page 169).

A popular Malacca dish is *satay celup*—skewered meats, seafood, and vegetables dipped in a boiling peanut sauce. It is also called steamboat *satay* (similar to the *lok-lok* or fondue). Malacca has many delectable desserts and sweet porridges, including their signature *sago gula Melaka* (chilled sago pearls, page 252), *kueh dadar* (coconut-filled crepes, page 250), and *pulut hitam* (sweet black rice pudding, page 256).

Johor

Johor is the southernmost state in Malaysia and its capital is Johor Bahru (JB). Its name originates from the Arab word *jauhar*, which means "precious stones." Johor is the first state where Bugis immigrants from Sulawesi arrived, and they had a powerful influence on the politics and culture of Johor. Johor also has a history of Arab traders who influenced many of the Malay dishes. In the nineteenth century, an influx of Chinese immigrants came to work on the black pepper and *gambier* (betelnut leaves) plantations. Johor Bahru is linked by a causeway to Singapore, with daily interaction across the border. Thus, there are many Singaporean dishes found in JB as well.

My sister Vas and her family lived in JB for years and whenever we visited them, she and her husband, Diva, took us out to experience local dishes and specialties. Because of its location on the water, JB has many Chinese al-fresco-style seafood restaurants (*makanan laut*). Once we went to an Indian Muslim stall and I had the most fragrant vegetable *nasi biryani* (an Arab-influenced rice dish, page 280), spicy fried chicken (page 165), and *murtabak* (egg and ground meat layered flatbread). My favorite in JB is *mee rebus* (page 142), a popular noodle dish sold by Mamak vendors.

Trishaw for transport

Another Johor specialty is *roti kirai* or *roti jala*, which is a perforated net-like pancake (or flatbread) made by Indian Muslim and Malay vendors. A ladle with a five-hole perforation or a mold is used to make the bread look like a fish net. It is usually eaten with spicy chicken curry or sweet *serawa*, which is made from boiled coconut milk, brown sugar, and pandan leaf. Johor has its special noodle dish, *laksa* Johor, which uses spaghetti instead of local noodles, with coconut milk, tamarind juice, and fish flakes, topped with mint leaves, cucumber, and bean sprouts. I found the local *satay* (an Arab-inspired dish) quite different from the others I had. The vendor basted the meat with coconut milk and oil, and used a lemongrass brush before and during grilling. This gave the *satay* a wonderful fragrance.

The town of Muar in Johor is located at the mouth of the Muar River, about 110 miles northwest of Singapore and a little over twenty-five miles south of Malacca. Muar's historical roots reach back to the fourteenth century, when it was part of the Indonesian Majapahit Empire and home to a succession of Malaysian royalty. Muar's name, bestowed by ancient Indian explorers, means "three rivers" in Sanskrit. According to legend, the explorers came looking for gold but found instead the confluence of the Muar, Serting, and Pahang rivers. Muar is dear to me as I spent my primary school years there. I remember its slower pace of life, rickshaw rides to movies with Ma and Vas, and the different food vendors who came to our home. Muar has many old Chinese coffee shops where we used to have meals on some weekends. I remember the local Chinese having *satay* for breakfast, which was an unusual sight. Today, Muar has not changed, and still has the same old charm, with time-worn coffee shops and restaurants.

The Chinese and Indian Muslim foods in Muar were my favorites. Cha (my father) would take us to the coffee shops as a treat to eat *wantan mee* (soy sauce braised noodles), *mee Bandung* (tomato-chile noodles, page 146), and *oh chien* (or *ojian*, fried oysters scrambled with eggs). The Mamak food vendors sold Ma's favorite *mee rebus* (noodles in sweet potato sauce, page 142), *roti prata* (layered flatbread), *nasi lemak* (page 117), and *mee goreng* (page 136). The Malay vendors specialized in *ikan bakar* (grilled fish), *satay* (page 65), and *otak-otak* (savory fish mousse or paste wrapped in banana leaves and grilled over a charcoal fire). The Chinese had simple dishes such as stir-fried rice vermicelli (page 148), claypot chicken, or fish-head curry with *roti boy* (light brown buns served warm).

Malay fruit vendor along the east coast near Kuantan

The Cuisine of East-Central Malaysia

East-Central Malaysia is less developed than the rest of the country, its tropical rivers and lush jungle-covered mountains making it more difficult for settlers to reach. It divides West Malaysia from the East. During my return visits to Malaysia, we took a couple of trips to see the hill resorts of Pahang, including Genting Highlands (and its famous casino), Cameron Highlands (with beautiful hillside tea plantations and English rose gardens), and Fraser's Hill (a family holiday resort). A long coastline of beaches gives the East Coast its natural beauty. Because of its relative isolation, the cuisine of East Malaysia has hardly been touched by outsiders.

Pahang

Pahang, called *darul makmur* or "abode of tranquility" by the Arabs, is the largest state on Peninsular Malaysia and occupies the Pahang River basin. In the north, it is bordered by Kelantan, the south by Johor, and the east by Terengganu and the South China Sea. The Orang Asli, Peninsular Malaysia's aboriginal people, were the original inhabitants of Pahang. Much later, Pahang's tin and gold prospects attracted conquerors, traders, and settlers who landed on its shores on the South China Sea.

In the rural areas there are the simple dishes of the Orang Asli, including boiled rice or tapioca, barbecued fish, boiled fern leaves, and tapioca leaves. One unique Orang Asli dish is *nasi periuk kera* (rice cooked in pitcher plant, a type of jar-shaped plant that preys on insects). Malay, Indian, and Chinese dishes are available in major towns. In the coastal town of Kuantan, you will also find typical Malay dishes from Terengganu state, such as *nasi dagang* (red rice cooked with coconut milk, shallots, and fenugreek seeds, page 128) and *nasi ulam* (herb rice, page 125). Malay-style *gulais* (curries) are prepared with coconut milk or toasted grated coconut, chilies, and fragrant roots.

Pahang is home to Malaysia's longest river, which provides an abundant variety of fish that are cooked in Malay, Chinese, or Indian styles. *Udang galah* (large freshwater shrimps), freshwater clams, and other fish are grilled, made into *sambals* (chile-based condiments, pages 101-103), *gulais*, and stir-fries. Traditional Malay dishes include *singgang ikan* (a tamarind-based fish soup eaten after Ramadan, page 81) and a spicy sour *ikan kelah assam rebus* (stewed brook carp with tamarind, chilies, and fragrant *laksa* leaves). Pahang is well known for *sata* (fish paste mixed with spices and toasted coconut and wrapped in banana leaves and grilled over charcoal), fried salted fish, and *otak-otak* (fish paste wrapped in banana leaves and grilled). Chinese dishes in Pahang are usually Cantonese, Hakka, or Hokkien, such as *yong tau foo*, soups, and many seafood dishes using local fish. Chinese and Malay-style noodle dishes worth mentioning are the *laksas* (noodles in spicy fish-and-coconut-based broths) and *mee pedas* ("spicy hot" noodles) made with yellow *mee* (wheat noodles) and doused in a spicy fragrant beef broth seasoned with star anise.

My first year of primary school was in Kuantan and I have many fond memories of the town. Cha took us to Chinese seafood restaurants and often brought home Malay *kuehs* after work, from vendors who came from nearby *kampungs*. The local sweets were often sold at the wet markets and stalls, including *dodol* (caramel-like sweet) and *kueh dadar* (coconut crepes, page 250). Fruits were plentiful and eaten fresh or made into porridges, snacks, jams, and drinks. I also enjoyed nibbling on crispy *keropok*, a popular snack made from fish paste and sago, which is dried and fried into crispy chips.

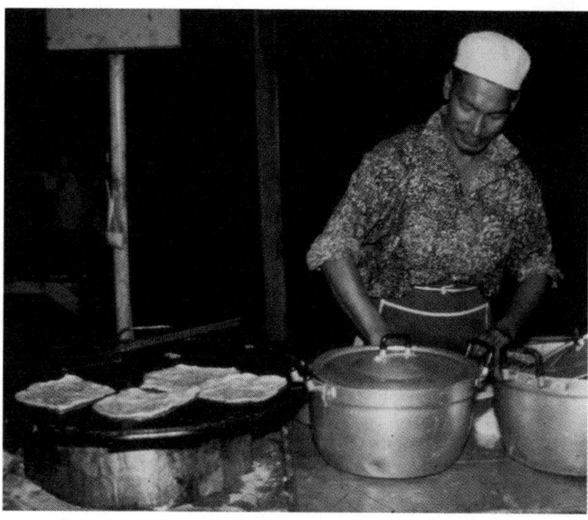

Roti canai vendor at night market, Kuala Terengganu

The Cuisine of Northeast Malaysia

The Malaysian states of the northeast coast, Terengganu and Kelantan, are less populated and industrialized than other states, and have had relatively few Chinese or Indians settlers. Thus, the culture is predominantly Malay.

Terengganu

Terengganu is bordered in the northwest by Kelantan, in the southwest by Pahang, and to the east by the South China Sea. Terengganu is known for sandy beaches and traditional fishing villages on its eastern shore, and mountains in the western region. Because of its proximity to the South China Sea, Terengganu has been trading with the world for centuries. Chinese merchants and seafarers reached Terengganu's shores in the early sixth century A.D. Like other Malay states, Terengganu practiced a Hindu–Buddhist culture with animist beliefs for hundreds of years before the arrival of Islam. However, it was the first to embrace Islam and has been given the honorific name *Darul Iman* ("Abode of Faith") in Arabic.

Over 90 percent of the Terengganu population is Malay, which is reflected in the cuisine. There is a strong Thai influence in its cooking because it is close to Thailand and at one time was ruled by Thailand (then called Siam). Coconut milk, lemongrass, pandan leaves, and fragrant roots, including galangal and turmeric, flavor the local dishes. Most dishes are accompanied by fresh or cooked *sambal belacan* (pages 101 or 102), hot and spicy condiments made of shrimp paste and chilies. Because of its long coastline, many locals are fishermen and seafood is a primary ingredient in most foods. *Singgang ikan* (a tamarind-based fish soup, page 81), *ikan percik* (grilled fish), and other grilled seafood served with *sambal tumis belacan* (page 102) are popular meals during Ramadan.

Terengganu is a rice growing region and offers many rice-based dishes: *Nasi dagang* (red rice cooked with coconut milk, page 128) is enjoyed with *kari ikan tongkol* (tuna curry, page 208) and *acar timun carot* (pickled cucumber carrot, page 99). *Nasi minyak* (ghee rice, page 121) is another typical rice dish eaten with *acar rampai* (pickled mixed vegetable salad, page 93) and chicken, egg, or beef curry. Like Pahang, Terengganu also has a unique *laksa* called *laksham*, typically eaten cold for breakfast. It is made from steamed rice and wheat flour, which is rolled, sliced, covered with a creamy white sauce of coconut milk and boiled mackerel, and served with *sambal belacan*.

Ulam is a typical Malay salad of raw vegetables and local fresh herbs that is popular for its health benefits. *Ulam* is eaten with cooked white rice or just dipped into a fiery *sambal belacan* (shrimp paste), *budu* (fermented baby anchovy sauce), or *tempoyak* (fermented durian paste). *Ulam* is also cooked with rice, called *nasi ulam* (page 125). Popular chicken dishes include spit-roasted chicken (*ayam golek* or *ayam percik*, page 166), spicy fried chicken (*ayam goreng berempah*, page 165), and chicken *kurma* (page 168) using *ayam kampung* (free-range chicken).

As you drive along the Terengganu coastal roads, you will find many vendors sitting under thatched-roof huts selling local fruits and an array of savory snacks. One of my favorite snacks is the chewy, spicy, and pungent *pulut lepa*. It is prepared from glutinous rice with a spicy fish filling seasoned with chilies, coconut, and onions, then wrapped in a banana leaf and grilled over a charcoal fire. Terengganu people have a sweet tooth and so desserts abound. *Ondeh-ondeh* (glutinous rice balls coated with shredded coconut, page 257), *pulut inti* (steamed glutinous rice topped with grated coconut and wrapped in banana leaves), and *lompat tikam* (coconut milk and rice flour flavored with pandan leaf) are a few that locals enjoy. On one of our visits to a local market, we saw a Malay vendor selling *putu piring*, an adaptation of the South Indian breakfast *putu*. Rice is steamed in hollow metal or bamboo tubes with a center of dark palm sugar, then topped with shredded coconut. In Terengganu, *putu piring* is made from rice and finely ground corn flour, unlike in Western Malaysia where only rice flour is used. After the *putu* is steamed, it is pushed out of the tube, broken up, topped with *gula Melaka* (palm sugar), and eaten piping hot.

Kelantan

Kelantan is bordered by Thailand to the north, Terengganu to the southeast, Perak to the west, and Pahang to the south. To the northeast of Kelantan is the South China Sea. Called *Darul Naim* in Arabic ("The Beautiful Abode"), it is the cradle of Malay culture. Like Terengganu, it has been isolated from the rest of the country and has had few Indian and Chinese immigrants. There are some Orang Asli, mostly Temiar people, who have lived in the forests of Kelantan and Perak for thousands of years.

Approximately 95 percent of Kelantan's population is ethnic Malay and its cuisine is predominantly Malay. The ethnic Thai inhabitants of Kelantan live primarily around the coastal town of Tumpat, where most of the Kelantan's Buddhist temples are located. Kelantan Thais are likely descendants of immigrants from Narathiwat, who came four centuries ago to what was then a sparsely populated Malay territory. The Kelantanese cuisine is heavily influenced by Thai cuisine and their curries are sweeter, richer, and creamier than those found in Western Malaysia.

Kelantanese favor rice dishes served with seafood. Many rice dishes are similar to those eaten in Terengganu but have greater Thai influence. *Nasi kerabu* (eaten with a dip made of fermented durian) is the state specialty, and similar to *nasi ulam* (herb rice, page 125) except it is tinted a bluish color from *bunga telang*, the flower of the butterfly pea. *Nasi tumpang* is rice packed in a cone-shaped banana leaf (like *nasi lemak*) with omelet, beef serunding (meat floss), and chicken curry. *Nasi berlauk* is a breakfast dish, a richer version of *nasi lemak* served with fish, beef *rendang* (spicy simmered beef, page 177), or *cili sotong* (chile squid, page 211).

Pulut, or glutinous rice, is very popular with locals, and generally cooked with coconut milk. There are many varieties: *pulut kuning*, savory yellow glutinous rice seasoned with turmeric; *pulut kacang*, sweet glutinous rice served with shredded coconut and beans; and my favorite, *pulut bakar* or *pulut lepa*. There are also many fish specialties—*ikan percik* (grilled fish) and *solok ladah* (fish fillet with coconut and chile stuffing) being my favorites. Savory snacks made from fish abound here. The local *keropok lekor* are fish crackers made from sago flour and pounded fish (generally mackerel and sardines) that are then steamed or deep-fried. They are also served for afternoon tea with a spicy, sweet and sour tamarind dip. *Solok ladah* are whole chilies stuffed with seasoned and cooked fish paste. *Keropok gote*, fish sausages made with fish and sago then cut into bite-sized pieces and deep-fried, are popular with schoolchildren.

Similar to Pahang and Terengganu, *ayam percik* (page 166) is a popular grilled chicken preparation. It is served with a sweet and spicy Thai chile dipping sauce called *cholek*. Kelantan, like Terengganu, has numerous sweet Malay *kuehs* including *che mek molek* (prepared with fried sweet potato and a syrup filling), *seri kaya* (custard made of eggs, sugar, and coconut milk), and *pengat pisang* (fried banana topped with a sweet coconut milk sauce, page 253).

In Kelantan, the Chinese see themselves as either *Cina Kampung* (village Chinese) or *Cina Bandar* (town Chinese). Cina Kampung cuisine is a melting pot of Chinese, Malay, and Thai flavors. Since herbs are grown abundantly and there is a strong Malay influence, herbs salads (*kerabu* or *ulam*) are popular, served with *budu*, an anchovy-based condiment. One of the signature dishes of Cina Kampung is *khau jam* ("mixed rice" in Thai), similar to the Malay *nasi ulam*. The rice is cooked in a mixture of juices blended from about thirty different leaves found around the garden. It is served during special occasions such as Chinese New Year and other Chinese festivals. The rice is eaten with finely sliced herbs with pounded grilled fish, *sambal*, *kerisik*, and the ubiquitous *budu*, which is used abundantly as a cooking ingredient and as a dip at the dining table.

Cina Kampung cook curry the Thai way. Instead of first frying the pounded ingredients in hot oil and then adding coconut milk, they add coconut milk first to the pot followed by the pounded ingredients. The mixture is allowed to simmer before the meats are added, giving a less oily but subtler flavor. As most of the Cina Kampung settlements are along the riverbanks, fish feature prominently in their daily diet. Fish is marinated in turmeric and either fried, grilled, prepared as *assam rebus* (hot and sour fish, page 205), or cooked *singgang*-style with dried chilies and tamarind (page 81). Pork is reserved for special occasions. Fern shoots (*pucuk paku*) are stir-fried with *budu*, or made into a salad.

The Cuisine of East Malaysia, on the Island of Borneo

Eastern Malaysia, which includes the states of Sarawak and Sabah on Borneo Island, has not been touched by the diverse immigration and cultural influences that Peninsular Malaysia has experienced (except for a small group of Chinese migrants). The population of Eastern Malaysia consists primarily of the various indigenous peoples who have lived there for thousands of years. Accordingly, the cuisine tends to be simple, using local ingredients, and is not heavily spiced as in Peninsular Malaysia.

Sarawak

Sarawak is located in the northwest of Borneo Island. Known as *Bumi Kenyalang* ("Land of the Hornbills"), it has a large tropical rain forest, national parks, and beautiful beaches. Sarawak has an abundance of natural resources—*padi*, palm oil, pepper, and sago. Pepper (black and white) is its cash crop and Sarawak is the fourth largest producer of pepper in the world.

Sarawak *kueh* vendor

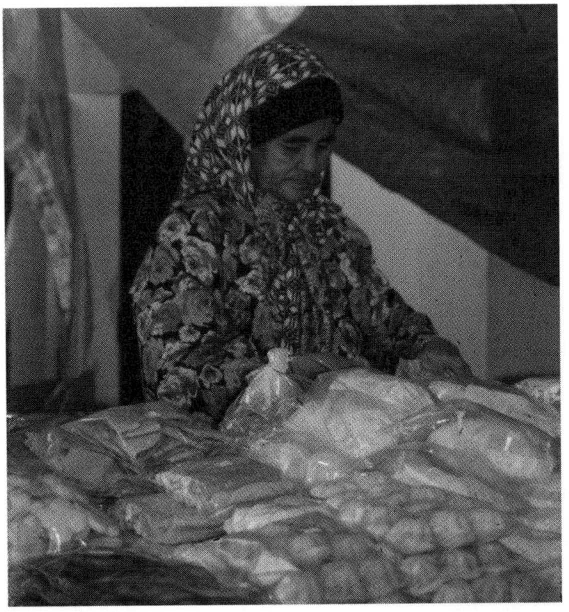

The indigenous peoples of Borneo speak languages belonging to the Austronesian family, which fall into more than twenty-five distinct ethnic groups. Most of these peoples came to Borneo thousands of years ago and are collectively referred to as the Dayaks. The largest ethnic group are the Ibans (roughly 29 percent of the population), Sea Dayaks who by legend were fierce headhunters. Other tribes include the Bidayuh or Land Dayaks (8 percent), the Melanaus (5 percent), and the Orang Ulu or "upriver people" (5.5 percent). The minorities are the Kenyahs, Kayans, Kedayans, Bisayahs, Kelabits, Berawans, and Penans. Many of the indigenous peoples continue to live a nomadic existence, while others have taken up farming and live in communal longhouses. Malays make up 21 percent of Sarawak's population, and are traditionally fishermen living on the banks of Sarawak's many rivers. The Chinese, who make up 29 percent of the population, first came to Sarawak as traders and explorers in the sixth century, and later as immigrants in the nineteenth and twentieth centuries. There is a small community of Indians who are professionals and merchants.

Sarawak food is not hot or spicy. White and black pepper, garlic, and ginger are the most frequently used seasonings for chicken, meats, or seafood. Forest ferns have a special place in the diet of the people, with the two most popular ferns, *midin* and the fiddlehead fern (*pucuk paku*), eaten as vegetables. They grow wild in the forests and today have become gourmet dishes prepared with *sambal belacan* (page 101).

Many of Sarawak's indigenous peoples still live by the river and forest fringes and cook over open fires. Bamboo is an essential cooking utensil for them. Rice, meat, fish, and vegetables are stuffed into hollow bamboo (which seals in flavor and creates tender finished products) and cooked over wood fires. A popular Iban dish is *ayam pansoh*, mildly seasoned chicken with lemongrass cooked in a hollow bamboo over an open fire. The bamboo is then cut open to release the cooked chicken pieces.

Sago palm, the staple food of the Melanaus and the nomadic Penans, is pounded to extract the starch or processed into granules or "pearls" or converted to flour. The Melanaus use sago flour to make sago cakes, biscuits, and other snacks. Ibans enjoy *tuak*, a sweet rice wine distilled from rice and sago that is served during festive occasions.

The numerous rivers of Sarawak provide abundant freshwater fish, including tilapia and catfish. Salted *ikan terubok* (shad) and *ikan assam pedas*, a tangy spicy fish, are Sarawak specialties. The signature dish of the Melanaus, who are skilled Sarawak fishermen, is *umai* (page 62), a pickled fish with lime juice, shallots, and chilies. *Kek lapis*, a layered cake, and *kueh celolot*, made of rice flour, coconut milk, and *gula apung* (local palm sugar), are two of Sarawak's sweets.

In Kuching, the capital, the food is influenced by its large Chinese community. One popular dish is *oh chien* (Teochew-style crispy oyster omelet) served with a pepper and fish sauce. The local tangy *laksa* combines blanched rice vermicelli, bean sprouts, omelet strips, and shrimp in a hot and sour broth. Noodle specialties include *kolok mee*, egg noodles tossed with slices of *char siew* (barbecue pork) or ground pork and flavored with black vinegar, and tomato *kueh teow*, seasoned with tomato sauce, chicken, vegetables, and shrimp.

Sabah

Sabah is located in the northeast of Borneo Island. Sabah is mountainous with a lush tropical rain forest, sandy beaches, and diverse flora and fauna. It has been referred to as the "Land Below The Wind" because it lies below the typhoon belt. It is also called "The Land Of The Sacred Mountain" because of Mt. Kinabalu, which is 4,101 meters high. Previously called North Borneo, it was ruled by the Philippines, then the British, and later joined the Federation of Malaysia as Sabah.

Sabah women in traditional attire

Sabah has over thirty different races speaking over eighty local dialects. The three main indigenous groups of Sabah are the Kadazan-Dusuns, the Muruts, and the Bajaus. The Kadazan-Dusuns are the largest group, making up about a third of the population. They are traditionally farmers practicing wet rice or hill rice cultivation. Muruts, or "Hill People," are mostly shifting cultivators (rice and tapioca) and hunters, and they live near the borders of Sarawak and Kalimantan. Many still reside in their traditional communal longhouses. Bajaus are skilled fishermen and rice farmers, and live mainly on the east and west coasts. The Chinese have settled in Sabah over the past century and are the largest non-indigenous group.

Sabah cuisine includes traditional indigenous foods and simple Chinese and Malay cooking. Traditional foods vary and depend on natural resources. Coastal dwellers tend to eat seafood while those living inland rely on freshwater fish and wild game. In the north, the staple foods include tapioca and rice. They also use a number of wild plants, including tubers such as yams and sweet potatoes, the tips of wild ferns, and tapioca and other edible leaves. *Ambuyat*, a gluey porridge made from sago is the main staple in some parts of Sabah. The Muruts favor tapioca-based porridges. Sabah cooks also add dried shrimp paste (*belacan*), dried tiny shrimp (krill), *ikan bilis* (baby anchovies), ginger, chilies, galangal, fresh turmeric root and leaves to their recipes.

The Kadazan Dusuns and the Muruts enjoy tart foods and thus limes, the pungent *bambangan* (wild mango), unripe mangoes, and *belimbing* (star fruit family) are used abundantly. They are made into many pickles and preserves with game, fish, wild roots and leaves. One of their favorites is *sayur manis* (Chinese flowering cabbage), which grows wild. The slopes of Mount Kinabalu produce a wide range of temperate climate vegetables, including asparagus and sweet green pea pods. The Muruts enjoy *jaruk*, made by packing pieces of wild boar or river fish with salt and cooked rice into a hollow bamboo tube. The bamboo is then sealed with leaves and left to ferment for several weeks, or even months. It is eaten as a condiment with cooked rice or tapioca starch.

The Kadazan Dusuns enjoy *hinava* (pickled fish like the *umai* of Sarawak, page 62), prepared with Spanish mackerel (*ikan tenggiri*), *bambangan*, red chilies, shredded ginger and sliced shallots drenched with lime juice which "cooks" the fish. The food of Sabah's Muslims is similar to Malay cuisine, except dry spices are rarely used. Instead, chilies and plenty of fragrant roots and leaves are added. Food is coated with pounded ingredients and sour tamarind juice, then wrapped in banana leaf and grilled over a fire. *Satay goreng* (page 178) using beef or chicken is popular at festivals and special occasions. Meat or chicken is stir-fried with spices, peanuts, and *belacan* instead of grilling it over charcoal fires. The local Chinese favor pork dishes with peppercorns, garlic, and ginger. Dark soy sauce and peppercorns are popular ingredients in meat and chicken dishes.

Many varieties of well-known tropical fruits and wild fruits are found in Sabah. Durian, the "king of fruits," has fifteen wild varieties found in Sabah. One unique variety has red flesh and lacks the distinctive fragrance of the typical durian. It is fried with onions and chilies and served as a side dish or *sambal*. Another fruit is the fragrant yellow-skinned passion fruit, usually made into juice. All of Sabah's non-Muslim groups make various types of rice wine from steamed glutinous rice or tapioca. *Tapai* is a locally-brewed sweet tapioca wine, a favorite of the Kadazan-Dusuns. Another is *lihing*, a popular golden rice wine. When added with ginger to chicken soup, it becomes a tonic for mothers after childbirth.

Sam Poh Temple, Perak

How This Cookbook Is Organized

Understanding Malaysia's collage of people and foods will help you understand my cookbook's organization. Like Malaysia's polyethnic culture, you will see recipes from different ethnic communities being intermingled. You may read about a Malay-inspired spicy sauce or *sambal*, preceded by a Nonya stir-fry, and followed by an Indian curry. My final chapter on "fusion" cooking demonstrates how you can add Malaysian zing to favorite American recipes and comfort foods.

However, I do try to bring some order to all of this mixing and intermingling. The book is organized by a general meal presentation. You are first introduced to Malaysian snacks and appetizers, then soups and stews, and then salads and condiments. Next are the rice and noodle chapters, because these two staples tend to serve as centerpieces of most Malaysian meals. The dishes considered "entrées" in the West are next—poultry, meats, and seafood—followed by the vegetable chapter. In Malaysia, vegetables are important and are served with the "entrée" dishes as sides or toppings around rice or noodle centerpieces. All Malaysians have a sweet tooth and my book finishes up with chapters on desserts and beverages. I have also included a chapter on Malaysia's colorful 'open house' festivities, and describe some of the unique celebrations where food plays a significant role. Those who seek to add a unique Asian touch to their comforting American foods will enjoy my chapter on Malaysian fusion cooking.

You can enjoy any of my recipes as part of an otherwise traditional Western meal, or alongside dishes from other Asian countries. I also help the reader who wishes to indulge in a complete Malaysian feast by providing suggestions for matching each dish with an appropriate rice or noodle dish, entrée, vegetable, and/or dessert and beverage. Finally, to further assist the home chef, I end the book with a glossary of Malaysian ingredients, which includes instructions on how to prepare ingredients that are essential to Malaysian cooking.

CHAPTER 1

SNACKS AND APPETIZERS: SPICY BITES

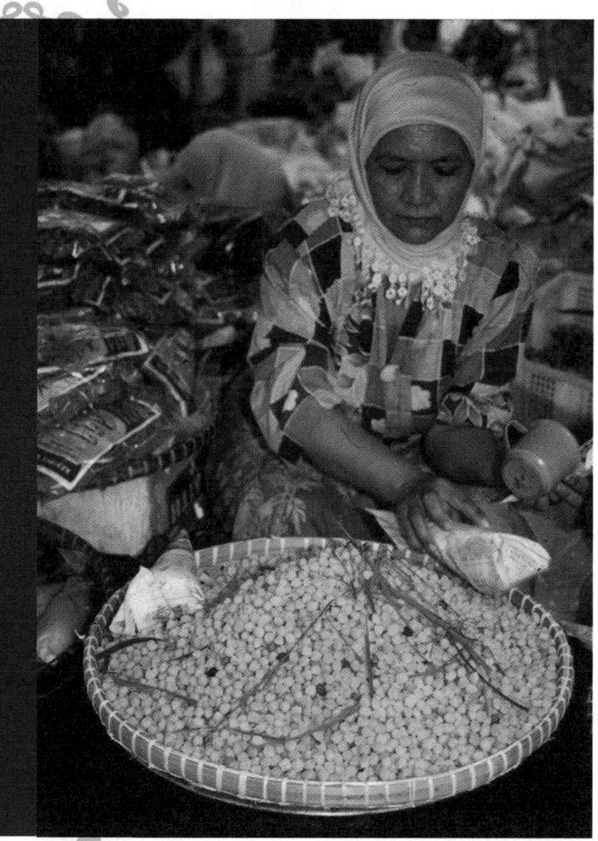

Malay snack vendor, Khatijah Market, Kota Bahru

Malaysians love snacking from morning till night, so snacks and appetizers are sold everywhere, by hawkers, coffee shops (*kopi kedai*), and restaurants. As kids, whenever we had a few cents left over from lunch, we would run to the shops behind our house in Petaling Jaya or to one of the local hawkers to buy our favorite snack after school. A snack we frequently enjoyed was *tauhu sumbat* (page 60), deep-fried tofu stuffed with fresh vegetables and topped with a spicy sweet chile sauce. Another Chinese favorite for us was *yong tau foo*, stuffed vegetables and tofu in a savory broth drizzled with a pungent spicy sweet sauce. We also loved *paus* (Chinese steamed buns), which we would sometimes buy on Saturdays as a late breakfast snack. Our favorite hawker for *paus* was a Chinese vendor at the PJ Old Town bus stop. His wooden baskets were always steaming with chicken, pork, and bean paste-filled buns. As children, we enjoyed peeling off the outer "skin," breaking it in half, and biting into the soft, spongy bun and sweet-savory filling.

At other times we snacked on savory flatbreads or *rotis* from the numerous *roti* stalls operated by Mamaks (Indian Muslims) and Indians. The chewy flaky *roti canai* (similar to *roti prata*) is Malaysia's most popular *roti*. In fascination, we often watched the *roti* vendor's special technique of tossing, spinning, and folding the dough to create the layered bread. Nowadays, they are available fresh and frozen from supermarkets and Asian grocery stores. *Roti canai* is often served with dhal curry, *dalcha*, chicken or mutton curry, *kurmas*, or our favorite as young adults, spread with sugar or condensed milk. There are other Mamak variations of layered breads—*murtabak*, stuffed with ground meat (generally mutton) and egg; *roti telor*, prepared with eggs; *roti bom*, small, thick *roti* served with fish curry (popular in Penang); and *roti tisu*, a paper-thin flaky *roti*, also referred to as "handkerchief" bread.

Some everyday snacks that we enjoyed after school were sour dried plums, hot spicy ginger strips, sweet tart mangoes, sunflower seeds, steamed sweet corn, chickpeas or peanuts, and freshly cut fruits like *jambu batu* (a firm variety of guava), jackfruit, and *rambutans*. Some days we would indulge in the sweet and savory glutinous rice-based snacks, such as the pungent and chewy *pulut panggang* (or *pulut udang*), stuffed with spicy dried shrimp and wrapped in banana leaf; *bubur kacang hijau* (green bean porridge, page 248); or chilled *cendol* (green pea flour noodle strips with palm sugar and coconut milk sauce).

While we often bought snacks from vendors, Ma preferred to entice us with homemade snacks like curry puffs (or as locals call them, *kari pap,* page 57), one of Malaysia's favorite snacks, fish cutlets (page 63), and fried sweet bananas (*goreng pisang manis*, page 67). The best were Ma's curry puffs, usually prepared for afternoon tea or on special occasions. These empanada-like pastries have a delicious savory filling of curried minced lamb or chicken, thinly sliced cabbage, and savory potatoes. Its shape and consistency varies with each cook, from a bite-size to a larger moon shape, and from soft to flaky textures. Another homemade favorite was Periama's (my grandmother) *thosai* (page 69), a fermented rice and lentil crepe that we usually enjoyed for a Sunday brunch.

Whenever I returned to Malaysia for a visit, Ma remembered my love for her snacks. Sometimes she would treat me to delicious *tauhu goreng*, thinly sliced tofu pieces rubbed with hot chile powder, a little curry powder, and salt and then deep-fried. I enjoyed them with Ma on quiet afternoons while we sat reminiscing about how she and Cha took us to an Indian coffee shop for tea and snacks on Sunday mornings. We feasted on *masala vadai* (spicy lentil cakes, page 61); *puttu* (steamed rice cakes with grated coconut topping); or *appam* (hoppers, also called *apom lenggang* by Malays and Indian Muslims), a bowl-shaped crispy-edged pancake served with grated coconut and sugar, *dalcha*, or curries. They were brought to Malaysia by immigrants from Sri Lanka.

Later in her life, Ma lived with my brother Sathee, and on trips home, we often stayed at his home in Subang Jaya, a suburb of Malaysia's capital, Kuala Lumpur. One year, Sathee took me on a short road trip to visit some of the towns of our youth.

In Malaysia, a regular loaf of bread is transformed into a sublime snack with delicious spreads. We often enjoyed *roti bakar* (toast spread with butter and *kaya*, a fragrant jam made with coconut milk, eggs, pandan juice, and sugar), and *roti sardine*, spread with coarsely mashed canned sardines and seasoned with tomato sauce, onions, lime juice, and chilies.

When Ma did not have time to make her English-style pancakes for us after school, we bought local-style pancakes from the vendors who came by our homes, especially when we lived in the more rural towns of Kuantan and Muar. *Roti jala* (lacy net-like pancake accompanied by curries, or sometimes stuffed with ground meats and chicken), *apom balik* (crispy pancake topped with crushed peanuts and sugar filling), *lempang bakar* (sweet banana pancake), and *roti syior* (coconut pancake served with curry or coated with sugar) are a few we enjoyed.

Along the way, we enjoyed not only our shared memories of the past but some of Malaysia's beloved foods as well. Our first stop was Kajang, Selangor, about a forty-minute drive from Subang Jaya. Most of the shop houses in Kajang's old commercial district, built in the 1920s and 1930s, have an antique look, with colonial and Chinese architecture. The ground floors of these shops was used for commercial activities, while the upper floors were reserved as living space for the families.

As a special childhood treat, our parents would make a thirty-mile Sunday drive to Kajang, known as "*Satay* Town." I remember the old Chinese coffee shops that served toasted bread with *kaya*, noodle soups, fried rice, and their delicious *satay* (page 65). These are thinly sliced seasoned chicken, beef, mutton, or pork skewered on bamboo or coconut leaf spines and grilled slowly over charcoal fires. It is served with *kuah kacang* (a spicy peanut sauce, page 66) and a side plate of cubed onions, cucumbers, and *ketupat* (a type of compressed rice, page 281).

Satay was brought by Javanese or Sumatran Malays to Malaysia, and has since become a Malaysian food icon. Malays concocted their own version of Arab kebabs using local ingredients—shallots, galangal, ginger, lemongrass, spices, and chilies. Each Malaysian region and ethnic group has a signature *satay* and peanut sauce. In Muar, Johor state, pork *satay* is most popular with the Chinese and is served for breakfast, while in Sarawak, pork *satay* is served with a spicy pineapple-based sauce. The Malays in Ipoh, Perak state, have *satay Endut* (named after a local Malay man) which they claim has a thicker, smoother sauce. Malacca specializes in *satay celup* or steamboat *satay*, a Chinese specialty. This unique *satay* is prepared by cooking raw or semi-cooked skewered chicken, seafood, meats, shrimp, fish balls, squid, and vegetables by dunking them in a hot pot of boiling peanut sauce and then dipping them in hot, tangy, and sweet sauces.

After feasting on *satay* in Kajang, Sathee and I headed to the West Coast town of Port Dickson (or "PD" as we called it), located on the Straits of Malacca about thirty-seven miles from Kuala Lumpur. White beaches shaded by palm, coconut, and banyan trees made it a favorite weekend retreat for locals and expatriates from nearby larger towns. We arrived around teatime and set out to find a snack from the local vendors. Malay vendors were selling warm deep-fried battered ripe bananas (*goreng pisang manis*, page 67), plantains, and jackfruit. Indian Muslim vendors offered their *cucok rode* (fritters of sweet yam, eggplant, green beans, and bean sprouts) and *cucuk udang* (fritters with seasoned shrimp); and Nonyas had *popiah* (fresh spring rolls), *lobak* (seasoned meat rolls), *paiti* (top hats), and numerous savory *kuehs* (bite-size cakes).

Sathee and I walked toward a roadside stall where a Malay lady was wearing a *tudong*, a colorful batik scarf covering her head, and standing behind a huge metal wok, frying some battered jackfruit, tapioca, and sweet yams. Speaking in fluent Malay, Sathee ordered some snacks while I watched her prepare them. She wrapped the fritters in newspaper and handed the package to him. I was truly surprised to note that they were not greasy, as I had imagined—instead they were crispy, moist, and delicious.

We sat near the beach and enjoyed our snacks against the cool ocean breeze, and reminisced about the days Cha brought us here on the weekends. He would drive around till he found a shady spot under a tree near the water. Cha was a great swimmer who grew up near the Indian Ocean, where as a boy he would swim through shark-infested ocean waters to see the big ships that anchored near Tellicherry on their route from the West to the Far East, and vice versa.

I smiled as I remembered us girls going into the water in our regular clothes (only Westerners wore bathing suits then!). We all enjoyed our cool swim in the water and then lunched on Ma's spicy sardine (cooked with onions and curry powder) and tomato sandwiches, and cool rose water and lemonade. She converted the plain tinned sardines into something delicious. As I was biting into the third jackfruit fritter, and thinking of our childhood, I heard Sathee hailing me from behind to continue our journey on to Muar (in Johor State). Back in our childhood days in Muar, our "take out" snacks were from food hawkers with push carts who came to our doorstep, a practice still found in some remote towns and *kampungs* (villages). Looking back, I remember the snack vendors being an integral part of our daily lives—the old Mamak *rojak* man, the skinny tanned *nasi lemak* Malay vendor, the younger *chee cheong fan* Chinese vendor who came on Sunday mornings, and the breadman, an older Indian Muslim. I could never forget the breadman who for years came on a daily basis at 4 pm on his bicycle (and later on a scooter) with all his trimmings hanging around him (breads, buns, pastries, cakes). I would be the first one to rush out and greet him, and sometimes if Ma allowed, to get my favorite cake with icing on top to have with my tea.

Indian curry puff vendor, Johor Bahru

Curry Puffs
Kari Pap

Makes 5 to 6 servings

Curry puffs are an iconic Malaysian snack. They come in different sizes and designs but still retain the original shape of a crescent moon. While the curry puff's pastry is Portuguese in origin, the filling is truly Malaysian. Every Indian and Malay vendor has his signature recipe, generally made with seasoned ground chicken, beef, or mutton and/or chopped vegetables or potatoes. You'll often find Malaysians enjoying curry puffs along with a cup of thick local coffee or tea with sweetened condensed milk. I especially enjoy them as an afternoon snack with Ma's addictive, sweet and frothy teh tarik *(Malaysian cappuccino). Ma and Periama (Grandma) worked late nights in the kitchen preparing curry puffs for special occasions like our birthdays and* Deepavali, *the Hindu Festival of Lights. Here is Ma's recipe. I have also made a delicious vegetarian* kari pap, *using tofu, potatoes, and cabbage.*

INGREDIENTS

Filling

1 tablespoon cooking oil
Heaping ½ cup finely chopped shallots or onions
1 pound ground chicken, lamb, or beef, cut into 1-inch cubes*
½ pound (1½ cups) potatoes, peeled and diced into ¼-inch pieces
1¼ to 1½ cups (3¾ to 4½ ounces) finely shredded cabbage
¾ teaspoon salt
¾ teaspoon sugar
¼ cup chopped coriander leaves (cilantro)

Spice Blend

1 teaspoon ground cumin
1 teaspoon ground coriander
½ teaspoon ground fennel seeds
½ teaspoon finely ground black pepper (use ¼ teaspoon for tofu)
½ teaspoon turmeric powder
¼ to ½ teaspoon chile powder
¼ teaspoon ground cinnamon
¼ teaspoon ground cardamom
⅛ teaspoon ground clove

Pastry**

1¼ cups all-purpose wheat flour
¼ teaspoon salt
1 tablespoon butter or margarine
¾ teaspoon freshly squeezed or bottled lime juice
cup water
Oil for deep-frying

DIRECTIONS:

1. Combine Spice Blend ingredients and set aside.
2. For filling: Heat oil in skillet or wok. Sauté shallots or onions for about 1 to 2 minutes till fragrant. Add Spice Blend and stir for about a ½ minute. Add chicken, lamb or beef and sauté for about 3 minutes. Add potatoes, cover, and cook for about 5 minutes. Then add cabbage and sauté for about 2 minutes, till limp. Add salt and sugar and cook another 2 to 3 minutes, till sauce becomes dry. Turn off heat and blend in chopped coriander. Set aside to cool.
3. If making your own pastry,** in a mixing bowl sift flour and salt. Work in the butter or margarine till flour looks like crumbled dough. Mix lime juice and ⅓ cup water and gradually add to dough. Knead dough lightly till it becomes smooth. Place dough on a lightly floured surface and roll out to ⅛-inch thickness. Cut the dough into 2¾ to 3-inch-diameter rounds. Cover with damp paper towel or cloth.
4. Place about 1 tablespoon filling on each dough round, fold over to form semicircles and enclose filling. Seal by pinching and/or fluting the dough with a fork. Cover with a damp paper towel or cloth.
5. Heat oil in pan or deep wok. Deep-fry curry puffs till golden brown. Drain on absorbent paper towels. (Or bake at 400°F for about 15 to 20 minutes till crust turns golden brown.)

***For a vegetarian filling:** Cut a 14-ounce package of tofu (*tauhu*) into 1-inch pieces and pan-fry in a dry non-stick skillet till they become light brown and firm. Set aside. Then follow steps 1 through 5, using tofu in place of meat and omitting sugar.

**Instead of making the pastry you can use ready-made refrigerated white (wheat flour) *empanada* dough, or a ready-made refrigerated pastry crust dough for a flakier crust.

Serve with tea, *teh tarik* (page 262), *teh masala* (page 259), coffee, beer, or wine.

Spicy Eggplant Dip

Sos Terong Berempah

Makes 4 to 5 servings

INGREDIENTS

- 3 medium or 1½ large eggplants (about 2 pounds), sliced in half lengthwise; or 13 cups unpeeled 1-inch cubes eggplant
- Optional: ⅛ teaspoon turmeric powder
- 1 tablespoon cooking oil
- ½ teaspoon black or dark brown mustard seeds
- 1-inch cinnamon stick
- ½ teaspoon cumin seeds
- 2 tablespoons sliced and crushed garlic cloves
- 1 tablespoon sliced and crushed fresh ginger
- ¾ cup coarsely chopped shallots or onions
- 1 fresh green chile (cayenne, jalapeno, Serrano, Thai, or New Mexican), sliced
- 1 cup (6 ounces) chopped tomatoes
- 1 tablespoon tamarind concentrate or juice from tamarind pulp (*see page 339*)
- ½ teaspoon salt

SPICE BLEND

- 1 tablespoon ground coriander
- ½ tablespoon ground cumin
- ½ teaspoon ground fennel seeds
- ¼ teaspoon turmeric powder
- ⅛ teaspoon ground fenugreek

When Ma passed away in January 2002, we flew to Malaysia for two weeks of ceremonial rites at my sister Vas's home in Johor Bahru. In keeping with Hindu tradition, only the men went to ceremonially scatter Ma's ashes into the flowing ocean. The next day, after prayers, a traditional vegetarian lunch would be served to family and guests. Ma was a perfectionist with cooking, and we wanted to have the best for her, as she did for us.

*While my sister and I were contemplating what to cook, an enticing aroma came from the kitchen. We found my sister-in-law Shanta busily stirring something in the wok. She let us try the most delicious eggplant (*brinjal *or* aubergine*) and tomato combination that we had ever tasted. Now I knew Ma would be pleased. Between Vas, Shanta, and I, we cooked some of her other favorites. Ma would have been happy with the feast laid out in her honor.*

I am sharing Shanta's eggplant recipe with you, but have reduced the heat and modified some spices. I also roasted the eggplant. It has become a vegetarian favorite at my home for special occasions.

DIRECTIONS:

1. Combine Spice Blend ingredients and set aside.
2. Brush eggplant halves with oil and place face down on oiled pan. Broil for about ½ hour or bake for about 45 minutes at 400°F (brushing with oil when necessary) till skin blisters and becomes soft. Then take out of oven and let cool at room temperature, or place in cold water. Peel and mash (discarding burnt pieces to avoid bitterness). (Alternately, bring 2 cups water to a boil, add the eggplant cubes and turmeric and mix well. Cover and simmer for about 15 to 20 minutes, till eggplant becomes somewhat soft.)
3. In a skillet or wok, heat 1 tablespoon oil, add mustard seeds, cover and cook till seeds "pop." When popping subsides, add cinnamon stick and cumin seeds and stir for ½ minute.
4. Add garlic and ginger, sauté for about ½ to 1 minute. Add shallots or onions, sauté for 1 to 2 minutes, then add chile and mix for another ½ to 1 minute.
5. Add Spice Blend and mix well for ½ minute.
6. Add tomatoes and sauté for about 3 minutes, till fragrant. Add cooked eggplant and sauté for about 3 to 4 minutes (mashing as necessary).
7. Stir in tamarind juice and salt and sauté for another 5 to 8 minutes (adding ½ to 1 cup water, depending on consistency desired).

A Malaysian version of the Middle Eastern *baba ganoush*, this is great with any kind of warm flatbread, such as *roti canai*, pita, soft taco, naan, *puri*, *chappati*, or even with a crusty piece of Italian or French bread. Enjoy it with a glass of cool wine, beer, or cold *lassi* (yogurt drink). Or serve as a side dish with cooked rice or ghee rice (page 121), dhal curry (page 231), spicy cucumber tomato salad (page 97) and spicy fried chicken (page 165), fish curry (page 198), *sambal* shrimp (page 204), chicken *kurma* (page 168), or mutton *peratil* (page 185).

Vegetable Fritters

Cucuk Sayur

Makes 4 to 5 servings

In Petaling Jaya, one of our neighbors was a Punjabi family. I was always intrigued by their foods, which were quite different from our home cooking or hawker Indian fare. Through the years, Punjabi foods have become trendy and are generally served at upscale North Indian restaurants. However, some popular dishes such as tandoori chicken *(traditionally baked in a clay oven called a* tandoor*),* naan*, and* chappati *are also found at Mamak joints. I particularly enjoyed my neighbor's* pakoras*, North Indian-style potato-and-pea fritters. Here I have created a Malaysian-style* pakora *appetizer, using a medley of vegetables my family enjoys, including broccoli, carrots, and zucchini, and I've added fresh chile peppers for a touch of heat and yam bean (*bengkuang*) for a crunchy mouthfeel.*

INGREDIENTS

1 tablespoon cooking oil
¼ teaspoon turmeric powder
¼ teaspoon ground paprika
1½ cups (about 5 ounces) cauliflower florets
1 cup (about 2 ounces) broccoli florets
1 cup (about 2 ounces) sliced zucchini (½-inch circular cuts)
1 cup (5 ounces) sliced carrots (2-inch-wide slices)
1 cup (4 ounces) sliced poblano, Anaheim, or bell peppers (3-inch-long pieces)
1 cup (about 5 ounces) peeled and sliced yam bean (½-inch by 2-inch pieces)
Oil for deep-frying

BATTER BLEND

2 cups chickpea flour (*besan*)
1¾ cups water
1 teaspoon salt
2 teaspoons ground cumin
1 tablespoon ground coriander
½ teaspoon turmeric powder
¼ teaspoon chile powder
¼ teaspoon baking powder
2 tablespoons freshly squeezed or bottled lime juice

DIRECTIONS:

1. Heat 1 tablespoon oil in a pan. Add turmeric and paprika and stir for about ½ minute. Add the vegetables and sauté for about 4 minutes, retaining the crisp texture of the vegetables. Set aside to cool.
2. Blend all batter ingredients and mix or whisk well till batter develops a smooth texture without lumps.
3. Heat oil in a deep skillet or wok. Dip vegetables in the batter blend, one at a time, letting any excess batter drip off, and deep-fry in heated oil. Fry till batter turns golden brown, turning when needed. Drain on paper towels.

Serve warm with tea, *teh tarik* (page 262), beer, or wine and a tamarind-based or mint-based dip or chutney.

Stuffed Tofu with Spicy Plum Sauce

Tauhu Sumbat dengan Sos Plum

Makes 4 to 5 servings

INGREDIENTS

1 package (14 ounces) firm tofu (*tauhu*), sliced into ¾ to 1-inch-thick by 3-inch-square pieces, then each square cut in half to create 2 triangular pieces
Optional: Oil for deep-frying
1 lettuce or Chinese cabbage leaf, shredded
½ cup (2 ounces) peeled, seeded, and shredded or julienned cucumber
¼ cup (about 1 ounce) shredded or julienned carrots
½ cup (about 1½ ounces) bean sprouts, rinsed or blanched

Spicy Plum Sauce

1 fresh red chile (cayenne, Fresno, jalapeno, Serrano, cherry, or Thai), chopped
1 teaspoon chopped garlic cloves
½ to ¾ cup (3 to 5 ounces) dried plums or apricots
6 tablespoons light brown sugar
2 teaspoons distilled white vinegar
1½ tablespoons freshly squeezed or bottled lime juice
½ teaspoon salt

Garnish

1 tablespoon toasted sesame seeds

I first tasted tauhu sumbat, a Hakka Chinese specialty, at the cafeteria of my primary school, St. Theresa's Convent, an all-girls school in Kuala Lumpur. Square slabs of tofu were deep-fried, sliced into triangular shapes, and arranged in neat rows on the counter. When I placed an order, the Chinese lady slit the tofu inside and stuffed it with thinly sliced cucumber, jicama, and bean sprouts. Before handing it to me, she topped it with a sweet spicy red chile sauce called Linggam's. I remember relishing the refreshing, crispy-crunchy vegetables along with the soft, chewy texture of tofu. It provided a warm, comfy feeling of satisfaction after a morning of stressful math classes.

Using crunchy vegetables is important when preparing this snack. In this recipe, I use a stuffing of vegetables commonly available in the U.S along with a spicy, sweet, fruity sauce that I created. This is a quick meal that you can enjoy with a cup of iced coffee, hot tea, or cold soymilk. Malaysians traditionally deep-fry tofu, but you can also pan-fry till they get light brown for a healthier version.

DIRECTIONS:

1. Pan-fry tofu till light brown in a non-stick skillet. (Alternately, heat oil and deep-fry tofu till golden brown. Drain and place on paper towels.)
2. Slit inside the long side of each tofu triangle creating a pocket. Stuff pockets with shredded lettuce, cucumber, carrots, and bean sprouts. Set aside.
3. To make spicy plum sauce, process chile, garlic, dried plums, and brown sugar with ¾ cup water to a smooth paste. In a saucepan or deep skillet, combine paste and remaining sauce ingredients, stir well, and bring to boil. Cool sauce.
4. Before serving, top stuffed tofu with spicy plum sauce and sprinkle with toasted sesame seeds. Serve at room temperature.

Serve with *teh masala* (page 259), regular tea, soymilk, beer, or wine.

Spiced Lentil Cakes
Masala Vadai

Makes 4 to 6 servings (17 to 18 cakes)

Periama (Grandma) loved deep-fried masala vadai *as a girl growing up in Coimbatore, South India. According to Periama,* masala vadai *are made from* channa dhal *(yellow split peas or split chickpeas) called* kadalai paripu *in Tamil, sometimes mixed with* urad dhal *(black lentils with skin and white when skinless). She also enjoyed the other* vadai, ulunthu vadai, *which she served with a fragrant coconut chutney or* sambhar *for breakfast.* Ulunthu vadai *are made solely from* urad dhal *and look like little doughnuts. I enjoy* masala vadai *for its crunchy smooth textures. In this recipe, I use* channa dhal *with chopped green and red chilies. In addition to the spices listed with the ingredients, you can also add a little ground fennel seeds, black pepper, or fenugreek to create a more intense flavor.*

INGREDIENTS

1 cup *channa dhal* (yellow split peas)
2 tablespoons diced shallots or onions (¼-inch pieces)
1 heaping teaspoon chopped fresh ginger
1 tablespoon chopped fresh green chilies (cayenne, jalapeno, Serrano, New Mexican, or Thai)
1 tablespoon chopped fresh red chilies (cayenne, Fresno, jalapeno, Serrano, cherry, or Thai)
1 teaspoon toasted and coarsely ground cumin seeds or ground cumin
⅛ teaspoon chile powder
⅛ teaspoon asafetida powder
1 tablespoon chopped fresh curry leaves or cilantro
¼ teaspoon salt
Oil for deep-frying

DIRECTIONS:

1. Soak *channa dhal* in 3 to 3¼ cups water for about 3 to 4 hours or overnight. Drain. This makes 2 cups soaked dhal. (Alternately, bring water to a boil, add dhal and cook till somewhat soft.)
2. Set aside ¼ cup cooked or soaked dhal and blend remaining 1¾ cups dhal with ¼ cup water to a coarsely blended batter.
3. Mix dhal batter with rest of the ingredients except the oil. Stir in the reserved ¼ cup cooked or soaked dhal.
4. Heat oil in pan. Spoon about 1 tablespoon batter at a time into the oil and deep-fry till golden brown. Drain on paper towels.

Serve with *sambar* (page 88), coconut or tamarind chutney, mint coriander dip (page 63), or plain yogurt.

Ma and Periama (my grandmother)

Spicy Pickled Fish
Umai

Makes 4 to 6 servings

INGREDIENTS

10 ounces fresh tuna fillet, sliced into 1-inch cubes
6 tablespoons freshly squeezed or bottled lime juice

SPICE PASTE

½ cup sliced shallots or onions
1 heaping tablespoon chopped garlic cloves
2 teaspoons sliced fresh ginger
1 fresh green chile pepper (jalapeno, Serrano, cayenne, Thai, or bird pepper), sliced
¼ teaspoon ground black pepper
⅛ to ¼ teaspoon turmeric powder
1 heaping teaspoon dried shrimp paste (*belacan*), toasted at 400°F for about 15 minutes (*see page 335*)
2½ tablespoons freshly squeezed or bottled lime juice

GARNISH

About ⅓ cup thinly sliced shallots or red onions
2 heaping teaspoons finely sliced fresh ginger
1 heaping tablespoon thinly sliced lime or lemon rind
1 fresh red chile (cayenne, Fresno, jalapeno, Serrano, Thai, or bird pepper), thinly sliced lengthwise
¾ teaspoon salt

I first tasted umai, *a much-loved, spicy pickled fish, when my family was vacationing in Sarawak, East Malaysia. It reminded me of Latin American ceviche.* Umai *is generally prepared with mackerel, fresh tuna, carp,* ikan piring, *swordfish, or trout (all high in omega 3 fatty acids). The local Melanau fishermen prepare* umai *for their meals at sea using fresh raw slices of white fish they catch (usually pomfret known locally as* duai*), and they eat it with sago. They marinate the* umai *with a local very sour fruit called* asam paya, *also referred to as* asam kelubi, *a fig-shaped wild palm fruit with a scaly reddish-brown skin found growing in the swampy areas of Sarawak. And then they season it with shallots, green peppercorns, and chilies.*

Most umai *recipes at food establishments call for the juice of musk limes, a local Malaysian lime (also called* kalamansi, *or* limau kasturi*), fiery* cili padi *(bird peppers), ginger, garlic, and turmeric. You can use Key lime (*limau nipis*), regular Persian lime, or bottled lemon or lime juice, or even vinegar. Serve* umai *over fresh greens or with cooked white rice. You can also use shrimp instead of fish. I use slightly more turmeric to give a beautiful color to the* umai.

DIRECTIONS:

1. Pour lime juice over fish and coat well. Refrigerate.
2. Process Spice Paste ingredients to a smooth paste, adding 2 to 4 tablespoons water as needed.
3. Coat marinated fish with the Spice Paste. Chill.
4. Before serving, toss with garnish and blend.

Serve with cooked white or brown rice, or yellow rice (page 118). Or place over salad greens. You can also serve as a spread on crusty slices of toast for a spicy tangy Malaysian-style bruschetta.

Fisherman of East Malaysia

Spicy Fish Cutlets

Ketulan Ikan Berempah

Makes 4 to 5 servings (16 to 18 cutlets)

Ma created these warm, soft, and spicy fish cutlets to introduce more fish in our diets. Depending on your taste, the cutlets can have a smooth or coarse texture. A firm white fish (swordfish, snapper, cod, bream, hake, grouper, sea bass, or haddock) is preferable. You can also use shrimp or crabmeat instead of fish. While my daughter Geeta was growing up, I made Ma's fish cutlets with sole or flounder, and sometimes added mashed tofu instead of breadcrumbs or potatoes. In this recipe given to me by my sister Vas, I have added a blend of spices that adds an extra boost of flavor.

INGREDIENTS

1 pound potatoes
14 ounces fillet of sole, flounder, or any other soft-fleshed fish
1 tablespoon cooking oil
1 heaping tablespoon crushed or chopped garlic cloves
1 heaping tablespoon crushed or chopped fresh ginger
¾ cup finely chopped shallots or onions
1 fresh red chile (cayenne, Fresno, jalapeno, Serrano, Thai, or bird pepper), chopped
½ cup coriander leaves (cilantro)
¾ teaspoon salt
2 teaspoons freshly squeezed or bottled lime or lemon juice
1 egg, beaten
½ cup dried breadcrumbs
1 to 2 tablespoons cooking oil

SPICE BLEND

¾ teaspoon ground cumin
¾ teaspoon ground coriander
¼ teaspoon ground fennel seeds
¼ teaspoon ground black pepper
¼ teaspoon turmeric powder
¼ teaspoon chile powder or ground paprika
⅛ teaspoon cinnamon powder
⅛ teaspoon ground fenugreek

MINT CORIANDER DIP

¼ cup mint leaves
¼ cup coriander leaves (cilantro)
1 fresh green chile (jalapeno, Serrano, cayenne, or New Mexican)
¼ cup chopped shallots or onions
¼ teaspoon salt
1 teaspoon sugar
2 tablespoons freshly squeezed or bottled lime or lemon juice

DIRECTIONS:

1. Bring water to boil in a medium pot, add potatoes and cook till done. Drain and cool (or rinse under cold running water). Peel skin and mash (about 1½ cups packed).
2. Combine Spice Blend ingredients and set aside.
3. To soften fish, cook or steam in a little water for about 2 minutes, or microwave for 60 seconds; then coarsely flake or mash.
4. Heat oil in a skillet or wok and sauté garlic and ginger for about ½ to 1 minute. Add shallots or onions and sauté another 1 to 2 minutes.
5. Add Spice Blend and stir for a ½ minute, then add chile and sauté another ½ minute. Add the flaked or mashed fish and sauté for 2 to 3 minutes.
6. Stir in the mashed potatoes and sauté for another 1 to 2 minutes. Add coriander leaves, salt, lemon juice, and half the beaten egg, and blend well for ½ minute. Remove from heat, cool, and refrigerate for about 30 minutes.
7. Roll fish mixture into balls the size of regular limes (about 2 inches in diameter) and flatten them into patties. Dip patties into remaining beaten egg and coat with breadcrumbs.
8. Pan-fry patties on both sides in a little oil about 4 minutes, till they turn golden brown (or you can deep-fry them).
9. Process all the ingredients for the Mint Coriander Dip with ¼ cup water to a smooth paste. Stir well before serving. Serve with the fish cutlets.

Serve with mint coriander dip or cooked *sambal belacan* (page 102), and beer, wine, or tea. Or serve over a bed of greens. You can also serve as a side dish with cooked white or brown rice, tomato rice (page 119), or vegetable *biryani* (page 280) with *sambar* (page 88) and a mixed vegetable *acar* (page 93).

Hot and Spicy Chicken Wings

Kepak Ayam Berempah

Makes 3 to 4 servings

INGREDIENTS

1 pound chicken wings
1 to 2 tablespoons cornstarch, rice starch, or tapioca starch
1 to 2 tablespoons cooking oil, or enough for deep-frying

MARINADE

1 tablespoon ginger juice, squeezed from 2 tablespoons crushed fresh ginger
1 teaspoon regular soy sauce
1 teaspoon honey or sugar
Optional: 1 teaspoon Worcestershire sauce
1 teaspoon ground coriander
1 teaspoon ground cumin
¾ teaspoon ground fennel seeds
½ teaspoon ground mustard
½ teaspoon ground chile pepper
½ teaspoon ground paprika
½ teaspoon sweet thick or double black soy sauce
½ teaspoon rice vinegar, rice wine, or distilled white vinegar
¼ teaspoon turmeric powder
¼ teaspoon finely ground black pepper
¼ teaspoon salt

GARNISH

Lime or lemon wedges
Slices of cucumber
Slices of tomato

In Malaysia, there are many different ways to prepare chicken wings, taking flavor cues from Chinese, Malays, Eurasians, Kristangs, or Indians. Chinese love to serve chicken wings, seasoned with oyster sauce, honey, sesame oil, and ginger, during their Chinese New Year. For their Sunday meals, the Kristangs of Malacca make chicken wings with Worcestershire sauce, white wine, mustard, and blend of spices, and serve them with rice, noodles, or breads. Malays and Indians enjoy a hot and spicier style.

This recipe is my own version of chicken wings with a little added "zing." I use Ma's technique for tenderizing the chicken—squeezing ginger juice over the chicken and allowing it to marinate for 1 hour before cooking. I like mine sautéed or stir-fried, which gives an equally delicious flavor as deep-frying. These spicy chicken wings are always a big hit as party hors d'oeuvres matched with a glass of wine or cold beer.

DIRECTIONS:

1. Combine Marinade ingredients and blend well.
2. Rub chicken wings with Marinade and set aside for at least 1 to 3 hours or overnight in the refrigerator.
3. If deep-frying: coat marinated chicken wings with the starch. Heat oil and deep-fry chicken wings for about 5 to 8 minutes till golden brown. Drain chicken wings on paper towels.
4. If sautéing: heat 1 to 2 tablespoons of oil in a skillet or wok, add chicken wings and stir for about 2 to 3 minutes till brown. Then add ¾ cup water, cover, and let cook for about 5 to 8 minutes. Uncover and cook another 15 minutes, stirring frequently, till wings are cooked. Add starch and continue stirring till sauce coats wings. (Another alternative is to bake the chicken wings at 450°F for about 30 minutes.)
5. Squeeze lime or lemon juice over wings and serve on a bed of cucumber and tomato slices.

Serve with beer or wine. Or for a meal serve with fried rice (page 123) or tomato rice (page 119); and cucumber pineapple *acar* (page 98), stir-fried okra, stir-fried cabbage (page 226), or braised spicy long beans (page 230).

Barbecued Chicken with Spicy Peanut Sauce

Satay Ayam dan Kuah Kacang

Makes 5 to 6 servings

While most Americans associate satay *with Thai cuisine,* satay *is really a Malaysian recipe with origins in Arab kebabs. Watching the* satay *man preparing this national specialty was always great fun. First he would place a dozen or so skewers of marinated chicken over a portable charcoal fire. He would then bruise a lemongrass stalk and crush it with the back of a knife. He then dipped the lemongrass "brush" in peanut oil and basted the chicken skewers (*satay*) while turning them. As we watched him in excited anticipation, fanning the* satay*, a waft of smoky delicious aroma drifted to our table, making our mouths water. The peanut sauce is essential to the true* satay *experience. You can substitute crunchy or smooth peanut butter for the unsalted roasted peanuts in this recipe, and the sauce tastes equally great.*

INGREDIENTS

1 to 2 tablespoons thinly sliced or chopped palm sugar or dark brown sugar (or use light brown sugar for a lighter color)
½ to ¾ teaspoon salt
1 teaspoon rice vinegar or distilled white vinegar
1½ pounds boneless chicken breasts, thinly sliced into 2-inch to 3-inch lengths**
Optional: 1 lemongrass stalk, bruised with the back of a knife (*to be used as a brush for basting*)
¼ to ½ cup cooking oil for basting

Satay Marinade

2 to 3 teaspoons sliced garlic cloves
½ teaspoon sliced fresh ginger
¾ cup chopped shallots or onions
1 lemongrass stalk, sliced into ¼-inch to ½-inch pieces (about ¼ cup)

Spice Blend

1 teaspoon ground coriander
½ teaspoon ground fennel seeds
½ teaspoon ground cumin
¼ to ½ teaspoon turmeric powder
¼ teaspoon ground chile powder

Garnish

Sliced shallot or onion rings
Sliced cucumbers

Spicy Peanut Sauce

(*see next page*)

DIRECTIONS:

1. Process Marinade ingredients with ¼ cup water to a smooth paste. Combine Spice Blend ingredients. Add Spice Blend, sugar,* salt, and vinegar to the marinade and mix well.
2. Rub chicken with the marinade paste to coat. Marinate for a minimum of 2 to 4 hours but preferably overnight in the refrigerator.
3. Skewer marinated chicken (if using wooden skewers, soak them first in warm water for about 20 to 30 minutes to soften).
4. Grill chicken (preferably over charcoal fire), basting occasionally with lemongrass brush or regular basting brush dipped in the oil or oil-sugar mixture.**

*Alternately, you can use ½ tablespoon of the sugar in the marinade and keep the remaining ½ tablespoon sugar to mix with the oil for basting the chicken.

**Alternately, you can cut the chicken into slices or small cubes, season with the marinade paste, and broil for about 8 to 10 minutes, turning after first 4 to 6 minutes.

Serve with spicy peanut sauce (page 66), compressed rice (page 281), sliced cucumbers, and sliced onion rings. You can also serve *satay* with fried rice (page 123), vegetable *biryani* (page 280), or spiced rice (page 120); and stir-fried mixed vegetables (page 224).

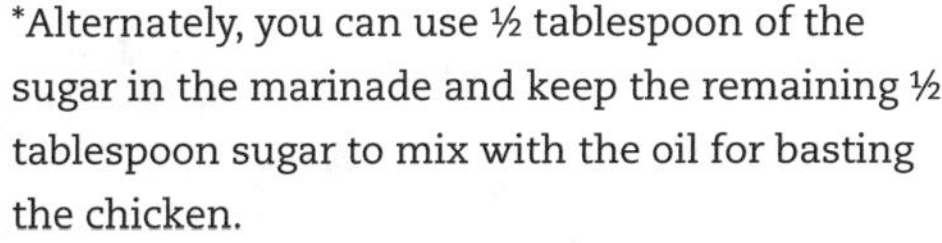

Kajang *satay* being grilled

Spicy Peanut Sauce
Kuah Kacang

Makes about 1½ cups sauce

INGREDIENTS

2 to 3 tablespoons cooking oil
¾ teaspoon ground coriander
½ teaspoon ground cumin
¼ teaspoon turmeric powder
2 tablespoons tamarind concentrate or tamarind juice extracted from pulp (*see page 339*)
¼ cup packed thinly sliced or chopped palm sugar or brown sugar
1 to 1¼ teaspoons salt
1 cup unsalted roasted peanuts, finely ground, or ½ cup crunchy peanut butter
¾ to 1 cup unsweetened coconut milk (*if roasted peanuts are used*), or ¼ cup (*if peanut butter is used*)

Spice Paste

2 teaspoons chopped garlic cloves
¼ cup chopped shallots or onions
1 teaspoon chopped fresh or frozen and thawed galangal or fresh ginger
1 to 3 dried chilies, soaked in hot water for 15 minutes, slit and deseeded; or ½ to 1 teaspoon *cili boh* (*see page 315*); or ¼ to ½ teaspoon bottled *sambal oelek*; or ¼ to ½ teaspoon chile powder (*depending on heat desired*)
¼ cup sliced lemongrass stalk (¼-inch to ½-inch pieces)
Optional: 1 teaspoon dried shrimp paste (*belacan*), toasted at 400°F for 15 minutes (*see page 335*)
¼ cup water

This makes a wonderful dipping sauce for the chicken satay *on page* 65.

DIRECTIONS:

1. Process Spice Paste ingredients to a smooth paste.
2. Heat 1 tablespoon of oil in a skillet or wok and sauté Spice Paste for 1 to 2 minutes, then add coriander, cumin, and turmeric and an additional 1 tablespoon of oil and sauté for another 4 to 6 minutes till fragrant, adding more oil if necessary.
3. Add tamarind juice, sugar, and salt and sauté for another 1 to 2 minutes.
4. Add peanuts or peanut butter, coconut milk, and 1¼ to 1½ cups water and stir continuously till oil seeps out from sauce, about 15 to 20 minutes.
5. Serve with barbecued chicken (*satay ayam*, page 65).

Satay with spicy peanut sauce, cubes of compressed rice and onions

FRIED SWEET BANANA FRITTERS

Goreng Pisang Manis

Makes 6 to 8 servings

When our family traveled by car, we often snacked on goreng pisang. *My father would stop at thatch-covered stalls along the roadside, where a Malay man would be standing over a huge metal wok filled with hot oil and sizzling bananas. Cha would order a bunch to go and they would still be warm when we snacked on them.*

Vendors usually set up stalls or carts on Malaysia's beaches and use makeshift fryers to deep-fry sweet bananas. As I watched my daughter Geeta playing on the beach sand, I usually enjoyed my goreng pisang, *or "hot-hot"* pisang *as vendors say, with a cup of milky sweet* teh tarik. *At these moments, it was easy to close my eyes and remember Ma standing over the frying pan making* goreng pisang *while Periama was busily boiling tea leaves to prepare her delicious tea.*

Nowadays, you can find vendors on many street corners or around shopping areas deep-frying bananas in large metal woks for the late afternoon snack break. As in my recipe, many restaurants serve goreng pisang *topped with vanilla ice cream or sweet pandan-flavored sauce. "Cooking bananas," such as* pisang mas *(small fragrant and sweet bananas),* pisang raja *(small sweet bananas),* pisang awak *(bananas with black seeds), and* pisang abu, *are sliced and coated with flour batter and fried to a crispy golden brown. Regular bananas or sweet ripe plantains popular in Latino cooking can also be used.*

INGREDIENTS

1 cup all-purpose flour (white wheat flour)
¼ cup rice flour
¼ teaspoon salt
¼ teaspoon baking soda
2 drops yellow food coloring
Oil for deep-frying
1 pound bananas (6 regular large yellow bananas or 12 small sweet yellow bananas), peeled and split in half lengthwise
1 to 2 tablespoons powdered sugar
1 teaspoon ground cinnamon

PANDAN SAUCE (SOS PANDAN)

6 tablespoons unsweetened coconut milk
1 knotted pandan leaf, or 2 or 3 drops of pandan-flavored paste, extract, or essence
¾ cup sweetened condensed milk
2 teaspoons cornstarch, rice starch, or tapioca starch mixed with 1 tablespoon water to create a paste

DIRECTIONS:

1. Sift both flours, salt, and baking soda, and mix well.
2. Mix yellow food coloring with ¾ to 1 cup water and blend.
3. Add this colored water to the dry flour mixture slowly, while whisking, to get a smooth batter.
4. Heat oil in a deep frying pan. Dip sliced bananas into batter, allow excess batter to drip off and deep-fry in heated oil till golden brown, about 6 to 8 minutes for large bananas and 3 to 4 minutes for small bananas. Drain on paper towels. Set aside.
5. Combine all pandan sauce ingredients except starch paste with ½ cup water in a saucepan and bring to a boil. Lower heat and simmer for 5 minutes. Add starch paste and cook for about 2 to 3 minutes longer till sauce thickens. Cool.
6. Drizzle pandan sauce over fried bananas or dust with powdered sugar blended with cinnamon. Serve while fritters are still crispy and warm.

Fried sweet bananas can also be served with vanilla, coconut, mango, or strawberry ice cream, frozen yogurt, or sorbet.

Preparing *Thosai* the Traditional Way

If I woke up early on Sunday morning, I could find Periama at the back of the house, sitting on a low stool next to our family's traditional wet grinder called an *atte kallu*. The *atte kallu* was a two-part, hand-operated grinding machine, similar to a mortar and pestle but much larger. The base of the *atte kallu* consisted of a large granite "mortar" with a large hole in the center. The hole was fitted with a second large cylindrical rock that worked as the "pestle." The pestle tapered to a handle which you would slowly turn in a circular motion with both hands to grind spices, lentils, or rice. In order for the *atte kallu* to work properly, it was critical to keep the interior surface of the 'mortar' rough. Because the grinding process would slowly smooth the stone surface over time, Ma would periodically have a vendor roughen the surface with a special chisel. Nowadays, most Indian families have replaced their *atte kallu* with an electric blender, but anyone who has tasted food prepared with the traditional hand grinder will swear that it tastes better.

To prepare her *thosai*, Periama would concoct her own special blend of cooked rice, skinned black lentils called *urad dhal*, fenugreek seeds, salt, and water, and allow it to ferment overnight. The next morning she poured it into the *atte kallu* and then slowly turned the handle of the grinding stone in a steady, circular motion. To ensure optimum texture for the finished *thosai*, she carefully added water to make the batter just right.

Periama (my grandmother)

Sometimes Periama allowed me to grind, but it was a slow process and I could not move the mortar as well, as I was only ten years old. She just smiled and told me that she grew up watching her cooks make *thosai* and that was how she learned to prepare *thosai* for us.

Once Periama prepared the batter to the correct consistency (smooth and slightly grainy), she went into the kitchen, scooped the batter with a ladle and placed it on a heated flat cast iron griddle. She then gently spread the batter outward with the bottom of the ladle, drawing concentric circles of batter till it spread into a large circular crepe with tiny 'holes' popping up. Then she flipped it and did the same on the other side till it turned light brown.

Savory Rice Lentil Crepes

Thosai

Makes 9 servings (18 medium crepes)

For our family, Sunday mornings provided a special culinary treat—Periama's (Grandma) crispy thosai *and her signature fragrant fish curry.* Thosai *is a crepe-like pancake made from a fermented batter of rice and* urad dhal *(black lentils, also called black gram).*

Periama had already prepared the fish curry and sambar *(spicy lentil sauce) which sat covered on the burners, the scent enticing me. Once she made the first* thosai, *she placed it on a plate, added a bit of* sambar *and fish curry next to it, and handed the plate to lucky me. The crepe looked pretty with small 'holes' all over. I enjoyed it while it was steaming hot, all the while watching her make more* thosai *for my sisters and brothers.*

Today in Malaysia, Malays, Chinese, and Indians throng to Indian coffee shops and restaurants to enjoy thosai *for lunch with chicken or fish curries,* sambars *or chutneys, or mutton* peratil *(dry-fried goat or lamb curry). Indian vegetarians enjoy* thosai *topped (or stuffed) with curried vegetables or potatoes. There are also other variations of* thosai *using wheat flour, semolina, or millet. Here is Periama's* thosai *recipe. They also serve well as an appetizer with beer, wine, soft drinks, or tea.*

INGREDIENTS

- 1 cup skinless split *urad dhal* (black lentil), washed and rinsed
- 3 cups long grain white rice, washed and rinsed
- 1½ teaspoons fenugreek seeds
- 1 teaspoon salt
- 2 tablespoons cooking oil

DIRECTIONS:

1. Place all ingredients except the oil in a bowl. Add 9 cups water and let soak overnight at room temperature to ferment (about 12 hours in warm weather and about 20 hours during colder weather).
2. Drain rice/dhal mixture, reserving soaking liquid. Place rice/dhal mixture in a blender with 2¼ cups of the soaking water and process till smooth.
3. Add the remaining soaking water and mix well. Place in a bowl, cover, and let ferment for about 2 to 3 hours at room temperature. The mixture will have a spongy and slightly grainy consistency with a slightly fermented pungent flavor. Set aside.
4. Heat an iron griddle or skillet and then lightly oil it.
5. Ladle about a ½ cup batter onto the griddle, and using the ladle or a large spoon spread the batter from its center outward, making concentric circles while thinning out the batter (bubbles will develop and tiny holes will be created) till *thosai* is about 7 inches in diameter with a crepe-like consistency. (You can make any size *thosai* you want. The thinner the batter, the crispier the *thosai*.)
6. Heat the *thosai* on medium heat for about 1 minute till it turns light brown on one side. Then flip over and heat another 1 minute till the other side turns light brown.

Serve while piping hot with fish curry (page 198), lamb *peratil* (page 185), chicken curry (page 171), *dalcha* (savory meat lentils, page 285), vegetable *kurma* (page 283), spicy dry curried okra (page 221), or *sambar* (page 88). Or serve stuffed with spice-infused potatoes (page 302), dry vegetable or meat curries, or spicy omelet with *keema* (page 305).

Indian Muslim Fresh Spring Rolls

Popiah Basah

Makes 6 to 8 servings (6 rolls; 1¼ cups sauce)

INGREDIENTS

Filling

1 cup (about 5 ounces) cubed firm tofu (*tauhu*) (½-inch pieces)
1 tablespoon cooking oil
1 heaping teaspoon chopped garlic clove
½ cup chopped shallots or onions
½ cup (about 4 ounces) peeled and deveined medium shrimp, chopped
½ teaspoon turmeric powder
½ teaspoon chile powder
¼ teaspoon ground white or black pepper
¾ cup (3¾ ounces) diced carrots
½ cup (2¼ ounces) sliced (crosswise) long beans or green beans
1 cup (5 ounces) julienned yam bean (*bengkuang*) or jicama (1-inch by ⅛-inch pieces)
¼ teaspoon salt

Apricot Date Sauce

½ cup (about 3 ounces) chopped dried apricots or plums
⅓ cup (about 2 ounces) chopped pitted dates
1 teaspoon chopped garlic cloves
2 teaspoons rice vinegar or distilled white vinegar
4 teaspoons light brown sugar
½ teaspoon salt
¼ teaspoon chile powder
½ teaspoon double black soy sauce
½ to 1 teaspoon freshly squeezed or bottled lime juice

(*continued next page*)

Popiah is Malaysia's spring roll. It comes fresh (called popiah basah *or wet* popiah*) and deep-fried (called* popiah kering*). The popiah skin is made from wheat or rice flour, and smeared with a sweet, fruity, and chile-based sauce, like hoisin, date sauce, and/or a sweet black sauce, then filled with fresh vegetables, tofu, and/or shrimp. Once folded, it is topped with a combination of sauces. There are different styles of* popiah *fillings depending on the ethnic group. The Chinese include vegetables as well as diced cooked pork belly, shrimp cooked in* taucheo *(preserved soybean paste),* lapcheong *(Chinese sweet sausage), shredded omelet, and fried minced garlic. The Nonyas use yam bean strips, bean sprouts, shrimp, crabmeat, and garlic paste. The Mamaks or Indian Muslims of Penang, influenced by Arab cooking, include a unique sweet date sauce flavored with fried shallots.*

This popiah *recipe is from my friend, Zubaidah, an Indian Muslim from Penang with Arab and Malay ancestry. I modified the recipe's spicing and use apricots with the dates so that it would appeal to a broader spectrum of tastes.*

DIRECTIONS FOR FILLING:

1. Heat non-stick skillet and pan-fry tofu pieces, stirring and turning them over till they turn light brown and firm. Remove from pan and set aside.
2. Heat oil in the skillet. Add garlic and sauté for ½ to 1 minute, then add shallots and sauté another 1 to 2 minutes till fragrant.
3. Add shrimp, turmeric, chile powder, and white or black pepper and sauté for about 1 minute.
4. Add carrots and long beans or green beans and stir for 1 minute. Add yam bean and stir another 4 to 5 minutes, maintaining the crispiness of vegetables.
5. Add pan-fried tofu and salt and stir for another 1 to 2 minutes. Remove from heat and set aside.

DIRECTIONS FOR APRICOT DATE SAUCE:

1. In a food processor or blender, process apricots, dates, and garlic with 1 cup water to a smooth sauce.
2. Heat saucepan. Add sauce, another 1 cup water, and remaining ingredients except lime juice and simmer for about 15 minutes till sauce becomes thick.
3. Add lime juice and stir for another 1 to 2 minutes.

A Teochew invention from Fujian, China, *popiah* has become a hawker specialty in Malaysia. The Indian Muslims or Mamaks have their own variation which is different from the Chinese or Nonyas. I remember the elderly Mamak vendor in Muar, who filled the rolls with sliced turnips, cucumber, tofu puffs, pineapple, and unripe guava, topped with bean sprouts and a drizzle of dark brown sauce.

POPIAH

6 spring roll skins (made from rice paper), soaked in warm or hot water for about 30 to 40 seconds, or use *popiah* skin (homemade), about 6 inches in diameter
6 lettuce leaves
¼ cup (about ¾ ounce) bean sprouts, rinsed or blanched
¼ cup chopped fresh mint or cilantro
Optional: ¼ cup fried shallots or onions (*see page 333*)
1 teaspoon chile sauce or bottled *sambal oelek*

DIRECTIONS FOR *POPIAH*:

1. Smear the inside of each spring roll or *popiah* skin with some apricot sauce.
2. Place a lettuce leaf on each skin, then add about 2 tablespoons of filling to each.
3. Garnish with a sprinkling of bean sprouts, mint leaves or cilantro, and fried shallots, if using.
4. Fold the *popiah* skins into the shape of a spring roll or egg roll.
5. Top each roll with a tablespoon of apricot sauce (and touch of *sambal oelek* or any chile sauce if desired) and cut the rolls into 2 or 3 pieces and serve.

Indian Muslim *popiah* vendor, Penang

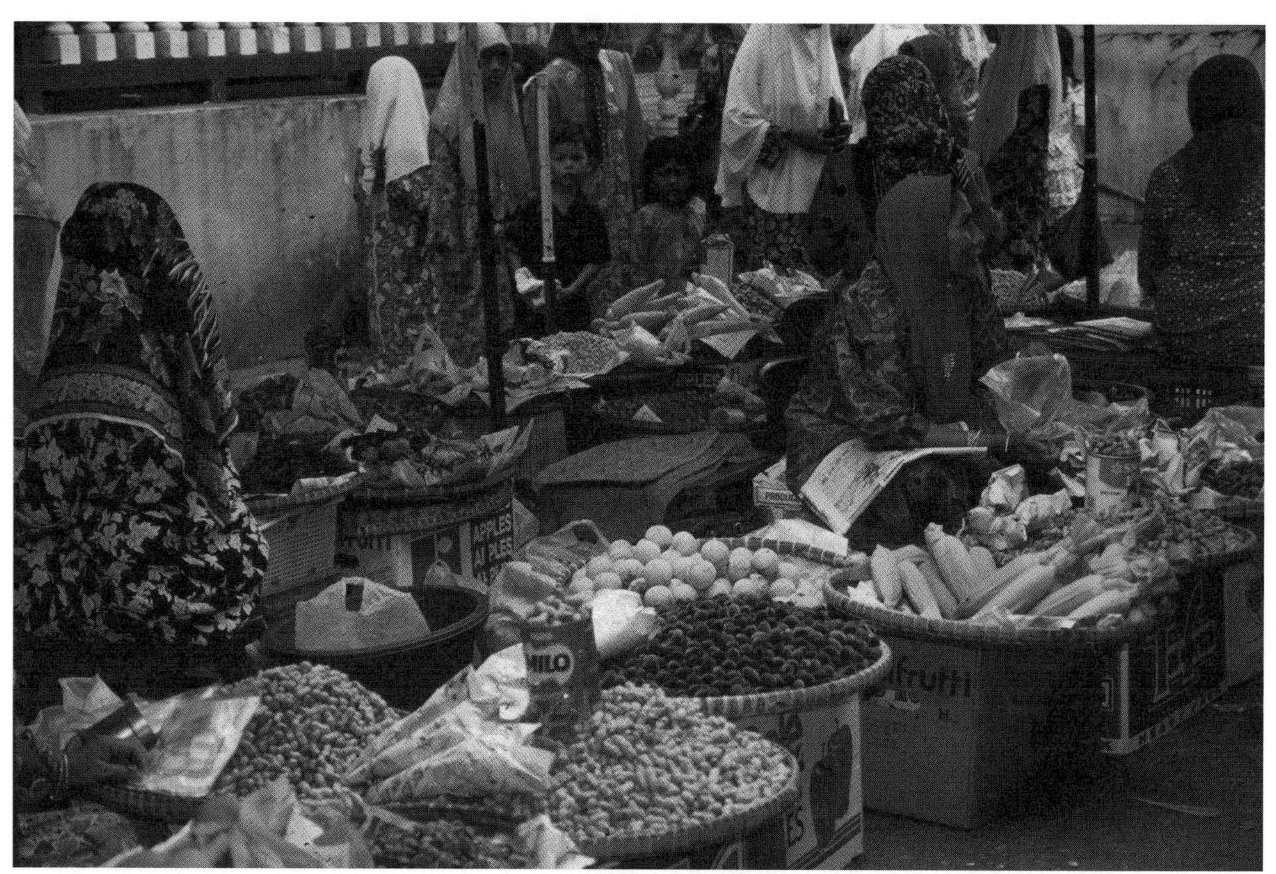

Khatijah Market snack vendors, Kota Bahru, Kelantan

CHAPTER 2

SOUPS AND STEWS: A RECIPE FOR COMFORT

Chee cheong fan vendor, Petaling Jaya

Malaysian soups come in a variety of forms—clear and hearty soups, noodle soups, rice porridges, curry stews, and herbal soups. Chinese cooks prepare innovative soups from all parts of the pig, poultry, or cow, and aromatic stocks or broths from shrimp shells or fish bones.

The Chinese in Malaysia, especially the Cantonese and Teochews, have created numerous noodle soups, light or dark—chicken noodle soup, claypot noodle soup, various seafood noodle soups, and *kway teow ting* (rice noodles in savory soup). Duck noodle soup is a favorite with Penang hawkers. For the Chinese and Nonyas, noodles represent long life and thus soups with noodles are often served on birthdays and on the first day of the Chinese New Year.

On damp rainy days, we especially enjoyed slurping steaming Chinese noodle soups. *Mee suah* (*meehoon* soup with rice vermicelli) or *sup mee* (page 83) with wheat flour and egg-based yellow noodles swimming in a clear savory broth, prepared with sliced fish balls or chicken and a bit of Chinese greens, was a comforting meal or snack for us.

While Chinese soups are served hot, Chinese Traditional Medicine says that some soups "warm" the body (yang soups) while others "cool" the body (yin soups). Ideally in a meal, foods are served to balance the body's yin and yang so as to achieve harmony, thus preventing ailments and sicknesses. Winter melon soup (*sup timun Eropah*, page 82) is a traditional Cantonese-style soup eaten as a yin or "cooling" soup. Another popular Chinese medicinal soup is *bakuteh* (pork rib soup, page 87), made with a rich broth of pork (including innards, belly, and/or knuckles) seasoned with Chinese herbs and spices, all simmered in a claypot till the meat falls off the bone.

Nonya soups and stews reflect their Chinese ancestry. They include *itek Tim* (duck cooked with pickled mustard greens called *kiam chye* and preserved plums), peppery

As children, we all loved *chee cheong fan* (steamed rolled rice noodles) with stuffed vegetables. Usually on a late Sunday morning, my brother Sree and sister Prema would sit on the porch and look out for the *chee cheong fan* vendor. When Sree heard him announce his arrival with a loud sing song "*chee cheong fan*" he would flag him down, while Prema would run into the kitchen to get a few plates from Ma. Using a pair of scissors, the vendor cut up the rolled steamed rice noodles and placed them on the plates. Next, he opened a container of vegetables stuffed with seasoned fish paste (also referred to as *yong tau foo*) and added them on the plate with some broth. Finally, he drizzled on a couple of different colored sauces, and topped it off with toasted sesame seeds. The combination of the sweet spicy flavors and varied textures was magnificent.

papaya soup, salted vegetable soup, and yam and chicken soup flavored with *taucheo*. Many Nonya hearty stews (cooked with noodles or rice) are themselves a complete meal. These dishes include the popular Nonya dish *pong teh* (prepared with pork or chicken with yam and seasoned with *taucheo*, page 188), spicy fish stew with vegetables and pineapples, and crabmeat and vegetable stew.

Eurasian stews and soups, derived from their Portuguese, Dutch, or English, and Chinese heritage, are slow cooked with meats and vegetables and flavored with Worcestershire sauce, vinegar, ketchup, spices, and hot chilies. They are sometimes thickened with wheat or corn flour, crushed biscuits, or breadcrumbs. The soup-loving community of Malacca, the Kristangs, prepare their soups (called *caldu*) and stews (*stius*) with seafood, pork, and beef and any leftover ingredients. Soups are generally served as the first course in a meal with crusty bread or rice, while elaborate stews are reserved for festive occasions and celebrations. Kristang soups are frequently spicy compared to traditional Portuguese soups. *Caldu pescador* (fisherman's soup), *caldu laler-laler* (baby mussels with lemongrass soup), *caldu bayam* (spinach fish ball soup), and *teem* (anise and cinnamon-flavored duck soup) are popular. Eurasians love stews and serve them for special occasions. *Semur*, a pork and beef oxtail and tongue stew, is served during Christmas. Other popular Eurasian stews include beef stew (like Irish stew), kidney beans and pork stew (similar to Brazil's *feijoada*), *feng* (a mix of different cuts of meat in a curry broth, similar to the Goan *sorpotel*), spicy sausage and potato stew, and mulligatawny soup (peppery soup with chicken and rice).

Malays enjoy spicy soups prepared with beef, mutton, chicken, fish, and fragrant roots. Malays believe that ox-tail soup helps blood circulation and even enhances male virility. *Mee soto*, a lunch favorite that originated in Java, Indonesia, has rice vermicelli or yellow noodles with chicken, hard-boiled eggs, and fried potatoes. Another popular Malay soup is *soto ayam* (similar to *sup ayam* recipe on page 78) prepared with shredded chicken, lemongrass, turmeric, and bean sprouts, accompanied by fried onions and a fiery *cili padi sambal*.

Indian Muslims (Mamaks) spice up various parts of the cow or goat to make interesting soups which they sop up with breads—*roti Bengali* (a crusty bread) or *roti bakar* (toasted bread). Indian Muslim vendors of Selangor and Penang have a signature soup called *sup tulang* or "bone soup" (a spicy sweet, long-simmering soup made with mutton bones or beef ribs). One popular variation is *sup kambing* (mutton soup spiced with cinnamon, cloves, and cardamom, page 79) created by Indian Muslim cooks for their colonial rulers during the British rule. Other variations include *sup bola* (prepared from bull testicles) and *sup torpedo* (prepared from bulls' genitals), both believed by Muslims to enhance male virility. I often used to wonder why my father frequented the Mamak soup stalls, although all he raved about was their *murtabak* (meat and egg stuffed flatbread)!

Malays and Indian Muslims also break their fasts during Ramadan month (also called *bulan puasa*) at home with soups and stews, because they are nutritious and easy-to-prepare communal meals for the whole family. *Singgang ikan* (page 81) is a hot, sour, and mildly sweet soup that originated in the eastern states of Terengganu, Kelantan, and Pahang. It is frequently served for Hari Raya, a festive celebration after Ramadan. In Sarawak, Muslims break their fast with *bubur pedas* (spicy porridge) containing beef or shrimp in a spicy coconut milk broth.

In the North because of Thai influences, the Thai hot and sour *sup tom yam* (page 80) is a local favorite. It has also become popular all over Malaysia and many vendors and restaurants now serve *tom yam*-based noodle soups, while the Chinese use *sup tom yam* as a base stock for their steamboat recipe called *lok-lok* (similar to the Mongolian hot pot), a Cantonese specialty. Pieces of cuttlefish, shrimp, scallops, crabsticks, chicken, meat, and fresh vegetables are cooked in a pot of boiling seasoned broth or soup placed at the center of the table. The cooked food is eaten with a variety of dipping sauces. When all the meats and vegetables are eaten, noodles are finally added to the broth and eaten.

Though soups are less prominent in Indian Malaysian meals, there are some that are still very popular, such as *rasam* and *sothi*. *Rasam* (page 76) is a spice-based soup that comes in several varieties. *Sothi* (page 77), the Malaysian version of the Thai *tom kha gha*, is a spicy coconut-milk-based soup that also becomes a complete meal with rice vermicelli, rice, or *iddiappam* (stringhoppers or extruded steamed rice vermicelli). Indians generally eat soups toward the end of their meal, to aid with digestion. Lentil-and-vegetable-based stews, such as *sambar* (page 88), are eaten with rice or used as a dip for *thosai* (rice-based crepes, page 69) and *idli* (steamed rice cake).

Indians add a variety of spices to soups for specific health considerations. *Rasam*, with its array of spices, is eaten to treat colds or promote proper digestion. Indians believe that the turmeric in *sothi* has multiple health functions, such as helping to offset the negative effects of the fat in coconut milk, and preventing liver disorders and tumors. Today, research is increasingly showing that turmeric has anti-inflammatory properties and can help prevent cancer and the onset of Alzheimer's disease.

Malaysians believe porridges are endowed with medicinal qualities, and so eat them to cure illness, renew strength after childbirth, ease digestion, and fortify the immune system. Soups and broths transform rice into *congee* (porridge), referred to as *bubur* (Malay and Nonya), *kanji* (Tamil), *moey* (Teochew), and *chok or jok* (Cantonese). These soothing soups, depending on the ethnic group, have slices of pork, shredded chicken or beef, pickled vegetables, preserved eggs, and fiery dips. On the East Coast, *nasi bubur* (rice porridge), served with fried fish, pickled garlic, and squid, is a popular meal with Malays. Malays also eat *bubur lambuk* to break their Ramadan fast. This fragrant porridge of ground or chopped beef, chicken, or shrimp cooked in coconut milk and flavored with ginger, fenugreek, cilantro, garlic, and fried shallots is considered soothing for the digestive system. Ma made us *nasi bubur* enhanced with ginger, fennel, and other spices when we fell sick as children. Although it tasted quite good, to this day porridge reminds me of the days when we had fevers and colds!

Spicy Sour Tomato Soup

Tomato Rasam

Makes 3 to 4 servings

INGREDIENTS

- 1 tablespoon cooking oil
- ½ teaspoon black or dark brown mustard seeds
- 2 to 4 dried whole red chilies (*depending on desired heat*)
- 3 or 4 fresh curry leaves
- ⅛ teaspoon turmeric powder
- ⅛ teaspoon asafetida powder
- 4 or 5 garlic cloves, crushed
- ½ heaping teaspoon crushed fresh ginger
- 2 tablespoons chopped shallots or onions
- ½ cup (3 ounces) chopped tomatoes
- 2½ to 3 tablespoons tamarind concentrate or juice from tamarind pulp (*see page 339*)
- ¾ to 1 teaspoon salt
- 2 tablespoons chopped coriander leaves (cilantro)

RASAM PODI*

- 1 tablespoon coriander seeds
- 1 teaspoon fennel seeds
- ¾ teaspoon whole black peppercorns
- ½ teaspoon cumin seeds
- ¼ teaspoon fenugreek seeds

**You can substitute ground spices for the whole spices when making this spice blend. Skip step one and add the ground spices in step 4.*

Rasam is a refreshingly spicy tart soup with South Indian origins. It comes in several flavors—tomato, garlic, and lime. In addition to these three basic flavors, the recipe for rasam *evolved as it traveled with the Indian diaspora. For example, the British adapted* rasam *to European tastes, creating a mild version called* mulligatawny *(from the Tamil words* mulliga thanni *or pepper water). Malaysians also use* rasam *as a base for vegetable, chicken, shrimp, or fish.*

Besides tasting good, rasam *is renowned as a restorative tonic believed to relieve cold symptoms. I especially appreciate a cup of warm and soothing* rasam *during the damp and dreary rainy seasons. Many pour* rasam *over rice at the end of a meal as a digestive aid. During one of my trips to Malaysia, when I experienced a bit of indigestion after indulging in a particularly rich* kurma *curry meal, my sister-in-law Shanta prepared tomato* rasam *for me. It cured my indigestion! In this adaptation of Shanta's recipe, I dry roast a blend of whole spices and then grind them to release a fresher and more aromatic flavor. This spice blend, called* rasam podi*, can be made in advance and kept in the freezer for later use.*

DIRECTIONS:

1. In a heated skillet, dry roast *rasam podi* ingredients about ½ minute, swirling skillet till spices get brown but not burnt. Cool and grind using a coffee grinder or mortar and pestle.
2. Heat oil in saucepan. Add mustard seeds, cover pan and let seeds pop. When popping subsides, add chilies and curry leaves and sauté for another ½ minute.
3. Add freshly ground *rasam podi*, turmeric, and asafetida, and sauté for about ½ minute.
4. Add garlic and ginger, sauté for ½ to 1 minute, and then add shallots or onions and sauté for another 1 to 2 minutes. (If using ground spices in place of the *rasam podi* add them here and sauté for about ½ minute.)
5. Stir in tomatoes and cook for 1 to 2 minutes. Add 4 cups water and bring to boil.
6. Lower heat and stir in tamarind juice and salt and simmer for 10 to 15 minutes.
7. Add coriander leaves and simmer for another 2 minutes.
8. Spoon into bowls and serve warm; or strain and serve the broth; or add a third of strained pulp back into soup and serve.

Rasam is generally eaten hot or warm, but it can also be served chilled with a wedge of lemon or cucumber. Serve with crusty bread or *roti*. You can also add cooked rice, noodles, or pasta, barley, carrots, cabbage, broccoli, and/or beans to create a more filling meal. In addition, for non-vegetarians you can add fish, shrimp, or chicken with a lemongrass stalk (at Step 5). Lemongrass gives an aromatic twist to the soup.

Spicy Coconut Soup
Sothi

Makes 3 to 4 servings

Sothi was brought to Malaysia by South Indian and Ceylonese (Sri Lankan) Tamils. This rich, aromatic soup is prepared with coconut milk, turmeric, tamarind juice, and other spices, and is reminiscent of tom kha gha, *the Thai coconut-lemongrass-based soup. In Malaysia,* sothi *is poured over rice or* iddiappam *(also called* putu mayam*). Keralites and Tamils prefer to serve* sothi *as a meal with fish, potatoes, beans, carrots,* murunggakka *(drumstick-shaped pod of the* moringa *tree), and eggs. The Sri Lankan version is generally made with vegetables and served as a side dish. Our family's* sothi *featured lemongrass, giving it a truly Malaysian taste.*

A rich soup, sothi *is frequently served on special occasions, such as Deepavali, the Hindu Festival of Lights, and at weddings. My sister-in-law Catherine (Kay) learned this Sri Lankan version from her father when she was a teenager. Kay adds rice vermicelli, chicken, and vegetables to make it into a complete meal for her family.*

INGREDIENTS

2 tablespoons cooking oil
1 heaping tablespoon crushed garlic cloves
1 cup diced shallots or onions
¼ teaspoon turmeric powder
1 or 2 fresh green chilies (cayenne, jalapeno, Serrano, Thai, or New Mexican), sliced in half lengthwise
1 cup (6 ounces) sliced or chopped tomatoes
1 lemongrass stalk, bruised or cracked with back of knife and knotted
1 Kaffir lime leaf (with 2 lobes) (*½ teaspoon of lime juice can be substituted for lime leaf but make sure milk does not get curdled*)
1 tablespoon tamarind concentrate or juice from tamarind pulp (*see page 339*)
¾ cup unsweetened coconut milk
¾ teaspoon salt
¼ teaspoon black or dark brown mustard seeds
4 to 6 fresh curry leaves

DIRECTIONS:

1. Heat 1 tablespoon of oil in saucepan. Add garlic and sauté for about ½ to 1 minute; add shallots or onions and sauté about 1 to 2 minutes.
2. Add turmeric powder and chilies, sauté ½ minute, then stir in tomatoes and sauté for 2 to 3 minutes.
3. Add lemongrass and lime leaf and sauté for ½ minute.
4. Mix in tamarind juice, and then coconut milk and 2 cups water and blend well. Bring to a boil. Lower heat, add salt, and simmer for 8 to 10 minutes, stirring occasionally, till sauce becomes aromatic.
5. In a separate skillet, heat remaining tablespoon of oil, add mustard seeds and curry leaves. Cover. When mustard seeds stop "popping" remove pan from heat.
6. Pour this savory oil mixture into the coconut milk broth and cook, with occasional stirring, for another 4 to 5 minutes. Discard lemongrass and lime leaves before serving.

Serve warm with cooked white or brown rice, *iddiappam* (stringhoppers), or warm crusty bread; and a light cucumber carrot *acar* (page 99) or green salad; and lamb *peratil* (page 185), fish curry (page 198), or chicken curry (page 171). Or you can add cooked noodles or pasta and chicken or shrimp to the soup and enjoy as a bowl meal.

Chicken Soup, Malay-style

Sup Ayam ala Melayu

Makes 3 to 4 servings

INGREDIENTS

1 pound chicken (drumsticks, thighs, or breasts)
⅛ or ¼ teaspoon turmeric powder
2 tablespoons cooking oil
1 tablespoon sliced and crushed garlic cloves
1 heaping teaspoon sliced and crushed fresh ginger
⅓ cup diced shallots or onions (¼-inch pieces)
1 fresh red chile (cayenne, Fresno, jalapeno, Serrano, Thai, or cherry), sliced and crushed; or ¼ teaspoon chile powder; or ½ teaspoon *cili boh* (*see page 315*); or ⅛ to ¼ teaspoon bottled *sambal oelek*
1 lemongrass stalk, bruised with back of knife and knotted
1 pound (3 cups) potatoes, halved or quartered
2 salam leaves or bay leaves, or 1 heaping tablespoon coriander leaves (cilantro)
¾ to 1 teaspoon salt
1 cup (5 ounces) sliced carrots (1 to 2-inch pieces) or whole baby carrots

Spice Blend 1

3 cardamom pods
2 cloves
1½-inch cinnamon stick
1 star anise

Spice Blend 2

1 teaspoon coriander seeds or ground coriander
1 teaspoon cumin seeds or ground cumin
½ teaspoon fennel seeds or ground fennel seeds
¼ teaspoon black peppercorns or ground black pepper

Chicken soup is a universal comfort food, and the different ethnic groups in Malaysia have their own special versions. Chinese make it mild, adding ginger and garlic as essential flavorings. Malays and Indian Muslims create fragrant chicken soups with lemongrass, chilies, cinnamon, clove, star anise, and many other spices. Most Malaysians use "kampung" (village) or free-range chicken because it is believed to be more nutritious and flavorful than commercially raised chicken.

Like all mothers worldwide, Ma made chicken soup for us when we fell sick. Likewise, I served it to my daughter Geeta, who enjoyed it during the cold, dreary winter months in New York. This soup reminds me of the spicy Javanese soto ayam *with shredded chicken, hard-boiled eggs, slices of fried potatoes, Chinese celery leaves, and fried shallots. In this recipe, I use cut-up chicken with potatoes and carrots seasoned with lemongrass stalk and spices.*

DIRECTIONS:

1. Cut chicken into 2 to 3-inch pieces. Rub turmeric on chicken pieces and set aside.
2. Dry roast the whole spices in Spice Blend 2 for about ½ to 1 minute. Cool and grind. Set aside. (Or if using ground spices, just combine.)
3. Heat 1 tablespoon oil in skillet, add Spice Blend 1 ingredients and sauté for about ½ to 1 minute. Add garlic and ginger and sauté for about ½ to 1 minute. Add shallots or onions and sauté for 1 to 2 minutes.
4. Add remaining oil and Spice Blend 2 and stir for about ½ minute. Add seasoned chicken and stir for 1 to 2 minutes to coat well with spice paste.
5. Add fresh chile, chile powder, *cili boh,* or *sambal oelek*, and lemongrass, and stir for about 1 minute.
6. Add 4 cups water and potatoes, and bring to a boil. Lower heat, add salam or bay or coriander leaves and salt, cover and simmer for about 15 to 25 minutes, till chicken and potatoes are almost cooked. Add carrots and simmer for an additional 5 to 10 minutes, till vegetables are tender.
7. Discard lemongrass before serving. Garnish with fried shallots or onions and coriander leaves or Chinese celery greens.

Serve with crusty bread or *roti*, or cooked white or brown rice, or spiced rice (page 120); and mixed vegetable *acar* or green salad; and a chile garlic dip (page 109).

Garnish

Optional: ½ cup fried (*see page 333*) or sautéed shallots or onions
1 to 2 tablespoons coriander leaves (cilantro), or Chinese celery greens (*daun sup*)

Indian Muslim Lamb or Mutton Soup

Sup Kambing

Makes 4 to 5 servings

Sup kambing *is an Indian Muslim specialty, a rich, thick, and spicy mutton soup generally served at Mamak stalls. Also called* sup tulang *(bone soup), it gets its intense flavor from the long simmering of mutton bones with a variety of spices. The most delicious* sup kambing *I ever had was from a Mamak vendor along a narrow side street in Penang.*

Many Indian cooks created beef and mutton soups for their British masters when they colonized Malaysia. Many of the cooks were Hindus, so they used chicken or mutton, while Chinese cooks used beef. Traditionally sup kambing *is prepared from goat meat, but it is also made with imported lamb meat. You can use lamb or mutton bones, but I prefer lamb shoulder or lamb ribs with some meat, so it becomes a complete meal when served with bread or rice and vegetables.*

INGREDIENTS

- 2 tablespoons cooking oil
- 1 pound lamb or mutton shoulder or ribs, cut into irregular pieces
- 1 tablespoon sliced and crushed garlic cloves
- 1 heaping teaspoon sliced and crushed fresh ginger
- ¾ cup diced shallots or onions
- 3 salam leaves or bay leaves
- 1 or 2 fresh green or red chilies (cayenne, Fresno, jalapeno, Serrano, cherry, or Thai), sliced in half lengthwise; or 2 whole dried chilies; or ⅛ to ¼ teaspoon chile powder
- ¼ teaspoon finely ground black pepper
- ⅛ teaspoon ground nutmeg
- 1 heaping cup (7 ounces) sliced tomatoes
- ½ teaspoon sugar
- ¾ to 1 teaspoon salt
- ¼ to ½ cup packed sliced spring onions (1-inch pieces); or 2 tablespoons to ¼ cup coriander leaves (cilantro) or Chinese celery greens (*daun sup*)

Spice Blend

- 8 black peppercorns
- 1½-inch to 2-inch cinnamon stick
- 2 cloves
- 2 green cardamom pods

Garnish

- 1 to 2 tablespoons sliced scallions or coriander leaves (cilantro) or Chinese celery greens (*daun sup*)
- ½ cup fried (*see page 333*) or sautéed shallots or onions

DIRECTIONS:

1. Heat 1 tablespoon of oil. Add lamb pieces and sauté till brown, about 4 to 5 minutes. Set aside.
2. Heat remaining 1 tablespoon of oil and sauté Spice Blend ingredients for about ½ minute.
3. Add garlic and ginger and sauté for about ½ to 1 minute, then add shallots or onions and sauté for another 1 to 2 minutes.
4. Add salam or bay leaves, chilies, black pepper, and nutmeg and sauté for another ½ to 1 minute.
5. Stir in lamb pieces, blend well, add tomatoes and stir for about 1 minute.
6. Add 4 cups water, sugar, salt, and spring onions, coriander leaves or Chinese celery greens and mix well for about 1 minute.
7. Bring to a boil. Lower heat, cover, and simmer for about 40 to 45 minutes, till lamb is cooked and tender. Skim off fat.
8. Garnish with scallions, coriander leaves, or Chinese celery greens and fried onions before serving.

Serve with crusty bread or *roti* or cooked white rice with a dip of chilies in soy sauce (page 104). You can also add carrots, celery, and/or potatoes for a complete meal; or add cooked noodles, pasta, or rice to the soup and serve as a bowl meal.

Malay-Style Thai Hot and Sour Soup

Thai Sup Tom Yam ala Melayu

Makes 4 to 5 servings

INGREDIENTS

- 2 tablespoons cooking oil
- 1 heaping tablespoon coarsely crushed garlic cloves
- 1 teaspoon sliced and pounded fresh or frozen and thawed galangal or fresh ginger
- ½ cup sliced shallots or onions (¼-inch-long strips)
- ¼ teaspoon coarsely pounded or ground black peppercorns
- ⅛ teaspoon chile powder
- 2 or 3 fresh green chilies (cayenne, jalapeno, Serrano, or Thai), sliced in half lengthwise
- 1 lemongrass stalk, bruised or cracked with blunt end of knife and knotted
- 1 Kaffir lime leaf (with 2 lobes)
- ½ cup (3 ounces) sliced tomatoes
- 2 tablespoons tamarind concentrate or juice from tamarind pulp (*see page 339*)
- 3 pieces *asam gelugor* or *asam keping* (sometimes labeled as tamarind skin), or an additional 1½ to 2 tablespoons tamarind juice
- 1 teaspoon freshly squeezed or bottled lime juice
- 1½ teaspoons white granulated sugar or light brown sugar
- 1 or 1¼ teaspoons salt
- ½ pound (about 1 cup) shelled and deveined shrimp, tails intact

For centuries, Thais have influenced Malaysian culture, particularly the northern states of Kelantan, Terengganu, Kedah, and Perlis. Today, Thai and Thai-influenced dishes have become very popular in Malaysia, whether at upscale restaurants or served by local Malay street vendors. Thai flavors have been incorporated into many local Malaysian dishes—soups, noodle dishes, steamboat stocks, fish, and chicken. Interestingly, Thai foods served in Malaysia taste quite different from Thai foods served in the U.S., with a more liberal use of spices and chilies.

My daughter Geeta loves Thai food, especially the hot and sour soup (tom yam goong), *not just for its great taste but as a remedy for colds and coughs. This is my adaptation of a Malay-Thai hot and sour soup with shrimp, popular in Malaysia. The first time I had it was about eighteen years ago from a Malay vendor in Kota Bahru, the capital city of Kelantan, which is in close proximity to Thailand. The soup was delicious and extremely hot, laden with fiery* cili padi *(bird peppers). In my recipe I have lessened the chilies.*

DIRECTIONS:

1. Heat 1 tablespoon of oil in a saucepan. Sauté garlic and galangal or ginger for about ½ to 1 minute, then add shallots or onions and sauté another 1 to 2 minutes.
2. Add remaining oil, black pepper, chile powder, chilies, lemongrass, lime leaf, and tomatoes, and stir for 1 minute.
3. Add tamarind juice, *asam gelugor*, lime juice, sugar, salt, and 5 cups water and bring to a boil. Lower heat and simmer for about 5 minutes.
4. Add shrimp and simmer for another 2 to 3 minutes, stirring occasionally. Discard lemongrass stalk and lime leaf before serving.

Serve hot with crusty bread or *roti* or cooked white or brown rice; and stir-fried *kailan* (page 222), or stir-fried Chinese greens (page 227); and green chilies in soy sauce dip (page 104). You can also add noodles, pasta, or rice, and hard-boiled eggs with vegetables to make a complete meal.

Tamarind Fish Soup

Singgang Ikan

Makes 3 to 5 servings

*Singgang ikan is a hot, sour, and sweet soup that originated in the northeastern Malaysian states of Terengganu, Kelantan, and Pahang. Fish, preferably mackerel or tuna fish head, is simmered in an earthen pot (*belanga*) in a broth of garlic, tamarind juice, galangal, and turmeric. This recipe is inspired by the singgang ikan I enjoyed at a Malay food stall in Kuantan on the East Coast (I spent my early primary school years there). The broth had a wonderful balance of sourness, pungency, and heat. I omitted the coconut milk but you can add ¼ to ½ cup coconut milk if you wish.*

Singgang ikan is typically served for occasions like Eid (or Hari Raya, a festive celebration after Ramadan, the fasting month for Muslims). Women prepare this dish one to two days before the festivities and leave the fish in the soup so the bones become soft. Coconut milk is added at the end. I enjoy this light spicy soup with cooked spaghetti or rice, along with a chile dip during the cooler months.

INGREDIENTS

1 pound tuna, haddock, swordfish, or halibut steak, sliced into 1 to 1½-inch pieces
⅛ teaspoon turmeric powder
1 tablespoon cooking oil
1½ tablespoons sliced and crushed garlic cloves
1 tablespoon sliced and crushed fresh or frozen and thawed galangal or fresh ginger
⅓ cup chopped shallots or onions
½ teaspoon coarsely crushed coriander seeds
¼ teaspoon coarsely crushed black peppercorns
1 fresh red chile (cayenne, Fresno, jalapeno, Serrano, cherry, or Thai), sliced lengthwise
1 lemongrass stalk, bruised or cracked with back of knife and knotted
1 Kaffir lime leaf (with 2 lobes)
2 tablespoons tamarind concentrate or juice from tamarind pulp (*see page 339*)
1 teaspoon salt

GARNISH

1 to 2 tablespoons chopped coriander leaves (cilantro)

DIRECTIONS:

1. Rub fish pieces with turmeric and set aside.
2. Heat oil in a saucepan, add garlic and galangal or ginger and sauté for about ½ to 1 minute. Add shallots or onions and sauté for another 1 to 2 minutes.
3. Add coriander seeds and peppercorns and saute for ½ minute. Add chile, lemongrass, and lime leaf, and sauté ½ minute; then add tamarind juice and 5 cups water and blend well. Bring to a boil, about 5 minutes, then lower heat, add salt and simmer for about 10 minutes.
4. Add fish pieces and let simmer for about 8 to 10 minutes.
5. Discard lemongrass and lime leaf and garnish with coriander leaves before serving.

Serve with crusty bread or *roti* or cooked white or brown rice; and a stir-fried mixed vegetable (page 224) and *sambal belacan* (page 101), or braised spicy long beans (page 230). You can also add cooked noodles, spaghetti, or other pastas, or rice and serve as a bowl meal.

Winter Melon Soup

Sup Timun Eropah

Makes 3 to 4 servings

INGREDIENTS

1 tablespoon cooking oil
1 heaping tablespoon sliced and coarsely crushed garlic cloves
2 teaspoons sliced and crushed fresh ginger
½ cup diced shallots or onions
1 fresh red chile (cayenne, Fresno, jalapeno, Serrano, cherry, or Thai), sliced crosswise
2 cups (9.5 ounces) peeled, seeded, and cubed winter melon (1 to 2-inch cubes)
1 lemongrass stalk, bruised or cracked with back of knife and knotted
2 Kaffir lime leaves (each with 2 lobes)
½ cup dried shiitake or other dried mushroom, soaked in warm water for 5 minutes, drained; or about ¾ cup fresh shiitake or other fresh mushrooms
1 cup (2 ounces) broccoli florets
⅓ cup (2 ounces) drained and sliced canned or fresh bamboo shoots
¼ cup chopped coriander leaves (cilantro)
¼ teaspoon sugar
¾ teaspoon salt

SPICE BLEND

¾-inch to 1-inch cinnamon stick
¼ teaspoon coarsely pounded peppercorns
¼ teaspoon coarsely pounded coriander seeds

Winter melon soup (called sup timun Eropah *by Malays) is a traditional Cantonese-style soup. While eaten hot, its property makes it a "cooling" (or yin) soup, according to Chinese Traditional Medicine. Thus it is popular as a comforting and healing soup to "cool" down fevers and coughs. There are many versions of winter melon soup using garlic, ginger, dried* longgan*, ginseng, mushrooms, and/or shredded chicken. Winter melon (also known as wax, ash, or white gourd, fuzzy melon, and* tong qwa *in Cantonese) is a large, oblong-shaped vegetable with white seeds and a heavy, green, waxy coat that gives it a frosty wintry look. It has a mild, sweet taste and absorbs the flavors of other ingredients in a recipe.*

Unlike the mild Cantonese version, my Malaysian winter melon soup includes spices—even chilies. "Cool" winter melon and cooling spices are balanced with "hot" chicken and "hot" spices. Here, I have created a twist to the Chinese version using lemongrass, cilantro, coriander seeds, and cinnamon that give a wonderful aroma to the soup. Chicken broth, pork broth, or shrimp broth can be used in the recipe instead of water.

DIRECTIONS:

1. Heat oil in a saucepan, add garlic and ginger and sauté for about ½ to 1 minute. Add shallots or onions and sauté for another 1 to 2 minutes.
2. Add chile and Spice Blend ingredients and stir for about ½ minute.
3. Add winter melon, stir for about ½ minute. Add 3 to 4 cups water, lemongrass, and Kaffir lime leaves, and bring to a boil. Lower heat and simmer for about 5 minutes, then cover and let cook for about 15 to 20 minutes, till winter melon becomes translucent and tender.
4. About 4 minutes before winter melon is translucent, add mushrooms, broccoli, bamboo shoots, and 2 tablespoons coriander leaves (don't overcook so as to retain broccoli's crispy texture).
5. Add sugar and salt and cook for another minute.
6. Discard lemongrass stalk and lime leaves and garnish with remaining 2 tablespoons coriander leaves.

Serve warm with crusty bread or *roti*. Or with cooked white or brown rice and a dip of green chilies in soy sauce (page 104) as a complete meal.

Noodle Soup
Sup Mee (or Meehoon)

Makes 4 to 5 servings with ⅔ cup dip

Chinese sup mee *was an integral part of my childhood years, from a meal in the school cafeteria to a quick lunch at a coffee shop (*kopi kedai*) or dining alfresco at a hawker's stall. For me, an essential part of eating* sup mee *is dipping each morsel into a chile-soy or chile-vinegar sauce—giving my bowl of* sup mee *a whole new depth of flavor. Chinese* sup mee *has pork, liver, gizzard, tofu, or fish balls. The Malay version, called* mee soto *has shredded chicken or sliced beef, fish cakes, potatoes, and eggs and is served with a fiery condiment.*

The basic recipe for sup mee *generally calls for* mee *(yellow wheat and egg-based fresh noodles) or* meehoon *(rice vermicelli), or broad rice noodles (*hor fun*), or a mix of* mee *and* meehoon*. The noodles are added to chicken stock flavored with garlic, ginger, soy sauce, and spices. Chinese mustard greens (*gai choy*) or Chinese cabbage and bean sprouts are added as garnish. My recipe is similar to the Malay or Indian Muslim-style. I also add lemongrass, which provides a fragrant note to the soup, and a generous amount of spices and chopped* cili padi *(bird peppers) for the dip. You can also substitute* meehoon *(rice vermicelli), wheat based vermicelli, or thin spaghetti for the noodles.*

INGREDIENTS

1 pound chicken (drumsticks, thighs, or breasts)
4 to 6 ounces Chinese flowering cabbage (*choy sam*), Chinese mustard greens (*gai choy*), or Chinese cabbage (*bok choy*)
2 tablespoons cooking oil
1½ tablespoons sliced and crushed garlic cloves
1 tablespoon sliced and crushed fresh ginger
½ cup diced shallots or onions
1 lemongrass stalk, cracked with back of knife and knotted
Optional: 1 fresh green chile (cayenne, jalapeno, Serrano, or Thai), sliced
½ teaspoon sugar
¾ to 1 teaspoon salt
8 ounces fresh *mee* (wheat egg-based noodles) or *meehoon* (dried rice vermicelli)
¾ to 1 cup (about 2¼ to 3 ounces) fresh bean sprouts, rinsed or blanched

Spice Blend

2 cloves
1 star anise
1-inch cinnamon stick
½ to ¾ teaspoon ground cumin
½ teaspoon ground fennel seeds
¼ teaspoon finely or coarsely ground white pepper

Garnish

1 fresh red chile (jalapeno, Fresno, Serrano, cayenne, or Thai), sliced
2 tablespoons chopped Chinese celery greens (*daun sup*)
Optional: ¼ teaspoon coarsely ground white peppercorns
Spicy Chile Soy Dip (page 84)

DIRECTIONS:

1. Combine Spice Blend ingredients. Cut chicken into 1-inch thick slices or cubes. Separate the Chinese flowering cabbage stalks from the leaves and cut into 1 to 2-inch pieces; cut leaves into 2 to 3-inch pieces.
2. Heat 1 tablespoon of oil in a saucepan, add garlic and ginger and sauté for about ½ to 1 minute, then add shallots or onions and sauté for about 1 to 2 minutes. Add Spice Blend and sauté ½ minute.
3. Add chicken and stir for 1 to 2 minutes, then add 5 cups water, lemongrass, and chile, if using, and bring to a boil. Lower heat, add sugar and salt and simmer for about 20 to 30 minutes till chicken is cooked. Add mustard greens about 3 minutes before chicken is done, adding stalks first and then after 1 minute adding the leaves. Mix well.
4. If using fresh *mee*, rinse in cold water or scald or cook in boiling water for a few seconds and rinse in cold water. If using dried *meehoon*, scald by steeping in boiling water and let sit for 3 to 5 minutes till softened. Drain and rinse under cold water.
5. Place the noodles, chicken, and bean sprouts in a bowl. Pour chicken stock over noodles. Garnish with sliced red chilies and Chinese celery greens. You can also garnish with coarsely ground white peppercorns to give it a wonderful finish. Discard lemongrass stalk before serving.

Serve the *sup mee* with spicy chile soy dip (page 84).

Spicy Chile Soy Dip

Cili Bersos Kicap

INGREDIENTS

3 to 4 tablespoons finely chopped scallions
6 tablespoons regular soy sauce
3 fresh green chilies (cayenne, Fresno, jalapeno, Serrano, cherry, or Thai) or *cili padi*, sliced (about 3 to 4 tablespoons)
2 tablespoons finely chopped shallots or onions
1 tablespoon cooking oil
1½ tablespoons crushed garlic cloves

This soy dip is used as a garnish for the Noodle Soup (Sup Mee) *on page 83.*

1. Mix the scallions, soy sauce, chilies, and shallots or onions in a small non-reactive bowl.
2. Heat 1 tablespoon of oil in pan. Add garlic and fry till golden brown.
3. Add the garlic-oil mixture to the bowl and mix well.

Chetawan Thai Buddhist temple, Petaling Jaya

Tofu Vegetable Soup

Sup Sayuran Tauhu

Makes 3 to 4 servings

I created this soup for tofu-vegetable lovers, including my daughter Geeta. It is spicy and tart, simulating the flavors of Chinese and Thai soups. I added taucheo *(preserved soybean paste) or black bean paste with ginger, garlic, soy sauce, sesame oil, and star anise as they are widely used as flavorings in Chinese soups. I also added tamarind juice for a slight tartness, and chile powder to spike its flavor.*

INGREDIENTS

- 1 tablespoon cooking oil
- 2 tablespoons crushed garlic cloves
- 2 teaspoons chopped fresh ginger
- 2 teaspoons regular soy sauce
- 2 teaspoons preserved soybean paste (*taucheo*, black version), or bean paste, or black bean sauce
- 2 teaspoons tamarind concentrate or juice from tamarind pulp (*see page 339*), or Chinese rice wine or vinegar
- 1 cup (5 ounces) carrot sticks (1½ to 2-inch long) or baby carrots, sliced in half lengthwise
- 1 package (14 ounces) firm tofu (*tauhu*), drained and cubed
- ½ cup sliced dried shiitake or other dried mushrooms, soaked in hot or warm water for 8 to 10 minutes and drained; or ½ cup sliced fresh Chinese mushrooms (shiitake, cloud ears, wood ears, or other)
- 3 ounces Chinese flowering cabbage (*choy sam*), Chinese mustard greens (*gai choy*), or Chinese cabbage (*bok choy*), stalks separated from leaves and sliced into 2-inch pieces
- ½ cup fresh or frozen and thawed petite peas
- Optional: ½ cup (1½ ounces) bean sprouts, rinsed or blanched
- ¼ to ½ teaspoon toasted sesame oil

Spice Blend

- 2 cloves
- 1-inch cinnamon stick
- 1 star anise
- ¼ teaspoon coarsely ground white peppercorns
- ¼ teaspoon chile powder

Garnish

- 1 scallion, sliced into ¼-inch pieces (about 2 tablespoons)

DIRECTIONS:

1. Heat oil in a saucepan, add garlic and ginger and sauté for about ½ to 1 minute, then add Spice Blend ingredients and sauté for another ½ minute.
2. Add soy sauce, soybean paste, and tamarind juice or rice wine or vinegar and 4 cups water and bring to a boil. Then lower heat, add carrots and simmer for about 5 minutes.
3. In a separate non-stick skillet, pan-fry tofu cubes till they become light brown and firm. Stir into soup. (Alternately, you can skip the pan-frying step and gently stir tofu cubes into soup.)
4. Add mushrooms and cook for another 2 to 3 minutes. Add Chinese cabbage or greens and peas and let simmer for 2 to 3 minutes.
5. Remove from heat and add bean sprouts, if using, and sesame oil and blend for 1 minute. Garnish with scallions before serving.

Serve as a complete meal with crusty bread or *roti*, or with cooked rice; and a dip with green chilies in soy sauce (page 104) or pickled green chilies (page 105).

Bakuteh's origins in Malaysia date back to the town of Klang (or Kelang), my birthplace, located about eighteen miles southwest of Kuala Lumpur. In the late 1800s, Klang was a bustling tin-mining center attracting many southern Chinese immigrants. These immigrant workers ate *bakuteh* as a cheap meal to boost their energy. Because most of the Chinese in Klang were Hokkiens, the soup became known by its name in the Hokkien dialect, *bakuteh* ("*ba*" for pork, "*kut*" for bone, and "*teh*" for tea).

There are numerous variants of *bakuteh*, based on who is preparing it. Hokkien *bakuteh* is saltier and darker in color because they add a dark soy sauce to their version. The Cantonese add medicinal herbs for a more intense flavor, while the Teochews add extra pepper for a spicier taste. A newer *halal* version, called *chikuteh*, uses chicken instead of pork so it can also be enjoyed by Muslims.

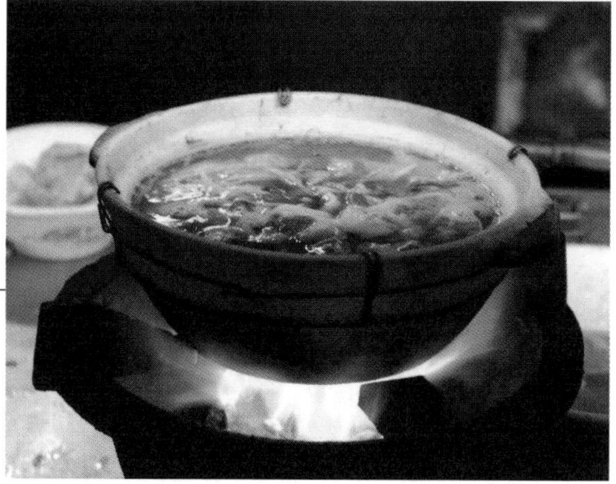

Bakuteh at Chinese food stall, Klang

Pork Rib Soup
Bakuteh

Serves 3 to 4

The popular bakuteh, *translated as "pork bone tea," is a mildly spiced Hokkien Chinese pork herbal soup. It contains pork ribs, pork loin, and/or offals seasoned with spices and Chinese medicinal herbs, tofu, and a variety of mushrooms. These ingredients are simmered for a few hours in a claypot and then traditionally served with a topping of crunchy lettuce and a sprinkling of fried shallots. It is accompanied with* ewe char kway, *slightly salted fried spongy dough sticks, to sop up the soup, and a soy sauce chile and fried garlic-based condiment as a dip for the pork pieces. Different kinds of teas are usually served with* bakuteh *to help digest the pork fat.*

Bakuteh *is believed to rid the body of toxins, boost the immune system, and strengthen the bones and kidneys. After a late night of clubbing, my younger brother, Suresh, took us to his favorite coffee shop serving* bakuteh. *He is addicted to it and swears by its restorative powers with hangovers.*

My recipe calls for lesser amounts of Chinese herbs but you can increase them if you desire. In Chinese traditional medicine, dong quai *(female ginseng) is eaten to lower high blood pressure and fight fatigue;* kei chee *(wolfberries) improves vision and prevents headaches; while* yok chok *(Solomon's seal) is eaten to prevent respiratory problems.*

INGREDIENTS

1 tablespoon cooking oil
1 pound pork loin back ribs, cut into 1½ to 2-inch-long pieces
¼ cup crushed garlic cloves
2 tablespoons regular soy sauce
1 to 2 teaspoons dark or thick soy sauce
½ teaspoon salt
2 tablespoons coriander leaves (cilantro)

Spice Blend

4 cloves
2 1-inch cinnamon sticks
1 star anise
½ teaspoon black peppercorns
½ teaspoon white peppercorns
½ teaspoon Szechwan peppercorns
½ teaspoon coriander seeds
½ teaspoon fennel seeds
½ teaspoon cumin seeds

Chinese Herb Blend

1 whole *dang gui* or *dong quai* or angelica root (about 4 to 5 grams), soaked in hot or warm water till soft and then sliced (about 1 tablespoon)
1 tablespoon *kei chee* (wolfberries or Chinese lycium), rinsed clean
5 slices (about 5 grams) *yok chok* (Solomon's seal rhizome or *yuzhu* in Japanese), rinsed clean

Garnish

2 or 3 pieces lettuce
1 tablespoon fried (*see page 333*) or sautéed shallots or onions

DIRECTIONS:

1. Place Spice Blend ingredients in a muslin pouch or cheesecloth (about 6 to 7 inches square) and tie closed.
2. Heat oil in a deep saucepan or Dutch oven pot, add pork and garlic and sauté for about 2 to 3 minutes. Add 5 cups water, mix well, and place the Spice Blend pouch among the ribs.
3. Place the Chinese Herb Blend ingredients in the pot and stir slowly to mix.
4. Bring to a boil, lower heat, add soy sauces and salt and simmer for about 1 hour, till ribs are cooked and tender. If using the optional tofu and mushrooms, add 15 minutes before cooking time is over.
5. Add coriander leaves and cook for another 2 minutes.
6. Before serving, remove the spice pouch and ladle soup with ribs into bowls. Garnish with pieces of lettuce and fried shallots or onions.

Serve with a chile garlic dip (page 109) and cooked white or brown rice or bread.

Optional

4 ounces (about ¾ cup) firm tofu (*tauhu*), cut into 1-inch cubes and pan-fried till light brown and firm (or use tofu puffs)
2 tablespoons fresh or dried shiitake mushrooms (if using dried, soak in warm water for about 10 to 15 minutes, drain)

Spicy Lentil Vegetable Stew

Sambar

Makes 4 to 5 servings

INGREDIENTS

1 cup *toor* or *toovar dhal* (yellow pigeon peas), washed and drained

¼ teaspoon turmeric powder

1 tablespoon cooking oil

¼ teaspoon black mustard seeds

2 teaspoons sliced and crushed garlic cloves

1 heaping teaspoon sliced and crushed fresh ginger

¼ cup chopped shallots or onions

2 dried whole red chilies, or ¼ teaspoon chile powder

Optional: ⅛ teaspoon ground asafetida

4 or 5 fresh curry leaves

½ cup (2½ ounces) diced carrots (¼-inch pieces)

½ cup (about 2¼ ounces) diced green beans (¼-inch pieces)

½ cup (3 ounces) chopped tomatoes (¼-inch pieces)

2 teaspoons tamarind concentrate or juice from tamarind pulp (*see page 339*)

¾ teaspoon salt

SPICE BLEND

3 teaspoons coriander seeds or ground coriander

1 teaspoon cumin seeds or ground cumin

½ teaspoon fenugreek seeds or ground fenugreek

Sambar or sambhar is a popular lentil and vegetable stew with Tamil (South Indian) origins. The lentil used is toor *or* toovar dhal *(also called yellow pigeon peas or* tuvaram paripu *in Tamil), cooked with tamarind juice, onions, garlic, vegetables, and spices. In Malaysia, Hindus of South Indian heritage generally serve it at temple functions, weddings, and religious festivals.*

Inspired by my husband Bob's affinity for sambar *and other South Indian fare, I decided to create a recipe (based on Ma's and with occasional tasting at the Ganesha Temple cafeteria in Queens, New York). Bob usually accompanies me when I go to the Ganesha Temple, and while he claims he enjoys participating in the religious ceremonies, he always insists that we stop by the Temple's cafeteria, which makes me wonder if he is motivated more by physical hunger than spiritual inspiration. But Bob reminds me—and the Ayurveda texts tell us—the path to a healthy mind and body is through the stomach!*

DIRECTIONS:

1. Bring 5 cups of water to boil in a deep saucepan, then add dhal and turmeric and stir well. Lower heat and simmer for about 20 minutes, till dhal gets a soft consistency.
2. While the dhal is cooking, prepare the Spice Blend: roast the coriander seeds, cumin seeds, and fenugreek seeds in a dry heated pan, stirring constantly till seeds get light brown, about 2 minutes. Cool and grind in a coffee grinder. (An alternative is to mix together ground equivalents of the coriander, cumin, and fenugreek.)
3. Heat oil in a deep saucepan. When hot, add mustard seeds and cover. When the popping sound subsides, add the garlic and ginger and stir for about ½ to 1 minute, then add shallots or onions and sauté for about 1 to 2 minutes. Add chilies or chile powder and sauté for about ½ minute.
4. Add Spice Blend, asafetida, if using, and curry leaves and stir for about ½ minute.
5. Add the cooked dhal, carrots, green beans, and 1 to 2 cups water, depending on consistency desired, and cook for about 5 minutes, stirring occasionally.
6. Stir in tomatoes and tamarind juice and cook for another 5 to 8 minutes while stirring. Add salt and cook for 1 minute more.

Optional: Heat 1 tablespoon oil in a skillet. Add 3 or 4 curry leaves and ½ teaspoon of crushed garlic and stir till brown. Swirl this mixture through sauce before serving. This gives a wonderful fragrance to the *sambar*.

Serve as a savory dip for *thosai* (page 69) and *vadai* (page 61). Or try *sambar* with pita, *roti*, *chappati*, or naan. *Sambar* is also great ladled on steaming cooked white or brown Basmati rice. You can also add your favorite vegetables to the *sambar*, including zucchini, squash, and cauliflower.

CHAPTER 3

SALADS, CONDIMENTS, SAUCES, AND DIPS: ADDING A LITTLE ZING

Indian Muslim *rojak* vendor, Petaling Jaya

SALADS

When I was growing up in Malaysia, "salad" was a Western concept with images of iceberg lettuce, sliced raw cucumbers, and tomatoes sitting coldly on a plate. In the intervening years, both Eastern and Western chefs have greatly transformed the notion of salad by combining fruits, vegetables, seasonings, and other ingredients in ever more creative ways. Within the expanded boundaries of today's nouvelle cuisine, many of the healthy and tasty foods I enjoyed in my youth can now be truly called salads. Referred to locally as *rojak, pasembor, acars,* and *kerabus,* these dishes offer a variety of fresh, pickled, or cooked vegetables, or fruits seasoned and layered with garnishes that add contrasting textures—crispy, crunchy, or chewy—and enticing visual appeal. They are drenched or drizzled with spicy, aromatic, and pungent sauces, resulting in a wonderful balance and harmony of flavors. These dishes are often enjoyed as snacks or side dishes.

Our most notable Malaysian salad, the *rojak* (which means "mixture of everything") or *pasembor* (similar to the *gado-gado* of Indonesia) contains freshly cut vegetables and/or seasonal fruits. The *rojaks* are generally prepared by Chinese or Indian Muslim vendors, who make quite different 'salads' using their signature ingredients and dressings. Indian Muslim salads or *Mamak rojak* include fried shrimp fritters and deep-fried fish cakes. They are tossed with a spicy sweet sauce made from mashed sweet potatoes, tamarind juice, chilies, and palm sugar, and topped with shredded cucumber and crushed peanuts. In Penang, the *Mamak rojak* (made with vegetables) is called *pasembor*, and *rojak buahan* (made with fruits) is simply referred to as *rojak*. In the south, in Johor state, Chinese *rojak* vendors add transparent mung bean noodles to the salad, which is then tossed with a sauce made from vinegar and dried shrimp.

My family lived for a few years in Muar, a sleepy town in the southern state of Johor. An Indian Muslim *rojak* mobile vendor would bicycle by our home every afternoon around the time we got home from school. As soon as he rang his bell, we ran out and hailed him. He was a somber man wearing a checked sarong and a batik shirt. We loved watching him prepare the *rojak*. He would place a bit of each of the ingredients in a bowl that Ma gave us—slices of fried tofu, bean sprouts, cubes of boiled potato, boiled green beans and sliced carrots, cucumber, and sliced hard-boiled egg. Then he spooned out a dark semi-thick sauce over everything, carefully blending them together without breaking or crushing the ingredients. We could tell that he took great pride in his work. We would take our bowls of *rojak* to the porch and savor it while Ma prepared the evening meal. Some days he would prepare the fresh fruit *rojak* using local fruits. This was a delicious snack before our dinner! And Ma was happy as the snack was healthy.

The Chinese in Penang prepare *rojak* using different ingredients—pineapple, white turnip or yam bean, cucumber, *tau pok* (deep-fried tofu), bean sprouts, and sometimes *kangkung* (water spinach). These ingredients are tossed in a dark, gooey, pungent, and mildly spiced sweet sauce made from thick dark shrimp paste (*hae koh*), chilies, sugar, and lime juice. Finally the *rojak* is sprinkled with roasted sesame seeds.

Acars (pickled vegetables and/or fruits) that have Indian Muslim origins are popular 'salads.' Unlike traditional Indian *acars*, which are rich and heavy with spices, Malaysian *acars* have a combination of light, sweet, sour, and spicy tastes. They are generally served with entrees as a condiment or as a side vegetable. They usually contain green mango (page 96), pineapple (page 98), green papaya (page 100), carrots, and/or cucumbers (page 99) drizzled with a dressing of lime juice or vinegar, sugar, chopped shallots, chilies, ginger, garlic, and/or turmeric.

Kerabus are popular along the predominantly Malay East Coast region. They usually contain fresh or pickled vegetables or fruits like jicama (yam bean or *bengkuang*), pineapple, and green mango topped with a hot and pungent dressing. Malaysian *acars* and *kerabus* are similar but have slightly different flavor twists, depending on whether they have Indian, Nonya, or Malay origins. One of my favorite is *acar rampai* (a sweet, sour, and spicy pickled salad of mixed vegetables, page 93), sometimes referred to as *acar kuning,* which combines flavors from the Indians (turmeric, ginger), Chinese (toasted sesame seeds, fresh garlic), and Malays (cayennes or *cili padi*, galangal, and *belacan*). *Acar timun nanas* (pickled cucumber and pineap-

My favorite salads are the Malay *acars*, as they are hot and pungent with fiery bird peppers (*cili padi*), *limau nipis* (a more acidic lime similar to key lime), or *limau kasturi* (musk lime, a more fragrant lime), galangal, toasted *belacan* (dried shrimp paste), and toasted grated coconut (*kerisik*). A milder sweet form is the Chinese *acar*, made with a dressing of vinegar, sugar, ginger, and garlic.

The Nonyas in Penang enjoy a Thai-type salad with green papaya, bean sprouts, dried shrimp, ginger flower, and tofu puffs drizzled with a dressing of *belacan* or *chinchaluk*. When I was in Sabah, I had a unique *acar* (*bambangan*), prepared with wild mango (also called *bambangan*), chilies, and salt.

ple with fresh cut chilies, page 98) is a Malay-style *acar* served with *nasi lemak* (coconut-infused rice, page 117), *nasi minyak* (ghee rice, page 121), or *nasi kemuli* (spiced rice, page 120).

Sambal ikan bilis

CONDIMENTS, SAUCES AND DIPS

Since Malaysians are flavor gourmands, condiments, sauces, and dips are must-haves with every meal. Without a condiment, the meal is simply incomplete. Their panoply of flavors personalizes meals and helps suit individual preferences. Spicy, hot, and pungent *sambals* (the *salsas* of Malaysia) add an exciting dimension to the eating experience, while dipping sauces provide a satisfying extra zing to the meal. Without a dip, the meal has something missing, an incomplete flavor. Malaysians need that extra punch, that special spicy, pickled, or pungent condiment or sauce to complement the dishes. Generally at home, our condiments are served in miniature bowls to perk up entrees, to provide an extra boost for soups, to satisfy individual tastes at the table, or simply to add another flavor dimension to our eating experience.

Pickled green chilies

When I first came to America, eating the comparatively bland foods for the first time was a torturous experience, and the standard tabletop condiments of mustard, ketchup, and sweet pickled relish did little to make American foods more palatable for me. As a consequence, I used to carry a bottle of Malaysian chile sauce with me everywhere I went, adding it to every dish. I'd get stares from the waiters and people around me, but I was only thinking of enjoying my meal. I treasured this bottle, carefully rationing it and taking only the small amount that I needed, as I was afraid I would run out of it before I could find a new supply. When I finally ran out of it, I made my own spicy concoctions, blending tomatoes, chilies, sliced onions, and lemon juice. I survived dining out in those days, thanks to my trusted chile condiment.

In Malaysia, a variety of basic dips are placed in the center of the meal table or in miniature bowls at individual place settings. During my childhood, when we dined out at coffee shops (*kedai kopi*) or hawker stalls, the first items the vendor placed on our table were miniature saucers of condiments appropriate for the meal. Popular condiments that we grew up with were various dipping sauces (called *sos* in Malay), including chile-ginger sauce for Hainanese chicken rice (page 126), and fiery pungent dressings or sauces made from dried shrimp paste (*belacan*) and chilies for freshly cut vegetables and fruit salads and noodle dishes.

Chilies in soy sauce

The varying flavor profiles of Malaysian condiments, sauces, and dips reflect their ethnic origins. Chinese foods are served with chopped pickled chilies (page 105), sliced green chilies in soy sauce (page 104), and a spicy sweet chile sauce (page 107). Favorite Chinese condiment combos include *Hokkien mee* or *kari mee* with a *belacan* chile paste dip (page 108), Hainanese chicken rice with a chile ginger garlic sauce (page 106), and fried rice or *sup mee* with a simple chile garlic and soy sauce dip (page 109).

Indians perk up their foods with green mango *acar* (page 96) or lime *acar*, cucumber *pachadi* (page 97), various spicy sweet chutneys, and many other vegetable pickles. Malay and Indian Muslim dishes are always accompanied by dips, a pungent chile paste, or *sambal belacan* (page 101) for noodles, or a spicy and sweet potato-based sauce for *rojak* (page 94).

The most widely used condiments in Malaysia are the aromatic tart, pungent, and fiery chile-based sauces or pastes called *sambals*. They are prepared fresh or cooked with shallots, red chilies, sugar, and salt. For Malaysians, *sambal* with or without *belacan* (dried shrimp paste made from shrimp-like crustaceans or krill, also called *geragau*) is a must, as a cooking sauce or table condiment. *Sambals* are the "soul" of a meal, served with wedges of small fragrant limes (*limau kasturi*) squirted over them before eating. Similar to salsa or ketchup, *sambal* is served as a side or topping to perk up our meals. Raw or cooked, *sambal* is a perfect accompaniment to cooked rice. Ingredients to make a *sambal* are traditionally pounded in a granite mortar and pestle (called *batu lesong*), but today's chefs use a blender or food processor to puree the chilies into a coarse or smooth paste. A favorite is *sambal ikan bilis* (page 103), made with fried baby anchovies, fiery *cili padi*, and *belacan*, served with *nasi lemak* for breakfast.

Cili boh, a coarse or smooth puree (or blended paste) of deseeded dried whole red chilies with water or oil, is found in every Malaysian pantry. It is used to make *sambals* or added to meat, seafood, and chicken dishes. *Sambal belacan* is a favorite with all Malaysians, with many flavor variations based on ethnic and regional preferences. A 'raw' *sambal belacan* (page 101) is made with *cili boh* or coarsely blended fresh red or green chilies, lime juice, chopped onions, sugar, and toasted *belacan*. Some ethnic groups also add chopped fresh fruits. A cooked *sambal belacan* (page 102) is prepared with similar ingredients, then slowly sautéed in hot oil with constant stirring, adding a little oil at a time to prevent it from scorching, till a point when the oil seeps out of the sauce and a fragrant aroma develops. This sauce now assumes a more intense flavor and a darker color. This technique is referred to as "*tumising*" in Malaysia. The process generally takes about 15 to 20 minutes, less or more depending on the amount of sauce and oil added. For health reasons, I use less oil in my recipes for *tumising* and still achieve similar flavor intensity without having the oil seep out.

Nonyas enjoy *sambals* made with *belacan*, salted fish, or dried shrimp, served with their *laksas*, stews, and soups. Chinese serve *sambal belacan* as a dip to enliven noodle dishes. For Kristangs, *sambals* are a must to offset the richness of coconut curries, to add flavor to soups, fried fish and rice dishes, or to add a zing to toast and sandwiches. *Sambal cili taucheo* (with preserved soybeans), *sambal gerago seccu* (with dried krill), *sambal belimbing* (with sour fruit), and *sambal bokra* (with candlenuts) are some *sambals* they enjoy.

The recipes in this chapter for a number of popular condiments, dips, and sauces that I grew up with will add wonderful flavor depth and balance to your Malaysian meals, and even some of your American meals!

Spicy Sweet Pickled Mixed Vegetable Salad

Acar Rampai

Makes 8 to 10 servings

Acar rampai or acar kuning (yellow) is a visually stunning spicy mixed pickled vegetable that has taken flavor cues from Malays, Indians, Nonyas, and Kristangs. It is popular with all Malaysians who enjoy its hot, sweet, and sour taste balanced with crunchy, crispy textures. Acar rampai *adds magic to plain cooked white rice and seasoned rice dishes, fried fish, curries, and barbecued meats.*

My sister-in-law Shanta makes the best acar *I have ever tasted. It has become my family's favorite. She serves it with vegetable* biryani, *chicken* kurma, *and* sambal *shrimp. It is quick to prepare and can be kept in the refrigerator for a week or more, with the flavors intensifying and the textures more appealing over time. Acar can be a great accompaniment to grilled or roast chicken and even hamburgers. Here I have substituted red, green, and/or yellow bell peppers for the chilies to make it less fiery than Shanta's version and to add more color as well.*

INGREDIENTS

- 2 medium cucumbers (about 1 pound), unpeeled, cored, cut into ¼-inch by 2-inch pieces (4 cups)
- 2 cups (10 ounces) baby carrots or carrot pieces, peeled, cut into ¼-inch by 2-inch pieces
- 2 cups (about 6½ ounces) cauliflower florets
- 1 red bell pepper, cut into ¼-inch by 2-inch pieces; or ¼ cup deseeded and chopped fresh red chilies
- 1 green bell pepper, cut into ¼-inch by 2-inch pieces; or ¼ cup deseeded and chopped fresh green chilies
- 1 heaping tablespoon salt

Sauce or Dressing

- 2 tablespoons cooking oil
- Heaping ¼ cup whole or halved garlic cloves
- ¼ cup sliced fresh ginger
- ¼ cup peeled and grated fresh turmeric root, or ½ teaspoon turmeric powder
- 1 cup thinly sliced shallots or red onions
- 2 tablespoons to ¼ cup *cili boh* (*see page 315*); or ½ to 1 tablespoon bottled *sambal oelek* (*depending on heat desired*)
- ⅔ cup distilled white vinegar or rice vinegar
- 3 tablespoons sugar

Garnish

- ½ cup toasted sesame seeds or coarsely ground unsalted peanuts

DIRECTIONS:

1. Mix the prepared vegetables with the salt and blend well. To remove liquid from the vegetables, let them sit in a colander weighted down by a plastic bag of water for about 15 to 20 minutes, till all liquid is drained. (Alternately, place vegetables in a non-reactive bowl, add 6 cups warm water or enough to cover, let sit for about 15 to 20 minutes. Drain in colander and gently squeeze excess water from vegetables.)
2. To prepare dressing, heat 1 tablespoon of oil in a large skillet or wok and sauté garlic, ginger, and turmeric (if using root) for about 1 minute, then add shallots or onions and sauté for another 1 to 2 minutes (don't let them get limp). Add remaining oil, *cili boh* or *sambal oelek*, and turmeric powder, if using, and sauté for about 3 to 4 minutes, adding more oil if necessary.
3. Add the drained vegetables to the dressing and stir well for about 1 minute. Add vinegar and sugar and blend well for about 1 to 2 minutes.
4. Remove from heat and let cool at room temperature for 15 to 20 minutes.
5. Before serving, garnish with toasted sesame seeds or coarsely ground unsalted peanuts.

Serve with cooked white or brown rice, ghee rice (page 121), or tomato rice (page 119); and chicken *kurma* (page 168), fish *kurma* (page 306), chicken *sambal* (page 161), chile chicken (page 163), beef *rendang* (page 177), grilled steak, or spicy fried chicken (page 165).

Spicy Vegetable Salad and Spicy Fruit Salad with Sweet Potato Dressing

Rojak and Rojak Buahan

Makes 5 to 6 servings

INGREDIENTS

Rojak Dressing

1 pound sweet potatoes
1 to 2 tablespoons cooking oil
2 teaspoons chopped garlic cloves
¼ cup chopped shallots or onions
3 or 4 dried whole red chilies, steeped in hot water for 5 minutes, slit and deseeded; or ¾ to 1 tablespoon *cili boh* (*see page 315*); or 1 to 1½ teaspoons bottled *sambal oelek* (depending on heat desired); or 1 or 2 slit and deseeded fresh red chilies
Optional: ½ to 1 teaspoon dried shrimp paste (*belacan*), toasted at 400°F for 15 minutes (*see page 335*)
1 tablespoon thinly sliced or chopped palm sugar or dark brown sugar
1½ to 2 tablespoons tamarind concentrate or juice extracted from tamarind pulp (*see page 339*)
4 teaspoons double black soy sauce
2 teaspoons thick or sweet soy sauce
¼ teaspoon salt
4 teaspoons freshly squeezed or bottled lime juice
¼ to ½ teaspoon toasted sesame oil

Spice Blend

⅛ teaspoon ground cumin
⅛ teaspoon ground coriander
⅛ teaspoon turmeric powder
⅛ teaspoon ground black pepper

Rojak, a Malay word meaning "hodgepodge" or "mixture," has spicy, sweet, and sour notes. With Indonesian origins, it is a salad of raw and cooked vegetables and/or fresh fruits, drenched or topped with a thick, pungent, and spicy sweet potato and peanut-based dressing.

My recipe is based on the Indian Muslim or Mamak version (called pasembor *in Penang) that I enjoyed as a youth. Its dressing, made with mashed sweet potato and seasoned with tamarind juice,* cili boh, belacan, *soy sauce, and lime juice, is traditionally slow cooked for few hours. In my recipe, I have reduced its pungency and the gooey sweetness.*

For Mamak rojak, *you can also use cabbage, broccoli, beans, zucchini, or carrots. The vegetables are topped with crispy shrimp and tapioca fritters, tofu puffs, and* sambal belacan. *Fruit rojak* (rojak buahan) *is traditionally topped with lime juice, chile powder, and* belacan *powder but you can omit these garnishes and just add what you prefer, including bean sprouts and thinly sliced cucumbers. Firm fruits and vegetables are always used, cut in varying sizes and shapes for visual effect.*

DIRECTIONS FOR *ROJAK* DRESSING:

1. Bring water to a boil in a deep saucepan. Add sweet potatoes and simmer for about 55 minutes till cooked and soft. Drain, run under cold running water and then peel and cut into small pieces. Process or blend pieces with 1 cup of water to a puree. Set aside.
2. Combine Spice Blend ingredients and set aside.
3. Heat 1 tablespoon oil in a small skillet. Sauté garlic for about ½ to 1 minute, then add shallots or onions and sauté for another 1 to 2 minutes. Add Spice Blend and stir for about ½ minute.
4. Add chilies, *cili boh*, or *sambal oelek* and remaining oil, if needed, and stir for another 1 to 2 minutes till fragrant.
5. Add pureed sweet potato, 2 cups water, dried shrimp paste, if using, palm sugar, tamarind juice, soy sauces, and salt and simmer at low heat for about 10 to 15 minutes, till sauce becomes slightly thick and pourable, adding more water if needed to get the desired consistency.
6. Add lime juice and cook another 2 minutes. Add sesame oil and stir for a minute. Allow to cool. When sauce cools, it may thicken slightly, so add a little warm water and then stir before serving.

Modern vegetable *rojak*

VEGETABLE ROJAK:

½ cup (2½ ounces) sliced carrots (1½-inch by ¼-inch pieces)
½ cup (2½ ounces) peeled and sliced jicama or yam bean (*bengkuang*) (1½-inch by ⅛-inch strips) or canned water chestnuts, drained
½ cup (about 2½ ounces) peeled, boiled, and quartered or cubed potatoes or sweet potatoes
1 cup (about 2 ounces) cooked broccoli florets
1 cup (about 5 ounces) cubed firm tofu (*tauhu*) (1-inch pieces), deep-fried or pan-fried (or use tofu puffs)
¼ cup (1 ounce) seeded and sliced cucumbers (1½-inch by ⅛-inch strips)
¼ cup (about ¾ ounce) bean sprouts, rinsed or blanched
Optional: shrimp fritters or tapioca fritters

FRUIT ROJAK

3 heaping cups any of the following fruits, sliced into 1-inch cubes, slices, or wedges: green mango, green apple, starfruit, green guava, pineapple, and/or green papaya or strawberries, apple, or melons

GARNISH

2 tablespoon toasted sesame seeds, or 2 heaping tablespoons coarsely ground peanuts
2 tablespoons chopped scallions

DIRECTIONS FOR ASSEMBLING THE *ROJAKS*:

To serve *rojak*, place vegetables or fruits in a bowl. Pour cooled dressing over. Garnish with toasted sesame seeds or ground peanuts and scallions.

Serve with tea or lemonade; or as a side with cooked white or brown rice or compressed rice (page 281); and roast chicken (page 297), spicy fried chicken (page 165), spicy baked or grilled fish (page 207), or spicy fried fish (page 206).

Pickled Green Mango Salad

Acar Mangga Hijau

Makes 3 to 4 servings

INGREDIENTS

1 heaping cup (about 6 ounces) peeled and sliced or cubed green mango (1½-inch by ½-inch pieces)

Dressing

2 teaspoons distilled white vinegar or rice vinegar
3 teaspoons sugar
½ teaspoon salt
1 tablespoon chopped mint leaves
1 to 3 fresh red chilies (cayenne Fresno, jalapeno, Serrano, Thai, or cherry), chopped

One of our favorite snacks during our school years was pickled and dried fruits, sour or salted, be they plums, mango, fresh ginger, or other local fruits. At home, we enjoyed cut-up green mango dipped in salt and chile powder or soy sauce. My younger sister, Rama, was addicted to sour fruits and hence her nickname, the "sour queen." Whenever Ma prepared pickled spicy green mango, Rama just hung around the kitchen. It is no wonder there was not enough of this pickled salad to share at dinnertime when she had been snacking on it while doing her homework in the kitchen!

Green mango acar *is a delicious accompaniment to Ma's fried fish,* dalcha, *chicken curry, or lamb* peratil. *It is light and refreshing and at the same time offsets the fiery heat of many dishes.*

DIRECTIONS:

1. Prepare mango and set aside.
2. In a non-reactive bowl, blend vinegar, sugar, and salt till sugar and salt dissolve. Add mint and chilies and mix well.
3. Pour this dressing over mango and let sit for at least 30 minutes, or chill overnight before serving.

Serve with ghee rice (page 121) or tomato rice (page 119); *dalcha* (page 285); and lamb *peratil* (page 185), spicy fried fish (page 206), grilled spicy chicken (page 166), or chicken curry *debal* (page 289).

Spicy Cucumber Tomato Salad

Pachadi Timun Tomato

Makes 5 to 6 servings

Pachadi originated with the South Indian immigrants, who prepare it with finely chopped and boiled vegetables and fruits (cucumber, squash, mango, tomato, onion, okra, eggplant, bitter gourd, and/or pineapple) which are then added to yogurt along with shredded coconut, green or red chilies, ginger, curry leaves, and mustard seeds. In Malaysia, Indian immigrants adapted the recipe with local techniques and ingredients to create lighter pachadis. *The vegetables are pickled first and then coated with the spicy dressing. Cucumber* pachadi *was a favorite at home, its cooling, gentle and spicy flavor balancing the other dishes.*

My father, who came from Kerala to Malaysia as a young boy, grew up enjoying pachadis *made with carrots, coconut, mango, and cucumbers. So he always enjoyed it whenever Ma prepared a cucumber and tomato* pachadi. *We ate it with cooked white rice, lentil curry, spicy chicken curry, shrimp* sambal, *or fish curry. Here is Ma's recipe.*

Cha (my father)

INGREDIENTS

- 2 medium (about 1 pound or 4 cups) cucumbers, peeled, cored, julienned into 2-inch by ¼-inch pieces
- ¾ to 1 teaspoon salt
- 1 heaping cup (about 7 ounces) cubed tomatoes (1-inch pieces)

DRESSING

- 1 to 1½ teaspoons cumin seeds, dry roasted and pounded or ground, or ground cumin
- 4 or 5 fresh green or red chilies (jalapeno, Fresno, Serrano, Thai, cherry, or cayenne), sliced and coarsely pounded (about ¼ cup)
- ¼ cup chopped shallots or red onions
- 2 cups plain yogurt
- ⅛ teaspoon turmeric powder, if color is desired

GARNISH

- 1 tablespoon cooking oil
- ¼ to ½ teaspoon black or dark brown mustard seeds
- 8 fresh curry leaves

DIRECTIONS:

1. Rub cucumber slices with salt and let sit in a colander with the cucumbers weighted down by a plastic bag of water for about 15 to 20 minutes, till all liquid is drained from cucumbers. (Alternately, place cucumbers in a non-reactive bowl, add 3 cups warm water or enough to cover, let sit for about 15 to 20 minutes. Drain in colander and gently squeeze out excess water.) Set aside.
2. Combine dressing ingredients and blend well. Add cucumber and tomatoes and coat well with the dressing.
3. Before serving, heat oil in a small skillet. When hot, add mustard seeds and curry leaves, cover and let seeds pop. When popping subsides, uncover and pour this savory mixture over the salad.

Serve with cooked white or brown rice or vegetable *biryani* (page 280); and vegetable dhal curry (page 231); and spicy fried fish (page 206), fish curry (page 198), *sambal* shrimp (page 204), chicken *varuval* (page 167), or lamb or mutton *peratil* (page 185).

Cucumber Pineapple Salad

Acar Timun Nanas

Makes 5 to 6 servings

INGREDIENTS

1 medium (about ½ pound) cucumber, sliced into 1½-inch by ¼-inch pieces (2 cups)
½ teaspoon salt
½ cup chopped or thinly sliced shallots or red onions
1½ cups (about 8 ounces) cubed or sliced fresh or canned pineapple (*if canned, drain juice before using*)

DRESSING

2 tablespoons freshly squeezed or bottled lime juice
2 tablespoons light brown sugar
½ teaspoon salt

GARNISH

1 fresh green or red chile (jalapeno, Fresno, cherry pepper, Serrano, Thai, or cayenne), sliced into ⅛-inch-thick pieces
1 tablespoon chopped mint leaves or coriander leaves (cilantro)

Malays and Nonyas have wonderful salad and pickled vegetable concoctions made with cucumbers and pineapples. At home, Ma usually served cucumbers as a side dish to 'cool off' the 'hot' foods, such as chicken, lamb, and chile sauces. The sweet and slightly tart pineapple pairs well with the crunchy cool cucumber, so they are a marriage made in heaven. A dressing of sugar, lime juice, and chopped shallots along with a topping of chilies gives the final touch to this combination.

DIRECTIONS:

1. Rub cucumber slices with salt and let sit in a colander with the cucumbers weighted down by a plastic bag of water for about 15 to 20 minutes, till liquid is drained from cucumbers. (Alternately, place cucumbers in a bowl, add 3 cups warm water or enough to cover cucumbers, and let sit for about 15 to 20 minutes. Drain in colander and gently squeeze out excess water from cucumbers.) Set aside.
2. Make the dressing by blending the lime juice, sugar, and salt in a non-reactive bowl.
3. Add the cucumbers, shallots or onions, and pineapple and coat well with dressing. Let sit for about 30 minutes or chill overnight before garnishing.
4. Garnish with chilies and mint or coriander leaves before serving.

Serve with ghee rice (page 121), vegetable *biryani* (page 280) or tomato rice (page 119); and chicken *kurma* (page 168), fish curry (page 198), Chettiar-style fiery shrimp (page 291), beef *satay goreng* (page 178), or beef *rendang* (page 177).

Pickled Cucumber and Carrot

Acar Timun Carot

Makes 5 to 6 servings

Cucumbers and carrots are another favorite pickle combination in Malaysia. This dish combines Indian and Malay flavor nuances to create a crunchy and delicious side dish for grilled chicken, stir-fried shrimp in sambal, *fried chicken, rich coconut-based curries, and rich rice dishes such as* biryanis, nasi minyak, *and* nasi dagang. *The light combination of cucumbers and carrots offsets the richness of the coconut milk and ghee in these dishes.*

INGREDIENTS

- 1 medium (½ pound) cucumber, sliced into 1½ to 2-inch-long by ¼-inch-wide pieces (2 cups)
- 1½ cups (7½ ounces) peeled and sliced carrots (1½-inch-long by ¼-inch-wide pieces)
- 1 cup sliced shallots or red onions (1-inch to 1½-inch by ⅛-inch pieces)
- 1 fresh red chile (jalapeno, Fresno Serrano, cayenne, Thai, or cherry), sliced into 1½-inch-long by ¼-inch-wide pieces
- 1 tablespoon salt

DRESSING

- 2 tablespoons rice vinegar or distilled white vinegar
- 7 teaspoons sugar
- Optional: 1 to 2 tablespoons sliced fresh ginger (1½-inch by ⅛-inch pieces)

OPTIONAL GARNISH

- 1 tablespoon cooking oil
- ¼ teaspoon black or dark brown mustard seeds
- ⅛ teaspoon chile powder
- ⅛ teaspoon turmeric powder

or

- 2 tablespoons roasted crushed unsalted peanuts or other nuts
- 1 or 2 fresh green chilies (jalapeno, cayenne, Serrano, or Thai), sliced

DIRECTIONS:

1. Rub cucumber, carrots, onions and chilies with salt and let sit in a colander weighted down by a plastic bag of water for about 15 to 20 minutes, till all liquid is drained. (Alternately soak the vegetables in water to cover for about 15 to 20 minutes. Then drain in colander and gently squeeze out excess water.)
2. Make the dressing by combining vinegar, sugar, and ginger, if using, in a non-reactive bowl. Add the vegetable mixture and coat well with the dressing.
3. Optional garnish: In a small skillet, heat oil, add mustard seeds, cover, and let seeds pop. When popping subsides, uncover, add the turmeric and chile powder and stir for a few seconds. Remove from heat and pour this savory oil mixture over the pickled salad. Or top the salad with peanuts and chilies.

Serve with *nasi dagang* (page 128), *nasi minyak* (page 121), beef or chicken *rendang* (pages 177 and 287), stir-fried shrimp (*sambal tumis udang*, page 204), or hot and sour shrimp (*udang assam pedas*, page 201).

Cucumber carrot *acar*

Pickled Green Papaya Salad
Acar Betik Hijau

Makes 5 to 6 servings

INGREDIENTS

1 pound (about 3 cups) green papaya, peeled and shredded or sliced (about 2-inch-long by ¼-inch-thick pieces)
1¼ cups (6¼ ounces) sliced carrots (about 2-inch-long by ¼-inch-thick pieces)
Optional: 1 tablespoon finely sliced garlic cloves
Optional: 1 tablespoon thinly sliced shallots or onion
2 to 3 teaspoons salt

Dressing

3 tablespoons freshly squeezed or bottled lime juice
1 tablespoon fish sauce or *budu*
1 tablespoon sugar
½ teaspoon *cili boh* (*see page 315*), or ¼ teaspoon bottled *sambal oelek*
Optional: ⅛ teaspoon ground coriander

Garnish

1 tablespoon coarsely ground peanuts or other nuts
1 tablespoon chopped coriander leaves (cilantro)

Green papaya salad (called somtam *in Thai) is a specialty of northern Malaysia, where the cuisine is influenced by Thai ingredients and flavors. Today, Thai-influenced foods have become popular all over Malaysia, especially in Kuala Lumpur and my hometown of Petaling Jaya where they are prepared by Malays or Mamaks who migrated from the states of Kelantan, Perlis, or southern Thailand. These vendors serve fiery dishes that have a mix of southern Thai and Malay flavors, quite different from the Thai foods served in Bangkok or Thailand. Chicken* padprik, tom yam sup, Pad Thai, *green papaya* acar, *or pandan-wrapped chicken are some specialties. Many Thai restaurants sprang up in the 1990s but their foods are not quite the same as the* tom yam *stalls. My daughter, Geeta, loves shredded pickled green papaya salad so I decided to include this recipe, which is popular in Malaysia as well as in the U.S.*

DIRECTIONS:

1. Rub papaya, carrot slices, garlic, and shallots or onion, if using, with salt and let sit in a colander weighted down by a plastic bag of water for about 15 to 20 minutes, till liquid is drained. (Alternately soak vegetable mixture in enough water to cover for about 15 to 20 minutes, drain in colander and gently squeeze out excess water.) Set aside.
2. To make dressing, combine lime juice, fish sauce, sugar, *cili boh* or *sambal oelek*, and coriander, if using. Mix well.
3. Before serving, drizzle papaya and carrot mixture with dressing and coat well. Cool for about 30 minutes or chill before adding garnish. Garnish with peanuts and/or coriander leaves.

Serve with cooked white or brown rice, ghee rice (page 121), yellow rice (page 118); and spicy fried fish (page 206), chicken curry (page 171), lamb chops in black pepper sauce (page 184), chile squid (page 211,) or *sambal* scallops (page 210).

Fresh Uncooked Sambal Belacan

Sambal Belacan

Makes 3 to 4 servings (about 1 cup)

Sambal belacan *for Malaysians is like salt and pepper in the U.S. It began as a "poor man's" seasoning for* kampung (village) *people to perk up plain cooked rice and tuber-based meals such as boiled tapioca (cassava) or sweet potato. For Malays and Chittys,* sambal belacan *is a must for their daily meals, as well as special functions.*

Sambal belacan *is served either fresh (uncooked) or cooked* (tumised, page 102)*. The fresh form is traditionally made from dried shrimp paste* (belacan)*, fresh chopped chilies, onions, palm sugar, salt, and lime juice blended in a mortar and pestle to a coarse paste. Some cooks add tamarind juice, tomatoes, or garlic to temper the chile heat. At restaurants* sambal belacan *is offered on the side, to add the extra perk to the meal. It is also used as a stuffing for grilled fish and as a base cooking sauce for many vegetable, meat, chicken, and seafood dishes.*

INGREDIENTS:

- 2 heaping teaspoons chopped garlic cloves
- 1 heaping cup chopped shallots or onions
- 2 fresh green chilies and 1 fresh red chile (jalapeno, Fresno, cayenne, Serrano, Thai, or bird peppers), sliced ¼ to ½ inch crosswise
- 4 to 6 teaspoons dried shrimp paste (*belacan*), toasted at 400°F for 15 minutes (*see page 335*)
- ¼ cup thinly sliced or chopped palm sugar or dark brown sugar
- ½ teaspoon salt
- ½ to ¾ teaspoon freshly squeezed or bottled lime juice

DIRECTIONS:

1. Pound garlic, shallots or onions, chilies, and shrimp paste in a mortar and pestle adding 1 to 2 tablespoons water if needed, or pulse in a food processor with ¼ to ½ cup water to a coarse paste.
2. Add the sugar and salt and blend well.
3. Add lime juice just before serving.

Serve with cooked white or brown rice or boiled potatoes; and roast chicken (page 297), spicy fried chicken (page 165), braised savory noodles (page 144), spicy baked or grilled fish (page 207), or pork *pong teh* (page 188); and vegetables in spicy coconut milk (page 223) or stir-fried bean sprouts (page 229).

Cooked Sambal Belacan

Sambal Tumis Belacan

Makes 3 to 4 servings

INGREDIENTS

½ cup coarsely pounded shallots or onions
40 whole dried red chilies, slit and deseeded and steeped in hot water for 5 minutes till soft; or ½ cup *cili boh* (*see page 315*); or ¼ to ⅓ cup bottled *sambal oelek*
¼ cup cooking oil
Optional: 1 teaspoon dried shrimp paste (*belacan*), toasted at 400°F for 15 minutes (*see page 335*)
½ cup tamarind juice or juice extracted from tamarind pulp (*see page 339*)
Optional: ⅛ to ¼ teaspoon sugar
1 teaspoon salt

Sambal tumis belacan *is a cooked aromatic condiment that is a favorite with all Malaysians.* Tumising *is a technique of stir-frying, where traditionally the* sambal *paste is slowly stirred in oil for about 15 to 20 minutes, till the oil starts seeping out of the paste and the paste becomes fragrant.* Sambal tumis belacan *is also a flavorful base sauce for* ikan bilis *(baby anchovies), squid, shrimp, chicken, fish, eggplant, asparagus, and okra.*

Ma prepared her sambal *without* belacan *and it was equally delicious. In those days,* belacan *was prepared along dusty roadsides, and being a health-conscious mom, she would not use it. Today it is manufactured under more sanitary conditions and made into pastes and powders.* Sambal tumis belacan *is a wonderful accompaniment for cooked white rice and fried or grilled chicken, fish, or shrimp.*

DIRECTIONS:

1. Process shallots or onions and chilies, *cili boh*, or *sambal oelek* with ¼ to ½ cup water to a coarse paste (use less water if using the liquid sauces). Set aside.
2. Heat 1 tablespoon oil in a skillet, add chile paste and stir for about 4 to 5 minutes till fragrant.
3. Add remaining oil and dried shrimp paste, if using, and stir for about 10 to 15 minutes, till oil seeps out of paste (add more oil if necessary) and paste becomes fragrant. (Alternately, you can use less oil and stir paste for about 6 to 8 minutes.)
4. Stir in tamarind juice and cook for 3 more minutes.
5. Add sugar, if using, and salt and cook for another minute.

Serve with cooked white or brown rice, coconut-infused rice (page 117), or yellow rice (page 118). Or add with cooked shrimp, squid, fried *ikan bilis* (baby anchovies), or spicy fried chicken (page 165). It is also great with fried rice (page 123), spicy pork ribs (page 190), roast chicken (page 297), savory meat lentils (page 285), and stir-fried rice noodles (page 139).

Baby Anchovy Sambal

Sambal Ikan Bilis

Makes 3 to 4 servings

Sambal ikan bilis is *my favorite condiment and I eat it with everything! It is generally used as the topping or side dish for* nasi lemak, *the national rice dish of Malaysia. It is made with chilies, shallots, tamarind juice, garlic, tomatoes, coconut milk, lime juice, belacan, sugar and fried baby anchovies (ikan bilis). There are some slight variations in the flavor of* sambal ikan bilis, *depending on whether a Nonya, Malay Chitty, Kristang, or Indian-Muslim prepares it. Malaysian children begin eating* sambal ikan bilis *as soon as they are able to eat solid food. It began as a poor man's relish to add zest to plain cooked white rice, especially among Kristang and Malay fisherman and rice farmers. Now it has become a trendy condiment at upscale restaurants and hotels for breakfast and lunch buffets, and is eaten with grilled or fried chicken or fish, or spooned over steamed vegetables. It even is used as a filling for sandwiches and pastries for breakfast and teatime.*

When I visited my Malaysian girlfriend Ratha Chitty, a Peranakan Indian, in San Francisco a few years ago, she served me the most delicious sambal ikan bilis. *She said it was her childhood favorite, served for everyday meals and special festivals like Parchu (a day for honoring and remembering ancestors). She gave me some to take back to New York. It should have lasted for two weeks, but I finished it in a few days! I started experimenting making my own* sambal ikan bilis *and arrived at this recipe. It can be kept in a refrigerator for up to 2 weeks (the flavor intensity getting better over time) or kept frozen.*

INGREDIENTS

½ cup (about 1¼ ounces) dried *ikan bilis* (baby anchovies), heads discarded
¼ teaspoon turmeric powder
2 tablespoons or ½ cup cooking oil (depending whether pan-frying or deep-frying method is used) plus additional ½ cup cooking oil
2 teaspoons tamarind concentrate or juice extracted from tamarind pulp (*see page 339*)
1 to 1½ teaspoons unsweetened coconut milk
2 teaspoons sugar
⅛ teaspoon salt
Optional: ¼ to ½ teaspoon freshly squeezed or bottled lime juice

SPICE PASTE

½ cup sliced shallots or onions
1 heaping tablespoon sliced garlic cloves
6 to 12 dried whole chilies, slit and deseeded and steeped in hot water for 5 minutes; or 1½ to 3 tablespoons *cili boh* (*see page 315*); or ¾ to 1½ tablespoons bottled *sambal oelek*
1½ cups (9 ounces) chopped tomatoes
1½ teaspoons dried shrimp paste (*belacan*), toasted at 400°F for 15 minutes (*see page 335*)
¼ cup water

DIRECTIONS:

1. Rinse and clean *ikan bilis*, pat dry and rub with turmeric. Marinate for 20 to 30 minutes.
2. Heat oil in a skillet and pan-fry (using 2 tablespoons oil) or deep-fry (using ½ cup oil) seasoned *ikan bilis* for about 2 to 3 minutes, till crispy. Set aside. (Alternately, if you prefer not to fry, add seasoned *ikan bilis* at step 5.)
3. Process Spice Paste ingredients to a smooth paste.
4. Heat ¼ cup oil in a skillet or wok. Add Spice Paste and simmer, stirring constantly, for about 10 to 15 minutes, till oil seeps out and paste becomes fragrant. (Alternately, add less oil and cook for about 8 minutes.)
5. Add seasoned *ikan bilis* (if not fried), tamarind juice, and ¼ cup water and stir for 5 minutes.
6. Add coconut milk and cook for about 5 minutes. Add sugar, salt, and fried *ikan bilis* and stir for another 1 minute. If desired, sprinkle with lime juice just before serving.

Serve with cooked white or brown rice, coconut-infused rice (page 117), spiced rice (page 120), or tomato rice (page 119); and chicken *kurma* (page 168), savory meat lentils (page 285), or a spicy omelet (page 305); and stir-fried mixed vegetables (page 224) or cucumber pineapple *acar* (page 98).

GREEN CHILIES IN SOY SAUCE

Cili Hijau Bersos Kicap

Makes 3 to 4 servings (about ½ cup)

INGREDIENTS

- 2 fresh green or red chilies (jalapeno, Serrano, cayenne, Thai), or 4 bird peppers (*cili padi*), sliced crosswise into ¼-inch-thick pieces
- 1½ to 2 tablespoons finely chopped garlic cloves
- 1 teaspoon finely chopped fresh ginger
- ½ cup regular soy sauce
- 4 teaspoons freshly squeezed or bottled lime juice

Simply referred to as cili kicap, this dip is hot, tart, and slightly sweet and is a must on Chinese hawker's tables for every meal, especially their noodle soups and noodle stir-fries. Eating noodles is not the same without this dip. It transforms plain soups into delectable meals. I also enjoy it with fried rice or grilled meat and seafood dishes.

DIRECTIONS:

1. Combine all ingredients in a non-reactive bowl and mix well.
2. Let dip sit for about 30 minutes or chill overnight before serving.

Serve with fried rice (page 123), stir-fried rice noodles (page 139), Cantonese-style noodles (page 140), grilled spicy chicken (page 166), peppercorn soy sauce beef (page 181), spicy fried chicken (page 165), or spicy fried fish (page 206).

About Chinese-Style Dips

The Chinese of Malaysia have delicious dips for every dish—noodles, rice, soup, chicken, meat, or seafood dishes. I remember those days after the rains, when my parents would sometimes take us to old PJ town for a bowl of steaming noodle soup, which would warm us immediately. What I most enjoyed at these meals were the side condiments served alongside the noodle soups. As a youngster, I was addicted to these simple dips of sliced red or green chilies in soy sauce or vinegar (generally called *cili kicap* or *jeruk cili* in Malay). These hot, spicy, sweet, pickled or pungent dips use different types and cuts of chilies, that are sliced, pounded, crushed, or blended with other ingredients, such as garlic, ginger, vinegar, lime juice, soy sauce, sugar, and toasted sesame oil. The Chinese also have created fragrant oils with pounded shallots, ginger, or garlic for their noodle, steamed chicken, or fish dishes.

Sweet Sour Pickled Green Chilies

Cili Berjeruk Masam Manis

Makes 3 to 4 servings (about ½ cup)

This is a mildly sweet and tart Chinese-style dip commonly served with fried rice or noodle dishes, such as wantan mee, tok tok mee *(in Penang), or soup noodles. It brings back memories of my high school years in Kuala Lumpur. Sometimes, after library hours on Saturdays, I would savor a plate of* wantan mee *on Petaling Street in Kuala Lumpur before I took the bus home. Cheong Kee restaurant (long gone now) served the best* wantan mee *in town. It came with a bowl of soup and the best part, the pickled green chile dip. What a treat after a hard day of studying!*

INGREDIENTS

- 2 fresh green chilies (jalapeno, Serrano, cayenne, or Thai), or 4 fresh bird peppers (*cili padi*), sliced crosswise into ¼-inch-thick rings
- ⅓ cup distilled white vinegar or rice vinegar
- 4 teaspoons sugar
- ¼ teaspoon salt

DIRECTIONS:

1. Combine all ingredients in a non-reactive bowl and mix well.
2. Let sit for at least 30 minutes before serving, or better still chill overnight.

Serve with fried rice (page 123), tomato rice (page 119), *sup mee* (page 83), hot and spicy chicken wings (page 64), or *yee mee* (page 140).

Pickled Chilies in Soy Sauce

Jeruk Cili Bersos Kicap

Makes 3 to 4 servings (about ½ cup)

Once, during a summer barbecue at home, I created this dip for grilled lamb using chilies and mint from my garden. It has a wonderful balance of sweetness, tartness, and a light minty taste. It is prepared with coarsely chopped chilies, garlic, and freshly chopped mint and complements roasts and grilled meats, especially lamb dishes.

INGREDIENTS

- 3 fresh green or red chilies (jalapeno, Serrano, cayenne, Thai), or 5 to 6 fresh bird peppers (*cili padi*), sliced crosswise into ⅛ to ¼-inch-thick rings
- 2 teaspoons coarsely chopped garlic cloves
- 1½ teaspoons distilled white vinegar or rice vinegar
- ½ teaspoon regular soy sauce
- 4 teaspoons sugar
- ½ teaspoon salt

GARNISH

- 1 tablespoon chopped fresh mint leaves

DIRECTIONS:

1. Pound chilies and garlic in a mortar and pestle to a coarse paste, or process to a coarse paste adding 1 to 2 tablespoons water.
2. Place chile-garlic paste in a non-reactive bowl and add the remaining ingredients and 3 tablespoons water and mix well. Let sit for at least 30 minutes or chill overnight.
3. Garnish with mint before serving and mix well.

Serve with noodle soup (page 83), spicy Indian Muslim stir-fried noodles (page 136), fried rice (page 123), spicy fried chicken (page 165), or grilled steak.

Chile Ginger Garlic Sauce

Sos Cili Halia Bawang Putih

Makes 3 to 4 servings (about ½ cup)

INGREDIENTS

3 fresh red chilies (Fresno, cherry, cayenne, jalapeno, or Serrano), sliced and deseeded
1 heaping tablespoon sliced garlic cloves
2 teaspoons sliced fresh ginger
2 tablespoons sugar
2 tablespoons freshly squeezed or bottled lime juice
½ teaspoon distilled white vinegar or rice vinegar
¾ teaspoon salt

This is a delicious and aromatic dip that is universally savored in Malaysia. It has a garlicky flavor that complements steamed dishes. Its flavor is similar to Thai Sriracha sauce, a popular condiment today with Americans. It also perks up fried chicken, fried fish, and roasts. Hainanese chicken rice would not be the same without it. It is also a great topping for pizzas and sandwich fillings.

DIRECTIONS:

1. Process or pound in a mortar and pestle the chilies, garlic, and ginger with ¼ cup water to a smooth paste.
2. Place the paste in a non-reactive bowl and add remaining ingredients and mix well.

Serve with Hainanese chicken rice (page 126) or fried rice (page 123) with grilled chicken, hot and spicy chicken wings (page 64), and spicy fried fish (page 206).

Pounded Ginger in Flavored Oil

Sos Halia Berminyak

Makes 3 to 4 servings (about ½ cup)

INGREDIENTS

4 heaping tablespoons finely chopped and crushed fresh ginger
2 teaspoons toasted sesame oil
½ teaspoon salt
1 teaspoon white granulated sugar
4 teaspoons chicken stock
1 teaspoon freshly squeezed or bottled lime juice
1 teaspoon regular soy sauce
¼ cup cooking oil

Indians fry whole spices—mustard seeds, curry leaves, coriander seeds, garlic cloves, and cumin seeds—in hot oil to obtain fragrant oils to season lentils, raitas, and meat dishes. Similarly, the Chinese have created aromatic flavored oils using shallots, Szechwan peppercorn, dried chilies, garlic, ginger, and many other spices.

This is another delicious dip especially for Hainanese chicken rice, an elaborate preparation for the Chinese New Year and other special occasions. This dip also complements fish dishes. It has a wonderful balance of ginger, soy sauce, and sesame oil.

DIRECTIONS:

1. Combine all ingredients well.
2. Let sit for at least 30 minutes before serving.

Serve with Hainanese chicken rice (page 126). By double dipping, you can get layers of flavor. First, dip the chicken pieces in this flavored ginger oil, then dip in chile ginger garlic sauce (above) and eat with seasoned rice (page 120).

Spicy Sweet Chile Sauce Dip

Sos Cili Manis

Makes 4 to 5 servings (1 cup)

This spicy sweet chile sauce dip with a slight tang is a favorite accompaniment to many foods, including steamed fish, roast lamb, chicken wings, and stewed or grilled meats. Growing up we were addicted to the Linggam's sweet and spicy chile sauce, the Malaysian version of the Thai sweet chile sauce that has become popular with Americans today. I remember adding it over cooked rice, fried fish, and fried chicken. Generally it comes as a smooth dip prepared with dried whole chilies or cili boh*, but I use coarsely ground fresh chilies, sugar, and soy sauce. It tastes like a spicy sweet version of the popular Latino condiment* chimichurri*, used for grilled meats and chicken.*

INGREDIENTS

5 small or 2 large fresh green or red chilies (Thai, cayenne, jalapeno, or Serrano), chopped
1 to 1½ heaping tablespoons chopped garlic cloves
1 teaspoon chopped fresh ginger
½ cup distilled white vinegar or rice vinegar
1 tablespoon white granulated sugar
½ teaspoon salt
Optional: 2 tablespoons regular soy sauce
3 teaspoons freshly squeezed or bottled lime juice

DIRECTIONS:

1. Process or pound in a mortar and pestle chopped chilies, garlic, and ginger with ¼ cup water to a coarse paste.
2. Place the paste in a non-reactive bowl and add remaining ingredients and mix well.
3. Let sauce stand for about 30 minutes before serving.

Serve with tomato rice (page 119) or fried rice (page 123); and hot and spicy chicken wings (page 64), spicy fish cutlets (page 63), spicy fried fish (page 206), pork *pong teh* (page 188), or spicy fried chicken (page 165).

Spicy sweet chili sauce dip served with herbs (*ulam*), cucumber, and *petai*

Dips for Noodles

The dips on the following pages are specifically used for noodle dishes. Noodles in Malaysia are always accompanied with a little saucer of dip or condiment. A condiment is a must, be it as a topping or side, and without these dips we do not enjoy eating noodles. Chilies are added when noodles are cooked, but these spicy condiments give that extra layer of flavor to the eating experience. Dips are created to complement the various noodle flavors. I have included here recipes for most of the popular noodle dips of Malaysia.

Belacan Chile Paste Dip for Curry Noodles

Sos Cili Belacan untok Kari Mee

Makes 3 to 4 servings (about ½ cup)

INGREDIENTS

- 3 to 4 tablespoons cooking oil (or use more oil, about ¼ to ½ cup, for longer frying or *tumising* time)
- 1 to 2 teaspoons dark brown sugar
- ¼ to ½ teaspoon salt
- ¼ teaspoon freshly squeezed or bottled lime juice

SPICE PASTE

- 1 teaspoon dried shrimp paste (*belacan*), toasted at 400°F for 15 minutes (*see page 335*); or 2 tablespoons whole dried small shrimp (krill), soaked in hot water for about 15 minutes to soften
- ¾ cup sliced shallots or onions
- 1 tablespoon sliced garlic cloves
- 4 to 6 fresh red chilies (Fresno, jalapeno, Serrano, Thai, cherry, or cayenne), or 8 fresh bird peppers (*cili padi*), sliced
- ¼ cup water

Belacan *chile paste dip is a very popular dip for a number of noodle dishes, including* kari mee *and* Hokkien mee. *A dollop of this spicy pungent* belacan *(dried shrimp paste) dip with chilies, shallots, dark brown sugar, and lime juice is a must for* kari mee, *noodles in a curry-based broth, a delicious concoction from the Chinese vendors in Kuala Lumpur and Penang. The Penang version is different from the Kuala Lumpur version. I prefer the Kuala Lumpur* kari mee, *which has a richer and stronger curry broth and generally comes with a* belacan-*based dip (Indian Muslim and Malay influences) instead of the dried whole small shrimp or krill-based dip, a specialty of the Nonyas.*

DIRECTIONS:

1. Process all Spice Paste ingredients to a smooth paste.
2. Heat oil in a small skillet or wok. Add Spice Paste, sugar, salt, and lime juice, and sauté for about 8 minutes (or longer if using more oil—about 15 to 20 minutes for oil to seep out), till sauce becomes fragrant.

Serve with curry noodles (page 149), braised savory noodles (page 144), stir-fried rice noodles (page 139), aromatic spicy noodles (page 142), or fried rice (page 123).

Chile Paste Dip for Laksa Lemak

Sos Cili untok Laksa Lemak

Makes 3 to 4 servings (about ½ cup)

Laksa lemak is a savory coconut-infused noodle dish that has its origins in Malacca. It is a Nonya specialty with Chinese and Malay flavorings. What gives it the "kick" is this hot and savory condiment.

INGREDIENTS

1 heaping cup chopped or sliced shallots or onions
6 whole dried red chilies, steeped in hot water for 5 to 8 minutes (slit and deseeded if you desire less heat), pounded or processed with ¼ cup water to a smooth paste; or 1 to 1½ tablespoons *cili boh* (see page 315); or ½ to ¾ tablespoon bottled *sambal oelek*
3 to 4 tablespoons cooking oil (or use more oil, about ¼ to ½ cup, for longer frying or *tumising* time)
4½ teaspoons sugar
1 teaspoon salt

DIRECTIONS:

1. Process shallots or onions, chilies, and ¼ cup water to a smooth paste.
2. Heat oil in a small skillet or wok and add chile paste, sugar, and salt and sauté for about 8 minutes (or longer if using more oil—15 to 20 minutes for oil to seep out), till sauce becomes fragrant.

Serve with coconut-based noodles (page 151), curry noodles (page 149), or other noodle dishes and soups.

Chile Garlic Dip for Soup Noodles

Sos Cili Bawang Putih untok Sup Mee

Makes 3 to 4 servings (about ½ cup)

This is another Chinese-style dip that accompanies steaming bowls of a simple noodle soup (with wheat-based noodles) or meehoon *soup (with rice vermicelli). It has a garlicky scallion flavor and is popular with Chinese and Nonya dishes. It also goes well with other light soups and stews and even the steamboat (called* lok-lok*).*

INGREDIENTS

6 fresh green chilies (jalapeno, Serrano, cayenne, or Thai), chopped; or 8 to 10 tablespoons chopped bird peppers (*cili padi*)
2 tablespoons chopped shallots or onions
2 to 4 tablespoons chopped scallions or spring onions
6 tablespoons regular soy sauce

GARNISH

1 tablespoon cooking oil
4 teaspoons crushed garlic cloves

DIRECTIONS:

1. Combine all ingredients in a bowl and mix well. Set sauce aside.
2. Heat oil in a small skillet or wok, add garlic cloves and saute till garlic gets golden brown.
3. Pour this hot garlic-oil mixture over sauce, let stand for about 20 minutes, and serve.

Serve with *sup mee* or *sup meehoon* (page 83).

Chile Oil Dip for Mee Siam

Sos Cili Berminyak untok Mee Siam

Serves 3 to 4 (about ½ cup)

INGREDIENTS

2 tablespoons tamarind concentrate or tamarind juice extract (*see page 339*)

4 to 6 dried whole red chilies, steeped in hot water for 5 to 8 minutes, slit and deseeded if less heat desired, and pureed to a smooth paste; or 1 to 1½ tablespoons *cili boh* (*see page 315*); or ½ to ¾ tablespoon bottled *sambal oelek*

1½ cups finely chopped shallots or onions

½ teaspoon sugar

¼ teaspoon salt

3 tablespoons cooking oil

This is a fiery tamarind-based fragrant oil dip for mee Siam, *a popular noodle dish in Northwest Malaysia, especially in Penang. The Penang Nonyas have taken flavor nuances from the Thais to create this rice vermicelli dish served for daily meals and birthdays.*

DIRECTIONS:

1. Combine all ingredients and 2 tablespoons water in a non-reactive bowl and mix well. Let stand for 30 minutes.
2. Serve as a topping or as a side dip.

Serve with Siamese noodles (page 138).

Kuan Yin Teng Temple, Penang

CHAPTER **4**

RICE: CENTERPIECE OF EVERY MEAL

Rice (*padi*) field, Kedah

Rice is central to Malaysian life, culture, and cuisine. Many of the ethnic groups have elaborate festivals and rituals to give thanks for a bountiful rice harvest. Rice is prepared in various ways—as entrees, sides, sweets, or beverages—and given as an offering to God, rice spirits, or the Sun God for blessings and prosperity. Rice dishes play a central role in food offerings for ancestral worship by Chinese, Malays, Nonyas, and Chittys, or as blessings at Indian and Malay religious ceremonies and weddings.

Malay traditional beliefs hold that the rice (*padi*) field is animated by the "spirit of life," called *semangat* in Malay, which bestows vitality to the *padi*. The *semangat padi* is treated with the utmost reverence in Malay culture, as reflected in ritual festivals carried out throughout the cycle of rice cultivation. During the ritual of the rice harvest, the rice field is considered a pregnant woman, and the first grain of harvested rice like a newborn child that must be protected and treated with care.

Undoubtedly, these beliefs and rituals are derived from the central role of rice as a stalwart against hunger in Malaysia and throughout Asia. The rituals reflect the community's fundamental need for a bountiful harvest. Similar rituals honoring the "Rice Mother," the goddess of the sacred grain, are prevalent throughout Asia. In Java, people call her "Sri Dewi." In Bengal, she is the Hindu goddess Annapurna, and in Japan, many shrines are dedicated to her. Accordingly, rice became a symbol of spirituality and life itself. Indeed, growing up in Malaysia, we were constantly reminded by our parents not to leave rice on our plates or throw away a grain of rice.

With modern rice harvesting techniques, these rituals are seen less often in Western Malaysia, but are still

Sacks of raw rice (*beras*)

prevalent in Sabah and Sarawak. Celebrated as Pesta Kaamatan and Gawai Dayak, these festivals mark the end of the rice harvest and thank the rice spirit for a bountiful harvest and ask for blessings for a new rice planting season. During this festival, *tuak* (rice wine) and many traditional foods are served, including glutinous rice roasted in bamboo and cakes made from rice flour, sugar, and coconut milk.

Malaysians of South Indian ancestry celebrate a rice harvest festival called Pongal (see Chapter 11 on festivals), and on this day, rice is boiled with fresh milk and jaggery (brown sugar) in new pots. The ritual of cooking rice is symbolic of good tidings and prosperity. The new boiled rice is offered to Nature during sunrise, giving thanks to the Sun and Nature, and then sprinkled around the house for blessings.

Rice also plays a dominant role for Parchu, a day of ancestral worship for the Chitty community in Malacca. At the altar, various rice dishes are placed in the center of banana leaves, including white rice, *nasi lemak* (rice cooked with coconut milk, page 117), and/or *nasi kemuli* (spiced rice, page 120), along with accompaniments.

The centrality of rice to Malaysian culture is also reflected in their diverse languages. In the Malay culture, the word "*nasi*" means cooked rice, but it is also the word for meal. Malaysians also commonly greet each other with the phrase "*sudah makan nasi?*" which means "have you eaten your meal?" Thus, for Malaysians a meal without rice is not considered a true meal.

At home or in restaurants, steamed white rice, called *nasi putih*, is a must with all meals. Many Malaysians eat plain cooked white rice with intensely flavored *sambal belacan* (page 101) or cooked *sambal tumis belacan* (page 102). The cooked white rice offsets the fiery *sambals* and other hot chile-based condiments. Each ethnic group in Malaysia adds its own basic flavoring to make *nasi putih* more fragrant or visually appealing. For example, Malays cook rice with stalks of lemongrass or pandan leaf tied into a knot, infusing the rice with their wonderful aromas. Indians add cloves, cumin seeds, and a pinch of turmeric or saffron to enhance the rice's flavor and to color it yellow. The Chinese add drops of sesame oil and broth to rice to produce an aromatic sensation.

TYPES OF RICE

A medium-grain to long-grain locally cultivated rice, referred to as "economy rice," is widely consumed in Malaysia. It is fluffy and not sticky. Imported long-grain rice, such as Jasmine or Basmati, is more expensive and is often reserved for special occasions, although today it is consumed on an increasingly larger scale. Long-grain and medium-grain rice are used for entrees, while short-grain rice is used for desserts and snacks. Most Chinese and Nonya dishes use long- or medium-grain rice that becomes slightly sticky while cooking and clumps as it cools.

Jasmine rice is a long-grain rice with a nutty aroma and a creamy pandan-like flavor. It is generally rinsed before cooking to rid it of extra starch. The grains cling together when cooked, although Jasmine rice is less sticky than glutinous rice because it has less amylopectin (a starch that makes rice "sticky" when released from the grain during cooking). Jasmine rice is used for festive occasions and increasingly by many cooks for daily meals such as *nasi lemak* (coconut-infused rice, page 117) or *nasi ayam* (Hainanese chicken rice, page 126).

Basmati rice has a delicate and fragrant aroma when cooked. Its grains are thin and longer than they are wide, and grow even longer as they cook. The grains are not sticky but stay firm and fluffy and separate after cooking because they are high in amylose (starch that does not gelatinize when cooked). Basmati rice comes both as white rice and brown rice. Brown rice, although high in vitamins, minerals, and fiber, is not as popular with Malaysians as white rice, because the latter soaks up curries, *sambals*, stir-fries, and stews better than brown rice. Pure white rice is also more visually appealing than brown rice and forms a better backdrop for the colorful curries and sauces. But with today's concern for a high fiber diet, many are incorporating brown rice into their diets at home. Festive rice dishes such as *biryanis, kembuli,* or *pullaos* also call for Basmati rice.

In the northern Malaysian state of Kelantan, locals enjoy a long-grain red rice with the bran intact called *beras nasi dagang.* Like brown rice, it is unpolished rice that is high in fiber, vitamins B1 and B2, iron, and calcium. *Beras nasi dagang* is traditionally steamed and eaten with a spicy, sweet, coconut-laden fish curry (*kari ikan tongkol,* page 208) or chicken curry (*kari ayam*, page 171). It is similar to "cargo rice" from Thailand, with a sweet, nutty, and chewy texture.

Short-grain rice (*beras pulut*), also called glutinous, sweet, or sticky rice, is made into compressed rice (page 281), which is eaten with *satay.* It is also used as a stuffing, fermented into wine, and ground into flour for noodles, dumplings, and confections. Nonyas and Malays prepare many desserts, cakes (*kuehs*), and snacks with short-grain glutinous rice, which gives them a soft, sticky texture.

MALAYSIAN RICE DISHES

In Malaysia, rice recipes are extraordinarily varied and reflect the diversity of ethnic groups and regional cooking styles. One of my favorite rice dishes is *nasi lemak* (page 117), said to be the national rice dish of Malaysia. It is a fragrant, savory rice dish cooked with coconut milk, pandan leaf (or lemongrass), and spices, and topped or accompanied with a fiery *sambal ikan bilis* (page 103). It is served with everything from anchovies to cuttlefish to chicken or beef *rendang* (pages 177 and 287). There is a wonderful mingling of flavors and textures when eating *nasi lemak*—creamy, hot, spicy, crunchy, and nutty.

Rice-based meals are particularly popular in Malaysia because they are complete, quick, and easy to prepare. In my home they were a common feature at dinner when Ma needed a quick preparation to feed all nine of us. Fried rice (*nasi goreng*, page 123) was our favorite. Though our family generally enjoyed the Chinese and Malays styles, Ma usually prepared her own version of it, adding our favorite meats, vegetables, and sliced tofu. From vendors, you can

Nasi campur (mixed rice) stalls run by roadside vendors, coffee shops, and restaurants offer *nasi campur* meals, steamed white rice or seasoned rice with accompaniments or sides. You can choose buffet-style from an array of curries, fried fish or chicken, vegetable stir-fries, shrimp or squid *sambal*, or *acars* to go with your rice. It is a popular rice combo meal for lunch crowds in Kuala Lumpur, my hometown of Petaling Jaya, and other southern states.

Nasi kandar is the Indian Muslim version of *nasi campur* and popular in street stalls in Penang and other northern states. *Roti canai*, *dalcha*, mutton or beef curry, fish head curry, *tandoori*, *kurma*, and eggplant are some sides. The term *kandar* refers to the practice of early vendors peddling their rice and curry dishes from home to home in large containers that they would balance on a long pole carried across their shoulders. Although the Indian Muslim vendors who originated it would just have a few dishes to go with the rice, today's *nasi kandar* stalls have elaborate and bountiful spreads.

get *nasi goreng biasa* (regular type) or *nasi goreng kampung ayam* (with free-range chicken) which is slightly more expensive.

Rice-based meals also made it easier for Ma to indulge in her favorite passion—watching movies. When we were growing up, there was no television at home, and even later when Cha (my father) reluctantly installed it, we could only watch it during the weekends. However, Ma was addicted to Tamil and Hindi movies. Since Cha did not share this passion, she took my sister Vas and me along with her. We felt grown up riding in the trishaw and staying up late at the movie theater (way past 11 p.m.!). It was also our chance to spend time alone with Ma. The challenge for my mother every time she wanted to see a movie was how to prepare a tasty and nutritious meal for her children and Cha before she left. The answer was fried rice (*nasi goreng*). It was quick and easy to prepare because she sometimes could use left-over cooked white rice, left-over meat or chicken, any fresh vegetables that were available at hand, and her magical ingredient—eggs!

During the movie, my mind sometimes wandered to "my share" of the fried rice that was hopefully waiting for me and not eaten by my brothers and their friends. On the ride back, I could almost taste the delicious fried rice alongside Ma's special condiment, green chilies and garlic in soy sauce (page 104).

Some of our rice-based meals were prepared at home by my Grandma, whom we fondly called Periama. Periama was born in Salem, a town near Coimbatore, South India. She was from a family of Chettiars, who were wealthy moneylenders. She told me how curious she was to see Malaysia, a land where everyone seemed to be going. So as a brave and adventurous teen, one day Periama packed her things and took a boat to visit some relatives who had moved to Malaysia, thinking it was just a stone's throw way and hardly expecting how far it really was. (I believe I received my adventurous spirit and love of travel from her.) While there she married out of her strict Chettiar caste to a military pilot, Kumaran, my Grandpa (whom we called Thatha), who hailed from Mahe, Kerala, a French enclave. She became an outcast with her own family and never returned to her homeland, not even for a visit.

On Fridays, Periama often took us to the Maha Mariamman Hindu Temple on Petaling Street in Kuala Lumpur. And on these days, she prepared *nasi sambar* (spicy vegetarian rice, page 124), which she generally made on our "non-meat" day of the week.

While an entire encyclopedia could be dedicated to Malaysian rice recipes, I present a number of extremely popular and easy-to-prepare rice dishes in this chapter. Hainanese chicken rice (nasi ayam, page 126) is a specialty from southern China. A lunch favorite, this rice dish is flavored with chicken broth and sesame oil and accompanied with a spicy sweet ginger-chile condiment. Sweet and savory Portuguese-style tomato rice (page 119) is traditionally made with diced tomatoes, star anise, and cinnamon. Six to eight varieties of herbs are added to *nasi ulam* (herb rice, page 125), a Malay-style favorite from the northeastern states of Malaysia. *Nasi kemuli* (spiced rice, page 120), of Arab origins, is a festive favorite for the Chittys of Malacca.

On special holidays or occasions, rice is seasoned with savory and sweet spices, sometimes wrapped in banana leaves, and grilled, stir-fried, or steamed. *Nasi bukhari* (page 278), an aromatic Malay wedding rice dish that has Arabic and Indian origins, contains meat seasoned with pandan leaf and a variety of spices, and is garnished with nuts and raisins. Claypot chicken rice, a Chinese favorite, is cooked with soy sauce, ginger, spring onions, and bits of tender chicken or salted fish in a claypot. Cooking in a claypot gives the dish a smoky and unique flavor. The rice on the very bottom of the pot singes into a gorgeous crisp layer, while meat at the top steams delicately, flavoring the rice with its juices. Rice is also comfort food for Malaysians. Whenever we fell sick or had a cold or fever, Ma served us a bowl of her 'healing' chicken *kanji* (porridge) with soft-boiled rice and shredded chicken flavored with ginger. Rice porridge is popular throughout Asia. In Malaysia, the Chinese have their version, called *congee*, prepared with chicken, pickled vegetables, ginger, and toasted sesame oil.

Rice in Ceremonies

For Malaysians, rice not only nourishes the body and soul but it plays a significant role in daily activities and special occasions. It holds a central and symbolic place in religious ceremonies and weddings, especially Malay and Hindu weddings. In the latter, rice is tossed on the bride and groom for good luck and prosperity.

For Hindu wedding banquets, cooked white rice is a must served on a banana leaf with varying accompaniments of vegetables, dhal curry, pickles, and *papadams*. I vividly remember my youngest brother Suresh's wedding, held at a Hindu temple. Attached to the temple is a community room where temple functions are held. It is here where a *mandabham* or dais is built for the wedding ceremony, and where the bride and groom are seated. When the wedding vows are taken at the end of the wedding ceremony, the bride and groom hold hands and walk in circles around the dais, and as they walk, the guests toss raw rice at the couple for fertility, longevity, and good luck.

PREPARING RICE

Rice, called *beras* in raw form and *nasi* when cooked, is a staple in every kitchen in Malaysia. *Nasi putih* is cooked white rice. The texture of cooked rice should not be too soft, hard, or soggy, but an al dente texture. And rice is always served steaming hot.

A high amount of starch clings to the rice grains, so many cooks wash or rinse the rice a couple of times in cold water before cooking it. This makes the rice fluffy and separate. Soaking it for half an hour before cooking makes the grains less likely to break during cooking and gives the rice a softer texture. Traditionally, Malaysians cook rice in a number of ways. One technique I remember Ma using early on was to boil the rice with a large amount of water till it was half cooked, then drain off the remaining water so the rice cooks in its steam. Another technique was to bring the water to a boil, then lower the heat, cover the pot, and let the rice steam in the pot till cooked. Later on, Ma bought a large rice cooker to cook enough rice for our big family. It was a lifesaver for her!

I use Basmati rice and Jasmine rice in my recipes. For Basmati rice, I use 1 cup rice to 2 cups water, and for Jasmine rice, 1 cup rice to 1¼ to 1½ cups water, depending on the desired texture. Initially I wash or rinse the rice by swirling it in cold water to remove any debris or starch dust. Generally, my recipes call for bringing water to a boil, adding rice and other ingredients, lowering the heat and covering the pot and then simmering the rice for 15 minutes. You then remove the pot from the heat and let the rice cook in its steam for about 10 minutes. If you enjoy rice dishes as much as I do, you may wish to purchase a rice cooker. Just place rice, water, and seasonings in the rice cooker and turn it on. It will shut off automatically when the dish is done. And this way, rice is kept warm till serving time.

Like most Malaysians, we ate *nasi lemak* for breakfast. I remember one Sunday morning during a trip home, my daughter Geeta and I were relaxing in my parents' living room in Petaling Jaya, or "PJ" as we call it. Morning hunger awakened my childhood memories of our favorite *nasi lemak* man from a nearby *kampung* (village). He wore a sarong with a white T-shirt and colorful *songkok* (batik hat), and balanced a bamboo pole across his shoulders with two covered baskets hanging from either end. One basket contained the prized banana leaf bundle of savory and spicy *nasi lemak* topped with *ikan bilis sambal* (dried baby anchovies in a spicy sauce) and garnished with half a hard-boiled egg, chopped roasted peanuts, and slices of cool cucumber. The other basket contained *kuih lapis*, a multi-layered, rainbow-colored glutinous rice custard, the perfect finale to a weekend brunch.

Just as I was daydreaming, I heard a melodious call, "*nasi lemak, nasi lemak* ..." in the distance. I ran out of the house and hailed the vendor, frantically waving my hands and hoping he would notice me! Others were hailing him too—I was afraid that there might not be enough for us! I was elated to see the friendly smile on his face as he walked toward our house and opened each basket to reveal his hidden delicacies. My family and I crowded around him to select our meals. I carefully but quickly picked up the biggest *nasi lemak* I could see, clutched it in my hands and seized a *kuih lapis*, layered in pink, green, and white. For the moment, I even forgot to pick food for Geeta and my Ma! Luckily for them, my brother did. We all gathered around the dining room table to enjoy the feast. As I eagerly unwrapped the banana leaf, I smelled the familiar, pungent aroma of the fish *sambal*, and the sweet, floral coconut rice. I hurriedly mixed the rice, *sambal*, and peanuts together with a spoon, cut the egg into bite-size pieces, and helped myself to a generous serving with the rice, balancing it with a bite of refreshing cucumber. What an explosion of flavors and textures in my mouth!

As I watched my Ma elegantly pick up her meal with her fingers and lift it to her mouth, I cast aside my spoon and followed suit. Now, it really tasted like *nasi lemak*! Then I carefully peeled away the layers of *kuih lapis*, just as I did as a child. How I relished the meal, very patiently letting each mouthful sink into my taste buds so I could savor every bit of it.

Malay-Style Rice with Coconut Milk

Nasi Lemak

Makes 3 to 4 servings

*N*asi lemak *is available on almost every street corner in Malaysia and in almost every restaurant serving Malaysian food. It is sold "to go"* (nasi lemak bungkus) *by street vendors, delis, and bakeries, and even found at the supermarket food counters in microwavable plastic containers. During our stays at my brother Suresh and Mala's home, I would look forward to the* nasi lemak *brunch with their daughter Davee, who like me, savored this meal before she went to school. Or I would sometimes enjoy a take-out* nasi lemak *after a late-night drink of beer or wine with my neice Priya, who is a nasi lemak addict.*

Today, nasi lemak *is served with fried chicken, beef* rendang*, or shrimp* sambal*. Even fancy five-star hotels serve* nasi lemak*, but for me nothing tastes better than a* nasi lemak bungkus *topped with spicy* ikan bilis sambal *and wrapped in banana leaf to go, purchased from a Malay vendor.*

In place of the Jasmine rice, you can also use what the locals use, economy rice, a medium- to long-grain fluffy rice.

INGREDIENTS

1 tablespoon cooking oil
2 teaspoons finely chopped, grated, or crushed fresh ginger
1 cup Jasmine rice, washed and rinsed
½ to ¾ cup unsweetened coconut milk
Pinch of salt
2 or 3 pandan leaves (fresh or frozen), raked with the tines of a fork and knotted; or 1 lemongrass stalk, bruised with back of knife and knotted

GARNISH

½ cup (1¼ ounces) deep-fried baby anchovies (*ikan bilis*) (*see page 323*)
1 hard-boiled egg, cut into 4 wedges
3 or 4 slices peeled cucumber
¼ cup roasted unsalted peanuts

DIRECTIONS:

1. Heat oil in a medium saucepan, add ginger and sauté for about ½ to 1 minute.
2. Add Jasmine rice and sauté for about 2 to 3 minutes.
3. Add 1¼ to 1½ cups water, coconut milk, salt, and pandan leaves or lemongrass, stir and bring to a boil. Then lower heat, cover, and simmer for about 15 minutes till all the liquid has been absorbed and rice is cooked. Remove from heat and let rice cook in its steam, covered, for another 10 minutes. (If using a rice cooker, use proportions for rice cooker based upon above quantities. Add the rice mixture to rice cooker, cover, and switch rice cooker on. Rice cooker automatically shuts off when rice is cooked.)
4. Fluff rice with a fork and remove pandan leaves or lemongrass stalk before serving. To serve this rice in the traditional way, place the rice on a platter and put garnish either on top of it or beside it.

Serve with baby anchovy *sambal* (page 103) or chicken or shrimp *sambal* (pages 161 and 204). You can also serve *nasi lemak* without garnishes with chicken curry (page 171), spicy baked or grilled fish (page 207), spicy fried chicken (page 165), curry chicken *debal* (page 289), or beef *rendang* (page 177); and spicy cucumber tomato salad (page 97), pickled green mango salad (page 96), or pickled green papaya salad (page 100).

Nasi lemak bungkus

Malay-Style Scented Yellow Rice

Nasi Kuning

Makes 3 to 4 servings

INGREDIENTS

1 tablespoon ghee, butter, or cooking oil
¼ to ½ teaspoon white peppercorns
½ teaspoon turmeric powder
1 cup Jasmine rice, washed and rinsed
½ cup unsweetened coconut milk
2 pandan leaves, bruised with the tines of a fork and knotted; or 1 lemongrass stalk, bruised with back of knife and knotted
1 lobe Kaffir lime leaf, crunched
1 piece *asam gelugor* (sometimes labeled tamarind skin), or ½ to ¾ tablespoon tamarind juice
½ teaspoon salt

GARNISH

¼ cup fried (*see page 333*) or sautéed shallots or onions
1 fresh red or green chile (Fresno, jalapeno, Serrano, cayenne, cherry, or Thai), sliced
Optional: 1 tablespoon roasted and crushed unsalted cashews or almonds
Optional: 1 tablespoon golden raisins

Nasi kuning *(yellow rice) or* kunyit *(turmeric rice) is a Malay-style rice preparation generally served for family get-togethers and festive occasions. In homes, it is traditionally prepared with glutinous rice, turmeric, white peppercorns, and coconut milk, and is frequently served with squid* sambal, *grilled chicken* (ayam percik), *beef* rendang, *or fried fish.* Nasi campur *or* nasi kandar *stalls also carry* nasi kuning *in addition to white rice, and prepared with economy rice as it is less expensive.*

Traditionally, when making nasi kuning, *Malays add lemongrass with pandan leaf and another local leaf called* daun salam, *also known as Indonesian bay leaf (its flavor is different from the Indian bay leaf generally used in North Indian cooking).* Nasi kuning *is topped with strips of scrambled egg and fried onions. The Nonyas of Penang have their own version flavored with* asam gelugor *(a sour, tamarind-like dried fruit) and served with chicken curries.*

DIRECTIONS:

1. Heat ghee, butter, or oil in a medium saucepan. Add peppercorns and fry for ½ minute, then add turmeric and stir for a few seconds.
2. Add rice and sauté for 1 to 2 minutes.
3. Add 1¼ to 1½ cups water, coconut milk, pandan leaves or lemongrass, Kaffir lime leaf, *asam gelugor*, and salt.
4. Stir, bring to a boil, then lower heat, cover, and simmer for about 15 minutes till all liquid is absorbed and rice is cooked. Remove from heat and let rice cook in its own steam, covered, for about 10 minutes. (If using a rice cooker, use proportions for rice cooker based upon above quantities. Add the rice mixture from step 3 to rice cooker, cover, and switch rice cooker on. Rice cooker automatically shuts off when rice is cooked.)
5. Remove pandan leaves, lemongrass, *asam gelugor*, and Kaffir lime leaf before serving. Garnish with fried shallots or onions and sliced green or red chile. Sprinkle with cashews and raisins to make it more festive.

Serve with chicken curry (page 171), chicken *vindaloo* (page 169), hot and sour shrimp (page 201), lamb *kurma* (page 282), *sambal* shrimp (page 204), beef *rendang* (page 177), spicy baked or grilled fish (page 207), or grilled spicy chicken (page 166); and spicy cucumber tomato salad (page 97), stir-fried cabbage (page 226), or vegetables in spicy coconut milk (page 223).

Tomato Rice

Nasi Tomato

Makes 3 to 4 servings

This unique fusion-style, sweet and savory rice dish combines flavor elements from the Portuguese, Indians, and Chinese in Malaysia. Its main ingredient, the tomato, brought to Malaysia by the Portuguese, provides tartness and balances to the chile's heat and the savory spices. Tomato rice complements grilled chicken, pork, and fish.

When we lived in Muar, Johor, I had my first taste of tomato rice at Leela's (my brother-in-law Diva's sister) home. Leela made her tomato rice with evaporated milk and Campbell's tomato soup because tomato puree, paste, sauce, and juice were not available in Malaysia then. In later years when we lived in Petaling Jaya, I enjoyed tomato rice from my neighbor, Mrs. Collar, a good friend of Ma's. They would often exchange recipes and dishes. Mrs. Collar was Portuguese Eurasian and she would serve her wonderful tomato rice with devil chicken curry (called kari ayam debal, *page 289). This recipe attempts to re-create the flavors I remember. I use tomato juice in this recipe as I found it easier to work with, but you can substitute tomato puree, sauce, paste, or even tomato soup like Leela! I usually serve tomato rice with a dry chicken or lamb curry.*

INGREDIENTS

- 1 tablespoon ghee, butter, or cooking oil
- 1 heaping teaspoon sliced and crushed garlic cloves
- 1 heaping teaspoon chopped and finely crushed fresh ginger
- ¼ cup finely chopped shallots or red onions
- ½ cup (3 ounces) finely diced tomatoes
- ⅓ cup tomato juice, or 2½ tablespoons tomato puree, or 1 tablespoon tomato paste, or 3½ tablespoons tomato sauce
- 1 cup Basmati or other long-grain rice, washed and rinsed
- ½ teaspoon salt

Spice Blend

- 2 cardamoms
- 2 cloves
- 1-inch cinnamon stick
- 1 star anise

Garnish

- 1 tablespoon golden raisins
- 1 heaping tablespoon crushed unsalted cashews or almonds
- 1 heaping tablespoon fried (*see page 333*) or sautéed shallots or onions
- 1 heaping tablespoon chopped coriander leaves (cilantro)

DIRECTIONS:

1. Heat ghee, butter, or oil in a medium saucepan. Add Spice Blend ingredients and stir for about ½ to 1 minute.
2. Add garlic and ginger and sauté for about ½ to 1 minute, then add shallots or onions and sauté for about 1 to 2 minutes, till fragrant.
3. Add diced tomatoes and cook and stir for about 2 minutes, till tomatoes soften. Add tomato juice, puree, paste, or sauce and stir for another ½ minute.
4. Add the rice and stir for about 1 minute, then add 1½ to 1⅔ cups water and the salt, stir well, and bring to a boil. Lower heat, cover, and let simmer for 15 minutes, till all liquid is absorbed and rice is cooked. Then remove from heat and let rice cook in its steam, covered, for another 10 minutes. (If using a rice cooker, use proportions for rice cooker based upon above quantities. Add the rice mixture to rice cooker, cover and switch rice cooker on. Rice cooker automatically shuts off when rice is cooked.)
5. Remove cinnamon stick and star anise before serving. Garnish with raisins, cashews or almonds, fried shallots or onions, and chopped coriander leaves.

Serve with chicken curry (page 171), lamb *kurma* (page 282), Captain's chicken curry (page 162), *sambal* chicken (page 161), fish with spicy preserved soybean sauce (page 212) or chicken *rendang* (page 287); and a green salad, or cucumber carrot *acar* (page 99), or spicy cucumber tomato salad (page 97). Also goes well with grilled spicy chicken (page 166), spicy fried chicken (page 165), grilled meats, and spicy fried fish (page 206).

Malay-Style Spiced Rice

Nasi Kemuli

Makes 3 to 4 servings

INGREDIENTS

- 1 cup low-sodium chicken broth (or if using regular chicken broth, decrease or omit salt in recipe)
- 1 tablespoon ghee, butter, or cooking oil
- 1 heaping tablespoon sliced and coarsely crushed garlic cloves
- 1 teaspoon sliced and coarsely crushed fresh ginger
- ¼ cup chopped shallots or red onions
- 1 cup Basmati or other long-grain rice, washed and rinsed
- 1 teaspoon sweet or thick soy sauce (or double black soy sauce and a little sugar)
- 1 teaspoon regular soy sauce
- ½ to 1 teaspoon sugar
- ¼ teaspoon salt

Spice Blend

- 3 cloves
- 3 cardamom pods
- 1½-inch cinnamon stick
- 1 star anise
- 1 tablespoon coriander seeds
- 1 teaspoon fennel seeds
- 1 teaspoon cumin seeds

Garnish

- 1 to 2 tablespoons golden raisins
- 1 tablespoon roasted unsalted cashews
- 1 to 2 tablespoons fried (*see page 333*) or sautéed shallots or onions
- Optional: 1 fresh green chile (cayenne, jalapeno, Serrano, Thai, or New Mexican), sliced
- 1 hard-boiled egg, cut in half

Nasi kemuli *(or* nasi kebuli*) is a fragrant rice dish, combining Indian, Malay, and Chinese flavorings. A variety of spices, ghee (clarified butter), and soy sauce are the main ingredients. While Nonya-style* nasi kemuli *calls for star anise, nutmeg, and poppy seeds, Chittys generally spice it with cinnamon, cumin, and coriander.*

In the kampungs *(villages), Malays serve* nasi kemuli *to guests on an oblong or triangle-shaped tray (a* nyiru*) made of bamboo or rattan, along with an array of curries,* rendangs*, and* sambals*. Malays, as well as Nonyas and Chittys who follow many Malay traditions, consider* nasi kemuli *a festive dish. They serve it for Sunday meals, when the whole family gathers to eat, and for special occasions, religious celebrations, and weddings. In fact,* nasi kemuli *is sometimes called wedding rice, and the Chittys in Malacca traditionally serve* nasi kemuli *to brides.*

DIRECTIONS:

1. Combine Spice Blend ingredients. Bring 2 cups water and chicken broth to a boil in a medium saucepan. Add Spice Blend and simmer for about 20 minutes. Strain and set broth aside (makes about 2 cups).
2. Heat ghee, butter, or oil. Sauté garlic and ginger for about ½ to 1 minute; add shallots or onions and sauté for 1 to 2 minutes.
3. Add rice and stir for about 2 to 3 minutes, then add soy sauces and sugar and mix well.
4. Add strained broth and salt and bring to a boil. Lower heat, cover, and simmer for 15 minutes, till broth is absorbed and rice is cooked. Then remove from heat and let rice cook in its steam for another 10 minutes. (If using a rice cooker, use proportions for rice cooker based upon above quantities. Add the rice mixture from step 3, broth and salt, cover and switch rice cooker on. Rice cooker automatically shuts off when rice is cooked.)
5. Remove cinnamon stick and star anise before serving. Garnish with raisins, cashews, and fried shallots or onions and/or sliced green chilies and hard-boiled egg halves.

Sabah woman pounding rice

Serve with beef *rendang* (page 177), chicken *rendang* (page 287), chicken, lamb, or vegetable *kurma* (pages 168, 282, or 283), *sambal* scallop (page 210), chicken *vindaloo* (page 169), or spicy tangy simmered fish (page 205); and cucumber pineapple *acar* (page 98), or stir-fried mixed vegetables (page 224).

Ghee Rice

Nasi Minyak

Makes 3 to 4 servings

When our family lived in Kuantan, the capital of Pahang state, I remember one day when my parents came home from a Malay wedding with beautiful baskets containing decorative hard-boiled eggs (called bunga telur *in Malay). These are symbols of fertility for the wedded couple and are given to family and friends to take home. They also brought home some chicken curry and yellow-tinted rice that was wonderfully fragrant. That was my first taste of* nasi minyak *(oil rice), better known by Indians as ghee rice.*

Originally, nasi minyak *was adapted from Arabic and Indian Muslim styles of cooking rice and thus resembles a* biryani*, but without the meats and vegetables. Now,* nasi minyak *is most readily found in the Malaysian states of Pahang, Terengganu, and Kelantan, which are predominantly Malay. Malaysians usually made this dish with evaporated milk because fresh milk was not available till recent times. Most Malaysians still use evaporated milk because of its rich flavor.* Nasi minyak *is often served with fried or grilled chicken,* rendangs, kurmas*, and curries.*

INGREDIENTS

1 to 2 tablespoons ghee, butter, or cooking oil
1 heaping tablespoon chopped or coarsely crushed garlic cloves
1 teaspoon chopped or coarsely crushed fresh ginger
¼ cup sliced shallots or onions (⅛-inch-thick pieces)
1 cup Basmati or other long-grain rice, washed and rinsed
⅛ teaspoon turmeric (for color)
1 lemongrass stalk, cracked or bruised with back of knife and knotted
1 or 2 pandan leaves, bruised with the tines of a fork and knotted
Optional: ¼ cup evaporated milk or fresh milk (to replace ¼ cup water)
½ teaspoon salt

SPICE BLEND

3 cloves
2 cardamoms
1½-inch cinnamon stick
1 star anise

GARNISH

1 tablespoon slivered almonds
2 tablespoons golden raisins
2 tablespoons fried (*see page 333*) or sautéed shallots or onions

DIRECTIONS:

1. Heat ghee, butter, or oil in a medium saucepan. Add Spice Blend ingredients and sauté for about ½ minute. Add garlic and ginger and sauté for about ½ to 1 minute, then add shallots or onions and sauté for another 1 to 2 minutes.
2. Add rice and turmeric and stir 2 to 3 minutes; add lemongrass, pandan leaves, and evaporated or fresh milk, if using, and stir for ½ minute. Add 2 cups water and the salt and bring to a boil.
3. Lower heat, cover, and cook for 15 minutes, till all liquid is absorbed and rice is cooked. Then remove from heat and let rice cook in its steam for an additional 10 minutes. (If using a rice cooker, use proportions for rice cooker based upon above quantities. Add the rice mixture from step 2, cover, and switch rice cooker on. Rice cooker automatically shuts off when rice is cooked.)
4. Before serving, remove cinnamon stick, star anise, lemongrass stalk, and pandan leaves. Garnish with almonds, raisins, and fried shallots or onions.

Serve with spicy fried chicken (page 165), spicy fried fish (page 206), chile chicken (page 163), chicken *satay* (page 65), grilled spicy chicken (page 166), spicy tomato chicken (page 284), or chicken curry *debal* (page 289); and cucumber pineapple *acar* (page 98), stir-fried okra or vegetables in spicy coconut milk (page 223).

Because of its rich flavors, *nasi minyak* is very popular at official functions and particularly at Malay weddings, so Malays often refer to it as *nasi kenduri* or celebration rice. Indeed, when an elderly Malay person asks a young person when she or he is going to serve *nasi minyak*, what the elder is really asking is, "When are you getting married?"

Lime Rice
Nasi Limau

Makes 3 to 4 servings

INGREDIENTS

1 tablespoon ghee, butter, or cooking oil
¼ teaspoon black or dark brown mustard seeds
3 or 4 fresh curry leaves
Heaping ¼ teaspoon *channa dhal* (yellow split peas) or *toovar dhal* or *toor dhal* (pigeon peas)
2 dried whole red chilies
1 teaspoon chopped or crushed fresh ginger
2 tablespoons thinly sliced shallots or onions
⅛ teaspoon turmeric powder
Optional: pinch of asafetida
1 cup Basmati or any long-grain rice, washed and rinsed
¼ cup fresh or frozen and thawed petite peas
1⅓ tablespoons freshly squeezed or bottled lime or lemon juice
¼ teaspoon salt

GARNISH

1 fresh green chile (jalapeno, Serrano, cayenne, or Thai), sliced
1 to 2 tablespoons fried (*see page 333*) or sautéed shallots or onions
1 tablespoon coriander leaves (cilantro)

Lime rice was a favorite rice meal for Periama (Grandma). It has South Indian origins and is a popular vegetarian rice dish for Hindu festive occasions, and is also served at Hindu temples for special functions. Periama served it with fried fish, dhal curry, and stir-fried cabbage or long beans. It has a tartness that is well balanced with the savory mustard seeds and spices. I would often go to the backyard to pick the curry leaves for Periama for the lime rice. When the aroma of the fried spices slowly pervaded the whole house from the kitchen, we knew Periama was cooking something special for us.

When Geeta and I visited my father at his relatives' home in Tellicherry in the coastal state of Kerala in Southwest India, the same aroma came from their kitchen one day. Curious, I went to the kitchen just as my cousin was adding peas to the finished rice. She served it with freshly caught fried fish. What a great combination! Using freshly squeezed lime juice tastes better than bottled lime juice. Malaysians generally use limau nipis *(Key limes) but you can use regular Persian limes or even lemon juice.*

DIRECTIONS:

1. Heat ghee, butter, or oil in a medium saucepan. Add mustard seeds, curry leaves, *channa dhal*, and dried chilies, cover and cook till mustard seeds start to "pop."
2. When popping subsides, add ginger and sauté for about ½ to 1 minute; add shallots or onions and sauté for 1 to 2 minutes. Add turmeric and asafetida, if using, and stir for 10 to 20 seconds. Add rice and stir for 1 to 2 minutes.
3. Add 2 cups water, peas, lime or lemon juice, and salt, stir and bring to boil. Lower heat, cover and simmer for 15 minutes, till all liquid is absorbed and rice is cooked. Then remove from heat and let rice cook in its steam, about 10 minutes. (If using a rice cooker, use proportions for rice cooker based upon above quantities. Add the rice mixture from step 2, and water, peas, lime or lemon juice, and salt, cover and switch rice cooker on. Rice cooker automatically shuts off when rice is cooked.)
4. Before serving, garnish with green chile, fried shallots or onions, and coriander leaves.

Serve with dhal or spicy lentil vegetable stew (page 88), spicy fried chicken (page 165), or chicken curry (page 171); and stir-fried cabbage (page 226), spicy curried pumpkin (page 225), spicy dry curried okra (page 221), or braised spicy long beans (page 230).

Malay-Style Fried Rice

Nasi Goreng ala Melayu

Makes 4 to 5 servings

*Eaten anytime—for breakfast, brunch, lunch, dinner, or as a late-night snack—fried rice (*nasi goreng*) is a favorite with Malaysians young and old alike. While rice is the main ingredient, several flavor variations have been created based on the various ethnic groups. Malays add* belacan *(dried shrimp paste), Chinese add fish balls or fish cake, and Indians add a little curry powder. Chinese fried rice is mild, while Malay, Nonya, and Indian styles are hot and fiery. Then there are also regional hawker variations. The ingredients for* nasi goreng *are limited only by the cook's imagination and the ingredients and seasonings that are on hand.*

Our family's favorite was a Malay-style fried rice with chicken, freshly cut vegetables, scrambled eggs, and fried tofu, served with a dip made with cili padi*. I have included* belacan *in my recipe because it adds that extra perk and makes it truly Malay.*

INGREDIENTS

- 1 cup Jasmine rice, washed and rinsed
- 1 to 2 tablespoons cooking oil
- 1 cup mixed fresh or frozen cut vegetables (½ cup chopped cabbage, ¼ cup peas, and ¼ cup either chopped carrots or green beans or snow pea pods)
- ⅛ teaspoon finely ground black pepper
- ¼ to ½ teaspoon double black, thick, or sweet soy sauce (*amount depending on the color desired*)
- ½ teaspoon thinly sliced or chopped palm sugar or brown sugar (*omit if using thick or sweet soy sauce*)
- ¼ teaspoon salt
- 1 egg, lightly beaten
- 2 teaspoons regular soy sauce

Spice Paste

- 1 or 2 dried or fresh whole red chilies (Fresno, jalapeno, Serrano, Thai, or cayenne); or ¾ to 1½ teaspoons *cili boh* (*see page 315*); or ½ to ¾ teaspoon bottled *sambal oelek*
- 3 tablespoons chopped shallots or onions
- 2 heaping teaspoons minced or chopped garlic cloves
- 2 teaspoons dried shrimp paste (*belacan*), toasted at 400°F for 15 minutes (*see page 335*)
- ¼ cup water

Garnish

- Optional: 1 fresh red chile, sliced
- ¼ cup fried (*see page 333*) or sautéed shallots or onions
- 1 to 2 tablespoons chopped coriander leaves (cilantro)

DIRECTIONS:

1. Prepare rice (preferably the day before), and then chill in refrigerator: Bring 1¼ to 1½ cups water to a boil, add rice, stir and bring to a boil again. Lower heat, cover, and simmer for about 15 minutes, till all liquid is absorbed and rice is cooked. Then remove from heat and let rice cook in its steam, covered, for 10 minutes. (If using a rice cooker, use proportions for rice cooker based upon above quantities. Add the rice and water, cover and switch rice cooker on. Rice cooker automatically shuts off when rice is cooked.)
2. Process Spice Paste ingredients to a coarse paste (if using dried red chilies, first steep in hot water for 5 to 8 minutes, deseed, and drain).
3. Heat oil in a large skillet or wok and sauté Spice Paste for about 4 to 5 minutes, till fragrant.
4. Add vegetables and stir-fry for about 3 to 4 minutes.
5. Add black pepper, double black, sweet, or thick soy sauce, sugar, if using, and salt and stir.
6. Push vegetable mixture to sides of skillet or wok and pour beaten egg in a corner or middle of the skillet or wok with a little oil and let cook till lightly scrambled. Then blend the egg with vegetable mixture and stir for 1 to 2 minutes.
7. Add the cooked rice and stir well with other ingredients. Toss with regular soy sauce and blend well.
8. Garnish with chile, fried shallots or onions, and coriander leaves. Serve warm.

You can also add chicken, beef, pork, or shrimp (before adding vegetables) for a complete meal. Or they can be cooked separately and added at the end. Serve warm with sliced green chilies in soy sauce (page 104); and spicy fried chicken (page 165), Chettiar-style fiery shrimp (page 291), spicy fried fish (page 206), or chile squid (page 211); and stir-fried mixed vegetables (page 224).

Spicy Vegetarian Rice
Nasi Sambar

Makes 4 to 6 servings

INGREDIENTS

½ cup *toovar* or *toor dhal* (pale yellow split peas or pigeon peas)
1 to 2 tablespoons ghee, butter, or cooking oil
1 teaspoon sliced fresh ginger
½ cup finely chopped shallots or onions
¼ teaspoon turmeric powder
⅛ teaspoon asafetida (or increase fresh ginger to 2 teaspoons)
½ cup (2½ ounces) chopped carrots (¼ to ½-inch pieces)
½ cup (2¼ ounces) chopped green beans (¼ to ½-inch pieces)
⅓ cup fresh or frozen and thawed petite peas
½ cup (3 ounces) diced tomatoes (½-inch pieces)
1 cup Basmati rice, washed and rinsed
¾ teaspoon salt
1 tablespoon tamarind concentrate or juice extract from tamarind pulp (*see page 339*)

SPICE BLEND 1 (SAMBAR PODI)

1½ teaspoons whole or ground coriander seeds
½ teaspoon whole or ground cumin seeds
¼ teaspoon whole or ground fenugreek seeds
Optional: ¼ teaspoon *urad dhal* (black lentils), skinned and white, and/or ¼ teaspoon *channa dhal* (yellow split peas)

SPICE BLEND 2

3 dried whole red chilies
2 cardamom pods
2 cloves
1-inch cinnamon stick
¼ teaspoon cumin seeds
¼ teaspoon black peppercorns
¼ teaspoon black or dark brown mustard seeds

Nasi Sambar *is an Indian-style aromatic vegetarian recipe with a blend of whole and ground spices. When Periama, my maternal grandmother, stayed with us in Kuantan, on the East Coast, she often cooked her vegetarian dishes for us and* nasi sambar *was one that she served with her favorite spicy bitter gourd. Today whenever I prepare this rice, I think of Periama.*

DIRECTIONS:

1. Bring 2½ to 3 cups of water (amount depending on the firmness of dhal you desire) to a boil in a medium saucepan. Add dhal and cook for about 30 to 40 minutes, till dhal is cooked and somewhat mushy (if you desire a smooth paste, cook longer with more water, or place cooked dhal in a blender and process to a smooth paste). Set aside.
2. If using the whole spices for Spice Blend 1, dry roast the ingredients in a skillet over medium heat till *urad dhal* turns light brown. Cool and grind coarsely. Set aside. (If using ground spices, combine and set aside.) Combine Spice Blend 2 ingredients in a separate bowl.
3. Heat 1 tablespoon ghee, butter, or oil in a large saucepan. Add Spice Blend 2, cover and cook till mustard seeds "pop." When popping subsides, uncover and stir in ginger and sauté for ½ to 1 minute; then add shallots or onions and sauté for 1 to 2 minutes, till fragrant. Add turmeric and asafetida, if using, and stir for a few seconds.
4. Add carrots and green beans and sauté for about 4 minutes, then add peas and tomatoes and sauté for about 1 minute.
5. Stir in rice and remaining ghee and stir for about 1 minute, then add cooked dhal and ground Spice Blend 1 and mix well for 1 minute. Add 2 cups water, salt, and tamarind juice and bring to a boil.
6. Lower heat, cover, and cook for 15 minutes, till all liquid is absorbed and rice is cooked. Then remove from heat and let rice cook in its steam for 10 minutes. (If using a rice cooker, use proportions for rice cooker based upon above quantities. Add the rice mixture from step 5, cover, and switch rice cooker on. Rice cooker automatically shuts off when rice is cooked.)
7. Remove cinnamon stick before serving. Garnish with coriander leaves.

Serve with mango chutney, or mango pickle, *pappadam*; and pickled green mango salad (page 96) or spicy cucumber tomato salad (page 97) as a vegetarian meal. For non-vegetarians, serve with chicken or fish curry (pages 171 or 198), chicken *varuval* (page 167), spicy egg curry (page 172), or spicy fried chicken (page 165); and cucumber carrot *acar* (page 99) or stir-fried Chinese greens (page 227).

GARNISH

1 heaping tablespoon chopped coriander leaves (cilantro)

Herb Rice
Nasi Ulam

Makes 3 to 4 servings

Malays sell a mix of herbs known as ulam *for a special salad dish,* ulam-ulam *or to prepare a fragrant herb rice called* nasi ulam. Nasi ulam *is particularly popular in the northeastern states of Kelantan and Terengganu, where they use a special mix of local herbs including: coriander leaves (cilantro), Vietnamese mint, basil, lemongrass, Kaffir lime leaves, turmeric leaves, Indonesian bay leaves, ginger flower, nasturtium leaves, and pennywort, as well as many others.*

At home in the U.S., I enjoy making nasi ulam *during the summer, when I can pick fresh herbs and leaves from my garden. It goes well with grilled chicken or fish and a spicy condiment. You can use herbs of your choice, and what is available at the market—basil, cilantro, dill, oregano, sage, thyme, arugula, watercress, celery leaves, or mint. For this recipe I also added some whole spices to give the* nasi ulam *a spicier and healthier twist. The herbs can be chopped and cooked with the rice, or mixed in when the rice is steaming, or served alongside the cooked rice so you and your guests can mix them with the rice at the table.*

INGREDIENTS

1 tablespoon cooking oil
1 teaspoon chopped or sliced and coarsely crushed fresh or frozen and thawed galangal or fresh ginger
½ cup finely chopped shallots or onions
1 teaspoon dried shrimp paste (*belacan*), toasted at 400°F for 15 minutes (*see page 335*)
1 fresh green chile (jalapeno, Serrano, Thai, or cayenne), sliced or coarsely pounded
1 cup rice, preferably Jasmine, washed and rinsed
1 lemongrass stalk, bruised with back of knife and knotted
2 pandan leaves, tined with fork and knotted
½ teaspoon freshly squeezed or bottled lime juice
⅛ teaspoon turmeric powder
½ teaspoon salt

Spice Blend

1 clove
1 star anise
1-inch cinnamon stick
¼ teaspoon black peppercorns
¼ teaspoon cumin seeds

Ulam (Mix of Herbs)

½ cup loosely packed chopped sweet basil
¼ cup loosely packed coarsely chopped coriander leaves (cilantro)
1 tablespoon coarsely chopped mint leaves
1 thinly sliced Kaffir lime leaf lobe (about 1 teaspoon)
1 tablespoon thinly sliced *laksa* leaf
1 teaspoon chopped dillweed
1 tablespoon chopped lemon verbena

DIRECTIONS:

1. Combine the *ulam* (herbs) in a small bowl and set aside.
2. Heat oil in a medium saucepan. Add Spice Blend ingredients and sauté for ½ minute. Add galangal or ginger and sauté for ½ to 1 minute; add shallots or onions and sauté for 1 to 2 minutes, then add dried shrimp paste and chile and stir for ½ to 1 minute.
3. Stir in rice, sauté for 2 minutes, add 1¼ to 1½ cups water, lemongrass, pandan leaves, lime juice, turmeric, and salt and mix well. Bring to a boil. Lower heat, cover, and simmer for 15 minutes, till all liquid is absorbed and rice is cooked. Remove from heat.
4. Immediately add the *ulam* (herbs), replace cover and let rice cook in its steam for another 10 minutes. (If using a rice cooker, use proportions for rice cooker based upon above quantities. Add the rice mixture from step 3, cover, and switch on rice cooker. Rice cooker automatically shuts off when rice is cooked.)
5. Remove lemongrass stalk, pandan leaves, cinnamon stick, and star anise before serving. Top rice with garnishes or place them on the side.

Serve with spicy fried chicken (page 165), grilled spicy chicken (page 166), chile chicken (page 163), spicy fried fish (page 206), vegetable *kurma* (page 283), dry beef curry (page 182), *sambal* scallop (page 210), or soy sauce fish (page 199) with spicy *sambal belacan* (page 101).

Optional Garnish

½ cup (2 ounces) cucumber slices, unpeeled or peeled (⅛-inch by 1½-inch pieces)
¼ cup green beans, sliced crosswise into 1-inch pieces, steamed or sautéed
1 tablespoon fried (*see page 333*) or sautéed shallots or onions
¼ cup (1¼ ounces) sliced fresh mango or grated green mango
¼ cup (1¼ ounces) grated green papaya

Hainanese Chicken Rice

Nasi Ayam

Makes 6 to 8 servings

INGREDIENTS

CHICKEN:

- 1 4½-pound whole chicken
- 1 to 2 tablespoons finely crushed fresh ginger
- 2 heaping tablespoons finely crushed garlic cloves
- ½ cup chopped scallions or spring onions
- ½ teaspoon freshly ground white pepper
- ½ teaspoon salt
- 2 teaspoons toasted sesame oil
- 2 teaspoons regular soy sauce

RICE

- 1 tablespoon cooking oil
- 1 tablespoon sliced and crushed garlic cloves
- 1 heaping teaspoon sliced and crushed fresh ginger
- Heaping ½ cup finely chopped shallots or onion
- 1 cup Jasmine rice, washed and rinsed
- 1½ cups reserved chicken stock (made when preparing chicken)
- ¼ teaspoon salt
- ¼ teaspoon toasted sesame oil
- 1 pandan leaf, tined with fork and tied into a knot

SOUP

- 4 cups reserved chicken stock (made when preparing chicken)
- 1 teaspoon salt
- ¼ to ½ teaspoon finely ground white pepper
- 1 teaspoon white granulated sugar
- Optional: 1 teaspoon chopped or coarsely crushed garlic cloves
- Optional: 1 teaspoon chopped or coarsely crushed fresh ginger

Chicken rice is a traditional Chinese dish that was brought to Malaysia by Hainanese immigrants. They modified the recipe using local flavors and ingredients, such as pandan leaf and coconut milk, and served it with spicy chile-based dips.

Although this dish is called chicken rice, the chicken is cooked (steamed or roasted) and served separately from the rice. It is a complete meal accompanied with a light soup, savory sticky rice, cool cucumber slices, and a couple of seasoned dips. The predominant flavorings for chicken rice are garlic, sesame oil, ginger, and soy sauce. Generally a whole chicken is used for this recipe, but you can also use breasts, thighs, or drumsticks.

Chicken rice brings back memories of my high school days in Malaysia. When we were growing up, the shopping area around the old Rex cinema in Kuala Lumpur was a center of student social activity. On weekends, my sister Vas and I would sometimes go to the Rex cinema to watch a western movie, one approved by our parents. Afterwards, we would go across the street from the Rex to our favorite coffee shop. I still remember those days, lingering at the table and savoring slices of sesame-scented chicken with rice and a sweet pungent gingery dip.

DIRECTIONS FOR CHICKEN:

1. Rinse chicken inside and out and pat dry. Stuff the cavity with 1 tablespoon each of ginger, garlic, and scallions. (You can also squeeze ginger and use its juice to rub the cavity.) Rub the whole chicken including cavity with white pepper and salt. Set aside.
2. Bring 13 cups of water to a boil in a large pot. Lower the heat and add remaining ginger, garlic, and scallions, and simmer 5 minutes.
3. Carefully place seasoned chicken into water making sure it is fully submerged. Bring to a boil, lower heat, and simmer for about 45 minutes. Turn off heat, cover, and let chicken steep in the hot stock for 15 to 20 minutes.
4. Remove the chicken from the pot, reserving stock for preparing the rice, soup, and dips.
5. If you will be serving the chicken cold, plunge the chicken into a pot of ice water and allow to sit for 20 to 30 minutes. Drain, allowing water to drip off chicken, and cool for 30 minutes. If you will be serving the chicken warm don't plunge into cold water but allow to cool to room temperature for about 30 minutes.
6. Brush chicken with sesame oil and soy sauce. Set aside. Before serving, cut chicken up into pieces.

DIRECTIONS FOR RICE:

1. Heat oil in a medium saucepan. Sauté garlic and ginger for about ½ to 1 minute, then add shallots or onions and sauté 1 to 2 minutes.

2. Stir in rice and sauté till translucent, about 2 to 3 minutes. Add 1½ cups reserved chicken stock, salt, sesame oil, and pandan leaf.
3. Bring to a boil. Lower heat, cover, and simmer for about 15 minutes, till all liquid is absorbed and rice is cooked. Remove from heat and let rice cook in its steam for about 10 minutes. (If using a rice cooker, use proportions for rice cooker based upon above quantities. Add the rice mixture from step 2, cover, and switch on rice cooker. Rice cooker automatically shuts off when rice is cooked.)

DIRECTIONS FOR SOUP:

1. Place all ingredients in a saucepan or pot, stir and bring to boil. Lower heat and simmer for about 1 to 2 minutes.
2. Garnish with scallions and serve with chicken, rice, and dips.

DIRECTIONS FOR DIPS:

1. Combine all ingredients for Dip 1 in a bowl and mix well. Let dip stand for 30 minutes before serving.
2. Prepare Dip 2 as directed on page 106.

Serve with chicken, soup, and the two dips, a complete meal with spicy cucumber tomato salad (page 97), stir-fried *kailan* (page 222), or stir-fried mixed vegetables (page 224).

GARNISH

1 stalk spring onions or scallions, chopped

DIP 1: SAVORY CHILE SAUCE / SOS CILI LEMAK

½ cup chicken stock
6 fresh red chilies (Fresno, jalapeno, Serrano, cayenne, Thai, or cherry peppers), finely chopped
1 heaping tablespoon chopped or crushed garlic cloves
1 tablespoon chopped or crushed fresh ginger
¾ teaspoon salt
3 teaspoons white granulated sugar
2½ teaspoons freshly squeezed or bottled lime juice
2 teaspoons cooking oil or fat skimmed from boiled chicken stock

DIP 2: POUNDED GINGER IN FLAVORED OIL

(*recipe on page 106*)

Chicken rice is eaten at any time of the day but is a favorite for lunch, and is served at stalls, by roadside vendors, coffee shops, food courts at malls, and in restaurants. These days it is even offered at school cafeterias (or canteens). This meal is especially comforting on a rainy day.

There are regional variations of Hainanese chicken rice. In Malacca, chicken rice is served with rice balls, and in the town of Ipoh, it is served with bean sprouts. Others serve it with tofu, chicken liver, or hard-boiled eggs. Steamed vegetables such *bok choy, choy sam* (Chinese flowering cabbage), *kailan* (Chinese broccoli), or other greens are generally served alongside chicken rice. There is even a Malay version with roast or fried chicken.

SAVORY RED RICE
Nasi Dagang

Makes 3 to 4 servings

INGREDIENTS

- 1 cup red Cargo rice or *beras nasi dagang*, soaked for 2 to 3 hours or overnight
- 1 tablespoon cooking oil
- 1 tablespoon thinly sliced and crushed garlic cloves
- 1 heaping teaspoon thinly sliced and crushed fresh ginger
- ½ cup thinly sliced or chopped shallots or onions
- 1½ cups unsweetened coconut milk, or 1 cup unsweetened coconut milk mixed with ½ cup water for less rich flavor
- 1 to 2 teaspoons ground fenugreek
- ¼ teaspoon salt

Nasi dagang *(trader's or traveler's rice) is a traditional steamed rice specialty from the East Coast of Malaysia. In the states of Terengganu, Kelantan, and Pahang,* nasi dagang *is made by cooking or steaming rice with fenugreek, ginger, onions, garlic, and coconut milk. It is served with tuna curry (*kari ikan tongkol*) or chicken curry, a spicy pickled salad (*kerabu*), and hard-boiled eggs, reflecting the Northeast preference for combining sweet, sour, and spicy tastes.*

On a trip to East Coast Malaysia, we drove from Tanjong Jara Beach near Kuala Terengganu to Kota Bahru, the capital of Kelantan state. Hungry and looking for a place to eat a late breakfast, I saw nasi dagang *scribbled on the menu board on a roadside food stall. I had never tried* nasi dagang *while growing up so decided to order the dish. It was made with a locally grown red unpolished rice (with bran on), called* beras nasi dagang*. It tasted rich and was filling!*

For this recipe, I asked my girlfriend Zubaidah, who hails from Penang, for her nasi dagang *recipe. I modified the seasonings and lessened the coconut milk. The rice can be steamed (the way it is traditionally cooked), or using the conventional method can be simmered in a saucepan, or cooked in a rice cooker.*

DIRECTIONS FOR CONVENTIONAL METHOD:

1. Drain rice. Heat oil in a medium saucepan. Sauté garlic and ginger for ½ to 1 minute; add shallots or onions and sauté 1 to 2 minutes. Stir in rice and sauté 1 to 2 minutes. Add coconut milk or coconut milk-water mixture, fenugreek, and salt and stir to blend.
2. Bring mixture to a boil. Then lower heat, cover, and simmer for 20 to 25 minutes, till all liquid is absorbed and rice is cooked. Remove from heat and let rice cook in its steam for about 10 minutes. (If using a rice cooker, use proportions for rice cooker based upon above quantities. Add the rice mixture from step 1, cover, and switch on rice cooker. Rice cooker automatically shuts off when rice is cooked.)

DIRECTIONS FOR STEAMING RICE:

1. Add rice to steamer and steam rice for 30 minutes.
2. Add garlic, ginger, shallots or onions, and fenugreek, and mix well. Steam for 15 minutes.
3. Add coconut milk or coconut milk-water mixture and salt and steam for 20 minutes, till the liquid is all absorbed and rice is cooked.

Serve with sweet and spicy tuna curry (page 208), spicy egg curry (page 172), chile squid (page 211), or chicken curry (page 171); and pickled cucumber and carrot *acar* (page 99) and sliced hard-boiled eggs.

CHAPTER 5

NOODLES: A HAWKER'S DELIGHT

Fresh noodles

It is generally agreed that the Chinese were the master inventors of noodles, and have been enjoying them for more than four thousand years. Noodles were first brought to Malaysia by early Chinese spice and silk traders, and later by the waves of immigrants arriving in Malaysia from southern China. Through the years, the Chinese in Malaysia have transformed many of their noodle dishes into flavor versions that are not found in their homeland. In Malaysia, noodles are prepared in endless exotic permutations and combinations. Malays, Nonyas, and Indians have taken noodles to new flavor heights by incorporating their favorite ingredients, including coconut milk, *belacan* (dried shrimp paste), galangal, curry powder, tamarind juice, and lemongrass. *Kari mee* (page 149) is a simple Chinese noodle soup transformed with Indian spices and Malay *rempah. Laksas*, a specialty of the Chinese Peranakans or Nonyas, are spicy, pungent, or tangy noodles, prepared with coconut-based, fish-based, or tamarind-based stocks. Malays can whip up a spicy stir-fried *mee goreng* (page 136) with chilies, *belacan*, and tomato, while Indian Muslims (Mamaks) offer their specialty, the mouth-watering *mee rebus* (page 142) in a spicy sweet-potato-based sauce.

From simple chicken-based or pork-based soup noodles and shrimp noodle stir-fries, to more complex coconut-based or fish-based broth noodles, Malaysian noodle dishes are unique and found nowhere else in the world. As these noodle dishes were transported across states and towns, they often took on new flavors with interesting accompaniments and toppings. *Yee mee* (also called *Cantonese mee*, page 140) and *Hokkien mee* (page 144) are Chinese specialties popular in Kuala

A quick way of preparing *mee goreng* that has become popular with Malay and Indian Muslim hawkers is using instant dried noodles (*Maggi mee*) or "*packet mee*" as locals call it. *Maggi mee goreng*, as it is called, is commonly served at Mamak food stalls in Malaysia and is a substitute for the regular yellow *mee*. For *Maggi mee goreng*, the *packet mee* is boiled and then stir-fried with bits of vegetables, eggs, tofu, *sambal belacan* (dried shrimp paste), and dark soy sauce. It is squirted with lime juice before serving. Some add a sunny-side-up egg (or as locals call it, *telor mata kerbau* or bull's eye egg) as a topping, while others stir the noodles with beaten egg.

Lumpur, Petaling Jaya, and Klang; *assam laksa* (page 153), *udang mee* (shrimp noodles), and *tok tok mee* (or *wantan mee*) are popular in Penang, which has a majority of Chinese and Nonyas, while *mee rebus* and *mee goreng* are favorites in Kedah, Kelantan, Terengganu, and Johor, where Indian Muslims and Malays predominate.

Growing up in Malaysia, I had a passion for noodle dishes. I would impatiently wait for the days when Ma would prepare them for dinner or get take-out noodle dishes. When dinner was noodles, I would clean my plate before anyone else, a surprise to my parents as I was a picky eater and usually the last one in the family to leave the dinner table. My daughter, Geeta, follows suit with her love for Malaysian noodles, her favorites being *mee goreng* (spicy stir-fried noodles, page 136), *char kway teow* (stir-fried flat broad rice noodles, page 139), and a simple noodle soup (*sup mee*, page 83) that I savored at school.

Malaysians are as passionate about noodles as Italians are about their pastas. I am happy to be one of them and I love to hunt for new noodle flavors, be it in a remote wet market, a coffee shop, or along the beach.

THE HAWKER-NOODLE CONNECTION

Noodles are the heart and soul of Malaysian hawker cuisine. They are freshly prepared on the spot by food vendors to provide a comforting and enjoyable on-the-run meal. Starch-based, inexpensive, and quick-to-prepare, many popular noodle dishes were originally created as energy-providing meals for the immigrant Chinese fishing, farming, and mining communities. When I was young, vendors on bicycle carts would come right up to our home and cook their noodles. It was great to eat a warm bowl of noodle soup for a Saturday brunch, or in the evenings, enjoy a plate of sizzling hot stir-fried noodles right from the *kwali* (wok).

When we craved noodles and the bicycle vendors were not around, Ma would send a couple of us to the Indian Muslim vendor in Brickfields, Kuala Lumpur, for *mee rebus* (page 142), as that was her favorite, or to old PJ town for our favorite, *char kway teow* (page 139). Before my sister Prema and I took the bus, Ma would hand us some eggs to add to our noodles. Eggs added protein and made the *char kway teow* a little healthier in Ma's mind. She also told us not to add the fried pork fat and cockles (*kerang*).

We had our favorite *char kway teow* vendor who was at the same spot, rain or shine. His mobile cart was located in a dark corner, next to some small grocery stores. He was an old Chinese man who stood hunched in front of his big worn-in black metal wok. He had a bright kerosene lamp hanging from his cart, but still I could never make out his face clearly because he was always bent over his cooking, never looking up to see who placed the order. His young assistant did that. First, he would heat the oil, and when the wok was really hot, he added some shrimp, stirred it for few seconds, then added the fresh *kway teow* noodles and *sawi* (greens), and tossed it around feverishly. Next, he pushed the noodles along the sides of the wok and broke the egg we gave him in the center of the wok and let it cook. (It was less expensive if we brought our own egg!) Then he tossed the noodles together with the egg and bean sprouts, and stirred for a minute. Before you knew it, he scooped the noodles from the huge steaming wok, and tossed portions on plastic-lined newspapers. His assistant neatly folded each one and tied them with plastic strings for us to carry. Its aroma was intoxicating and I could not wait to eat it. The bus ride back home with the warm packages of *char kway teow* was torture. Many years later, after I returned home from college abroad, I sought him out again, but he was gone. For me, *char kway teow* never tasted the same again!

Be it breakfast, brunch, lunch, teatime, dinner, or even after the movies or club hopping, there are noodle hawkers everywhere, serving their specialty noodles just to satisfy your hunger. Today, noodles are also popular on menus at trendy restaurants, and some Western-style hotels even have themed "noodle rooms" for tourists, where decorative hawker-style carts serve a variety of noodles.

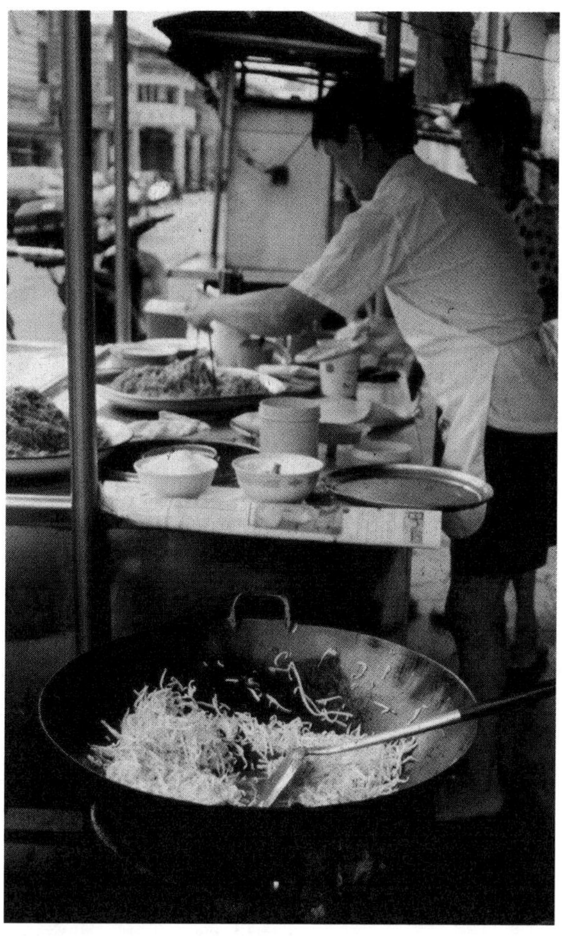

Chinese vendor preparing *char kway teow*, Ipoh

VARIETIES OF NOODLES

There are many types and shapes of fresh and dried noodles, generally made from wheat or rice, and prepared in various styles. In Malaysia, noodle dishes generally have Cantonese and Hokkien names. Let me share with you some of my favorites: The most common types are the yellow fresh noodles called *mee*, made from wheat flour and/or eggs. They can be thick or thin. My other favorites are the dried translucent rice vermicelli called *meehoon* (or *bihun*), and *kway teow*, fresh chewy flat rice noodles. Others include *wantan mee* (coiled thin egg and wheat-based dried noodles); mung bean noodles (*soohon* or *tunghoon*) also called cellophane noodles, which become transparent after soaking in water; *hor fun*, broad chewy dried or fresh rice noodles; and *laksa* noodles, thick and opaque white rice noodles used in *assam laksa.* More details on all these noodles are in the recipe section.

PREPARING AND ENJOYING NOODLES

Wet or fresh noodles are sold precooked or uncooked in the supermarket refrigerated section and are yellow (with color additives) or pale gold (without color additives). For precooked or ready to eat noodles, just rinse noodles in cold running water to get rid of oil, or scald in boiling water for few seconds and then rinse in cold water. For uncooked noodles, cook in boiling water for 3 to 5 minutes (depending on the noodle dimensions), drain and then rinse under cold water. Toss with a little oil to prevent sticking. With fresh *kway teow* noodles, rinse first with cold running water to remove the oil before cooking them. With all dried noodles, scald them in hot water for 10 to 15 minutes till they soften, then drain and rinse under cold running water and toss with a little oil to prevent sticking. You can also cook dried noodles in boiling water anywhere from 3 to 5 minutes, depending on the noodles, till they soften. Then drain and rinse under cold running water and toss with oil, if desired. For *yee mee* (page 140), a pan-fried-noodle dish, fresh thin, precooked wheat and egg noodles (also called Hong Kong-style pan-fried noodles) are used.

Noodles are cooked in many different ways—stir-fried, added to soups or curries, simmered, braised, or pan-fried and stirred with oyster and soy sauces. Braised noodles, like *Hokkien mee* (page 144) and *yee mee* (page 140), tend to absorb more flavors since the noodles are simmered in a thick seasoned sauce. Stir-fried noodles, lightly stirred with spice pastes, have an aromatic flavor. Noodles that are pan-fried or deep-fried and topped with a flavorful sauce (like *wantan* or *yee mee*) have crispy textures. Soup noodles provide comforting meals and come in a clear chicken-based, shrimp-based, or pork-based broth, curry-flavored broth, or *tom yam*-seasoned broth.

For the Chinese, a bowl or plate of noodles is not just a satisfying meal, but a symbol of long life (because of their length); noodles also denote happiness, commitment, and friendship. Since they represent longevity, noodles are served for birthdays, and are never cut before cooking. *Lam mee* also called "birthday noodles" by Penang Nonyas, is a Hokkien-style *mee* in a fragrant and thick five spice, soy sauce, and shrimp-based broth, topped with pinkish-red strips of omelet (colored red for good luck), served with a *sambal belacan*-lime dip.

Apart from their signature dishes, the local Chinese have also created many simple noodle dishes among their own communities. The Cantonese in Kuala Lumpur enjoy *char hor fun*, stir-fried with egg, seafood, or chicken and seasoned with oyster and soy sauce, and *loh shu fan*, either with chicken stock, or a "dry" version, cooked in a claypot with shredded pork and dark soy sauce and topped with an uncooked egg while the claypot is still steaming hot. *Pan mee*, a favorite in Seremban and Ipoh, is a flat broad slippery noodle generally handmade from wheat flour and eggs, and mixed with dark soy sauce, fried garlic, sweet potato leaves, *fucuk* (deep-fried tofu skin), and topped with fried crispy anchovies, ground meat, and Chinese black mushrooms.

Being a noodle addict, on my trips back to Malaysia I go hunting to discover noodle vendors in all corners of Malaysia. It is an endless adventure for me. *Hailam* is a simple noodle dish that I discovered in an office cafeteria in my hometown. A large population of Chinese from Foochow, China, settled in Sibu, Sarawak, where they introduced Foochow noodles. So when I visited Sarawak, I tried their steamed Foochow noodles prepared with thick black soy sauce, oyster sauce, spring onions, garlic, and white pepper. Another simple favorite, *kolo mee*, is blanched in a sauce of garlic, shallot oil, and vinegar and topped with minced pork or *char siew*. Once in Ipoh, on the way to see my father at Lumut, I had Hakka *mee*, which is quite similar to *wantan mee*, prepared with thin yellow noodles, ground chicken, barbecued pork, and wood ear mushrooms, and topped with a dark soy sauce.

The excitement of eating noodles is not only the way they are prepared, but the delectable dips or condiments (see Chapter 3) they come with, which add a further flavor dimension to the eating experience. Dips are an integral part of the noodle experience. For *Hokkien mee*, the dip is *belacan* and chile-based (page 108), and for *char kway teow* the dip is sliced green chilies in soy sauce (page 104) or pickled green chilies in a vinegar sauce (page 105). Another way to truly enjoy noodles is to eat them with chopsticks. When I was ten, I had my first lesson with chopsticks. Ma cooked some spicy *mee goreng* for lunch, and placed a pair of wooden chopsticks on the side of each plate. She felt we were ready to use chopsticks and believed that they were the best vehicle to get the most flavor experience when eating noodles. I looked around me and saw that my sisters and brothers were busily grabbing the chopsticks and hungrily lifting the noodles into their mouths. Some were more successful than others. It was quite chaotic! Finally, I did it because there was no other way to eat the noodles. After some practice, I became adept at it and would eat noodles no other way. There is a certain "added" flavor when you use wooden chopsticks that forks do not give, and Ma knew that!

ETHNIC AND REGIONAL NOODLE DISHES

Eating noodles in Malaysia is a cultural adventure, with each noodle dish reflecting ethnic and regional influences. They are prepared dry (stir-fried) or wet (sauce or broth) versions. Wherever the Chinese settled in Malaysia, they created simple noodle dishes. For example, *mee suah* is a comforting and filling Chinese noodle soup prepared with rice vermicelli (*meehoon* or *bihun*) or wheat flour egg noodles in a broth (*sup mee*, page 83) with fish balls. Lunch was my favorite time at high school at Bukit Nanas Convent School in Kuala Lumpur. While listening to the last lecture before lunch, my mind often wandered to the neatly laid out bowls with noodles and garnishes sitting on the lunch counter at the school cafeteria. I patiently waited for the school bell to ring. At this point, it was a struggle to hear the teacher, as I pictured the steaming bowl of noodles placed in front of me with their savory pungent flavors. I rushed out at the sound of the bell. There were two flavors to choose from—one with yellow egg noodles with chewy fish balls, *choy sum*, and crispy fried onions, and the other was a spicy *meehoon* (rice vermicelli) in a tamarind-flavored fish broth prepared with slices of tofu, pieces of shrimp, and bean sprouts. It was truly a treat for me, savoring each noodle with wooden chopsticks, and then drinking the broth with a porcelain spoon. For me, this was something to look forward to every day at school. *Wantan mee* (also known as *kon loh mee*) is a popular breakfast or lunch meal in Malaysia. For us, it was a favorite snack after school, or a late lunch after a noon movie. Pan-fried coiled thin wheat flour-egg noodles are topped with sliced roast pork (*char siew*) and Chinese mustard greens, dressed with oyster sauce, garlic oil, and soy sauce-flavored sauces. It is accompanied with a bowl of clear *wantan* (dumpling) soup and a pickled green chile dip. In Penang it is known as *tok tok mee*, its name

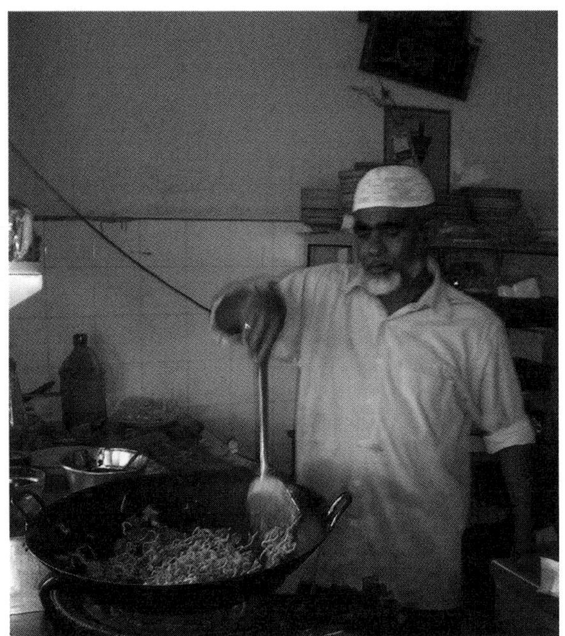

Mamak vendor preparing *mee goreng*, Petaling Jaya

being derived from the sound made by the food hawker as he hits the side of the bowl with chopsticks. The Malacca version has *wantans* added to the noodles.

Mee goreng (stir-fried noodles, page 148) is an all-time favorite in Malaysia, and an addiction with Bob, Geeta, and me. My first taste of *mee goreng Mamak* (Indian Muslim-style) was with my grandfather, Thatha. He had his favorite *Mamak mee* vendor in PJ town. I remember holding Thatha's hand and standing in front of a kerosene lamp-lit cart that was parked on the roadside. Thatha greeted a man in a colorful sarong and tee shirt, who stirred yellow noodles in a big black *kwali* (wok) over big flames. It smelled so good that I wanted to eat it then and there. While I waited, I looked up at the containers of ingredients, spice pastes, and condiments neatly arranged along the top of the cart. He ladled from these containers small amounts of shrimp, boiled peeled potatoes, bean curd, soy sauce, and Chinese broccoli, and kept stirring each time. Finally he added some red chile paste on Thatha's request, then quickly emptied the noodles from the wok onto a banana leaf-lined newspaper. His assistant garnished it with fried onions, sliced scallions, and green chilies, then folded it neatly and tied it with a string. I could smell the *Mamak mee* all the way home and it made for a long bus ride.

Chee cheong fun is a popular Chinese-style breakfast fare. Steamed, flat rice noodles are rolled up and cut into little pieces, then topped with a spicy sweet and pungent sauce and sprinkled with toasted sesame seeds. *Chee cheong fun* has many regional variations. I grew up with the Kuala Lumpur version that has steamed or fried *yong tau foo* (tofu and vegetables stuffed with fish paste).

Whenever I go shopping in Kuala Lumpur, I usually take a break and enjoy a bowl of *kari mee* (page 149). *Kari mee* has *mee* or *meehoon* in a spicy curry-coconut broth served with a dollop of chile paste or *sambal belacan*. I enjoy this break much more than the shopping! Sometimes *kari mee* is referred to as *kari laksa* (referring to *laksa lemak*, page 151) although it is quite different from *laksa lemak*. Unlike *laksa*, *kari mee* broth has the profile of a curry, so it has a more intense curry flavor than *laksa lemak* .

Laksas are unique to Malaysia, as they assimilate the flavors of all the ethnic groups to truly represent a "soulful creation." Generally they are a Nonya specialty, and the two most popular ones are *laksa lemak* (with coconut milk broth, page 151) and *assam laksa* (with fish-tamarind broth, page 153). *Laksas* are topped with shredded chicken, shrimp, deep-fried tofu, fish cake, and strips of omelet, with fragrant toppings of *laksa* leaves (or *daun kesum*, also known as Vietnamese coriander or Vietnamese mint), *bunga kantan* (torch ginger bud), bean sprouts, and shredded cucumber. And all are accompanied with pungent fiery dips.

The name *laksa* comes from the Sanskrit word *laksha*, meaning "many," a reference perhaps to the many ingredients used to make the famous dish. While the origins of the *laksa* are unknown, it may have arrived on Malaysian shores with Indian-Muslim and Chinese traders. The different ethnic groups claim their own style and every state has its own special recipe. In fact, it seems as though every cook in Malaysia claims to have his own version using special "secret ingredients." Ultimately, the secret of *laksa* is in the savory broth or gravy (as Malaysians call it), each having its own characteristic flavorings.

On one of my trips home, I went *laksa* hunting. I was familiar with the two famous laksas—*laksa lemak* and *assam laksa*—but I was curious about the other not as well known regional *laksas*. We drove all the way across the golden *padi* fields of Kedah to the northwestern tip, to Perlis state. We sat at a Malay hawker stall and savored their *laksa*, which contained handmade noodles in a spicy and tangy broth, topped with a slice of hard-boiled egg. In the northeast state of Terengganu, we had a bowl of *laksa putih* (or white *laksa*) from the Malay lady at the wet market. It had white noodles in a sauce seasoned with black peppercorns. While we drove down south to Pahang, we stopped by a local vendor to taste their spicy seafood-based, chile-based, and coconut-based rice noodle *laksa*. I was sweating in the heat, but it was delicious! Kelantan had an unusual type called *laksham*, which has thick chunks of noodle rolls in a savory sauce of pureed fish, coconut milk, dried shrimp paste, and tamarind juice. As I watched the local Malays eating it with their hands (like rice), I too followed suit.

When we drove down south to see my sister Vas in Johore Bahru, we tried their local *laksa*. I was surprised to see spaghetti instead of noodles in a rich and creamy fish broth seasoned with coconut milk, curry, lemongrass, and *kerisik* (toasted grated coconut). It had a creamy and strong fish flavor. Sarawak was my final stop for discovering new *laksas*. One morning at the hotel breakfast buffet I saw bowls of rice vermicelli and colorful toppings on plates. I was excited. I picked up a bowl, topped it with sliced cucumbers, bean sprouts, and chilies and ladled spicy seafood-based broth from a saucepan onto my bowl of vermicelli. It smelled a bit fishy and I was hesitant. Then I added a dollop of *sambal* paste, squeezed some lime juice over it, and sat down to eat it. I was pleasantly surprised. What a melding of flavors!

Spicy Indian Muslim Stir-Fried Noodles

Mee Goreng Mamak

Makes 5 to 6 servings

INGREDIENTS

2 to 4 tablespoons cooking oil
½ pound (about 1 cup) shelled and deveined shrimp or thinly sliced chicken
8 ounces (about 1½ cups) firm tofu (*tauhu*), cubed (1½-inch by ½-inch pieces) and deep-fried or pan-fried till light brown
6 to 8 ounces Chinese flowering cabbage (*choy sam*) or Chinese mustard greens (*gai choy*) or Chinese cabbage (*bok choy*), stalks separated from leaves and rinsed to remove stones and dirt
1 pound fresh precooked yellow noodles, rinsed under cold water; or fresh uncooked noodles, cooked for 3 to 5 minutes in boiling water, drained, rinsed with cold water and coated with oil; or thin wheat and egg dried noodles or thin spaghetti, cooked and drained
1 egg, beaten
1 cup (3 ounces) bean sprouts, rinsed or blanched

Spice Paste 1

1½ tablespoons sliced garlic cloves
6 dried red whole chilies, steeped in hot water for 5 to 8 minutes and deseeded; or 1½ tablespoons *cili boh* (*see page 315*); or ¾ tablespoon bottled *sambal oelek*
Optional: 1 tablespoon dried shrimp paste (*belacan*), toasted at 400°F for 15 minutes (*see page 335*); or dried tiny whole shrimp (krill), soaked in hot water for about 10 to 15 minutes to soften and then drained
¼ cup water

Mee goreng Mamak (also called Mamak mee) is a unique spicy sweet noodle preparation enjoyed by all Malaysians. Fresh yellow Chinese noodles are stir-fried with soy sauce, chilies, sawi (greens), scrambled egg, bean sprouts, Chinese cabbage, fish cake, squid, and slices of tomato. Ketchup and sweet soy sauce provide a sweet touch. Sometimes slices of boiled potato are added. It is topped with slices of red chilies, crispy fried shallots, and shrimp fritters, and squirted with lime juice before serving.

I first learned how to prepare mee goreng *while on vacation with my family in Penang. We strolled along Batu Feringgi (Foreigner's Rock) Road, where the restaurants and cafes are, scouting for a place to eat. One evening, we discovered the tiny open-air AB café, owned by chefs Bala and Shankar. The chef brought me back to his small kitchen and showed me how he prepared his* mee goreng. *Once ingredients were cut, he added his secret ingredients—*satay *sauce and ketchup—and then took only a few minutes to stir the noodles. The end product was delicious. When we returned to Penang a few years later, we looked for the AB café but sadly it was gone.*

Here is my own recipe for mee goreng Mamak *(developed after watching many street vendors on my trips home). Unlike Bala and Shankar, I don't use tomato ketchup, but instead use a tomato paste or tomato sauce, and sometimes even pureed fresh tomatoes. I also add* belacan, *another of my favorite ingredients, or you can use fish sauce.*

DIRECTIONS FOR *MEE GORENG MAMAK*:

1. Process Spice Paste 1 ingredients to a coarse paste. In a separate bowl, combine Spice Paste 2 ingredients.
2. Heat 2 tablespoons of oil in a wok or skillet; add Spice Paste 1 and sauté for about 3 to 5 minutes, adding more oil if needed. Stir in Spice Paste 2 and remaining oil and sauté for about 2 to 3 minutes, till fragrant.
3. Add chicken or shrimp and stir-fry till cooked. Add fish cake, if using, tofu, and Chinese cabbage stalks and cook 1 minute; add noodles and stir with sauce.
4. Add Chinese cabbage leaves, cover, and cook for another minute, till greens start to wilt. Uncover, mix well, make a space in center of pan and pour in the beaten egg. Let sit for about 1 to 2 minutes, then blend in with the noodles so the egg coats noodles. Add bean sprouts and stir well for about 1 minute, till egg is cooked. Don't let noodles get mushy.
5. Garnish with boiled potatoes and red chilies. Squeeze lime juice over cooked *mee goreng* and serve hot.

Variation: You can use julienned carrots or sliced cabbage and tofu for a vegetarian *mee goreng*.

Serve with a chile paste dip (page 109) or pickled chilies in soy sauce dip (page 105).

Mee goreng Mamak is a simple and delicious preparation that you can indulge in at a busy lunchtime coffee shop in Kuala Lumpur, or while strolling through the bustling night market (*pasar malam*) of the north-eastern town of Kota Bahru. For me, it is a wonderful lunch with *teh tarik*, while enjoying the warm sea breeze at the beach in Penang.

SPICE PASTE 2

2 tablespoons tomato paste, or 4 tablespoons tomato puree, or 6 tablespoons tomato sauce
¼ cup water
3 tablespoons regular soy sauce
2 tablespoons double black, sweet, or thick soy sauce
½ teaspoon turmeric powder
¼ teaspoon finely ground white pepper
1 teaspoon sugar (lessen or omit if using sweet or thick soy sauce)
¼ teaspoon salt
Optional: ½ teaspoon chile powder (if more heat is desired)

GARNISH

Optional: ½ pound (1½ cups) potatoes, peeled, boiled, and sliced into 1-inch by 1-inch pieces
1 fresh red chile (Fresno jalapeno, Serrano, cayenne, Thai, or cherry), sliced
1 *kasturi* lime, or ½ regular Persian lime

FISH CAKES (OPTIONAL)

1 tablespoon dried whole shrimp, pounded till smooth
¼ cup (¾ ounce) chopped bean sprouts, rinsed or blanched
1 tablespoon chopped onions
2 tablespoons chopped scallions
3 tablespoons all-purpose flour
¼ teaspoon sugar
¼ teaspoon salt

DIRECTIONS FOR FISH CAKES:

1. Combine all ingredients and ½ cup water and mix well.
2. Drop mixture by spoonfuls into hot oil and fry till they turn light brown. Drain and cool.
3. Slice into 1-inch to 1½-inch pieces. Set aside to serve with *mee goreng.*

Note: You can prepare these before hand and freeze till needed. Or you can also buy ready-made fish cakes and just slice and use.

Siamese Noodles

Mee Siam

Makes 3 to 4 servings

INGREDIENTS

- 8 ounces *meehoon* (dried rice vermicelli)
- 2 to 3 tablespoons cooking oil
- 1½ heaping tablespoons crushed garlic cloves
- 2 tablespoons preserved soybean paste (*taucheo*, black version) or bean sauce or black bean sauce
- 1 tablespoon regular soy sauce
- 3 tablespoons tamarind concentrate or tamarind juice extract (*see page 339*)
- 1 teaspoon sugar
- ¼ teaspoon salt
- 8 ounces (about 1 cup) shelled and deveined shrimp
- 7 ounces (about 1½ cups) firm tofu (*tauhu*), cubed or cut into 1½-inch by ½-inch slices, deep-fried or pan-fried till light brown
- 1½ cups (4½ ounces) bean sprouts, rinsed or blanched

Spice Paste

- ¼ cup sliced or chopped shallots or onions
- 4 to 6 dried whole red chilies, steeped in hot water for 5 to 8 minutes, slit and deseeded; or 1 to 1½ tablespoons *cili boh* (*see page 315*); or ½ to ¾ tablespoon bottled *sambal oelek*
- 1 heaping teaspoon chopped fresh or frozen and thawed galangal or fresh ginger
- 1 lemongrass stalk, sliced into ¼ or ½-inch pieces
- 2 heaping tablespoons dried whole shrimp, soaked in hot water for about 10 to 15 minutes to soften and then drained
- ¼ cup water

Mee Siam is a signature noodle dish from Penang now popular throughout Malaysia, As with most noodle dishes, it has slight flavor variations, depending on whether you eat it at an Indian, Malay, Nonya, or Chinese hawker stall. Like many other soup-based or gravy-based noodle dishes, mee Siam *is usually eaten for breakfast. There is also a dry version of* mee Siam.

My recipe is a wet version, with rice vermicelli (meehoon), *preserved soybean paste* (taucheo), *lemongrass, and tamarind juice. Some chefs use a prepared fish, shrimp, or chicken stock. However, I did not use any broth but relied on the natural juices from the added ingredients. It is garnished with hard-boiled egg, spring onions, lime leaves, and coriander leaves (cilantro) and served with a fiery* sambal, *a typical condiment of a Malay or Nonya meal.*

DIRECTIONS:

1. Process Spice Paste ingredients to a smooth paste. Cook *meehoon* in boiling water for 3 to 5 minutes or scald in hot water for 10 to 15 minutes till soft, then drain.
2. Heat 1 tablespoon of oil in a wok or skillet; add garlic and sauté for about ½ to 1 minute. Stir in Spice Paste and sauté for about 4 to 6 minutes till fragrant, adding remaining oil as needed.
3. Add soybean paste, mash it with wooden spoon to a coarse paste, then add soy sauce, tamarind juice, sugar, salt, and ¼ cup water and cook for another 1 to 2 minutes.
4. Add shrimp and stir for about 2 to 3 minutes, then add tofu and stir for another 1 to 2 minutes.
5. Stir in cooked *meehoon* and coat well with sauce, mixing for about 1 to 2 minutes, then add bean sprouts and stir for another minute.
6. To serve, place cooked noodles in a bowl, add first three garnishes, and drizzle with chile oil. You can also serve the chile oil as a dip on the side.

Garnish

- 2 Chinese chive stalks (*kuchai*) or scallions, sliced into ¼-inch pieces
- 1 *kasturi* lime, or ½ regular Persian lime, cut into wedges
- 1 hard-boiled egg, quartered
- Chile oil dip (*see page 110*)

Ethnic Thai foods and flavors have influenced Malaysian cooking for hundreds of years, particularly in the North. *Mee Siam*, a Thai-inspired noodle dish (Siam is previous name for Thailand) from northwest Malaysia, is particularly popular in Penang where it is considered a Nonya dish. It combines Chinese ingredients, such as *taucheo*, soy sauce, and scallions, with Malay flavorings, such as galangal and lemongrass, as well as Thai flavors, including tamarind and Kaffir lime leaves.

Chinese Stir-Fried Rice Noodles

Char Kway Teow

Makes 5 to 6 servings

Char kway teow *is an iconic Malaysian-Chinese dish, a specialty of the Teochows who settled in Ipoh town. It is prepared with broad fresh rice noodles and seasoned with sweet soy sauce, garlic, and shrimp. It is enjoyed steaming hot with a smoky chile dip. The best tasting* char kway teow *is usually prepared with pork lard or fried pork fat, which gives that extra aroma and flavor to the dish, but vendors have gradually deleted these ingredients due to health concerns. Penang* char kway teow *includes duck's eggs (for a richer taste) and crabmeat (for extra sweetness). And to meet the religious requirements of the Muslim population, many cook it halal-style, with shrimp and without pork products.*

My last meal with my youngest sister Prema was in Penang, sitting alfresco-style outside a Chinese restaurant along the beachside. Prema, like me, devoured all kinds of noodles, her favorites being Chinese-style stir-fries and noodle soups when young but later enjoying the spicier Malay and Mamak styles as well. This recipe is in memory of Prema, who always savored a plate of char kway teow *on her visits home, and the many times we spent eating noodles together.*

INGREDIENTS

- 2 to 3 tablespoons cooking oil
- 1 tablespoon crushed garlic cloves
- 8 ounces (about 1 cup) shelled and deveined shrimp or thinly sliced chicken
- 2 tablespoons double black, thick, or sweet soy sauce
- 2 tablespoons regular soy sauce
- 1 teaspoon finely pounded white peppercorns, or ½ teaspoon finely ground white pepper
- ½ to ¾ teaspoon white granulated sugar (*use less if using thick or sweet soy sauce*)
- 6 to 8 ounces Chinese flowering cabbage (*choy sam*) or Chinese mustard greens (*gai choy*) or Chinese cabbage (*bok choy*), stalks and leaves separated and rinsed to remove dirt and stones
- 14 ounces fresh, flat rice noodles, already cut or cut into ½-inch wide strips, rinsed in cold water to remove excess oil, or dried *hor fun* noodles, cooked and drained
- 2 eggs, beaten
- 1½ cups (4½ ounces) bean sprouts, rinsed or blanched

SPICE PASTE

- 6 whole dried red chilies, steeped in hot water for 5 to 8 minutes and then deseeded; or 1 to 1½ tablespoons of *cili boh* (*see page 315*); or ½ to ¾ tablespoon bottled *sambal oelek*
- Optional: 1½ to 2 teaspoons dried shrimp paste (*belacan*), toasted at 400°F for 15 minutes (*see page 335*); or whole dried shrimps, soaked in hot water for 5 to 8 minutes till soft, then drained
- ¼ cup water

DIRECTIONS:

1. Process Spice Paste ingredients to a smooth paste. Set aside.
2. Heat 1 tablespoon oil in a wok or skillet and sauté garlic for about ½ to 1 minute, till light brown and fragrant. Add Spice Paste and remaining oil and sauté for about 4 to 5 minutes, till fragrant (adding more oil if necessary).
3. Add shrimp or chicken and stir-fry for about 3 minutes for shrimp or 6 minutes for chicken, till cooked.
4. Stir in soy sauces, white pepper, sugar, and Chinese cabbage stalks, and stir for about 1 to 2 minutes. Add noodles and coat well with sauce for about 1 minute. Add Chinese cabbage leaves, cover, and cook for about 1 minute, till greens start to wilt.
5. Uncover, push noodles towards edge of skillet/wok, add a little oil in center, add beaten egg and let set 1 to 2 minutes, then lightly scramble the egg till cooked and blend with noodles so egg coats noodles.
6. Toss in the bean sprouts, blend well and stir for another minute or two. (Don't overcook, as noodles will get mushy if cooked too long.)
7. Garnish with Chinese chives and chilies and serve hot.

Serve with green chilies in soy sauce dip (page 104).

GARNISH

- ⅓ cup sliced Chinese chives (*kuchai*) or spring onions
- 1 or 2 fresh red chilies, sliced

Pan-fried or Braised Cantonese-style Noodles

Makes 5 to 6 servings

Yee Mee

INGREDIENTS

½ to ¾ pound (1 to 1½ cups) pork or chicken, sliced into 1-inch-long thin strips; or shrimp, shelled and deveined; and/or squid, sliced into 1-inch pieces
1 tablespoon toasted sesame oil
1½ tablespoons sliced and coarsely crushed garlic cloves
1 tablespoon sliced and coarsely crushed fresh ginger
6 to 8 ounces Chinese flowering cabbage (*choy sam*) or Chinese mustard greens (*gai choy*) or Chinese cabbage (*bok choy*), stalks and leaves separated and rinsed to remove dirt and stones; or a mix of snow peas, carrots, and green beans, sliced into 1½-inch-long by ¼-inch-thick pieces
¼ cup dried shiitake, cloud ear, or other Chinese mushrooms, soaked in warm water for 5 minutes, drained and/or squeezed to remove water; or ½ cup fresh mushrooms
1 egg, lightly beaten
1 teaspoon cornstarch mixed with 1 tablespoon water
1 pound fresh, thin, precooked wheat and egg noodles (also called Hong Kong-style pan-fried noodles)*

MARINADE

1 teaspoon preserved soybean paste (*taucheo*, black version), bean sauce, black bean sauce, or oyster sauce
¼ teaspoon toasted sesame oil
¼ teaspoon sugar
¼ teaspoon regular soy sauce

Yee mee or yee mein is a Cantonese Chinese specialty, using thin mee *(wheat- and egg-based noodles) or* meehoon *(rice vermicelli), or a mix of both. It is simmered in mildly thick seafood-and-egg-based sauce in a claypot (braised) or pan-fried to a crispy texture and topped with sauce. As with all Cantonese cooking,* yee mee *highlights the textures, colors, freshness, and natural flavors of the ingredients, so only fresh ingredients are used, including chicken, pork, shrimp, or mixed seafood and an assortment of vegetables. It is flavored with* taucheo *(preserved soybean paste), oyster sauce, soy sauce, sesame oil, and garlic.*

My sister-in-law Catherine (or Kay as we call her), who is married to my younger brother, Sathee, is adept at making yee mee*. Kay learned to make Chinese dishes from her Chinese mother, and Indian dishes from her father, who is of South Indian ancestry. This recipe was handed down from her mother. In this recipe, I have modified the ingredients somewhat to mimic the hawker take-out I had several times on our home visits. I also substitute bean sauce or* taucheo *for oyster-flavored sauce. You can also use cooked thin spaghetti instead of wheat and egg noodles.*

DIRECTIONS:

1. Combine Marinade ingredients and rub on pork, chicken, or shrimp. Set aside to marinate for about 30 minutes.
2. Combine Sauce Paste ingredients and set aside.
3. Warm sesame oil in a wok or skillet and sauté garlic and ginger till fragrant, about ½ to 1 minute.
4. Add marinated pork, chicken, or shrimp and stir-fry over high heat for about 8 to 10 minutes for pork and chicken or 3 to 4 minutes for shrimp.**
5. Add the Sauce Paste (and if using vegetables other than Chinese cabbage or mustard greens, add them now) and cook while stirring for another 2 to 3 minutes.
6. Add Chinese cabbage or mustard green stalks, stir about 1 minute, then add the cabbage or mustard green leaves and shiitake mushrooms, cover, and cook for about 1 to 2 minutes, till leaves start to wilt.
7. Push meat and vegetable mixture toward edge of skillet/wok, add a little oil in center, add lightly beaten egg, let set for 1 to 2 minutes and then lightly scramble the egg till cooked and blend well with rest of mixture.
8. Lower heat, add cornstarch paste while stirring, and cook till sauce thickens, about 1 minute. Keep warm.
9. In a separate pan, add a little oil, add noodles and pan-fry, turning them over till they become crispy and brown, being careful not to burn noodles. Place pan-fried noodles on a plate or in a bowl, and pour the sauce over. (Alternately, when using the blanched noodles, pan-fry as in directions and then add to sauce in wok or skillet, cover, and simmer for 3 to 5 minutes, uncover, and stir noodles for about 1 minute, till sauce becomes slightly thick.)

10. Garnish with freshly ground white peppercorns.

*Alternately you can use the braising method for the noodles, using thin wheat and egg-based dried noodles (*mee*): bring pot of water to boil, add dried noodles, and blanch for about 2 minutes till semi-soft, drain and plunge in or rinse under cold water. Drain again and set aside. Pan-fry and braise as in directions.

**You can also stir-fry or braise the pork, chicken, or shrimp separately and steam or stir-fry the vegetables separately as well and add to the pan-fried noodles before pouring the sauce over them. The sauce softens the noodles, and as you eat the noodles, there is a combined texture sensation of crispiness and softness.

Serve with pickled green chilies (page 105).

Sauce Paste

1 teaspoon double black soy sauce
4 teaspoons preserved soybean paste (*taucheo*, black version), bean sauce, black bean sauce, or oyster sauce
½ teaspoon sugar
¼ teaspoon white peppercorns, finely pounded, or ⅛ teaspoon finely ground white pepper
¾ cup chicken stock or broth
1 cup water
¼ teaspoon toasted sesame oil

Garnish

¼ teaspoon coarsely ground white peppercorns

Braised *yee mee*

Yee mee can be served with chile-based condiments, but is especially good with the sweet and hot, pickled green chilies in soy sauce. This noodle dish is absolutely delicious and can be found all over Kuala Lumpur and Petaling Jaya at hawker stalls. This was one of our favorite take-outs in later years.

Aromatic Spicy Noodles

Mee Rebus

Makes 4 to 5 servings

INGREDIENTS

1 pound sweet potatoes
Optional: 1 cup chicken stock or shrimp stock (*to replace 1 cup of water*)
1 to 2 tablespoons cooking oil
1 tablespoon tomato paste, or 2 tablespoons tomato puree, or 3 tablespoons tomato sauce
1 to 1½ tablespoons tamarind concentrate or tamarind juice (*see page 339*)
2 teaspoons sugar
¼ cup unsweetened coconut milk
1½ teaspoons salt
1 pound fresh precooked yellow noodles, rinsed in cold water or scalded or cooked in boiling water for a few seconds and then rinsed in cold water*
½ cup (about 4 ounces) cooked shrimp or sliced or shredded cooked chicken
4 ounces (about 1 cup) firm tofu (*tauhu*), cubed or cut into 1½-inch by ½-inch slices, deep-fried or pan-fried till light brown
1 large or 2 medium potatoes (about ½ pound), boiled, peeled, and quartered
6 to 8 ounces Chinese flowering cabbage (*choy sam*) or Chinese mustard greens (*gai choy*) or Chinese cabbage (*bok choy*), steamed or cooked in a little oil
2 hard-boiled eggs, quartered
½ cup bean sprouts (1½ ounces), rinsed or blanched

Mee rebus, a variation of mee Jawa (popular in Penang) has Javanese origins. Mee rebus translates as "boiled noodles," meaning the stock or sauce is simmered before adding the noodles. It is another noted Indian Muslim (Mamak) dish. Mee rebus is well known in Kedah, Selangor, and other areas where there is a significant number of Indian Muslims. Mee rebus is also sold by Chinese vendors in Penang and many other towns with a large Chinese population.

On Sunday mornings, Ma would take my sister Vas and I to see the oldie Hindi movies at the Lido cinema, located in Brickfields Road in Kuala Lumpur. Mee rebus was Ma's favorite noodle dish, and she would buy it as a late lunch after the movie from an Indian Muslim vendor who had a mobile cart located near Lido.

Sweet potatoes are rich in antioxidants and vitamins A and C, and help prevent stomach ulcers and colon cancer. They are also high in fiber with a low glycemic index, thus protecting the heart. Their anti-inflammatory effect helps alleviate arthritis.

I have added tomato paste to this recipe and like the Mamak man by the Lido cinema, I left out the crushed peanuts!

DIRECTIONS:

1. Cook sweet potatoes in water for 50 to 55 minutes till soft; then peel and cut into small cubes. Process or blend cooked sweet potatoes with 1 cup of the water to a smooth puree. Set aside.
2. Process Spice Paste ingredients to a smooth paste. Set aside. Combine Spice Blend 2 ingredients and set aside.
3. In a wok or skillet, heat 1 tablespoon of oil and add Spice Blend 1 ingredients and sauté for about ½ to 1 minute. Add Spice Paste and sauté for about 4 to 5 minutes, till fragrant, adding remaining oil as needed.
4. Add Spice Blend 2 and stir for about ½ to 1 minute.
5. Stir in pureed sweet potatoes, 2 cups of water (or 3 cups if stock not used), chicken or shrimp stock, if using, tomato paste, tamarind juice, and sugar and bring to a boil. Lower heat and simmer for about 15 to 20 minutes, till sauce becomes slightly thick. Stir in coconut milk and more water, if needed to get the right consistency, and mix well. Cook, stirring, for another 5 minutes. Add salt and stir.
6. Remove cinnamon stick and star anise before serving. To serve, place noodles in a bowl, add shredded or sliced cooked shrimp or chicken, tofu, potatoes, Chinese cabbage or mustard greens, eggs, and bean sprouts. Ladle sauce to just about cover all ingredients in bowl. Top with garnishes and squeeze lime juice over.

*Alternately you can use fresh uncooked noodles and cook for 3 to 5 minutes, rinse in cold water and coat with oil. Or use dried thin wheat and egg-based dried noodles or thin spaghetti, cooked and drained.

Serve with a hot spicy *belacan* chile paste dip (page 108).

Mee rebus is prepared with fresh yellow noodles (wheat flour and egg-based) in a spicy and slightly tangy and sweet potato-and-peanut-based sauce. It is topped with sliced hard-boiled eggs and fried tofu, prawn fritters, fish cake, lime wedge, fried shallots, and chilies.

Bukit Nanas Convent, Kuala Lumpur, my secondary school

Spice Paste

1 heaping tablespoon sliced garlic cloves
2 teaspoons sliced or chopped fresh or frozen and thawed galangal or fresh ginger
⅓ cup sliced shallots or onions
3 dried whole red chilies, steeped in hot water for about 5 to 8 minutes to soften (slit and deseed if less heat is desired); or ¾ to 1¼ tablespoons *cili boh* (*see page 315*); or 1 to 2 teaspoons bottled *sambal oelek*
¼ cup water

Spice Blend 1

1 star anise
1-inch cinnamon stick
2 cloves

Spice Blend 2

3 teaspoons ground coriander
1½ teaspoons ground cumin
¾ teaspoon ground fennel seeds
¼ teaspoon finely ground black pepper
¼ teaspoon turmeric powder, or ¾ teaspoon peeled and grated fresh or frozen and thawed turmeric root

Garnish

2 tablespoons fresh mint leaves
1 fresh green chile, sliced
1 fresh red chile, sliced
¼ cup fried (*see page 333*) or sautéed shallots or onions
1 to 2 *kasturi* limes, or ½ to 1 regular Persian lime, halved

Braised Savory Noodles
Hokkien Mee

Makes 5 to 6 servings

INGREDIENTS

½ pound (about 1 cup) shelled and deveined shrimp
½ pound pork, thinly sliced (about 1-inch-long pieces)
¼ teaspoon finely pounded white peppercorns, or ⅛ teaspoon finely ground white pepper
6 teaspoons regular soy sauce
2 to 3 tablespoons cooking oil
2 heaping tablespoons sliced or chopped garlic cloves
6 dried whole red chilies, steeped in hot water for about 5 to 8 minutes (slit and deseeded if less heat is desired), pounded or processed with ¼ cup water to a smooth paste; or 1 to 1½ tablespoons *cili boh* (*see page 315*); or ½ to ¾ tablespoons bottled *sambal oelek*
4 tablespoons preserved soybean paste (*taucheo*) or black bean sauce or oyster sauce
2 tablespoons double black, thick, or sweet soy sauce
2 teaspoons sugar (*use less if using thick or sweet soy sauce*)
½ teaspoon salt
1 teaspoon cornstarch mixed with 1 tablespoon water
1 pound fresh precooked yellow noodles, rinsed in cold water or scalded in boiling water for a few seconds and then rinsed in cold water*
6 to 8 ounces Chinese flowering cabbage (*choy sam*) or Chinese mustard greens (*gai choy*) or Chinese cabbage (*bok choy*), stalks and leaves separated and rinsed well to remove dirt and stones
1 cup (3 ounces) bean sprouts, rinsed or blanched

*H*okkien mee *simmered in a dark savory sauce is another favorite noodle dish of mine. Immigrants from the Fujian (or Fukien) Province in southeast China brought* Hokkien mee *to Malaysia, where it has taken on a different flavor dimension, far from its origins. Small cubes of crispy fried pork fat are added to the sauce which gives it its characteristic aroma and flavor, though it is now less commonly added due to health concerns.*

On my trips home, I always go to the Chinese hawker who set up shop by a hotel near my brother Sathee's house in Subang Parade, Petaling Jaya. I have enjoyed watching the cook as he prepared Hokkien mee. *Even cleaning the wok is an art. Using a large ladle, he threw some water into the 'aged' steel wok, placed over high flames, and cleaned it by moving the wok around and finally dumping the water out with his ladle. Then he would add some oil and scoop out bits of seasonings from plastic containers arranged neatly on his cart. As the wok sizzled, he added the squid, pork, or shrimp and stirred them, then added the yellow noodles, stirring them continuously with flames flaring underneath the wok and steam rising from the top of the noodles. Then he added some stock and covered the noodles to cook in the flavored broth. He uncovered it and threw in some greens while stirring. By this time, it smelled delicious, and I wanted to just sit there and then and eat it. Before I knew it, he scooped the noodles up and placed it on plastic wrap over a newspaper. Finally, he topped the dish with bean sprouts, chilies, and half a* kasturi lime *with* sambal belacan *on the side. Forget nutrition and healthy eating. They became distant thoughts as I savored my noodles.*

In my recipe presented here I have substituted the oyster sauce with taucheo *(preserved soybean paste) and some additional sugar.*

DIRECTIONS:

1. Season shrimp with ⅛ teaspoon white pepper and 1 teaspoon regular soy sauce. Season pork with ⅛ teaspoon white pepper and 1 teaspoon regular soy sauce. Set both aside.
2. Heat 1 tablespoon oil in a wok or skillet, and sauté garlic for about ½ to 1 minute. Add chile paste, *cili boh,* or *sambal oelek* and sauté for about 4 to 5 minutes, till fragrant, adding remaining oil if necessary.
3. Add soybean paste or oyster sauce, double black, thick or sweet soy sauce, remaining 4 teaspoons regular soy sauce, sugar, salt, and ¼ cup water, and simmer for 1 to 2 minutes. Add seasoned pork, cook for about 4 to 5 minutes, then add seasoned shrimp and cook for 2 minutes.
4. Lower heat, add cornstarch paste while stirring, and cook till sauce thickens, about 1 minute.
5. Add noodles and ¼ cup water, cover, and simmer in sauce for about 4 to 5 minutes. Then add Chinese cabbage or mustard green stalks and cook about 1 minute. Add Chinese cabbage or mustard green leaves, cover, and cook another 1 to 2 minutes, till greens start to wilt.

6. Uncover and add bean sprouts and stir for about 1 minute. Noodles should be well coated with sauce.
7. Garnish with chilies and scallions and serve warm.

*Alternately, you can use fresh uncooked noodles and cook them in boiling water for 3 to 5 minutes, then rinse in cold water and coat with oil. Or use dried noodles (thin egg and wheat-based) or thin spaghetti, cooked and drained before use.

Serve with *belacan* chile paste dip (page 108).

GARNISH

1 or 2 fresh red chilies, sliced
2 scallions or spring onions, sliced (about ¼ cup)

In Malaysia, there are two types of *Hokkien mee*: *Hokkien hae mee* (soupy shrimp noodles) and *Hokkien char mee* (braised noodles). Hokkien *char mee*, popular around Klang, Petaling Jaya, and Kuala Lumpur, is my favorite, made with thick, yellow noodles braised in thick, dark soy sauce and oyster sauce, with pork, squid, fish cake, and Chinese cabbage. Hokkien *hae mee*, a Penang specialty, is a soupier version, prepared in a rich-flavored dark shrimp-based stock with fresh and dried shrimp as well as pork or chicken and topped with *kangkung* (Malaysian water spinach), *taugeh* (bean sprouts), sliced pork, fish cake, and/or sliced shrimp. In Kuala Lumpur it is referred to as *mee yoke*.

Savory Tomato Shrimp and Chile Noodles

Mee Bandung

Makes 5 to 6 servings

INGREDIENTS

½ pound (about 1 cup) shelled and deveined shrimp
2 to 3 tablespoons cooking oil
¼ cup dried shrimp, soaked in hot water for about 10 minutes to soften and drained (or use commercially ground dried shrimp); or 1 teaspoon dried shrimp paste (*belacan*), toasted at 400°F for 15 minutes (*see page 335*)
2 or 3 dried whole red chilies, steeped in hot water for about 5 to 8 minutes (slit and deseeded if less heat is desired); or 1 to 1½ teaspoons *cili boh* (*see page 315*); or ½ to ¾ teaspoon bottled *sambal oelek*, depending on heat desired
3 cloves
1-inch cinnamon stick
1½ heaping tablespoons sliced and crushed garlic cloves
1 heaping tablespoon sliced and crushed fresh ginger
Heaping ½ cup sliced shallots or onions
¼ teaspoon finely or coarsely ground white pepper
½ cup (3 ounces) sliced tomatoes
6 tablespoons tomato puree, or 3 tablespoons tomato paste, or 9 tablespoons tomato sauce
Optional: ½ cup chicken or beef broth (*to replace ½ cup water*)
1 teaspoon sugar
½ teaspoon salt
1 egg
1 pound fresh precooked yellow noodles, rinsed in cold water or scalded in boiling water for a few seconds and then rinsed in cold water*

Mee Bandung *was popular with Chinese vendors in Muar, a quiet little seaside town in Johor state where our family spent some years and which holds fond memories for me as I spent my early school years there. Muar also has numerous coffee shops (*kedai kopi*), located on the ground level of old Chinese shop houses where people come and socialize over a cup of coffee or tea and a snack or meal. These coffee shops extend out onto the sidewalks where chairs and tables were placed. Of course, there was no air conditioning and everyone ate alfresco-style. These were our restaurants and where I first tried their local specialty,* mee Bandung. *Cha would have his cold Tiger beer in a tall glass, Ma her iced coffee, and we children ordered our cold drinks—lychee drink,* cincau *(with black jelly), lime juice, or Fanta orangeade.*

I revisited Muar and drove around my old neighborhood and school, recapturing those early years. Then we stopped at the waterfront indoor stalls for mee Bandung. *I watched the vendor add noodles in a simmering savory broth of ground dried shrimp, ketchup,* cili boh, *and egg (poached earlier in the broth). It smelled so good. This recipe for* mee Bandung *has a flavor quite similar to* mee udang *(shrimp noodles) from Penang, prepared with tomato ketchup, chilies, and dried shrimp paste (*belacan*). You can also replace the dried shrimp or* belacan *flavor with shrimp stock which can be used instead of the chicken or beef stock. But the intensity of the sauce is not as good.*

DIRECTIONS:

1. Combine Marinade ingredients and rub on shrimp. Heat 1 tablespoon oil in a wok or skillet and stir-fry shrimp for about 2 to 3 minutes. Set aside.
2. Process soaked and drained dried whole shrimp (or *belacan*) and dried whole chilies with ¼ cup water to make a coarse paste.
3. Heat 1 tablespoon oil in the wok or skillet. Add cloves and cinnamon stick and stir for ½ to 1 minute, then add garlic and ginger and sauté for about ½ to 1 minute. Add shallots or onions and sauté for another 1 to 2 minutes.
4. Add white pepper and tomato slices and sauté for about 1 to 2 minutes, then add tomato puree, paste, or sauce, dried shrimp and chile paste (or *belacan* and *cili boh*), and sauté for 4 to 5 minutes, till fragrant, adding remaining 1 tablespoon of oil if necessary.
5. Stir in chicken broth, if using, and 2 cups water (1½ cups if using broth), and bring to boil, then lower heat, add sugar and salt and simmer about 10 minutes. Break the egg (keeping yolk intact) and slowly add egg into the simmering broth to poach the egg. Then let sauce simmer for another 5 minutes longer till sauce thickens slightly (total simmering time is anywhere from 15 to 20 minutes).
6. To serve, place cooked noodles in a bowl, top with cooked shrimp, Chinese cabbage or broccoli and bean sprouts, and pour sauce over to just about cover noodles. Garnish with chile and spring onions. Squeeze lime juice over and serve while hot.

*Alternately you can use fresh uncooked noodles and cook them in boiling water for 3 to 5 minutes, rinse in cold water and coat with oil (or you can rinse the noodles and add to simmering sauce after the egg is poached and let simmer for another 3 to 5 minutes). Or use dried noodles (thin wheat and egg-based) or thin spaghetti, cooked and drained.

Serve with chile paste dip (page 109) or *belacan* chile paste dip (page 108).

Mee Bandung

6 ounces Chinese cabbage (*bok choy*) or Chinese broccoli (*kailan*), steamed or sautéed

¾ cup (2¼ ounces) bean sprouts, rinsed or blanched

MARINADE

3 to 5 dried whole red chilies, steeped in hot water for about 5 to 8 minutes (slit and deseeded if less heat is desired), pounded or processed with ¼ cup water to a smooth paste; or ½ to 1 tablespoon *cili boh* (*see page 315*); or ¼ to ½ tablespoon bottled *sambal oelek*

1 teaspoon tomato puree, or ½ teaspoon tomato paste, or 1½ tablespoons tomato sauce

⅛ teaspoon salt

GARNISH

1 fresh red chile, sliced

1 tablespoon sliced Chinese celery (*kunchoy* or *daun sup*) or spring onions

1 *kasturi* lime, or ½ Persian regular lime

Bandung is a city in western Java, Indonesia, and is a center of the Sundanese population. The Sundanese are a Muslim-Malay people, some of whom migrated throughout the Malay Archipelago, including present-day Malaysia. *Mee Bandung*, which combines Chinese and Malay flavors, is a savory and pungent dried shrimp and chile tomato-based noodle dish that was probably brought to Malaysia by the Sundanese or Chinese merchants from Bandung, which also has a large Chinese population.

Stir-Fried Rice Vermicelli

Meehoon Goreng

Makes 5 to 6 servings

INGREDIENTS

8 ounces dried *meehoon* (rice vermicelli)
1 tablespoon cooking oil
1 heaping tablespoon sliced and crushed garlic cloves
½ teaspoon tomato paste, or 1 teaspoon tomato puree, or 1½ teaspoons tomato sauce
3 tablespoons regular soy sauce
Optional: ½ teaspoon dried shrimp paste (*belacan*), toasted at 400°F for 15 minutes (*see page 335*)
½ cup (about 4 ounces) peeled and deveined shrimp or sliced chicken
Optional: ½ cup chopped ham
4 ounces (1⅓ cups) shredded cabbage or Chinese flowering cabbage (*choy sam*) or Chinese mustard greens (*gai choy*), stalks separated from leaves
6 ounces (1¼ cups) cubed firm tofu (*tauhu*) (¼-inch pieces), deep-fried or pan-fried till golden brown
1 egg, lightly beaten
½ cup (1½ ounces) bean sprouts, rinsed or blanched

SPICE BLEND

1 teaspoon ground coriander
¾ teaspoon ground cumin
½ teaspoon turmeric powder
¼ teaspoon ground fennel seeds
⅛ teaspoon finely ground black pepper

GARNISH

1 fresh red chile, sliced
2 tablespoons sliced spring onions or scallions
1 *kasturi* lime, or ½ regular lime

Stir-fried meehoon (or bihoon) *is a Chinese hawker's favorite all over Southeast Asia and is on many take-out menus in Chinese restaurants and food courts in the U.S., as* Singapore mein *or curry noodles. Curry spices are added to Chinese rice vermicelli, giving it a yellow tinge and a wonderful aroma. Again, like many noodle dishes, there are regional variations with respect to flavor and color.*

Stir-fried meehoon *is a light, mildly flavored quick and easy-to-prepare family meal. Ma prepared this noodle dish for us when she wanted to make a quick meal before she went out for a movie or dinner. She added leftover ingredients—shrimp, chicken, pork, shredded cabbage, and/or slices of omelet—and served it with a chile-soy dip. Here is my version of her recipe.*

DIRECTIONS:

1. Combine Spice Blend ingredients. Soak the *meehoon* in boiling water for 10 to 15 minutes or cook in boiling water for 3 to 5 minutes, till softened; drain and rinse with cold water.
2. Heat oil in a wok or skillet and sauté garlic for about ½ to 1 minute. Add Spice Blend and sauté another ½ to 1 minute.
3. Add tomato paste, puree or sauce, soy sauce, and shrimp paste, if using, and stir for 1 minute. Add shrimp or chicken and/or ham and cook for 2 minutes for shrimp or 5 to 6 minutes for chicken.
4. Add cabbage and stir-fry for about 2 to 3 minutes (if using Chinese cabbage or mustard greens, first add the stalks and stir for 1 minutes, then add the leaves, cover, and cook for 1 minute till leaves start to wilt).
5. Stir in tofu, sauté for 1 minute; add cooked *meehoon* and mix well for 1 minute.
6. Uncover, push *meehoon* towards edge of skillet or wok, add a little oil in center, add beaten egg and let it set for 1 to 2 minutes, then scramble till cooked. Mix well with *meehoon*.
7. Toss in the bean sprouts, mix well and stir-fry for another 1 to 2 minutes.
8. Add garnishes and squeeze lime juice over dish. Serve warm.

Serve with a dip of chopped pickled chilies in soy sauce (page 105).

The Nonyas of Penang transform stir-fried *meehoon* into a rice vermicelli salad with Malay and Thai touches called *kerabu bihoon*. Dried rice vermicelli (*meehoon*, also called *bihoon*) is boiled, strained, and stir-fried with shrimp, bean sprouts, and strips of cucumber, and tossed with a hot *sambal* dressing flavored with *kerisik* (toasted grated coconut), *belacan*, ginger flower, lime juice, and lemongrass. The noodles are topped with hard-boiled eggs, mint leaves, and fried tofu.

Curry Noodles
Kari Mee

Makes 4 to 5 servings

Kari mee *has assimilated many local flavors—Chinese, Indian, and Malay. It is prepared with coconut milk, curry spices, and a chile-flavored broth.* Kari mee *uses yellow wheat-and-egg-based noodles (*mee*), which are my favorite, but many also prefer* meehoon *(rice vermicelli) or a mix of both. Many hawkers add chicken stock to flavor the broth. It is served with a fiery chile paste dip made of chilies, garlic, shallots,* belacan, *dark brown sugar, and lime juice.*

There are many versions of kari mee, *depending on the cook. My favorite* kari mee *was served at a Kuala Lumpur food stall run by a Chinese lady who added her "secret curry-based broth." Another* kari mee *I enjoyed was from a hawker on Gurney Drive in Penang, who made a lighter and sweeter* kari mee *with coriander, peppercorns, and coconut water. He said he used "a special ingredient that only Penang hawkers use." The traditional Chinese* kari mee *has fresh cockles or cuttlefish and fried pig's blood.*

Here is my kari mee *recipe, with my "secret spices" and a touch of* belacan. *I use less coconut milk to give a lighter stock but you can increase it (replacing some water) to give a richer stock.*

INGREDIENTS

- 1 pound fresh precooked yellow *mee**
- 2 to 3 tablespoons cooking oil
- 1 or 2 lemongrass stalks, bruised with back of knife and tied in knot
- Optional: 1 cup chicken broth (*in place of 1 cup water*)
- ½ cup unsweetened coconut milk
- 2 teaspoons light brown sugar or white granulated sugar
- 1½ to 1¾ teaspoons salt
- 1 cup (about ½ pound) shelled and deveined shrimp or sliced chicken
- 4 ounces (¾ cup) firm tofu (*tauhu*), cubed or cut into 1½-inch by ½-inch slices, deep-fried or pan-fried till light brown; or sliced tofu puffs
- ¾ cup (2¼ ounces) bean sprouts, rinsed or blanched

Spice Paste

- 1½ tablespoons sliced garlic cloves
- 1 heaping tablespoon chopped fresh or frozen and thawed galangal or fresh ginger
- ¾ cup sliced shallots or onions
- 3 to 5 dried whole red chilies, steeped in hot water for about 5 to 8 minutes (slit and deseeded if less heat is desired); or ½ to 1 tablespoon *cili boh* (*see page 315*); or ¼ to ½ tablespoon bottled *sambal oelek*
- Optional: 1 teaspoon dried shrimp paste (*belacan*), toasted at 400°F for 15 minutes (*see page 335*)
- ¼ cup water

DIRECTIONS:

1. Process Spice Paste ingredients to a smooth paste. Set aside. Rinse precooked yellow *mee* in cold water or blanch in boiling water for a few seconds; drain and then rinse with cold water.*
2. If using whole spices for the Spice Blend, dry roast them (except for the 3 optional ingredients) for about 30 seconds, cool, and grind. (If using ground spices, combine.) Add cinnamon stick, cloves, and cardamom pods, if using, and set Spice Blend aside.
3. Heat 2 tablespoons of oil in a wok or skillet and sauté Spice Paste for about 4 to 5 minutes, till fragrant, adding remaining oil as needed. Add Spice Blend and sauté for about ½ to 1 minute. Add lemongrass and sauté for about 30 seconds.
4. Add chicken broth, if using, and 4 cups water (3 cups if using chicken broth) and bring to a boil. Stir in coconut milk, sugar, salt, and chicken, if using, and lower heat and simmer for about 25 to 30 minutes, till stock is fairly thick. Add shrimp, if using, about 4 minutes before stock is cooked. (Or you can precook the chicken or shrimp and add to bowl for serving.)
5. Remove lemongrass stalk and cinnamon stick (if using) before serving. In a bowl, place noodles, then top with shrimp or chicken, tofu, and bean sprouts and pour stock over to just about cover noodles. Garnish with chilies and mint leaves. Squeeze lime juice over and serve while warm.

*As an alternative use dry *meehoon* (rice vermicelli) soaked in boiling water for 15 minutes or cooked in boiling water for 3 to 5 minutes till it softens; drained and rinsed with cold water and coated with oil. Or use an equal mix of both noodles.

Serve with *belacan* chile paste dip (page 108).

(*continued on next page*)

(CONTINUED) CURRY NOODLES

Kari Mee

SPICE BLEND

4 teaspoons coriander seeds or ground coriander
2 teaspoons cumin seeds or ground cumin
1 teaspoon whole or finely ground fennel seeds
½ teaspoon white or black peppercorns or finely ground white or black pepper
½ teaspoon turmeric powder
¼ teaspoon chile powder or paprika powder
Optional: 1-inch cinnamon stick
Optional: 2 to 3 cloves
Optional: 2 cardamom pods

GARNISH

2 fresh red chilies, sliced
½ cup fresh mint leaves
1 *kasturi* lime, or ½ regular lime

Kari mee with condiments, as served at a Kuala Lumpur food stall

Malacca Nonya's Savory Coconut-based Noodles

Laksa Lemak

Makes 4 to 5 servings

My favorite laksa *comes from the Nonyas of Malacca. Called* laksa lemak, Nonya laksa, *or sometimes* curry laksa, *it has some flavor variations depending on who prepares it—Nonyas, Chinese, or Malays. Laksa lemak has a sweet creamy and pungent flavor with a base stock of rich coconut milk, pungent galangal and* belacan, *and lemongrass thickened with candlenuts. Fresh yellow (wheat and egg) noodles or dried* meehoon *(rice vermicelli) are used, topped with tofu puffs, fish cake, shrimp, wild ginger bud (*bunga kantan*), chilies, and* daun kesum *or* laksa *leaf (Vietnamese mint). Like all noodles, it is served with a spoonful of fiery* belacan *chile paste and* kasturi *limes.*

I had a delicious bowl of laksa lemak *at the restaurant in Tanjong Bidara Beach resort, twenty kilometers northwest of Malacca. After our swim, my sister Prema and I ordered a late afternoon snack of* laksa lemak. *Each colorful bowl of* laksa *was served with a tiny saucer of chile paste and half a* kasturi *lime. We could not wait to dig into it with our chopsticks and porcelain spoons. It tasted wonderful, with a fragrant minty citrusy flavor.*

Here is my version of this wonderful laksa lemak *of Malacca. I use less coconut milk to give a lighter stock but you can increase it (replacing some water) to give a richer stock.*

INGREDIENTS

2 to 3 tablespoons cooking oil
1 tablespoon ground coriander
1 or 2 lemongrass stalks, bruised with back of a knife and tied into a knot
2 ginger bud petals (*bunga kantan*), thinly sliced (¼ inch wide)
6 to 10 Vietnamese mint leaves (*laksa* or *daun kesum* leaves) or regular mint leaves
1 lobe Kaffir lime leaf
Optional: 1 cup chicken stock or broth (*in place of 1 cup water*)
½ cup unsweetened coconut milk
1¼ teaspoons sugar
½ cup (about 4 ounces) shelled and deveined shrimp or sliced chicken
½ cup tofu puffs, or 4 ounces (¾ cup) firm tofu (*tauhu*), cubed or cut into 1½-inch by ½-inch slices and deep-fried or pan-fried till light brown
1½ to 1¾ teaspoons salt
1 cup (3 ounces) bean sprouts, rinsed or blanched
1 pound fresh precooked yellow noodles, rinsed in cold water or scalded in boiling water for a few seconds and then rinsed in cold water*

SPICE PASTE

1 cup chopped shallots or onions
1½ tablespoon chopped fresh or frozen and thawed galangal or fresh ginger
3 dried whole red chilies, steeped in hot water for about 5 to 8 minutes (slit and deseeded if less heat is desired); or ½ tablespoon *cili boh* (*see page 315*); or ¾ teaspoon bottled *sambal oelek*

(*continued on next page*)

DIRECTIONS:

1. Process Spice Paste ingredients (except turmeric powder, if using) to a smooth paste. Heat 2 tablespoons of oil in a wok or skillet and sauté Spice Paste for about 4 to 5 minutes, till fragrant.
2. Add remaining oil, coriander, and turmeric powder, if using, and stir for about ½ minute. Add lemongrass, ginger bud petals, mint leaves, and lime leaf and stir for about 1 minute.
3. Add chicken stock or broth, if using, 4 cups water (3 cups if using chicken stock or broth) and bring to a boil. Then lower heat, add coconut milk, sugar, and chicken, if using, and simmer for about 25 to 30 minutes, till stock becomes fairly thick. If using shrimp, add towards end of cooking, about 4 minutes before simmering is completed. (Or you can precook chicken or shrimp and add to bowl before serving.)
4. Add tofu puffs and salt and cook for another 1 to 2 minutes.
5. Remove lemongrass stalk and lime leaf before serving.
6. In a bowl, place noodles, then top with shrimp or chicken and bean sprouts, and pour stock over to just about cover noodles. Garnish with mint leaves and chilies. Squeeze lime juice over and serve while warm.

*As an alternate use fresh uncooked noodles and cook in boiling water for 3 to 5 minutes, rinse in cold water and coat with oil. Or use dried noodles (thin wheat-and-egg-based) or thin spaghetti, cooked and drained.

Serve with a dollop of chile paste dip (page 110).

(continued) Malacca Nonya's Savory Coconut-based Noodles

Laksa Lemak

1 teaspoon fresh or frozen and thawed turmeric root, peeled and chopped, or ½ teaspoon turmeric powder
1 teaspoon dried shrimp paste (*belacan*), toasted at 400°F for 15 minutes (*see page 335*)
4 to 5 candlenuts or macadamia nuts
¼ cup water

Garnish

8 Vietnamese mint leaves (*laksa* leaves or *daun kesum*) or regular mint leaves
1 fresh red chile (Fresno, jalapeno, Serrano, cayenne, Thai, or cherry), sliced
1 *kasturi* lime, or ½ regular lime

Baba Nonya diningware

Penang Nonya's Tamarind and Fish-Based Noodles

Assam Laksa

Makes 4 to 5 servings

Assam laksa is *a popular* laksa *from the north. It has a clear tamarind* (asam jawa) *and fish-based stock (sometimes with pineapple juice added). The Penang* assam laksa *is hot and tangy and uses soft white and opaque noodles (called* laksa noodles, *made from non-glutinous and glutinous rice flour). Ingredients include poached flaked fish, usually mackerel* (ikan kembong), *shredded lettuce, cucumber, pineapple, chilies, lemongrass, galangal, and onions. Dried slices of tamarind-like fruit, called* asam keping *or* asam gelugor, *give that tangy flavor to the stock. Pink* bunga kantan *(wild ginger bud) and* laksa leaves *or* daun kesum *(Vietnamese mint) give it a fragrant aroma. A topping of the thick sweet and pungent black shrimp paste* (udang petis *or* hae-ko) *reflects the flavors of the Hokkien immigrants of Penang.*

The intense sour and hot flavors of assam laksa *are a Thai influence, while* belacan, *ginger bud, and fish flavors are typical of Malay cooking. You can adjust the sourness based on your preference, and you can also use a chile* belacan *dip instead of the* hae ko *dip.*

INGREDIENTS

1 pound mackerel (you can also use sardine, tuna, or other oily fish)
1 or 2 lemongrass stalks, bruised with back of a knife and tied into a knot
1 pound *laksa* noodles or dried rice vermicelli (*meehoon*)
2 to 3 tablespoons cooking oil
3 tablespoons tamarind concentrate or tamarind juice (*see page 339*)
3 pieces dried *asam gelugor* or *asam keping* (sometimes labeled tamarind skin), or 1½ to 2 tablespoons additional tamarind juice
2 ginger bud petals, sliced
1 teaspoon sugar
½ teaspoon salt
6 Vietnamese mint leaves (*laksa* leaves or *daun kesum*) and 6 regular mint leaves, or 12 regular mint leaves

Spice Paste

2 teaspoons chopped garlic cloves
1 tablespoon chopped fresh or frozen and thawed galangal or fresh ginger
1 cup chopped shallots or onions
1 or 2 lemongrass stalks, sliced into ¼-inch pieces
2 to 4 dried whole red chilies, steeped in hot water for about 5 to 8 minutes (slit and deseeded if less heat desired); or ½ to ¾ tablespoon *cili boh* (*see page 315*); or ½ to ¾ teaspoon bottled *sambal oelek*
2 fresh green chilies (jalapeno, Serrano, cayenne, Thai), sliced
1 teaspoon peeled and chopped turmeric root, fresh or frozen and thawed, or ¼ to ½ teaspoon turmeric powder

DIRECTIONS:

1. Clean mackerel and slice into 2-inch pieces. Bring 5 cups of water to a boil. Add fish pieces and lemongrass stalk to boiling water and bring back to a boil. Lower heat and simmer for about 10 minutes. Remove fish pieces and strain and reserve stock. Debone fish, cool, and flake. Set aside.
2. Process Spice Paste ingredients (except for turmeric powder, if using) to a smooth paste. Set aside.
3. If using *laksa* noodles, scald them for 3 to 4 minutes in boiling water, drain, and rinse with cold water. If using dried vermicelli, soak in boiling-hot water for 15 minutes or cook in boiling water for 3 to 5 minutes, till softened, then drain and rinse with cold water. Set aside.
4. Heat oil in a wok or saucepan and sauté Spice Paste for about 4 to 5 minutes till fragrant; add reserved fish stock, tamarind concentrate, *asam gelugor*, if using, ginger bud petals, sugar, turmeric powder, if using, and salt, and bring to a boil. Lower heat, add both kinds of mint leaves and simmer for about 20 minutes. Add half of fish flakes to the stock and simmer for 3 more minutes.
5. Remove lemongrass and *asam gelugor* from sauce. Place noodles in a bowl, top with garnishes and pour sauce over to just about cover noodles. Top with remaining fish flakes and 1 tablespoon of *hae ko* paste or *belacan* chile paste dip (page 108).

(*continued on next page*)

(continued) Penang Nonya's Tamarind and Fish-Based Noodles

Assam Laksa

1 teaspoon dried shrimp paste (*belacan*), toasted at 400°F for 15 minutes (*see page 335*)
¼ cup water

Garnish

½ medium cucumber (about 4 ounces), cored and grated or julienned (1 cup)
1 cup (5½ ounces) julienned pineapple
½ cup thinly sliced onion
¼ cup loose Vietnamese mint leaves (*laksa* leaves or *daun kesum*) or regular mint
3 or 4 ginger bud petals, finely sliced
1 fresh red chile, sliced

Hae ko paste

4 tablespoons *hae ko* (dark thick small shrimp or krill paste) mixed with ¼ to ⅓ cup water

Thai Buddhist temple (Wat Chayamangkalaram), Penang

CHAPTER 6

POULTRY AND EGGS: THE DELICIOUS FAVORITES

Ma's mobile vendor

FOOD MARKETS (*PASAR MAKAN*) IN MALAYSIA

Buying food in Malaysia can be an adventure. While Western-style supermarkets (*pasar raya*) are quickly becoming popular in urban areas, Malaysians traditionally do their food shopping at "wet" markets (*pasar basah*), at night markets (*pasar malam*) that are held on special days of the month, from local farms, or from mobile food vendors, particularly in small towns and more rural areas.

Ma did not have time to go grocery shopping because she was running a large household, so like many housewives, she usually did her food shopping from her favorite mobile vendor, a Chinese man who came everyday on his motorbike with a cart attached to it (or later in a big van). It was a mini mobile supermarket. Cha preferred to go to the wet markets, especially the big market near Foch Avenue (now called *Jalan Tun Tan Cheng Lock*) in Kuala Lumpur, today occupied by Central Market, a souvenir retail center for tourists. These shopping markets were called "wet" markets because all the foods sold were fresh, and in addition, the floors were hosed down daily for clean up, particularly where fish and meats were butchered. Wet markets and night markets thrive today in rural areas because of their fresh appeal and also because they are less expensive than buying from a middleman, like the mobile vendor, or from a supermarket. The wet markets also offer greater variety.

Cha enjoyed going to the wet market on a Sunday morning after breakfast, and on occasions he took me along. At the market, there were rows and rows of vendors, women generally, some selling wares outside under canopies, while others were indoors sitting on

Ma's favorite mobile vendor would drive right up to our porch late mornings. Whenever I was at home, I could hear his loud high-pitched voice as his bike turned into the entrance to our street. Upon hearing the familiar voice at our front entrance, Ma would hurriedly walk up to the front door to greet him. Their daily encounters led to friendship, and after initial greetings, they would chat a bit about their families while Ma looked over his wares. Then he would ask Ma what she was cooking that day. He sold fresh chicken, meats, fish, fresh vegetables and fruits, *belacan*, all kinds of small snacks including dried fruits, packaged dried salted fish, and fried tofu, all hanging around his cart. It was amazing how much his small cart held.

He organized his meats, poultry, and other household goods (or sundries as Malaysians call them—soaps, detergents, milk powder, kitchenware, cutlery, or strainers) packed tightly inside and around his cart. As years went by, his cart slowly evolved into a big van. If Ma needed any household goods or a cleaner, he had it or would bring it the next day. He kept a notebook in which he tallied up the costs and Ma paid him on a monthly basis.

stools next to built-in stalls. They were selling fresh vegetables, fruits, spices, and other foods, all laid out for us to see, touch, smell, and choose. I lingered at the vegetable, fruit, and spice sections with their colorful displays and wonderful smells. The colors, textures, movements, gossip, and bargaining were endlessly fascinating.

I was drawn to an Indian Muslim vendor selling fresh red and green chilies. I could not resist standing and staring at his stall. It was so colorful. He used a container to scoop up the chilies and weigh them. I also enjoyed the bustle around us, with women in *tudongs* calling out as we walked around the rows of batik sarongs, tee-shirts, small appliances, toys, mats, brooms, and other housewares on display. Malay food vendors were serving freshly prepared *halal* foods, including *satay* (page 65), fried fish, *sambal* chicken (page 161), *kangkung belacan* (page 228), *nasi goreng* (fried rice, page 123), and beverages, including spiced lime juice (page 263), and sugarcane juice.

While I loved many parts of the wet market, I always walked at a faster pace when Cha and I reached the seafood sections. I did not want to look at the freshly cut and gutted fish laid out all over the concrete, but this was Cha's favorite section and he would eagerly pick out his favorite fish for our meals for the week. When he was done we would move to the next stop, the chicken and meat areas, which were not a happy place for me as a child either. Here, the chickens were slaughtered on the premises and all the blood dripping and hanging organs were too much for me. The first time I went with Cha I nearly fainted! When I went home I could not eat chicken or meat for a couple of weeks. After that, I avoided the chicken, meat, and seafood sections on my shopping ventures with Cha.

Years later, whenever I traveled to Malaysia, I enjoyed visiting the wet markets again, sometimes with Cha, where much of the color and sense of shopping adventure I experienced as a youth still remained. My daughter Geeta had the same reaction to the sight of slaughtered meats and chicken that I had, so I just whisked her past them. However, on one family trip to a wet market in Kuching, Sarawak, she was intrigued by the vendor selling live chickens. Each customer would examine the chickens and pick one. Next, the vendor would tie the chicken's feet together, then take a plastic shopping bag (like the ones you get from the supermarket today), cut a small hole in the bottom, and slip the chicken into the bag, head first. The customer then took his prize chicken home in the shopping bag with the poor chicken's head sticking out through the hole in the bottom of the bag, squawking all the way!

CHICKEN

Chicken (*ayam* in Malay), also referred to as fowl, is the most popular meat in Malaysia. Religious strictures prevent Muslims from eating pork and Hindus from eating beef. However, everyone enjoys chicken and there are endless ethnic and regional chicken preparations in Malaysia.

Preparing Chicken

In Malaysia, chicken is prepared in many delicious ways. It is slow-cooked in coconut milk-based *rendangs*; simmered with spice-laden curries; braised in a sweet mild *taucheo* and star anise sauce; stewed Kristang-style in a tangy tomato-vinegar sauce; marinated and deep-fried; wrapped in banana leaf and grilled (*bakar*) and served with *sambal* and other chile-based condiments.

Chinese generally steam or braise chicken, seasoned with sesame oil, soy sauce, star anise, or five spice. Nonyas use a combination of Chinese and Malay techniques and flavor the chicken with *taucheo* (preserved soybean paste), *cili padi* (bird peppers), ginger, candlenuts, or *belacan* (dried shrimp paste). Malays have a three-step cooking process for chicken that adds layers of flavor. First, the chicken is marinated with coriander, lemongrass, galangal, or pureed chilies, then simmered or stewed in seasoned stock, and finally, deep-fried or grilled. Indians generally dry-fry chicken in seasoned oil (called *varuval*), or simmer it with spices, resulting in intensely aromatic wet sauces (curries) or dry sauces (*peratils*).

Ma usually prepared her dishes with free-range *kampung ayam* (village chicken). She preferred them as they are more flavorful, low-fat, and generally considered to have higher nutritional value. *Kampung ayam* are small and lean chickens with less body fat than their farmed counterparts (which in the U.S. are bred to overproduce breast meat). So whenever a family member had a fever or was sick, Ma would prepare *kampung ayam* as soup or porridge. I miss the wonderful taste of *kampung* chicken, although even mass-produced chickens in Malaysia are smaller and have more flavor than the U.S. chickens.

When Malaysians cook chicken, they usually cut them up into small pieces with bones and all so the flavor gets deep into every piece of chicken when cooked. Ma would not eat chicken without bones. She also felt that to fully enjoy cooked chicken, it was best to use your hands, not a fork and knife. Even today, I follow Ma's way of cooking when I make a Malaysian-style chicken dish.

Ma made delicious wet and dry chicken curries, *sambal*-style or seasoned with spices and deep-fried. I can still smell her cooking in the kitchen, with the *sambal* aroma permeating the whole house. Nothing could keep me away from her aromatic chicken *sambal* (page 161), not even playtime with friends. Growing up, my idea of a *sambal* dish was the way Ma prepared it, which was without *belacan* (dried shrimp paste). She did not like the idea of adding *belacan* as she had seen how they dried the shrimp in the villages in those days, spreading dried shrimp on the busy roads and stomping them with their bare feet. Thus, she did not use it till much later when *belacan* became commercially manufactured. So our early tastes of *sambal* with *belacan* were only at friends' homes or at Malay food stalls. One thing is for sure, I became addicted to using *belacan* in *sambal* chicken, as that truly gave an added intensity to the dish.

Every time we visit Malaysia, Shanta, my sister-in-law, makes us her chicken *kurma* (page 168). Even my daughter, who did not like chicken or meat dishes then, fell in love with Shanta's chicken *kurma*. On one of my visits, Shanta showed me how to make it. Geeta and I helped her and watched her cooking in her enclosed porch attached to her kitchen. It had large windows, and this is where she did almost all her cooking, in a *kwali* atop a small gas-operated stove. Many homes in Malaysia have this extra small airy room attached to their kitchen. I often wondered why she did not use her kitchen stove to cook meals, but later it made sense. This way the cook does not mess up the kitchen, especially with local cooking in which high heat and heavy stirring is sometimes involved, and the strong aromas of *belacan* or curry pastes did not seep through the whole house. It was also a smaller place and easier to clean or hose off after food preparation. Many families have maids or cooks who prepare their meals in this small naturally ventilated space. It has the concept of a "wet" kitchen.

Shanta prepared, chopped, and blended the ingredients in her kitchen and then started her cooking in the porch kitchen. She is one of the fastest cooks to watch, and before you know it, she has made a number of mouth-watering dishes. She never measures anything, just takes a handful of shallots, a bunch of mint and cilantro, a few chilies, a little turmeric, and a pinch of pepper, and adds them all into the *kwali*. Shanta does not own any measuring cups or spoons and I had to bring these to get measurements for her recipes. Watching Shanta cook made the recipes look so easy to prepare.

My sister-in-law Shanta in her porch kitchen

A popular chicken curry (page 171) all Malaysians enjoy has influences from the three major ethnic groups—Indian, Malay, and Chinese. Each ethnic group has their signature chicken recipes that also have crossover appeal, such as chicken *kurma* (page 168), chile chicken (page 163), or chicken *sambal* (page 161). Malay favorites include *ayam percik* (grilled spicy chicken, page 166), *ayam masak merah* (chicken in spicy tomato sauce, page 284), and *ayam rendang* (chicken simmered in a coconut milk, page 287). Nonya specialties are *kari ayam Kapitan* (Captain's chicken curry, page 162), *ayam pong tey* (stewed chicken), and *inchee kabin* (spicy sweet fried chicken). Eurasians have their tangy hot *debal* (devil's) curry (page 289), chicken *vindaloo* (page 169), and pot roast chicken. In the East Malaysian states of Sabah and Sarawak, Malay and Chinese-influenced recipes prevail. Chicken is roasted in bamboo, stewed in rice wine, soy sauce, and sweet spices, or lightly curried. The Iban (or Sea Dayaks of Sarawak)

rub chicken pieces with salt, pepper, and garlic, place them in hollow bamboo cylinders, and roast them over charcoal fires. The Bidayuhs (or Land Dayaks of Sarawak) have wonderful Chinese-influenced stews, seasoned with ginger, garlic, and lemongrass. The Kadazans of Sabah have healing chicken soups and stews, flavored with rice wine, black pepper, and ginger, or light chicken curries with candlenuts, tamarind juice, and coconut milk.

Kaya is an addictive coconut-egg jam, our favorite spread for toasts while growing up. It is also a sweet topping for many Nonya and Malay desserts and snacks made with glutinous rice. To make *kaya*, eggs are mixed with coconut milk and boiled for a while at low heat, till the sauce thickens and caramelizes into a brown jam-like mixture. Sometimes, pandan juice is added to flavor *kaya*.

EGGS

Our family was not alone in our love for eggs, as they are popular with most Malaysians. For the Chinese, Nonyas, and Malays, eggs represent good luck and fertility, so are served as symbolic dishes for weddings, birthdays, and other festive occasions. Chinese distribute red eggs on birthdays as a symbol of prosperity and happiness. *Bunga telor* (colored eggs decorated with flower designs) are given at Malay weddings for guests to take home. Hard-boiled eggs and omelet strips are used extensively in Malaysian cooking as garnishes and toppings for rice and noodle dishes. Many working Malaysians begin their day with eggs. I remember as we walked to school, passing by *kopi kedai* or *kopi tiam* (coffee shops) where men sat and sipped coffee with condensed milk and ate thick slices of white bread toasted over charcoal wth butter and *kaya* and soft-boiled eggs sprinkled with black or white pepper and topped with slices of red chilies and soy sauce.

When we lived in Kuantan, on the East Coast of Malaysia, Ma raised chickens for meat and eggs. She was quite an entrepreneur in those days and wanted to have her own egg business, along with running a household of nine children. We had a huge enclosed back porch where the chickens would sometimes roam. At first we were scared of the hens, but slowly got used to them. Eventually, we would chase the hens and roosters around and play with the baby chicks, allowing them to walk over our heads and hands. Thus we grew to adore the chickens and would not eat them. So Ma abandoned the idea of raising them for meat and kept them for eggs. When the eggs were laid we would collect them for her and enjoyed holding the warm eggs in

Chinese hawkers love eggs and add them as a sauce or garnish for noodles, and scramble them with oysters to make *oh chien*. They also pickle or season eggs for soups and stews and make many rich custards and sweets. Malays cook them in a spicy chile tomato-based sauce or top their *nasi goreng* (fried rice) and soups with a sunny-side-up egg. The Malay *tom yam* stalls serve *nasi Pattaya* (Pattaya rice), fried rice wrapped inside an omelet and garnished with chile sauce. *Telur bistik*, a ground beef omelet in a sweet and sour sauce served with cooked white rice, is a favorite fast food lunch or dinner item from Mamak vendors in Kuala Lumpur.

our hands. She made a small business of selling the eggs to neighbors and vendors. When we moved to Petaling Jaya, a suburb of Kuala Lumpur and a thriving industrial center, she continued her egg business for a few more years, even selling to the door-to-door vendor, but eventually gave it up as we got older.

Ma also made delicious scrambled eggs with tomatoes, onions, chilies, and seasonings, and a wonderful egg curry (page 172) using hard-boiled eggs. It was a legacy from her mom, Periama, a Chettiar. She modified the recipe adding Malay flavors and local ingredients. Like many Hindu Indians, Ma set aside one day of the week for prayers and vegetarian foods, but Cha and us children did not observe this as strictly as Ma did. So for us, Ma also cooked egg curries and egg *sambals* with lentil and vegetable dishes. *Murtabak*, a flaky flatbread prepared with ground meat and egg, a Mamak specialty, reminds me of my father. It was his favorite and a must when a visitor was being introduced to Malaysian fare.

Chinese and Nonyas also enjoy duck eggs and their favorites include salted duck eggs and century eggs. Cooked salted eggs (soaked in brine and encased in salted mud and straw) are popular condiments for porridge and for stir-fried crab or shrimp dishes. The black Century eggs (called thousand year eggs) coated in salt, wood ash, and lime, are added to porridge or eaten with ginger pickles.

DUCK

Duck (*itek*) is not commonly eaten in Malaysia except in Chinese and Nonya households. The Chinese generally steam and braise duck, flavoring it with thick and sweet soy sauce (*kicap*), *taucheo*, and spices like clove, cinnamon, and star anise. They also add duck to soups and stews, such as *itek tim* (duck with salted vegetables), *itek sioh* (duck simmered with coriander, cloves, cinnamon, and black soy sauce), or a Teochew-style braised duck. Kristangs raise ducks in their backyards and enjoy a spicy baked duck for Sunday meals with *sambal belacan*. In Sabah and Sarawak, duck is also plentiful, left to graze in the farm fields, and roasted or braised with Chinese and Malay spicing. The ethnic Ibans cook duck with lemongrass, soy sauce, and sweet spices, or boil it with spices and then roast it.

Fragrant Chile Tomato Chicken

Sambal Ayam

Makes 3 to 4 servings

Sambal ayam *was a favorite with all of us at home and Ma prepared it without using dried shrimp paste* (belacan). *For those like me, who like the wonderful background flavor that* belacan *provides, it can be an optional ingredient in the recipe. For Malaysians,* sambals *are indispensable chile-based cooking sauces prepared in an endless variety of ways (see Chapter 3) using* belacan *(dried shrimp paste), krill, salted fish, lemongrass, garlic, ginger, galangal, tomatoes, tamarind juice, and/or soy sauce.*

While there are numerous sambal *variations, a basic* sambal *has sliced shallots and red chilies, flavored with sugar, salt, and lime juice. The additional ingredients vary depending on application and ethnic and regional preferences. Malays, Nonyas, Chittys, and Kristangs have* sambals *almost daily, made with chicken, fish, shrimp, baby anchovies, or squid. My favorite is a Malay-style* sambal, *fiery, pungent and slightly tart with lime juice. The longer you stir the sauce in this recipe the more fragrant it becomes. So here I add more oil to achieve optimum* tumising, *when the oil seeps out of the sauce. A* sambal *is not a* sambal *till this is done. But for those health-conscious cooks you can add less oil and stir in less time and still get a delicious* sambal.

INGREDIENTS

- 1 pound chicken (breasts, thighs, or drumsticks), cut into 1-inch to 1½-inch pieces
- 1 teaspoon salt
- 1 teaspoon turmeric powder
- Optional: ½ teaspoon chile powder
- ¼ cup cooking oil
- 1-inch to 1½-inch cinnamon stick
- 1 star anise
- 1 teaspoon ground fennel seeds
- Heaping ½ cup (3 ounces) chopped tomatoes
- 2 tablespoons tomato paste, or ¼ cup tomato puree, or 6 tablespoons tomato sauce
- 1 teaspoon sugar
- ½ teaspoon freshly squeezed or bottled lime juice

Spice Paste

- ½ cup diced shallots or onions
- 1 heaping tablespoon sliced cloves garlic
- 1 lemongrass stalk, sliced into ¼-inch to ½-inch pieces
- 15 to 20 dried whole red chilies, steeped in hot water for 5 to 8 minutes, slit and deseeded; or about ¼ cup *cili boh* (*see page 315*); or 2 tablespoons bottled *sambal oelek*; or ¼ to ½ teaspoon chile powder (*depending on desired heat*) with 1 teaspoon ground paprika for color
- Optional: ½ to 1 teaspoon dried shrimp paste (*belacan*), toasted at 400°F for 15 minutes (*see page 335*)
- ¼ cup water

Garnish

- 1 to 2 tablespoons sliced spring onions or chopped coriander leaves (cilantro)

DIRECTIONS:

1. Rub chicken with ½ teaspoon of salt, turmeric, and chile powder, if using. Set aside for a minimum of 30 minutes. Brown chicken in a skillet with 1 tablespoon oil. Set aside.
2. Process Spice Paste ingredients to a smooth paste. Set aside.
3. Heat 1 tablespoon oil in a wok or skillet and fry cinnamon stick and star anise for ½ minute. Add 2 tablespoons of oil and Spice Paste and sauté for about 10 to 15 minutes, till sauce becomes fragrant, gradually adding remaining oil.
4. Add ground fennel seeds, tomatoes, tomato paste, puree, or sauce, sugar, and ½ cup water and stir for about 5 minutes. Add chicken and sauté for 2 minutes, then add another ½ cup water and remaining ½ teaspoon salt and continue to stir till sauce becomes thick and fragrant and chicken is cooked, about 10 to 15 minutes.
5. Add lime juice and stir another minute. Garnish with spring onions or coriander leaves.

Serve with coconut-infused rice (page 117), tomato rice (page 119) or cooked white or brown rice; and cucumber carrot *acar* (page 99), stir-fried mixed vegetables (page 224), or a green salad.

Captain's Chicken Curry

Kari Ayam Kapitan

Makes 6 to 8 servings

INGREDIENTS

- 1½ to 2 pounds chicken (breasts, thighs, or drumsticks or a mix), cut into 1-inch to 1½-inch pieces
- ¼ teaspoon turmeric powder
- ¼ teaspoon finely ground black pepper
- 2 to 3 tablespoons cooking oil
- 1 teaspoon lemon juice
- ½ teaspoon light brown sugar or white granulated sugar
- 2 tablespoons unsweetened coconut milk
- ¼ teaspoon salt

SPICE PASTE

- ½ to ¾ cup sliced shallots or onion
- 2 heaping tablespoons sliced garlic cloves
- 1 teaspoon sliced fresh ginger or fresh or frozen and thawed galangal
- 1 or 2 lemongrass stalks, sliced into ¼-inch to ½-inch pieces
- 2 to 4 whole dried red chilies, steeped in hot water for 5 to 8 minutes, slit and deseeded; or ½ to 1 tablespoon *cili boh* (*see page 315*); or ¼ to ½ tablespoon bottled *sambal oelek*
- ½ teaspoon dried shrimp paste (*belacan*), toasted at 400°F for 15 minutes (*see page 335*)
- 2 candlenuts or macadamia nuts
- ¾ cup water

GARNISH

- 2 tablespoons crispy fried (*see page 333*) or sautéed shallots or onions
- 2 tablespoons chopped fresh mint leaves or sliced Kaffir lime leaves

Kari ayam Kapitan, *or simply* kari Kapitan, *is a rich and spicy chicken curry generally served for special occasions with* biryanis *or* nasi kemuli. *Indians, Malays, and Kristangs have contributed to its flavor, adding chilies, turmeric root, mint, cilantro, and coconut milk.*

The origins of kari Kapitan *are open to debate, and the dish is so popular in Malaysia that a number of groups claim its ownership. Nonyas add* belacan *and candlenuts to thicken the sauce, and have two regional versions, a Malacca version with a more intense spicing, and a tart Penang version with tamarind juice and Kaffir lime leaves and using less spices. Chinese have their own version adding* taucheo *(preserved soybean paste), chilies, tamarind juice, and white peppercorns.*

Here is my version of this popular dish, taking cues from my sister-in-law Shanta as well as flavor hints from Nonya and Kristang cooks.

DIRECTIONS:

1. Rub chicken with turmeric and black pepper. Set aside.
2. Process Spice Paste ingredients to a smooth paste.
3. Heat 1 tablespoon oil in a wok or skillet and sauté the Spice Paste for 8 to 10 minutes till fragrant, gradually adding remaining oil.
4. Add the seasoned chicken and stir for about 3 minutes, then add ¾ cup water and simmer, stirring, for about 15 minutes, till chicken is cooked.
5. Add lemon juice and sugar and mix well. Stir in coconut milk and let cook for about 5 minutes, then add salt and stir for another 1 minute.
6. Garnish with crispy fried shallots or onions and mint or lime leaves.

Serve with cooked white or brown rice, ghee rice (page 121), or yellow rice (page 118); with mixed vegetable *acar* (page 93), green mango *acar* (page 96), or eggplant and pineapple *pajeri* (page 232).

There are many fabled stories attached to *kari Kapitan*. In one story, a Dutch captain in Penang asked an Indonesian mess boy what was for dinner and he answered, "*kari … Kapitan*!" ("curry … Captain") and thus its name was born. Another story is from the Nonyas of Malacca. When the old trading port of Malacca was a bustling spice, tea, and silk bazaar and the Chinese had an imperial presence, it is said *kari Kapitan* was created in honor of an important Chinese captain.

Chile Chicken
Cili Ayam

Makes 3 to 4 servings

When we were young, Ma used to make spicy crispy deep-fried chicken pieces that would simply melt in your mouth! Ma made her recipe with bite-size pieces of chicken, bone and all. I missed Ma's cili ayam *when I stayed at the women's hostel in Bombay (now Mumbai) while attending college, so I would order a take-out chicken dish that was called "chilly (or chili) chicken." It did not taste the same as Ma's, but I enjoyed it anyway. There are a few Indian restaurants in New York City that serve foods prepared in Chinese restaurants in India, called Indo-Chinese cuisine, and chilly chicken is a favorite.*

Below is a cili ayam *recipe from my sister Vas that we all love. She serves it as a main course with fried rice and a salad of cool sliced cucumbers and tomatoes. I sometimes serve* cili ayam *as an appetizer with cold beer and wine. You can also grill or bake the chicken, but deep-frying produces the best flavor and texture. If you prefer stir-frying, slice chicken thin, but again flavor does not match the deep-fried chicken.*

INGREDIENTS

1 pound chicken (breasts or breast tenders, thighs, or drumsticks, or a mix), cut into 1-inch pieces
1 heaping tablespoon corn flour or rice flour
Oil for deep-frying

MARINADE

Juice squeezed from 1 to 2 tablespoons crushed ginger
½ teaspoon turmeric powder
½ to 1½ teaspoons chile powder (*depending on heat desired*)
½ teaspoon paprika (for color)
¼ teaspoon finely ground black pepper
¾ teaspoon ground cumin
½ teaspoon ground fennel seeds
Optional: ½ to 1 teaspoon ground mustard
½ teaspoon salt

GARNISH

½ teaspoon freshly squeezed or bottled lime juice
2 tablespoons fresh coriander leaves (cilantro)

DIRECTIONS:

1. Combine Marinade ingredients and rub on chicken. Marinate for a minimum of 30 minutes to 1 hour, preferably 3 to 5 hours or overnight in the refrigerator.
2. Coat chicken pieces lightly with corn flour or rice flour.
3. Heat oil in a deep pan and deep-fry chicken pieces for 8 to 15 minutes, till golden brown, about 5 minutes for breast tenders and about 15 minutes for thighs or drumsticks; or bake at 400°F for 30 to 40 minutes, or grill, or broil. Drain on paper towels.
4. Sprinkle lime juice over chicken and garnish with coriander leaves.

Serve on a bed of tomato and cucumber slices, with fried rice (page 123), tomato rice (page 119), or vegetable *biryani* (page 280). Or simply enjoy with cold beer or wine.

Vas and her daughter Priya

Malaysian *cili ayam* has a blend of sweet and savory spices mixed with sweet thick soy sauce that forms the basis of its flavor. Corn or rice flour gives it crispiness. This recipe incorporates Indian, Chinese, Nonya, and even Eurasian flavorings. It is light and spicy and has a different flavor and texture from the chicken I had in India, which was coated with egg batter, deep-fried and doused in a sweet sauce. The Kristang recipe for *cili ayam* calls for the chicken to be marinated in Worcestershire sauce, ground mustard, and sweet spices.

Tamarind Coriander Chicken

Ayam Sioh

Makes 3 to 4 servings

INGREDIENTS

- 1 tablespoon coriander seeds, dry roasted in small skillet, cooled, and finely ground; or 1 tablespoon ground coriander
- ¼ teaspoon finely ground black pepper
- 2 tablespoons tamarind concentrate or tamarind juice extracted from pulp (*see page 339*)
- 1 teaspoon turmeric powder
- ¼ to ½ teaspoon chile powder
- 2 teaspoons sweet soy sauce or regular soy sauce (if less sweetness is desired)
- 1 tablespoon preserved soybean paste (*taucheo*, light brown version with whole or crushed beans)
- 1 to 2 teaspoons sugar
- 1 tablespoon rice vinegar, cider vinegar, palm vinegar, or distilled white vinegar
- ¼ teaspoon salt
- About 1 pound chicken (breasts, drumsticks, thighs, or mix), cut into 1½-inch pieces
- 1 to 2 tablespoons cooking oil

Spice Paste

- 1½ to 2 heaping tablespoons sliced garlic cloves
- 1 cup sliced shallots or onions
- 1 dried whole red chile, steeped in hot water for 5 to 8 minutes, drained; or ¾ teaspoon *cili boh* (*see page 315*); or ¼ teaspoon bottled *sambal oelek*
- ¼ cup water

Garnish

- 1 to 2 tablespoons chopped coriander leaves (cilantro)

*Ayam Sioh is a sweet, spicy, and tangy tamarind-and-coriander-based chicken stew, a specialty from the Malacca Nonyas who serve it for their New Year. Preserved soybean paste (*taucheo*, the light brown version), sweet soy sauce, chile pepper, and rice wine are its basic flavorings. Since duck is a popular meat with the Chinese and Nonyas, this dish is also prepared with duck and called *itik Sioh* (or duck Sioh). I had my first taste of *ayam Sioh* in Malacca, at an open-air stall along the muddy Malacca River, the muggy and salty air adding to the ambience. We ordered Nonya fried rice and a tomato cucumber salad to go along with it.*

*Traditionally, there are a number of cooking steps to prepare *ayam sioh* that intensifies its flavor. Chicken is first marinated and then simmered in a tamarind-based sauce. Then the sauce is drained from the chicken and reduced, and the chicken is sautéed, pan-fried, or grilled. Before serving, the chicken is topped with the reduced sauce.*

DIRECTIONS:

1. Process Spice Paste ingredients to a smooth paste. Add the remaining ingredients except chicken and oil to Spice Paste and mix well.
2. Rub chicken with sauce and let marinate in refrigerator 1 to 3 hours or preferably overnight.
3. Drain chicken from sauce, reserving sauce.
4. Heat oil in a wok or skillet, add the sauce and sauté for about 4 to 5 minutes, till fragrant, then add chicken and stir for 2 to 3 minutes. Add ½ to ¾ cup water and stir to blend.
5. Cover and cook chicken for 5 to 8 minutes, stirring occasionally. Uncover and stir chicken till it is cooked and sauce thickens, about 10 minutes. (Alternately as in traditional method, after adding water, let chicken cook till nearly done, then take out and let sauce cook and thicken, about 5 to 8 minutes; meanwhile grill, broil, or sauté chicken till cooked.)
6. Top chicken with reduced sauce and garnish with coriander leaves before serving.

Serve with cooked white or brown rice, yellow rice (page 118) or tomato rice (page 119); and a spicy cucumber pineapple salad (page 98), green papaya salad (page 100), or braised spicy long beans (page 230). Or serve with tofu vegetable soup (page 85) and mixed vegetable *acar* (page 93).

Interior decor of Baba Nonya cafe, Malacca

Spicy Fried Chicken

Ayam Goreng Berempah

Makes 3 to 4 servings

Fried chicken is a favorite everywhere, and Malaysia is no exception. In Malaysia, fried chicken comes with flavor versions from the different ethnic groups. To add even more flavor, it is accompanied by spicy dips using chilies, soy sauce, lime juice, and/or Worcestershire sauce.

One day, my Eurasian neighbor and friend Betty invited me for lunch and prepared fried chicken with sweet spices, ground mustard, and soy sauce. Her dip had white wine, lemon juice, and soy sauce. It was mild tasting and delicious. Betty told me the recipe was handed down through her family, who were of Dutch and local ancestry.

Chinese season theirs with soy sauce, toasted sesame oil, and ginger. The Nonyas of Penang have their signature crispy fried chicken called inchee kaybin, *which is chicken marinated with coconut milk and spices and deep-fried. The Kristangs serve fried chicken with a dip prepared with Worcestershire sauce, ground mustard, pureed chilies (cili boh), and soy sauce. I have created a recipe that captures the* inchee kaybin *flavor and Betty's fried chicken. In this recipe, I use larger chicken pieces and they still retain the same delicious flavor. You can substitute with smaller pieces.*

INGREDIENTS

½ teaspoon sugar
½ teaspoon salt
1 pound chicken (thighs, breasts, and/or drumsticks), cut into 2-inch to 2½-inch pieces (if using drumsticks, leave as is)
Oil for deep-frying

Spice Paste

¼ cup sliced shallots or onions
1 teaspoon sliced fresh ginger
2 or 3 dried whole chilies, steeped in hot water for 5 to 8 minutes, slit and deseeded; or ½ to ¾ tablespoon *cili boh* (*see page 315*); or ¾ to 1 teaspoon bottled *sambal oelek*
¼ cup water

Spice Blend

1 tablespoon ground coriander
1 teaspoon ground cumin
1 teaspoon ground fennel seeds
1 teaspoon ground mustard
½ teaspoon finely ground black pepper
½ teaspoon turmeric powder
¼ teaspoon ground cinnamon
¼ teaspoon ground paprika

Dip

1 tablespoon Worcestershire sauce
½ teaspoon freshly squeezed or bottled lime juice
1 teaspoon regular soy sauce
½ teaspoon sugar, or 1 tablespoon honey
¼ to ½ teaspoon *cili boh*, or ¼ teaspoon bottled *sambal oelek*
¼ teaspoon salt

Garnish

1 fresh red or green chile, thinly sliced lengthwise
1 to 2 tablespoons coriander leaves (cilantro)

DIRECTONS:

1. Process Spice Paste ingredients to a smooth paste.
2. Combine Spice Blend ingredients and add to the Spice Paste along with the sugar and salt and mix well. Rub chicken with this marinade and refrigerate for 3 to 5 hours or preferably overnight.
3. Combine all the dip ingredients and mix well. Let sit for about 30 minutes before serving.
4. Heat oil in a wok or deep pot and deep-fry chicken pieces for about 10 to 15 minutes, turning them over till they become golden brown. Drain on paper towels.
5. Garnish chicken with chile slices and coriander leaves and serve with dip.

Serve with fried rice (page 123) or lime rice (page 122); and a green papaya salad (page 100) or mixed vegetable *acar* (page 93). It also goes great with plain cooked white or brown rice with vegetable dhal curry (page 231) or savory meat lentils (page 285). Or serve with cold beer and wine as an appetizer.

Grilled Spicy Chicken

Ayam Percik

Makes 5 to 6 servings

INGREDIENTS

2 to 3 tablespoons cooking oil
¼ cup unsweetened coconut milk
Optional: ¼ teaspoon dried shrimp paste (*belacan*), toasted at 400°F for 15 minutes (*see page 335*)
1 tablespoon tamarind concentrate or tamarind juice extracted from pulp (*see page 339*)
1 tablespoon thinly sliced or chopped palm sugar or dark brown sugar
½ teaspoon salt
1¼ pounds chicken (breasts, thighs, and/or drumsticks), cut into 2-inch pieces (if using drumsticks, use whole)
1 teaspoon turmeric powder
Optional: ¼ to ½ teaspoon chile powder

Spice Paste

½ cup sliced shallots or onions
2 heaping tablespoons sliced garlic cloves
1 teaspoon sliced fresh ginger or fresh or frozen and thawed galangal
3 to 5 dried whole chilies, steeped in hot water for 5 to 8 minutes, slit and deseeded; or ¾ to 1¼ tablespoons *cili boh*; or ⅓ tablespoon bottled *sambal oelek*; or ¼ to ½ teaspoon chile powder, depending on heat desired
2 lemongrass stalks, sliced into ¼-inch to ½-inch pieces
5 to 6 candlenuts (*kemiri*) or macadamia nuts
¼ cup unsweetened coconut milk

Ayam percik is a Malay-style grilled chicken, a delicacy from Kelantan, located on the northeast coast of Malaysia. It is sold by roadside vendors all along the East Coast. Chicken is marinated and cooked in a spicy, sweet, lemongrass, coconut milk, and palm-sugar sauce, and grilled over a charcoal fire. During Ramadan, ayam percik *is cooked in many Malay households, and sold by Malay vendors in Muslim neighborhoods.*

On a trip to the East Coast of Malaysia, we visited the huge colorful Khatijah Central Market (a wet market) in Kota Bahru. There we passed by many Malay women in front of makeshift stalls under large umbrellas, basting chicken pieces with a lemongrass brush. An intoxicating smoky aroma beckoned us, so we walked over and bought a few pieces of ayam percik *for lunch. It came with* lontong *(cubed compressed rice wrapped in banana leaves) and a spicy dipping sauce. We found a shady spot and sat down to enjoy this irresistible chicken.*

DIRECTIONS:

1. Process Spice Paste ingredients to a smooth paste.
2. Heat 1 tablespoon of oil in a wok or skillet and sauté the Spice Paste for about 4 to 6 minutes, till fragrant, adding remaining oil as needed. Add coconut milk, *belacan*, if using, tamarind juice, sugar, salt, and 1 cup water and bring to a boil. Lower heat and simmer till sauce reduces and becomes thick, about 5 to 6 minutes. Remove sauce from heat and allow to cool.
3. Rub chicken with turmeric, chile powder, if using, and half of the cooked sauce and refrigerate a minimum of 1 to 2 hours, or preferably overnight.
4. Grill chicken, basting with remaining half of sauce mixed with about ¼ cup oil at intervals till chicken is cooked. Or place chicken and the remaining half of sauce in a wok or skillet and cook on the stove-top, stirring till chicken is cooked and sauce is heated through (adding more water if necessary).

Serve with cooked white or brown rice, *lontong* or compressed rice (page 281), herb rice (page 125), or yellow rice (page 118) with eggplant and pineapple *pajeri* (page 232), vegetables in spicy coconut milk (page 223), spicy water spinach (page 228) or green mango salad (page 96). Or serve with cold beer or wine.

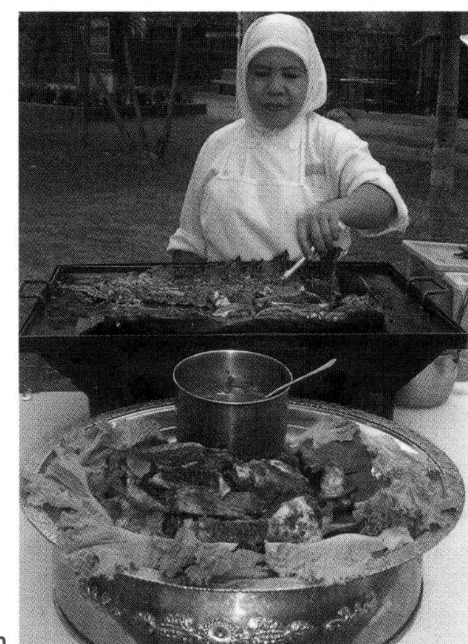

Malay vendor grilling chicken

Chicken Varuval

Ayam Varuval

Makes 8 to 10 servings

Varuval in Tamil means "dry fry," and this cooking technique is typical of South Indian and Sri Lankan Tamil immigrants. Chicken is stirred continuously in a small amount of seasoned oil till it is cooked and well-coated. The resulting chicken is intensely flavored with a delicious, rich aroma. Some cooks slow-simmer the chicken in water first and then stir the cooked chicken in the oil and spices (dry-fried). This gives a melt in your mouth "texture."

My maternal grandmother, Periama, was a Chettiar (from Tamil Nadu) and was adept at cooking chicken, seafood, meat, and vegetarian varuvals. *She was born a vegetarian and made great vegetable* varuvals *but slowly converted to eating fish when she married my grandfather and cooked chicken when we were growing up. Watching her make a chicken* varuval *was like watching an artist paint from a palette. She first fried the spices in hot oil, then added ginger and garlic, followed by onions, and when they turned light brown and translucent she added her spices, then chicken pieces, and stirred the pieces in the fragrant oil mixture. She stirred and cooked till the chicken was done, then she finally topped it with an aromatic finish—fresh curry leaves fried in oil! Ma added soy sauce to give a unique twist to the* varuval. *My whole family unanimously voted that I should have a chicken* varuval *dish in my cookbook, as a reminder of Periama and our Chettiar heritage.*

INGREDIENTS

- 2 pounds chicken (breasts, thighs, and/or drumsticks), cut into 1½-inch to 2-inch pieces
- ¼ teaspoon turmeric powder
- 1 teaspoon plus 1 to 1½ tablespoons regular soy sauce
- 2 to 3 tablespoons cooking oil
- 1½-inch cinnamon stick
- 1 star anise
- 1 teaspoon fennel seeds
- 2 to 4 dried whole red chilies
- 1½ tablespoons tomato paste, or 3 tablespoons tomato puree, or 4½ tablespoons tomato sauce
- ¾ teaspoon sugar
- ⅛ to ¼ teaspoon salt

SPICE PASTE

- 2 teaspoons sliced fresh ginger
- 1 heaping tablespoon sliced garlic cloves
- ½ cup sliced shallots or onions
- ¼ cup water

SPICE BLEND

- 2½ teaspoons ground coriander
- 1½ teaspoons ground cumin
- 1½ teaspoons ground fennel seeds
- 1 teaspoon finely ground black pepper
- ¼ teaspoon turmeric powder
- ¼ teaspoon ground cardamom
- ⅛ teaspoon ground cloves
- ⅛ teaspoon ground nutmeg
- ⅛ teaspoon ground mace

GARNISH

- 1 tablespoon cooking oil
- 5 or 6 fresh curry leaves

DIRECTIONS:

1. Rub chicken pieces with turmeric and 1 teaspoon soy sauce. Set aside.
2. Process Spice Paste ingredients to a coarse paste and set aside. Combine Spice Blend ingredients and set aside.
3. Heat 1 tablespoon of oil in a wok or skillet, add cinnamon stick, star anise, fennel seeds, and whole chilies, and stir for about ½ to 1 minute.
4. Add the Spice Paste and sauté for about 5 to 8 minutes till fragrant (adding more oil when needed). Add Spice Blend to sauce and sauté for about ½ minute. Add marinated chicken and stir for about 3 minutes, coating well with seasoned paste.
5. Add tomato paste, puree or sauce, 1 to 1½ tablespoons soy sauce, sugar, and salt and blend well. Cover and cook for about 4 to 5 minutes with occasional stirring. Uncover and continue to cook, stirring chicken continuously for about 10 to 15 minutes, till it is cooked and sauce becomes dry.
6. Remove cinnamon stick and star anise before serving. For the garnish, in a separate small skillet, heat 1 tablespoon oil and fry curry leaves for about ½ minute. Add this fragrant mixture to cooked chicken just before serving.

Serve with cooked white or brown rice, *sambar* rice (page 124), spiced rice (page 120), or yellow rice (page 118); and stir-fried okra or cabbage (page 226) or stir-fried bean sprouts (page 229).

Chicken Kurma

Ayam Kurma

Makes 7 to 8 servings

INGREDIENTS

3 to 4 tablespoons cooking oil, ghee, or butter
2-inch cinnamon stick
1 or 2 star anise
5 cardamom pods
2 cloves
½ cup sliced onions
Heaping ½ cup (3 ounces) diced tomatoes
2 pounds chicken (breast and/or drumsticks), cut into 1-inch pieces
Heaping 1¼ cups (7 ounces) peeled, quartered, or halved potatoes
½ cup unsweetened coconut milk
½ heaping cup (3 ounces) sliced carrots (1-inch to 2-inch pieces)
½ teaspoon salt
¼ to ½ teaspoon freshly squeezed or bottled lime juice

SPICE PASTE

½ cup sliced shallots or onions
¼ cup sliced garlic cloves
1 tablespoon sliced fresh ginger
2 to 5 fresh green chilies (jalapeno, Serrano, cayenne, or Thai), sliced
½ cup packed fresh mint leaves
½ cup packed coriander leaves (cilantro)
¼ cup slivered almonds or unsalted cashews
¼ cup water

SPICE BLEND

1 tablespoon ground cumin or cumin seeds
1 tablespoon ground or whole fennel seeds
1 teaspoon finely ground white pepper or white peppercorns
½ teaspoon ground coriander or coriander seeds

Chicken kurma *has origins in the creamy, rich Mughlai* korma *dishes of North India that were brought to Kerala in the south by Muslims. In Kerala, coconut milk was substituted for the cream or yogurt used in North India. When Indian Muslim immigrants from South India came to Malaysia, many intermarried with Malay women and new curries were created. Chicken* kurma *is one of them. It is generally served for festive occasions.*

I learned to make a delicious kurma *with Indian and Malay spicing from my sister-in-law Shanta. She fries the spices and spice paste in ghee (clarified butter), which gives her* kurma *a rich flavor. Whenever we visit her home, Shanta and her daughter Previna lay out a feast for us!*

DIRECTIONS:

1. Process Spice Paste ingredients to a smooth paste. Set aside. If using whole spices for the Spice Blend, dry roast them, allow to cool, and then finely grind. (If using ground spices, combine all ingredients.) Set aside.
2. Heat 1 tablespoon of oil or ghee in a wok or large skillet. Add cinnamon stick, star anise, cardamom, and cloves and fry for about ½ to 1 minute. Add onions and sauté for about 1 to 2 minutes.
3. Add the Spice Paste and 2 tablespoons oil or ghee and stir for about 4 minutes, till paste gets fragrant, adding more oil or ghee when needed. Add Spice Blend and sauté for about ½ minute, then add tomatoes and stir another 2 minutes.
4. Add chicken and stir for about 3 minutes and coat well with paste. Stir in ½ cup water and add potatoes and stir for 2 minutes.
5. Stir in coconut milk, cover, and cook for about 5 minutes. Uncover, add carrots and salt and cook, stirring occasionally, till chicken and potatoes are done, about 10 to 15 minutes. Stir in lime juice and cook for another minute.
6. Garnish with fried shallots or onions, mint or coriander leaves, and sliced chilies, if using.

Serve with cooked white or brown rice, yellow rice (page 118), or lime rice (page 122); and stir-fried mixed vegetables (page 224) or spicy curried pumpkin (page 225). Or serve as a dip for *roti canai*, *roti jala*, or other flatbreads with spicy sweet mixed vegetable *acar* (page 93).

GARNISH

¼ cup fried (*see page 333*) or sautéed shallots or onions
1 tablespoon chopped fresh mint or coriander leaves (cilantro)
Optional: 1 fresh red chile and 1 fresh green chile, slice in half lengthwise

Chicken Vindaloo

Ayam Vindaloo

Makes 3 to 4 servings

In the colonies of Goa and Malacca, the Portuguese developed a dish they called "vinha d'alhos" (meat with wine and garlic, referred to by Kristangs as "vinhu de arlu" or pickled garlic meat in wine). This dish, now commonly known as "vindaloo," has no wine or alcohol, only vinegar, chilies, and spices. Over time, some cooks interpreted the "aloo" in vindaloo as the Indian Urdu word "aloo" meaning potato and thus began adding potatoes to the original recipe. In Malaysia, vindaloo is a favorite with the Eurasian communities.

My first taste of vindaloo was during a vacation on the beach in Goa, India, and later in England when I went for further studies. In Malaysia, we grew up with a vindaloo that had a fiery, sour and slightly sweet flavor that is quite unlike the Indian vindaloo. *I started making this vindaloo for my heat-loving American husband. Bob first tasted vindaloo at a hotel café in Malacca, owned by Portuguese Eurasians, and ever since it's been a favorite with him. It takes influences from the Portuguese (tomato, vinegar, potatoes), Indians (spices), and Malays (lemongrass, galangal, chilies).*

INGREDIENTS

- 1 pound chicken (drumsticks, thighs, and/or breasts), cut into 1½-inch pieces
- 2 to 3 tablespoons cooking oil
- ¼ teaspoon dark brown mustard seeds
- ½-inch cinnamon stick
- 3 petals of star anise
- 1 cardamom pod
- 2 to 3 fresh curry leaves
- ½ cup water or chicken stock
- ¼ teaspoon salt
- ¾ teaspoon freshly squeezed or bottled lime juice

SPICE PASTE

- 1 teaspoon chopped fresh ginger
- 1½ teaspoons chopped garlic cloves
- ¼ cup sliced shallots or onions
- 2 to 3 dried whole red chilies, steeped in hot water for 5 to 8 minutes, drained (slit and deseeded if less heat is desired); or ½ to ¾ tablespoon *cili boh*; or ¼ to ½ tablespoon bottled *sambal oelek*
- ½ lemongrass stalk, sliced (about 2 heaping tablespoons)
- 1 candlenut, macadamia nut, or almond

MARINADE

- 3 to 3½ tablespoons distilled white vinegar
- 1½ to 2 teaspoons ground cumin
- 1½ to 2 teaspoons ground coriander
- ¾ teaspoon ground fennel seeds
- ¼ to ½ teaspoon turmeric powder
- ¼ teaspoon finely ground black pepper
- ¼ to 1 teaspoon ground paprika
- ⅛ teaspoon ground cinnamon
- Pinch ground cloves
- ¼ teaspoon ground mustard
- ¼ teaspoon chile powder

DIRECTIONS:

1. Process Spice Paste ingredients to a smooth paste.
2. Combine Marinade ingredients and ¼ of the Spice Paste. Rub chicken with this marinade and let sit for 30 minutes to 1 hour.
3. Heat 1 tablespoon oil in a wok or skillet, add mustard seeds and cover till they "pop." When popping subsides, add cinnamon stick, star anise, cardamom pod, and curry leaves and sauté for about ½ minute.
4. Add remaining Spice Paste and 1 to 2 tablespoons oil and stir for about 4 minutes, till fragrant.
5. Add marinated chicken and stir for about 5 minutes, coating well with sauce.
6. Stir in water or stock. Cover and cook for about 3 to 5 minutes, stirring occasionally. Uncover and cook, stirring constantly, till chicken is done, about 8 to 10 minutes.
7. Add salt and lime juice and stir for another 1 to 2 minutes. Remove cinnamon stick before serving.

Kristang chicken *vindaloo*

Serve with cooked white or brown rice, tomato rice (page 119), spiced rice (page 120), or yellow rice (page 118); and braised spicy long beans (page 230), stir-fried Chinese greens (page 227), or spicy cucumber tomato salad (page 97).

Black Peppercorn Chicken

Ayam Berlada Hitam

Makes 3 to 4 servings

INGREDIENTS

1 pound boneless chicken breasts, thinly sliced into 1½-inch to 2-inch-long strips, or mix of breasts and drumsticks, cut into 1-inch pieces
1 tablespoon cooking oil
1 teaspoon sliced and coarsely crushed garlic cloves
1 teaspoon sliced and coarsely crushed fresh ginger
½ cup sliced shallots or onions
1 fresh green or red chile (Fresno, jalapeno, Serrano, Thai, or cayenne), sliced
2 tablespoons unsweetened coconut milk or yogurt
¾ to 1 teaspoon tamarind concentrate or tamarind juice extracted from pulp (*see page 339*)
1 teaspoon regular soy sauce
¼ to ½ teaspoon salt
½ to 1 teaspoon freshly squeezed or bottled lime or lemon juice

SPICE BLEND

1 teaspoon ground coriander
1 teaspoon coarsely ground or cracked black peppercorns
½ teaspoon ground cumin
½ teaspoon ground fennel seeds
¼ teaspoon turmeric powder
¼ teaspoon salt

GARNISH

1 tablespoon chopped coriander leaves (cilantro)
1 fresh red chile, sliced in half lengthwise
Optional: 1 tablespoon coarsely chopped cashews or almonds

Malaysians have created a number of delicious dishes using black peppercorns, a spice that is indigenous to Sarawak. One of them is a black peppercorn chicken.

Ma created this recipe for Cha, who came as a little boy from Kerala, India, where peppercorns also abound. She created a simple, quick-to-prepare and delicious 'dry' pepper chicken with soy sauce and tamarind juice. You can substitute yogurt, low-fat yogurt, or lite coconut milk for the coconut milk, for those watching their cholesterol levels.

DIRECTIONS:

1. Combine Spice Blend ingredients and rub over chicken. Refrigerate for at least 1 hour and preferably 3 to 5 hours or overnight.
2. Heat oil in a wok or skillet and sauté garlic and ginger for about ½ to 1 minute. Add shallots or onions and sauté for 1 to 2 minutes. Add chile and sauté another ½ minute.
3. Add marinated chicken and stir for about 3 to 4 minutes. Add coconut milk, tamarind juice, soy sauce, and ½ cup water, if needed. Cover and cook for about 4 to 5 minutes, stirring occasionally. Uncover and cook another 5 to 10 minutes (depending on cut of chicken), stirring constantly, till chicken is done and sauce thickens to coat chicken.
4. Add salt, mix well for 1 minute, then add lime or lemon juice and blend well for another minute.
5. Garnish with coriander leaves, chile, and cashews or almonds, if using.

Serve with cooked white or brown rice, tomato rice (page 119), yellow rice (page 118), or vegetable *biryani* (page 280); and spicy dry curried okra (page 221), spicy curried pumpkin (page 225), stir-fried cabbage (page 226), or spicy cucumber tomato salad (page 97).

There are many versions of peppercorn chicken in Malaysia, depending on the ethnic group. The Chettinand Indians or Chettiars prepare it with poppyseeds, tomatoes, and curry leaves. The Keralites add vinegar and coconut milk, while the Chinese add black bean sauce and toasted sesame oil. Indian Muslims make a delicious peppercorn chicken with soy sauce and spices. Peppercorn chicken is generally eaten with cooked white rice or rich *biryanis* and seasoned vegetable *acars* (pickles).

Traditional Chicken Curry

Kari Ayam Tradisional

Makes 10 to 12 servings

Curries in Malaysia came from the South Indian and Sri Lankan immigrants. Curries vary greatly, depending on the application (chicken, fish, vegetables, or beef) and who is preparing it. Typically, a combination of dry and wet spices is used. The wet spice paste is generally a blend of galangal or ginger, shallots, garlic, chilies, and lemongrass.

I have created for you this "traditional" Malaysian chicken curry, a reflection of its multicultural heritage. It takes a bit from each ethnic culinary tradition: star anise, white pepper and other spices, cooked with coconut milk, chilies, tomatoes, soy sauce, and sugar. Many Malaysian restaurants overseas serve a similar flavored curry as an entree or as a dip for roti canai, *our national bread.*

INGREDIENTS

3 pounds chicken (breasts, thighs, and/or drumsticks), cut into 1½-inch pieces
3 to 4 tablespoons cooking oil
9 ounces (about 1¾ cups) peeled and halved or quartered potatoes
1 tablespoon tomato paste, or 2 tablespoons tomato puree, or 3 tablespoons tomato sauce, or 1 small tomato, chopped
1½ to 2¼ teaspoons regular soy sauce
1½ teaspoons sugar
Optional: 1 tablespoon poppy seeds
½ cup unsweetened coconut milk
¾ teaspoon salt

SPICE PASTE

1½ heaping tablespoons chopped or sliced garlic cloves
2 teaspoons sliced fresh ginger
1½ cups diced shallots or onions
¼ cup water

SPICE BLEND 1

6 fresh curry leaves
3 cloves
3 cardamom pods
2-inch to 3-inch cinnamon stick
2 star anise

SPICE BLEND 2

2 tablespoons ground cumin
1 tablespoon ground coriander
2 teaspoons ground fennel seeds
1 teaspoon turmeric powder
¾ to 1½ teaspoons chile powder (depending on heat desired)
½ teaspoon ground white pepper

DIRECTIONS:

1. Process Spice Paste ingredients to a smooth paste. Coat chicken pieces with ¼ cup of Spice Paste and allow to sit for about 30 minutes.
2. Combine Spice Blend 2 ingredients and set aside.
3. Heat 1 tablespoon of oil in a wok or skillet and fry Spice Blend 1 ingredients for about ½ minute.
4. Add 2 tablespoons of the oil and remaining ¾ cup Spice Paste and sauté for about 5 to 6 minutes till fragrant (adding more oil if necessary).
5. Add Spice Blend 2 and sauté for about ½ minute. Add marinated chicken and stir for about 3 minutes.
6. Add potatoes, tomato paste, soy sauce, sugar, and 1¾ cups water and bring to a boil. Lower heat, add poppy seeds, if using, and simmer, stirring occasionally, till chicken and potatoes are cooked and sauce thickens a bit, about 10 to 15 minutes.
7. Add coconut milk and cook for about 4 more minutes, then add salt and stir for about 2 minutes.

Serve with cooked white or brown rice or ghee rice (page 121); and spicy water spinach (page 228), mixed vegetable *acar* (page 93), or stir-fried Chinese greens (page 227). Or use as a dip for *roti canai*, *roti jala*, or other flatbreads. This curry can be served with almost any rice dish but goes best with cooked white or brown rice.

Every ethnic group in Malaysia has their traditional chicken curry that reflects their tastes, borrowing ingredients and flavors from each other. Malays and Nonyas usually add *belacan*, galangal, star anise, lemongrass, and coconut milk to make a spicy pungent curry. Chinese add soy sauce and sugar for a sweet curry, while Kristang curries are slightly tart with tamarind juice, vinegar, or lime juice. Then there are also regional variations, with Kelantanese curries being distinct from Penang, Negeri Sembilan, or Johor curries.

Spicy Egg Curry

Kari Telor

Makes 3 to 5 servings

INGREDIENTS

1 tablespoon cooking oil
¼ teaspoon black or dark brown mustard seeds
¼ teaspoon fenugreek seeds
2 teaspoons sliced and crushed garlic cloves
2 teaspoons thinly sliced fresh ginger
¼ cup sliced shallots or onions
1 fresh green chile (jalapeno, Serrano, Thai, or cayenne), sliced
½ cup (3 ounces) diced tomatoes
1½ cups (½ pound) potatoes, peeled or unpeeled, halved or quartered
½ teaspoon tomato paste, or 1 teaspoon tomato puree, or 1½ teaspoons tomato sauce
5 hard-boiled eggs, cooled, peeled, sliced in half
½ teaspoon salt

Spice Blend

1 teaspoon ground coriander
½ teaspoon ground cumin
¼ teaspoon ground fenugreek
¼ teaspoon turmeric powder
¼ teaspoon coarsely ground black peppercorns
¼ teaspoon ground fennel seeds
⅛ teaspoon ground cardamom
⅛ to ¼ teaspoon chile powder (depending on heat desired)

Garnish

1 to 2 tablespoons chopped coriander leaves (cilantro)

Eggs are popular meals for many, even on days when many don't eat meats and chicken for religious reasons, or simply when there is no meat, chicken, or fish at hand. Eggs are prepared into delicious curries and sambals *with potatoes, eggplant, or okra, and even with* sawi *(greens). Our family observed vegetarian day at least once a week on a Monday or Friday when Ma would visit the Hindu temple. Before she left, she would prepare a delicious egg curry (with hard-boiled eggs), stir-fried vegetables, and dhal curry. When our grandmother, Periama, made egg curry, she added fenugreek seeds,* ikan bilis *(baby anchovies), and sliced potatoes.*

My younger sister Rama, who resides in Macclesfield, England, remembers enjoying lunch time with Periama with steaming hot rice, spicy egg curry, and homemade pickled green mangoes. Rama got hooked on egg curry and learned to make it from Periama and Ma, and then later taught her younger son, Adam. He says his great-grandmother's recipe helped him through the dreary winter months of his college days, when he had to survive on little money but found warmth in the egg curry. Here is Rama's recipe with some slight modifications.

DIRECTIONS:

1. Combine Spice Blend ingredients and set aside.
2. Heat oil in a wok or skillet and add mustard seeds and fenugreek seeds, cover and cook till mustard seeds "pop." (Be careful not to burn fenugreek seeds, or you can add them after mustard seeds stop popping and stir for about ½ minute.)
3. When popping subsides, add garlic and ginger and sauté for about ½ to 1 minute. Add shallots or onions and sauté for about 1 to 2 minutes.
4. Add the Spice Blend and sauté for ½ minute. Add chile, sauté for ½ to 1 minute; add tomatoes and stir for about 2 minutes.
5. Add potatoes, tomato paste, puree, or sauce, and 1¼ to 1½ cups water and bring to a boil. Lower heat and cook for about 10 minutes, stirring occasionally, till potatoes are cooked. Add hard-boiled eggs and salt, and cook, stirring, for another 4 to 5 minutes, till sauce gets slightly thick and coats eggs well. Garnish with coriander leaves.

Serve with cooked white or brown rice or yellow rice (page 118); and stir-fried cabbage (page 226), stir-fried bean sprouts (page 229), or stir-fried mixed vegetables (page 224); and a vegetable dhal curry (page 231).

Spicy Pickled Fish (*Umai*), page 62

Spicy Sweet Pickled Mixed Vegetable Salad
(*Acar Rampai*), page 93

Assorted condiments (*sos, acars, and sambals*), pages 96-110

Malay-style Spiced Rice (*Nasi Kemuli*), page 120

Left: Cooked Sambal *Belacan* (*Sambal Tumis Belacan*), page 102

Below: Herb Rice (*Nasi Ulam*), page 125

Spicy Indian Muslim Stir-fried Noodles
(*Mee Goreng / Mamak Mee*), page 136

Curry Noodles (*Kari Mee*), page 149

Captain's Chicken Curry (*Kari Ayam Kapitan*), page 162

Stewed Beef, Eurasian-style (*Daging Semur*), page 180

Lamb or Mutton *Peratil* (*Kambing Peratil*), page 185

Fish Curry, Indian-style (*Kari Ikan ala India*), page 198

Stir-fried Sambal Shrimp *(Sambal Tumis Udang)*, page 204

Spicy Water Spinach (Kangkung Belacan), page 228

Pineapple Tarts (*Kueh Tat*), page 254, with cup of black coffee (*kopi-o*)

Sweet Glutinous Rice Balls (*Ondeh-Ondeh*), page 257

Malay fruit vendor along the East Coast near Kuantan

Garlanded trishaw for transport

Durians and mangosteens

Khatijah Central Market (*Pasar Besar Siti Khadijah*),
Kota Bharu, Kelantan state

CHAPTER 7

MEATS: FESTIVE FAVORITES

Lamb or mutton *peratil*

In years past, meats were a luxury for Malaysians and reserved primarily for festive occasions. However, Malaysia's economy has grown dramatically over the last twenty-five years, and most Malaysians enjoy meat (called *daging* in Malay) prepared in different ethnic styles. Malays prefer beef, Chinese and Nonyas enjoy mostly pork, and Indians like mutton or lamb. Religion plays a significant role in these preferences. Hindu Indians and Chittys don't eat beef (as the cow is sacred to them); Muslims don't eat pork as pork is *haram* (unlawful or forbidden); while Chinese, Nonyas, and Eurasians have no restrictions with regard to meats, although some Buddhists are pure vegetarians.

Under Muslim dietary laws, all meats and poultry must be *halal* (meaning "permitted") and slaughtered by a Muslim in the prescribed Islamic way. And because the large Muslim population requires this prescription, many Chinese, Indian, Nonya, and Eurasian restaurants use *halal* meats on their premises.

Malaysians enjoy thinly cut marinated meats that are well seasoned and prepared in many different ways—stir-fried, stewed, braised, pan-fried, barbecued, or curried.

BEEF

Beef, called daging lembu or simply referred to as *daging* in Malay, is a forbidden meat for Hindu Indians, Chittys, and some Buddhists, but enjoyed by other groups. Beef is frequently slow simmered or cooked for a long time, which makes the meat tender and moist. Thus *rendangs*, curries, and stews are popular methods of cooking beef. Beef is also stir-fried, pan-fried, braised, roasted, grilled, cooked with rice (as in *biryanis* prepared by Indian Muslims), made into soups, or added to noodle dishes.

Malays prepare aromatic rich beef dishes to celebrate weddings and other festivities. They savor all parts of the cow in soups (sup tulang or ox-tail soup) and stews. Beef cuts are made into spicy floss (*serunding*), curries, and *rendangs* which call for braising and slow cooking the beef in coconut milk spiked with chilies and spices. There are many types of *rendangs* but when Malaysians refer to *rendang*, they generally mean beef *rendang* (page 177). Additional Malay beef favorites include beef curry (*kari daging*), beef *satay*, *daging assam* (beef in spicy tamarind sauce), and *daging kerutuk* (dry beef curry, page 182). Historically, Indian Muslim cooks created flavorful beefsteaks (*bifstiks*) with sweet soy sauce, black pepper, chilies, and tomato ketchup in the kitchens of their colonial masters. Chinese enjoy their beef thinly cut and stir-fried with soy sauce, five spice blend, and *taucheo*. A special Eurasian dish for a Sunday meal or wedding is *daging semur* (page 180), a braised beef stew cooked with vinegar, spices, chilies, red wine, Worcestershire sauce, and potatoes. It is generally eaten with warm bread and fiery *sambal belacan*. Apart from the regular roast beef, pot roast, meatballs, or beef Wellington, there are some unique beef dishes enjoyed by Kristangs and other Eurasians, including *satay daging goreng* cooked with *belacan*, peanuts, and chilies (page 178); *feng*, a curry with beef, oxtail, and tongue (similar to the *sorpotel* from Goa); and thinly sliced steak seasoned with soy sauce, peppercorns, and Worcestershire sauce (page 181).

Ma never cooked beef at home and we also did not eat beef when we ate out. Cha dined out often with his British, Chinese, and Malay colleagues and ended up eating the "forbidden" meat, but never told Ma or us till much later. I guess he believed that religion (he was a Hindu) should not dictate his taste buds. He just enjoyed eating and tasting different foods and influenced us to try all kinds of foods, which I did later in life when food became my career. When I was in graduate school at Reading University, England, I lived in the dormitory and ate at the cafeteria, where roast beef, beef stew, and beef-filled pies were the norm. Then I worked in Latin America, where beef was one of the primary meats. Like my father, I decided to join the crowd and experiment with all meats, including the game meat *gibnut* (also called *paca* or *agouti*) that lives on plants near forested areas where I worked in Belize, Central America. During my years in the U.S., I occasionally ordered a beef dish when we went out to eat, but it always had to be thinly cut, well-seasoned, and well done, so Hispanic steaks became my favorites. It has been many years since I have eaten beef, so I had my husband and friends help me in tasting the recipes.

MUTTON — LAMB AND GOAT

Lamb and goat meat (called *daging kambing* in Malay) are collectively referred to as mutton. The English usually use the term lamb for meat from a less-than-year-old sheep and mutton for meat from a mature sheep more than 2 years old. Usually mutton has a stronger flavor, darker color, and less-tender flesh than lamb. In Malaysia, mutton is usually eaten and is popular with Indian immigrants, both Hindus and Muslims, who have created many different styles of mutton curries, biryanis, mutton soups (*sup kambing*), stews, and seasoned mutton or lamb chops.

Roast pork with noodles

In Malaysia, we grew up with goat meat, as goats were raised locally while lamb was imported. Indians who emigrated from South India brought their technique of making dry curries with meats. The result is the delicious and addictive goat meat curry called *kambing peratil* (page 185). It is mutton stirred in seasoned oil with tomatoes and a little water to produce a dry curry. I learned to make mutton peratil from Ma, who added star anise and tomato paste to my grandmother's recipe. Instead of ghee, Ma used vegetable oil as she found ghee too rich.

On one of my visits home, my youngest brother, Suresh, took us to a friend's lunch joint in Kuala Lumpur—a temporary makeshift stall set up in a canvas-roofed tent with aluminum sides. As I entered, I saw a ramshackle small space with long wooden benches and tables. Initially, I could not believe that executive office workers had business lunches at such a place, but Suresh promised me I would enjoy it. As the owner seated us, I asked where the kitchen was and he took me to the back, where I saw his wife and several other women scurrying around, cooking, cutting, or washing. His wife was preparing mutton *peratil* in a big pot and frying fish in a *kwali* set on a portable stove under the open sky. The place looked neat and clean.

I returned to the table and Suresh ordered a few dishes. The waiters placed clean banana leaves in front of each of us and scooped a mound of cooked white rice onto them. Next came plates and small containers of spicy fried fish (page 206), mutton *peratil* (page 185), vegetable dhal curry (page 231), spicy cucumber tomato salad (page 97), and crispy *pappadam* (lentil wafers). Suresh waited and closely watched my expression as I started to taste each item. Every dish had its own wonderful taste and I enjoyed every morsel! Forget my calories for the day. The mutton peratil had fiery roasted spice notes and a great depth of flavor. We ended with a cup of cool comforting *morru* (or *lassi*, Indian-style buttermilk) that helped us to digest our meal, especially the rich mutton *peratil*.

PORK

Pork, called *daging khinzir* or *babi* in Malay, is *haram* (forbidden) for Muslims in accordance with Islamic dietary laws. However, pork is enjoyed by Chinese, Nonyas, Kristangs, Eurasians, and other Christians.

Not all Indians enjoy pork, but those that do create spicy recipes with it. In our home, Ma cooked a delicious pork dish, chile pork (*cili khinzir*, page 186) that we all still remember, and yet one that Ma never savored. She sliced the pork and slowly stirred it with ground chile powder, ginger, and tamarind juice. I remember one afternoon I could not go home for lunch as I had French language homework and had to stay behind to finish it. I knew Ma was cooking chile pork for lunch and with a large family, unless you were at the table when lunch was served everything was gone before dinner. I was upset when I got home at 5 p.m., having missed out on one of my favorite meals. As I sat at the table to have my afternoon tea, Periama (my grandmother) beckoned me to the kitchen cupboard. She smiled as she opened it and took a bowl out for me. It was my share of Ma's chile pork! Was I happy! I had an early dinner before the others, eating chile pork with cooked white rice and Chinese vegetables. I savored every piece and relished my meal. Although Periama never ate pork, she sat next to me and enjoyed watching me eat.

In Malaysia, the Chinese are the biggest consumers of pork. Most soups, noodle dishes, and even vegetable dishes contain some bits of pork—whether the meat, belly, tongue, liver, gizzards, intestines, or the fat made into crispy lard croutons (like the Latin American *chicharrón*). Most Chinese vendors in those days also used lard as cooking oil, which contributed to the wonderful flavor of noodles and soups. Today, because of health concerns, many cooks have switched to using vegetable-based cooking oils. Some family favorites are *bakuteh* (page 87), a traditional Chinese spicy herbal soup prepared with pork ribs and accompanied by a fiery chile-based dip; pork with black and white peppercorns (page 187); a spicy Chinese-inspired chile pork (page 186); and spicy pork ribs (page 190).

The Nonyas, like the Chinese, enjoy pork cooked Chinese-style but on a spicier level with ginger, *taucheo*, and aromatic spices. Some popular ones are se bak (pork loin marinated overnight with herbs and spices and simmered over a slow fire); fried *assam* pork (pork marinated in tamarind juice, soy sauce, and palm sugar); *babi chin* (pork cooked with *taucheo*, black soy sauce, and coriander); and pork floss, which, unlike the Malay beef floss, is mild and sweet with cloves, star anise, peppercorns, and sugar.

Pork *pong teh* (stewed pork, page 188), a Nonya specialty from Malacca, is prepared with pork and potatoes and seasoned with *taucheo*, cinnamon, dark soy sauce, and sugar. On a visit to Malacca with my sister Vas and her daughter Prita, we had lunch at a pub-like café along the historic Malacca River. As the waiter set the dish down, it looked like a hearty Irish stew with chunks of pork and potatoes in a light brown sauce. It smelled savory and slightly sweet. I looked around for some chile sauce, but all I could see were ketchup bottles and Tabasco sauce on every table. Upon my request, the waiter happily brought me a *sambal belacan* dip, which put a smile on my lips. I spooned the pork with its sauce and let its subtle flavor blend in with the mound of rice.

While I enjoyed my meal, I gazed at the muddy water beneath the restaurant's balcony and took in the old colonial Portuguese and Dutch buildings around us. Across the river were fishing boats with weather-beaten Kristang fishermen pulling in their nets after a catch. For a moment, I began to daydream about when Malacca was a bustling trading port and the air was filled with the intoxicating scent of spices (the catalyst for this daydream, as I momentarily closed my eyes, must have been the spicy scents wafting up from my *pong teh*) and the bazaars were filled with busy traders, buying and selling the treasures of the East—spices, silks, and teas. Dreamily lost in the aromas, I was jolted back to my meal by a question from my sister Vas. Unlike the past, there was quietness in the air around us. Except for the diners chatting and the tourists in the streets, Malacca seemed to have become a somewhat sleepy monument to the past.

Beef Rendang

Rendang Daging

Makes 3 to 4 servings

Beef rendang (rendang daging) is *an intensely aromatic and rich, slow-simmered braised beef preparation. It came with the immigrants from Sumatra in Indonesia and has become a favorite with Malays, who like it fiery. Malays prepare it for weddings, birthdays, and Hari Raya Puasa, the festival that celebrates the end of their fasting period, Ramadan. Hindus don't eat beef, so they make* rendang *with chicken and shrimp.*

The flavor of rendang *varies depending on how much coconut milk and dried chilies are added. Once when my sister Rama and her boys, Daniel and Adam, visited us, my husband Bob, to impress us, spent half a day preparing his masterpiece* rendang. *It was delicious! But we had to gulp down tons of water as we were eating it as it was fiery hot! I decided to add this recipe as it is Bob's and a Malaysian favorite. In my recipe, I lessened the chilies and added a blend of spices, a flavor closer to the* rendang tok, *a specialty from the state of Perak. I braise the meat and cook it slowly in coconut milk till the sauce becomes slightly dry and thick, and the meat extremely tender and dark.*

INGREDIENTS

4 to 5 tablespoons cooking oil
1 pound beef chuck, rump, loin, or sirloin steak, cut into 1½-inch to 2-inch pieces
5 teaspoons tamarind concentrate or tamarind juice extracted from pulp (*see page 339*)
1 lemongrass stalk, bruised with back of knife and tied into a knot
1 Kaffir lime leaf with 2 lobes
¼ to ½ cup unsweetened coconut milk
2 teaspoons thinly sliced or chopped palm sugar or dark brown sugar
½ teaspoon salt
¼ cup toasted grated coconut (*kerisik*) (*see page 319*)

Spice Paste

1 tablespoon sliced garlic cloves
1 heaping tablespoon chopped fresh or frozen and thawed galangal or fresh ginger
¾ cup sliced shallots or onions
10 to 15 dried whole red chilies (*depending on heat desired*), steeped in hot water for 5 to 8 minutes, slit and deseeded; or 2½ to 3¾ tablespoons *cili boh* (*see page 315*); or 1¼ to 1¾ tablespoons bottled *sambal oelek*
½ cup unsweetened coconut milk

Spice Blend 1

2 cloves
2 cardamom pods
1¼-inch cinnamon stick
1 star anise (or 3 petals)

Spice Blend 2

1 teaspoon ground coriander
1 teaspoon ground cumin
1 teaspoon ground fennel seeds
½ teaspoon turmeric powder
¼ teaspoon finely ground black pepper

DIRECTIONS:

1. Process Spice Paste ingredients to a coarse paste. Combine Spice Blend 2 ingredients and set aside.
2. Heat 1 tablespoon of oil in a wok or skillet and fry Spice Blend 1 ingredients for about ½ minute. Add Spice Paste and another 2 tablespoons oil and cook, stirring, for about 4 to 5 minutes, till fragrant. Add Spice Blend 2 and remaining oil and sauté for another 2 minutes.
3. Add beef and stir for about 1 to 2 minutes, coating well with paste. Add tamarind juice, lemongrass, lime leaf, and coconut milk, and cook, stirring continuously, for 5 minutes.
4. Add sugar and salt and continue to cook, stirring constantly, for about 30 minutes, till beef becomes tender, sauce thickens, and oil starts seeping out. (Be sure to keep stirring to prevent sauce or beef from sticking to wok.)
5. Add toasted desiccated coconut, blend well and simmer, stirring continuously, for about 5 to 10 minutes, till beef gets darker and sauce becomes dry and coats the beef. Remove lemongrass, lime leaf, cinnamon stick, and star anise before serving.

Serve with cooked white or brown rice, yellow rice (page 118), coconut-infused rice (page 117), or compressed rice (page 281); and cucumber carrot *acar* (page 99), vegetables in spicy coconut milk (page 223), or eggplant and pineapple *pajeri* (page 232). For a festive occasion, serve with festive rice (page 278), spiced rice (page 120), or ghee rice (page 121).

Fried Beef Satay

Satay Daging Goreng

Makes 3 to 4 servings

INGREDIENTS

- 1 pound beef chuck, beef top, bottom round, beef rump, skirt steak, or sirloin tips, thinly sliced into about 1½-inch pieces
- ½ teaspoon finely chopped or pounded, fresh or frozen and thawed turmeric root, or ¼ teaspoon turmeric powder
- 2 teaspoons light brown sugar or white granulated sugar
- 2 to 4 tablespoons cooking oil
- 4 teaspoons ground cumin
- 4 teaspoons ground coriander
- ¾ cup coarsely ground peanuts or crunchy peanut butter
- 1 tablespoon tamarind concentrate or tamarind juice extracted from pulp (*see page 339*)
- ¼ cup coconut milk (*when using ground roasted peanuts*), or 2 tablespoons (*when using crunchy peanut butter*)
- ¼ to ½ teaspoon salt

SPICE PASTE

- 1½ heaping tablespoons sliced garlic cloves
- ½ cup sliced shallots or onions
- 1 lemongrass stalk, sliced into ½-inch pieces (about ¼ cup)
- 3 to 6 dried whole red chilies, steeped in hot water for 5 to 8 minutes, slit and deseeded; or ¾ to 1¼ tablespoons *cili boh* (*see page 315*); or ¾ to 1½ teaspoons bottled *sambal oelek*
- ¼ cup water

GARNISH

- ¼ cup shallot or red onion rings
- ¼ cup julienned cucumber, peel on
- A few lettuce leaves or greens

Satay goreng *is a stove-top version of grilled* satay. *Generally beef or chicken is used, but the Chinese from the East Malaysian state of Sabah also use pork.* Satay goreng *is also popular with the Malacca Kristang community, who add* belacan, candlenuts, *and curry powder to their recipe. They serve it for Sunday lunch or for family gatherings after church.*

Norizah Abidin, former deputy director at the Malaysian Tourism office in New York City and now posted at the Tourism office in Malaysia, says that it is a favorite dish with Malays from Sabah. Norizah, who hails from Sabah, learned to make her grandmother's satay goreng *from her mother, Rosnah. It originated with her great-grandmother, Dayang Aminah, who hailed from Brunei and was married to an Indian Muslim. This unique and wonderful recipe from Norizah reflects her multicultural heritage. In Norizah's family,* satay goreng *is prepared for festive occasions, including Hari Raya Puasa, weddings, and other* kenduris *(ceremonial gatherings).*

In this recipe I have reduced the sugar and added coriander and cumin to give a truly delicious sauce with coconut milk and crunchy peanut butter.

DIRECTIONS:

1. Toss beef with turmeric and sugar and marinate for about 1 to 3 hours or preferably overnight.
2. Process Spice Paste ingredients to a smooth paste.
3. Heat 1 tablespoon of oil in a wok or skillet and add Spice Paste, cumin, and coriander and saute for about 6 to 8 minutes, till fragrant, gradually adding remaining oil.
4. Add marinated beef, stir for about 1 to 2 minutes, then add peanuts or peanut butter, tamarind juice, coconut milk, salt, and ½ cup water, and blend well. Cook about 10 to 15 minutes, stirring continuously, till beef is cooked and oil separates out of sauce and sauce becomes somewhat thick and coats beef.
5. Garnish with shallot or onion rings and cucumber slices and serve on a bed of lettuce or greens.

Serve with cooked white or brown rice, compressed rice (page 281), yellow rice (page 118), or ghee rice (page 121); and stir-fried mixed vegetables (page 224), spicy water spinach (page 228), or braised spicy long beans (page 230).

Stir-Fried Beef Steak
Bifstik Goreng

Makes 3 to 4 servings

During my youth, Cha, my Father, like many Malaysians, socialized and enjoyed meals at pubs and office clubs. Their cooks were Chinese and Indian Muslims who took western foods such as steaks, chicken chops, or lamb chops and made flavorful local versions not found in England. Today, most of these colonial hangouts are gone, but you'll still find a few where expatriates and locals who have a touch of nostalgia for the Colonial era continue to go to reminisce about the "good old days."

On a few occasions, my father would take us for a meal to the renowned Coliseum Café in Kuala Lumpur (see pages 30-31). Today, when I walk into the Coliseum Café or an "old" pub for a meal, they remind me not only of the British era but especially of Cha. Here is a recipe for stir-fried beef steak which will take you "back" to the Coliseum Café era.

INGREDIENTS

1 pound beef (sirloin tips or skirt steak), thinly sliced into 1½-inch pieces
1 tablespoon toasted sesame oil
1 tablespoon sliced garlic cloves
3 dried whole red chilies, steeped in hot water for 5 to 8 minutes till they soften, either left whole or coarsely pounded
1 tablespoon preserved soybean paste (*taucheo*, black version) or black bean sauce or bean sauce
1 teaspoon regular soy sauce
1 teaspoon thick or sweet soy sauce
Optional: ⅛ to ¼ teaspoon salt
1 cup sliced shallots or onions (1-inch by 1½-inch pieces)
½ cup (2 ounces) sliced green bell peppers (1-inch by 2-inch pieces)
½ cup (2 ounces) sliced red bell peppers (1-inch by 2-inch pieces)

MARINADE

1 tablespoon ginger juice squeezed from 2 tablespoons sliced and coarsely crushed fresh ginger
1 teaspoon sugar
1 teaspoon regular soy sauce
¼ teaspoon rice wine
¼ teaspoon ground mustard
2 teaspoons corn, rice, or tapioca flour

SPICE BLEND

¼ teaspoon ground fennel seeds
¼ teaspoon chile powder
⅛ teaspoon ground star anise
⅛ teaspoon ground cinnamon
⅛ teaspoon ground cloves
⅛ teaspoon finely ground black pepper

DIRECTIONS:

1. Combine Marinade ingredients. Combine Spice Blend ingredients and add to Marinade and mix well. Rub marinade mixture on beef and let sit for at least 1 hour, preferably 2 to 3 hours or overnight in refrigerator.
2. Heat sesame oil in a wok or skillet, sauté garlic for about ½ to 1 minute. Add chilies and sauté for another ½ minute.
3. Add marinated beef and stir 3 minutes to brown on both sides, then add soybean paste, soy sauces, salt, if needed, and ¼ cup water and blend well. Stir till beef is cooked, about 5 to 8 minutes.
4. Add shallots or onions and bell peppers and stir-fry for another 2 to 3 minutes.

Serve with tomato and spice-infused potatoes (page 302), stir-fried broccoli rabe (page 301), or cooked white or brown rice; and vegetables in spicy coconut milk (page 223), green papaya salad (page 100), or stir-fried mixed vegetables (page 224).

Stewed Beef, Eurasian-Style

Daging Semur

Makes 3 to 4 servings

INGREDIENTS

1 pound boneless beef (chuck or top or bottom round), cut into 1½-inch pieces
2 teaspoons coarsely ground black peppercorns
2 tablespoons double black, thick, or sweet soy sauce (if using double black add ¼ teaspoon sugar)
1 tablespoon Worcestershire sauce
1 tablespoon cider vinegar or distilled white vinegar
2 to 3 tablespoons cooking oil
1 tablespoon chopped garlic cloves
2 teaspoons chopped fresh ginger
½ cup sliced shallots or onions (2-inch by ¼-inch pieces)
1 heaping cup (about 6 ounces) halved or quartered potatoes
½ cup (2½ ounces) sliced carrots (about 2-inch by ½-inch pieces)

Spice Blend 1

5 cloves
3 cardamom pods
2-inch cinnamon stick
1 star anise

Spice Blend 2

½ teaspoon ground paprika
¼ teaspoon chile powder, or 1 teaspoon *cili boh* (*see page 315*), or ½ teaspoon bottled *sambal oelek*
⅛ teaspoon ground nutmeg

Garnish

1 heaping tablespoon chopped coriander leaves (cilantro)

Daging semur is *a Dutch-inspired beef stew, popular in Malacca (now Melaka) and other Dutch colonies. Each place has its own version of the stew using local ingredients and flavorings. It has become a staple with all Eurasians in Malaysia, including the Portuguese Eurasians (Kristangs). Beef is stewed in sweet soy sauce and sweet spices, including star anise, cardamom, cinnamon, cloves, nutmeg, and black pepper. Pork can be substituted for beef. The Kristang community at the Portuguese settlement (*Kampung Portugis*) in Malacca, generally prepare this fragrant stew for their Christmas meal, using pork or beef, oxtail, and ox tongue. They flavor it with spices, red wine, vinegar, and Worcestershire sauce. Vegetables, including potatoes, carrots, yams, cabbage, and beans are also added, and it is thickened with crushed biscuits, crackers, or breadcrumbs.*

DIRECTIONS:

1. Mix beef with black pepper, soy sauce, Worcestershire sauce, and vinegar and marinate for at least a ½ hour, preferably 1 to 2 hours in the refrigerator.
2. Combine Spice Blend 2 ingredients and set aside.
3. Heat 1 tablespoon oil in a wok or skillet. Add Spice Blend 1 ingredients and fry for about ½ minute.
4. Add garlic and ginger and sauté for about ½ to 1 minute; add shallots or onions and sauté 1 to 2 minutes, adding another tablespoon of oil if needed. Add Spice Blend 2 and stir for about ½ minute.
5. Drain marinated beef (set any marinade aside) and add beef to skillet and cook for about 4 to 5 minutes, stirring occasionally and adding remaining oil if needed.
6. Add in the marinade juice, 2 cups water, and potatoes and bring to a boil. Lower heat and simmer for about 10 to 15 minutes till beef and potatoes are cooked; add carrots and cook another 3 to 5 minutes, till sauce thickens slightly and coats beef pieces.
7. Remove cinnamon stick and star anise before serving. Garnish with chopped coriander leaves.

Serve with cooked white or brown rice or crusty bread; and stir-fried mixed vegetables (page 224), spicy water spinach (page 228), or braised spicy long beans (page 230); and *sambal belacan* (page 101).

The Dutch call this dish *smoore* and serve it with cooked white rice or a loaf of crusty white bread and a spicy *sambal* or *acar* (pickled salad). Sometimes the beef is cooked pot roast-style and sliced at the table.

Peppercorn Soy Sauce Beef

Daging Kicap Berlada Hitam

Makes 3 to 4 servings

Indian Muslims (or Mamaks) enjoy beef cooked in many styles, incorporating Western, Chinese, and Indian flavors. Traditionally they worked as cooks at British homes and clubs, preparing foods the British enjoyed but flavoring them with local ingredients. Indian Muslim hawkers in Penang, Kuala Lumpur, Sarawak, and Sabah whip up delicious beef steak (bifstik) seasoned with thick soy sauce, black peppercorn, rice wine, chilies, and ketchup.

Daging kicap is also a favorite at many Western-style restaurants and pubs run by Chinese. There cooks add rice wine, soy sauce, sweet spices, Worcestershire sauce, and tomato ketchup to create aromatic steak pieces. Indian Muslim vendors also use mutton or lamb steaks for those who don't consume beef or pork. In Ipoh town, with a predominantly Chinese population, Mamak hawkers also create delicious steaks seasoned with Chinese and Indian spices and seared at high heat. My recipe incorporates both Mamak and Chinese flavors.

INGREDIENTS

2 tablespoons sliced and crushed garlic cloves
1 teaspoon sliced and crushed fresh ginger
1 pound beef (top or bottom round steak, sirloin tips, or skirt steak), sliced thin (2-inch by ¼-inch pieces)
2 tablespoons cooking oil
½ cup sliced shallots or onions (1-inch by 1-inch pieces)
1 tablespoon double black soy sauce (*or use thick or sweet if you want a slight sweetness*)
1 tablespoon tomato paste, or 2 tablespoons tomato puree, or 3 tablespoons tomato sauce
2 teaspoons Worcestershire sauce
Optional: ½ teaspoon granulated white sugar
¼ teaspoon salt
1 fresh red chile (Fresno, jalapeno, Serrano, Thai, or cayenne), sliced

MARINADE

1 tablespoon double black, thick, or sweet soy sauce
½ teaspoon coarsely ground black peppercorns
2 teaspoons rice wine
1 teaspoon tomato paste, or 2 teaspoons tomato puree, or 1 tablespoon tomato sauce
⅛ teaspoon chile powder
⅛ teaspoon turmeric powder

SPICE BLEND

2 cardamom pods
2 cloves
1-inch cinnamon stick
1 star anise

GARNISH

¼ cup sliced raw shallots or red onions, or fried (*see page 333*) or sautéed
1 tablespoon peas (fresh and cooked, or frozen and thawed)
1 small tomato, sliced or chopped

DIRECTIONS:

1. Combine Marinade ingredients, ¼ teaspoon of the crushed garlic, and ¼ teaspoon of the crushed ginger. Rub beef with marinade mixture and let sit for at least 1 hour, preferably 2 to 3 hours or overnight in refrigerator.
2. Heat 1 tablespoon of oil in a skillet or wok at high heat and sear marinated beef for 2 to 3 minutes on both sides. Remove from skillet and set aside.
3. Heat remaining 1 tablespoon oil in skillet. Add Spice Blend ingredients and fry for about ½ minute. Add the remaining garlic and ginger and sauté for ½ to 1 minute; add shallots or onions and sauté for another 1 to 2 minutes.
4. Add soy sauce, tomato paste, puree, or sauce, Worcestershire sauce, sugar, if using, and salt and stir for 2 to 3 minutes.
5. Add chile and seared beef to skillet and sauté while stirring till beef is cooked and sauce thickens and coats beef pieces, about 4 to 5 minutes.
6. Remove cinnamon stick and star anise before serving. Garnish with shallots or onions, peas, and tomato.

Serve with cooked white or brown rice, tomato and spice-infused potatoes (page 302), or crusty bread; and stir-fried mixed vegetables (page 224), stir-fried *kailan* (page 222), stir-fried Chinese greens (page 227), or stir-fried bean sprouts (page 229).

Dry Beef Curry, Malay-Style

Daging Kerutuk

Makes 3 to 4 servings

INGREDIENTS

1 pound beef (sirloin tips, beef chuck, top or bottom round, or skirt steak), cut into 1½-inch by ½-inch pieces or 1-inch cubes
2 to 3 tablespoons cooking oil
2 pandan leaves, tined with a fork and knotted
1 piece *asam gelugor* or *asam keping* (sometimes called tamarind skin), or ½ to ¾ tablespoon tamarind juice
2 salam leaves or bay leaves
¼ cup toasted grated coconut (*kerisik*) (*see page 319*)
¼ cup unsweetened coconut milk
1 to 2 teaspoons thinly sliced or chopped palm sugar or dark brown sugar
¾ teaspoon salt

SPICE BLEND 1

1 tablespoon ground coriander
1½ teaspoons ground cumin
1½ teaspoons ground fennel seeds
1 teaspoon finely ground black pepper

SPICE PASTE

1 cup sliced shallots or onions
1½ tablespoons sliced garlic cloves
2 teaspoons sliced fresh ginger or fresh or frozen and thawed galangal
1 lemongrass stalk, sliced (¼-inch to ½-inch pieces)
2 dried whole red chilies, steeped in hot water for 5 to 8 minutes and slit and deseeded, if desired; or ½ tablespoon *cili boh* (*see page 315*); or ¼ tablespoon bottled *sambal oelek*

(continued on next page)

Daging kerutuk *is a traditional Malay-style dry spiced beef curry from the eastern state of Kelantan, served with cooked white rice,* nasi dagang *(red bran rice), or* nasi minyak *(ghee rice). It is also found in Terengganu where it is served with* lontong *(compressed glutinous rice) or* lemang *(glutinous rice flavored with coconut milk). It is prepared with coconut milk, dried chilies, cumin, star anise, cloves cinnamon,* belacan*, lemongrass, palm sugar, and* asam gelugor.

I had tasted chicken kerutuk *only a couple of times, once on the East Coast of Malaysia, but its flavor lingered with me all these years. One afternoon when we stayed at a beach along the East Coast near Kuantan, we walked to a local Malay food stall and ordered* ayam *(chicken)* kerutuk *and* daging *(beef)* kerutuk. *The vendor served it with cooked white rice, a cucumber and pineapple* acar, *and* sayur lodeh. *It was fiery and delicious, and had a wonderful depth of flavor. Here is a recipe I created for* daging kerutuk *that has a similar flavor to the Malay vendor's. If you prefer, you can use chicken in this recipe.*

DIRECTIONS:

1. Combine Spice Blend 1 ingredients. Rub on beef and let marinate for a minimum of 30 minutes and up to 2 hours.
2. Process Spice Paste ingredients to a smooth paste. Set aside.
3. Heat 1 tablespoon oil in a wok or skillet and sauté Spice Blend 2 ingredients for about ½ minute.
4. Add Spice Paste and remaining oil and sauté for about 5 minutes, till fragrant. Add pandan leaves and sauté for another ½ minute.
5. Stir in marinated beef and sauté for about 1 to 2 minutes. Add *asam gelugor* or tamarind juice, salam or bay leaves, and *kerisik* and sauté for about 2 to 3 minutes.
6. Add coconut milk, sugar, salt, and ½ cup water, and cook, stirring constantly, for about 6 to 10 minutes, till beef is cooked and sauce thickens.
7. Remove pandan leaves, *asam gelugor*, cinnamon stick, and star anise before serving. Garnish with chopped coriander leaves.

Serve with cooked white or brown rice, ghee rice (page 121), red rice in coconut milk (page 128), or festive rice (page 278); and mixed vegetable *acar* (page 93), cucumber pineapple *acar* (page 98), spicy water spinach (page 228), or vegetables in spicy coconut milk (page 223).

½ teaspoon dried shrimp paste (*belacan*), toasted at 400°F for 15 minutes (*see page 335*)
¼ cup water

SPICE BLEND 2

2 cardamom pods
2 cloves
1-inch to 1½-inch cinnamon stick
1 star anise

GARNISH

1 heaping tablespoon chopped coriander leaves (cilantro)

Malay rural home (*rumah kampung*)

Lamb in Black Pepper Sauce

Kambing Berlada Hitam

Makes 2 to 3 servings

INGREDIENTS

6 baby lamb chops, or 1 pound boneless lamb steak, thinly sliced into 3 to 4-inch pieces ¼-inch thick
2 to 3 tablespoons cooking oil
2 to 3 teaspoons coarsely ground black peppercorns
1½ tablespoons chopped garlic cloves
½ cup chopped shallots or onions
1½ tablespoons preserved soybean paste (*taucheo*, black version) or black bean sauce or bean sauce
1 teaspoon sugar (*use only ¾ teaspoon if using thick or sweet soy sauce*)

MARINADE

1 tablespoon double black, thick, or sweet soy sauce
1 teaspoon rice vinegar, cider vinegar, or distilled white vinegar
1 teaspoon all-purpose or rice flour

SPICE BLEND

4 cardamom pods
3 cloves
1-inch cinnamon stick

GARNISH

3 stalks spring onions or scallions, cut into 1-inch pieces crosswise
Optional: ¼ cup petite peas (fresh and cooked, or frozen and thawed)
Optional: ¼ cup fried (*see page 333*) or sautéed shallots or onions

For Malaysians, 'chops' of lamb, chicken, pork, or steak are European-style dishes also favored by many Indians and Chinese who frequent clubs and pubs. They are generally battered and cooked with black pepper, onions, and garlic, and served with a dollop of ketchup. Sometimes they are flavored with soy sauce, preserved soybean paste, and sweet spices.

My father sometimes used to take us to his office clubs in the different towns that we lived in. As we entered many of these clubs, I immediately felt I was in a bygone era—with rattan furniture, ceiling fans, and aged waiters in white uniforms. The air in the bar section would be filled with smoke and the smell of alcohol. Women were not allowed at the bars in clubs (and even today are forbidden in most of them). Women may drink, but at the seated section where food is being served. I generally ordered the lamb chops, as it was my favorite. My Father and most of my brothers and sisters enjoyed the chicken chop, while Ma usually opted for some battered fish. All the foods were mild tasting, as they were cooked for Europeans living and serving in Malaysia since World War II.

This recipe for lamb chops with peppercorns, soy sauce, and taucheo *will take you to that bygone era. You can also make it with pork chops or chicken chops, or even boneless, thinly cut steaks.*

DIRECTIONS:

1. Combine Marinade ingredients and coat lamb. Allow to marinate for about 30 minutes.
2. Heat 1 tablespoon oil in a skillet and using high heat, pan-sear lamb on both sides about 6 minutes, till brown on both sides. Remove lamb from skillet and set aside.
3. Heat another tablespoon of oil in the skillet and add Spice Blend ingredients and sauté for about ½ minute, then add black peppercorns and stir for another ½ minute.
4. Add garlic and sauté for about ½ to 1 minute, and then add shallots or onions and sauté for another 1 to 2 minutes, adding more oil if necessary.
5. Add soybean paste, sugar, and ½ cup water, and stir for about 3 minutes.
6. Add seared lamb to sauce, cover and cook for 2 minutes, then uncover and stir for another 4 minutes, turning the chops over till lamb is cooked and sauce thickens and coats the lamb.
7. Remove cinnamon stick before serving. Garnish with spring onions, peas, and fried onions, if using.

Serve with tomato and spice-infused potatoes (page 302), curried spaghetti (page 307), fried rice (page 123), or cooked white or brown rice; and stir-fried bean sprouts (page 229) or stir-fried *kailan* (page 222); and spicy cucumber tomato salad (page 97) or a green salad.

Lamb or Mutton Peratil

Kambing Peratil

Makes 3 to 4 servings

Lamb or mutton peratil *is a dry fragrant curry that has become an addiction with our family. It has also become popular with our American friends. Ma used to make a terrific* mutton peratil *to serve for our dinner and special celebrations such as Deepavali. Whenever I visited Malaysia, it was the first dish I wanted to savor, and if Ma was busy, I ordered take-out from a local Indian restaurant. The cooks there usually prepared* peratil *in ghee, and finished off the flavor by sprinkling it with aromatic spices (garam masala) fried in ghee. Some cooks season the lamb lightly and cook in water till water is reduced and lamb becomes tender, then they stir the lamb continuously in seasoned oil till it coats the lamb and a fragrant aroma develops.*

In the U.S., my younger brother Sree always asks me to cook lamb peratil *for our yearly Deepavali party. He takes the leftovers 'to go'* (tau pau)*, and enjoys them for the next few days. Over the years I have fiddled with and improved my recipe, and here is the result! I use less oil and no ghee. I add the lamb pieces to the seasoned oil, tomatoes, and onions, and keep stirring till the lamb becomes fragrant and dry.*

INGREDIENTS

2 to 3 tablespoons cooking oil
1 tablespoon chopped or coarsely crushed garlic cloves
1 heaping teaspoon chopped or coarsely crushed fresh ginger
½ cup sliced or chopped shallots or onions
2 dried whole red chilies
1 fresh green chile (jalapeno, Serrano, Thai, or cayenne), sliced
1 pound lamb or mutton, cut into 1 to 1½-inch by ¼-inch to ½-inch pieces
¼ cup (1½ ounces) sliced tomatoes
½ teaspoon freshly squeezed or bottled lime or lemon juice
½ teaspoon salt
Optional: 4 or 5 fresh curry leaves

Spice Blend 1

4 or 5 fresh curry leaves
2 cardamom pods
2 cloves
1 star anise
1-inch cinnamon stick
¼ teaspoon coriander seeds
¼ teaspoon cumin seeds
¼ teaspoon fennel seeds
⅛ teaspoon black or dark brown mustard seeds

Spice Blend 2

1½ teaspoons ground coriander
1½ teaspoons ground cumin
1½ teaspoons ground fennel seeds
½ teaspoon ground cardamom
¼ teaspoon turmeric powder
⅛ to ½ teaspoon chile powder (*depending on heat desired*)

DIRECTIONS:

1. Combine Spice Blend 1 ingredients and set aside. Combine Spice Blend 2 ingredients and set aside.
2. Heat 1 tablespoon of oil in a wok or skillet, add Spice Blend 1, cover, and fry for about ½ minute, till mustard seeds pop.
3. When seeds stop popping, add garlic and ginger and sauté for about ½ to 1 minute; then add shallots or onions and red and green chilies and sauté another 1 to 2 minutes.
4. Add Spice Blend 2 and remaining oil and stir for about ½ minute.
5. Add lamb or mutton and stir for about 1 minute, coating well with spice paste. Add tomatoes, cover and let cook for about 4 to 5 minutes. Uncover and cook, stirring constantly, till lamb is done and sauce gets dry and aromatic, about 15 to 20 minutes.
6. If using curry leaves, in a separate skillet, add 1 tablespoon oil and when oil is hot, add curry leaves and fry till crispy, about ½ minute. Remove from heat.
7. Add lime or lemon juice and salt to the lamb mixture and stir another 1 minute. Add the curry leaves in oil and stir another 1 minute.
8. Remove cinnamon stick and star anise before serving.

Serve with cooked white rice or yellow rice (page 118); and mixed vegetable *acar* (page 93), stir-fried okra, or stir-fried cabbage (page 226). For festive occasions, serve with vegetable *biryani* (page 280), festive rice (page 278), or spiced rice (page 120).

CHILE PORK
Cili Khinzir (Babi)

Makes 3 to 4 servings

INGREDIENTS

1 pound pork, thinly sliced into 1½-inch by ½-inch pieces
Juice squeezed from 1½ tablespoons crushed fresh ginger
½ teaspoon rice wine
1 teaspoon regular soy sauce
1 fresh red chile (Fresno or cherry), deseeded and sliced, or ¼ cup sliced red bell pepper
10 to 20 dried whole red chilies (*depending on heat desired*), steeped in hot water for 5 to 8 minutes, drained, slit and deseeded, and processed with ¼ cup water to a smooth paste; or 2½ tablespoons to ⅓ cup *cili boh* (*see page 315*); or 1¼ to 2½ tablespoons bottled *sambal oelek*
2 to 3 tablespoons cooking oil
2 teaspoons sliced or coarsely crushed garlic cloves
¾ teaspoon double black, thick, or sweet soy sauce
½ teaspoon sugar (*use less if using thick or sweet soy sauce*)
½ teaspoon tamarind concentrate or tamarind juice (*see page 339*)
¼ teaspoon salt
¼ cup chopped spring onions (scallions) or Chinese chives (*kuchai*)

Ma did not eat pork, but she created this mouth-watering chile-and-soy-sauce-based pork preparation called cili (chilly or chilli) pork that we all savored. She also flavored it with rice wine and ginger juice which tenderized the pork.

I remember at the meal table, we used to fight for a larger share of cili pork. So to be fair, Ma would place our share right on our plates before we sat down to eat. My siblings and I unanimously voted for this dish to be in the cookbook, a strong reminder of Ma and our meals together. This was truly a challenge for me, to re-create Ma's recipe. And the end result will take us down memory lane and surely put a smile on all our lips!

DIRECTIONS:

1. Mix pork with ginger juice, rice wine, and soy sauce and marinate for 15 to 20 minutes.
2. Process fresh chile or bell pepper, dried chilies, and ¼ cup water to a smooth paste. Heat 1 tablespoon of oil in a wok or skillet and sauté garlic for about ½ to 1 minute. Add chile paste, *cili boh,* or *sambal oelek* and remaining oil and sauté for 8 to 10 minutes. Add double black, thick, or sweet soy sauce and stir for 1 minute.
3. Add marinated pork and stir for about 1 to 2 minutes, then add sugar, tamarind juice, and salt, cover and let cook for about 5 minutes. Uncover and stir for another 5 to 6 minutes, till pork is done and sauce becomes thick and coats the pork.
4. Add spring onions or chives and stir for 1 minute.

Serve with cooked white or brown rice, yellow rice (page 118), or vegetable *biryani* (page 280); and stir-fried cabbage (page 226), stir-fried Chinese greens (page 227), or stir-fried bean sprouts (page 229).

Mixed Peppercorn Pork

Khinzir (Babi) Berlada Hitam Putih

Makes 3 to 4 servings

Since peppercorns abound in Sarawak (East Malaysia) many dishes are cooked with peppercorns, both black and white. During one of my trips to Malaysia, we visited Sarawak to take in its culture, food, and beach. One morning, we went to the amazing colorful Sunday market at Kuching filled with all kinds of local vegetables, poultry, and fruits brought into town by indigenous farmers.

While in town, we enjoyed a lunch of Chinese-style peppercorn pork that reminded me of a dish my Ma used to make, inspired by a radio cooking show. I vividly remember Ma listening attentively to the radio cooking programs (TV was not available then) and taking down notes. Even during her last few years, when she was in a wheelchair and less active in the kitchen, she would watch the cooking shows on TV with a passion. Here is Ma's inspirational recipe for peppercorn pork using a blend of black and white pepper.

INGREDIENTS

- 1 pound pork, thinly sliced into 2-inch by ½-inch pieces
- 1 tablespoon cooking oil
- 1 heaping tablespoon sliced garlic cloves
- 2 teaspoons sliced fresh ginger
- ½ cup sliced shallots or onions
- ¼ teaspoon coarsely ground white peppercorns
- ¾ teaspoon coarsely ground black peppercorns
- 2 teaspoons regular soy sauce
- 1 teaspoon double black, thick, or sweet soy sauce
- ¼ teaspoon toasted sesame oil
- ⅛ teaspoon salt

MARINADE

- ½ teaspoon rice wine
- ½ teaspoon regular soy sauce
- ½ teaspoon cornstarch, rice starch, or tapioca starch
- ¼ teaspoon coarsely pounded or crushed black peppercorns
- ¼ teaspoon coarsely pounded or crushed white peppercorns

GARNISH

- 1 stalk spring onions or Chinese chives (*kuchai*), chopped
- Optional: ¼ cup sliced shallots or red onions, sautéed for 2 to 3 minutes

DIRECTIONS:

1. Combine Marinade ingredients and rub on pork. Let sit for about 30 minutes.
2. Heat oil in a wok or skillet. Add garlic and ginger and sauté for about ½ to 1 minute. Add shallots or onions and sauté for another 1 to 2 minutes. Add peppercorns and stir for about ½ minute.
3. Stir in marinated pork and sauté for about 2 minutes to brown the pork.
4. Add soy sauces and cook, stirring constantly, till pork is done and sauce becomes thick and coats pork, about 8 minutes.
5. Add sesame oil and salt and stir for another 1 minute.
6. Garnish with spring onions or Chinese chives and, if using, sautéed shallots or onions.

Serve with cooked white or brown rice, yellow rice (page 118), or tomato rice (page 119); and green mango *acar* (page 96), stir-fried *kailan* (page 222), spicy water spinach (page 228), or stir-fried Chinese greens (page 227).

The dishes from Sabah and Sarawak are simple and not as heavily spiced as in Western Malaysia. Because of the Chinese and Malay influences, the primary ingredients in Sarawak cooking are soy sauce, sesame oil, spring onions, galangal, cumin, coriander, lemongrass, coconut milk, and chilies.

Pork Pong Teh

Khinzir (Babi) Pong Teh

Makes 3 to 4 servings

INGREDIENTS

- 1 pound pork loin or boneless chops, cut into 1 to 1½-inch pieces
- 1 teaspoon regular soy sauce
- ⅛ to ¼ teaspoon finely ground black pepper
- 2 tablespoons cooking oil
- 1-inch cinnamon stick
- 1½ tablespoons sliced garlic cloves
- ¾ cup diced shallots or onions
- 1 to 1½ tablespoons preserved soybean paste (*taucheo*, black version) or black bean sauce or bean sauce
- 1 tablespoon double black, thick, or sweet soy sauce
- ¼ teaspoon white granulated sugar (*omit if using thick or sweet soy sauce*)
- 1 fresh red chile (Fresno, jalapeno, cherry, Serrano, Thai, or cayenne), sliced
- 1 heaping cup (6 ounces) peeled, sliced or quartered yams, sweet potatoes, or potatoes (1-inch pieces)
- ¼ to ½ cup fresh shiitake mushrooms; or dried shiitake mushrooms, soaked in hot water for 8 to 10 minutes till tender, drained and moisture squeezed out

GARNISH

- 1 tablespoon chopped coriander leaves (cilantro)

During my regular visits home, I make it a point to go to Malacca (now called Melaka) to take in its historic walkways, buildings, and antique Chinese Peranankan cafes, and it's cuisine. Malacca was once a bustling spice bazaar with merchants and traders coming here from all over the world.

I learned to make pork pong teh *from a culinary instructor in Malacca of Nonya background many moons ago when my brother Sathee accompanied me to Malacca. I cooked* pong teh *in a clay pot that the instructor said enhanced the dish's slightly sweet pungent notes. My recipe takes the flavors from the cooking class as well as captures the ambience of the* pork pong teh *I had in a café overlooking the winding Malacca River.*

DIRECTIONS:

1. Rub pork with regular soy sauce and black pepper and marinate for 30 minutes.
2. Heat 1 tablespoon of oil in a wok or skillet and fry cinnamon stick for ½ minute, then add garlic and sauté for ½ to 1 minute, then add shallots or onions and sauté for another 1 to 2 minutes.
3. Stir in marinated pork and remaining oil and sauté for about 2 minutes to brown.
4. Add soybean paste, double black, thick, or sweet soy sauce, sugar, if using, and chile and sauté for about 2 minutes. Add 1 cup water and potatoes and cook, stirring occasionally, till pork and potatoes are done, about 15 minutes, adding an additional ¼ cup water if necessary.
5. Add shiitake mushrooms and cook till sauce thickens, about 2 to 3 minutes.
6. Remove cinnamon stick before serving. Garnish with coriander leaves.

Serve with cooked white or brown rice, stir-fried *kailan* (page 222), stir-fried mixed vegetables (page 224), stir-fried bean sprouts (page 229), cucumber carrot *acar* (page 99), or eggplant and pineapple *pajeri* (page 232).

During one of our visits to Malacca, we took the riverboat ride up the meandering muddy river that passes along the back of the shops and houses, with chicken coops, women washing their utensils, and weather-beaten fishermen hauling in their nets after the day's catch. After the ride, we walked in the historic district and found a simple café overlooking the river. It appeared to be a meeting place for artists, writers, and Western tourists looking for a bit of colonial nostalgia. The menu offered both Western and local Nonya dishes. My sister Vas and niece Prita ordered spaghetti and pizza, a change from their local fare, although the spaghetti sauce had some Malaysian flavors. However, I wanted a local specialty and ordered pork *pong teh*. It was delicious!

Malacca River

Spicy Pork Ribs

Tulang Rusuk Khinzir (Babi) Berempah

Makes 3 to 4 servings

INGREDIENTS

1 pound pork ribs, excess fat trimmed off
2 tablespoons cooking oil
1½ teaspoon double black, thick, or sweet soy sauce (*if using double black add ¼ teaspoon sugar*)
½ teaspoon regular soy sauce
½ to ¾ teaspoon thinly sliced or chopped palm sugar or dark brown sugar
¼ teaspoon salt
½ teaspoon toasted sesame oil

SPICE BLEND

½ teaspoon ground coriander
½ teaspoon ground cumin
½ teaspoon ground fennel seeds
¼ teaspoon finely ground black pepper
¼ teaspoon ground star anise
⅛ teaspoon turmeric powder
Optional: ⅛ teaspoon ground cinnamon
Pinch of ground cloves

MARINADE

1 teaspoon rice wine
½ teaspoon regular soy sauce
½ teaspoon double black, thick, or sweet soy sauce (*if using double black add ¼ teaspoon sugar*)

SPICE PASTE

1 tablespoon sliced garlic cloves
2 teaspoons sliced fresh ginger or fresh or frozen and thawed galangal
¾ cup chopped shallots or onions
4 to 5 dried whole red chilies, steeped in hot water for 5 to 8 minutes, slit and deseeded; or 1 to 1¼ tablespoons *cili boh (see page 315)*; or ½ to ¾ tablespoon bottled *sambal oelek*
¼ cup water

Chinese enjoy pork ribs prepared with ginger, soy sauce, and sweet spices. Nonyas go a step further, adding cumin, coriander, turmeric, chilies, and coconut milk. Our family's favorite ribs are a spicy version prepared by my younger sister Rama whose home is in Macclesfield, England.

Whenever we visit her home, her spicy pork ribs are a must for us as it is a favorite with her sons, Daniel and Adam. She serves them with steaming cooked white rice and a stir-fried cabbage or a green salad. I have slightly modified her recipe adding rice wine, sweet soy sauce, and additional spices. You can enjoy this recipe with beef ribs as well.

DIRECTIONS:

1. Combine Spice Blend ingredients and set aside. Combine Marinade ingredients. Mix marinade and Spice Blend and rub on pork ribs. Allow to marinate for at least 1 hour and preferably 3 to 5 hours or overnight in refrigerator.
2. Process Spice Paste ingredients to a coarse paste.
3. Heat oil in a wok or skillet and sauté Spice Paste for 4 to 5 minutes, till fragrant.
4. Add marinated ribs and stir to coat well with sauce. Add soy sauces and stir for 2 minutes.
5. Add ½ to ¾ cup water and sugar, and cook for about 20 minutes, stirring occasionally, till ribs are cooked and sauce coats ribs. Add salt and sesame oil and cook another 1 to 2 minutes.
6. Garnish with spring onions or Chinese chives.

Serve with cooked white or brown rice, fried rice (page 123), or coconut-infused rice (page 117); and cucumber pineapple *acar* (page 98), stir-fried broccoli rabe (page 301), or spicy cucumber tomato salad (page 97).

GARNISH

2 stalks spring onion or Chinese chives (*kuchai*), sliced into 1 to 1½-inch pieces (about ½ cup)

CHAPTER **8**

SEAFOOD: THE BOUNTIFUL CATCH

Ikan bilis (dried baby anchovies)

Malaysia is surrounded by water, so seafood is abundant. It is caught fresh off the coasts, from rivers, and even from rice fields. Fish is *halal* (permitted) under Islamic law and is a staple in the daily diet for Malays, especially in rural areas, and is served with cooked white rice, vegetables, and fiery *belacan*-based condiments. Seafood dishes are also popular with the Chinese and served at many seafood restaurants (called *makanan laut*). Most Malaysians eat fish daily because it is less expensive than meat and more readily available.

The Gente Kristang or Kristang community in Malacca (of Portuguese descent) are also fishermen by trade. They love seafood, whether baked, grilled, curried, cooked with *sambals*, or added to soups and stews. Chinese Peranakans (Nonyas and Babas) of Chinese and Malay heritage also enjoy seafood dishes cooked in tamarind juice, coconut milk, chilies, and/or *belacan*, or stuffed with spicy paste and grilled or fried. Indians make fragrant seafood curries that are well-seasoned with an array of spices, chilies, tomatoes, coconut milk, and/or tamarind juice.

TYPES OF SEAFOOD

Malaysians prefer flavor-rich oily fish, including mackerel, tuna, sardines, and anchovies. There are a great variety of marine and freshwater fish (called *ikan* in Malay). They include *ikan bawal* (pomfret), *ikan tenggiri* (Spanish mackerel), *ikan kembong* (chubb or Indian mackerel, the common mackerel), tuna, *ikan merah* (red snapper), *ikan parang* (wolf herring), *ikan kerapu* (grouper), *ikan kurau* (threadfin), *ikan siakap* (sea bass), tilapia, *ikan pari* (stingray), catfish, bream, shad, and sea

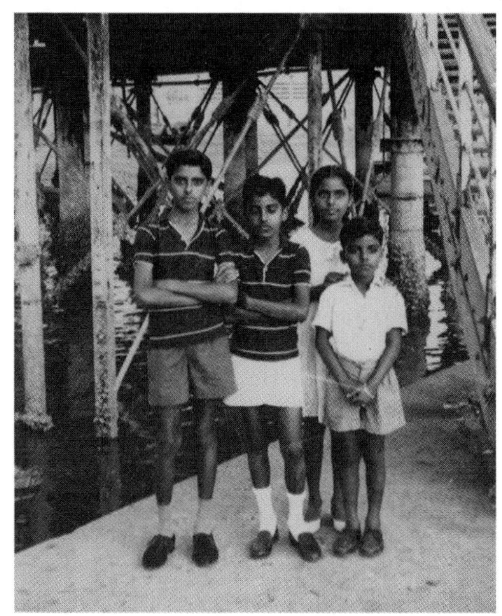

My younger siblings at Port Kelang (*from left to right*: Sathee, Sree, Prema, and Suresh)

perch. Freshwater fish such as carp, perch, trout, or tilapia are caught from rivers, streams, and ponds. Imported fish such as salmon or cod are generally bought frozen. We grew up only knowing Malay names for the different fish and not the English translations, and this posed some issues for me when I went to the supermarkets in the U.S or to the wet markets in New York's Chinatown. Sometimes I had difficulty researching for this cookbook as even today there is some confusion about exact English translations. However, I was able to get translations for most of the popular fish consumed in Malaysia.

A simple peasant meal in Malaysia features cooked white rice, seasoned deep-fried dried salted mackerel or *sambal ikan bilis* (baby anchovies), and a pickled vegetable. Dried salted fish are also used in condiments, curries, and soups. Dried salted whole *ikan bilis* are marinated with chile powder and turmeric and deep-fried to add as garnishes or enjoyed as snacks. Many cooks pound it to flavor vegetables and curries. In many countries, "low status" foods are emerging as "comfort foods" and trendy dishes. While *ikan bilis* is still a poor man's meal for some Malaysians, today, fried *ikan bilis* has become a gourmet spicy nibbler with cold beer at bars. They are also served by many local vendors and at many up-scale hotel restaurants as a crunchy topping for *nasi lemak* (page 117). In northeast Malaysia, in Kelantan and Terengganu, *ikan bilis* is salted and fermented for *budu*, a pungent salty sauce similar to Thai fish sauce or Vietnamese *nuoc mam*. It is enjoyed with boiled white rice, fresh vegetables, and as a dip for fish or shrimp crackers.

Dried fish (*ikan kering*)

Shrimp (*udang*) are enjoyed everywhere in Malaysia. The more expensive large shrimps are called prawns, while the small ones are referred to as shrimp. Shrimp is prepared in many ethnic styles—*sambals* and curries or stir-fried with chilies, oyster sauce, *taucheo*, or tomato sauce. Boiled shrimp becomes a topping for noodles and fried rice, while

Ma sometimes desalted the pieces of salted fish and added it to potato and vegetable curries. Or she would rub the fish slices and baby anchovies (*ikan bilis*) with chile and curry powder and deep-fry them. She served them with tomato *rasam* (page 76), stir-fried Chinese greens (*sawi,* page 227), and plain cooked white rice. It was a simple meal, but a delicious one that I treasured in my youth. Ma called it a "poor man's meal." I still remember biting into the crunchy *ikan bilis* and picking a handful of savory *sawi* with rice. The tomato *rasam* paired perfectly with fried *ikan bilis*. *Ikan bilis* and other fish are major sources of protein for Malaysians in rural settings.

shrimp fritters are added as garnish for *rojak* or *pasembor* (local salads). *Sambal tumis udang* (shrimp stir-fried in a fragrant tomato-chile sauce, page 204), *udang assam pedas* (shrimp in spicy tamarind sauce, page 201), and fiery shrimp with *cili padi* (bird peppers) were some of our favorite Malay shrimp dishes growing up. Shrimp with pineapples, shrimp in *taucheo*, and sweet sour shrimp are popular Chinese dishes, served especially during their New Year. Nonya favorites are *assam* shrimp (spicy tangy shrimp), shrimp fritters, and shrimp cooked in *sambals*.

Dried small shrimp or shrimp-like crustaceans (krill) called *udang kering*, are also referred to as *geragau* or *gerago*. They are used whole or ground to flavor many Malaysian dishes. It is a ubiquitous seasoning for Nonya, Malay, and Kristang dishes. On family trips across states, and driving through *kampungs*, I remember seeing these tiny shrimp being dried on large mats under the scorching sun. They are then fermented with salt in large earthenware jars. The fermented mush is ground into a smooth paste and again dried under the sun. The dried paste is shaped into blocks or cylinders, dried again, and then packaged as *belacan*. *Belacan* comes as pale pink to dark reddish brown pastes or blocks. When the *belacan* package is opened or toasted, it gives off a strong, pungent fishy smell, but when cooked with sauces and spice pastes, it gives a wonderful aroma and a flavor intensity to *sambals*, sauces, or stir-fries that is truly unique.

Belacan to Malaysians is like fish sauce to Thais. Its flavor is closer to *gapi*, the moist Thai shrimp-like paste. You can toast *belacan* wrapped in aluminum foil by holding it with a tong or bamboo skewer over an open flame till the surface is slightly charred; or you can flatten the wrapped *belacan* and toast it in a toaster oven at 400°F for about 15 minutes, as I do. Cha did not like the strong, pungent, fishy smell of toasted *belacan* seeping into the living room, so when our Malay cook did occasionally make her homemade *sambals* for us, she opened both windows and the back door of the kitchen. In the U.S., toasting *belacan* might get tricky for those living in closed apartments or in homes where windows are shut during winter months. So I suggest following my method for toasting *belacan* in a toaster oven, with the exhaust fan on.

Gerago is traditionally caught in nets from deep-sea fishing platforms (*kelongs*) off the Straits of Malacca. Kristangs mix *gerago* with steaming boiled rice and salt that is then fermented. This fermented mixture, called *cincalok*, is mixed with lime juice, shallots, and chilies and used to perk up soups and stews, and used as a staple condiment for Nonya and Kristang meals. Kristangs also savor seasoned and battered deep-fried *gerago* (called *gerago pikkadel*) as snacks.

Ma liked squid and usually prepared it spicy with chilies and spices as a dry curry or as a *sambal* (page 211). Unlike squid, Ma was not a fan of some shellfish, such as oysters, clams, and mussels, so they were generally not served at home. While these shellfish sometimes appear as ingredients in Malay-style rice, *sambals*, and curries, and in Chinese, Kristang, and Nonya soups, stews, and stir-fries, they are not particularly popular as meals. However, *kerang* (cockles) are an important flavoring in Chinese cooking. They add zest to many soups and stir-fried noodles, including *kari mee* (page 149) and *char kway teow* (page 139). Because Ma did not like the flavor of *kerang*, she always asked the food hawker to omit them and add an egg instead. So as a child I was not familiar with *kerang*. Later on, as my taste for *laksas* and *kari mee* increased, I started to enjoy these tiny cockles.

On a visit to Malaysia, my elder brother Prasnan and his wife, Shanta, took us out to eat at a local stall near our home to try *oh chien*. It is a Chinese-style oyster omelet preparation brought by Hokkien immigrants which has become a popular hawker food in Malaysia. Egg is combined with tiny oysters (called *tiram* in Malay) and seasoned with ground coriander, garlic, shallots, chilies, and scallions. When the Chinese vendor brought the oyster omelet to our table, I did not know what to make of it. Prasnan and Shanta dug into it, enjoying its flavor. I followed suit and picked a piece up with my chopsticks. It tasted kind of chewy, savory, and in the end, quite delicious.

PREPARATION OF SEAFOOD

Malaysians have created numerous delicious recipes with seafood, especially fish. Mackerel, tuna, red snapper, and pomfret are popular fish made into hot curries, stuffed with *sambal belacan*, or marinated with curry and *cili* powder and deep-fried. *Ikan bawal putih* (white pomfret) is a delicate fish, lightly seasoned and pan-fried till it turns golden brown. *Ikan tenggiri* (Spanish mackerel) is braised, stewed, or cooked in a more heavily seasoned coconut-based curry. Malays and Nonyas also stuff mackerel with pungent *sambal belacan* (dried shrimp paste) and grill it. Red snapper (*ikan merah*) has a subtle flavor that works well with a sweet-sour or chile sauce.

Ma simply seasoned her favorite fish with a chile-turmeric paste and deep-fried it (page 206) and for Cha, she curried it with coconut milk (page 198). Kristangs, similar to Malays, have fish *singgang*-style (cooked with tamarind juice, chilies, and galangal). Some Kristang preparations I enjoyed in Malacca were a spicy pickled fish cooked in vinegar with chilies, *escebeche*-style, and fish cooked in tamarind and chile sauce called *pesce tambrinhu*. I am addicted to the Malay style of cooking fish in fiery *tumised sambals* or wrapped in banana

On one of our regular visits to Malacca, we decided to explore the unique Portuguese (Kristang) fishing community at Ujong Pasir. As we entered the village, we passed small colorful wooden houses with children running around playing ball. We walked toward the water, passing wooden stores that sold candies, vegetables, fruits, cigarettes, and other household items. The place was quiet and it felt peaceful. We came across an old fisherman taking a smoke and relaxing near the water. I could not resist taking his photo as he smiled at me. His weather-beaten tanned face reflected the mix of Portuguese and Malay cultures of the community. We walked by the local residents sitting outside their homes and chatting, and came to Medan Portugis, a simple square containing a few restaurants with plastic tables and chairs out in front. We ate at Restoran de Lisbon. The hospitable owners, Albert and Julie, allowed me in their kitchen and answered my questions about the menu. They brought out a few of their signature dishes—*pesca assa* (whole fish seasoned with spices, lemongrass, chile paste, tamarind juice, and soy sauce wrapped in banana leaves and grilled or baked, page 207), *sambal* scallops (page 210), chicken curry *debal* (page 289), the smoky *otak-otak* (pureed fish wrapped in banana leaves), and a *sambal belacan* dip (page 101). This was truly a Malaysian feast, dining al-fresco-style on fresh seafood caught by local Kristang fisherman, prepared with Indian, Malay, and Chinese seasonings and cooking styles and accompanied with fiery pungent condiments. What a delicious feast of flavors!

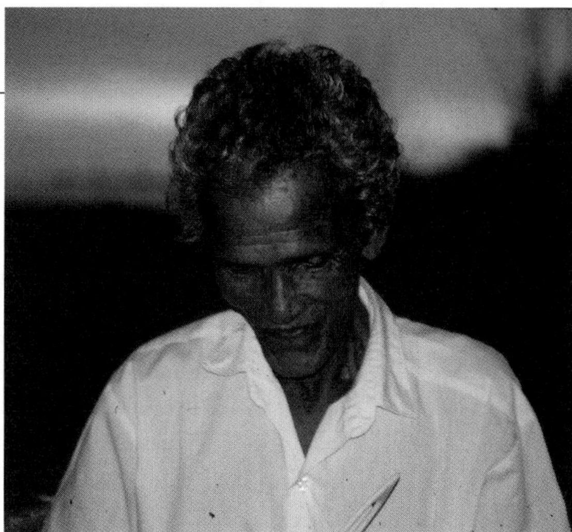

Kristang fisherman at Kampung Portugis (Portuguese settlement) in Ujong Pasir

leaf and grilled. Sarawak has an unusual preparation for fish, "cooked" with lime juice and chilies (*umai*, page 62). Nonya and Chinese boil fish and use the stock for soups, stews and *laksas* (page 153).

Indians make delicious dry shrimp curries or *varuvals* (page 203) and luscious fish curries with an array of spices. The Chinese and Nonyas generally steam or braise it with ginger, soy sauce, oyster sauce, or *taucheo*. *Kicap ikan* (soy sauce fish, page 199) is a unique fish preparation I had from an Indian Muslim vendor in Penang, who said it was handed down from his grandfather, a recipe that combined Chinese, Indian, and Malay seasonings.

Ma also had a "double cooking" method for her fish recipes (like her chicken recipes) that added another layer of flavor to them. After she seasoned the fish, she initially pan-seared it, then she curried, braised, or grilled it, or added it to *sambals*. Malaysians do not use fish fillets but prefer cooking the whole fish or whole fish cut up into pieces with bones and skin intact.

ETHNIC AND REGIONAL SEAFOOD DISHES

Since Malays enjoy fish as a staple, they have created numerous fish delicacies, also adopting flavors from other ethnic groups and neighboring cultures. Some well-known dishes are *gulai ikan pedas* (hot and sour fish curry with Arab and Chinese touches from the southern state of Johor); *ikan masak lemak* from Malacca (fish cooked in a savory coconut curry with Nonya influences); *ikan masak lemak cili padi* (fish cooked in coconut milk, tamarind juice, and fiery bird peppers with strong Minangkabau influences); and Kelantan's *ikan panggang* (stuffed fish wrapped in banana leaves and grilled over charcoals) with Thai influences.

A dish I enjoyed from a Portuguese friend of my mother is *ikan chuan-chuan* (page 212), a crispy fried whole fish with Malay and Chinese seasonings. The fish (usually Spanish mackerel or snapper) is marinated and deep-fried, then topped with a sauce of *taucheo* or thick soy sauce, black pepper, chilies, ginger, and vinegar (or tamarind juice). As a healthier alternative, I pan-sear the fish and then add the sauce and garnishes.

Because of Cha's love of seafood, Ma prepared fish often and in a variety of ways, including his favorite style, fish cooked with coconut milk and black peppercorns. But in my view, Grandma made the best fish curry. She seasoned Spanish mackerel with her special spice paste (*rempah*) and we enjoyed it with her delicious *thosai* (page 69) for Sunday brunch. My other favorite fish recipe is Ma's spicy fried fish (slices of *ikan tenggiri* that she marinated with turmeric, chilies, and lime juice and deep-fried, page 206). She served it with stir-fried Chinese greens (*sawi tumis*, page 227) and vegetable dhal curry (page 231), a perfect combination!

To Ma's pleasure, my husband, Bob, loved her curried crab and chile crab dishes (page 213) and always licked his fingers when he finished his plate! Ma's skills for creating her delicious crab dishes developed in her birthplace of Klang (now called Kelang), formerly the capital of the Selangor State and the old royal capital. We lived in Klang till I was five years old, so it holds special memories for me. It is close to Port Swettenham (now called Port Kelang), once a major seaport for Kuala Lumpur and other inland towns. It was a busy port in those days, located on the Straits of Malacca, receiving oceanliners and large ships as well as fishing boats. Sumatra in Indonesia is a stone's throw away by boat and many Indonesians immigrated to Malaysia through this port. Today, Port Kelang is a sleepy old town with old fishing boats and nets drying in the sun, and aged, worn buildings and shops. Klang has many Chinese (especially Hokkien) immigrants and is renowned for its seafood, especially black pepper crab and chile crab dishes.

The last time I was in Port Kelang was with Cha, who enjoyed its tranquil seaside atmosphere and slow-paced life. Retired and in his 70s, he sometimes took the bus there just to spend the day and have tea or an early dinner. He enjoyed walking on the covered pier to the water's edge and sometimes took a boat ride to the nearby fishing island between Sumatra and Malaysia called *Pulau Ketam* or Crab Island. (It also had wonderful Chinese seafood restaurants.) In Port Kelang, as we sat and sipped our beer and lemonade at a restaurant facing the water, waiting for our crab dish to come, my father spoke nostalgically of his youth, his job, stories of us growing up, and his great love of the ocean.

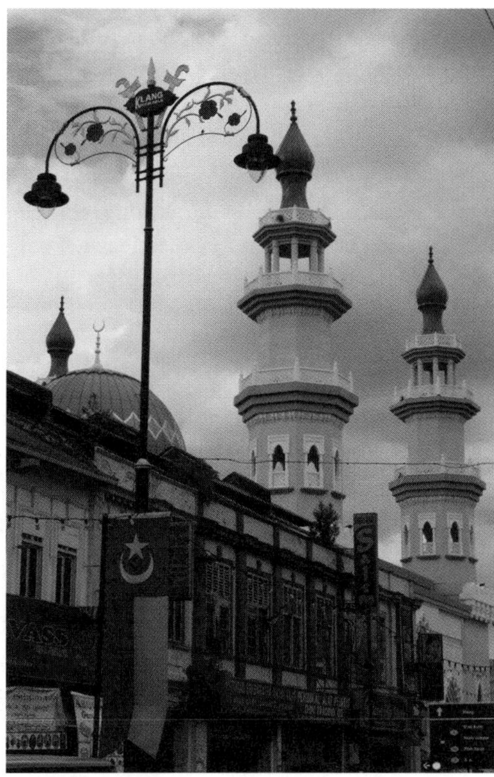

Klang (Kelang) town and mosque

Fish Curry, Indian-Style

Kari Ikan ala India

Makes 6 to 7 servings

INGREDIENTS

18-ounce whole mackerel, sardine, tuna, swordfish, or trout, cleaned and cut into 1-inch pieces, or fish steaks cut into 1-inch pieces
¼ teaspoon turmeric powder
¼ teaspoon chile powder
1 to 2 tablespoons cooking oil
1½-inch cinnamon stick
1 teaspoon fenugreek seeds
3 dried whole red chilies
6 to 8 fresh curry leaves
2 teaspoons sliced garlic cloves
1½ tablespoons sliced fresh ginger
¾ cup diced shallots or onions
1½ cups (9 ounces) sliced tomatoes
1 tablespoon tamarind concentrate or tamarind juice extracted from pulp (*see page 339*)
1⅓ cups (about 5 ounces) okra (*bendi*) or eggplant (*aubergine*)
¾ teaspoon salt

Spice Blend

4½ teaspoons ground coriander
2 teaspoons ground cumin
1½ teaspoons ground fennel seeds
½ to ¾ teaspoon turmeric powder
½ teaspoon finely ground black pepper
¼ to ½ teaspoon chile powder

Periama, my maternal Grandma, often stayed with us when Ma needed help. I remember she made the best seafood curries, filling the house with their delicious aromas. Our favorite was her fish curry that she served with thosai *for Sunday brunch. She cut up the whole fish into smaller pieces and added sliced eggplant or okra. I remember Periama telling me that the spice mix, especially the fenugreek seeds, gave that extra edge to its flavor. And she told me to always rub the fish with a little turmeric paste in order to remove the fishy odor. This technique is common with Indians and Malays.*

I have yet to taste any dish that surpasses Periama's fish curry. However, Ma's fish curry comes close, and I am sharing it here.

DIRECTIONS:

1. Rub fish with turmeric and chile powders. Marinate for a minimum of 30 minutes.
2. Combine Spice Blend ingredients and set aside.
3. Heat 1 tablespoon oil in a wok or skillet and add cinnamon stick, fenugreek seeds, chilies, and curry leaves and stir for about ½ to 1 minute.
4. Add garlic and ginger and sauté for about ½ to 1 minute, then add shallots or onions and sauté for about 1 to 2 minutes.
5. Add Spice Blend and remaining oil, if needed, and sauté for about ½ minute, then add tomatoes and sauté another 1 to 2 minutes.
6. Stir in 1½ to 2 cups water, tamarind juice, okra or eggplant, and salt, and bring to boil. Lower heat and cook for about 10 to 15 minutes, stirring occasionally. Add marinated fish and cook for 5 to 7 minutes, stirring occasionally (gently so as not to break up fish), till sauce thickens slightly and fish is cooked. Remove cinnamon stick before serving.

Serve with cooked white or brown rice, yellow rice (page 118), stir-fried cabbage (page 226), spicy dry curried okra (page 221), or spicy curried pumpkin (page 225); and savory meat lentils (page 285) or spicy lentil vegetable stew (page 88); and tomato *rasam* (page 76).

Roti canai and fish curry

Soy Sauce Fish

Kicap Ikan

Makes 3 to 4 servings

The term kicap *means soy sauce in Malay, and there are a variety of soy sauces available in Malaysia. In addition to regular soy sauce, there are many dark, thick, and sweet soy sauces to flavor fish and other seafoods.*

We used the sweet, thick soy sauce (called kicap manis*) the way American children use ketchup—over everything—over rice, noodles, and especially over fried eggs instead of salt and pepper. Malaysian children still have this habit today, although many turn to ketchup and hot Tabasco sauce. In this recipe, I combine a couple of soy sauces,* taucheo*, and tomato paste with chilies and black pepper to create a delicious fish dish that is reminiscent of Indian Muslim and Chinese hawker dishes.*

INGREDIENTS

- ¾ pound fish fillets or steaks (tilapia, red snapper, mackerel, pomfret, kingfish, tuna, trout, or swordfish), cleaned and sliced into ½-inch-thick pieces
- ¼ teaspoon turmeric powder
- 2 tablespoons cooking oil
- 1 to 1½ tablespoons sliced garlic cloves
- 2 teaspoons sliced fresh ginger
- 1 cup thinly sliced shallots or onions
- ⅛ teaspoon finely ground black pepper or coarsely ground black peppercorns
- ½ teaspoon sugar
- ¼ teaspoon salt
- 1 fresh red chile (Fresno, jalapeno, Serrano, cayenne, or cherry), thinly sliced
- ¾ cup (4½ ounces) quartered tomatoes

SAUCE BLEND

- 1 tablespoon tomato puree, or ½ tablespoon tomato paste, or 1½ tablespoons tomato sauce
- ¼ cup water
- 2 teaspoons preserved soybean paste (*taucheo*, black version) or black bean sauce or bean sauce
- 1 teaspoon double black soy sauce
- 1 teaspoon regular soy sauce
- 1 teaspoon distilled white vinegar, rice vinegar, or rice wine

GARNISH

- 1 fresh green chile (jalapeno, Serrano, cayenne, or Thai), sliced
- ½ to ¾ cup (2 to 3 ounces) peeled, seeded, and julienned cucumber
- 1 tablespoon chopped spring onions or Chinese chives (*kuchai*)

DIRECTIONS:

1. Rub fish with turmeric. Marinate for about 15 minutes.
2. Combine Sauce Blend ingredients and set aside.
3. Heat 1 tablespoon of oil in a wok or skillet and pan-fry seasoned fish for about 8 to 10 minutes (4 to 5 minutes on each side); or you can deep-fry the fish. Remove from pan and set aside, keeping warm.
4. Heat remaining oil in the wok or skillet and add garlic and ginger and sauté for ½ to 1 minute; add ½ cup of the shallots or onions and sauté for about 1 to 2 minutes.
5. Add Sauce Blend and stir for about 2 minutes, then add black pepper, sugar, salt, and chile, and stir for another minute.
6. Add tomatoes and remaining ½ cup shallots or onions and sauté another minute. (Don't overcook tomatoes and onions, so their texture does not get too soft.)
7. When ready to serve, place fish on plate and pour sauce over fish. Top with garnishes.

Note: Instead of pan-frying or deep-frying the fish ahead of time you can steam it in the sauce till cooked.

Serve with cooked white or brown rice, tomato rice (page 119), spiced rice (page 120), or fried rice (page 123); and cucumber pineapple *acar* (page 98), stir-fried mixed vegetables (page 224), stir-fried *kailan* (page 222), or stir-fried Chinese greens (page 227).

Shrimp with Preserved Soybeans

Udang Taucheo

Makes 3 to 4 servings

INGREDIENTS

1 pound shelled and deveined shrimp, tails intact
1 tablespoon cooking oil
2 teaspoons sliced and coarsely crushed garlic cloves
1 fresh green chile (jalapeno, Serrano, Thai, or cayenne), sliced and coarsely crushed
2 heaping tablespoons preserved soybean paste (*taucheo*, light brown version) or black bean sauce or bean sauce
½ teaspoon double black, thick, or sweet soy sauce
½ teaspoon dark brown sugar (*use less if using thick or sweet soy sauce*)
Optional: ⅛ teaspoon salt
½ cup (2 ounces) mix of diced red and green bell peppers (1-inch-square pieces)
½ cup diced shallots or onions (1-inch-square pieces)
1 fresh green chile (cayenne, serrano, jalapeno, or Thai), sliced

MARINADE

1 teaspoon rice wine or palm vinegar
1 teaspoon regular soy sauce

GARNISH

1 to 2 tablespoons chopped spring onions, Chinese chives (*kuchai*), or coriander leaves (cilantro)

Taucheo *is preserved or fermented soybean paste with discrete whole or chunky soybean pieces. It generally comes in two versions, a dark blackish brown (or deep reddish black) and a light brown version. The black* taucheo *has a pungent and salty taste while the lighter brown version is slightly sweeter and less salty. Both are featured in many of the Chinese and Nonya dishes. In many recipes that call for oyster sauce, I substitute* taucheo, *thick soy sauce, and sugar.*

This shrimp dish is a simple Nonya favorite with its spicy, sweet, and pungent taste from the combined effect of salted soybeans, rice wine, garlic, soy sauce, and green chilies.

DIRECTIONS:

1. Mix Marinade ingredients and toss with shrimp. Marinate shrimp for 30 minutes.
2. Heat oil in a skillet or wok. Sauté garlic and crushed chile for ½ to 1 minute.
3. Add soybean paste and sauté for another minute.
4. Add marinated shrimp and stir for 1 to 2 minutes, then add soy sauce, brown sugar, and salt and cook for about 2 to 3 minutes, stirring continuously, till shrimp is cooked.
5. Add bell peppers, shallots or onions, and sliced chile and sauté for about 1 to 2 minutes. Top with garnish.

Serve with cooked white or brown rice, coconut-infused rice (page 117), yellow rice (page 118), or fried rice (page 123); and stir-fried *kailan* (page 222), stir-fried bean sprouts (page 229), or stir-fried mixed vegetables (page 224).

Hot and Sour Shrimp

Udang Assam Pedas

Makes 3 to 4 servings

This is a favorite seafood preparation with the Penang Nonyas, the Malays from Kedah, and the Muslims of the Northeast. It is hot and spicy prepared with tamarind juice, belacan, *lemongrass, turmeric root, galangal, palm sugar, and Vietnamese mint. The lavish use of tamarind gives it its tanginess and* cili padi *(bird peppers) its fiery heat. Nonyas also add pounded dried shrimps, a touch inherited from their Chinese ancestors. The Indian and Chinese versions of* udang assam pedas *are not as tangy as the Malay version which has Thai influences.*

I had my first taste of this dish at a Malay restaurant in Kedah, the rice bowl of Malaysia. As we drove through the state, we were captivated by its gorgeous scenery—golden stalks of rice swaying against the wind. Here I have given you a recipe that embodies the cooking of Malays and Nonyas.

INGREDIENTS

1 pound (about 2 heaping cups) shelled and deveined shrimp, tails intact
2 to 3 tablespoons cooking oil
Optional: 1 teaspoon ground or pounded tiny whole dried shrimp (*udang kering*), steeped in hot water for about 10 minutes to soften; or pounded or ground dried baby anchovies (*ikan bilis*)
7 tablespoons tamarind concentrate or tamarind juice extracted from pulp (*see page 339*)
½ teaspoon tomato paste, or 1 teaspoon tomato puree, or 1½ teaspoons tomato sauce, or ½ small tomato
Optional: ½ cup okra (*bendi*) (about 2 ounces) or eggplant slices (1¼ ounces)
¼ cup Vietnamese mint leaves (*daun kesum*) or regular mint leaves
1 teaspoon thinly sliced or chopped palm sugar or dark brown sugar
1 fresh red chile (Fresno, cayenne, jalapeno, Serrano, cherry, or Thai), sliced
1 fresh green chile (cayenne, jalapeno, Serrano, cherry, or Thai), sliced
¼ teaspoon salt

MARINADE

1 tablespoon tamarind concentrate or tamarind juice extracted from pulp (*see page 339*)
½ to 1 teaspoon peeled and pounded fresh or frozen and thawed turmeric root, or ¼ to ½ teaspoon turmeric powder
¼ teaspoon chile powder

(*continued on next page*)

DIRECTIONS:

1. Combine Marinade ingredients and rub on shrimp. Let sit for 30 minutes to 1 hour.
2. Process Spice Paste ingredients to a smooth paste.
3. Heat 1 tablespoon of oil in a wok or skillet and sauté Spice Paste for about 5 minutes, till fragrant, adding remaining oil if needed.
4. Add dried shrimp or baby anchovies, if using, stir for about 1 to 2 minutes, then add tamarind juice, tomato paste, puree, or sauce, okra or eggplant, if using, 3 tablespoons of the mint leaves, sugar, and ½ cup water and stir for about 3 minutes.
5. Add marinated shrimp and stir for about 3 to 4 minutes, then add half of the sliced red and green chilies and salt and stir well for about 1 minute.
6. Garnish with remaining 1 tablespoon mint leaves and remaining red and green chilies.

Serve with cooked white or brown rice, or crusty bread; and spicy simmered cabbage (page 290), cucumber carrot *acar* (page 99), or green papaya *acar* (page 100). Or add cooked rice, noodles, or spaghetti to make a bowl meal and serve with a spicy *belacan* chile paste dip (page 108).

(CONTINUED) HOT AND SOUR SHRIMP

Udang Assam Pedas

SPICE PASTE

- 1 teaspoon sliced fresh or frozen and thawed galangal or fresh ginger
- 1 tablespoon sliced garlic cloves
- ¼ cup sliced shallots or onions
- 5 to 8 dried whole red chilies, steeped in warm or hot water for 5 to 8 minutes, slit and deseeded; or 1¼ to 2 tablespoons *cili boh* (*see page 315*); or ½ to 1 tablespoon bottled *sambal oelek*
- 1 lemongrass stalk, sliced into ¼ to ½-inch pieces
- 1 teaspoon dried shrimp paste (*belacan*), toasted at 400°F for 15 minutes (*see page 335*)
- ¼ cup water

Shanta's hot and sour shrimp

Shrimp Varuval

Udang Varuval

Makes 3 to 4 servings

Varuval in Tamil means dry-fried in oil, and this technique has its origins from South India and Sri Lankan Tamils. Shrimp is stir-fried in seasoned oil, resulting in an intensely flavored dish. Some cooks toss masala *(spices) over the dish before serving, creating a more intense aroma at the table. Traditionally, ghee (clarified butter) is used to make* varuvals *to obtain a rich taste and aroma but I prefer oil. Ma also added soy sauce to give it a local twist.*

One of our neighbor's was a Ceylonese (or Sri Lankan) Tamil with a large family like ours. She and Ma shared a common passion for cooking, visiting each other's homes and exchanging recipes and cooking techniques. This is one of Ma's recipes to celebrate and honor her Sri Lankan neighbors and friends.

INGREDIENTS

1 tablespoon cooking oil
1½ tablespoons sliced garlic cloves
1 tablespoon sliced fresh ginger
¼ cup sliced shallots or onions
1 to 1½ teaspoons tomato paste, or 2 to 3 tablespoons tomato puree, or 3 to 4½ tablespoons tomato sauce
1½ teaspoons regular soy sauce
¼ teaspoon double black soy sauce
1 pound (about 2 heaping cups) shelled and deveined shrimp, tails intact
⅛ teaspoon salt

Spice Blend 1

2 or 3 dried whole red chilies
1 star anise
½ teaspoon fenugreek seeds
½ teaspoon fennel seeds

Spice Blend 2

1 teaspoon ground coriander
½ teaspoon ground fennel seeds
¼ teaspoon ground cumin
¼ teaspoon turmeric powder
¼ teaspoon chile powder

Garnish

4 to 6 fresh curry leaves, fried in 1 tablespoon of oil for ½ minute
Optional: ¼ cup fried (*see page 333*) or sautéed shallots or onions

DIRECTIONS:

1. Combine Spice Blend 2 ingredients and set aside.
2. Heat oil in a wok or skillet. Add Spice Blend 1 ingredients and sauté for about ½ minute.
3. Add garlic and ginger and sauté for about ½ to 1 minute; add shallots or onions and sauté for another 1 to 2 minutes.
4. Add Spice Blend 2 and sauté for another ½ minute, then add tomato paste, puree, or sauce and soy sauces and sauté for another minute.
5. Add shrimp and stir-fry for about 3 minutes, then add salt and stir-fry for another 1 or 2 minutes, till shrimp are cooked.
6. Garnish with fried curry leaves and oil mixture and fried shallots or onions before serving.

Serve with cooked white or brown rice, spiced rice (page 120), yellow rice (page 118), lime rice (page 122), or *sambar* rice (page 124); and stir-fried cabbage (page 226), vegetables in spicy coconut milk (page 223), or spicy cucumber tomato salad (page 97). Or for a festive occasion you can serve with vegetable *biryani* (page 280) or festive rice (page 278) with spicy dry curried okra (page 221) or spicy curried pumpkin (page 225).

Stir-Fried Sambal Shrimp

Sambal Tumis Udang

Makes 3 to 4 servings

INGREDIENTS

1 pound (about 2 heaping cups) shelled and deveined shrimp, tails intact
¼ teaspoon turmeric powder
¼ cup cooking oil
1 cup (6 ounces) chopped and pureed tomatoes, or ½ cup tomato paste, or 1½ cups tomato sauce
2 tablespoons tamarind concentrate or tamarind juice extracted from pulp (*see page 339*)
3 to 4 teaspoons sugar
½ teaspoon salt

Spice Paste

2 tablespoons sliced garlic cloves
1 teaspoon sliced fresh ginger
2 cups sliced shallots or onions
12 to 20 whole dried red chilies (depending on desired heat), steeped in hot water for 5 to 8 minutes, slit and deseeded; or 3 to 5 tablespoons *cili boh* (*see page 315*); or 1½ to 2½ tablespoons bottled *sambal oelek*
4 to 6 fresh red chilies, preferably mild or deseeded (Fresno, cayenne, or cherry), sliced
1 lemongrass stalk, sliced into ¼-inch to ½-inch pieces
Optional: 1 teaspoon dried shrimp paste (*belacan*), toasted at 400°F for 15 minutes (*see page 335*)
¼ cup water

Spice Blend

2 teaspoons coarsely pounded or ground fennel seeds
1 star anise
1-inch cinnamon stick

Sambals are the ubiquitous chile-based sauces of Malaysia and for most Malaysians the "soul" of a meal. Sambal tumis udang *is one of our family's favorite Malay dishes. To make it, shallots are a must and Ma or Periama would sit for hours in the kitchen peeling them. When I asked Ma why she didn't use big onions so there was less to peel, she would say that the dish would not taste the same, but you can use regular onions in this recipe. Ma 'tumised' the ingredients in oil, a slow-stirring technique that takes away the raw notes, and releases a wonderful aroma to the sauce.*

Although it is frequently served with nasi lemak *(coconut rice), Ma served it with cooked white rice,* kankung belacan *(spicy water spinach), and a cucumber tomato salad. Ma balanced the spicy shrimp* sambal *with "cooling" spices, such as fennel, star anise, cinnamon, and turmeric. These spices made her recipe a truly unique* sambal tumis udang *with Indian and Malay touches. I have added* belacan, *but it is optional. You can also use fish for this recipe.*

DIRECTIONS:

1. Rub shrimp with turmeric. Set aside. Process Spice Paste ingredients to a coarse or smooth paste.
2. Heat 1 tablespoon of oil in a wok or skillet and sauté the Spice Blend ingredients for about ½ minute.
3. Add remaining oil and the Spice Paste and cook, stirring, for about 10 to 15 minutes, till the oil seeps out. (Note: This is when the spice paste gets to its optimum fragrance. But you can always add less oil and stir for less time and still achieve a wonderful flavor.)
4. Stir in the tomato puree, paste, or sauce (if using paste add 2 to 4 tablespoons of water), tamarind juice, sugar, and salt and sauté for another 3 to 5 minutes.
5. Add the seasoned shrimp and stir for about 4 minutes, till shrimp are cooked and coated well with sauce.
6. Garnish with coriander leaves or Kaffir lime leaves.

Serve with cooked white or brown rice, coconut-infused rice (page 117), spiced rice (page 120), yellow rice (page 118), ghee rice (page 121), or tomato rice (page 119); and spicy cucumber tomato salad (page 97) or stir-fried mixed vegetables (page 224).

Garnish

1 tablespoon chopped coriander leaves (cilantro) or thinly sliced Kaffir lime leaves

Spicy Tangy Simmered Fish

Ikan Assam Rebus

Makes 3 to 4 servings

Ikan assam rebus *is fish boiled in a broth seasoned with tamarind, coriander seed, and chilies. This recipe for* ikan assam rebus *was provided by Aliza Mansor, Senior Assistant Director International Marketing, Tourism Malaysia, based in Kuala Lumpur. Aliza typifies Malaysia's melting pot. She was born in Kuala Lumpur, her mom is from Penang and has Nonya heritage, while her grandmom is from Ipoh (in Perak state) and has a Chinese background. Aliza also inherited Malay and Indian influences on her paternal side from Kedah. So as a result of growing up in an ethnically mixed parentage, her family celebrated both the Malay Hari Raya Puasa and Chinese New Year and other festivals. Her husband, Nasir, is from Kelantan so Aliza has also become well-versed in Kelantanese cooking. Aliza is an adept cook, having learned cooking from her mother who would often bring her to the kitchen, and from her paternal grandmother.*

This ikan assam rebus *recipe is a unique celebration of Malaysia's multiculturalism, handed down by Aliza's family through generations. In this recipe, I have modified some of the seasonings slightly to suit a spectrum of tastes, but still maintained its authenticity.*

INGREDIENTS

- 1 pound swordfish, seabass, tuna, salmon, haddock, or mackerel fillets or steaks, cut crosswise into ½-inch-thick pieces
- ⅛ to ¼ teaspoon turmeric powder
- 2 tablespoons cooking oil
- 1 lemongrass stalk, bruised with back of knife and knotted
- 7 teaspoons (2⅓ tablespoons) tamarind concentrate or tamarind juice extracted from pulp (*see page 339*)
- 1 medium (about ½ pound or 2 cups) cucumber, deseeded and thickly sliced (about 1½-inch by 1-inch pieces)
- 1 teaspoon sugar
- ¼ teaspoon salt
- 2 or 3 teaspoons rice grains, dry roasted in a skillet over medium heat to a light brown color, cooled, and ground to a powder

Spice Paste

- ¾ cup sliced shallots or onions
- 5 to 6 fresh red chilies (jalapeno, Fresno, Serrano, cayenne, Thai, or cherry), sliced
- 1 teaspoon dried shrimp paste (*belacan*), toasted at 400°F for 15 minutes (*see page 335*)
- 2 teaspoons coriander seeds
- ¼ cup water

Garnish

- 1 heaping tablespoon chopped coriander leaves (cilantro)

DIRECTIONS:

1. Rub fish with turmeric and set aside for 30 minutes. Heat 1 tablespoon of oil in skillet and pan-fry fish pieces on both sides till brown, about 2 to 3 minutes on each side. Set aside.
2. Process Spice Paste ingredients to a smooth paste.
3. Heat 1 tablespoon oil in a wok or skillet and sauté Spice Paste for about 4 to 5 minutes, till fragrant Add lemongrass, stir for a minute, and stir in tamarind juice and 1 cup water and simmer for about 8 to 10 minutes, stirring occasionally.
4. Add seasoned fish, cucumber, sugar, and salt and stir for 1 minute. Cover and let fish cook for about 3 to 4 minutes. Uncover and stir till fish is cooked, another 3 to 5 minutes depending on fish and whether it was pan-fried first.
5. Stir in ground rice and stir slowly for 1 minute to thicken sauce.
6. Remove lemongrass stalk before serving. Garnish with coriander leaves.

Serve with cooked white or brown rice or yellow rice (page 118); and eggplant pineapple *pajeri* (page 232), stir-fried cabbage (page 226), or braised spicy long beans (page 230).

Spicy Fried Fish
Ikan Goreng Pedas

Makes 3 to 4 servings

INGREDIENTS

1 teaspoon regular soy sauce
1 teaspoon crushed fresh ginger (or just the juice squeezed out of it)
¼ teaspoon salt
1 tablespoon water
¾ to 1 pound fish steaks or fillets (kingfish, red snapper, haddock, mackerel, tuna, swordfish, or salmon) or small to medium whole fish (white pomfret, sardine, or trout), cut into ½-inch-thick pieces
Oil for deep-frying

SPICE BLEND

½ teaspoon turmeric powder
¼ to ½ teaspoon chile powder
¼ teaspoon ground paprika
¼ teaspoon ground cumin
¼ teaspoon ground coriander
¼ teaspoon ground fennel seeds
¼ teaspoon ground fenugreek

GARNISH

¼ cup sliced shallots or onions (⅛-inch-thick rings)
5 or 6 fresh curry leaves, fried in 1 tablespoon hot oil and crushed
1 lemon or lime, cut into wedges

When I first went to graduate school at the University of Reading, England, the cafeteria served poached or boiled fish with no seasonings except salt and pepper. Even when I came to the U.S., the restaurants prepared fish with little seasoning. It was plain broiled or baked and served with lemon wedge or tartar sauce or breaded and deep-fried. I had grown up with intensely flavorful fish dishes so found these dishes quite unappetizing.

One fish dish that I especially enjoyed was Ma's fried fish. She seasoned it with turmeric, chile powder, other fragrant spices, and soy sauce. You can also bake, grill, or barbecue it, or wrap in banana leaves before cooking. This is one of my favorite fish recipes that I inherited from Ma. You can use whole fish such as kingfish, snapper, mackerel, or pomfret, or firm fish steaks like tuna, salmon, or swordfish. Like me, you can also season the fish pieces and pan-fry them.

DIRECTIONS:

1. Combine Spice Blend ingredients. Mix with soy sauce, ginger or juice, salt, and water. Rub fish with this paste and marinate for 30 minutes.
2. Heat oil in a deep wok or skillet. When oil is hot, add seasoned fish slices and deep-fry 2 to 4 minutes on each side till brown. You can also bake at 350°F for about 20 to 35 minutes; or like I do, pan-fry in 1 to 2 tablespoons of oil in a skillet for about 3 to 5 minutes on each side (depending on thickness of fish), till cooked. Place on paper towels to remove excess oil.
3. Garnish with shallot or onion rings and curry leaves and squeeze on lime or lemon juice before serving.

Serve with cooked white or brown rice, fried rice (page 123), yellow rice (page 118), or vegetable *biryani* (page 280); and savory meat lentils (*dalcha*, page 285); and spicy cucumber tomato salad (page 97) or cucumber carrot *acar* (page 99).

Portuguese Spicy Baked or Grilled Fish

Pesca Assa

Makes 3 to 4 servings

This is a popular fish preparation from the Genti Kristang (Christian People), descendants of sixteenth-century Portuguese settlers who married Malay or other local women. They are a fishing community, so fish is a mainstay of their daily diet, served with rice, curries, and sambals. The Kristangs have created a truly unique cuisine by combining the Portuguese tradition of marinating seafood with vinegar or lime or lemon juice and using local spices and ingredients.

When we visit Malacca, we usually make a trip to the Portuguese settlement and have a simple meal at a café at the Medan Portugis (which has a great potential for cafes and restaurants serving Kristang food). One of our favorite dishes is this spicy fish called pesca assa. *Seasoned fish is wrapped in banana leaf and baked or grilled. Serve it with spicy dry curried okra or spicy long beans and cool watermelon juice and you have the perfect meal!*

INGREDIENTS

- 4 to 5 tablespoons cooking oil
- 1 teaspoon double black, thick, or sweet soy sauce (if using double black add ¼ teaspoon sugar)
- ⅛ teaspoon finely ground black pepper
- ¼ teaspoon ground paprika
- ¼ teaspoon turmeric powder
- ½ teaspoon sugar
- ½ teaspoon salt
- 2 tablespoons tamarind concentrate or tamarind juice extracted from pulp (*see page 339*)
- 1 banana leaf, rinsed with water and patted dry (if frozen, let thaw first and pat dry)
- 1-pound whole fish (red snapper, bream, rock cod, tilapia, or threadfish), cleaned; or tilapia, sole, cod, haddock, or salmon fillets
- 1 finely shredded Kaffir lime leaf (with 2 lobes)
- ½ teaspoon freshly squeezed or bottled lime or lemon juice

SPICE PASTE

- ¾ cup chopped shallots or onions
- 1½ tablespoons sliced garlic cloves
- 1 tablespoon sliced fresh or frozen and thawed galangal or fresh ginger
- 3 to 5 dried whole red chilies, steeped in hot water for 5 to 8 minutes till they soften, slit and deseeded; or ¾ to 1¼ tablespoons *cili boh* (*see page 315*); or ¼ to ½ tablespoon bottled *sambal oelek*
- 1 lemongrass stalk, sliced into ¼-inch to ½-inch pieces
- ½ teaspoon dried shrimp paste (*belacan*), toasted at 400°F for 15 minutes (*see page 335*)
- 2 candlenuts or macadamia nuts, or 1 teaspoon almonds
- ¼ to ⅓ cup water

DIRECTIONS:

1. Process Spice Paste ingredients to a smooth paste. If baking fish, heat oven to 350°F.
2. Heat 2 tablespoons oil in a wok or skillet and sauté Spice Paste for about 4 to 5 minutes.
3. Add soy sauce, black pepper, paprika, turmeric, sugar, salt, tamarind juice, and ¼ cup water and stir for about 5 minutes, till fragrant. Cool sauce.
4. Place banana leaf on aluminum foil (you can brush the aluminum foil with oil, if desired). Make 3 or 4 slits across both sides of the fish. Then place fish in center of banana leaf and rub it on both sides with some of the cooked sauce including the slits and the cavity. Top with shredded lime leaf. Wrap the fish in banana leaf and foil: first gently bring together the top and side of the banana leaf ends (leaving some space between fish and leaf) and secure with toothpicks; then fold the foil over the top and sides to seal the fish.
5. Bake at 350°F for about 40 to 45 minutes, or grill for 8 to 10 minutes. Then open foil and bake or grill for another 15 to 20 minutes, till water around fish dries up.
6. Before serving, remove lime leaves and sprinkle lime or lemon juice on fish. Warm or heat remaining cooked sauce and pour over fish.

Note: If whole fish is not desired, use 3 to 4 fish fillets, but cut baking time to 8 to 10 minutes or grilling time to 4 to 5 minutes.

Serve with cooked white or brown rice, tomato rice (page 119), yellow rice (page 118), or coconut-infused rice (page 117); and spicy dry curried okra (page 221), braised spicy long beans (page 230), or a green salad.

Sweet and Spicy Tuna Curry

Kari Ikan Tongkol

Makes 3 to 4 servings

INGREDIENTS

1 pound tuna steaks or any firm-fleshed fish steaks such as swordfish, trout, cod, or kingfish, cut into 1-inch to 1½-inch-thick pieces
¼ teaspoon salt
⅛ teaspoon turmeric powder
Optional: 1 tablespoon flour (rice, tapioca, corn, or all-purpose white)
2 to 3 tablespoons cooking oil
1 cup unsweetened coconut milk
2 pieces *asam gelugor* or *asam keping* (sometimes labeled tamarind skin), or 1 to 1½ tablespoons tamarind juice
¾ pound (about 5 cups) Oriental or other small eggplant, sliced (1½-inch-thick slices)
1 to 1½ teaspoons sugar
¼ teaspoon salt
Optional: ½ teaspoon dried *ikan bilis* (baby anchovies) stock granules or finely pounded dried *ikan bilis*, steeped in hot water for about 10 minutes to soften, then drained and patted dry

SPICE PASTE

½ cup sliced shallots or onions
1½ tablespoons sliced garlic cloves
1 heaping teaspoon sliced fresh or frozen and thawed galangal or fresh ginger
1 lemongrass stalk, sliced into ¼ to ½-inch pieces
2 to 4 dried whole red chilies, steeped in hot water for 5 to 8 minutes, slit and deseeded; or ½ to 1 tablespoon *cili boh* (*see page 315*); or ¾ to 1½ teaspoons bottled *sambal oelek*; or ¼ teaspoon chile powder
¼ cup water

Kari ikan tongkol *is a mild, creamy, and sweet fish curry that is a favorite of Kelantan and Terengganu Malays. The curry is made with tuna fish (called* ikan tongkol*; also known as* kari ikan aya *or* kari ikan kayu*) cooked with spices, coconut milk, sugar, and tamarind. It is traditionally eaten with steamed* nasi dagang *(red bran rice), a pickled vegetable, and hard-boiled egg.*

My friend Zubaidah, an Indian Muslim from Penang, shared her recipe for kari ikan tongkol *with me. I have made some modifications with regard to heat, amount of coconut milk, and spicing.*

DIRECTIONS:

1. Rub fish slices with salt, turmeric, and flour, if using.
2. Heat 1 tablespoon oil in a skillet and pan sear fish for about 2 minutes on each side till brown. Set aside.
3. Process the Spice Paste ingredients to a smooth paste and set aside. Combine the Spice Blend ingredients and set aside.
4. Heat 1 tablespoon oil in a skillet and sauté the Spice Paste for about 5 minutes, till fragrant, then add the Spice Blend and sauté for ½ to 1 minute, adding remaining oil.
5. Add ½ cup water, coconut milk, *asam gelugor*, and eggplant and bring to a boil. Then lower heat and simmer, stirring occasionally, for about 15 to 20 minutes, depending on the desired firmness of eggplant (don't let eggplant get mushy).
6. Add pan-seared fish, sugar, salt and *ikan bilis*, if using. Stir well and cook for another 3 minutes. Remove *asam gelugor* before serving.

Serve with cooked white or brown rice, red rice in coconut milk (page 128), or herb rice (page 125); and cucumber carrot *acar* (page 99), stir-fried cabbage (page 226), or spicy water spinach (page 228).

SPICE BLEND

1 tablespoon ground coriander
½ teaspoon ground cumin
½ teaspoon finely ground black pepper

One morning, while visiting Kota Bahru in Kelantan, we went to visit the noted wet market, *pasar Khatijah*. What a colorful and amazing sight, with vegetables, fruits, herbs, chilies, fresh fish, and poultry on display! Many Malay women vendors were selling prepared Malay delicacies—*nasi lemak* (coconut rice), *ayam percik* (grilled chicken), *nasi ulam* (herb rice), and *kari ikan tongkol* with *nasi dagang*.

After a few hours of walking around and taking photographs, we went back to have lunch—but the *kari ikan tongkol* vendor was gone! I was disappointed. Next morning for breakfast at our hotel, I ordered *kari ikan tongkol* with *nasi dagang*. It tasted rich and slightly sweet, and filled me up instantly. The waiter explained to me that it was a regular breakfast fare in Kelantan state. Now I understood why it was gone by lunch!

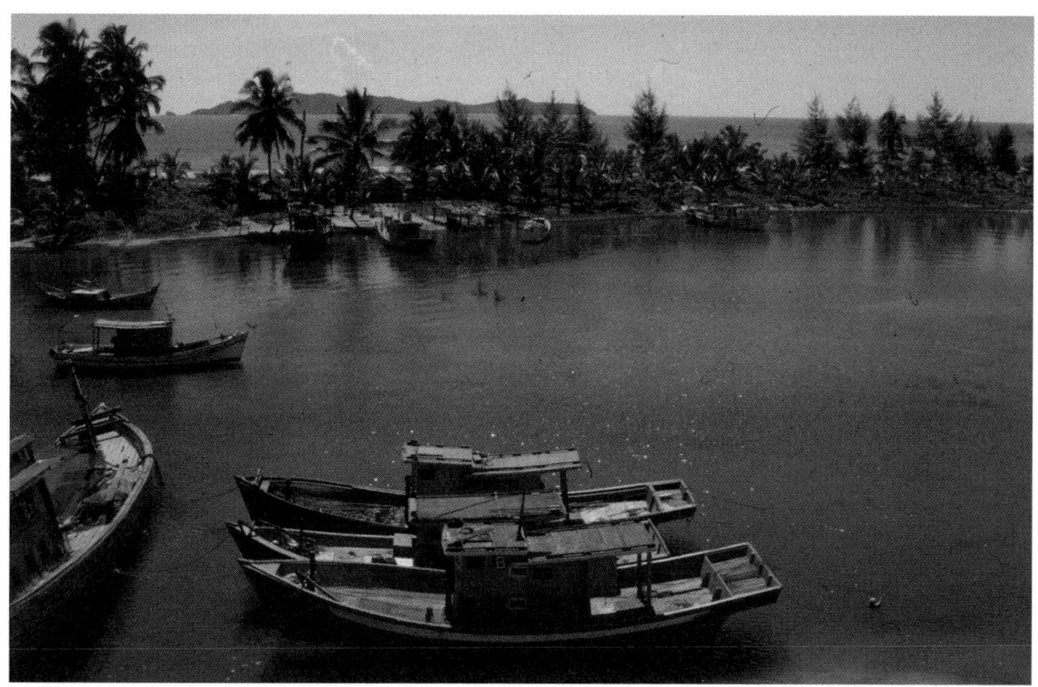

Fishing boats, Kelantan

Scallops in Aromatic Chile and Tomato Sauce

Sambal Scallop

Makes 3 to 4 servings

INGREDIENTS

1 pound bay scallops, rinsed, drained, and patted dry
2 to 3 tablespoons cooking oil
¾ cup (4½ ounces) chopped tomatoes
1 tablespoon tomato paste, or 2 tablespoons tomato puree, or 3 tablespoons tomato sauce
¼ teaspoon sugar
½ teaspoon regular soy sauce
¼ teaspoon salt
¼ teaspoon freshly squeezed or bottled lime or lemon juice

Spice Blend

½ teaspoon ground coriander
½ teaspoon ground cumin
½ teaspoon ground fennel seeds
¼ teaspoon turmeric powder
¼ teaspoon finely ground black pepper

Spice Paste

1½ tablespoons sliced cloves garlic
½ heaping cup diced shallots or onions
2 to 4 dried whole red chilies, steeped in hot water for 5 to 8 minutes, slit and deseeded; or ½ to 1 tablespoon *cili boh* (*see page 315*); or ¾ to 1½ teaspoons bottled *sambal oelek*; or ¼ teaspoon chile powder
1 heaping tablespoon sliced lemongrass stalk (¼-inch to ½-inch pieces)
¼ cup water

Garnish

2 tablespoons chopped coriander leaves (cilantro)

In Malaysia, scallops are prepared with light spicy sauces as compared to in the U.S. where cooks use rich butter and wine-based sauces. Chinese, Nonya, and Kristangs season scallops with soy sauce, ginger, taucheo, *and oyster sauce. Malays add chilies,* belacan, *tamarind juice, coconut milk, and garlic to create wonderful* sambals.

One memorable scallop preparation that I especially enjoyed was made by an Indian Muslim vendor in an alleyway in Penang. I discovered him while taking a walking tour of historical Penang. He combined spices with chile paste, lemongrass, garlic, and shallots. Then he heated a large kwali *and sautéed the spice paste, spooning in a little tomato ketchup and soy sauce. He continued stirring the spice paste in oil at high heat till a wonderful aroma suddenly burst into the air around us. Then he added bay scallops and coated them with the fragrant sauce. I could not wait to eat! He served the scallops with coconut-infused rice (*nasi lemak*) and a pickled cucumber* acar. *We sat on rickety stools that he had placed around his mobile cart and enjoyed the meal under the dim lights.*

In this recipe, I use tender, tiny bay scallops but you can also use larger sea scallops. It will transport you to Penang and the hawker special I enjoyed there.

DIRECTIONS:

1. Combine the Spice Blend ingredients. Rub scallops with 1 teaspoon of Spice Blend and marinate for 30 minutes.
2. Process Spice Paste ingredients to a smooth paste.
3. Heat 1 tablespoon oil in a skillet, add scallops and pan-sear about 1 minute on each side till brown. Remove from skillet and set aside.
4. Heat remaining oil in the skillet and sauté Spice Paste for about 5 minutes, till fragrant, then add the remaining Spice Blend and sauté another ½ to 1 minute.
5. Stir in tomatoes and sauté for about 1 to 2 minutes. Add ½ cup water, tomato paste, puree, or sauce, sugar, soy sauce, and salt and cook, stirring, for about 3 to 5 minutes, till sauce becomes thick.
6. Add pan-seared scallops and sauté for about 2 to 3 minutes, till scallops are done and coated well with sauce. (Be careful not to overcook otherwise scallops will become tough and bitter.)
7. Add lime or lemon juice and stir for ½ minute. Garnish with coriander leaves.

Serve with cooked white or brown rice, coconut-infused rice (page 117), lime rice (page 122), or yellow rice (page 118); and cucumber carrot *acar* (page 99), spicy water spinach (page 228), or stir-fried Chinese greens (page 227).

Chile Squid
Cili Sotong

Makes 3 to 4 servings

Sotong is the Malaysian term given to squid and its close relatives, cuttlefish and octopus. Sotong *is prepared in many styles by Chinese, Malays, and Indian Muslims. Indian Muslims generally cook* sotong *in a curry sauce with chilies, or in* sambal *and serve it with* nasi minyak *(ghee rice) or* nasi biryani. *In Penang,* sotong *is served with cooked white rice, as a side for a* nasi kandar *meal. In Kuala Lumpur and Petaling Jaya, the towns I grew up in, many Malay-operated* nasi campur *stalls almost always have* sambal *or* cili sotong *served with steamed white rice, vegetables, and spicy* acars. *Chinese prepare* sotong *with soy sauce, vinegar, sugar, lime juice, turmeric, and/or chilies.*

Ma did not cook sotong *often so I am no expert on* sotong *dishes, though I enjoyed them occasionally when our Malay cook Zaiton prepared them with chilies. This is my favorite* sotong *recipe, taking some cues from Ma who had watched her cooking. It is prepared with chilies and spices, tempered with tomatoes, and garnished with cilantro and fried onions. This recipe is for the fiery loving cooks, but you can reduce the chilies if you want.*

INGREDIENTS

- 2 tablespoons cooking oil
- 1½-inch cinnamon stick
- 2 or 3 cloves
- 1 lemongrass stalk, bruised with back of knife and knotted
- 2 tablespoons tamarind concentrate or tamarind juice extracted from pulp (*see page 339*)
- 1 to 2 teaspoons sugar (*just use 1 teaspoon or less if using thick or sweet soy sauce*)
- 2 to 3 teaspoons double black, thick, or sweet soy sauce
- ½ teaspoon salt
- 1 pound squid, cleaned, rinsed, cut into 1½-inch pieces
- ¼ to ½ teaspoon fresh or bottled lime or lemon juice

Spice Paste

- 2 tablespoons sliced garlic cloves
- 2 teaspoons sliced fresh ginger
- 1 cup chopped shallots or onions
- 15 to 20 dried whole red chilies, steeped in hot water for 5 to 8 minutes, slit and deseeded; or ¼ to ⅓ cup *cili boh* (*see page 315*); or 2 to 2½ tablespoons bottled *sambal oelek*
- ¼ cup water

Garnish

- 2 tablespoons chopped coriander leaves (cilantro)

DIRECTIONS:

1. Process Spice Paste ingredients to a coarse paste. Set aside.
2. Heat 1 tablespoon oil in a wok or skillet and fry cinnamon stick and cloves for about ½ minute.
3. Add remaining oil and Spice Paste, and sauté for about 5 minutes, till fragrant, adding more oil if necessary.
4. Add lemongrass, tamarind juice, sugar, soy sauce, and salt and sauté for 1 to 2 minutes.
5. Stir in squid and sauté for about 4 to 5 minutes; add lime or lemon juice and cook another minute, taking care not to overcook as squid will get chewy.
6. Remove lemongrass and cinnamon stick before serving. Garnish with coriander leaves.

Serve with cooked white or brown rice, ghee rice (page 121), vegetable *biryani* (page 280), or yellow rice (page 118); and spicy water spinach (page 228), eggplant and pineapple *pajeri* (page 232), or vegetables in spicy coconut milk (page 223).

Fish with Spicy Preserved Soybean Sauce

Ikan Chuan-Chuan

Makes 3 to 4 servings

INGREDIENTS

- ¾ to 1 pound fish steaks (cod, tuna, mackerel, swordfish, or other firm-fleshed fish), or 12-inch-long whole fish (red snapper, threadfin, pomfret, or bream), cleaned and tail discarded, cut into ½-inch-thick slices
- ¼ teaspoon finely ground black pepper
- ⅛ teaspoon chile powder
- ⅛ teaspoon turmeric powder
- 2 to 3 tablespoons cooking oil
- 1 heaping tablespoon sliced or chopped garlic cloves
- 4 teaspoons sliced or chopped fresh ginger
- 1 cup sliced or diced shallots or onions (⅛-inch-thick slices)
- 1 fresh green chile (jalapeno, Serrano, cayenne, or Thai), sliced or diced
- ¼ teaspoon thick or sweet soy sauce
- 1 teaspoon regular soy sauce
- 2 teaspoons mashed preserved soybean paste (*taucheo*, black version) or bean sauce or black bean sauce
- 1 teaspoon distilled white vinegar, rice vinegar, or palm vinegar

GARNISH

- 2 tablespoons sliced spring onions or Chinese chives (*kuchai*)

Ikan chuan-chuan is *a well-known Penang Nonya fish preparation with Chinese Hokkien origins. The Kristangs of Malacca also lay claim to it. Fresh whole fish such as Spanish mackerel, threadfin, or red snapper is sliced and marinated with black pepper and salt and deep-fried. When I had* chuan-chuan *in a Kristang restaurant, whole fish was used instead of fillets or steaks. A sauce is prepared separately with preserved soybean paste* (taucheo), *soy sauce, ginger, garlic, chilies, and vinegar. The fish is then simmered in the sauce or the sauce is poured over the cooked fish. Some cooks dip the fish in flour before frying. Some use tamarind juice instead of vinegar.*

In my recipe, I have added some extra ingredients to the marinade, including turmeric and chile powder. When using taucheo *or bean sauce, mash the beans before adding to the saucepan. I also prefer to pan-sear the fish instead of deep-frying.*

DIRECTIONS:

1. Rub fish with black pepper, chile powder, and turmeric, and let marinate for about 15 to 30 minutes.
2. Heat 1 to 2 tablespoons oil in a skillet and when hot, add fish and pan-sear till brown, about 3 to 5 minutes on each side (depending on whether using steaks or whole fish and their thickness). Remove fish from pan and set aside and keep warm.
3. Heat 1 tablespoon oil in the skillet and sauté garlic and ginger for about ½ to 1 minute; add shallots or onions and sauté for about 1 to 2 minutes, then add chile and sauté another ½ minute.
4. Add ¼ cup water, soy sauces, and soybean paste and stir for about 2 minutes. Add vinegar and stir for another minute, till sauce becomes thick.
5. Pour sauce over fish and garnish with spring onions or Chinese chives.

Serve with cooked white or brown rice, yellow rice (page 118), or tomato rice (page 119); and stir-fried mixed vegetables (page 224), spicy cucumber tomato salad (page 97), stir-fried bean sprouts (page 229), or stir-fried *kalian* (page 222).

Chile Crab
Ketam Cili

Makes 5 to 6 servings

Chile, chili, and chilli are the Western terms for chile peppers, while cili *is the Malay term. Chile crab is an aromatic, spicy, sweet crab dish popular with Malaysians and Singaporeans. It is usually served at Chinese seafood restaurants but many Malays also prepare spicy chile crabs using* cili padi *(fiery bird peppers) and sometimes even add* belacan*. Some cooks make it sweeter with more sugar, while others add galangal, turmeric root, or preserved soybean paste* (taucheo) *to make it pungent. The original recipe calls for beaten egg but I omit it to cut out its richness. Ketchup is usually added as the tomato substitute but I prefer to add pureed tomato, tomato paste, or tomato sauce. I like mine a little spicy and pungent but light tasting. I also prefer it with less sugar, but you can add more to make it sweeter.*

INGREDIENTS

- 2 to 3 teaspoons rice wine
- 2 pounds crab legs (regular, king, or snow), cut into 1½-inch pieces, or Dungeness crabs, cleaned and quartered
- 2 to 3 tablespoons cooking oil
- 2 tablespoons regular soy sauce
- 2 to 3 teaspoons sugar
- ½ teaspoon coarsely ground black peppercorns
- ¾ to 1 cup tomato puree, or ⅓ to ½ cup tomato paste, or 1 to 1½ cups tomato sauce
- ½ cup sliced spring onions or Chinese chives (*kuchai*)

SPICE PASTE

- 3 heaping tablespoons sliced garlic cloves
- 4 teaspoons sliced fresh ginger
- 7 to 12 dried whole red chilies (*depending on heat desired*), steeped in hot water for 5 to 8 minutes till softened, slit and deseeded; or 1¾ to 3 tablespoons *cili boh* (*see page 315*); or ⅔ to 1½ tablespoons bottled *sambal oelek*
- 1 to 2 lemongrass stalks, sliced crosswise into ¼ to ½-inch pieces (½ to ¾ cup)
- 1¾ to 2 tablespoons preserved soybean paste (*taucheo*, black version) or black bean sauce or bean sauce
- ¼ to ½ cup water

DIRECTIONS:

1. Process Spice Paste ingredients to a coarse paste (if using black bean sauce or bean sauce add to Spice Paste at step 3). Set aside.
2. Mix rice wine with 1 tablespoon of the Spice Paste and 1 to 2 tablespoons water. Coat crab pieces with this marinade and marinate for about 1 hour in the refrigerator.
3. Heat 2 tablespoons oil in a wok or skillet and sauté the remaining Spice Paste for about 5 to 8 minutes, till fragrant, adding remaining oil if needed.
4. Add soy sauce, sugar, black pepper, and tomato puree, paste, or sauce, and stir for about 5 minutes.
5. Stir in 1 cup water, add crabs, bring to a boil, lower heat and stir for 1 minute. Cover and simmer for about 5 minutes, then uncover and simmer, stirring constantly, an additional 12 to 15 minutes, till sauce becomes thick.
6. Add spring onions or Chinese chives and stir another minute.

Serve with cooked white or brown rice, yellow rice (page 118), spiced rice (page 120), or vegetable *biryani* (page 280); and spicy water spinach (page 228), stir-fried *kailan* (page 222), or cucumber carrot *acar* (page 99). You can also serve with naan, *roti*, or pita, or like the Malaysians, with toasted bread to sop up the sauce!

My siblings, Vas, Ravee, Prasnan, and myself (on right)

CHAPTER 9

VEGETABLES: FRESH OFFERINGS

Vegetable vendors at wet market, Kuching, Sarawak

Malaysians prepare vegetables (called *sayur* in Malay, *marakari* in Tamil, and *choy* in Cantonese) in a multitude of ways to accompany entrees and rice—curried with coconut milk; stir-fried with garlic and chilies; pounded with dried shrimps; dry braised with *belacan*; or simply steamed with garlic, toasted sesame oil, and soy sauce. Malaysians traditionally buy fresh vegetables at wet markets or *pasar malam* (night markets) where all varieties are piled in colorful displays. Today more Malaysians are patronizing supermarkets, which also enticingly display fresh vegetables and fruits for sale.

TYPES OF VEGETABLES IN MALAYSIA

In most Malaysian homes, cooked greens (*sawi-sawi*) are an everyday dish, savored for their crispy crunchy textures and health benefits. When buying greens that have small flowers, make sure there is no profusion of flowers as that indicates they are not fresh. Generally, greens are used the same day or within a few days before the leaves wilt or yellow. When you walk around open-air markets, it is wonderful to see numerous varieties of fresh greens of different shapes and sizes displayed all over, some with bright flowers. There are Chinese mustard greens (*sawi*, *kadugu kira*, or *gai choy*) with broad deep-green leaves and a pungent, peppery and mustard-like flavor; Chinese flowering cabbage (*choy sam* or *yu choy*, *sawi bunga*, or *sawi manis*) with long stalks and thin deep green leaves; Chinese broccoli (*kailan* or *gailan*) with thick round stems and green leaves and white flowers; Chinese cabbage or *pak choy* (*sawi putih*) with thin stalks, green leaves, and bright yellow flowers; Chinese spinach (*por choy* or *bayam*); and the slender dark green water spinach (*kangkung* or *ong choy*). (*See Glossary on Asian greens, page 311.*)

Asian greens must be cleaned thoroughly before cooking. Gently dunk and swirl them in a large pot of water to dislodge the sand or dirt, making sure not to bruise the leaves. This should be done a few times. Alternatively, like my Ma, you can wash each stem separately, making sure that there is no sand lodged in between the stems. Also break the base of the stem as dirt and sand can be lodged inside. Then pat dry (or use a salad spinner) before cooking, so greens will not get soggy during cooking. When cooked, greens lose at least half of their volume, so use double the amount you need when preparing them.

Store greens in tightly sealed plastic bags in the refrigerator. Make sure there is no moisture as moisture accelerates spoilage. Don't wash them before storage or if you do, pat dry and wrap with paper towels to absorb any moisture. If stored too long, leaves will turn yellow or become slimy due to moisture.

Petai vendor

The taste and texture of greens take on new levels when prepared quickly and with certain seasonings. *Pak choy* becomes sweeter when cooked with a simple garlic-ginger-soy sauce. *Kailan* (Chinese broccoli), prepared Chinese-style or Nonya-style, becomes delicious when steamed, blanched, or braised with fried garlic and oyster sauce and tossed with toasted sesame oil. *Kangkung* (water spinach) cooked with *belacan* becomes an addictive dish (page 228). Its leaves are pointed or round and light to dark green with a reddish center. Since *kangkung* has a high moisture content, it is generally cooked soon after purchase.

Malays make wonderful *sambals* using four angled beans or winged beans (*kacang botol*) and stink beans (*petai*, also called *sataw* or *yongchak*) cooked with *belacan*, garlic, bird peppers, and shrimp or baby anchovies. *Petai*, broad edible bright green beans enclosed in pods, are from the genus Parkia of the Fabaceae family. *Petai* is a "cooling" vegetable and Malays eat it for its many health benefits, especially for energy, lowering blood pressure, and for the heart, as it is believed to cut strokes by as much as 40 percent. It has a strong smell and a taste that lingers.

Arabs and Indians introduced okra, eggplant, lentils, and beans to Malaysia. Lentils (dhals) are popular with Indians, prepared in South Indian, Ceylonese (Sri Lankan), Punjabi, and Gujarati styles. *Toovar dhals* (smaller than yellow split peas) are translucent with an earthy flavor. They are simmered till soft and are made into dhal curry, mashed for *sambar*, or dry roasted and added for textural effect to cabbage, bitter gourd, and other vegetable dishes. *Urad dhal* has a black skin and white interior. They are dry roasted and added to curries and Indian stir-fries for textural effect. They are also fermented with rice and fenugreek seeds and then ground into a smooth paste to make *thosai* and *idli*.

ETHNIC PREPARATION STYLES

With vegetables, particular cooking styles and flavorings suit certain vegetables. Okra tastes good when curried, water spinach is delicious stir-fried with *belacan* and chilies, *choy sum* is good with dried shrimp and soy sauce, and *kailan* is delicious steamed with garlic and oyster sauce. The Chinese invented the art of stir-frying vegetables with garlic, ginger, and soy sauce, a technique that adds flavors yet retains the crispy crunchy textures of the vegetables. It works well with most greens and vegetables. A simple stir-fried mixed vegetable is popular in every home in Malaysia with each ethnic group adding their favorite ingredients. Nonyas and Kristangs have *chap chye*, a transparent mung bean noodle prepared with shredded yam bean, cabbage, wood ear mushrooms, dried lily buds, dried shrimp, and/or *taucheo* (see recipe for Chinese-style mixed vegetables without the noodles, page 224). My first exposure to the wonderful Chinese cooking styles with greens was at the homes of my high school classmates Yew Ying and Adeline, both of Chinese ancestry. I have fond memories of our get-togethers for Chinese New Year and birthdays. I remember clearly one year in Yew Ying's home being served braised *kailan*, vegetable soups, seafood dishes, and different kinds of colorful shredded steamed and stir-fried crispy vegetables, and a number of sauces to make delicious *popiah basah* (fresh spring rolls).

Europeans brought potatoes, cabbage, carrots, cauliflower, sweet bell peppers, and cucumbers to Malaysia. Broccoli, button mushrooms, peas, Brussels sprouts, artichokes, and celery are more recent introductions at supermarkets. Other more exotic local vegetables include *paku pakis* (wild ferns), notably the *pucok paku* or wild fiddlehead fern, which is stir-fried with *belacan* and chilies by the ethnic tribes of Sarawak and Sabah. When we were at the open market in Kuching, Sarawak, I saw bunches of these ferns being laid out on the ground for display. The women selling them told me they gathered them from the forests nearby. At the hotel where we stayed, the chef prepared them as a stir-fry. It had a unique taste and texture that I was not accustomed to.

There are many unusual vegetables or parts of plants that are used to flavor or provide a textural effect in Chinese, Malay, Kristang, and Nonya dishes. Dried lily buds, sweet potato leaves, sweet pumpkin flower, blue pea flower (*bunga telang*), and hibiscus flowers are a few of them.

Bitter gourd

Besides stir-frying, there are many ways in which Malaysians prepare vegetables, such as braising, simmering, steaming, or currying. Nonyas and Kristangs add fresh or pickled vegetables to enrich soups and stews. A Nonya mixed vegetable soup, *chap chai t'ng*, has pork belly and dried squid with cabbage, yam bean, carrots, and shiitake mushrooms. Salted Chinese mustard greens (*kiam chye*) are rinsed several times in water to remove excess salt and added to Chinese, Nonya, and Kristang soups and stews. Winter melon (wax gourd), another cooling vegetable, is candied or added to Chinese soups (page 82).

Sweet spicy pickled sides (*acars*) with cucumbers, carrots, yams, cauliflower, cabbage, or long green beans are extremely popular with all Malaysians (see Chapter 3). Pickled or shredded vegetables also garnish soups and noodle dishes. Nonya *acars* are spicy, sweet, and sour, particularly in the north, where tamarind juice or lime juice is added with chilies and spice pastes (*rempah*). Nonyas and Kristangs also add pieces of salted fish and dried shrimp to flavor bean sprouts, *kalian*, or cabbage. Kristangs and Eurasians add fresh shrimp or pieces of meat to their vegetables. *Ambilar kacang* is a popular preparation with Kristangs and Nonyas, using long beans, pieces of beef, eggplant, tamarind juice, and curry paste.

Indians usually curry their vegetables or add them to lentil-based curries and stews. Many also prepare vegetables as Ma did, stir-frying them with spices, dried shrimp, soy sauce, or *belacan*. In our home, it was common to serve curried or spicy stir-fried vegetables at a meal that also included a lentil curry. Our family favorites included stir-fried bean sprouts (*taugeh*, page 229), stir-fried shredded cabbage with scrambled egg (page 226), and long green beans braised in *sambal belacan* (page 230). Ma sometimes added an egg to her stir-fried vegetables, especially when she was not serving meat, chicken, or seafood.

While we were in Kuantan in Pahang state, along the East Coast, there were times when my grandparents came to stay with us. Ma had a vegetable garden at the back and grew some of the vegetables she enjoyed—long green beans, cucumbers, eggplants, tomatoes, greens, bitter gourd, and chilies. I remember vividly my grandmother's visits because of her drumstick curry and spicy bitter gourd, both of which were not our favorites but she ate them for their health benefits as well. Like typical children everywhere, we did not like eating vegetables that had a strong taste or were slightly bitter. One morning, as usual, my two older brothers, Prasnan and Ravee, and my younger sis, Vas, and I climbed up the *jambu batu* tree (firm guava) behind our house to pick the fruits. I was eight then. Hearing Periama's (my grandmother) call, I climbed down and picked two bitter gourds from the vegetable garden and gave them to her. I decided to sit and watch Periama prepare her famous dry bitter gourd curry. She was wearing her typical home attire, a simple floral cotton *saree* blouse with a cotton batik sarong. Her hair was always neatly combed and tied in a bun behind her head. She wore large earrings of precious red stones, her favorite. I noticed the green tattoos of Hindu Gods on both her lower arms that she received when she was a little girl in her hometown in Salem, South India.

First Periama sliced the bitter gourd. Then she toasted some mustard seeds in hot oil. I watched the seeds pop, some out of the pan. After the noise subsided a bit, she added turmeric powder and some curry powder and stirred for a couple of minutes. (Periama blended her own curry powders for different dishes, which she kept marked in silver containers in the kitchen cupboard.) She then put this mixture aside while she stir-fried the garlic and shallots. Then she added the fragrant cooked spice paste, the bitter gourd slices, and boiled lentils. After stirring for a few minutes, she added some water, covered the pan and let it cook. Finally, she added some sliced red chilies and curry leaves. As she lifted the cover, I got a whiff of its aroma . . . delicious! She took a spoonful of it and gave it to me to taste. It smelled so good and looked so appetizing. But the bitter flavor overwhelmed me as I bit into the gourd slices. She smiled as she watched me. She said that in order to stay healthy, she balanced the different tastes—bitter, spicy, sweet, sour, and astringent. She had a much higher tolerance for bitterness than I did!

Periama would often reminisce about her past—about her family and how she came to Malaysia. These were our times together and I always loved her stories. I asked her about my grandfather, whom we called Thatha—how she met him and about her wedding. To this question, she sighed and said that since it was performed locally, none of her family members attended. She said it was a simple ceremony and never gave the details, but I saw the sadness on her face. Later on Ma told me Periama was an outcast with her family because she married outside her wealthy Chettiar community. I don't think Periama ever went back to India to see her family but she always encouraged me to visit her family home in Coimbatore in South India.

In Malaysia there are Chinese vegetarian restaurants that specialize in mimicking chicken, meat, and seafood dishes, both visually and in flavor. They are made solely from vegetarian ingredients—soy protein, tofu, wheat gluten, mushrooms, and other vegetables. You can get vegetarian roast "pork," spicy and sweet "shrimp," whole steamed "fish," or "chicken" drumsticks. They are amazing works of art and science.

My favorite vegetable dish was Periama's stir-fried Chinese greens (*sawi tumis*, page 227), which she sometimes made with fresh shrimp or beaten eggs for us. Unlike the Chinese, who cook *sawi* as whole intact leaves, Periama would cut the greens in ½-inch thickness. Ma cooked it the same way, and always concerned about nutrition, broke an egg towards the end to scramble with the *sawi*. Sometimes she would add fresh shrimp for flavor. We enjoyed eating the crunchy *sawi* with cooked white rice and Ma's *sambal* shrimp.

Malays (especially in the Northeast region of Malaysia) and Nonyas enjoy an *ulam* meal that consists of blanched green vegetables, including *petai*, long green beans, and/or slices of

Malays consider an *ulam* meal healthy because the different herbs provide therapeutic healing for the body. *Petai* cleanses the urinary system and promotes healthy function of the kidneys, stabilizes blood sugar levels, and reduces the effects of PMS among women. Nasturtium leaves aid digestion; turmeric leaves help with the irregularities in the digestive system; mint leaves relieve colds and coughs; and basil prevents stomach disorders and cramps.

cucumbers with an array of fresh herbs. *Ulam* is accompanied by steaming hot rice and spicy grilled or fried fish with fiery *sambals*. Some add the *ulam* to cooked rice (*nasi ulam*, page 125). *Sayur lodeh* (page 223) is a well known East Coast Malay vegetable dish with cabbage, long green beans, and carrots simmered in coconut milk and flavored with dried shrimp paste, galangal, and other spices. The Nonya version, called *sayur lemak*, has bean curd and dried shrimp in coconut milk thickened with candlenuts.

Shredded crispy yam beans and long green beans are boiled for Indian Muslim *rojak* or *pasembor*. Bitter gourd is relished by Malays who *tumis* it with dried shrimp and add it to omelets. The Chinese stuff bitter gourd with fish paste for a dish called *yong taufoo*. Yam bean or jicama (*sengkuang* or *bengkuang*) is a mildly sweet and crispy tuber eaten raw in salads or shredded and used as a stuffing in Nonya *popiah* (fresh spring rolls).

When I first traveled to England as a student, I was lost without the delicious vegetable dishes that I enjoyed while growing up. I had to adjust to new vegetables like potatoes, broccoli, Brussels sprouts, beets, asparagus, and French beans. I didn't enjoy the way they were prepared—boiled and not seasoned except for salt and pepper, and sometimes served with butter or cream. They were rich and heavy with no texture or flavor. So my vegetable diet consisted of very little, because the preparation lacked the intense flavors and distinct textures I grew up with. I added whatever spices or sauces I could get my hands on at the dining table, and practically gulped down the vegetables with a glass of water!

When I came to the U.S it was the same experience for me. I lived close to major cities like Washington D.C. and New York, so I often went to the markets in Chinatown during weekends to get Asian greens and other fresh vegetables to prepare them the way I liked. Slowly through the years, as North American tastes for spicy flavor profiles and crispy textures emerged, more Indian, Chinese, Thai, and Vietnamese vegetable and salad dishes became popular. Flavorful and textured vegetables have come a long way! Today, Asian and many mainstream supermarkets carry a variety of Asian vegetables and greens, even in the suburbs.

In the recipes in this chapter, vegetarians can omit the dried or fresh shrimp, shrimp paste, or eggs.

Spicy Dry Curried Okra

Kari Bendi

Makes 3 to 4 servings

Okra, also called bendhi, vendikai, *or* lady's fingers, *is a popular vegetable with Indians, Malays, and Nonyas. At home, Periama prepared okra frequently, adding it to fish curries or making a robust dry curried okra dish that I enjoyed. Ma, like her Malay help, sometimes added dried shrimps or* belacan *to give that extra oomph to the okra dish.*

On one of our recent trips to Malaysia, after my Ma passed away, my sister Vas invited me to lunch at her home in Petaling Jaya. She prepared a delicious dry okra curry, one of my favorites, that Ma used to make for me whenever I visited home. We plopped down on her front porch with the bowl of okra and rice amidst the beautiful garden of tropical flowers while feeling the hot humid afternoon weather. As I bit into the okra, memories of Ma flooded back. And we reminisced about our times with Ma, especially going to the movies.

Vas used her own blend of spices for the okra that is out of this world. I could not resist adding a little belacan *to her recipe, and it does take the flavor to a whole new level. So here it is, and Vas … hopefully you will enjoy it too.*

INGREDIENTS

- 2 to 4 tablespoons cooking oil
- 3 cups (about 11 ounces) okra, washed and patted dry
- 1 teaspoon cumin seeds
- 2 teaspoons sliced and coarsely crushed garlic cloves
- 1 tablespoon chopped or crushed fresh ginger
- ¾ to 1 cup thinly sliced shallots or onions
- Optional: 1 teaspoon dried shrimp paste (*belacan*), toasted at 400°F for 15 minutes (*see page 335*)
- 1 fresh green chile (cayenne, jalapeno, Serrano, or Thai), sliced
- 1 tablespoon tamarind concentrate or tamarind juice extracted from pulp (*see page 339*)
- Heaping ¼ cup (about 1½ ounces) sliced tomatoes
- Optional: 4 or 5 fresh curry leaves

Spice Blend

- ½ teaspoon turmeric powder
- ½ teaspoon ground cumin
- ¼ to ½ teaspoon chile powder
- ¼ teaspoon ground fennel seeds
- ¼ teaspoon ground coriander
- ⅛ teaspoon ground cinnamon
- ⅛ teaspoon ground cloves

DIRECTIONS:

1. Combine Spice Blend ingredients and set aside.
2. Heat 1 tablespoon of oil in a wok or skillet. Add okra and cook, stirring, for about 8 to 10 minutes, till okra gets a little brown and drier, adding another tablespoon oil if necessary. Set aside. (As an alternative, you can deep-fry the okra.)
3. Heat 1 tablespoon oil in the wok or skillet and fry cumin seeds for about ½ minute; add garlic and ginger and sauté for about ½ to 1 minute. Add shallots or onions and sauté for 1 to 2 minutes; add dried shrimp paste, if using, and another tablespoon oil, if needed, and stir for another ½ to 1 minute, mashing in the shrimp paste to get a smooth mixture.
4. Add green chile and Spice Blend and sauté for about ½ minute.
5. Add cooked okra and tamarind juice and sauté for about 2 minutes; add tomatoes and sauté for 3 to 4 minutes, till mixture becomes aromatic.
6. Add curry leaves and sauté for another minute. (Or fry curry leaves in 1 tablespoon hot oil in a separate skillet and add this fragrant oil mixture to cooked okra and mix well.)

Serve with cooked white or brown rice, yellow rice (page 118), or lime rice (page 122); and shrimp *varuval* (page 203), lamb *peratil* (page 185), lamb chops in black pepper sauce (page 184), or spicy egg curry (page 172). Or serve with naan, pita, or any flatbread with vegetable dhal curry (page 231) or spicy lentil vegetable stew (page 88).

There are many ethnic and regional recipes for okra. For example, in Malacca, the Nonyas add dried shrimp, *belacan*, and candlenuts, while the Kristangs add vinegar and *belacan* to give it a slightly sour taste. I like the way the Malays prepare it, with a spicy and pungent taste using hot bird peppers (*cili padi*) and *belacan*.

Stir-Fried Chinese Broccoli

Kailan Tumis

Makes 4 servings

INGREDIENTS

1 tablespoon cooking oil
2 teaspoons sliced and crushed garlic cloves
1 teaspoon crushed fresh ginger
¼ cup thinly sliced shallots or onions
1 heaping teaspoon chopped and pounded dried tiny whole shrimp, soaked in ¼ cup hot water for 10 minutes to soften, then drained
4 heaping teaspoons preserved soybean paste (*taucheo*, black version) or black bean sauce or bean sauce
½ teaspoon thick or sweet soy sauce
¼ teaspoon rice wine
¼ teaspoon sugar
⅛ teaspoon salt
½ pound Chinese broccoli (*kailan*), bottom stems trimmed about 1 to 2 inches, then rinsed and swirled in water a few times to dislodge sand and dirt
¼ teaspoon toasted sesame oil

Optional Garnish

1 fresh red chile (cayenne, Fresno, cherry, jalapeno, Serrano, Thai, or cili padi), sliced (¼-inch pieces)

Kailan *(Chinese broccoli) when mature is a slightly bitter, leafy vegetable with thick stems and dull gray-green leaves. Baby* kailan *is tender with bright green leaves and slender stems. The leaves, stems, and flowers are all eaten. Baby* kailan *is generally stir-fried with ginger and garlic, and mature* kailan *is steamed or blanched and topped with seasoned oyster sauce.* Kailan *is a must for me whenever I visit home or when I go to Chinatown in New York City. I first tasted* kailan *at the home of Yew Ying, my childhood friend and schoolmate. I enjoyed it so much that my Ma learned to prepare it the same way, with oyster sauce and sesame oil.*

In my recipe, I use baby kailan *as it is fresher and sweeter, and in place of the oyster sauce, I use a blend of smooth black* taucheo *(preserved soybean paste) or bean sauce, thick soy sauce, and pounded dried shrimp. It still tastes light and delicious and has also become*

DIRECTIONS:

1. Heat oil in a wok or skillet and sauté garlic and ginger for about ½ to 1 minute; add shallots or onions and sauté for another 1 to 2 minutes.
2. Add pounded shrimp and stir for about 2 to 3 minutes.
3. Stir in soybean paste, soy sauce, rice wine, sugar, and salt. Blend well.
4. Add *kailan* and cook for about 2 to 3 minutes, till leaves wilt, turning over using a pair of tongs to coat well with sauce.
5. Add sesame oil and blend well for 1 minute.
6. Garnish with chile, if using, before serving.

Serve with cooked white or brown rice or fried rice (page 123); and tamarind coriander chicken (page 164), stir-fried beef steak (page 179), chile pork (page 186), mixed peppercorn pork (page 187), stir-fried *sambal* shrimp (page 204), fish with spicy preserved soybean sauce (page 212), or soy sauce fish (page 199).

The name *kailan* is derived from the Cantonese word *gailàhn*. *Kailan* belongs to the mustard family and is from the same species as broccoli and kale, *Brassica oleracea*. Thus, it is also commonly called Chinese broccoli or Chinese kale. However, *kailan* has a stronger aftertaste than broccoli.

Vegetables in Spicy Coconut Milk

Sayur Lodeh

Makes 5 to 6 servings

Sayur lodeh is a vegetable medley simmered in coconut milk and spices. A Malay and Nonya specialty with Indian influences, it is sometimes called masak lodeh *or* masak lemak*, depending on where in Malaysia the dish is prepared. Its color varies from a creamy yellow to a yellowish brown. The vegetables used also vary, depending on the cook, and can include long green beans (or green or string beans), cabbage, carrots, eggplant, yams, pumpkin, or cauliflower. Nonyas, with their Chinese heritage, add tofu pieces, fresh or dried shrimp, and yams to their* sayur lodeh.

My first taste of sayur lodeh *was at a Terengganu night market, referred to locally as* pasar malam. *The state of Terengganu is in the northeast of Malaysia, with a largely Malay population. A Malay lady with a* tudong *(a veil or headscarf) ladled out* sayur lodeh *from a huge pot on a stove. It had a delicious aroma of curried stew and contained green beans, cabbage, and eggplant. She served it with cubes of* lontong *and a small saucer of* sambal belacan. *It reminded me of the coconut-milk-based vegetable curries of Kerala, except that it had a wonderful pungency from galangal and pounded dried shrimps. She said that galangal, dried shrimp, and* cili padi *were a must for her* sayur lodeh.

My recipe combines traditional Malay and Nonya flavors, and I have added vegetables that my family enjoys.

INGREDIENTS

- 1 package (14-ounce) firm tofu (*tauhu*), cut into 2-inch by ½-inch pieces
- 1 or 2 tablespoons cooking oil
- 1 heaping tablespoon thinly sliced garlic cloves
- 1 teaspoon thinly sliced fresh or frozen and thawed galangal or fresh ginger
- ¾ cup sliced shallots or onions
- 1 heaping tablespoon chopped or coarsely pounded tiny dried whole shrimp, soaked in ¼ cup hot water for 10 minutes to soften, then drained
- 1 fresh red chile (cayenne, Fresno, jalapeno, Serrano, cherry, or Thai), deseeded if less heat is desired, sliced into ¼-inch pieces
- ¾ cup unsweetened coconut milk
- 1 cup (5 ounces) sliced carrots (2-inch-long by ¼-inch-thick slices)
- 1 cup (4½ ounces) sliced green beans (1 to 1½-inch-long pieces)
- 1½ cups (4½ ounces) sliced cabbage (cut criss-cross into 1½-inch pieces)

SPICE BLEND

- 1 teaspoon ground coriander
- ½ teaspoon ground cumin
- ¼ teaspoon turmeric powder
- ¼ teaspoon finely ground black pepper
- ¼ teaspoon chile powder

DIRECTIONS:

1. Pan-fry tofu pieces in a non-stick skillet (or in a regular skillet with 1 tablespoon oil) till light brown, about 5 minutes. Remove from pan and set aside. (Alternately, you can skip this step and add tofu pieces in step 7 with the cabbage.)
2. Combine Spice Blend ingredients and set aside.
3. Heat 1 tablespoon oil and sauté garlic and galangal or ginger for ½ to 1 minute; add shallots or onions and sauté for 1 to 2 minutes.
4. Add pounded shrimp and stir for about 2 to 3 minutes.
5. Add Spice Blend and stir for ½ minute, then add sliced chile and sauté another ½ minute. Stir in coconut milk and ½ cup water, bring to a boil, then lower heat and simmer for about 5 minutes.
6. Add carrots and green beans and another ½ cup water, cover, and simmer about 3 to 4 minutes (being careful to retain crunchy texture of carrots and beans).
7. Add cabbage, cover, simmer another 2 to 3 minutes. Uncover and add tofu pieces and cook 2 to 3 minutes, blending well without breaking up the tofu (don't overcook).

Serve with cooked white or brown rice, yellow rice (page 118), ghee rice (page 121), crusty bread, or *lontong* (compressed rice cubes); and chicken *kurma* (page 168), lamb *kurma* (page 282), beef *rendang* (page 177), fried beef *satay* (page 178), shrimp *varuval* (page 203), or chicken *rendang* (page 287).

Stir-Fried Mixed Vegetables

Sayur Campur Tumis

Makes 5 to 6 servings

INGREDIENTS

1 tablespoon cooking oil
1 tablespoon sliced or crushed garlic cloves
1½ teaspoons sliced or crushed fresh ginger
¾ cup chopped shallots or onions
2 tablespoons coarsely chopped or pounded dried tiny whole shrimp, soaked in ¼ cup hot water for 10 minutes to soften and then drained
1 tablespoon preserved soybean paste (*taucheo*, black version) or black bean sauce or bean sauce
1 tablespoon regular soy sauce
¼ teaspoon sugar
1 dried whole red chile, steeped in hot water for 5 to 8 minutes (slit and deseeded, if less heat is desired), pureed with ¼ cup water to a smooth paste or just coarsely crushed; or ¾ teaspoon *cili boh* (*see page 315*); or ⅓ teaspoon bottled *sambal oelek* *
½ teaspoon finely ground black pepper
1¼ cups (6¼ ounces) julienned carrots (about 2-inch-long pieces)
1 cup (4½ ounces) sliced green beans (1½ to 2-inch-long pieces)
2 heaping cups (6.5 ounces) sliced cabbage (1½-inch to 2-inch pieces)
Optional: ¾ cup dried shiitake mushrooms, soaked in hot or warm water for about 15 minutes, then drained and squeezed; or 1¼ cups sliced fresh shiitake mushrooms
½ teaspoon salt
½ teaspoon toasted sesame oil

OPTIONAL GARNISH

1 fresh red chile, sliced
1 to 2 tablespoons sliced spring onions (½-inch pieces)

The Chinese stir-frying technique is a flavorful, quick, and healthy way to incorporate a variety of vegetables into our diets. Basic stir-fry flavorings include garlic, ginger, soy sauce, and sesame oil. Every household in Malaysia makes a simple preparation of mixed vegetables for their meals. Chinese typically add tofu, fook choy *(dried soybean skin), dried lily buds, mushrooms, bamboo shoots,* taucheo, *or oyster sauce. Other ethnic groups add their favorite seasoning—Nonyas use dried shrimp, Indians prefer spices, while Malays enjoy their essential ingredient, dried shrimp paste (*belacan*).*

My sister-in-law Shanta prepares a delicious Chinese-style mixed vegetable stir-fry with thinly sliced carrots, cabbage, and cauliflower. It balances the fiery flavors of her chicken kurma, *spicy shrimp, and rich* biryani. *Here is her recipe with some minor additions.*

DIRECTIONS:

1. Heat oil in a wok or skillet and sauté garlic and ginger for about ½ to 1 minute; add shallots or onions and sauté for another 1 to 2 minutes.
2. Add dried shrimp and sauté for about 2 to 3 minutes.
3. Stir in soybean paste, soy sauce, sugar, chile, black pepper, and ¼ cup water, and sauté for about 2 to 3 minutes.
4. Add carrots and green beans and stir for about 2 to 3 minutes; add cabbage, stir for another 2 minutes till vegetables are cooked but still slightly crunchy. Add shiitake mushrooms, if using, and stir for another 2 to 3 minutes.
5. Add salt and sesame oil and stir to blend well for about 1 minute.
6. Garnish with sliced chile and spring onions, if using.

***Note:** You can also use fresh red chile instead of dried or you can simply add sliced fresh chilies after vegetables are added.

Serve with cooked white or brown rice, yellow rice (page 118), ghee rice (page 121), or tomato rice (page 119); and lamb or mutton *peratil* (page 185), chicken *kurma* (page 168), vegetable *biryani* (page 280), fish curry (page 198), spicy tangy simmered fish (page 205), or chicken curry (page 171).

Spicy Curried Pumpkin

Kari Labu

Makes 5 to 6 servings

Pumpkin is popular with Indians of Kerala origin, Chinese, and Eurasians, who add it to soups, stews, curries, desserts, or simply serve it mashed and seasoned. Keralites prepare pumpkin curry with cumin, mustard seeds, and curry leaves to celebrate Onam (Harvest festival). Eurasians enjoy it mashed as a side dish for Christmas. Chinese serve a delicious savory pumpkin dessert.

My sister Vas and her daughters, Priya and Prita, laid out a delicious feast of curried pumpkin with curried crabs and spicy fried chicken on one of my visits to her home. I enjoyed the pumpkin's sweet and spicy flavor, which was far better than the mashed potatoes. Vas showed me how to make it before I left. Some cooks dry roast urad *or* toovar dhal *and toss them over the finished dish to add some crunchiness. You can substitute butternut squash (which has a similar sweet flavor) for the pumpkin. On a snow day last winter, I converted this recipe into a wonderful fragrant soup by adding more water to it and letting it simmer.*

INGREDIENTS

2 tablespoons cooking oil
¼ to ½ teaspoon black or dark brown mustard seeds
½ teaspoon cumin seeds
2 teaspoons sliced and coarsely crushed garlic cloves
1 tablespoon sliced and coarsely crushed fresh ginger
½ cup diced shallots or onions
1 pound peeled and deseeded pumpkin or butternut squash, cut into ¾-inch pieces
Optional: 2 teaspoons tomato puree, or 1 teaspoon tomato paste, or 1 tablespoon tomato sauce
½ teaspoon salt
1¼ teaspoons freshly squeezed or bottled lime juice
4 fresh curry leaves

SPICE BLEND

1 teaspoon ground cumin
½ teaspoon turmeric powder
½ to 1 teaspoon chile powder (*depending on heat desired*)

DIRECTIONS:

1. Combine Spice Blend ingredients and set aside.
2. Heat 1 tablespoon of oil in a wok or skillet. Add mustard seeds, cover, and fry till they "pop." When popping subsides, add cumin seeds and fry for about ½ minute.
3. Add garlic and ginger and sauté for about ½ to 1 minute, then add shallots or onions and sauté another 1 to 2 minutes.
4. Add Spice Blend and sauté for ½ minute, then stir in pumpkin or squash and sauté 1 to 2 minutes. Add 2 cups water, tomato puree, if using, salt, and lime juice and let cook, stirring constantly, till pumpkin is cooked and becomes soft and somewhat mushy and sauce thickens, about 25 to 30 minutes.
5. Heat remaining tablespoon of oil in a wok or skillet and add curry leaves. Fry for ½ minute till crispy and then add this mixture to cooked pumpkin and mix well.

Serve with cooked white or brown rice, yellow rice (page 118), or vegetable *biryani* (page 280); and spicy fried chicken (page 165), spciy fried fish (page 206), lamb *peratil* (page 185), or chicken *varuval* (page 167), Chettiar-style fiery shrimp (page 291), and savory meat lentils (page 285). Or use as a dip for flatbreads.

Stir-Fried Cabbage

Kobis Tumis

Makes 5 to 6 servings

INGREDIENTS

1 to 2 tablespoons cooking oil
¼ teaspoon black or dark brown mustard seeds
1 tablespoon thinly sliced garlic cloves
1 tablespoon thinly sliced fresh ginger (about 1-inch-long by ⅛-inch-thick pieces)
1 pound (5⅓ cups) shredded cabbage (2-inch-long by ½-inch-thick pieces)
1½ cups (9 ounces) sliced tomatoes
2 or 3 fresh green chilies (jalapeno, Serrano, Thai, or cayenne), sliced
½ to ¾ teaspoon salt
1 to 2 teaspoons regular soy sauce
Optional: 1 egg, lightly beaten

Spice Blend

½ teaspoon ground coriander
¼ to ½ teaspoon turmeric powder
¼ teaspoon ground cumin
⅛ teaspoon finely ground black pepper

Garnish

¼ cup thinly sliced shallots or onions, sautéed till light brown
1 tablespoon coriander leaves (cilantro), or 4 or 5 fresh curry leaves

Ma would cook stir-fried white cabbage at least once a week and serve it with my favorite spicy chile pork. When I make it, I think of Ma in the kitchen, stirring her cabbage in a large wok. Sometimes she would add an egg or two to provide more protein in our diet. It is a favorite for Tamils, Malayalees, and Chettiars from Southern India, each using a slightly different preparation. My sister-in-law Shanta, of Tamil background, adds pan-fried or dry roasted toovar dhal *for a crunchy feel.*

When my daughter Geeta and I visited my father's relatives in Tellicherry (now called Kozhikode), India, I learned to make a Kerala-style cabbage seasoned with turmeric, green chilies, and mustard seeds. It was served with a fish curry simmered in a clay pot. As I watched my cousin preparing the cabbage, I remembered how Ma prepared hers—taking cues from her mom-in-law and adding some Chinese and Malay ingredients as well, so the flavor was not quite the same as the Kerala version. Along with spices she would add a little soy sauce, tomatoes, and sometimes pounded dried shrimp. And like the Malays, she garnished it with fried or sautéed onions.

DIRECTIONS:

1. Combine Spice Blend ingredients and set aside.
2. Heat 1 tablespoon oil in wok or skillet. Add mustard seeds, cover, and fry till seeds "pop," about ½ a minute. When popping subsides, add garlic and ginger and sauté for about ½ to 1 minute, then add Spice Blend and stir for ½ minute.
3. Add cabbage and remaining oil and stir for about 3 minutes.
4. Add tomatoes and chilies and sauté for about 4 to 5 minutes, blending well, till cabbage is cooked but still has a slight crunch.
5. Add salt and soy sauce and stir for another 1 minute.
6. If adding egg, push aside the vegetables, add a little oil in center of wok or skillet, and add beaten egg. Cook till egg is partially set, 1 to 2 minutes, and then blend well with the cabbage and cook till set.
7. Garnish cabbage with sautéed shallots or onions and coriander or curry leaves.

Serve with cooked white or brown rice; and chile pork (page 186), fish curry (page 198), spicy fried fish (page 206), shrimp *varuval* (page 203), or Chettiar-style fiery shrimp (page 291); and savory meat lentils (page 285).

Stir-Fried Chinese Greens

Sawi Tumis

Makes 6 to 8 servings

All ethnic groups have embraced greens in their daily diets in Malaysia, as they are not only healthy but also inexpensive compared to many other vegetables. In our home, we enjoyed greens prepared in many different styles. Ma would prepare greens quite often and served them with dhal curry and chicken varuval *or fried fish. I would watch with amazement as Ma painstakingly washed each leaf to make sure there was no dirt or sand or other defects before she cooked them.*

Ma probably learned her recipe from my grandmother (Periama), as Periama enjoyed preparing all kinds of vegetables. Now my sister Vas prepares greens the way Ma did. When I eat them, I visualize Ma in our kitchen, standing over the sizzling wok, and stirring the sawi *while chatting with Zaiton, our Malay help, with Periama nearby, quietly peeling the shallots for her fish curry. Ma sliced the greens into ¼-inch to ½-inch strips and sometimes added fresh shrimp. I prefer a larger cut and add the tiny whole dried shrimp (krill also known as* geragau*) in my recipe. Again you can omit the shrimp to make it truly vegetarian.*

INGREDIENTS

1 to 2 tablespoons cooking oil
1 tablespoon sliced and crushed garlic cloves
1 teaspoon sliced and crushed fresh ginger
1 heaping cup sliced shallots or onions
1½ tablespoons coarsely pounded dried whole shrimp, steeped in hot water for 10 minutes to soften and then drained
½ teaspoon turmeric powder, or 1 teaspoon chopped fresh or frozen and thawed turmeric root
1 teaspoon ground cumin
1 fresh red chile (cayenne, Fresno, jalapeno, Serrano, cherry, or Thai), sliced lengthwise
1 bunch (about 1¼ pounds) *sawi* or Chinese mustard greens (*gai choy*), bottom stems trimmed and swirled in water a few times to remove and dislodge dirt and sand, leaves separated from stalks, leaves sliced into 1-inch to 1½-inch pieces and stalks sliced into 1-inch pieces
4 teaspoons regular soy sauce
¼ to ½ teaspoon salt
Optional: 1 egg, lightly beaten

SPICE BLEND

½ teaspoon *urad dhal* or skinned black dhal
¼ teaspoon black or dark brown mustard seeds
¼ teaspoon cumin seeds
⅛ teaspoon fenugreek seeds

DIRECTIONS:

1. Combine Spice Blend ingredients. Heat 1 tablespoon oil in a wok or skillet. Add Spice Blend, cover, and cook till the mustard seeds "pop" and *urad dhal* turns a light brown color.
2. When popping subsides, add garlic and ginger and stir for about ½ to 1 minute; then add shallots or onions and stir for about 1 to 2 minutes.
3. Add dried shrimp and remaining oil and stir for about 2 minutes; add turmeric and cumin and sauté for about ½ minute. Add chile and stir for another ½ minute.
4. Stir in the *sawi* stalks and stir for about 1 minute, then add the *sawi* leaves, cover and cook for 2 minutes; uncover and cook for another 2 to 3 minutes, turning leaves over often (using pair of tongs) and coating them well with seasoning till leaves turn a bright green and wilt (making sure stalks are still crispy and leaves not over cooked).
5. Add soy sauce and salt and mix well for 1 minute.
6. If adding egg, push aside the *sawi*, add a little oil in center of pan and add beaten egg. Cook till egg is partially set, 1 to 2 minutes, and then blend well with the sawi and cook till set.
7. Garnish with sliced red chile, if desired.

Serve with cooked white or brown rice, yellow rice (page 118), savory meat lentils (page 285), or vegetable dhal curry (page 231); and lamb or mutton *peratil* (page 185), chile squid (page 211), spicy egg curry (page 172), black peppercorn chicken (page 170), or chicken *kurma* (page 168).

Spicy Water Spinach

Kangkung Belacan

Makes 3 servings

INGREDIENTS

2 to 3 tablespoons cooking oil
¼ teaspoon ground coriander
⅛ teaspoon turmeric powder, or ½ teaspoon chopped fresh or frozen and thawed turmeric root (¼-inch to ½-inch piece)
1 teaspoon regular soy sauce
1 tablespoon tamarind concentrate or tamarind juice extracted from pulp (*see page 339*)
1 small bunch (about 6 to 8 stalks with leaves; 8 ounces) *kangkung* (water spinach), bottom stems trimmed about 1 to 2 inches and washed in water, swirling a few times to remove and dislodge dirt and sand
Optional: ⅛ teaspoon salt

Spice Paste

¼ cup sliced shallots or onions
1 heaping tablespoon sliced garlic cloves
½ teaspoon sliced fresh or frozen and thawed galangal or fresh ginger
1 to 3 fresh red chilies, (cayenne, Fresno, jalapeno, Serrano, Thai, or cherry), sliced
½ teaspoon dried shrimp paste (*belacan*), toasted at 400°F for 15 minutes (*see page 335*); or 1 heaping teaspoon dried whole shrimp, soaked in hot water for 10 minutes to soften and then drained
¼ cup water

Kangkung, *also known as water spinach or water convolvulus, has long narrow leaves with thin stems.* Kangkung *grows wild in Malaysia wherever there is water (and thus is also called "swamp cabbage"), and Malay farmers pick it alongside rice fields. There are many varieties of* kangkung *and they do not taste or look like our Western spinach. They can be found in Chinese supermarkets sold as* ong choy *or Chinese watercress. They wilt easily and lose their texture, so it is best to cook them as soon as possible after purchase.*

Kangkung belacan *is served at food courts, restaurants, and even at upscale hotel restaurants as it has become an icon vegetable preparation in Malaysia. On one of my trips back to Malaysia, my American girlfriend Pat Nazzo came with me and we stayed in Johor Bahru across from Singapore. My sister Vas and her hubby, Diva, took us to an outdoor food mall to sample local dishes. Out of curiosity, Pat ordered* kangkung belacan *and it has since become her favorite. My family was surprised to see an American get hooked not only to a local vegetable but a local flavor,* belacan, *which is an acquired taste. Here is my recipe that hopefully will make you a fan of* kangkung belacan *as well.*

DIRECTIONS:

1. Process Spice Paste ingredients to a coarse paste.
2. Heat 1 tablespoon oil in a wok or skillet and sauté Spice Paste for about 5 to 6 minutes, till fragrant, adding 1 to 2 more tablespoons oil if needed. Add ground coriander and turmeric and stir for another ½ to 1 minute.
3. Add soy sauce and tamarind juice and stir for about 1 minute.
4. Add *kangkung* and stir for about 4 minutes, turning the leaves over often (using tongs) and coating well with sauce, till leaves wilt and become bright green with stems still retaining their crispiness. Add salt if needed.

Serve with cooked white or brown rice; and stir-fried *sambal* shrimp (page 204), or *sambal* chicken (page 161), spicy fried fish (page 206), chile crab (page 213), spicy tomato chicken (page 284), or lamb in black pepper sauce (page 184).

Kangkung belacan is a Malay peasant preparation but has evolved to become a trendy dish. Prepared with dried shrimp paste (*belacan*), it is traditionally eaten in villages with cooked white rice or *nasi lemak* and hot fiery *sambal belacan*. Nonyas add dried shrimp, candlenuts, and ground *ikan bilis* (baby anchovies) to their recipe.

Stir-Fried Bean Sprouts

Taugeh Tumis

Makes 3 to 4 servings

INGREDIENTS

- ½ pound (1½ cups) cubed firm tofu (*tauhu*) (½-inch to ¾-inch pieces)
- 1 to 2 tablespoons cooking oil
- 1 heaping tablespoon crushed garlic cloves
- 1 teaspoon thinly sliced fresh ginger
- ¼ cup diced shallots or onions
- 1 tablespoon chopped dried shrimp, soaked in hot water for 10 minutes to soften and then drained
- ¼ to ½ cup dried shiitake mushrooms, soaked in hot water for about 15 minutes, then drained and squeezed to remove water; or ½ cup fresh shiitake mushrooms
- 3½ to 4 cups (10½ to 12 ounces) bean sprouts, rinsed or blanched
- 2 tablespoons regular soy sauce
- 2 spring onions or Chinese chives (*kuchai*), sliced into 1-inch pieces
- 1 fresh red chile (cayenne, Fresno, jalapeno, Serrano, cherry, or Thai), sliced (¼-inch pieces)
- ⅛ teaspoon coarsely pounded black or white peppercorns
- ½ teaspoon salt

Bean sprouts (taugeh) *are generally added as toppings to provide crunchiness for noodles, soups, salads, and many other dishes. But Chinese and Nonya cooks have transformed the simple bean sprouts into flavorful side dishes by seasoning them with salted dried fish* (ikan kurau), *dried* ikan bilis, *dried shrimp or fresh shrimp, roast pork* (char siew), *scrambled eggs, and/or cockles* (kerang).

This is another vegetable Ma served regularly, with tofu pieces, salted fish, or fresh or dried shrimp and Chinese chives (kuchai). *The crunchiness of the bean sprouts balances well with the chewy tofu. I have provided Ma's recipe here which uses chopped dried shrimp. However, you can omit them if you want a purely vegetarian dish. You can also add toasted sesame oil and toasted sesame seeds. Use mung bean sprouts and not soybean sprouts or other sprouts. Make sure you use bean sprouts as soon as possible after purchase as they lose their crispiness and get mushy within a few days.*

DIRECTIONS:

1. Place tofu pieces in a non-stick skillet or wok (or add 1 tablespoon oil to a skillet or wok) and pan-fry till light brown and firm, about 5 to 6 minutes, turning often to cook evenly. Remove from skillet or wok and set aside.
2. Heat 1 tablespoon oil in skillet or wok, add garlic and ginger and sauté for ½ to 1 minute; add shallots or onions and continue to stir for 1 to 2 minutes. Add dried shrimp and stir for 1 to 2 minutes.
3. Add shiitake mushrooms and tofu and stir for about 2 minutes. Add bean sprouts and stir for about 1 minute. Add soy sauce and stir for another minute.
4. Add spring onions or Chinese chives and chile and sauté 1 minute, then sprinkle in pepper and salt and sauté another 1 minute, mixing well.

Serve with cooked white rice, *sambar* rice (page 124), or lime rice (page 122); and chicken curry (page 171), chicken curry *debal* (page 289), soy sauce fish (page 199), spicy sweet shrimp (page 286), chile crab (page 213), peppercorn soy sauce beef (page 181), stir-fried *sambal* shrimp (page 204), or fish curry (page 198).

Nonyas in Penang make wonderful salads with bean sprouts, flavored with shallots, chopped ginger flower (*bunga kantan*), toasted grated coconut (*kerisik*), lime juice, and *belacan*. Kristangs from Malacca season bean sprouts with slices of beef, *taucheo* (preserved soybean paste), and thick soy sauce.

Braised Spicy Long Beans

Kacang Panjang Tumis

Makes 3 to 4 servings

INGREDIENTS

1 to 2 tablespoons cooking oil
2 cups (8 ounces) long beans or green beans, cut into 1½-inch-long pieces
4 teaspoons regular soy sauce
¼ teaspoon salt

SPICE PASTE

1 heaping tablespoon sliced garlic cloves
1 tablespoon sliced fresh ginger
½ cup diced shallots or onions
1 fresh red chile (cayenne, Fresno, jalapeno, Serrano, Thai, or cherry), sliced
½ lemongrass stalk, sliced into ½-inch pieces (2 tablespoons)
½ teaspoon dried shrimp paste (*belacan*), toasted at 400°F for 15 minutes (*see page 335*)
¼ cup water

OPTIONAL GARNISH

2 tablespoons coarsely ground peanuts, or 1 teaspoon toasted sesame seeds

Long beans are frequently prepared with belacan *(dried shrimp paste), oyster sauce,* taucheo, *pork fat, scrambled eggs, or fresh prawns, depending on whether the recipe is Malay, Nonya, Chinese, or Kristang.*

This was another vegetable Ma would cook regularly, dicing the beans into ½-inch pieces and sometimes adding scrambled eggs or fresh shrimp. I also enjoy the beans with belacan *and lemongrass, a Malay-style preparation. You can also substitute French beans or green beans for the long beans. Instead of* belacan, *you can use* taucheo, *the black version, or black bean sauce for a purely vegetarian version.*

DIRECTIONS:

1. Process Spice Paste ingredients to a smooth paste.
2. Heat 1 tablespoon of oil in a wok or skillet and sauté the Spice Paste for about 4 to 5 minutes, till fragrant, adding remaining oil.
3. Add long beans or green beans and stir for 2 to 3 minutes, then add ½ cup water and soy sauce and stir for about 2 minutes. Lower heat, cover, and let cook, stirring occasionally, till beans become tender but are still slightly crunchy, about 4 minutes.
4. Uncover, add salt and stir till aromatic and sauce thickens and coats beans, about 2 to 3 minutes. Add garnish, if desired.

Serve with cooked white or brown rice, tomato rice (page 119), or spiced rice (page 120); and pork *pong teh* (page 188), dry beef curry (page 182), chile squid (page 211), spicy tomato chicken (page 284), chile crab (page 213), or spicy egg curry (page 172).

Ma at porch

Long beans, called *kacang panjang hijau* in Malay, *tau kok* in Chinese, and *paithang kai* in Tamil, is a widely used vegetable in Malaysia. They are also called yard long beans, Chinese long beans, garter beans, cowpeas, or snake beans. When choosing long beans, pick firm, thin, deep green beans without softness or yellowing and use them as soon as possible as they lose texture and shrivel up if kept too long. Snip off the ends before using.

Vegetable Dhal Curry

Kari Dhal Sayuran

Makes 3 to 5 servings

Periama, my grandmother, made a wonderful lentil and vegetable preparation on Fridays, the day Ma tried to observe as a vegetarian day for health and religious reasons. The spicy dhal went well with warmly made thosai*, Periama's specialty, but was also delicious with rice or bread, such as* chappati, roti canai, *or naan.*

When my husband, Bob, first visited Malaysia, he tagged along with my younger brother, Sathee, to an Indian restaurant behind our home to enjoy roti canai *and dhal curry for a late breakfast. Addicted to this combo, on future visits Bob would regularly sneak off early in the morning to a Mamak shop near Sathee's home in Subang Jaya to enjoy it before we all woke up. And when we asked him where he went, he would reply "for an early morning brisk walk before Ma's breakfast." He thought he had us fooled!*

Vegetable dhal curry is generally made with toovar/toor dhal *(pale yellow split lentils). I usually use* masoor dhal *(pink, split, skinned variety) or* toovar dhal *to make my dhal curry. But you can also use your favorite lentils to make this curry.*

INGREDIENTS

- 1 cup dry *toovar* or *masoor dhal*
- ½ teaspoon turmeric powder
- 1 tablespoon cooking oil
- ¼ teaspoon black or dark brown mustard seeds
- 2 teaspoons crushed or chopped garlic cloves
- 1 heaping teaspoon crushed or chopped fresh ginger
- ¾ cup diced shallots or onions
- 2 dried whole red chilies
- 1 cup (6 ounces) sliced tomatoes
- 1 cup (5 ounces) diced carrots (¼-inch to ½-inch pieces)
- ½ cup diced green beans or okra or eggplant (¼-inch to ½-inch pieces)
- ¼ cup petite peas (fresh and cooked, or frozen and thawed)
- ½ teaspoon salt

Spice Blend (Sambar Podi)

(Note: this spice mixture can also be used for dhal curry)

- ½ teaspoon cumin seeds
- ½ tablespoon *urad dhal* (skinned black gram)
- ¼ teaspoon black or dark brown mustard seeds
- ⅛ teaspoon fenugreek seeds

Garnish

- 1 tablespoon cooking oil
- 5 fresh curry leaves, or 2 tablespoons coriander leaves (cilantro)
- 1 or 2 cloves garlic, sliced in half

DIRECTIONS:

1. Place the Spice Blend ingredients in a small skillet and dry-roast for about 4 minutes, stirring constantly, till mustard seeds cease to pop. (Be careful not to burn or it becomes bitter.) Cool and grind to a fine powder. Set aside.
2. Bring 4 cups water to a boil in a saucepan. Add dhal and turmeric, return to a boil, lower heat and simmer for about 10 to 15 minutes, depending on consistency desired, smooth or with some discrete pieces of dhal. (Scoop out and discard white froth as it appears on dhal.) Set aside.
3. Heat oil in a wok or skillet and add mustard seeds, cover and cook till seeds pop. When popping subsides, add ground Spice Blend and stir for about ½ to 1 minute. Add garlic and ginger and sauté for about ½ to 1 minute; add shallots or onions and sauté for another 1 to 2 minutes. Stir in chilies and sauté ½ to 1 minute.
4. Stir in tomato, vegetables, cooked dhal, and ¼ to ½ cup water (depending on desired consistency), and bring to a boil. Then lower heat and cook for about 6 to 8 minutes, stirring occasionally so dhal does not stick to bottom of pan.
5. Add peas and salt and cook about 1 to 2 minutes.
6. Prepare garnish: heat oil in skillet, add curry or coriander leaves and garlic and sauté till garlic turns light brown and crispy. Pour this fragrant oil mixture over the dhal curry just before serving.

Serve with cooked white or brown rice, lime rice (page 122), or vegetable *biryani* (page 280); and chicken curry (page 171), lamb or mutton *peratil* (page 185), Chettiar-style fiery shrimp (page 291), spicy fried chicken (page 165), black peppercorn chicken (page 170), or spicy fried fish (page 206); and spicy cucumber tomato salad (page 97). For a vegetarian meal, serve with spicy dry curried okra (page 221), stir-fried cabbage (page 226), or spicy curried pumpkin (page 225). Or serve with *roti canai*, *chappati*, or naan.

Spicy Eggplant and Pineapple Curry

Pajeri

Makes 4 to 5 servings

INGREDIENTS

2 to 3 tablespoons cooking oil
1 pound (about 6½ cups) Japanese or Chinese eggplant, sliced (3-inch-long by ½-inch-thick pieces)
2 tablespoons tamarind concentrate or tamarind juice (*see page 339*)
½ teaspoon thinly sliced or chopped palm sugar or dark brown sugar
1¼ cups (about 7 ounces) fresh or canned pineapple chunks (¾-inch to 1-inch pieces; if using canned, drain juice before using)
¼ cup toasted grated coconut (*kerisik*) (*see page 319*)
2 fresh green or red chilies (jalapeno, Fresno, Serrano, cayenne, cherry, or Thai), sliced lengthwise into quarters (deseeded if less heat is desired)
½ teaspoon salt

SPICE PASTE

1 heaping cup sliced shallots or onions
1 teaspoon chopped garlic cloves
1 heaping teaspoon chopped fresh ginger
2 to 3 heaping tablespoons dried whole shrimp, soaked in ¼ cup hot water for 10 minutes and drained
¼ cup water

SPICE BLEND 1

2 cardamom pods
1-inch cinnamon stick
1 star anise

SPICE BLEND 2

1½ teaspoons ground coriander
1¼ teaspoons ground cumin
½ teaspoon ground fennel seeds
½ teaspoon chile powder
¼ teaspoon turmeric powder

Pajeri or pajri is a mild and slightly sweet curry made with eggplant and pineapple chunks seasoned with turmeric, coriander, cumin, fennel, and chilies. It has a hint of tartness from the tamarind juice and pungency from dried shrimp. Malays add kerisik *(toasted grated coconut) to complete its flavor. The Nonyas and Kristiangs call this dish* pajelis *or* pachree *and have their own versions. Nonyas add star anise, turmeric, coriander, chilies, and coconut milk, but generally leave out the curry powder. Kristiangs enjoy it with salted fish, shrimp paste, pineapple, and chilies. For Malay weddings and Nonya festive meals, pajeri is made using pineapples with sweet and savory spices.*

When I was in high school, I had my first taste of pajeri at my Malay girlfriend's home, served with steaming cooked white rice and sambal tumis. *I have since modified it somewhat to suit my family's taste, but at the same time keeping its authenticity. Use the slender and sweet purple Japanese or Chinese eggplants instead of the more bitter dark purple Western varieties.*

DIRECTIONS:

1. Process Spice Paste ingredients to a smooth paste. Set aside.
2. Combine Spice Blend 2 ingredients and set aside.
3. Heat 1 tablespoon of oil in a wok or skillet and add Spice Blend 1 ingredients and stir for about ½ to 1 minute.
4. Add Spice Blend 2 and stir for about ½ minute, then add Spice Paste and remaining oil and stir for about 5 minutes, till fragrant.
5. Add eggplant and sauté for about 2 minutes; add 1 cup water, tamarind juice, and sugar and cook for about 20 minutes, stirring occasionally, till eggplant becomes somewhat mushy.
6. Add pineapple chunks, coconut, chilies, and salt and cook, stirring, for another 10 minutes. Remove cinnamon stick and star anise before serving.

Serve with cooked white or brown rice, yellow rice (page 118), vegetable *biryani* (page 280), or spiced rice (page 120); and grilled spicy chicken (page 166), spicy tomato chicken (page 284), spicy tangy simmered fish (page 205), soy sauce fish (page 199), hot and sour shrimp (page 201), *sambal* scallops (page 210), beef *rendang* (page 177), or chile squid (page 211).

Tofu Curry

Kari Tauhu

Makes 3 to 4 servings

On one of our visits to Malaysia, my youngest brother's wife, Mala, brought us a couple of nibblers that tasted spicy and hot. While we were enjoying them, Mala said they were tofu and mushrooms. My hubby was shocked as he does not eat tofu or mushrooms yet he enjoyed them.

Since my sister-in-law Mala became a vegetarian, she has added more recipes with vegetables and tofu to her collection. Of Sri Lankan (or Ceylonese) ancestry, Mala grew up a non-vegetarian. My brother Suresh and their children are lovers of meat and chicken, and so at times Mala also cooks delicious Sri Lankan-style chicken and seafood dishes, recipes she learned from her mom and sisters. When they visited us a few years ago, I learned this curried tofu dish from Mala, a dish she prepared in just a few minutes. I share her recipe here, with some modifications so you too can enjoy it, vegetarian or not.

INGREDIENTS

- 1 package (14 ounces) firm tofu (*tauhu*), cubed (½-inch to ¾-inch pieces)
- 2 to 3 tablespoons cooking oil
- 1 heaping tablespoon sliced or crushed garlic cloves
- 2 teaspoons sliced or crushed fresh ginger
- ½ cup chopped shallots or onions (½-inch pieces)
- 1 or 2 dried whole red chilies, steeped in hot water for 5 to 8 minutes, drained, deseeded, and pounded; or ½ to 1 teaspoon *cili boh* (*see page 315*); or ¼ to ½ teaspoon bottled *sambal oelek*; or ⅛ to ¼ teaspoon chile powder
- 1 teaspoon tomato paste, or 2 teaspoons tomato puree, or 1 tablespoon tomato sauce, or ¼ cup chopped tomatoes

SPICE BLEND 1

- 1-inch cinnamon stick
- 1 star anise
- ¼ teaspoon black or dark brown mustard seeds

SPICE BLEND 2

- ½ teaspoon ground cumin
- ½ teaspoon ground fennel seeds
- ½ teaspoon ground coriander
- ¼ teaspoon ground fenugreek
- ¼ teaspoon finely ground black pepper
- ¼ teaspoon turmeric powder

GARNISH

- 1 heaping tablespoon chopped coriander leaves (cilantro)

DIRECTIONS:

1. In a non-stick skillet, pan-fry tofu pieces till light brown and firm, about 5 to 6 minutes, turning often so as to cook evenly. (Or add a tablespoon oil to wok or skillet and pan-fry tofu.) Set aside.
2. Combine Spice Blend 2 ingredients and set aside.
3. Heat 1 tablespoon oil in a wok or skillet, add Spice Blend 1 ingredients, cover, and fry till mustard seeds "pop."
4. When popping subsides, add garlic and ginger and sauté for about ½ to 1 minute; add shallots or onions and sauté for about 1 to 2 minutes; add chilies and stir for ½ minute.
5. Add remaining oil and Spice Blend 2 and stir for about ½ minute, then add tomato paste, puree, sauce, or chopped tomatoes and blend well. Add tofu pieces and stir for about 3 to 4 minutes, coating well with paste and adding 2 tablespoons to ¼ cup water if necessary.
6. Garnish with chopped coriander leaves. Remove cinnamon stick and star anise before serving.

For a vegetarian meal, serve with cooked white or brown rice, yellow rice (page 118), or vegetable *biryani* (page 280); and vegetable dhal curry (page 231); and spicy dry curried okra (page 221), spicy eggplant dip (page 58), or a cucumber carrot *acar* (page 99).

Tofu is widely consumed in Malaysia. Chinese cook tofu in a mildly seasoned sauce with soy sauce, garlic, and sesame oil. Malays, Nonyas, and Kristangs have taken tofu to a spicier level, adding *belacan* and chilies to create *sambals* and unique stir-fries. Nonyas deep-fry tofu and top it with a spicy sweet *taucheo* and chile-based sauce. Many Indian vegetarians have also taken a liking to tofu and add spices to make delicious tofu curries and stir-fries, creating yet another flavor dimension to tofu.

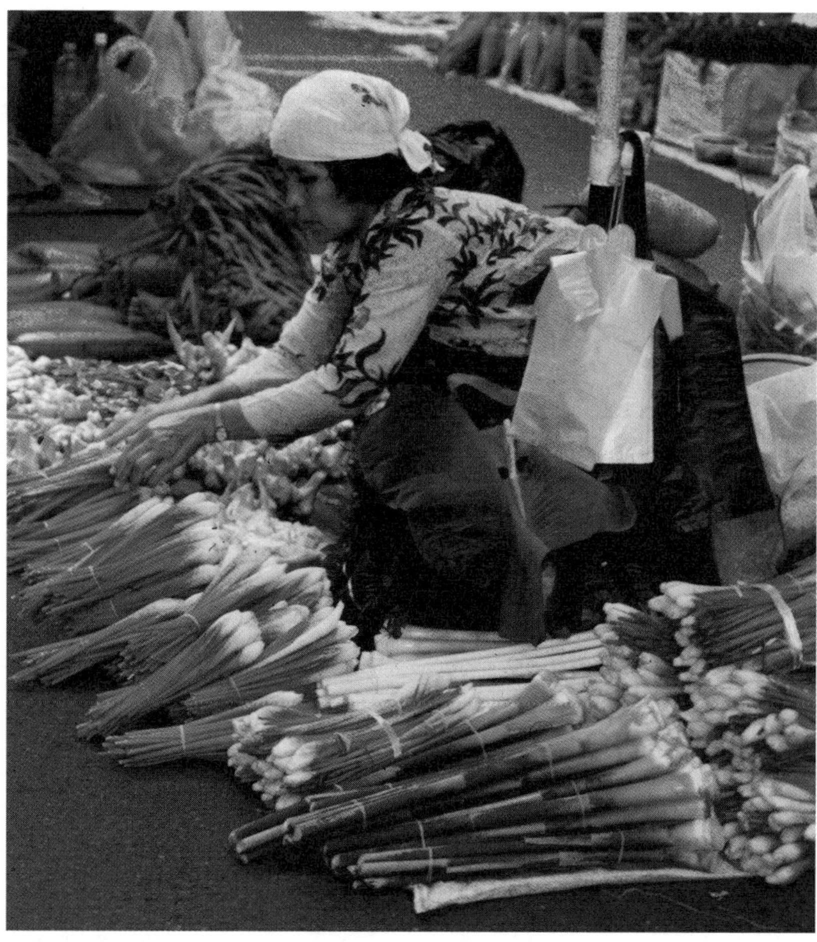

Outdoor wet market, Kuching, Sarawak

CHAPTER 10

DESSERTS AND BEVERAGES: SWEET DELIGHTS

Drinks in plastic bags

FRUITS

Malaysia abounds in a wonderful array of tropical fruits and its desserts and drinks reflect this bounty. Fruits also are the principle flavorings in many savory dishes. As you drive along Malaysia's roads, especially in rural settings and along the East Coast, you pass by make-shift *atap* (thatched roof) sheds where bunches of fruits are hung—mangosteens, guavas, papayas, *longgans* (also called *mata kuching* or cat's eyes), *duku-langsat*, rambutan, mango, pineapple, lychee, jackfruit, dragon fruit (*pitaya*), *cikoo*, and durians.

Malaysians love fruits so much that many families in urban areas plant fruit trees in their yards if space allows, and in rural villages fruit trees are plentiful. In our rural home settings in Muar and Segamat in Johor state, and Kuantan in Pahang state, we had many fruit trees. I especially remember the guava (*jambu batu*, a firmer type of guava; *batu* is Malay for "stone"), and water apple (*jambu air*, also known as Malay apple or rose apple). Our *jambu air* tree was visually stunning when its red and pink fruits appeared. As youngsters, we used to climb up and pick the rose-scented fruit and enjoyed snacking on them dipped in dark soy sauce with sliced green chilies. When ripe, *jambu air* had a watery and crispy bite, a real thirst quencher for us. We also had mango, lime, papaya, and custard apple trees.

When our family moved to Petaling Jaya, a suburb of Malaysia's capital of Kuala Lumpur, we had a rambutan tree and mango tree in our yard. Our grandparents had planted these trees before we moved in. I still remember bunches of red rambutans hanging by our dining room windows. It was a beautiful sight! After Cha retired, he used to take long walks after breakfast and before din-

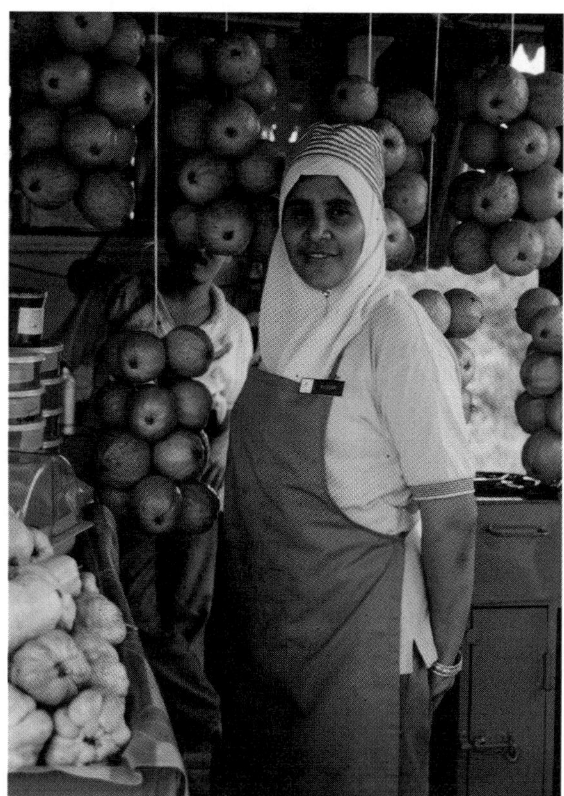

Indian Muslim guava vendor, Seremban

ner, and always returned with bunches of seasonal fruits from fruit vendors or wet markets, papaya and bananas being his favorites. Fruits were our typical after-meal 'desserts' since by custom, cakes, biscuits, and other sweets were served during teatime, from 4 to 6 p.m., for special occasions, or as snacks between meals.

As a proper introduction to Malaysian desserts and beverages, an understanding of some of our favorite Malaysian fruits is necessary.

Malaysian Fruits

In Malaysia, bananas, or *pisang* as locals call them, are a popular fruit and a common part of the regular diet. In fact, it is believed that the banana plant originated in Malaysia which has the greatest diversity of bananas in the world. Indian Muslim traders brought them from Malaysia to India (now the world's largest producer of bananas) and from there bananas were eventually transplanted around the world. There are numerous banana varieties that vary in shape, size, skin color, flavor, and texture. Some varieties are eaten fresh while others are made into fritters, puddings, and porridge, or baked into cakes and cookies.

Cempedak, a Malay favorite, is eaten fresh or cooked when it is semi-ripe. Its taste is similar to jackfruit—custard-like, sweet, and mild with a hint of durian flavor. Custard apple (*buah nona*) or soursop is a knobby, greenish or brown fruit with a pulpy flesh encasing brownish-black seeds. Ma sometimes placed unripe custard apples in our rice container so they would ripen faster. (I checked the container frequently to see if they were ready to eat!) The *langsat*, *duku*, and *duku langsat* are familiar fruits for us. They are closely related, all with white fleshy interior. We enjoyed *duku* more as it was sweet while *langsat* is generally sour. *Duku langsat* is a hybrid that captures the best of both.

When I was growing up in Malaysia, we did not have the Western concept of after-meal desserts. Rather, we enjoyed fruit after meals. Many fruits are seasonal and so we enjoyed different fruits throughout the year. Because of their abundance, freshly cut and chilled fruits could be readily bought from hawkers, particularly during lunch and snack hours.

Colorful gelatins, made from watermelon and other fruit juices with pandan essence or coconut milk, were very popular with us as children. It was great to have these chilled jellies after school as a cool treat after walking back home in the hot humid afternoons. Ma also had watermelon jellies for our birthdays.

Guava (*guayaba*) is a popular fruit with the locals, especially the firmer type referred to as *jambu batu*. It has a strong sweet vanilla-like flavor when ripe with hints of rose, though some varieties can be tart. The sweet ones are eaten fresh or made into juice. Two common forms are the yellow ones and pink-fleshed ones. Malaysians enjoy eating the slightly unripe *jambu batu* with a seasoning of salt and chile pepper or *asam boi* (a tangy mixture of preserved plums).

Another popular Malay fruit and one of my favorites growing up is jackfruit (*nangka*), known as breadfruit in the Caribbean. This is an enormous watermelon-size fruit with a sweet aroma. When the smooth, thick, and pimply rind is sliced open, the inside has a large number of bright orange-yellow segments that are firm and crunchy, and which enclose large, creamy seeds. Fruit stall vendors often skewer several *nangka* segments together. Because of its fragrant flavor, Malays stew or boil them and add them to salads and fish curries. As a youngster, I used to enjoy the roasted seeds prepared by our Malay cook.

There are several types of citrus referred to as "limes" that are grown in Malaysia: *limau nipis* (a thin skinned lime, similar to Key lime), *limau kasturi* (musk or calamansi lime), and Kaffir lime. *Limau nipis* is very acidic with a strong lemony aroma and a thin rind. It is more tart and bitter than the Persian lime, the common lime used in the U.S. *Limau kasturi* is the local favorite, a fragrant and less sour lime with a flavor between a lemon and a Mandarin orange. The Kaffir lime is a small, bumpy, green fruit that hardly produces any juice, although its rind is occasionally used in cooking. But its leaves are very aromatic and are a ubiquitous flavoring in northern Malaysian cooking.

Lychee (*laici*) with an inner sweet, translucent white flesh is an extremely popular fruit, particularly among the Chinese of Malaysia. It is my favorite juice drink from the stalls even today.

Mango comes in many varieties, like most other fruits. When ripe and aromatic, it is eaten freshly sliced or juiced. The unripe fruit is sour and is made into a beverage or into pickles or salads. During my childhood years, I remember always seeing a jar of pickled green mangoes on the dining table but don't remember having them often, as my youngest sister, Rama, the "pickle queen," the lover of sour foods in our family, usually finished them before we could get to them at dinner!

Mangosteen (*manggis*) is called the "queen of fruits" in Malaysia, rightfully so as it is eaten with durian, the "king of fruits." It has a dark purplish-red outer skin that opens to reveal clusters of pure white segments of juicy pulp that have a delicious aromatic and sweet flavor.

Pomelo is a large version of a grapefruit or orange, measuring up to one foot in diameter and weighing as much as twenty pounds. The fruit appears from a light yellow to a green color. Its flavor ranges from sweet and spicy to tart, similar to grapefruit but drier. Pomelos are particularly popular during Chinese festive seasons such as Chinese New Year and Moon Cake Festival.

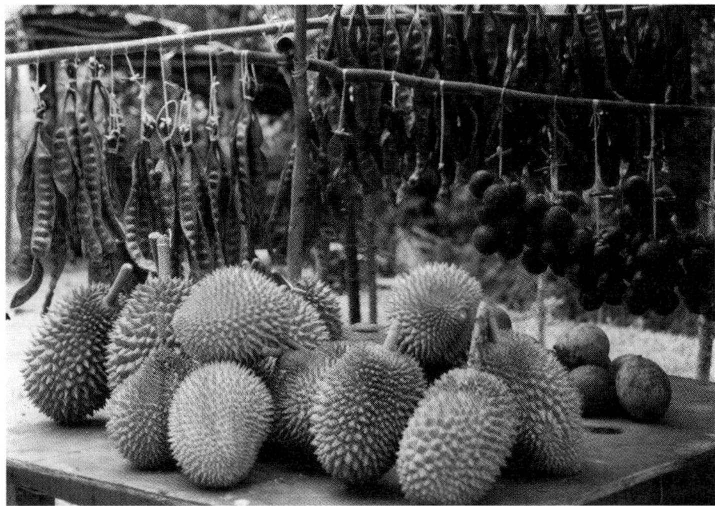

Durians and mangosteens

For many years, I could not get my husband, Bob, to try durian. However, during one visit, my older brother Prasnan drove us around for several hours searching for the perfect fruit for Bob. Indeed, for those who love durian, selecting one is like choosing a fine wine. It was durian season and hawkers had their carts and trucks parked by the roadsides loaded with the ripe fruits. Like other savvy customers, Prasnan stopped and examined each hawker's wares. The hawker selected his best fruit, made an incision with a sharp knife, and allowed Prasnan to savor its aroma. Prasnan made at least a half-dozen stops before he found a couple of perfect durians. Now Bob was trapped! Given Prasnan's efforts on his behalf, Bob felt that the least he could do was give durian a try. As Bob placed the pulp reluctantly into his mouth, I could see his face contort. Too bad for Bob, but I didn't mind as there was now more for me to savor!

Papayas, with their juicy, sweet flavor and fragrant aroma, are another Malaysian favorite. The green or unripe papaya is thinly sliced or shredded to make salads and pickles that are popular in Malaysia's Northeast states. Pineapples, referred to as *nanas* in Malaysia, come in many varieties. They are generally enjoyed fresh, but are also added to balance the heat in many Malay, Nonya, and Indian Muslim savory dishes and stews, such as *pajeri* (page 232) and *rojak* (page 94), as well as in jams and fillings for tarts (page 254) and other desserts.

Rambutans come in bunches and are the size of small limes and covered in soft red spines or hair (*rambut*). The hairy red or yellow skin is removed to reveal the cool flesh around a pit or seed. *Belimbing* (or *bilimbi*), a close relative of *carambola* (starfruit), is a green-colored fruit resembling a miniature-size cucumber. It is refreshingly crunchy with a tart and slightly sweet taste. Malays sometimes use it instead of tamarind, and also make a jam from it. Water apple (*jambu air* in Malay) is a colorful rosy red, pink, or pale green fruit that has a juicy and crunchy texture. Also called rose apple or wax apple, they are found growing in many rural home gardens.

Finally, how can I not talk about the durian, Malaysia's "king of fruits"? It is a large, oval fruit, covered with sharp, pointed spikes or thorns. This hard exterior protects the fruit when it ripens and falls from the tree from great heights. To harvest durians, villagers wait to collect the fruit after it falls, or place nets around the bottom of trees to catch the falling durians. Reportedly, collecting durians in more remote jungle areas can be dangerous, as locals say that the Malaysian tiger also has a liking for the ripe fruit!

To eat a durian, you must first break through its hard, spiny exterior (*duri* means thorns) to find the inner segments, lined neatly with the rich creamy or yellow custard-like pulp that enclose dark brown seeds. The pulp has a strong smell that many, particularly tourists, find sulfury and overpowering, though not for many Malaysians! Its odor lingers, so durians are not permitted at hotels, airports, or even in rental cars.

Durian is eaten raw, added to puddings, cakes, confectionary, and ice creams, and made into jams. For me, as with many Malaysians, once you get over the overpowering odor (which generally is not an issue for us), the creamy sweet flesh is simply divine. Durian is a fruit that brings out people's passions—one is either for or against it. My entire family has always loved durian. I remember during the durian season, my father would bring home durians in the trunk of his car or would buy them on the way to our weekend stay at the beach in Port Dickson. He would sit on the house porch and open them himself with the palm of his hand, while Ma would take the creamy fleshy seeds from the open compartments and place them on a dish for us. No one ever commented on its smell, we just enjoyed them. Cha would also bring mangosteens with the durian as Ma wanted us to eat them after eating the durians. She said the durians gave too much "heat" to our bodies and the mangosteens would "cool" us off, thereby counteracting the negative "heat" that might give rise to fevers and coughs.

Malays believe durians have powerful aphrodisiac properties, which adds to their popularity. Malays and Nonyas also make durian into stews, thick porridges called *pengat*, *tempoyak* (fermented durian pulp eaten with sambal and fish curry), and as *dodol*, a dark brown chewy sweet prepared with coconut milk and palm sugar.

DESSERTS AND KUEHS

Malays and Monyas prepare an incredible array of bite-size cakes, custards, cookies, and pastries called *kueh-kueh* (or *kuehs*) or *kuih-kuih* (or *kuihs*). The concept of cakes and pastries in Malaysia is very different than that in the West. They are savory as well as sweet, and are steamed more frequently than baked. Their flavor, texture, and appearance are also very different from Western-style cakes and pastries. *Kuehs* are generally made from glutinous rice flour, tapioca and/or sago pearls, pandan juice, *gula Melaka* (palm sugar), coconut milk, and local fruits. They have gelatinous or custard-like consistencies with multiple layers and neon-like colors—bright blue, pink, purple, yellow, red, or green. They come in many different shapes, including triangles, ovals, balls, and even as decorative flowers.

Today, many upscale restaurants are adopting Western-style menus with a dessert or *kueh* at the end of a meal. For us, *kuehs* were not after-meal desserts, but were served as snacks throughout the day, particularly at teatime. Outside the home, hawkers sell *kuehs* around office buildings during lunch or from 3 to 4 p.m. when workers take a tea break. After office hours, many people also *bungkus* (pack to go) sweets or cakes to take home. When we visit my family in Malaysia, my elder brother, Prasnan, often brings home *kesari* (semolina cake, page 247), fried sweet banana fritters (page 67), a bag of *ondeh-ondeh* (sweet rice balls, page 257), or pineapple tarts (page 254) after work for tea.

There are also sweet porridges that I enjoyed during my youth. The taste of *cendol* and

Kuehs play an important role in religious ceremonies, such as temple offerings. For example, during *Cheng Beng*, when Nonya families get together to pay homage to their ancestors, they make offerings of colorful cupcakes made with sweet rice and coconut juice called *huat kueh*; pink, tortoise-shaped flour cakes (*mi koo*); and ceremonial sweet broths or *pengkat*, made with sweet potato, taro, banana, yam, sweet coconut milk, and pandan sauce. During Ramadan, Malays break their fast at the end of the day with *kuehs*.

bubur cha-cha remains with me to this day. These sweet snacks were invented by Malays of Javanese descent and Nonyas, and have become favorites at hawkers' carts. My recollection as a youngster was buying them from an Indian Muslim vendor who came by our home in the late afternoons during the week. They were a great treat after a spicy lunch and a perfect antidote to the sweltering afternoon heat. The sweet, creamy, and addictive *cendol* has short, green strands made from tapioca flour and colored with pandan juice. *Cendol* is served in a sauce made with coconut milk and *gula Melaka* (palm sugar) that is chilled with shaved ice. Optional ingredients include red beans, grass jelly, and corn.

In the small towns where we lived, Chinese vendors also came by our home selling sweet porridges. They were a special treat for us after school. These porridges are made from pumpkin, tapioca, adzuki beans, black glutinous rice, taro, and/or jackfruit, and flavored with coconut milk and/or condensed milk, palm sugar, sago pearls, and pandan leaves. A sweet porridge called *bubur cha-cha* was my first creation in home economics class (then a required course for girls in primary school). It is made with a hotchpotch of ingredients—taro, sweet potatoes, bananas, black-eyed peas, pieces of colored jelly, and sago pearls—that swim in a pandan-flavored coconut milk broth. It can be served either warm or chilled. I can still recall the rave reviews Ma gave my dish when I excitedly brought it home and proudly presented it to her.

Another popular sweet that we regularly enjoyed at home was *bubur kacang hijau* (page 248) that has Chinese origins. It is made with green mung beans, coconut milk, palm sugar, and pandan leaf. We also enjoyed *pulut hitam* (page 256), a sweet porridge prepared by our Malay help, Zaiton, who added black or purple sticky rice, *longgan* fruit, and pandan leaves. She said it was a specialty from her *kampung* (village).

A shaved ice dessert called *ais kacang* (iced beans), also known as *air batu campur* or simply *ABC* (page 246), is a sweet, milky dessert made from an assortment of ingredients. Red beans, sweet corn, colored tiny tapioca balls and jellies, and *cincau* (grass jelly) are buried in a cone of shaved ice and doused with red and brown syrup and condensed or evaporated milk.

I also cannot forget the canned fruitcake from England, a residue of Cha's nostalgia with the Colonial era. For every birthday (our parents had nine birthdays to celebrate in a year!) Cha brought a tin of fruitcake and placed a candle on the cake for us to blow out. With birthday fruitcakes to eat nine times each year, it is no wonder I cannot even look at a fruitcake now!

Today, the concept of a sweet dessert is catching on with Malaysians, and many hotel and fancy restaurants serve sweet puddings, cakes, custards, and pastries after meals.

Ethnic Desserts

While each ethnic group has their own favorite sweets, their recipes have been adapted, modified, and blended by Malaysia's melting pot culture over the years. With many of the *kuehs* and sweet porridges it is sometimes hard to say which ethnic group created them, although for many popular desserts, everyone lays claims to having invented them!

Malaysian Indians love their sugary sweets and puddings, which they brought from both North and South India. Some traditional sweets include *gulab jamun* (syrupy fried flour-milk balls), *ladoo* (lentil flour and ghee), *palgoa* (milk, sugar, and ghee), *kesari* (with semolina, sugar, ghee, raisins, and almonds), and carrot *halwa* (grated carrots with milk, ghee, spices, and cashews). South Indians also brought their sweet puddings (*payasams*) to Malaysia, prepared with semolina, chickpeas, green peas, or rice vermicelli. Many of these puddings have taken on local flavorings. My favorite is *sago payasam* (page 249) with sago pearls spiced with cardamom, ginger, and rose essence.

Chinese desserts are often chewy, jellied, or soupy, and made with soybean curd, rice flour, sweet *adjuki* beans, mung beans, and sweet potatoes. *Tong sui* is a sweet soup-like tonic dessert enjoyed at Chinese coffee shops, served hot or cold and made with peanuts, red beans, sago pearls, gingko, barley, and sweet potatoes. The *tau foo fah* Chinese vendor was a familiar sight at most street corners. His sweet, soft milky curdled soybean doused in syrup or *gula Melaka* (palm sugar) was Ma's favorite. She enjoyed it warm, but it is also served cold. *Nin gao* is a sweet, chewy, and sticky rice cake served during Chinese New Year. Mooncakes are decorative little cakes filled with bean paste and duck egg yolk and enjoyed during the Chinese mid-Autumn Festival (see Chapter 12). Another Chinese New Year favorite of mine is the zodiacal animal-shaped cookies made with arrowroot flour. I loved the way they melted in my mouth.

Pulut or glutinous rice is made into legendary Malay desserts, flavored with sweet fruits—mango, durian, banana, or coconut—and even with savory fillings such as spicy dried shrimp. They are rural favorites, especially in Northeast Malaysia. Many prepare them for Hari Raya Puasa, which celebrates the end of Ramadan, a month-long fast. Another favorite is a sweet *pengkat* made with bananas, durian, or jackfruit. *Pengkat pisang* (bananas in a sweet pandan sauce, page 253) is my addiction. Malays and Nonyas make it slightly different but use sweet bananas as the base ingredient.

A popular Malay *kueh* that I enjoyed for Hari Raya celebrations at my Malay friends' homes was *ondeh ondeh* (page 257), a sweet glutinous rice flour ball stuffed with palm sugar and then boiled and rolled in shredded coconut. I also enjoyed in my youth *kueh lapis*, made from steamed glutinous rice flour, coconut milk, and pandan leaves. It has an orange-red top layer and nine layers of alternating pink and white, and we enjoyed peeling off each layer as we ate it.

Nonyas have a sweet tooth like the Malays and have artfully crafted desserts that combine Chinese and Malay ingredients. On our visits to Malacca, we usually end up on Jonkers Street where elaborate afternoon teas are offered inside tiled cafes and set inside antique shops (once beautiful Chinese Peranakan homes). It is a treat to sit down and sample Nonya *kueh* and delicacies while enjoying the surrounding architecture and decor. Our favorites are *sago gula Melaka* (sago pearl pudding doused with palm sugar and coconut milk, page 252), *kueh dadar* (green-colored crepes with sweet grated coconut filling, page 250), and *kueh bangkit* (arrowroot flour cookies). *Sago gula Melaka* is a great "cooling off" snack in the afternoon when the heat and humidity are at a peak.

In our home, Ma generally prepared pineapple tarts and her special biscuits and cookies for festive occasions and when guests came. But we especially remember Ma's special cakes for tea—marble cake with chocolate, green, and pink swirls, and Madeira cake, a golden-yellow English cake that is similar to pound cake. We knew when Ma baked her cakes, as the house was filled with a delicious, sweet aroma!

The Kristangs, like their Portuguese ancestors, have an array of sweet custards, pies, and cakes, referred to as *boca doce* (sweet treats), that have assimilated Malay, Indian, and Nonya flavors. Banana cake and *sugee* cake (semolina cake with eggs, lemon rind, almond, vanilla, and rose essence) are favorites with all my Eurasian friends. I used to enjoy a slice of pandan-flavored banana cake or pineapple tarts (page 254) with afternoon tea at one of my Eurasian neighbor's home. We have adopted this everyday ritual of afternoon teas and cakes as part of our daily lives.

My daughter Geeta drinking fresh coconut water at Batu Caves

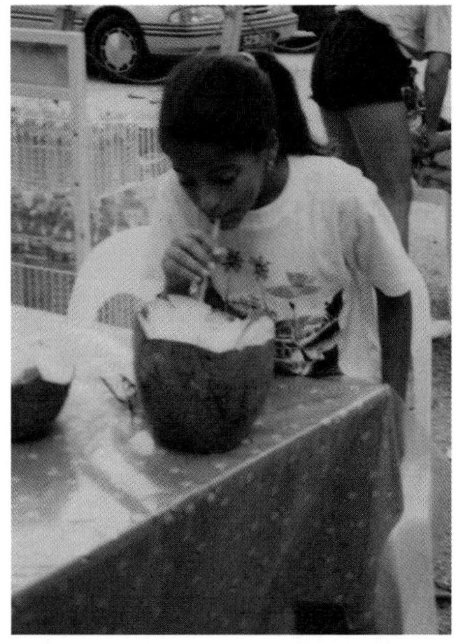

I enjoyed making some of the desserts—*sago gula Melaka*, *kueh dadar,* and *kueh tat* (pineapple tarts)—with my good friend Pat Nuzzo, who had traveled with me to Malaysia a few years ago and got hooked on them. Today she regularly makes *kueh tat* for her friends for holiday festivities or parties.

DRINKS AND BEVERAGES

Fruit juices, fresh or processed, are probably the most popular Malaysian beverages. Freshly made fruit juices (*jus* in Malay) are sold everywhere, especially by hawkers. Our favorites were *jus limau* (lime juice), *jus jambu* (guava juice), *jus* watermelon (*buah tembikai*), and *jus laici* (lychee or litchi juice). Many hawkers will display three or four fruit drinks in plastic containers on a push cart without labeling them, but locals know what they are by their colors. Lime juice is freshly squeezed from *kasturi* limes (*limau kasturi*), a quite different flavor from our regular Persian limes. Malaysian lime juice has a taste that is closer to lemonade. Another Malay favorite is *jus assam Jawa* (tamarind juice) that is delicious when drunk chilled.

A refreshing drink I enjoyed when we were at the beaches in Malaysia is coconut water or juice, called *air kelapa*, while watermelon juice or lime juice mixed with some sugar were my daughter Geeta's and her cousins Daniel and Adam's favorites. These drinks quenched their thirst and enabled them to cope with the heat and high humidity. Processed fruit juices

Usually on our trips back home, my older brother Prasnan and his wife Shanta would take us to Batu Caves, a natural limestone cave located a few miles outside of Kuala Lumpur. I remember the last trip when we took along Ma who was in a wheelchair. Batu Caves also has one of the most popular Hindu shrines in the world, dedicated to Lord Muruga. It is the site of Malaysia's annual Thaipusam festival that attracts more than 1.5 million pilgrims from all over Malaysia, both Hindus and peoples of other religions (see Chapter 12).

Visiting the temple inside Batu Caves requires a climb up 272 steep steps. While Ma stayed down, Geeta and I walked up to visit the temple. Then we climbed down and walked around the stores. It was a muggy afternoon and we were thirsting for a cool drink. We came to a stack of green coconuts and an Indian man in a sarong was slicing away the kernel husk with a *parang*. We ordered our coconut water. He asked us if we wanted the "flesh" with it and we said yes, and he immediately took two young coconuts, removed their husks, and cut open the kernels. Then he placed a spoon and straw in each and handed them to us. It was just what I was looking for! In between, I scooped its soft, white, tender flesh with the spoon and it melted in my mouth—refreshing!

and drinks are also sold in cans and packages (the latter referred to locally as "packet drinks"). Most Malaysians grew up with the deep purple-colored Ribena or black currant juice drink, especially drunk to prevent colds and flus as it has a high added vitamin C content.

Ma did not allow us to drink sodas or gaseous carbonated drinks such as orangeade or cherryade very often, as she thought they were not good for us, and it got expensive with nine of us! But it was a treat to have cold ginger ale when we got sick. Years later, the demand has grown for Coke, Pepsi, and other popular Western and Asian sodas including Fanta Orange, Sarsi, Kickapoo (grapefruit and strawberry), Sprite, and Seven-Up.

Malted drinks, such as Milo, Horlicks, and Ovaltine were very popular hot drinks. I remember Ma giving us a warm glass of Ovaltine or Horlicks before we went to bed or as a pick-me-up in between meals. Today, when we go to eat at food stalls or homes, I often order a cold glass of Milo which surprisingly goes well with a spicy plate of *mee goreng*.

A popular drink Malaysians grow up drinking almost every day is soybean milk. Freshly made by Chinese hawkers or sold as packet drinks, it is sweetened and sometimes flavored with pandan leaf. When chilled, it is the perfect antidote to the hot, humid weather. Another cooling drink is *lassi*, cultured milk seasoned with salt, cumin, and pepper or with sugar, pureed mango, and rose water, generally served with Indian meals and snacks.

There are many energy and healing drinks that Malaysians enjoy on a daily basis. Ma was a believer in Ayurvedic and Chinese traditional medicine and thus practiced its many principles and diets when she could. I remember Ma making barley water, another 'cooling' drink that she often made for us when we had a fever. She sometimes flavored it with *limau kasturi* juice but always served it warm, not chilled. It is also a popular packet drink that many Chinese enjoy. *Tongkat ali*, an aphrodisiac tonic drink (made from a special herb, sometimes with *panax ginseng* and/or ginkgo biloba), is popular with Malay men to boost sexual energy and also used to lower high blood pressure. It was traditionally prepared and sold at coffee shops, but today is also sold as a processed drink. Many energy drinks that are imported are also popular with the young locals. My niece Shobana was hooked on Vitagen when she was younger, a cultured milk drink popular with the young and taken to aid digestion. It comes in tiny plastic bottles with many flavors, such as strawberry, lime, chocolate, and vanilla. My sister-in-law Kay introduced me to a jelly drink called *air cincau* that is a black drink with strips of black jelly made from *agar-agar* or seaweed, flavored with pandan leaf and sugar. She said that it is an herbal tonic that 'cools' down the body. Kay's mother was Chinese and this was a favorite drink with the Chinese and Nonyas.

Like other cultures around the world, Malaysians enjoy both coffee (*kopi*) and tea (*teh*) from their favorite hawker, Mamak café, or coffee shop. Like the British, Malaysians enjoy their tea with milk, but usually use condensed milk, evaporated milk, or milk powder rather than fresh milk or cream. When we were growing up, fresh milk was not available. But even today, with the availability of fresh milk, the same practice follows as Malaysians feel fresh milk does not enhance tea as condensed milk does. *Teh tarik* (pulled tea, page 262) is the "national drink" of Malaysia. It is a specialty tea prepared by the Mamaks that is enjoyed by all. It is named after the theatrical "pulling" motion that is used to pour it. Of Mamak origin, this display of pulling action has become a tourist attraction, and many hotels now have someone on the premises making *teh tarik*, not only at teatime but also at breakfast, lunch, or dinner.

Ma made the best tea, an opinion voiced by many of our friends and relatives. I remember one of our cousins, Basi, who would somehow always appear at our doorstep during teatime. He finally confessed that he could not resist her tea. Ma boiled the tea leaves in water, strained them, and then added condensed milk, which gave her tea a rich, smooth flavor. Even after living many years in the U.S. and never adding sugar to my teas, whenever I went home, I fell prey to Ma's sweet, creamy tea. She just smiled to see me enjoy her tea again.

Regular tea with condensed milk or evaporated milk and sugar is called *teh*. Other tea variations are *teh o* or *teh kosong* (black with sugar but no milk), *teh ais* or *teh peng* (iced with condensed milk), and *teh o ais* (iced tea without milk). Drinking tea with no sugar at all is considered odd, but asking for *kurang manis* (less sugar) will ease the pain. Packet teas—chrysanthemum, winter melon, chamomile, peppermint jasmine, green tea, ginger, and masala teas—are also readily available.

Traditionally, for coffee (*kopi*) lovers in Malaysia, coffee is mixed with condensed milk or enjoyed as black coffee (*kopi-o*) or as *kopi peng* (iced with condensed milk). When we lived in small towns, like Muar and Kuantan, I remember locals buying coffee to go in a condensed milk tin or a plastic bag and not in paper cups as we do in the U.S. Vendors sell drinks in plastic bags with a straw, and display them in large containers or hanging from their cart. In those days, Cha frequented coffee shops with his Chinese friends for a cup of coffee and toast. Coffee was piping hot, so Cha and his friends poured the coffee onto their saucers to cool it and then sipped from the saucers. Today, Malaysia has Starbucks, The Coffee Bean and Tea Leaf, and other trendy coffee and tea chains that are growing fast to cater to the youth market.

Another peculiar local coffee favorite is the *kopi tongkat ali ginseng*, which is a mixture of coffee, a local aphrodisiacal root, and ginseng served with condensed milk. It's touted as a super combination of Viagra and Red Bull and is advertised with a picture of a bed broken in half!

Malaysia is officially an Islamic country, and under Sharia (Islamic Law), alcohol is *haram* (forbidden). However, because Malaysia is a multicultural society, the government permits the sale of alcohol to non-Muslims. However some states, such as Kelantan and Terengganu, place considerable restrictions on sales by and to Muslims, and even in busy Kuala Lumpur, you will occasionally see signs reminding Muslims that the consumption of alcohol is forbidden. Beer (*bir*) is popular, particularly the locally brewed brands, as well as imported beers from Europe and neighboring Southeast Asian countries. Traditionally, wine was not popular, but today demand for wine is growing. It is generally sold at supermarkets, although the selection is limited by Western standards and substantially more expensive. Locally home-brewed alcoholic drinks made from rice, coconut palm or other palms, such as toddy, made from fermented coconut sap, and *tuak*, a sweet, fruity rice wine made from the Iban tribes of Borneo, are also popular with the rural communities.

Shaved Ice Dessert

Air Batu Campur (ABC)

Serves 2 to 3

INGREDIENTS

Optional: 1 to 2 heaping tablespoons sago or small tapioca pearls
1 heaping tablespoon whole kernels sweet corn (no salt added)
1 heaping tablespoon cooked sweet red beans (*adzuki*)
½ cup diced mixed fruits (lychee, *longgan*, mango, and/or pineapple, or mix of berries) (¼-inch pieces)
Optional: 1 tablespoon basil seeds, soaked in ¼ cup warm water for 5 minutes and then drained
1 tablespoon crushed unsalted roasted peanuts
1 tablespoon golden raisins
1 heaping tablespoon cubed fruit-flavored jello or jelly (¼-inch pieces)
2 cups shaved ice (crush ice in a blender or use shaved ice maker)

SAUCE

¼ cup thinly sliced or chopped palm, dark brown, or light brown sugar
2 teaspoons condensed milk or evaporated milk
1 teaspoon rose syrup

Air batu campur *(translated as "mixed ice") is an addictive shaved ice dessert usually sold by hawkers. Malaysians simply refer to it as "ABC." Traditionally, this sweet, milky dessert has savory ingredients—red beans, sweet corn, sago or tapioca pearls, colorful jellies (jello), and* cincau *(grass jelly). Today, many prepare it with fruits. All these ingredients are buried in a cone of shaved ice and topped with red rose syrup, brown palm sugar syrup, and condensed or evaporated milk. When we were growing up, it was called* ais kacang *(iced beans) as it contained small red beans (*adzuki *called* kacang*). It was a wonderful cool treat and thirst quencher for us during the hot, humid afternoons after school.*

You can add your favorite fruits and use light brown sugar instead of palm sugar. My friend Nurul Huda Tmimi, from Tourism Malaysia in New York, provided me with a recipe which I modified somewhat to suit American palates, but still retaining its flavor. Basil seeds become gelatinous when soaked in water. Malays add them for their health benefits, but adding them is optional.

DIRECTIONS:

1. If using sago or tapioca pearls, place in a sieve and rinse under cold running water to remove excess starch between pearls (or soak the pearls in water for 15 minutes and drain). Then place in a saucepan with water to cover and simmer till translucent. Drain.
2. Make sauce: Boil sugar and ¼ cup water in a small saucepan till sugar is completely dissolved; allow to cool. Combine sugar syrup with the condensed or evaporated milk and rose syrup.
3. Mix all ingredients in a non-reactive bowl except shaved ice and sauce.
4. Place shaved ice on top of the ingredients. Drizzle sauce over the shaved ice and serve.

Cardamom-Scented Semolina Cake

Kesari

Makes 8 to 10 servings

Kesari is of South Indian origin and has become part of our Deepavali celebrations in Malaysia. Ma made it using semolina (called suji *in Malaysia), ghee (clarified butter), evaporated milk, cashews, raisins, and freshly ground cardamom. When its aroma filled the house, we children would dash into the kitchen and wait for a taste.*

On our visits to Malaysia, we enjoy going to my older brother Prasnan's home because we know that my sister-in-law Shanta will spread out a feast for us, and the finale will be kesari*! To make a healthier version, I decreased the amount of ghee and sugar, and substituted skim or non-fat milk for regular milk. I still add a little ghee, because without ghee, the* kesari *is not the same.*

INGREDIENTS

- 1 to 2 tablespoons ghee, or part ghee and part olive or other vegetable oil, plus an additional ¼ cup, if desired
- Heaping ⅓ cup unsalted, roasted, and coarsely chopped cashews
- Heaping ⅓ cup golden raisins
- 1 cup fine semolina (*suji* or farina)
- ½ cup milk (regular, low fat, or skim)
- 1 teaspoon saffron threads dissolved in ¼ cup hot or warm water for about 8 to 10 minutes; or 3 or 4 drops yellow food coloring
- ½ teaspoon ground cardamom, preferably freshly ground (about 10 cardamom pods, crushed and seeds removed and ground)
- ¾ cup light brown sugar (*increase or decrease amount depending on desired sweetness*)
- ¼ teaspoon salt

DIRECTIONS:

1. Heat a wok or saucepan over medium heat. Add ghee and melt. Add cashews and raisins and stir till cashews turn light brown and raisins puff up, about 2 to 3 minutes.
2. Add semolina and toast for about 4 to 5 minutes with constant stirring, till semolina becomes light brown. Remove from heat and set aside.
3. In a separate wok or saucepan, bring 1¾ cups water and the milk to a boil. Add coloring (saffron or yellow food coloring), cardamom, sugar, and salt, and stir till sugar dissolves completely.
4. Sprinkling in a little at a time and stirring continuously, add the toasted semolina mixture to the milk mixture till it blends in and a grainy consistency (with no lumps) is obtained.
5. Keep stirring (adding more ghee or oil if desired) till *kesari* mixture thickens and comes easily off the sides of the wok or saucepan, about 8 to 10 minutes. Place the *kesari* mixture into an 8-inch square greased (glass or metal) container or baking pan (preferably with 2-inch depth). Spread mixture evenly and smooth the top while it is still hot. Allow to cool and then cover and refrigerate.
6. Before serving, cut into small blocks or triangles (or any desired shape).

Serve with hot tea or coffee, *teh masala* (page 259), or wine; or with a dollop of vanilla or chocolate ice cream.

Green Bean Porridge

Bubur Kacang Hijau

Makes 6 to 9 servings

INGREDIENTS

1 cup mung beans or whole green lentils
½ cup sago or small tapioca pearls, placed in a sieve and rinsed under running water or soaked in water for about 15 minutes and drained (to remove excess or adhering starch between pearls)
¾ cup unsweetened coconut milk
½ to 1 cup light brown sugar (or less if desired)
2 fresh or thawed frozen pandan leaves, tined with fork and knotted
1-inch cinnamon stick, or 1 star anise
Juice squeezed from ½ teaspoon coarsely crushed fresh ginger
½ teaspoon salt
Optional: sliced fruits (blueberries, bananas, strawberries, jackfruit, mangoes, plums, and/or peaches)

In Malaysia, porridges (called bubur *in Malay) are a comforting snack. Sweet porridges are made with fruits and/or lentils and tubers flavored with pandan leaves and doused with coconut milk and palm sugar (*gula Melaka*). The Kristangs have their version served during the feast of St. John (*Festa de San Juang*). Malays and Nonyas add jackfruit or durian pulp or pieces.*

Bubur kacang hijau *was Ma's favorite and she prepared it as a snack after school from a recipe she learned from Periama (my grandmother). Ma added sago pearls, star anise, and pandan leaf to give it a local touch. It tastes great when chilled and you can also add fruits of your choice.*

DIRECTIONS:

1. Optional: Soak mung beans in 2 cups water (or enough to cover) for at least 1 hour or overnight. Strain.
2. Bring 6 cups of water to a boil in a saucepan and add mung beans. Cover and boil for about 25 to 30 minutes if beans were soaked or 40 to 45 minutes if not soaked, till beans get soft and tender (even less cooking time is needed if soaked overnight).
3. Add sago or tapioca pearls and simmer, stirring continuously, for about 8 to 10 minutes, till the pearls get translucent and swollen.
4. Add coconut milk, sugar, pandan leaves, cinnamon stick or star anise, ginger juice, and salt, and bring to a boil. Lower heat and simmer for about 5 minutes, stirring continuously.
5. Remove pandan leaves and cinnamon stick or star anise before serving. Serve lukewarm or chilled.
6. Optional: Add fresh fruits before serving, or add fruits and simmer another minute.

Kristang children at Portuguese settlement in Malacca (Melaka)

Fragrant Vermicelli Sago Milk Pudding

Vermicelli Sago Payasam

Makes 4 to 6 servings

*South Indian immigrants brought a variety of sweet puddings (*payasams*) to Malaysia—*paal *(milk)* payasam*, rice* payasam*, vermicelli and* sago payasam*,* kadala paripu *(chickpea)* payasam*, and green pea* payasam*. They are generally rich and filling, flavored with evaporated or condensed milk (and today with fresh milk), cardamom, ghee, rose essence, and ginger.*

Ma usually prepared vermicelli sago payasam *to celebrate Deepavali (Festival of Lights) and Onam (Harvest Festival for Keralites). My sister-in-law Shanta showed me her version that I am pleased to share with you. You can substitute ½ cup cooked chickpeas for the vermicelli. I have decreased the milk and semolina for a slightly thinner and less rich pudding. And you can omit the evaporated milk and just use fresh milk.*

INGREDIENTS

1 tablespoon ghee or cooking oil
¼ cup unsalted roasted cashews
¼ cup raisins
½ to ¾ cup (2 to 3 ounces) dried wheat-based vermicelli broken into 3-inch pieces
1½ cups fresh milk (whole, low fat, or skim)
¼ cup evaporated milk
2 tablespoons sago or small tapioca pearls, placed in sieve and rinsed under running water or soaked in water for about 15 minutes and drained (to remove excess or adhering starch to separate pearls)
1 tablespoon fine semolina (*suji*)
¼ cup light brown sugar or white granulated sugar
¼ teaspoon salt
5 green cardamom pods, crushed, seeds removed and finely pounded, or ¼ teaspoon ground cardamom
⅛ teaspoon ground ginger
Optional: ½ teaspoon rose essence

DIRECTIONS:

1. Heat ghee or oil in a small skillet. Add cashews and raisins and stir till cashews turn light brown and raisins puff up, about 2 to 3 minutes. Set aside.
2. In a dry saucepan or wok, pan-fry vermicelli till it turns golden brown, stirring continuously and being careful not to burn.
3. Add ½ cup water, milks, and sago or tapioca pearls and bring to a boil.
4. Lower heat and simmer till sago gets translucent and swollen, about 10 minutes.
5. Sprinkle semolina slowly into the pudding while stirring to dissolve evenly. Add sugar and salt and cook till sugar dissolves completely.
6. Add cardamom, ginger, and rose water, if using, and cook for another 2 to 3 minutes.
7. Serve warm or chilled. If the *payasam* thickens after chilling, you can add more water and blend well before serving.

Serve with *teh masala* (page 259), *teh tarik* (page 262), or regular tea or coffee.

Hindu Keralites make *paal payasam* with rice and fresh milk as a *prasadam* or offering to Gods. *Paal payasam* is believed to be the favorite dessert of Lord Krishna. On Janamashtami, Lord Krishna's birthday, *paal payasam* is offered at Krishna temples in Kerala, India. Keralites also prepare these rich, filling desserts to celebrate their New Year, called Vishu.

Sweet Coconut Crepes

Kueh Dadar

Makes 3 to 4 servings

INGREDIENTS

CREPES

⅔ cup all-purpose flour
⅛ teaspoon salt
1 egg, beaten
1 cup unsweetened coconut milk
¼ teaspoon pandan extract, essence, or paste

FILLING

¼ cup thinly sliced or chopped palm sugar or dark brown sugar
1 tablespoon white granulated sugar
¼ cup water
1 fresh or frozen and thawed pandan leaf, tined with a fork and knotted
1 cup grated or shredded fresh coconut (or use dried unsweetened grated or shredded coconut, soaked in warm water for 5 minutes to rehydrate, then drained and patted dry)
Optional: 1-inch cinnamon stick or 1 star anise
1 teaspoon tapioca or cornstarch dissolved in 1 to 2 teaspoons water

COCONUT SAUCE TOPPING

½ cup unsweetened coconut milk
2⅓ tablespoons white granulated sugar
⅛ teaspoon salt
2 teaspoons tapioca or cornstarch dissolved in 2 to 3 teaspoons water

OPTIONAL GARNISH

Chopped toasted walnuts or almonds
Ground cinnamon

My first exposure to kueh dadar *was at a small beach hotel on Pangkor Island. After retirement, my father (Cha) worked as an engineer at the Malayan Flour Mill in Lumut, a sleepy fishing community on the western Malaysian coast across from Pangkor Island. Cha invited us to spend a few days with him at Pangkor beach. Early one evening, as we sat on the porch of our tiny chalet near the water, Cha ordered tea with* kueh dadar, *a local specialty. It is a rolled crepe with a sweet coconut filling topped with a coconut milk sauce. The sea was still, the sun was setting, and the horizon was turning breathtaking shades of orange, red, gold, and purple. We enjoyed our evening snack of* kueh dadar *and watched the sun go down against a backdrop of swaying branches of coconut trees and children running back home along the beach. My daughter, Geeta, only two years old then, was gleefully running around in the garden picking flowers and munching on her cookie.*

Today, whenever I make kueh dadar, *it brings back wonderful memories of those happy times with Cha. In my recipe, I add pandan extract (instead of boiling pandan leaves in water to extract their juice) to give a more intense lime green color for the crepe portion.*

DIRECTIONS FOR CREPES:

1. Sift or mix flour and salt in a medium bowl and set aside.
2. Mix remaining crepe ingredients and ⅓ cup water in a separate bowl.
3. Pour liquid ingredients slowly into the flour while whisking or stirring till a smooth batter is obtained.
4. Heat a 5-inch to 6-inch skillet or shallow non-stick pan (if using a regular pan, add a tablespoon of oil). Add 2 tablespoons batter and swivel it around in pan till an even layer of batter coats the bottom of the pan. Cook crepe on both sides till tiny bubbles appear and crepe turns light brown. Set crepe aside. Repeat with remaining batter.

DIRECTIONS FOR FILLING:

1. Place all filling ingredients except tapioca or cornstarch in a saucepan and stir over low heat for about 3 to 4 minutes till sugar dissolves completely and blends well with coconut.
2. Stir in tapioca or cornstarch paste and cook, stirring constantly, for another 4 to 5 minutes, till sauce thickens. Remove pandan leaf and cinnamon stick or star anise, if used, before serving.

DIRECTIONS FOR TOPPING:

1. Place all ingredients for topping, except tapioca or cornstarch, in a small saucepan and mix well.
2. Bring to a boil, lower heat, add tapioca or cornstarch and cook while stirring till sauce thickens, about 3 to 5 minutes.

TO ASSEMBLE CREPES:

1. Place 2 tablespoons filling in center of each crepe, tuck in edges and fold over into rolls.
2. Top with sweet coconut sauce.
3. If desired, sprinkle with chopped toasted walnuts or almonds and/or cinnamon powder.

Pangkor Island fishing village

Sago Pudding with Palm Sugar

Sagu Gula Melaka

Makes 8 servings

INGREDIENTS

1 cup sago or small tapioca pearls, placed in sieve and rinsed under running water or soaked in water for about 15 minutes then drained (to remove excess or adhering starch to separate pearls)

COCONUT MILK SAUCE

1 cup thinly sliced or chopped palm sugar or dark brown sugar
¼ cup white granulated sugar
2-inch cinnamon stick
2 or 3 pandan leaves, tined with fork and knotted
¾ to 1 cup unsweetened coconut milk
½ teaspoon salt

Sago gula Melaka *is a sinfully delicious dessert unique to Malaysia. It is found at most hawker stalls and cafes, and even at hotel restaurants. While originally a Nonya dish, the Malays, Chinese, and Indian Muslims (or Mamaks) also make this sago pudding topped with a sweet palm sugar and coconut milk sauce. A great cooling refresher after a spicy meal, it is also served at weddings and parties. Bob and I are addicted to it and make it a point to try it at most places we visit in Malaysia. Our favorite was at a Nonya café in Malacca where we went for a delicious cup of tea and* sago gula Melaka *with my sister Vas and her husband, Diva. It was a wonderful antidote to the hot humid weather.*

Gula Melaka *(called* gula Jawa *by Indonesians) is also the Malay name for palm sugar, the sap derived from the flower buds of the palm (Palmyra) tree. A golden brown sugar, it is sold as paste, in tubes, or as blocks. Sago (or* sagu *in Malay) is a starch derived from the trunk of the sago palm, which is widely cultivated in Sarawak. Small tapioca pearls can be subsituted for sago pearls if they are unavailable.*

DIRECTIONS:

1. Bring 4 to 5 cups water to a boil in a saucepan. Add sago or tapioca pearls, stir, and bring back to a boil. Lower heat and simmer while stirring, for about 8 minutes, till pearls become translucent and swollen.
2. Place in ½ cup molds or small bowls or in one large bowl, and chill to set.
3. To make the sauce, combine 1½ cups water, the sugars, cinnamon stick, and pandan leaves in a small saucepan. Stir to dissolve sugars. Add coconut milk and salt and bring to a boil. Lower heat and simmer till sauce thickens. Let sauce cool. Remove pandan leaves and cinnamon stick before serving.
4. To serve, unmold sago or tapioca pudding into a bowl or plate. Drizzle with sauce. Optional: You can also add sliced fruits, such as ripe mango, tangerines, or melon.

BANANAS IN A SWEET PANDAN SAUCE

Pengat Pisang

Makes 5 servings

For Malays, pengat pisang *is a traditional sweet snack eaten at teatime. It is also popular during Hari Raya Puasa. Nonyas add steamed sweet potatoes and taro to the pandan-scented coconut milk broth. They usually prepare it for ceremonial occasions and especially enjoy it on the fifteenth day of their New Year, during Chap Goh Meh festival.* Pengat pisang *can be served warm or chilled.*

On a recent trip to Malaysia's East Coast, during a rainy evening brought on by the Northeast monsoon, I stopped by a Malay stall in a Kelantan village to enjoy a bowl of warm sweet pengat pisang *with hot tea. In my recipe, I reduce the sugar and coconut milk and add cardamom and diced mango. You can add melon or other fruits to make a mixed fruit* pengat pisang*. Some cooks also use ripe plantains and simmer it longer.*

INGREDIENTS

1 tablespoon sago or small tapioca pearls

1 cup unsweetened coconut milk

¼ cup thinly sliced or chopped palm sugar or dark brown sugar

2 fresh or frozen and thawed pandan leaves, tined with a fork and tied into a knot

3 green cardamom pods, crushed, seeds removed, and pounded or ground, or ⅛ teaspoon ground cardamom

⅛ to ¼ teaspoon salt

5 (14 ounces) ripe peeled bananas, sliced on the diagonal into ½-inch pieces (*slice just before cooking or serving to prevent discoloration*)

1 cup (5 ounces) peeled and cubed ripe mangoes or honeydew melon (½-inch cubes)

DIRECTIONS:

1. Place sago or tapioca pearls in a sieve and rinse under running water, or soak in water for about 15 minutes and then drain (this is to remove excess or adhering starch to separate pearls).
2. In a pot, place the sago or tapioca pearls, 1½ cups water, coconut milk, sugar, pandan leaves, cardamom, and salt and bring to a boil stirring frequently.
3. Lower heat and simmer for about 8 minutes, till sago or tapioca pearls become translucent and swollen.
4. Add bananas and mangoes or melon and simmer for about 1 to 2 minutes, taking care not to let bananas get mushy. (Or place bananas and mango or melon in a bowl and pour sauce over.) Discard pandan leaves before serving.

Serve with tea or coffee, *teh masala* (page 259) or *teh tarik* (page 262).

Pengat pisang usually has sliced *pisang raja* (King bananas, sweet small bananas) simmered in coconut milk with sago pearls, palm sugar (*gula Melaka*), and pandan leaves. Malays enjoy different fruit-based and tuber-based *pengats* using durian, jackfruit, yam, tapioca, or pumpkin.

Pineapple Tarts

Kueh Tat

Makes 8 to 10 servings (25 to 30 tarts)

INGREDIENTS

PASTRY*

1½ cups all-purpose flour
¼ teaspoon salt
6 tablespoons unsalted chilled butter
1 egg, beaten
1 tablespoon lemon juice
1 teaspoon vanilla extract

PINEAPPLE JAM FILLING

¼ to ⅓ cup (*depending on desired sweetness*) firmly packed light or dark brown sugar
½ to ¾ cup (*depending on desired sweetness*) white granulated sugar
⅛ to ¼ teaspoon ground nutmeg, or 1-inch cinnamon stick
⅛ to ¼ teaspoon ground cloves, or 3 to 4 whole cloves
⅛ to ¼ teaspoon ground star anise, or 4 segments of whole star anise
3 cups (about 1 pound) canned pineapple chunks, drained, or fresh pineapple chunks

Pineapple tarts, also referred to locally as jam tart or kueh tat, *are a local twist to a classic Portuguese sweet snack. Ma learned to make pineapple tarts watching her Portuguese friend and neighbor Mrs. Collar prepare them and from listening to the radio cooking programs. She generally served them for our afternoon tea as well as for special celebrations. I have also enjoyed them at many Malaysian homes during their festive occasions.*

I first made pineapple tarts for my daughter's primary school function and they turned out to be a great success and were enjoyed by children and parents alike. You can make pineapple tarts in many interesting shapes and sizes or even as a whole pie, especially for family functions. My friend Pat Nuzzo, who is a creative baker, helped me make this recipe and enjoyed it so much that since then she has prepared them for her get-togethers at home.

DIRECTIONS FOR PASTRY:*

1. In a bowl, sift flour and add salt and mix well. Slice chilled butter into pieces and add to flour. Mix with fingers till dough has a crumbly texture.
2. In a small bowl, beat egg with lemon juice and vanilla. Add this mixture to the crumbly dough and knead till dough gets soft and pliable. (Chill dough, if desired.)
3. Roll dough on a floured board into ⅛-inch thickness.
4. Cut dough into 2-inch diameter circles using a cookie or tart cutter or mold. Shape the dough into cup-like forms, or place dough circles in greased mini cupcake pans, and flute edges with fork. Set aside or refrigerate till ready to use.

DIRECTIONS FOR FILLING:

1. In a small bowl, mix sugars and spices and mix well.
2. Grate or coarsely process pineapple chunks.
3. Place pineapple in a saucepan, add the sugar mixture and stir.
4. Cook for about 10 to 15 minutes over low heat, stirring constantly so mixture does not burn, till all the liquid evaporates and mixture thickens and becomes a golden brown color.
5. Remove whole spices if used. Cool or chill jam filling for about 30 minutes before filling pastry. (You can prepare pineapple jam filling ahead of time and keep refrigerated or frozen. When ready to use, add some water and blend the filling well before use.)

* In place of homemade pastry you can use ready-made refrigerated pie crust (2 sheets, 15 ounces). Follow pastry directions for Step 3 and 4.

Each ethnic group in Malaysia claims that jam tarts are theirs. They are specially favored during celebrations. Chinese and Nonyas prepare them for their New Year, while Malays and Indian Muslims prepare them for Hari Raya. For Eurasians and Kristangs, they are a treat for Christmas, and Indians and Chittys prepare them for Deepavali.

TO ASSEMBLE TARTS:

1. Heat oven to 350°F. Add about 1 heaping teaspoon pineapple filling in center of each pastry cup. Flute rims with fingers or fork.
2. Optional: decorate or criss-cross top of filling with 2 or 3 strips of dough about ½ inch long and ⅛ inch wide, or roll tiny balls of dough and place one on top of filling.
3. Brush top and sides of pastry with egg whites before baking.
4. Bake tarts at 350°F for 25 to 30 minutes, till crust turns golden. Cool before serving.

Shanta's pineapple tarts served with a cup of black coffee (*kopi-o*)

Sweet Black Rice Pudding

Pulut Hitam

Makes 4 to 5 servings

INGREDIENTS

Rice Pudding

1 cup black sticky rice, washed and drained
3 pandan leaves, tined with fork and knotted; or 3 drops of pandan extract or flavored paste or essence
¾ cup light brown sugar
Optional: ½ cup peeled fresh or dried *longgan* (if dried, soak in water for about 15 minutes and remove skin)
Optional: mango and/or lychee slices

Coconut Milk Sauce

1 cup unsweetened coconut milk (regular or lite)
¼ cup water
¼ teaspoon salt
Optional: 1 teaspoon rose essence

Pulut hitam *was one of our family favorites—a magical and visually appetizing combination of creamy coconut milk melding with deep purple rice.* Longgans *(referred to as dragon's eye or eyeball, or* mamoncillo chino*) are traditionally added to the pudding. Longgan is also called the 'little brother of the lychee' but does not have the sweetness or bouquet of the lychee. Its flesh is whitish and translucent and it has a musky flavor.*

In my recipe I also add rose essence to the coconut milk, which blends well with the purple rice. Since fresh longgans *are hard to find, I added dried* longgans *to the recipe. You can also substitute sliced lychees or mangos for the* longgans *before serving, as I do.*

DIRECTIONS:

1. Place 6½ cups water and rice in a saucepan and let sit for 30 minutes.
2. Bring rice mixture to a boil. Lower heat, add pandan leaves or extract, sugar, and *longgan*, if using. Cover and simmer for about 45 minutes, till rice becomes tender and chewy. Take off heat and cool. Set aside.
3. To make sauce, in a separate saucepan, mix coconut milk, water, and salt and simmer for about 2 to 3 minutes, stirring constantly. Add rose essence, if using, and blend well for ½ minute.
4. Remove pandan leaves before serving. To serve, place rice pudding into bowls and top each serving with about 3 to 4 tablespoons coconut milk sauce. If not using *longgan*, top with mango or lychee slices before serving.

Sweet Glutinous Rice Balls

Ondeh-Ondeh

Makes 5 to 6 servings (30 balls)

Ondeh-ondeh *are sweet glutinous rice balls filled with palm sugar (*gula Melaka*) and coated with finely shredded coconut. As you bite into one, the melted palm sugar inside bursts into your mouth, creating a wonderful sweet flavor sensation against the chewy texture of glutinous rice.*

I got this recipe from my friend and wonderful source of information Nurul Huda Rahim-Tmimi, marketing executive at Tourism Malaysia in New York. Her father is from Malacca and her mother is from the neighboring state of Johor. Her paternal ancestors can be traced to Quandong in southern China, and her maternal roots are Bugis (from Sumatra) and Bengali. Nurul loved to watch her mother make ondeh-ondeh*. She'd wait for the rolled-up dough balls to pop up in the boiling water when they were done cooking. She was in charge of scooping the balls from the pot and rolling them in the grated coconut.*

In this recipe, I add green coloring to pandan juice to give a more intense green color. I also added pandan-flavored extract with the pandan juice to intensify its flavor and to add to its nice green color. Making ondeh-ondeh *is fun when two people work on them, and it could become a fun-filled activity with your children.*

INGREDIENTS

1 cup finely grated or shredded fresh coconut (or use dried unsweetened grated or shredded coconut, soaked in warm water for 5 minutes to rehydrate, then drained and patted dry)
⅛ plus ¼ teaspoon salt
4 pandan leaves, fresh or frozen and thawed, cut into 1-inch pieces
Optional: 5 to 6 drops green food coloring
Optional: ⅛ teaspoon pandan-flavored paste, or 4 to 5 drops of pandan extract or essence
½ to 1 teaspoon vanilla extract
2 cups glutinous rice (sweet rice or sticky rice) flour
¼ cup thinly sliced or chopped palm sugar or dark brown sugar

DIRECTIONS:

1. Spread fresh or rehydrated coconut on a small baking sheet and dry in warm toaster oven for a few minutes to toast. Place in a bowl and sprinkle with ⅛ teaspoon of salt.
2. Place pandan leaves and ½ cup water in food processor and pulse till leaves are pulverized, about 1 minute. Pour this mixture through a sieve and squeeze the mixture to get juice. Add food coloring and/or pandan-flavored paste, if using, and vanilla extract to liquid and mix well.
3. Add ¼ teaspoon salt to glutinous rice flour in a medium bowl and mix well. Add the pandan mixture and another ½ cup water and mix till you get a smooth dough with no lumps. Dough should not stick to hand (adjust water and flour as needed).
4. Pinch dough into small pieces (about 1 tablespoon) and roll into balls between your palms.
5. Flatten balls slightly and press thumb into middle of balls to make an indentation. Place sugar (about ¼ teaspoon each) in the indentations in the balls. Pinch the dough around the palm sugar to seal it. Roll dough between palms again to create a ball and cover the palm sugar well (so it will not leak during cooking). Cover *ondeh-ondeh* with plastic wrap if waiting for water to boil.
6. Bring a large pot of water to a boil and drop the balls into the water. Make sure they are separate from each other and that they don't stick to bottom of pot (you may have to cook in batches).

(*continued on next page*)

(CONTINUED) SWEET GLUTINOUS RICE BALLS
Ondeh-Ondeh

7. After about 4 minutes simmering, the balls will rise and float on the surface of the water, at which point they are cooked.
8. Scoop the balls out with a perforated ladle or slotted spoon and roll them in the shredded coconut till evenly coated. Transfer to a plate and cool before serving. (Do not refrigerate as they will become too hard to eat. Store at room temperature for not more than 2 to 3 days.)

Serve with tea or coffee, *teh masala* (page 259) or *teh tarik* (page 262).

Ondeh-ondeh (sweet glutinous rice balls)

Spiced Pandan Tea

Teh Masala

Makes 2 servings (about 2 cups)

Spiced pandan tea is Malaysia's answer to India's chai which has become popular in the U.S. It is made by brewing tea with a mixture of aromatic spices. There are many ways of preparing spiced tea. The most traditional method is by boiling loose tea leaves with whole spices in a mixture of milk and water. Alternatively tea leaves and spices are steeped in hot water, strained, and then milk and sugar are added. Some combine all the ingredients together, bring them to a boil, then strain and serve, others leave the mixture to simmer for a while and then strain. Or it can be prepared like my Ma. She would boil the tea leaves, add spices, allow them to sit for several minutes, then strain the tea and add milk and sugar.

*I go a step further and add star anise and pandan leaf, which makes it truly Malaysian! The pandan leaf (*daun pandan*) adds a sweet, vanilla, and rose accent to the tea. You can drink the spiced tea black, but I present a recipe that calls for milk and sugar which balances the bitterness of the tea leaves. You can add fresh, evaporated, or condensed milk.* Teh masala *is a warming and soothing brew that is also a great digestive aid after meals.*

INGREDIENTS

1 teaspoon chopped and crushed fresh ginger
3 cardamom pods, crushed
2 cloves
1-inch cinnamon stick
4 petals star anise
1 black peppercorn, crushed
1 fresh or frozen and thawed pandan leaf, tined with fork and knotted
2 black tea bags, or 2 to 3 teaspoons loose black tea
½ to 1 teaspoon sugar
8 teaspoons fresh milk

DIRECTIONS:

1. Bring 2½ cups water, ginger, remaining spices, and pandan leaf to a boil. Lower heat and simmer for about 2 to 3 minutes.
2. Turn heat off, add tea bags, and let steep for another 2 to 3 minutes, then strain. Drink black or add sugar and/or milk. For 1 cup tea, add ¼ to ½ teaspoon sugar (more if desired) and 4 teaspoons fresh milk. Mix well and serve.

Serve with semolina cake (page 247), banana cake, cheesecake (page 310), pineapple tarts (page 254), biscuits, pastries, or cookies. You can also serve with sandwiches, fried sweet banana fritters (page 67), curry puffs (page 57), spiced lentil cakes (page 61), *thosai* (page 69), spicy fish cutlets (page 63), spicy pickled fish (page 62), or *samosas*.

Ginger Drink
Minuman Halia

Makes 2 to 3 servings (2¼ cups)

INGREDIENTS

- 2 to 3 tablespoons chopped and crushed fresh ginger
- ½-inch cinnamon stick
- 2 cloves
- 4 petals star anise
- 2 cardamom pods, crushed
- 2 teaspoons dried hibiscus flowers (*calyces*)
- Optional: 1 to 2 teaspoons sugar
- Optional: 2 mint leaves, freshly chopped, or ¼ teaspoon dried mint leaves

Malaysians generally drink ginger drink or tea to alleviate stomach pains or discomfort. Ginger is simmered with water or added to tea. Ma believed in the magical powers of ginger and whenever we felt sick, she would give us ginger ale, ginger tea, or a warm ginger drink. She would squeeze ginger juice and add boiling water, then strain and serve it warm, as she said we should not have any drink cold, even water, so we do not "shock" our body. I don't remember going to doctors for colds and flus, but taking Ma's home remedies were our cures.

I have given a twist to Ma's ginger drink by adding mint leaves and dried hibiscus flowers (roselles), actually the calyces (which are the sepals of the flower) of the sorrel plant, Hibiscus sabdariffa *(Malvaceae family). This is different from the* Hibiscus rosa-sinensis *or* Bunga Raya, *the national flower of Malaysia. The chilled warm ginger melding with the acidic flavor of roselle is a particularly refreshing drink for the hot summer months.*

DIRECTIONS:

1. In a medium saucepan, bring 3 cups water to a boil. Add ginger and spices, then lower heat and simmer for about 3 minutes.
2. Turn off heat, add dried hibiscus and let steep in hot water for about 3 to 5 minutes, depending on the strength you want.
3. Strain, and serve warm or chilled, with or without sugar and mint leaves.

Serve with curry puffs (page 57), hot and spicy chicken wings (page 64), vegetable fritters (page 59), or fried sweet banana fritters (page 67).

Roselles are new to Malaysia. A variety of roselle, known locally as *asam paya* or *asam susur,* was introduced in the early 1990s in the Northeast state of Terengganu. The calyces and leaves are acidic in flavor. The bright red roselle calyces (often called flowers) are made into a health drink (rich in vitamin C and anthocyanins), preserves, and sweet pickles. Roselle is reported to be used as a treatment for hypertension and urinary tract infections.

BARLEY DRINK
Minuman Barli

Makes 3 to 4 servings

Barley water has been touted as a medicinal drink since Hippocrates' times and through the years has been drunk as a soothing tonic for the stomach. Barley water is usually flavored with lemon or other fruits by the British. Sometimes it is mixed with milk when given to children.

Ma made barley drink quite often, kept it in the refrigerator, and warmed it whenever she wanted it. She drank it because she said it was healthy. I decided to add it to the beverage section because of its benefits. You can add lemon rind or juice, as the British do. I like pandan leaf and rose essence as they add a wonderful fragrance to the drink. It can also be eaten as porridge by adding less water.

INGREDIENTS

½ cup barley pearls
Heaping ½ teaspoon chopped or sliced and crushed fresh ginger
2 fresh or frozen and thawed pandan leaves, tined with fork and tied into a knot
Optional: ½ to 1 tablespoon sugar
Optional: ¼ teaspoon rose essence

DIRECTIONS:

1. Combine 5 cups water and all ingredients except rose essence in a saucepan and bring to a boil.
2. Lower heat and simmer for about 30 minutes, till barley pearls are cooked and become soft and chewy, adding rose essence, if using, 2 to 3 minutes before done.
3. Cool at room temperature or chill before serving. Add more water if barley water becomes thick.

The barley grain originated in Ethiopia and Southeast Asia and has been cultivated for more than 10,000 years. Barley's dietary fiber is four times that of oatmeal, and it is a great source of selenium, phosphorus, copper, and manganese. Its high beta glucan lowers cholesterol and its selenium reduces the risk of colon cancer. It is also believed to prevent gallstones and breast cancer. Its niacin content provides protection against cardiovascular disease.

Sweet Frothy Mamak Tea

Teh Tarik

Makes 2 servings

INGREDIENTS

2½ cups water

2 to 3 teaspoons loose black tea, or 2 black tea bags

2 to 3 tablespoons sweetened condensed milk

Teh tarik *("pulled" tea) is a Malaysian-style cappuccino. It is similar in appearance to a tea latte. Malaysians love* teh tarik *and enjoy it throughout the day—for breakfast with* roti canai, *with* kuehs *for afternoon tea, or as a late evening beverage before dinner. Every time I visit Malaysia, I cannot keep away from this really sweet tea, even though I don't take sugar in my tea. What I especially enjoy is watching the Mamak vendors preparing it.*

Teh tarik *is named after the act of the vendor's "pulling" motion used to pour it. Tea prepared with sweetened condensed milk is poured into a light metal container with a handle. Then, using another similar container, the vendor pours the hot tea between the two containers through a distance of more than 3 or 4 feet. This action is repeated a few times till a layer of froth appears on the tea. Then he pours the contents in a glass or cup. This "pulling" action also cools the tea a bit.*

Here is my Ma's recipe for afternoon tea, and I am including directions for the "pulling" action to create teh tarik. *You can decrease the sweetened condensed milk but you may not get the same "intoxicating flavor" effect!*

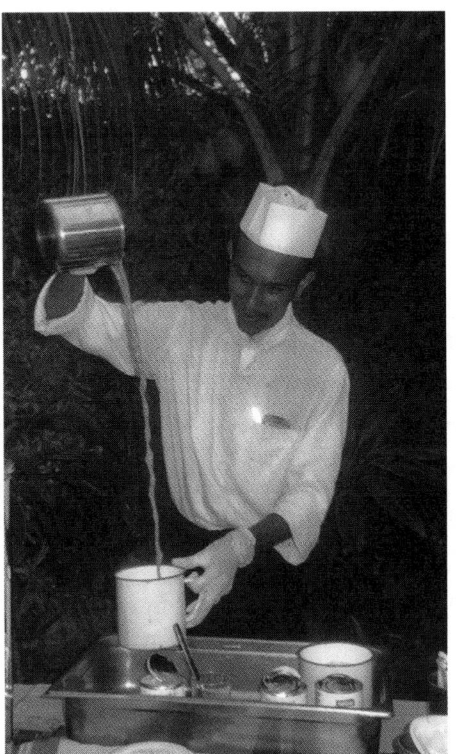

Teh tarik vendor

DIRECTIONS:

1. Bring water to a boil. Remove from heat and add tea leaves or bags and let steep for about 2 to 3 minutes.
2. Strain tea leaves or remove tea bags and discard. Add sweetened condensed milk and stir well.
3. Using two metal containers with handles, pour the tea into one container. Then holding the each container by the handle, one with tea and the other empty, carefully pour the tea back and forth about 4 times, till froth appears on the tea.
4. Place the tea in a cup or mug and enjoy it before the froth disappears.

Serve with curry puffs (page 57), sandwiches, sweet rice balls (page 257), sago pudding (page 252), spiced lentil cakes (page 61), stuffed tofu (page 60), fried sweet banana fritters (page 67), or pineapple tarts (page 254); and entrees like stir-fried noodles (page 136), fried rice (page 123), or *satay* (page 65).

Spiced Lime Juice
Minuman Jus Limau

Makes 4 servings (4 to 4½ cups)

In Malaysia, lime juice is prepared from small yellow-green limes called limau kasturi *(or calamansi lime) that have a fragrant sweet and slightly tart taste, or the regular limes in Malaysia called* limau nipis *(similar to Key limes) that give a more intense sour note. You can use the regular limes you get in the U.S., the Persian limes, if these are not available. On a trip to Malaysia, while we drove along the East Coast I came across a Malay vendor (of Sumatran background) who made me a delicious cooling lime juice that had a wonderful aroma of sweet spices, lemongrass, and ginger. Sometimes he said he added milk and a touch of salt as well. He said the drink was called* bandrek *in Indonesia and explained that his family drank it warm at night, or to get rid of sore throats and colds. I fell in love with this spiced lime juice.*

In my recipe, I use freshly squeezed lime juice like the Malaysians, and I've added lemongrass, cinnamon, star anise, and ginger to give a sweet spicy twist to the lime juice. I omitted the clove but you can add 1 or 2 cloves if you like the flavor. You can use bottled lime juice and omit the spices if you want a plain lime juice, but then you will be missing the Malaysian touch.

INGREDIENTS

1 to 2 teaspoons sliced and crushed fresh ginger
2-inch cinnamon stick
Optional: 1 or 2 cloves
1 star anise
1 or 2 lemongrass stalks, bruised with back of a knife and tied into knot
1 to 3 tablespoons sugar (*depending on the limes you use as well as your taste*)
½ cup freshly squeezed or bottled lime juice
2 teaspoons chopped fresh or dried mint leaves, or 2 sprigs whole mint leaves

DIRECTIONS:

1. Bring 4½ to 5 cups water to a boil. Add ginger, cinnamon stick, clove, if using, star anise, and lemongrass, and simmer for about 5 minutes.
2. Remove from heat and let sit for about 1 to 2 minutes. Strain, add sugar and lime juice and mix well.
3. Chill or add ice cubes, and garnish with mint leaves before serving.

Serve with fried rice (page 123), stir-fried noodles (page 136), vegetable fritters (page 59), coconut-infused rice (page 117), spicy fried fish (page 206), chicken curry *debal* (page 289), chicken *rendang* (page 287), or curry noodles (page 149).

Lemongrass Lychee Martini

Martini Serai Laici

Makes 1 serving

INGREDIENTS

Lemongrass syrup

(*makes enough for about 5 martinis*)

1 cup sugar

1 cup water

3 or 4 lemongrass stalks (depending on their size), bruised with back of knife and tied into a knot

Martini mix (for 1 serving)

Cracked ice

2 ounces vodka

1 ounce lemongrass syrup

½ ounce lychee syrup (from canned lychees in syrup)

½ teaspoon freshly squeezed or bottled lime juice

1 lychee (from canned lychees in syrup)

My husband, Bob, makes wonderful martinis and he has learned to make a delicious lychee martini using lychee syrup, vodka, cassis, and lychee fruit (called laici locally). For this recipe, he decided to use lemongrass syrup to make it truly Malaysian, and knowing my love for lemongrass. Lemongrass has a wonderful bouquet of a rose-like lemony flavor without the tanginess of lemon. It is becoming the 'in' flavor today in many restaurants and bars.

Bob combines equal parts sugar and water with bruised lemongrass stalk, and simmers them together for a fragrant lemongrass syrup. For the martini, he also adds some lime juice. You can substitute pomegranates for the lychee fruit and add a touch of ginger juice if you prefer.

DIRECTIONS:

1. To make lemongrass syrup, mix sugar, water, and lemongrass in a saucepan. Bring to a boil, then lower heat and simmer for 10 minutes, till sugar is dissolved. Strain and refrigerate till chilled.
2. To make martini, chill martini glass in freezer. Then fill cocktail or martini shaker with cracked ice. Add vodka, lemongrass syrup, lychee syrup, and lime juice and shake till well mixed and chilled.
3. Place lychee in chilled martini glass and pour martini mix over it.

Serve with hot and spicy chicken wings (page 64), curry puffs (page 57), chile chicken (page 163), spicy pickled fish (page 62), spicy fried chicken (page 165), spiced lentil cakes (page 61), or spicy eggplant dip (page 58).

Martinis have become trendy drinks, and you can find all kinds of flavors. Generally I am not fond of hard drinks but when I tasted a lychee martini at a French Thai restaurant in New York City, I was hooked. Lychees (or *litchis*) are one of my favorite fruits and this lychee martini has become my favorite cocktail drink.

CHAPTER **11**

FESTIVALS AND FEASTS OF MALAYSIA: CELEBRATING FLAVOR

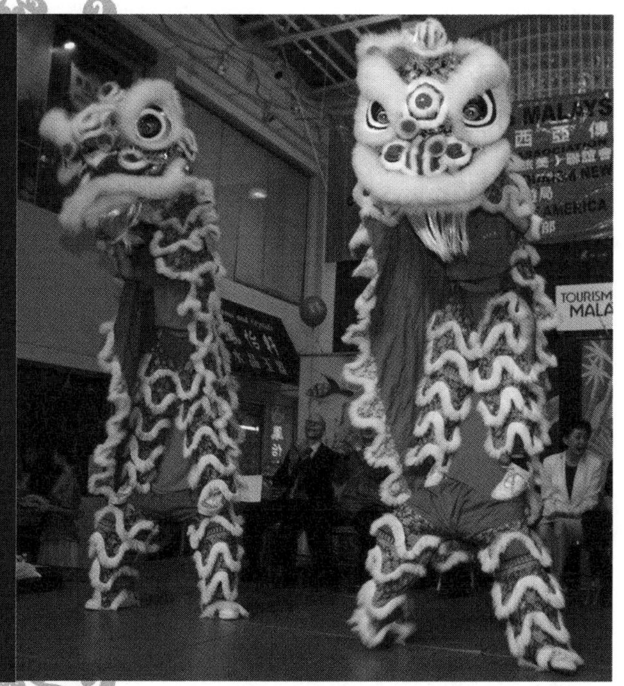

Chinese New Year dragon dance

Throughout the year, Malaysians celebrate many religious holidays and festive occasions that reflect their beliefs and culture. One common, significant characteristic of all Malaysian festivities is *rumah terbuka* or "open house." Whether the celebration is Malay, Chinese, or Indian, friends and neighbors of other faiths and ethnicities are welcomed into the family home to share the lavish and plentiful festival foods.

Malay and Indian Muslim Festivals

Hari Raya Puasa

Hari Raya Aidilfitri, known elsewhere in the Islamic World as Eid, and popularly as Hari Raya Puasa in Malaysia, is a major festival for Malays and Indian Muslims. It marks the end of Ramadan, the month of fasting (*puasa*). Each year, fasting starts in a different month according to the moon and Muslim calendar. It is a joyous occasion for all Muslims, signifying purification and renewal through self-restraint. Family members pray at the mosque in the morning, and then later say prayers for the departed souls of loved ones. Afterwards, they come to their decorated homes, light oil lamps, and open their doors to celebrate with relatives, friends, and neighbors.

Many Malay and Indian Muslim homes prepare their favorite family recipes, handed down through generations. *Ketupat* or *nasi impit* (page 281), beef *rendang* (page 177), and *ayam masak merah* (page 284) are a few special dishes for Hari Raya Puasa, usually served with beef floss (*serund-*

ing daging), *satay* (page 65) or *satay goreng* (page 178), and *acars* (see Chapter 3). Rice is symbolic for Malays so a variety of rice dishes abound during Malay festivities, including *nasi minyak* (ghee rice, page 121), *nasi kuning* (yellow rice, page 118), *nasi dagang* (red rice in coco nut milk, page 128), *ketupat pulut* (glutinous rice wrapped in palm leaves), or *lemang* (glutinous rice cooked in hollow bamboo).

My friend Zubaidah, who now lives in New Jersey, is an Indian Muslim from Penang. She shared with me her memories of Hari Raya Puasa and the foods she remembers for the special day. She remembers having *pulut kaya* (steamed glutinous rice with a rich custard topping) for breakfast, *ketupat* with peanut *satay* sauce and *serunding* for lunch, and a variety of dishes for dinner. Curry puffs (page 57) are a must she says. *Nasi tomato* (tomato rice, page 119), *nasi biryani* (page 280), and *roti jala* (a net-like crepe) served with chicken curry (page 171) or chicken *kurma* (page 168), *ayam masak merah* (page 284), beef *rendang* (page 177), *dalcha* (savory meat lentils, page 285), and a spicy stir-fry of string beans with chicken livers or gizzards, and eggplant and pineapple *pajeri* (page 232) are some dishes she savors. These dishes reflect the Indian and Malay heritage of Indian Muslims (or Mamaks) in Penang and elsewhere.

Colorful arrays of sweet and savory *kuehs* (little cakes, custards, and cookies) are an important part of Hari Raya festival foods. They are generally made from glutinous rice flour, palm sugar, pandan leaf, coconut milk, and many local fruits—durian, banana, coconut, jackfruit, and pineapple.

Chinese and Chinese Peranakan Festivals

Chinese New Year

Chinese New Year, also referred to as Lunar New Year, is the most important celebration for the Chinese and Chinese Peranakans. It begins on the first day of the first lunar month in the Chinese calendar and ends on the fifteenth day, so is usually observed in January or February. On the eve, there is a family reunion dinner when spirits are appeased and food offerings are made to gods, including *Kuan Yin*, the goddess of Mercy. The married and family elders give unmarried youngsters *ang pow*, red packets that hold gifts of money. Homes are decorated with oranges, plum blossoms, and kumquat trees for good luck. Firecrackers are exploded to ward off evil spirits. Non-Chinese friends often pay a visit and offer greetings of *gong hee fatt choy*. On the fifteenth night of Chinese New Year, which is called *Chap Goh Meh*, unmarried women throw oranges into the sea to wish for prospective good husbands and celebrate by eating rice dumplings. New Year celebrations end on the fifteenth day with Shang Yuan Jie, the festival that honors the Lords of Heaven, Earth, and Water.

On New Years' Eve, foods that symbolize long life, joy, togetherness, children, and prosperity are served. Buddha's Delight (vegetarian dish), steamed whole fish (signifying abundance), curried noodles (for longevity), sticky rice (signifying sustenance), egg rolls (for wealth), eggs (for fertility), sweet sesame seed balls, turnip cakes, and fruits are served. Vegetarian and fish dishes are prepared on the first day of the New Year as slaughtering animals is considered bad luck. So spicy sweet shrimp (symbolizing happiness, page 286) and fish dishes are popular. Depending on the homes, New Year's day meal may consist of *popiah*, shark fin soup, fried rice in lotus leaf, roast chicken, sesame and honey chicken, fragrant duck, braised Chinese mustard greens with seaweed, *kailan* with crabmeat sauce, and boiled dumplings. Hainanese chicken rice (page 126) served with a light chicken broth, sesame-scented rice, and a chile ginger dip (page 106) is a traditional meal served in many homes.

Sweets and cakes are essential for the New Year, including almond cookies, pineapple tarts, water chestnut cake, semolina cake, peanut puffs, and butter cookies. Also during this time, a traditional household offers candy, honey, and sticky rice cake to the House Gods or Deities (protectors of the home) and ancestors.

Chinese Peranakans (Baba-Nonyas) also celebrate the Lunar New Year. Although of a mixed Chinese and Malay heritage, they identify themselves as Chinese, observing their many festivities and religious and ancestral rites. They speak Malay and the women dress in Malay attire, but they have remained Chinese, retaining their "traditional" Hokkien customs. But unlike the Chinese, their foods have a strong Malay influence, prepared with chilies, *rempah* (spice pastes), spices, lemongrass, coconut milk, and *belacan* (dried shrimp paste). Following their Chinese identity, they prepare and serve foods based on their symbolism. Their choice of ingredients and dishes for festivities derives from Chinese traditions and the concept of yin and yang. Some of their festive dishes include chicken curry (page 171); *chap chye* (mixed vegetables with mung bean noodles); *inchee kabin* (similar to the spicy fried chicken on page 165); *ayam sioh* (tamarind coriander chicken, page 164); *nasi lemak* (coconut-infused rice, page 117); and spicy *laksas* (pages 151 and 153) with fiery *sambal* condiments.

Every Nonya household offers a great variety of delectable *kuehs* and sweets. *Kueh kapit* (love letters), *seri muka* (glutinous rice custard), *kueh lapis* (layered custard), *kueh kosui* (steamed rice custard), and *kueh bangkit* (snow-white arrowroot flour cookies) are some they enjoy. For *Chap Goh Meh*, the fifteenth and final day of the Lunar New Year period, Nonyas enjoy *pengat* (page 253), a sweet porridge prepared with sweet potatoes, taro, and/or bananas flavored with coconut milk and pandan leaf, a true reflection of their mixed heritage.

The Mid-Autumn or Mooncake Festival

The Mid-Autumn or Mooncake Festival is celebrated by Chinese and Chinese Peranakans in mid to late September, when the moon is at its fullest and brightest, to celebrate the abundance of the summer's harvest. It is also called the Lantern Festival, for the many decorative paper lanterns that are hung in front of homes. Traditionally, on this day, family members and friends will gather to admire the bright mid-autumn harvest moon and have tea with mooncakes that come in a variety of flavors. Mooncakes are rich and heavy with a thin crust and a thick filling typically made from black bean paste (*tou-sha*), brownish lotus paste (*lien-yung*), or yellow bean paste (*tou-yung*). Today, they are also prepared with pandan, durian, and green tea flavors. Traditional mooncakes have Chinese characters for longevity or harmony printed on top. To the Chinese, the round palm-size shape of mooncakes symbolizes family unity.

Prayers are offered with the customary lighting of joss sticks and red candles. After prayers, there is feasting and merrymaking with children carrying lighted paper lanterns around the neighborhood, sometimes joined by their non-Chinese friends, to celebrate the evening.

Vesak—Buddhist Festival

Vesak is celebrated by the Buddhists (Chinese and Sri Lankan Sinhalese) and is the most holy time in the Buddhist calendar. The exact date of Vesak, informally called "Buddha's Birthday," is in the fourth month in the Chinese lunar calendar, coinciding with the first full moon of that month. It encompasses the birth, enlightenment (Nirvana), and passing (Parinirvana) of Gautama Buddha. On Vesak day, Buddhists assemble at their temples before dawn for the ceremonial hoisting of the Buddhist flag and the singing of hymns in praise of the holy triple gem: the Buddha, the Dharma (His teachings), and the Sangha (His disciples). Devotees bring simple offerings of flowers, candles, and joss-sticks to place at the feet of Buddha. These symbolic offerings remind Buddha's followers that just as the beautiful flowers wither away after a short while, and candles and joss-sticks soon burn out, so too is life subject to decay and destruction. Devotees make a special effort to refrain from killing of any kind on that day, so are encouraged to eat vegetarian food for the day. Foods are generally prepared on this day without spices, garlic, onions, or ginger, which are believed to be stimulating for the mind.

Indian Festivals

Deepavali

Deepavali or Diwali, known as the Festival of Lights, is an important festival for Hindu Indians, who celebrate it during the seventh month of the Hindu solar calendar, usually at the end of October or early November. As light signifies goodness in Hinduism, *deeps* (earthen oil or ghee lamps) are burned throughout the day and into the night as a sign of celebration and to ward off darkness and evil. On this day, Hindu Malaysians welcome fellow Malaysians of different races and religions to their homes to celebrate the festival.

I have wonderful memories of our Deepavali celebration with the family. Ma and Periama (my grandmother) began their food preparations a few weeks earlier, cleaning the home, getting new curtains and sofa covers, designing a *kolam* at our front entrance, and placing flowers on the eve to welcome Mahalaxmi, the goddess of prosperity and wealth, at midnight. This was the time we all got new clothes to wear and show-off. I remember the activity in the kitchen, long into the early hours of morning, with Ma and Periama preparing all kinds of sweets and snacks, such as rose *kueh* (rose-shaped cookie), icing-coated wheat-based cruellers, *murukku*, and other shelf stable sweets that were stored in containers for the special day. This began the Deepavali mood for me. I would always try to sneak into the kitchen and taste some of the sweets and snacks being prepared.

On the eve of Deepavali, offerings and prayers are made to ancestors and deceased family members and many go to temples to pray. On the night before the great day, our excitement

Kolam for Deepavali

kept us awake. The next morning we would wake up at sunrise to take our baths. Traditionally, oil was applied on our heads (a ritual known as *ganga-snanam*, which was done to cleanse the impurities of the past year) and we would dress in new attire to mark the special day. By 9 a.m., the house was already filled with aromas coming from the kitchen, where Ma and Periama had begun to prepare the dishes. Later, prayers were held at the family altar, after which the family gathered before the elders to receive their blessings. Some families also gave yellow packets with money to the children, adopting the Chinese red *ang pow* tradition.

While Ma and Periama spent the morning busily preparing delicious dishes, we would sit in the living room, waiting anxiously for our friends. The celebrations began as soon as they arrived. We started with snacks that included curry puffs (page 57), *murruku* (made with rice flour and *urad dhal*), and *masala vadai* (spiced lentil cakes, page 61) or rose *kueh* (crispy rose-shaped cookies). Then came the *iddiappam* (extruded rice-based stringhoppers), ghee rice (page 121), chicken *kurma* (page 168), vegetable *biryani* (page 280), mutton *peratil* (page 185), stir-fried mixed vegetables (page 224), and spicy sweet shrimp (page 286). Lastly the sweets, both homemade and store-bought—cakes, cookies, *kesari* (page 247), *sago payasam* (page 249), *laddu* (sweet wheat-based balls), *Mysore pak* (chickpea flour and ghee-based sweet), or *jalebi* (bright orange pretzel-shaped sweets).

Once our friends left late in the afternoon, the celebration began for our parents and their friends and colleagues. So Ma once again was in the kitchen preparing more dishes or heating up dishes. We helped serve foods for Cha's and Ma's friends, this time with beer and liquor for Cha's friends.

Harvest Festivals

Most Indian immigrants in Malaysia are from South India and Sri Lanka, and so their festivals are widely celebrated, particularly the harvest festivals and New Year. Harvest festivals are not only observed by farmers but by urbanites as well.

Thai Pongal is a Tamil harvest festival celebrated when the first rice grains are gathered. The Sun God is worshipped on the first day of the Tamil month of *Thai* (January 14th or 15th) to help in the growth of rice and other crops. Ma adopted the custom of celebrating this holiday from Periama. Ma designed a beautiful *kolam* (decorative design made with colored rice powder) at the entrance of our home. And she would follow the Hindu customs for the day. Sweet rice in a decorated clay pot is placed on firewood in the center of the *kolam*. Jasmine flowers,

Milk boiling over in a Pongal pot at Vas's home

ginger and turmeric leaves are placed around the pot. The rice is boiled with milk and jaggery (unrefined brown sugar) till the milk spills over (the Tamil word *pongal* meaning to boil or spill over), which represents prosperity and a good year to come. Cashews and raisins are also added. The moment the rice and milk bubbles out of the vessel, the tradition for the family standing around the claypot is to shout "*pongalo pongal*" three times and blow the *sangu* (a conch). This proclamation announces that the year will be blessed with happiness. The new boiled rice is offered to the Sun and Earth at sunrise, symbolizing thanks to the Sun and Earth for providing prosperity. Sugarcane, turmeric sprigs, and sweet potatoes are also offered to the Sun God. After the offering, everyone takes a little cooked rice and sprinkles it around the house. This ritual asks God to bless their home. Then the rice is served to the family members present. Other foods offered are curried eggplant (page 232), *sambar* (page 88), *masala vadai* (page 61), *idli* (steamed rice and lentil dumpling), and *payasam* (page 249) on a fresh new banana leaf. My sister Vas continues this tradition in her home, with their daughters, Prita and Priya, creating beautiful *kolams* each year.

Onam is a harvest festival celebrated by the Malayalees who migrated from the Indian state of Kerala. All Malayalees celebrate Onam, irrespective of their religion—Hindu, Christian, Muslim, or Jew. It falls during the month of Chingam (August/September), the first month of the Malayalam calendar, and lasts for ten days. Houses are cleaned and decorated with flowers and traditional lamps. At the entrance to homes, blossoms of different tints are made into a decorative design called *pookalam*. On Cha's (my father) side, his uncle and aunt celebrated it with new clothes and a sumptious spread of dishes. Traditionally his aunt cooked white rice, coconut-laden fish curries, *sambar* (page 88), *avial* (vegetables cooked in yogurt and coconut), and *thoran* (cabbage, raw jackfruit, bitter gourd, or beans cooked with grated coconut). They were served with spicy pickled mango or lime, *papadum*, buttermilk, and banana or plantain chips. The meal ended with *pradhaman* (quite similar to *payasam*, page 249), made with jaggery and coconut milk and served with rice, mung beans, jackfruit, or rice vermicelli.

Tamils celebrate their calender year or New Year by honoring the Hindu God Brahma, the Creator of the world. It falls on the first day of the Tamil month of *Chitthirai* (April 13th or 14th), the anniversary of the day the earth was created. The Sikhs celebrate their New Year (*Vaisakhi*) on April 14th, the first day of the *Vaisakh* month, which also marks their new harvest season.

Lord Murugan at Batu Caves, near Kuala Lumpur

Thaipusam

Thaipusam is a religious Hindu festival celebrating the birthday of Lord Murugan or Subramaniam (younger son of Lord Shiva and Goddess Parvati and the brother of Lord Ganesha). *Thai* is the Hindu month that falls between January 15th and February 15th and *pusam* refers to a star that is at its brightest during this period. A popular festival in Tamil Nadu and Sri Lanka, it was brought to Malaysia by Tamil immigrants. It is celebrated for three days at Batu Caves, a phenomenal limestone cave located outside Kuala Lumpur. A chariot procession carrying Lord Murugan is carried from the Maha Mariamman temple in Kuala Lumpur to the caves, culminating in a climb of 272 steps to the entrance to Batu Caves and the shrine inside. It is a day of penance, fulfilled by various forms of self-mortification or by simply carrying a pot of milk. Vegetarian dishes, sweet rice, and sweets are served on this day.

Peranakan Indian (or Melaka Chittys) Festivals

The Peranakan Indian or Chitty community of Gajah Berang in Malacca (now Melaka) are descendants of early South Indian traders married to Malay women, and also some, to Nonyas. Chittys look Malay, speak in Malay, dress in Malay attire, but are Hindus and celebrate Hindu festivals, rituals, and customs. Like other Hindus, they celebrate Deepavali, Hindu (Tamil) New Year, and Pongal but also have their own special and unique festivals based on Hindu traditions, including Bhogi, Parchu, and Sadangku (fertility ceremony).

Chitty girls in Indian attire at a Sadangku celebration

Pongal and Bhogi

Chittys celebrate Pongol and Bhogi (which falls on the eve of Pongol) to give thanks to the Sun God for helping crops grow and ripen. Traditionally they commemorate the first day of Pongol by destroying old clothes and materials, setting them on fire, and wearing new clothes and using new kitchen utensils. Similar to the Tamils, they draw a colorful *kolam* in front of their homes. After early morning prayers, the lady of the house places red hibiscus flowers on the front and rear doors of her home and waits for the sun to rise and the hibiscus buds to open, at which point they are thrown on the roof. During this day the Chittys also pay homage to their ancestors, a tradition taken from their Indian and Malay ancestry.

Parchu or Padayal

Parchu (or Padayal) is the day when Chittys pay homage to ancestors, similar to Catholics' All Souls Day, Mexican Cinco de Mayo, or Chinese Cheng Beng. They visit the graves of their forbearers and then come home and eat sweet rice and cakes. My girlfriend Radha Pillay is a Melaka Chitty. Radha told me about her own family's Parchu customs. Photos of ancestors are dusted and cleaned and placed on a raised platform on a matted floor. Jasmine garlands are placed over the photos and a brass standing lamp is lit. Coconuts, betel leaves, areca nuts, slaked lime, and seven banana leaves, their tips facing the sea, are placed before the photos. (The Chittys believe that souls enter the sea to find their way to Lord Shiva's home.) Seven cups of tea and seven cups of coffee are neatly arranged on the mat (the number seven being an auspicious number for them). Personal items of the ancestors are also included. The family prays at the altar and asks for blessings from the ancestors.

After prayers, the family prepares their ancestors' favorite foods. Chitty dishes have Malay and Indian flavors, but are generally referred to by Malay names. During the ceremony, rice is placed in the center of banana leaves, surrounded by meats, chicken, seafood, vegetables, and condiments. Steamed *nasi lemak* (coconut-infused rice, page 117), *nasi kemuli* (spiced rice, page 120), and cooked white rice are generally prepared, accompanied by salted eggs, *sambal tumis udang* (stir-fried sambal shrimp, page 204), mutton curry, *lauk belimbang udang* (tamarind-based shrimp curry), fried chicken, pineapple *pachadi*, cabbage cooked with shrimp and coconut milk (page 290), water spinach with shrimp, cucumber carrot *acar* (page 99), radish and salt (for souls to add to food as the cook does not taste the food), coffee, and tea. *Sambal belacan* (page 101) is a must side dish for the Parchu ceremony. Sweets include *kuehs*, tarts, *agar-agar* (jello), and many Indian sweets. At sunset, the family places the food on banana leaves and waves incense at the doorway and outside the house. The head of the household addresses the ancestors in their spoken language, Malay, to allow their souls to come and eat the meal. Afterwards, the family re-enters the home, offers prayers, and then eats the meal from the banana leaves.

Eurasian Festivals

Fiesta de San Pedro

The Portuguese-Eurasian settlement of Malacca, called Kristangs, is a tightly knit community which retains traditions, rituals, and customs dating back almost five hundred years. The community is staunchly Catholic, and they celebrate many of their religious festivals, including Intrudo (splashing of water the Sunday before Ash Wednesday), Fiesta de San Juan (Feast of St. John), Fiesta de Santa Cruz, Fiesta de Assunta, Natal (Christmas), and many more. They celebrate Fiesta de San Pedro (Feast of St. Peter), the patron saint of fishermen, with a week-long celebration beginning June 29th. The festivities include the blessing of the boats and a procession with the statue of St. Peter carried around the settlement, reflecting the community's prayers for God's grace and a bigger and better catch for fishermen, who depend on the sea for their livelihood. Candles are also lit to signify the Light of Christ to guide them safely through the storms at sea and of life on land at their homes.

Christmas

Christmas is a big festival for all Eurasians and Christians of other ethnic groups. Like many places around the world, Christmas has become a holiday celebrated with a decorated tree, lights, and gifts for the family. Many shopping malls and hotels create a festive look and offer popular local dishes. Eurasians prepare Western-style meals, often with local touches—roast chicken, lamb, beef, or turkey with rice stuffing, baked or mashed potatoes, pumpkin, carrots and peas, beef Wellington, chicken pot roast, duck ala orange, Shepherd's pie, or fish cutlets. Desserts include mincemeat pies, gingerbread cookies, almond bars, pudding with rum sauce, semolina cake, fruit cocktail, or fruitcake.

The Kristangs of Malacca prepare spicier meals, unlike the other Eurasians, that include spicy oxtail stew, *teem* (cinnamon and anise-flavored duck soup), spicy *satay goreng* (fried *satay*, page 178), beef in soy sauce, *assam* beef, *debal curry* (page 289), *feng* (mixed meats curry), and hot fiery *sambals*. Pineapple tarts (page 254), coconut ice cream and cakes, *agar-agar*, and coconut rice granules (called *sersagung*), a unique dish that I had in Muar, are their favorite desserts. Some Kristang homes also prepare elaborate rice and noodle dishes, including *arroz gordu* (jumbo rice with sausages, chicken, vegetables), *arroz Macau* (rice with chicken, mushrooms, scallions, ginger, garlic, and eggs), *nasi lemak* (coconut-infused rice, page 117), and *laksa lemak* (noodles in spicy coconut milk, page 151).

East Malaysian Festivals

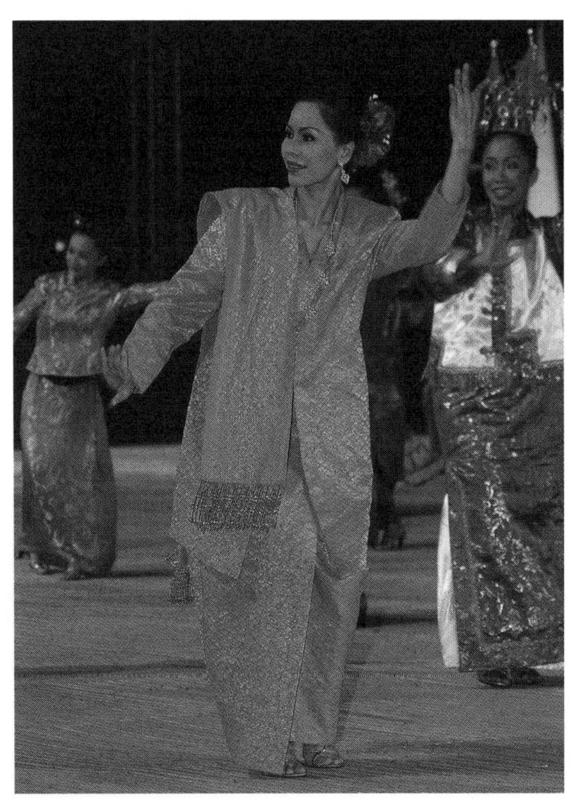

Malay dancers

Pesta Kaamatan

The Kadazan Harvest Festival or Pesta Kaamatan is celebrated at the end of May by all Sabahans. During this festival, known locally as Tadau Ka'amatan, Sabah natives wear their traditional costumes and enjoy a carnival atmosphere the whole day. Most native Sabahans consider rice to be more than just a staple of their diet. There is a sacredness attached to it as Sabahans believe that rice was given to them by Kinoingan, the Almighty Creator, so they will never go without food. According to legend, Kinoingan sacrificed his daughter Huminodun and from her body *padi* (rice) grew. Sabahans repay Kinoingan by conducting ceremonies to honor Huminodun whose spirit is embodied in rice. As part of their celebrations, indigenous Sabahans enjoy rice wine in bamboo cups. The thanksgiving ceremony, called Magavau, is conducted by the *Bobohizan* or high priestess, who invokes the rice spirit with prayer chants and offerings of foods served on banana leaves. The offerings include chicken, meat, eggs, betel leaves, *pinang* (areca nut), *kirai* or *rokok gulung* (rolled up cigars), but the important customary dish is the *hinava*. *Hinava* (similar to *umai*, page 62, or ceviche) is thinly sliced local fish marinated with turmeric, lime juice, onions, and fragrant local leaves. It is accompanied by their local drink, *lihing* (a sweet sherry-like rice wine) made from fermented glutinous rice (*pulut*) and natural yeast called *sasad*. Another popular wine beverage— a party drink for the Muruts—is *tapai*, brewed from cassava or tapioca.

Gawai Dayak

In Sarawak, Gawai Dayak or Dayak Festival is a major celebration on June 1st for the Dayak people. The Ibans (also known as Sea Dayaks) and the Bidayuhs and other groups (referred to collectively as the Land Dayaks) were animists but most are now Christians and some Muslims, though some still observe their traditional festive ceremonies. Like the Sabahans, the Dayaks also celebrate by giving thanks to their gods and spirits for a bountiful harvest and to ask blessings for the new rice planting season. They feast with friends and family who live communally in longhouses. In the longhouses, new mats are laid out on the *ruai* (an open porch that runs through the length of the longhouse). A ceremony is performed to cast away the bad spirits and bad luck. Each family member drags a *chapan* or winnowing basket to their room to throw unwanted or old articles into it. Then the unwanted articles are tossed to the ground from the end of the longhouse for the spirit of bad luck. In the evening, the *miring* (offering ceremony) takes place, followed by dinner.

Iban's traditional foods are called *pansoh*-style, which means food (meat, chicken, fish, vegetables, and rice) is seasoned with lemongrass, chilies, and ginger, and placed in a hollow bamboo stem which is put over an open flame to cook. Eggplant, greens, and ferns are also local favorites. *Penganan* (cakes made with rice flour, sugar, and coconut milk) and *tuak* (brewed rice wine) are served along the *ruai* or veranda of the longhouses. The homes of the Dayaks are opened to visitors who are served *tuak* before they enter.

Wedding Festivals

Malaysian wedding ceremonies are elaborate and involve weeks of preparation and festivities. The wedding rituals among Malaysia's ethnic groups have many similarities, especially the Hindu Indian and Malay or Muslim weddings. Before the advent of Islam, Hinduism was the prominent religion practiced in Malaysia and the rest of Southeast Asia, so many of the Hindu practices were adopted as part of the Malay wedding ceremonies. Thus, in some respects the traditional Malay wedding ceremony bears similarities to the Hindu Indian wedding ceremony. Hindu Indians have differences in their ceremonies based on their Indian ethnicity, whether Tamil, Malayalee, Ceylonese Tamil, Punjabi, or Telegu.

In a traditional Malay wedding, after signing the *akad nikad* (the wedding contract or vows) in the presence of an *imam* (priest) at the mosque (*surau*), the bridegroom walks under a decorative yellow umbrella leading his procession with the sound of drums to the bride's home (similar to Hindu weddings). The bride greets him with a kiss on his hand and they are led away to the *bersanding* ceremony where the couple is blessed. The *bersanding* ceremony is similar to the use of a *mandapan* in Indian weddings. This is when the couple become king and queen for the day, sitting on a decorated dais (*pelamin*) where they can be viewed by guests. Blessing takes place, anointing the couple's upturned palms with *tepung tawar* (pounded rice flour with betel leaves), scented water, pandan potpourri, and rice to protect and ward off evil. For Hindu weddings, the sprinkling of rice grains mixed with turmeric and flowers (called *atchathai*) by family (especially by the elderly) and guests symbolizes prosperity, abundance, and fertility. Just as rice seeds sprinkled on earth take root and create bountiful rice fields, so the couple will produce wonderful children. For the Malays, decorated flowers called *bunga telur* (flower eggs) are placed at the bottom of their feet and then are given as gifts to the guests. Traditionally, *bunga telur* is a plastic flower with a hard-boiled egg attached to it in a net. The egg symbolizes fertility and a request for Allah's blessing to bestow many children upon the couple. The design of the *bunga telur* has evolved over the years. Nowadays, the *bunga telur* includes a plastic flower with chocolates or cookies attached to it in a net, sweets stuffed in decorated eggcups, jewelry purses with potpourri, and tea sachet boxes. Guests, especially relatives, then bless the couple with the sprinkling of *beras kunyit* (yellow rice, similar to the Hindus), scented *bunga rampai* (mix of flower petals and thinly cut pandan leaves), and rose water.

Indians and Malays both have the cleansing ceremony, *nallangu* or *mandi lulur,* before the wedding day. Indians rub turmeric and scented oils on the bride and bridegroom's bodies in each of their homes and milk baths are taken to rid them of ill luck and any evil eye cast on them. Similarly, the Malay bride and groom often use a special bath scrub which includes turmeric powder. Additionally, Malay and Hindu weddings have ceremonies for brides, for example, applying decorative henna to hands and feet (called *majlis berinai* and *mehndi* respectively). These designs are meant to ward off evil.

The wedding feast (*kenduri*) then begins. Guests wash their hands in a little red pot of water before eating the food. Dishes are rich and prepared with meats and/or chicken, generally cooked with ghee. Rice is important, prepared in a variety of ways *nasi minyak* (page 121), *nasi kuning* (page 118), *nasi biryani* (page 280), or *nasi bukhari* (page 278). Beef *rendang* (page 177) is a must, with different states having their own unique flavors. *Pajeri* (eggplant pineapple curry, page 232), *ayam masak merah* (chicken in spicy tomato sauce, page 284), pickled mixed vegetable salad (page 93), and *sambal tumis belacan* (page 102) are some accompaniments.

For traditional Hindu weddings, a strictly vegetarian diet several days before and on the day of the wedding is observed. But today vegetarianism is observed only when the wedding is conducted on temple premises. Later in the evening, rich non-vegetarian foods (including favorite Malay and Chinese dishes) are prepared, such as chicken and mutton *peratil* (page 185), chicken *rendang* (page 287), and chicken *kurma* (page 168) or mutton *kurma* (page 282), shrimp *sambal* (page 204), and *nasi biryani* (page 280). Vegetarian foods prepared from tofu, wheat gluten, mushrooms, and/or seasoned vegetable pickles, and tofu or eggplant *rendangs* are getting trendy for Hindu weddings. Generally for sweet dishes, *payasam* (page 249), traditional Indian desserts, and other local Malay and Nonya *kuehs* are served.

The Indian bride wears a colorful saree of yellow, red, orange, blue, and green as those colors are believed to bring good luck and blessings to the occasion. White and black, considered to be mourning colors, are avoided. Based on the ancient Vedic customs, a traditional Hindu (Tamil) wedding involves extensive prayers and the circumambulation of fire (in a man-made fire pit called a *homa*) which symbolizes God as a witness to the marriage. The groom ends the ceremony with the tying of the *thali* (blessed turmeric-rubbed string or gold chain) on his bride's neck, an act greeted with loud traditional music, clapping, and congratulations from the guests. They then take seven steps around the *homa* as husband and wife, a ritual with each step signifying their togetherness and unification in their life ahead. The guests take home sweets as a blessing for the couple.

For traditional Chinese weddings, the color red, which symbolizes prosperity for the Chinese, fills the house of the bride. The wedding tea ceremony at the bride's home is significant, especially for her parents. The bride offers tea to both her parents to give thanks for having raised her. Once this ceremony is completed, the groom arrives and the wedding begins. It is much simpler than the Hindu or Malay weddings, with no priest involved. The bride and groom pay respects to gods of Heaven and Earth, the Kitchen God, and family ancestors and ask for their blessings. This is followed by a tea ceremony between the newlyweds and the groom's parents which basically completes the wedding. Then their feast is laid out!

Chinese New Year celebration dancers

Aromatic Festive Rice

Nasi Bukhari

Makes 3 to 4 servings

INGREDIENTS

Chicken

1 pound chicken (mix of drumsticks and breasts), cut into 1½-inch pieces
1 teaspoon freshly squeezed or bottled lime juice
2 to 3 tablespoons ghee, butter, or cooking oil
¼ teaspoon salt

Spice Paste

1 heaping teaspoon sliced garlic cloves
1 teaspoon sliced fresh ginger
¼ cup diced shallots or onions
2 or 3 dried whole chilies, steeped in warm or hot water for 5 to 8 minutes, slit and deseeded; or ½ to ¾ tablespoon *cili boh* (*see page 315*); or ¼ to ½ tablespoon bottled *sambal oelek*
¼ cup fresh or evaporated milk

Spice Blend 1

3 teaspoons coriander seeds or ground coriander
1 teaspoon cumin seeds or ground cumin
1 teaspoon whole or ground fennel seeds
¼ teaspoon black peppercorns or finely ground black pepper
1 star anise, or ¼ teaspoon ground star anise
¼-inch cinnamon stick, or ⅛ teaspoon ground cinnamon
¼ teaspoon turmeric powder
1 clove, or ⅛ teaspoon ground clove
1 cardamom pod, or ⅛ teaspoon ground cardamom

I had my first taste of nasi bukhari, *a fragrant rich Malaysian version of a* biryani *at a* Hari Raya Puasa *celebration at the home of one of my Malay classmates. It has Arab and Indian origins and is well known in Johor state in the South and in Northeast Malaysia, where Arab influences are strongest. It is a traditional dish for Malay weddings and festivities. Rice is cooked with chicken, beef, or mutton in ghee, a variety of spices, pandan leaf, dried chilies, fresh or evaporated milk, and tomato sauce.*

*When we were growing up, our parents would take us on some rare occasions as a treat to Bilal, a noted Indian Muslim restaurant on Ampang Road in Kuala Lumpur, for their specialty—*biryanis. *They were prepared with chicken, beef, or mutton. For us, it was a special place, and I remember the blue and white tiles at the entrance and men in checkered sarongs waiting at tables.*

DIRECTIONS FOR CHICKEN:

1. Process Spice Paste ingredients to a smooth paste. Set aside.
2. If using the whole spices for Spice Blend 1, place in skillet (except turmeric powder) and dry roast. Cool and grind together to a fine powder and mix in turmeric. (Or if using ground spices, combine them together.) Set aside.
3. Mix chicken with 1 tablespoon Spice Paste, 1 tablespoon Spice Blend 1, and lime juice till well coated. Set aside to marinate for a minimum of 30 minutes.
4. Heat 1 tablespoon ghee, butter, or oil in a wok or skillet and add remaining Spice Paste and sauté for about 4 to 5 minutes, till fragrant, adding remaining ghee or oil. Add remaining Spice Blend 1 and sauté another 1 minute.
5. Add marinated chicken and stir for about 1 to 2 minutes, then add ¼ cup water and the salt and cook, stirring constantly, till sauce becomes dry and fragrant, about 15 to 20 minutes.

DIRECTIONS FOR RICE:

1. Heat 1 tablespoon of ghee or oil in a saucepan and sauté garlic and ginger for about ½ to 1 minute, then add shallots or onions and sauté for about 1 to 2 minutes.
2. Add Spice Blend 2 ingredients and stir for about 1 minute. adding more ghee or oil if needed; then add rice and pandan leaf and stir for about 1 to 2 minutes. Add 1¾ to 2 cups water, milk, tomato puree, paste, or sauce, rose water, if using, and salt. Blend well and bring to a boil. Turn to very low heat, add cooked chicken and mix.
3. Cover and simmer for 15 to 20 minutes, till all liquid is absorbed and rice is cooked. Remove from heat and let rice cook in its steam for about 10 minutes. (If using a rice cooker, use proportions for rice cooker based upon above quantities. Add the rice mixture from step 2, cover and switch rice cooker on. Rice cooker automatically shuts off when rice is cooked.)

My sister-in-law Shanta's aromatic festive rice

RICE

1 to 2 tablespoons ghee, butter, or cooking oil
1 heaping teaspoon sliced and coarsely crushed garlic cloves
1 teaspoon sliced and coarsely crushed fresh ginger
¼ cup chopped shallots or onions
1 cup Basmati or any long grain rice, rinsed and drained
1 fresh or frozen and thawed pandan leaf, tined with a fork and tied into a knot
¼ cup fresh or evaporated milk
1 tablespoon tomato puree, or ½ tablespoon tomato paste, or 2 tablespoons tomato sauce
Optional: 1 teaspoon rose water
¼ teaspoon salt

SPICE BLEND 2

3 petals star anise
½-inch cinnamon stick
1 clove
1 cardamom pod

4. Remove pandan leaf and whole spices before serving.

Serve with a spicy cucumber tomato salad (page 97), braised spicy long beans (page 230), eggplant and pineapple *pajeri* (page 232), or vegetables in spicy coconut milk (page 223); and chicken *kurma* (page 168), beef *rendang* (page 177), stir-fried *sambal* shrimp (page 204), spicy tangy simmered fish (page 205), fish curry (page 198), spicy fried fish (page 206), or spicy fried chicken (page 165); and savory meat lentils (page 285) or vegetable dhal curry (page 231).

Vegetable Biryani

Biryani Sayuran

Makes 3 to 4 servings

INGREDIENTS

1 to 2 tablespoons ghee or cooking oil
2 teaspoons thinly sliced garlic cloves
2 teaspoons thinly sliced fresh ginger
½ cup sliced shallots or onions
1 lemongrass stalk, bruised with back of knife and tied into a knot
1 fresh green chile (cayenne, jalapeno, Serrano, or Thai), sliced
¾ cup (4½ ounces) chopped tomatoes
1 tablespoon tomato puree, or ½ tablespoon tomato paste, or 2 tablespoons tomato sauce
½ cup (2½ ounces) chopped carrots (¼-inch pieces)
½ cup (2¼ ounces) chopped green beans (¼-inch pieces)
1½ cups Basmati or any long grain rice, rinsed and drained
¼ cup evaporated or fresh milk (whole, low-fat, or skim)
¼ teaspoon saffron threads, steeped in ¼ cup water for 5 minutes
½ teaspoon salt
¼ cup petite peas (fresh and cooked, or frozen and thawed)
Optional: ½ teaspoon rose water

SPICE BLEND

2 cardamom pods
2 cloves
1-inch cinnamon stick
1 star anise

GARNISH

¼ cup roasted cashews or almonds
¼ cup golden raisins
2 tablespoons chopped fresh mint or coriander leaves (cilantro)
2 tablespoons fried (*see page 333*) or sautéed shallots or onions

Hindus traditionally observe a strict vegetarian diet on the days prior to a wedding, on the wedding day, and at the reception, and this is a perfect dish for those times. Here is a sweet and savory recipe for a light vegetable biryani *with Malaysian touches that we enjoy during Deepavali celebrations at my home. You can add vegetables of your choice, and it goes with any entrée. I generally serve it with* acars *and vegetable* kurma *but it also complements spicy shrimp* varuval*, fried chicken, and mutton* peratil*. I also add rose essence to give a touch of aroma and festivity. You can add half a teaspoon toasted whole cumin seeds to increase its savory notes.*

DIRECTIONS:

1. Heat 1 tablespoon of ghee or oil in a medium saucepan and sauté Spice Blend ingredients for about ½ to 1 minute. Add garlic and ginger and sauté for about ½ to 1 minute, then add shallots or onions and sauté 1 to 2 minutes.
2. Add lemongrass and chile and stir for 1 minute. Add tomato and tomato puree, paste, or sauce, and stir for 1 to 2 minutes, adding more oil if needed. Add carrots and green beans and sauté for about 3 minutes. Add rice and stir for about 1 to 2 minutes, then add 1½ cups water, milk, saffron water, and salt and bring to a boil.
3. Turn to low heat, cover, and simmer for about 15 minutes, till all liquid is absorbed and rice is cooked, adding peas 3 minutes before done. Remove from heat and let rice cook in its steam for another 10 minutes. (If using a rice cooker, use proportions for rice cooker based upon above quantities. Add the rice mixture from step 2, cover and switch rice cooker on. Rice cooker automatically shuts off when rice is cooked.)
4. Remove lemongrass stalk, cinnamon stick, and star anise before serving. Sprinkle with rose water, if desired, and top with garnishes.

Serve with chicken curry (page 171), dry beef curry (page 182), lamb *peratil* (page 185), shrimp *varuval* (page 203), or Captain's chicken curry (page 162); and cucumber carrot *acar* (page 99), stir-fried okra, stir-fried Chinese greens (page 227), or spicy curried pumpkin (page 225). For a vegetarian meal, serve with stir-fried cabbage (page 226), stir-fried Chinese greens (page 227), spicy eggplant dip (page 58), spicy dry curried okra (page 221), tofu curry (page 233), vegetable dhal curry (page 231), or spicy lentil vegetable stew (page 88).

Compressed Rice

Nasi Impit

Makes 3 to 4 servings

Compressed rice is a very popular meal with Malays during their festivities, especially Hari Raya Puasa and Hari Raya Haji (celebrating a Muslim's pilgrimage to Mecca). Nasi impit, lontong, ketupat, *and* lemang *are various forms of compressed rice, generally prepared with broken rice grains or short grain rice wrapped in banana or coconut leaves.*

Nasi impit *is cube-shaped and wrapped in banana leaf.* Lontong *comes as a roll wrapped in banana leaf and is cut into pieces before serving.* Ketupat *is in a dumpling form wrapped in coconut fronds or palm leaves.* Lemang *is prepared with short grain rice and coconut milk, and cooked for many hours over an open charcoal fire in a long hollow bamboo tube lined with banana leaves. I have given a recipe for* nasi impit *here as it is the easiest to prepare. I use long grain rice but you can use medium or short grain (sticky) rice.*

INGREDIENTS

1 cup medium, short grain, or long grain rice
1 fresh or frozen and thawed pandan leaf, tined with a fork and tied into a knot
¼ teaspoon salt

DIRECTIONS:

1. Place 10 to 12 cups water (depending on type of rice used) and all ingredients in a saucepan and bring to a boil, about 4 to 5 minutes. Lower heat, cover, and simmer for about 40 to 50 minutes, till most liquid evaporates and rice becomes soft with a porridge-like consistency. Uncover, remove pandan leaf and stir well till remaining liquid reduces and rice becomes drier. Remove from heat and allow to cool.
2. Place cooled rice on a shallow oiled baking tray (or a tray lined with banana leaf or wax paper), compress or press the rice firmly using wax paper or by placing a heavy object on top, to a depth of ½ to 1 inch. Refrigerate for a few hours.
3. Invert rice onto a plate, slice into cubes (1½ to 2 inch) using a knife dipped in water.

Serve with *satay* (page 65), fried beef *satay* (page 178), beef *rendang* (page 177), *sambal* chicken (page 161), spicy tomato chicken (page 284), *sambal* scallops (page 210), or stir-fried *sambal* shrimp (page 204); and vegetables in spicy coconut milk (page 223), cucumber pineapple *acar* (page 98), or eggplant and pinapple *pajeri* (page 232).

LAMB OR MUTTON KURMA

Kurma Kambing

Makes 5 to 6 servings

INGREDIENTS

2 to 3 tablespoons cooking oil
1¼ pounds mutton (lamb or goat) or boneless lamb shoulder, cut into 1 to 1½-inch pieces
1 to 2 fresh green chilies (cayenne, Serrano, jalapeno, or Thai), sliced into ¼-inch pieces
Heaping ¾ cup (4½ ounces) diced tomatoes
¼ cup unsweetened coconut milk
¼ to ½ teaspoon sugar
½ to ¾ teaspoon salt
1 teaspoon freshly squeezed or bottled lime or lemon juice

SPICE PASTE

¾ to 1 cup sliced shallots or onions
1 heaping tablespoon sliced garlic cloves
1 tablespoon sliced fresh ginger
1 lemongrass stalk, sliced into ¼-inch to ½-inch pieces
½ cup coriander leaves (cilantro)
¼ cup slivered almonds
¼ cup mint leaves
¼ cup water

SPICE BLEND 1

3 cardamom pods
2 cloves
1 star anise
1½-inch cinnamon stick

SPICE BLEND 2

2 teaspoons ground coriander
2 teaspoons ground fennel seeds
2 teaspoons ground cumin
¼ teaspoon finely ground black pepper
¼ teaspoon ground cardamom
¼ teaspoon turmeric powder
⅛ teaspoon ground cinnamon

A favorite with Malays, Indian Muslims, and Indians, mutton kurma *is prepared for Hari Raya Puasa or Deepavali, usually using goat meat. It is a rich, very aromatic dish cooked with coconut milk and spices. Ma cooked the most delicious mutton* kurma *for us at Deepavali, and she served it with* iddiappam *(extruded rice vermicelli).*

Indian Muslims brought kurma *(a mild creamy and rich curry made with yogurt or cream and almonds, a specialty of the Mughlai cooks in north India) to Malaysia. In Malaysia, Indian Muslim and Malay cooks have transformed it to yet another flavor level, adding coconut milk, lemongrass, star anise, and cilantro. The recipe I give here is an Indian Muslim-style, similar to one that I enjoyed in Penang. It reminds me of Thai green curry or a spicier version of Italian pesto. However, since goat meat has a flavor that is too strong for many Westerners, I have substituted lamb in this recipe.*

DIRECTIONS:

1. Process Spice Paste ingredients to a smooth paste and set aside. Combine Spice Blend 2 ingredients and set aside.
2. Heat 1 tablespoon of oil in a wok or skillet and sauté Spice Blend 1 ingredients for about ½ to 1 minute.
3. Stir in Spice Paste and another tablespoon of oil and sauté for about 4 to 5 minutes, till fragrant, adding remaining oil if needed. Add Spice Blend 2 and sauté for ½ to 1 minute.
4. Add lamb or mutton pieces and coat well with sauce. Cook, stirring occasionally, for about 3 minutes. Add chilies and tomatoes and sauté for about 2 minutes.
5. Add coconut milk and ¾ cup water and stir 1 to 2 minutes. Add sugar and cook, stirring constantly, till lamb is done and sauce becomes thick and coats lamb pieces, about 20 to 25 minutes.
6. Add salt and lime or lemon juice and stir for another 1 to 2 minutes.
7. Remove cinnamon stick and star anise before serving. Garnish with mint or cilantro.

Note: You can add quartered potatoes (4 to 5 small or 2 medium) with lamb if you want. Add more water if needed to cook potatoes.

Serve with ghee rice (page 121), yellow rice (pge 118), vegetable *biryani* (page 280), or plain cooked white or brown rice; and stir-fried mixed vegetables (page 224), spicy long beans (page 230), spicy eggplant and pineapple curry (page 232), or spicy water spinach (page 228); and savory meat lentils (page 285) or vegetable dhal curry (page 231). You can drink some *rasam* (page 76) at the end of the meal to offset the richness of this dish.

GARNISH

1 to 2 sprigs fresh mint or coriander (cilantro)

Vegetable Kurma

Kurma Sayuran

Makes 4 to 5 servings

Here is a vegetarian version of lamb kurma *which Ma prepared for festive occasions at our home. Indians and Indian Muslims also serve it at restaurants as a dip for* thosai *(rice-lentil crepe) and* roti canai *(flaky layered flatbread). Generally string beans, cauliflower, carrots, eggplants, potatoes, and/or cabbage are used. Unlike Indian vegetable* kormas *that use cream to thicken their sauce, Malaysians use coconut milk and add tomato, green chilies, cilantro, and mint leaves.*

My sister-in-law Shanta makes a delicious vegetable kurma *that she taught me on one of our "eating marathons" at her home. She served it with* biryani *rice, crispy fried chicken, and a mixed vegetable stir-fry.*

INGREDIENTS

- 2 to 3 tablespoons cooking oil
- 2 tablespoons coarsely crushed garlic cloves
- 1 tablespoon sliced and coarsely crushed fresh ginger
- ¼ cup diced or thinly sliced shallots or onions
- ½ pound (1½ cups) potatoes, halved or quartered
- 1 cup (5 ounces) sliced carrots (1½-inch by ¼-inch pieces) or whole baby carrots
- ¾ cup sliced green beans (1-inch to 1½-inch pieces)
- 2½ heaping cups (about 8 ounces) cauliflower florets
- ½ cup unsweetened coconut milk
- 1¼ cups (7½ ounces) sliced tomatoes
- ¾ teaspoon salt

Spice Blend 1

- 2 cardamom pods
- 2 cloves
- 1-inch cinnamon stick
- 1 star anise

Spice Blend 2

- 1 teaspoon ground cumin
- 1 teaspoon turmeric powder
- 1 teaspoon ground fennel seeds
- ¼ teaspoon finely ground white pepper
- ⅛ teaspoon ground cloves

Spice Paste

- ½ cup sliced shallots or onions
- 1 fresh green chile (cayenne, jalapeno, Thai, or Serrano), sliced
- ¼ to ½ cup mint leaves
- ¼ to ½ cup coriander leaves (cilantro)
- ¼ cup almonds or unsalted cashews
- ¼ cup water

DIRECTIONS:

1. Combine Spice Blend 2 ingredients and set aside. Process Spice Paste ingredients to a smooth paste and set aside.
2. Heat 1 tablespoon oil a saucepan and sauté Spice Blend 1 ingredients for ½ minute. Add garlic and ginger and stir for about ½ to 1 minute, then add shallots or onions and sauté for about 1 to 2 minutes. Add Spice Paste and 1 tablespoon oil and sauté for another 4 to 5 minutes, till fragrant, adding remaining oil if needed. Add Spice Blend 2 and sauté for about ½ minute.
3. Add potatoes and 1½ cups water and bring to a boil. Then lower heat and simmer for about 8 to 10 minutes. Add 1 more cup of water and vegetables and simmer, stirring occasionally, for about 4 to 5 minutes.
4. Stir in coconut milk and cook for about 4 to 5 minutes, then add tomatoes and salt and cook another 2 to 3 minutes. Remove cinnamon stick before serving.

Serve with vegetable *biryani* (page 280), tomato rice (page 119), or *iddiappam* (extruded rice vermicelli also called stringhoppers); and mixed vegetable *acar* (page 93), spicy cucumber tomato salad (page 97), spicy dry curried okra (page 221), tofu curry (page 233), or vegetable dhal curry (page 231).

Spicy Tomato Chicken

Ayam Masak Merah

Makes 4 to 5 servings

INGREDIENTS

1 pound chicken (drumsticks and breast), cut into 1½ to 2-inch pieces
⅛ teaspoon turmeric powder
⅛ teaspoon chile powder
2 to 3 tablespoons cooking oil
⅓ cup tomato puree; or ⅔ cup tomato sauce plus 2 tablespoons tomato paste; or 1 small tomato, finely chopped
2 tablespoons tamarind concentrate or tamarind juice extracted from pulp (*see page 339*)
2 teaspoons sugar or honey
Optional: ¼ cup unsweetened coconut milk or evaporated milk or regular milk (to replace ¼ cup of the water)
¼ to ½ teaspoon salt

SPICE PASTE

¼ cup sliced shallots or onions
1 tablespoon chopped garlic cloves
1 heaping teaspoon chopped fresh ginger or fresh or frozen and thawed galangal
1 lemongrass stalk, sliced into ¼-inch to ½-inch pieces
3 dried whole red chilies, steeped in hot water for 5 to 8 minutes, slit and deseeded; or ¾ tablespoon *cili boh* (*see page 315*); or 1 teaspoon bottled *sambal oelek*
¼ cup water

SPICE BLEND 1

2 cardamom pods
1-inch cinnamon stick
1 or 2 cloves

SPICE BLEND 2

½ teaspoon ground fennel seeds
½ teaspoon ground cumin
¼ teaspoon finely ground black pepper

Ayam masak merah *is a traditional favorite with Malays. It is prepared for Muslim feasts (*kenduris*) celebrating Hari Raya Puasa, weddings, and other festive occasions.* Ayam masak merah *translates to "red cooked chicken," from the recipe's tomato and chile-based sauce. Some recipes do not add any spices but cook chicken in tomato sauce or ketchup with chilies, giving it a flavor that is quite similar to a* sambal *recipe. It is also a popular accompaniment at many Malay and Indian Muslim* nasi campur *stalls.*

During the summer months, it is a favorite dish of mine. I usually barbecue the chicken coated with the spicy tomato sauce, and serve it with sliced cucumber pieces and white or brown rice or even fried rice.

DIRECTIONS:

1. Rub chicken pieces with turmeric and chile powder and marinate for about 20 to 30 minutes.
2. Heat 1 tablespoon oil in a wok or skillet and sauté chicken till brown, or broil or grill for 2 to 3 minutes. Set aside.
3. Process Spice Paste ingredients to a smooth paste and set aside. Combine Spice Blend 2 ingredients and set aside.
4. Heat another tablespoon oil in a wok or skillet and sauté Spice Blend 1 ingredients for about ½ to 1 minute. Add Spice Blend 2 and sauté for about ½ minute. Stir in Spice Paste and sauté for about 4 to 5 minutes, till fragrant, adding remaining oil if needed.
5. Stir in tomato puree or paste, or tomatoes, tamarind juice, sugar or honey, and 1 cup water (¾ cup if using milk), and stir for 2 to 3 minutes. Add chicken pieces and sauté for about 15 minutes, till cooked.* Add coconut or evaporated milk, if using, and salt and stir for another 3 to 4 minutes. Remove cinnamon stick before serving.

*Alternately, just add the milk, if using, and salt to the sauce and rub over chicken, keeping aside some sauce for basting. Let sit for about 30 minutes and then grill chicken, basting often with the reserved sauce mixed with a little oil, till cooked.

Serve with cooked white or brown rice, ghee rice (page 121), vegetable *biryani* (page 280), fried rice (page 123), tomato rice (page 119) or *roti jala*; and stir-fried Cinese greens (page 227), vegetables in spicy coconut milk (page 223), green papaya *acar* (page 100), or mixed vegetable *acar* (page 93).

Savory Meaty Lentils

Dalcha

Makes 4 to 5 servings

Dalcha is a unique Malaysian dish that has origins with Indian Muslim immigrants from Kerala. It is prepared with dhal (lentils), usually channa dhal, *and meat or chicken bones (with some meat and cartilage and fat) that add a wonderful flavor to the lentils. For me it is a comforting meal with pickled vegetables and fried chicken. It offsets fiery* sambals *and curries and is a wonderful accompaniment to spicy dry chicken, beef, or mutton curries.*

Viji, a tour guide and cooking instructor of Keralan heritage, shared one of his favorite recipes with me, mutton dalcha, *which he says is normally cooked for weddings and other festive occasions. Some cooks also add vegetables, including eggplant, carrots, potatoes, and tomatoes along with curry leaves, yogurt, or tamarind juice. Since most people find goat meat too strong, I substitute lamb and have slightly modified the dish to suit current tastes. Mutton* dalcha *is not a spicy dish and is generally served with cooked white rice.*

INGREDIENTS

- 4 cups water
- 1 cup *channa dhal* (yellow split peas)
- 1 pound lamb bones, shoulder, shank, or ribs
- ½ teaspoon turmeric powder
- 1 to 2 tablespoons cooking oil
- 1-inch cinnamon stick
- 1 star anise
- 3 cardamom pods
- ¾ teaspoon salt
- 2 tablespoons coriander leaves (cilantro)
- 1 to 2 teaspoons freshly squeezed or bottled lime or lemon juice

Spice Paste

- ¾ cup sliced shallots or onions
- 2 tablespoons sliced garlic cloves
- 1 heaping tablespoon sliced fresh ginger
- ¼ cup water

Spice Blend

- 1 teaspoon ground cumin
- 1 teaspoon ground coriander
- ½ teaspoon finely ground black pepper
- ¼ teaspoon chile powder

DIRECTIONS:

1. Bring 3 cups of water to a boil, add *channa dhal* and cook for about 20 to 25 minutes, till somewhat soft but still retaining their shape and form. Remove from heat.
2. In a separate pot, place 1 cup water, lamb bones (if you want to remove fat, refrigerate lamb bones so fat solidifies, then remove), and turmeric powder. Bring to a boil, lower heat and simmer for about 15 to 20 minutes, till lamb is cooked.
3. Process Spice Paste ingredients to a smooth paste. Combine Spice Blend ingredients. Set aside.
4. Heat 1 tablespoon oil in a large saucepan and sauté cinnamon stick, star anise, and cardamom for about ½ to 1 minute. Add Spice Paste and sauté for about 2 to 4 minutes, till fragrant, adding remaining oil if needed. Add Spice Blend and sauté for about ½ minute.
5. Stir in cooked dhal, cooked lamb, and ½ cup water, and simmer for 10 minutes. Add salt, stir and cook 1 to 2 minutes; add coriander leaves and lime or lemon juice, blend well for another minute. Remove cinnamon stick and star anise before serving.

Serve with cooked white or brown rice, ghee rice (page 121) or yellow rice (page 118); and beef *rendang* (page 177), lamb *peratil* (page 185), spicy fried chicken (page 165), stir-fried *sambal* shrimp (page 204), or spicy fried fish (page 206); and cucumber pineapple *acar* (page 98), stir-fried bean sprouts (page 229), stir-fried Chinese greens (page 227), or mixed vegetable *acar* (page 93).

SPICY SWEET SHRIMP

Udang Manis Berempeh

Makes 4 to 5 servings

INGREDIENTS

- 1 tablespoon cooking oil
- 1 tablespoon chopped garlic cloves
- 1 heaping tablespoon chopped fresh ginger
- Heaping ¼ cup sliced or diced shallots or onions
- 1 fresh red chile (Fresno, jalapeno, cayenne, Thai, or cherry), sliced
- 3 tablespoons tomato puree, or 2 tablespoons tomato paste, or 6 tablespoons tomato sauce
- ½ to 1 teaspoon sugar
- 1 teaspoon Worcestershire sauce
- 1 teaspoon cooking wine
- 1 pound (about 2 heaping cups) shelled and deveined shrimp, with tails intact
- 1 teaspoon roasted sesame oil
- 1 teaspoon cornstarch mixed with 2 tablespoons water

GARNISH

- 2 tablespoons sliced spring onions or Chinese chives (*kuchai*)

For Chinese New Year, generations of a family get together and celebrate for two weeks. Seafood dishes are important, as they are symbolic of prosperity and good luck. Serving fish (yee) symbolizes always having extra money in your hands, shrimp (ha) symbolizes happiness and laughter, and oysters (ho) bring good business.

During one Chinese New Year, at the home of one of my schoolmates, Adeline, I had wonderful spicy, sweet, and almost pinkish jumbo shrimps with shells on. Many a Chinese New Year I would visit her home, but through the years of studying and living overseas, I lost touch with her. My memory of her and our mutual friends at Bukit Nanas Convent School in Kuala Lumpur has not faded, as I still treasure those wonderful times together. I created this shrimp dish that reminds me of Adeline's open house Chinese New Year celebrations and the wonderful times with my friends.

DIRECTIONS:

1. Heat oil in a skillet or wok and sauté garlic and ginger for about ½ to 1 minute; add shallots or onions and sauté another 1 to 2 minutes.
2. Add chile and sauté ½ minute, then add 1 cup water, tomato puree, paste, or sauce, sugar, Worcestershire sauce, and cooking wine, and stir for about 1 to 2 minutes.
3. Add shrimp and sauté for 3 minutes, till cooked.
4. Add sesame oil, stir for ½ minute, then add cornstarch paste and blend well for about 1 minute.
5. Garnish with spring onions or Chinese chives.

Serve with cooked white or brown rice, fried rice (page 123), yellow rice (page 118), or spiced rice (page 120); and stir-fried mixed vegetables (page 224), stir-fried *kailan* (page 222), stir-fried bean sprouts (page 229), or stir-fried Chinese greens (page 227).

Chicken Rendang

Ayam Rendang

Makes 3 to 4 servings

Rendang originated with the Minangkabau people of Sumatra, Indonesia, and has become a national dish of Malaysia. It is traditionally prepared at Malay homes for Hari Raya Puasa (Eid), weddings, or other festive celebrations. Rendang is generally made with beef and chicken, but depending on ethnic and regional preferences also with mutton, water buffalo meat, duck, tofu, hard-boiled eggs, or vegetables. Depending on the region, rendang *is served with plain cooked rice,* ketupat, lontong, *or* lemang *(glutinous rice cooked in bamboo tubes over a charcoal fire).*

*In my recipe, chicken is slow-cooked or simmered in coconut milk with toasted grated coconut (*kerisik*), chilies, and spices till all the liquid is gone and the chicken just cooks in the fragrant coconut oil. I add spices to my recipe to take this dish to an even more flavorful level. You can reduce the spices by half if you prefer a less spicy rendang. I also added less chilies than the locals would add.The final chicken becomes coated in a dry spicy and intensely flavored sauce. It has a delicious aroma and tender texture that almost melts in your mouth. For a saucier dish, you can add some water and cook till sauce becomes thick and coats chicken.*

INGREDIENTS

- 3 to 4 tablespoons cooking oil
- 1 pound chicken (breast, thighs, and/or drumsticks), cut into 1½-inch to 2-inch pieces
- 1 cup unsweetened coconut milk
- 1 to 1½ tablespoons tamarind concentrate or tamarind juice extracted from pulp (*see page 339*)
- 1 Kaffir lime leaf (2 lobes)
- 1 teaspoon thinly sliced or chopped palm sugar or dark brown sugar
- ¾ to 1 teaspoon salt
- ½ cup toasted grated coconut (*kerisik*) (*see page 319*)

SPICE PASTE

- 2 tablespoons sliced garlic cloves
- 1½ tablespoons sliced fresh or frozen and thawed galangal or fresh ginger
- ¾ cup sliced shallots or onions
- 6 to 8 dried whole red chilies (*depending on heat desired*), steeped in warm or hot water for 5 to 8 minutes, slit and deseeded; or 1½ to 2 tablespoons *cili boh* (*see page 315*); or ¾ to 1 tablespoon bottled *sambal oelek*
- 1 or 2 lemongrass stalks, sliced into ¼-inch pieces (½ cup)
- ¼ cup water

SPICE BLEND 1

- 2 cardamom pods, whole or cracked
- 2 cloves
- 1½-inch cinnamon stick
- 1 star anise

(*continued on next page*)

DIRECTIONS:

1. Process Spice Paste ingredients to a smooth paste. Set aside. Combine Spice Blend 2 ingredients and set aside.
2. Heat 1 tablespoon of oil in a large wok or skillet and sauté Spice Blend 1 ingredients for about ½ to 1 minute, then add Spice Blend 2 and sauté for ½ minute. Add Spice Paste and 2 to 3 tablespoons of oil and stir for about 5 to 6 minutes, till fragrant.
3. Add chicken pieces and stir 1 to 2 minutes coating well with paste. Add coconut milk, tamarind juice, Kaffir lime leaf, sugar, and salt and sauté, stirring occasionally, for about 15 to 20 minutes.
4. Add grated coconut and cook, stirring constantly, another 5 to 10 minutes, till sauce dries up and chicken gets darker. (If you like a saucier finish, add ¼ to ½ cup water with the coconut milk and stir till sauce thickens and coats the chicken.) Remove lime leaves, cinnamon stick, and star anise before serving.

Serve with cooked white or brown rice, yellow rice (page 118), tomato rice (page 119), cococonut-infused rice (page 117), or compressed rice (page 281); and cucumber carrot *acar* (page 99), braised spicy long beans (page 230), or vegetables in spicy coconut milk (page 223).

(CONTINUED) CHICKEN RENDANG

Ayam Rendang

SPICE BLEND 2

1 teaspoon ground coriander
1 teaspoon ground cumin
½ to ¾ teaspoon turmeric powder, or 1 to 1½ heaping teaspoons chopped fresh or frozen and thawed turmeric root
½ teaspoon finely ground black pepper
¼ teaspoon ground fennel seeds

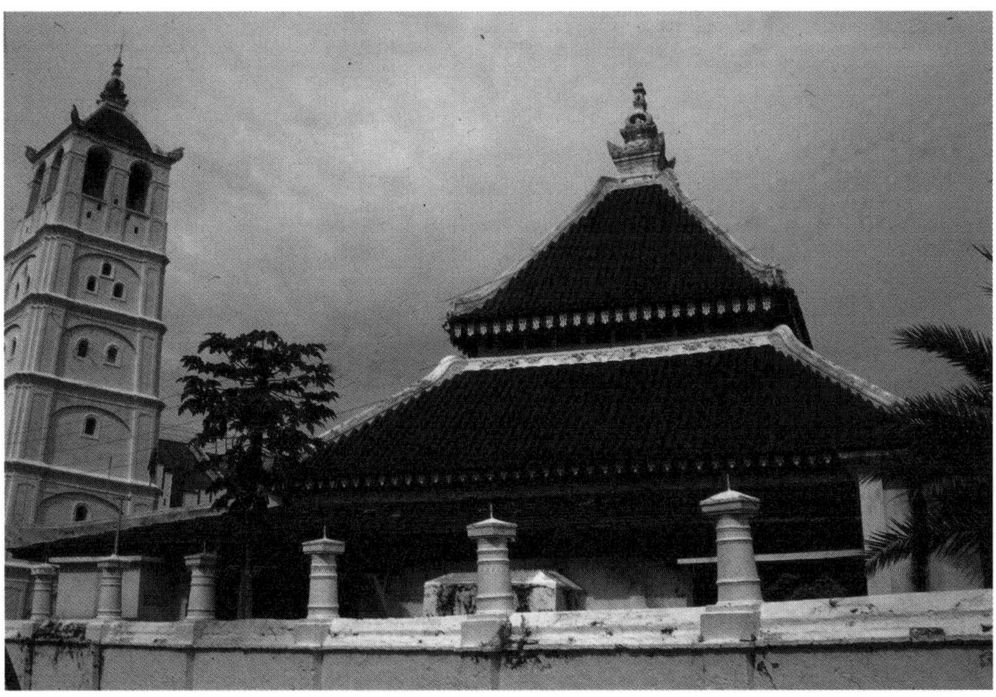

Sumatran Minangkabau-style mosque

FIERY PORTUGUESE CHICKEN CURRY

Kari Ayam Debal

Makes 4 to 5 servings

Wherever the Portuguese traded or settled, they greatly influenced the local cooking. Debal or 'devil' curry, so called because of its fiery vinegary taste, is popular with the Kristangs. Growing up I would return from school and quite often see Ma and Mrs. Collar, Ma's Eurasian neighbor pal, enjoying their afternoon chats on our porch. On some days Mrs. Collar would surprise us with her famous fiery debal *curry. We could not wait for dinner time!*

The Kristangs from the Portuguese settlement located in Melaka (formerly Malacca) traditionally add vinegar, ground mustard, and a mix of fresh chilies and chile powder to give that extra touch of tanginess and heat that they enjoy. The Malay, Chinese, and Nonya influences are prominent, with the use of galangal, lemongrass, cili padi, candlenuts, soy sauce, and sugar. Their use of mustard seeds in a curry is an Indian touch. Kari debal *with less heat is also a favorite with the Eurasian community of Malaysia as a whole, and generally is prepared for Christmas meals.*

The traditional way of preparing curry debal *is to cook it in a seasoned, round-bottomed earthenware or clay pot called a tezaler (in the Cristao language). It is served in this* tezaler *with cooked white rice or bread, mixed vegetables (*bredu chapchye*), salad, or stir-fried eggplant or okra.* Kari debal *will definitely challenge those who desire a fiery flavor. You can lessen or add more heat if you desire.*

INGREDIENTS

- 1 pound chicken (drumsticks, thighs, and/or breasts), cut into 1½-inch pieces
- 2 to 3 tablespoons cooking oil
- 2 teaspoons thinly sliced or julienned fresh ginger
- ½ cup thinly sliced shallots or onions
- 1 to 2 fresh red chilies (Fresno, jalapeno, cayenne, Thai, cherry, or Serrano), sliced in half lengthwise
- ½ to 1 teaspoon coarsely pounded dark brown mustard seeds
- ¼ teaspoon chile powder
- ⅛ teaspoon turmeric powder
- 1 heaping cup (about 6 ounces) halved or quartered potatoes
- 1 tablespoon distilled white vinegar
- ¼ teaspoon sugar
- ½ teaspoon salt

MARINADE

- 1 teaspoon thick or sweet soy sauce
- 1 teaspoon distilled white vinegar

SPICE PASTE

- ½ cup sliced shallots or onions
- 2 teaspoons sliced garlic cloves
- 1 teaspoon sliced fresh or frozen and thawed galangal or fresh ginger
- 1 lemongrass stalk, sliced into ¼-inch to ½-inch pieces
- 7 dried whole red chilies, steeped in hot water for 5 to 8 minutes, slit and deseeded; or 1¾ tablespoons *cili boh* (*see page 315*); or ¾ to 1 tablespoon bottled *sambal oelek*
- 2 candlenuts or macadamia nuts
- ¼ cup water

DIRECTIONS:

1. Mix chicken with Marinade ingredients and set aside to marinate for about 30 to 60 minutes.
2. Heat 1 tablespoon oil in a small skillet and sauté ginger for about ½ to 1 minute; add shallots or onions and chilies and sauté for about 1 to 2 minutes. Remove from heat and set aside.
3. Process Spice Paste ingredients to a smooth paste.
4. Heat another tablespoon oil in a wok or skillet and sauté Spice Paste for about 4 to 5 minutes, till fragrant, adding more oil if necessary. Add mustard seeds, chile powder, and turmeric, and stir for ½ minute.
5. Stir in marinated chicken and stir for about 2 to 3 minutes, coating well with spice paste.
6. Add potatoes and 1 to 1½ cups water and bring to a boil. Lower heat, add vinegar, sugar, and salt and simmer till chicken and potatoes are done, about 15 to 20 minutes.
7. Stir in the sautéed ingredients from step 2 and stir another 1 to 2 minutes.

Serve with cooked white or brown rice, tomato rice (page 119), yellow rice (page 118), coconut-infused rice (page 117), or vegetable *biryani* (page 280); and braised spicy long beans (page 230), stir-fried mixed vegetables (page 224), mixed vegetable *acar* (page 93), or spicy water spinach (page 228).

Spicy Simmered Cabbage

Kobis Rebus Berlada

Makes 5 to 6 servings

INGREDIENTS

1 to 2 tablespoons cooking oil
2 teaspoons sliced garlic cloves
2 teaspoons thinly sliced fresh ginger
½ cup diced shallots or onions
4 ounces (about ½ cup) shelled and deveined shrimp
1 pound (5⅓ cups) cabbage, cut criss-cross into 1½-inch pieces
¼ to ½ cup unsweetened coconut milk
½ teaspoon salt

SPICE BLEND 1

6 fresh curry leaves
½ teaspoon black or dark brown mustard seeds
¼ teaspoon fenugreek seeds
¼ teaspoon fennel seeds

SPICE BLEND 2

1 tablespoon ground coriander
1½ teaspoons ground cumin
¾ teaspoon turmeric powder
¾ teaspoon finely ground black pepper
¼ teaspoon chile powder

This is a recipe given to me by my friend Radha Pillay, who is from the Chitty community of Malacca and has settled in the U.S. It was one of the many dishes her mom prepared for her Sadangku ceremony (a cleansing ceremony for coming of age, also referred to as a fertility ceremony for girls, and also celebrated by Hindus). She continues to celebrate the festivals she grew up with: Hindu New Year, Deepavali, Pongol, Parchu (homage to ancestors), and Sadangku. She often goes back to Malaysia to participate in her family's celebration of Parchu and Sadangku, and even took her daughter recently to celebrate Sadangku with her family.

This recipe uses both whole and ground spices. I have modified the spices somewhat and use less coconut milk.

DIRECTIONS:

1. Combine Spice Blend 2 ingredients and set aside.
2. Heat 1 tablespoon oil in a wok or skillet and sauté garlic and ginger for about ½ to 1 minute. Add shallots or onions and sauté 1 to 2 minutes.
3. Add Spice Blend 1 ingredients and stir for about 1 minute; add Spice Blend 2 and stir for about ½ minute.
4. Add shrimp and stir for about 1 to 2 minutes. Add cabbage and stir for about 1 to 2 minutes.
5. Add coconut milk and ¼ cup water and cook, stirring, for about 5 minutes, till sauce becomes drier. Add salt and blend well for another minute.

Serve with cooked white or brown rice, coconut-infused rice (page 117), or spiced rice (page 120); and fish curry (page 198), chicken *varuval* (page 167), Chettiar-style fiery shrimp (page 291), chile squid (page 211), or lamb *peratil* (page 185).

Chettiar-Style Fiery Shrimp

Udang Tumis Berlada ala Chettiar

Makes 3 to 4 servings

The Chettiars, whose cooking style is referred to as Chettinand, were bankers from Tamil Nadu who came to Malaysia during the nineteenth and twentieth centuries. They set up moneylending and banking institutions, especially around Kuala Lumpur and Penang. My maternal grandmother was a Chettiar. She had an adventurous spirit and came as a teenager to Malaysia. She married an English and French-speaking Keralite and raised her family in Malaysia.

We looked forward to Periama's visits as we enjoyed her intensely flavored Chettiar dishes. One of our favorites was her spicy shrimp dish. Periama ate her food spicy hot but in this recipe, I reduced the chilies. When we were children, shrimp was not prepared often as it was expensive. Imagine making shrimp for nine of us children! So we generally enjoyed it on some weekends or for special occasions.

In this recipe, you can use less chilies or substitute sweet bell peppers or use a blend of chilies and bell peppers if you want less heat.

INGREDIENTS

1 to 2 tablespoons cooking oil
1½ tablespoons sliced or crushed garlic cloves
2 teaspoons sliced fresh ginger
1 cup sliced shallots or onions
2 teaspoons ground coriander
½ to 1 teaspoon chile powder
¼ to ½ teaspoon turmeric powder
1½ to 2 cups (9 to 12 ounces) sliced tomatoes
2 to 3 teaspoons tamarind concentrate or tamarind juice extracted from pulp (*see page 339*)
1 pound (about 2 heaping cups) shelled and deveined shrimp, tails intact
¼ teaspoon salt
1 fresh red chile (Fresno, jalapeno, serrano, cayenne, cherry, or Thai), deseeded and sliced lengthwise; or 2 heaping tablespoons sliced red bell peppers (½-inch-long pieces)
1 fresh green chile (jalapeno, Serrano, cayenne, or Thai), deseeded and sliced lengthwise; or 2 tablespoons sliced green bell peppers (½-inch-long pieces)

SPICE BLEND

6 dried whole red chilies
½ teaspoon fennel seeds
½ teaspoon cumin seeds
½ teaspoon fenugreek seeds
½ teaspoon black or dark brown mustard seeds

GARNISH

1 tablespoon cooking oil
6 to 8 fresh curry leaves

DIRECTIONS:

1. Combine Spice Blend ingredients. Heat 1 tablespoon oil in a wok or skillet. Add Spice Blend ingredients and cover till mustard seeds pop, about ½ minute.
2. When popping subsides, add garlic and ginger and sauté for about ½ to 1 minute; add shallots or onions and sauté for about 1 to 2 minutes.
3. Add remaining oil, if needed, coriander, chile powder, and turmeric and stir for about ½ minute.
4. Stir in tomatoes, tamarind juice, and ¼ cup water and sauté for 2 to 3 minutes, till fragrant.
5. Add shrimp and cook for about 3 to 4 minutes, stirring constantly, till sauce thickens and shrimp are cooked and coated with sauce. Add salt and chile or bell peppers, and stir for 1 minute.
6. Prepare garnish: heat 1 tablespoon oil in a small skillet, add curry leaves and fry till crispy. Pour this fragrant mixture over the shrimp before serving.

Serve with cooked white or brown rice, ghee rice (page 121), vegetable *biryani* (page 280), or yellow rice (page 118); and vegetable dhal curry (page 231), or savory meat lentils (page 285), and stir-fried okra, stir-fried cabbage (page 226), or stir-fried eggplant.

Hindu temple

CHAPTER 12

FUSION MALAYSIAN: A HARMONY OF FLAVORS

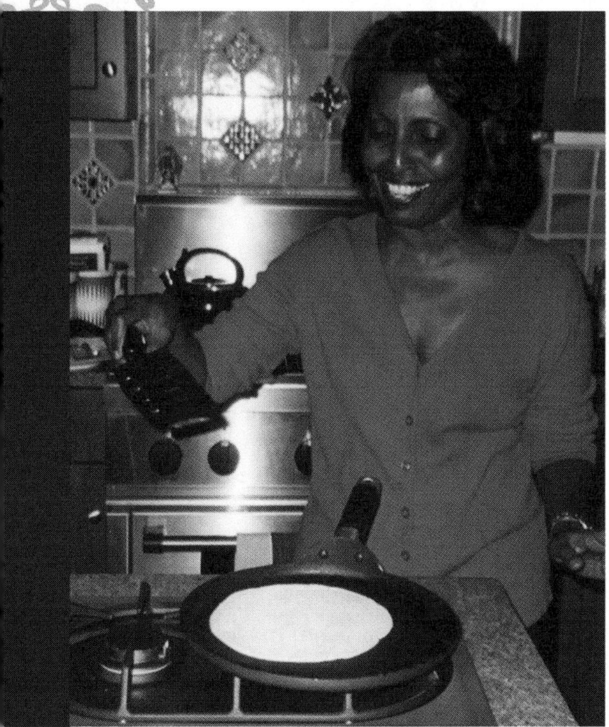

Cooking fusion fare in my New York home

The United States has become increasingly diverse in its population, and this has been affecting how we eat. For example, Asians and Hispanics are the fastest-growing ethnic groups in America and their cuisines have become an integral part of our social fabric. In the coming years, Asian foods will take center stage in America because they have variety, intense flavors, and vivid textures. Asian ingredients and cooking techniques create flavorful and healthy foods as well. They also adapt well to other preparations and enhance their flavors and textures as a whole. One of the most important trends has been fusion cooking. Fusion dishes have been created by combining ingredients and/or cooking techniques of two or more ethnic cuisines. Fusion cooking adds an ethnic flair to many American foods, for example, adding *masala*, *sambal*, or lemongrass to roast chicken, pasta, or potatoes.

The cuisines of India, the Caribbean, the United States, and Malaysia, among others, evolved from the mixing of multiple cultures. And new flavors will continue to evolve wherever cultures are transported. In the U.S., *laksas*, fried rice, *rendangs*, or *sambals* can easily take on new flavors to meet the demands of second-generation and third-generation Asians who have adapted to an American lifestyle and want flavors of both worlds. Fusion cooking is also a great way to introduce Americans to Malaysian flavors. Cooks must, however, be careful to use compatible ingredients and preparation methods that effectively fuse the components. For this, first we have to understand Malaysia's authentic cooking methods and ingredients.

Consumers are looking for exotic flavors that are also familiar, and Malaysian cuisine can fulfill this demand. It has the familiar notes of South Indian, Chinese, or Thai, as well as the exotic flavors of Indian Muslim, Malay, Nonya, and Kristang cooking. Many cuisines derive their flavors from oil, fat, sugar, salt, and butter. In my recipes, I reduce or eliminate these less healthy ingredients and use the healthier flavor sources—intense spices and other natural flavorings. Additionally, I have given flavorful recipes that are easy to prepare, sometimes taking less than 30 minutes, and that have healthy alternatives. Alternately, you can use my spice blends under the brand name Taste of Malacca (www.tasteofmalacca.com) for the many recipes in this book, to create authentic recipes, or to give flavorful twists to local cooking.

Many Americans still long for their comfort foods—spaghetti, roast chicken, burgers, fish, omelets, salads, potatoes, sandwiches, and even cheesecake—these can be transformed into exotic versions with Malaysian spicing. And many second-generation and third-generation Asians are beginning to enjoy many of America's comfort foods but want some Asian flavors. I began blending Malaysian flavors with American foods to get my American-born daughter, Geeta, and her schoolfriends to enjoy Malaysian flavors. My first attempt was with spaghetti, her favorite. I created a delicious curried spaghetti with spices and tomato sauce that Geeta and her friends enjoyed. I also learned a fusion spaghetti dish from my older brother Ravee, who resides in Puerto Rico. Ravee would open a can of *pulpo* (octopus), add tomato sauce or pasta sauce, a bottled curry sauce, a bit of *sambal oelek* and soy sauce and simmer them for few minutes with water. He would toss this sauce over spaghetti to make a quick Malaysian meal. It was delicious! I have eaten many spicy *pulpo*-spaghetti meals for lunch since.

I also enjoy adding Malaysian flavors to traditional American holiday meals such as Thanksgiving, Christmas, and Easter dinner. I did not grow up celebrating American or Christian holidays, but have enjoyed celebrating them since I moved to America, especially once I brought a bit of home to the table. Since most of my family lives overseas, we usually invite friends over for Thanksgiving each year. One year, I seasoned the turkey with an aromatic Malaysian paste of spices, lemongrass, and soy sauce, and added sautéed chopped cilantro, shallots, and jalapeno to the stuffing. Instead of serving gravy, I created some light, spicy dips.

For summer barbecues, I always add a touch of Malaysian flavor to chicken, burgers, or shrimp, using a traditional curry blend, *sambal*, spicy *rendang*, or *ayam masak merah* (red curry paste) served with Malay-style fried rice or herb rice made with herbs from my garden, and a cooling salad of mango, pineapple, and cucumber. Likewise, young Malaysians are also looking for something new and different to incorporate with their delicious flavors, whether roast chicken, noodles, hamburgers, rice dishes, potatoes, or salads.

When I was a student in England at Reading University, I offered to create "Malaysia day" at our dormitory cafeteria and I organized the other Asian students to help in the kitchen so we could enjoy some seasoned Asian foods. We'd had enough of plain English meats, boiled vegetables, and bland soups. So I blended together the meager spices that were available and created a Malaysian roast chicken and a spicy lentil. Once I moved to a dormitory with kitchen facilities the following year, I started cooking simple pasta dishes using spicier Asian seasonings and sauces. Slowly, I added more fusion dishes to my collection. Lamb is an English favorite, and once I splurged on lamb chops. I added an aromatic Malaysian twist to it, with black peppercorn, star anise, and other spices, fresh red chilies and coconut milk, which was enjoyed by all of my friends. Of course that was years ago. Today, Indian foods are an Englishman's favorite, so Indian foods and ingredients are plentiful everywhere.

After my graduate studies, I went to work in Belize, Central America, and lived on *empanadas*, rice and beans, tamales, fish *escabeche*, and stewed chicken. Sometimes I would eat hot dogs, sandwiches, and salads at an American cafe, and I also frequented the only Chinese restaurant in Belize City. I missed the foods of home. So I bought available spices, including cumin, chile powder, and coriander, and incorporated them into Belizean cooking to create simple chicken, vegetable, and rice dishes that reminded me of home.

Here are some of my favorite fusion recipes including curried roast chicken (or turkey) for Thanksgiving, a spicy omelet for a brunch menu, peppercorn lamb chops, and spice-scented hamburgers for the summer barbecue. The recipes for curried spaghetti, stir-fried broccoli rabe, and pan-seared spicy fish are my daughter Geeta's favorites. I hope you will enjoy them as much as we do!

Please go to the www.tasteofmalacca.com website for further information on Malaysian spice blends and recipes.

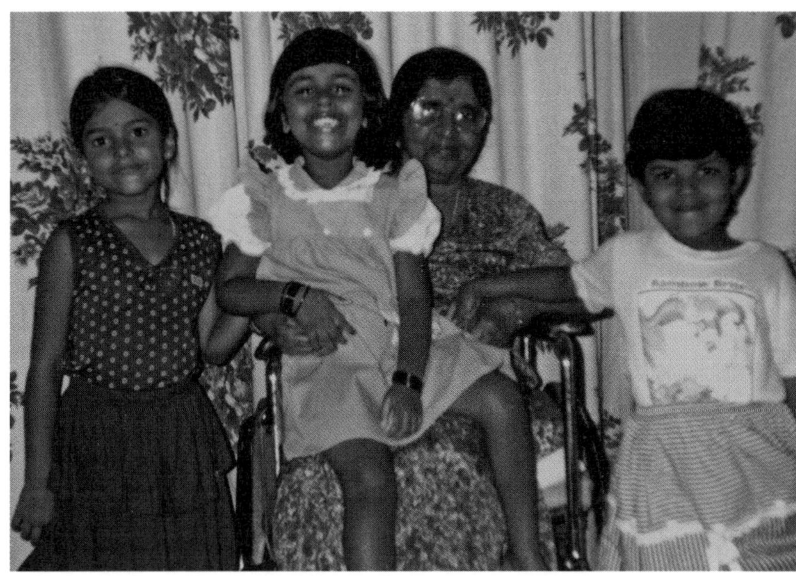

Ma with her granddaughters (from left to right: Geeta, Previna, and Prita)

Sambal Chicken Sandwich

Makes 6 servings

INGREDIENTS

2 to 3 tablespoons cooking oil
½ teaspoon chopped garlic cloves
¼ cup chopped red onions
2 tablespoons tomato paste, or ¼ cup tomato puree, or 6 tablespoons tomato sauce
1 teaspoon regular soy sauce
1 teaspoon tamarind concentrate or juice from tamarind pulp (*see page 339*)
¼ teaspoon sugar
⅛ teaspoon salt
1¼ pounds boneless chicken breast, thinly sliced (1½-inch to 2-inch pieces)
6 sandwich rolls

Spice Blend

½ teaspoon ground fennel seeds
½ to ¾ teaspoon chile powder
¼ teaspoon turmeric powder
¼ teaspoon ground paprika
¼ teaspoon finely ground black pepper
¼ teaspoon ground cumin
¼ teaspoon ground mustard

Toppings

1 pound thinly sliced Havarti cheese
1 sweet bell pepper, sliced into 1-inch to 1½-inch pieces and sautéed lightly in oil or grilled
1 red onion, sliced ⅛-inch thick and sautéed in 1 tablespoon cooking oil till caramelized
12 fresh basil leaves

The standard American sandwich has been transformed with different fillings, breads, and garnishing. Naan, panini, thosai, pita, tortilla wraps, and other flatbreads have become the trend as sandwich breads. Some wonderful fusion creations have emerged, including tandoori *panini, spicy potatoes in wraps, and rolls with Vietnamese grilled beef.*

In this recipe, I have taken the sambal, *a traditional Malaysian sauce, and created a sandwich with Havarti cheese, caramelized onions, and fresh basil. You can substitute Swiss cheese for the Havarti or if you like a smoky flavor, you can use smoked gouda. You can use a roll or slices of bread or slice up the chicken and add it as a filling for a panini, pita, wrap, or other flatbreads.*

DIRECTIONS:

1. Combine Spice Blend ingredients and set aside.
2. Heat 1 tablespoon of oil in a saucepan or wok and sauté garlic for about ½ to 1 minute. Add onions and sauté another 1 to 2 minutes.
3. Add Spice Blend and stir for about ½ minute. Add tomato paste, puree, or sauce, soy sauce, tamarind juice, sugar, salt, and ½ cup water, and simmer, stirring constantly, for about 5 to 8 minutes, till sauce thickens. Set aside 2 to 3 tablespoons of the *sambal* sauce for the sandwiches.
4. Heat remaining 1 or 2 tablespoons oil in a skillet. Dip chicken slices in the rest of the *sambal* sauce and then sauté in oil till cooked on both sides, about 5 to 6 minutes. Set aside. (You can also broil or grill the seasoned chicken pieces, basting with the sauce.)

TO ASSEMBLE SANDWICH:

For 1 serving, place 2 to 3 slices (about 3 ounces) chicken on a roll, add some of the reserved *sambal* sauce (you can spread *sambal* sauce on both slices of rolls if you want), 2 to 3 slices of Havarti cheese, 2 slices of sweet bell peppers, few pieces of caramelized onions, and 2 fresh basil leaves. Top with other half of roll or bread, cut in half and serve.

LEMONGRASS 'N' SPICE SCENTED ROAST CHICKEN

Makes 4 to 5 servings

On Thanksgiving Day, like everyone else we have roast turkey or chicken with stuffing, sweet potatoes, and vegetables. I season the roast and stuffing with Malaysian seasonings and have a peppered gravy or sometimes a light dipping sauce for the meat. Bob and Geeta look forward to this special meal every year. Sometimes I serve the roast with ghee rice, fried rice, or a vegetable biryani. *My daughter, Geeta, grew up with this different yet unique Thanksgiving meal that she enjoys to this day. Here, I am giving you here a recipe for one of the roasts I prepared recently, followed by recipes for its accompaniments.*

INGREDIENTS

1 4-pound whole chicken
2 to 3 tablespoons plus ¼ to ½ cup cooking oil
1 to 2 tablespoons honey
¼ teaspoon salt
1 to 1½ tablespoons regular soy sauce
1 teaspoon rice wine or vinegar, cider vinegar, or distilled white vinegar

SPICE BLEND 1

2 cloves
1 star anise
1-inch cinnamon stick

SPICE PASTE

¼ cup diced shallots or onions
1 heaping tablespoon sliced garlic cloves
1 heaping tablespoon sliced fresh ginger
2 tablespoons sliced lemongrass stalk (¼-inch to ½-inch pieces)
1 fresh red chile (Fresno, cayenne, jalapeno, Serrano, Thai, or cherry), sliced (deseeded if less heat is desired)
¼ cup water

SPICE BLEND 2

1 teaspoon ground coriander
½ teaspoon ground fennel seeds
½ teaspoon ground cumin
¼ teaspoon turmeric powder
Optional: ⅛ to ¼ teaspoon chile powder (if not using fresh red chile)

DIRECTIONS:

1. Clean chicken and cavity and pat dry. Place Spice Blend 1 ingredients in cavity and close. Set aside.
2. Process Spice Paste ingredients to a smooth paste. Combine Spice Blend 2 ingredients. Set aside.
3. Heat 1 tablespoon of oil in a small wok or skillet and sauté Spice Paste for 5 to 6 minutes, till sauce becomes fragrant, adding 1 or 2 tablespoons oil or more as needed. Add Spice Blend 2 and sauté another 2 minutes, till fragrant. Remove from heat and allow to cool.
4. Once cool, combine this cooked sauce with the honey, salt, soy sauce, and rice wine or vinegar. Rub chicken with 2 tablespoons of this marinade. Marinate in the refrigerator for at least 1 hour, preferably 3 to 4 hours or overnight.
5. Add ¼ to ½ cup oil to remaining marinade, blend well and set aside to use to baste chicken.
6. Heat oven to 350°F. Place chicken on rack in a roasting pan, add about 1 inch of water to pan. Roast for 1 hour, basting with the basting sauce every 15 minutes, till it becomes golden brown (adding additional water to pan if it evaporates).* Then cover chicken with aluminum foil and roast for about 30 more minutes, till chicken is done, basting with sauce after 15 minutes. (You can increase oven temperature to 375°F to shorten cooking time.) Reserve remaining basting sauce to make sauce for chicken.

***Note:** While chicken is in oven, prepare the stuffing (page 298), sauce (page 298) and/or dipping sauce (page 299).

Serve with the stuffing and two sauces and fried rice (page 123), ghee rice (page 121), tomato rice (page 119), or vegetable *biryani* (page 280); and sweet potatoes, cucumber pineapple *acar* (page 98), stir-fried mixed vegetables (page 224), and/or a green salad.

Stuffing for Roast Chicken

INGREDIENTS

1 tablespoon cooking oil
¼ cup chopped shallots or onions
1 to 2 heaping teaspoons chopped fresh green chilies (jalapeno, Serrano, cayenne, or Thai)
1 tablespoon unsalted butter
1 (6-ounce) box stove-top stuffing mix
1 tablespoon chopped coriander leaves (cilantro)
Optional: ¼ cup diced chorizo or other spicy sausage, chopped and sautéed for 3 to 4 minutes

DIRECTIONS:

1. Heat oil in a small skillet or wok and sauté shallots or onions for about 1 minute; add chilies and sauté another ½ minute. Set aside.
2. Bring 1½ cups water and butter to a boil in a saucepan. Add stuffing mix, sautéed shallot or onion mixture, coriander leaves, and chorizo, if using. Stir, cover, and remove from heat. Let stand for 5 minutes, then uncover and fluff with fork.

Serve with roast chicken (page 297).

Sauce for Roast Chicken

Makes about 1 cup

INGREDIENTS

Reserved basting sauce from roast chicken (page 297)
½ cup chopped shallots or red onions

DIRECTIONS:

1. Skim off as much oil as possible from the top of the reserved basting sauce.
2. Add a little oil to a small saucepan. Add the shallots or onions and sauté for about 1 minute. Add reserved basting sauce and ¾ to 1 cup water and bring to a boil. Lower heat and simmer for 4 to 5 minutes, till sauce gets slightly thick (or thicken with corn, rice, or tapioca starch). Skim off any oil or fat before using.

Serve with roast chicken (page 297).

Dipping Sauce for Roast Chicken

Makes about ½ cup

INGREDIENTS

- 1 fresh red or green chile (Fresno, jalapeno, Serrano, cayenne, Thai, or cherry), finely chopped or pounded
- 2 teaspoons finely chopped or crushed garlic cloves
- 1 teaspoon finely chopped or crushed fresh ginger
- 3 tablespoons freshly squeezed or bottled lime juice
- 1 teaspoon toasted sesame oil
- 2 tablespoons sugar
- ½ teaspoon salt
- 1 teaspoon regular soy sauce

DIRECTIONS:

Combine all ingredients in a non-reactive bowl and mix well. Let sit for about 30 minutes before using.

Serve with roast chicken (page 297).

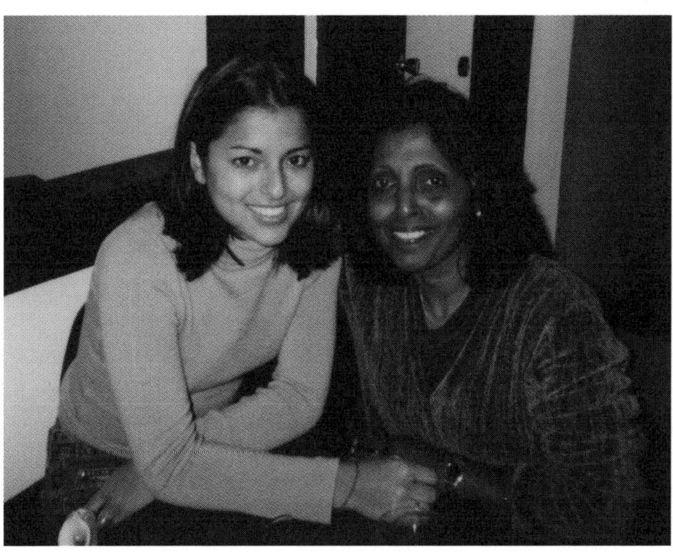

My daughter Geeta and me

Lemak Rice and Beans

Makes 3 to 4 servings

INGREDIENTS

- 1 tablespoon cooking oil
- Heaping ½ teaspoon chopped garlic cloves
- ½ cup chopped shallots or onions
- ½ cup (3 ounces) chopped tomatoes
- 1 cup Basmati or other long-grain rice
- 1 lemongrass stalk, bruised with back of knife and tied into a knot
- 1 tablespoon unsweetened coconut milk
- ½ teaspoon salt
- ¾ cup drained canned black beans (or dried beans cooked per package directions)
- 1 to 2 tablespoons chopped coriander leaves (cilantro)

Spice Blend

- ¼ to ½ teaspoon ground coriander
- ¼ to ½ teaspoon ground cumin
- ¼ teaspoon chile powder
- ¼ teaspoon turmeric powder

One of my favorite dishes is rice and black beans, a staple in many Hispanic homes. It was my daily meal when I worked in Belize, Central America. During my travels to the Caribbean and Mexico, rice and beans is a must for me and I ate my favorite one at an outdoor café in Havana, Cuba, listening to jazz music and watching the locals dance. I learned to make rice and beans from my Latina friend Maria Bejarano with whom I have shared many a Latino meal in her kitchen or at restaurants. I add a Malaysian twist with spices, tomato, and coconut milk. I also add lemongrass stalk which complements the coconut milk, both of which are staples in preparing flavored rice dishes in Malaysia.

This lemak *(savory) rice dish has wonderful flavors that complement roast chicken, burgers, or any of the entrees in this book, including beef simmered in coconut milk (beef* rendang*), grilled spicy chicken (*ayam percik*), fried chicken (*ayam berempah*), chile-based shrimp (*sambal tumis udang*), or spicy fried fish. You can substitute red beans or pigeon peas (*gandules *or* toor dhal*) for the black beans.*

DIRECTIONS:

1. Combine Spice Blend ingredients and set aside.
2. Heat oil in a skillet or saucepan and sauté garlic for about ½ to 1 minute. Add shallots or onions and sauté for about 1 to 2 minutes. Add Spice Blend and sauté another ½ minute.
3. Add tomatoes and stir for 2 minutes, then add rice and sauté 2 minutes. Add 2 cups water, lemongrass, coconut milk, and salt and stir to combine. Add beans and stir to mix.
4. Bring to a boil. Lower heat, cover, and simmer for about 15 minutes, till all liquid is absorbed and rice is cooked. Remove from heat, add coriander leaves, cover and let rice cook in its steam for another 10 minutes. (If using a rice cooker, use proportions for rice cooker based upon above quantities. Add the rice mixture from step 3, cover and switch rice cooker on. Rice cooker automatically shuts off when rice is cooked.)
5. Remove lemongrass stalk before serving.

Serve with roast chicken (page 297), spicy fried fish (page 206), spicy chicken burgers (page 303), or spicy tomato chicken (page 284); and mixed vegetable *acar* (page 93), spicy cucumber tomato salad (page 97), stir-fried broccoli rabe (page 301), spicy water spinach (page 228), or a simple green salad.

Stir-fried Spicy Broccoli Rabe

Makes 3 to 4 servings

My daughter, Geeta, and I enjoy Asian and other greens prepared in a variety of styles, especially Asian-style. Broccoli rabe has florets and leaves that somewhat resemble broccoli and belongs to the Brassica family. It is rich in vitamins A, C, K, folic acid, and phytochemicals, including sulforaphane and indoles that protect against cancer. Generally it is sautéed in olive oil or steamed by Westerners. Broccoli rabe goes well with garlic, ginger, sesame oil, soy sauce, and chile peppers. I have given you a recipe here that is easy to prepare and delicious. Crunchy bean sprouts pair well with broccoli rabe and mellow its bitterness.

INGREDIENTS

- 1 tablespoon cooking oil
- 2 tablespoons sliced and crushed garlic cloves
- 1 tablespoon sliced and crushed fresh ginger
- 1 fresh green or red chile (Fresno, jalapeno, Serrano, cherry, or cayenne), sliced and crushed
- ¼ teaspoon coarsely ground black peppercorns
- 1 tablespoon preserved soybean paste (*taucheo*, black version) or black bean sauce, or bean sauce
- 1 teaspoon regular soy sauce
- 1 bunch (about ¾ pound) broccoli rabe, cut into 2-inch pieces, stems discarded, and washed or rinsed by swirling in a pot of water to dislodge and remove sand and dirt
- Optional: 1 cup (3 ounces) bean sprouts, rinsed or blanched
- 1 teaspoon toasted sesame oil

DIRECTIONS:

1. Heat oil in a wok or skillet. Add garlic and ginger and sauté for about ½ to 1 minute. Add chile and sauté another ½ minute.
2. Add black peppercorns, soybean paste, and soy sauce and stir.
3. Add broccoli rabe and cover and let cook for about 2 minutes, till broccoli rabe gets limp. Uncover, add bean sprouts, if using, and sesame oil and cook for another minute.

Serve with cooked white or brown rice or yellow rice (page 118), or vegetable *biryani* (page 280); and roast chicken (page 297), spicy fried chicken (page 165), chicken *kurma* (page 168), tofu curry (page 233), or vegetable dhal curry (page 231).

Tomato and Spice-Infused Potatoes

Makes 4 servings

INGREDIENTS

½ teaspoon salt
1 pound (about 3 cups) potatoes, peeled and cubed
1 to 2 tablespoons cooking oil
1 teaspoon chopped garlic cloves
1 teaspoon chopped fresh ginger
¼ cup thinly sliced red or white onions
Optional: 1 fresh green or red chile (cayenne, jalapeno, Serrano, or New Mexican), chopped
2 teaspoons regular soy sauce
¾ teaspoon tomato paste, or 1½ teaspoons tomato puree, or 2¼ teaspoons tomato sauce
¼ cup water or olive or canola oil
Optional: ½ cup petite peas (fresh and cooked, or frozen and thawed)
½ teaspoon lemon juice

SPICE BLEND

¾ teaspoon ground coriander
¾ teaspoon turmeric powder
½ teaspoon ground cumin
¼ teaspoon ground fennel seeds

GARNISH

2 tablespoons chopped coriander leaves (cilantro)

I did not cook potatoes for my family because I did not grow up eating them in Malaysia. But my daughter Geeta used to enjoy them at her friend's homes and in restaurants in many forms—mashed, scalloped, baked whole with butter, and fried. I still remember when Geeta was four or five, her coming from my neighbor Joyce Pezzola's home and asking if we were having baked potatoes for dinner. I looked at her with surprise! She had enjoyed the potato and pasta dishes at Joyce's. I had no idea how to even bake a potato, much less create a mashed potato dish!

Initially I bought the store packaged mashed and scalloped potatoes. Feeling sorry for me, Geeta tolerated this, but she said they tasted different from Joyce's homemade potatoes. So one day, I decided to work on potato dishes but with Malaysian touches, and prepared a spicy potato dish for dinner, incorporating spices and emulating the potato filling of the masala thosai*. Another day I made a spicy potato dish similar to the Malay* bergedil*. She enjoyed them both. I am including a recipe for you here so you can serve it as a change from your regular potato dishes. You can also add peas and/or cauliflower to it, if desired.*

DIRECTIONS:

1. Bring 3 cups water to boil in a medium saucepan, add salt and cubed potatoes and simmer for about 10 to 15 minutes, till potatoes are cooked (firm and not mushy). Drain and set aside.
2. Mix Spice Blend ingredients and set aside.
3. Heat oil in a wok or skillet and sauté garlic and ginger for about ½ to 1 minute; add onions and sauté for about 1 to 2 minutes till fragrant. Add chile, if using, and sauté for another ½ minute.
4. Add Spice Blend and sauté for about ½ minute. Add soy sauce, tomato paste, puree, or sauce, water or olive oil or canola oil, and salt and stir for another ½ to 1 minute.
5. Lower heat and add the cooked potatoes and coat well with paste, without breaking up the potatoes, adding more oil or water if neccesary. Add peas, if using, and stir for about 1 minute. (If you desire a mashed consistency, add about ½ cup more water and cook for another 3 to 5 minutes till the potatoes become slightly mushy and sauce dries up somewhat.)
6. Sprinkle with lemon juice and stir for another minute. Garnish with coriander leaves.

Serve with cooked white or brown rice, vegetable dhal curry (page 231), or spicy lentil vegetable stew (page 88); and/or chicken curry (page 171), roast chicken (page 297), chicken *sambal* (page 161), Chettiar-style fiery shrimp (page 291), or mutton *peratil* (page 185). Or use as a filling for *thosai* (page 69) or other flatbreads (as vegetarian wraps).

Nonya-Style Chicken Burgers

Makes 4 to 5 servings

My husband enjoys burgers, generally made with ground beef. Since I have stopped cooking beef at home, he has switched to chicken and turkey burgers. I usually season the burgers before I pan-fry or grill them. For one summer barbecue with friends, we made chicken burgers and served them with a light salad, using vegetables from our garden, and curried spaghetti. For the burgers, I made a Nonya-style seasoning and combined it with Worcestershire sauce, lemon juice, and soy sauce and added chopped red onions and tomatoes. We also added fresh chopped cilantro from our garden. Bob found it delicious … especially since it had a spicy bite!

INGREDIENTS

1 pound ground chicken or turkey (or you can use ground beef or lamb)
1 tablespoon Worcestershire sauce
1 teaspoon regular soy sauce
½ teaspoon lemon juice
½ cup chopped onions
½ cup (3 ounces) chopped tomatoes
¼ cup chopped coriander leaves (cilantro)
½ to ¾ teaspoon salt
1 tablespoon oil

Spice Blend

1 tablespoon ground coriander
1 teaspoon ground cumin
1 teaspoon ground fennel seeds
1 teaspoon ground mustard
½ teaspoon turmeric powder
½ teaspoon finely ground black pepper
¼ teaspoon ground cinnamon
¼ teaspoon ground paprika
¼ teaspoon chile powder

DIRECTIONS:

1. Combine Spice Blend ingredients. In a bowl, mix the Spice Blend with the rest of the ingredients except oil, and mix well.
2. Divide into 4 to 6 portions. Roll each into a ball, then flatten into a patty, about ¼-inch or less thickness.
3. Heat oil in a skillet, add patties and cook on each side for about 4 to 6 minutes; or grill.

Serve with a green salad, cucumber carrot *acar* (page 99), or green papaya *acar* (page 100); and vegetable *biryani* (page 280), yellow rice (page 118), curried spaghetti (page 307), or tomato and spice infused potatoes (page 302).

Fragrant Peppercorn Lamb

Makes 4 to 5 servings

INGREDIENTS

2 teaspoons distilled white vinegar or rice vinegar or rice wine
½ to 1 teaspoon sugar
1 pound lamb, thinly sliced into 1½-inch to 2-inch pieces, or lamb chops
1 to 2 tablespoons cooking oil
2 teaspoons chopped garlic cloves
⅓ cup chopped onions
1 fresh green or red chile (Fresno, jalapeno, Serrano, cayenne, cherry, or Thai), chopped
Optional: ¼ cup unsweetened coconut milk
¼ teaspoon salt
2 teaspoons lemon juice (if not using coconut milk, increase to 5 teaspoons)

SPICE BLEND

2 teaspoons ground coriander
1 teaspoon coarsely ground black peppercorns or cracked black pepper
1 teaspoon ground cumin
½ teaspoon ground fennel seeds
½ teaspoon ground star anise
¼ teaspoon ground cinnamon
¼ teaspoon ground cardamom
¼ teaspoon ground mustard
⅛ teaspoon ground cloves
Optional: ⅛ teaspoon each of turmeric, ground nutmeg, and chile powder

GARNISH

2 tablespoons sliced spring onions or chopped coriander leaves (cilantro)

I enjoy lamb dishes, especially the well-seasoned lamb preparation I grew up with. During my college years in England, I also relished their mildly flavored roast lamb with mint sauce. After many years, I took Bob and Geeta, who was a teen then, to see my old college haunts in Reading, London, and other nearby towns. I was amazed at the growth of Indian cuisine everywhere, including highway rest stops and pubs. We had a wonderful meal at an upscale Indian fusion restaurant in London, a meal of masala roast *lamb shank with* pulao *rice. It was a great fusion meal!*

The Indian Muslims in Malaysia have created truly delicious mildly seasoned lamb dishes. I have eaten steak on rare occasions in the past and a preparation I enjoyed was steak au poivre. While I was not fond of the heavy cream sauce, I liked its peppery flavor. I took this concept and prepared a delicious lamb dish using coarsely ground black peppercorns, star anise, and fennel seeds. Instead of cream, you can add coconut milk as its sweetness balances well with the peppercorn. When I prepare lamb chops, I prefer not to add coconut milk but instead increase the amount of lemon juice which adds a wonderful balance to the spiced lamb.

DIRECTIONS:

1. Combine the Spice Blend ingredients. Mix the Spice Blend with the vinegar and sugar in a non-reactive bowl. Add the lamb and coat well. Set aside in the refrigerator for a minimum of 30 minutes or 2 to 3 hours or overnight.
2. If using lamb chops, pan sear chops at high heat in a skillet till brown, about 3 minutes on each side, adding 1 tablespoon oil if needed. Set aside.
3. Heat 1 tablespoon oil in a wok or skillet and sauté garlic for about ½ to 1 minute. Add onions and sauté another 1 to 2 minutes. Add chile and sauté another ½ minute.
4. Add marinated lamb pieces or chops and stir. Cover and let cook for about 3 minutes for pieces or 2 minutes for lamb chops. Uncover and cook an additional 5 to 7 minutes for pieces or 4 minutes for chops, stirring occasionally, till lamb is cooked and coated with sauce.
5. Stir in coconut milk, if using, and salt, and let cook for another 2 to 3 minutes.
6. Add lemon juice and stir for 1 or 2 minutes more. Garnish with spring onions or coriander leaves.

Serve with cooked white or brown rice, herb rice (page 125), or lime rice (page 122); and spicy cucumber tomato salad (page 97), stir-fried bean sprouts (page 229), stir-fried *kailan* (page 222), or stir-fried Chinese greens (page 227).

Mamak-style Omelet with Keema

Makes 5 to 6 servings

Ma made flavorful omelets with chopped onions, tomatoes, and chilies. She sliced them into pieces, like pizza slices, and served them with dalcha *or* dhal *curry and a tomato cucumber salad. For Ma this was a light meal that she served sometimes for dinner. One morning, for breakfast at my home, I went a step further and added leftover spicy ground curried lamb to make an omelet for my brother Sree, who enjoys meat, even for breakfast. Ground meat (called minced meat in Malaysia) curry is called* keema *curry in Malaysia and is generally made from lamb or beef depending on whether prepared by Hindu Indians or Muslim Indians. Keema curries are a specialty of Indian Muslims, especially of Hyderabad in Andhara Pradesh, India. Like Latin cultures who add chopped chorizo or hot sausage to omelets, I sometimes use my left-over curried* keema *(or even chop other dry curried meat or chicken) for omelets or scrambled eggs. The tomatoes, chilies, and bell peppers (called* capsicums *by Malaysians) add a wonderful balance to it.*

Here I use ground turkey as a change for a less fatty omelet. The curried turkey spices up the omelet and goes well with plain toast. Generally ghee is used as the cooking fat to give an aromatic finish to the keema*, but I use olive or canola oil in my recipe to create a lighter* keema*. You can also use ground chicken, lamb, or beef.*

INGREDIENTS

Chicken or Turkey Keema:

- 1 tablespoon ghee or cooking oil
- 1½ teaspoons chopped fresh ginger
- 1½ teaspoons chopped garlic cloves
- 1 cup diced shallots or red onions
- 2 fresh green chilies, sliced lengthwise
- ¾ cup (4½ ounces) chopped tomatoes
- 1 pound ground or minced chicken or turkey (you can also use beef or lamb)
- ½ to ¾ teaspoon salt
- ¾ cup petite peas (fresh and cooked, or frozen and thawed)
- ¼ teaspoon lemon juice
- Optional: 2 tablespoons chopped coriander leaves (cilantro)

Spice Blend

- 1 tablespoon ground cumin
- 1 tablespoon ground coriander
- ¼ to ½ teaspoon turmeric powder
- ¼ to ½ teaspoon chile powder
- ⅛ to ¼ teaspoon finely ground black pepper

Omelet

- 1 tablespoon cooking oil
- 1 cup chopped shallots or red onions
- 1 cup (6 ounces) chopped tomatoes
- ½ cup (2 ounces) diced sweet bell peppers
- Optional: 1 or 2 fresh chilies (cayenne, Fresno, jalapeno, Serrano, Thai, or cherry), sliced
- 6 eggs, beaten
- ¼ teaspoon salt

Garnish

- 2 tablespoons chopped coriander leaves (cilantro)

DIRECTIONS FOR KEEMA:

1. Combine Spice Blend ingredients. Set aside.
2. Heat oil in a skillet. Add ginger and garlic and sauté for about ½ to 1 minute, then add shallots or onions and sauté another 1 to 2 minutes.
3. Add Spice Blend and sauté for about ½ minute. Add chilies and tomatoes and sauté another 1 to 2 minutes.
4. Add ground meat and cook, stirring, for about 10 minutes, till done. Add salt and peas and stir for about 1 minute. Add lemon juice and coriander leaves, if using, and blend well.

DIRECTIONS FOR OMELET OR SCRAMBLED EGGS:

1. In a skillet, heat oil and sauté shallots or onions for 1 to 2 minutes. Add tomatoes and cook for 1 minute. Add bell peppers and stir for about 1 to 2 minutes.
2. Add 1 to 2 cups cooked meat mixture (*keema*) and chilies, if using. Stir well for about 1 to 2 minutes.
3. Pour in beaten eggs and let sit till set. Sprinkle on salt. Fold in half for an omelet. (Another option is to cook the eggs like scrambled eggs.) Garnish with coriander leaves.

Serve with toasted bread, bagel, panini, naan, or other flatbreads or as a wrap. Or you can eat it as an entrée with cooked white or brown rice or yellow rice (page 118) with a green salad, spicy cucumber tomato salad (page 97), stir-fried cabbage (page 226), or stir-fried Chinese greens (page 227).

Aromatic Malay-style Fish Kurma

Makes 4 to 5 servings

INGREDIENTS

2 to 3 tablespoons cooking oil
1 pound fish steak (red snapper, haddock, mackerel, cod, sole, salmon, swordfish, or tuna); or 1 whole fish (red snapper, bream, pomfret), cleaned, tail discarded, cut into ½-inch pieces
1½ teaspoons chopped garlic cloves
1 teaspoon chopped fresh ginger
½ cup diced shallots or red onions
1 or 2 fresh green chilies (cayenne, jalapeno, Serrano, or Thai), sliced
½ cup (3 ounces) diced tomatoes
¼ cup unsweetened coconut milk or yogurt
½ teaspoon freshly squeezed or bottled lime juice
¼ teaspoon salt

SPICE BLEND

½ teaspoon ground fennel seeds
½ teaspoon ground cinnamon
½ teaspoon ground cardamom
¼ teaspoon ground cumin
¼ teaspoon ground coriander
¼ teaspoon turmeric powder
¼ teaspoon finely ground white pepper
¼ teaspoon ground star anise
¼ teaspoon ground mustard
⅛ teaspoon ground cloves

GARNISH

¼ cup chopped coriander leaves (cilantro)
¼ cup chopped mint leaves
Optional: ¼ cup slivered almonds

One of my daughter Geeta's favorite dishes at Indian restaurants is chicken kurma. *And she especially enjoys her Aunt Shanta's chicken* kurma *during her visits to Malaysia. For Easter dinner, I generally prepare fish for my family. One Easter, when Geeta came home from college, I made a Malay-kurma-style red snapper. I used the flavors Shanta used and modified the spices to complement the fish. I made a side dish of vegetarian* paella *and a simple stir-fry that offset the richness of the* kurma. *Geeta and everyone loved it!*

DIRECTIONS:

1. Combine the Spice Blend ingredients. Add 1 tablespoon of oil or water and rub fish with this paste. Heat 1 tablespoon of oil in a skillet and pan-fry fish on both sides till brown. Set aside.
2. Heat another tablespoon of oil in the skillet and sauté garlic and ginger for about ½ to 1 minute. Add shallots or onions and sauté another 1 to 2 minutes.
3. Add chile and tomatoes and sauté for about 2 to 3 minutes.
4. Add coconut milk or yogurt and ¼ cup water and cook and stir for about 2 to 3 minutes.
5. Add pan-fried fish, cover and let simmer for about 3 to 4 minutes till cooked.
6. Uncover, add lime juice and salt, and stir for 1 to 2 minutes till sauce thickens. Add garnishes and cook another minute.

ALTERNATE DIRECTIONS:

1. Combine the Spice Blend ingredients. Set aside. Heat 1 tablespoon of oil in a skillet and pan-fry fish on both sides till brown. Set aside.
2. Process garlic, ginger, onions, chilies, tomatoes and the coriander and mint leaves and almonds to a smooth paste.
3. Heat 1 tablespoon of oil in a wok or skillet, add paste and stir for about 4 minutes till fragrant, adding more oil if needed. Add Spice Blend and stir for 1 minute.
4. Add coconut milk or yogurt and ¼ cup water, and cook for 2 to 3 minutes. Add pan-fried fish and salt and stir till cooked, about 3 to 4 minutes. Add lime juice and mix well.

Serve with cooked white or brown rice, tomato rice (page 119), lime rice (page 122), or *sambar* rice (page 124); and green papaya *acar* (page 100), stir-fried broccoli rabe (page 301), or spicy dry curried okra (page 221).

Curried Spaghetti

Makes 3 to 4 servings

Whenever I have guests coming and don't have much time to cook, I turn to this recipe. It is an aromatic, lime-infused, curried tomato pasta that is a favorite at my home. It was also a great meal to prepare when my daughter Geeta and her friends came home for a "surprise" dinner! It can be served as a side dish or bowl meal. Add seasoned shrimp, chicken, or tofu, chopped tomatoes, sliced snowpea pods, or shredded cabbage for a complete meal. Alternatively, you can add diced ham, sliced omelet, and peas. It also goes well with grilled or roast chicken, pan-fried fish, or burgers. During summer months, sometimes I use penne instead of spaghetti and serve cold. The curry flavor comes through beautifully on the cold penne.

INGREDIENTS

- 2 to 4 tablespoons olive oil or other cooking oil
- 1 teaspoon chopped garlic cloves
- ½ to 1 fresh green chile (cayenne, jalapeno, Serrano, Thai, or New Mexican), sliced into ¼-inch pieces
- 4 teaspoons regular soy sauce
- ½ teaspoon tomato paste, or 1 teaspoon tomato puree, or 1½ teaspoons tomato sauce
- ⅛ to ¼ teaspoon salt
- 2 teaspoons freshly squeezed or bottled lime juice
- 8 ounces spaghetti or penne or your favorite pasta, cooked al dente and drained

Spice Blend

- 2 teaspoons ground coriander
- ½ teaspoon ground cumin
- ½ teaspoon ground paprika
- ½ teaspoon turmeric powder
- ¼ teaspoon ground fennel seeds
- ¼ teaspoon finely ground black pepper
- ¼ teaspoon ground ginger
- ⅛ teaspoon chile powder

Garnish

- ½ heaping cup (about 3½ ounces) diced tomatoes, or cherry tomatoes cut in half, or diced sun-dried tomatoes
- ¼ cup chopped coriander leaves (cilantro)

DIRECTIONS:

1. Combine Spice Blend ingredients. Set aside.
2. Heat 1 tablespoon oil in a skillet or wok. Add garlic and stir for about ½ to 1 minute, then add chile pieces and stir another ½ minute.
3. Add remaining oil and Spice Blend and stir ½ to 1 minute. Add soy sauce and tomato paste, puree, or sauce, and cook another minute to get a fragrant paste.
4. Take off heat, add salt and lime juice and blend well. Add to cooked spaghetti and coat well.
5. Toss with tomatoes and coriander leaves before serving.

FOR A COMPLETE MEAL

Season 8 ounces chicken, shrimp, or pan-fried tofu with 2 teaspoons of Spice Blend, 1 teaspoon regular soy sauce, ¼ teaspoon tomato paste, and 1 teaspoon oil. Heat 1 tablespoon oil and stir the seasoned chicken, shrimp, or tofu till cooked. (Optional: add shredded cabbage or snowpea pods and stir till cooked, about 3 minutes.) Add to seasoned spaghetti and mix well.

Chile Turmeric Tofu

Makes 3 to 4 servings

INGREDIENTS

- 1 package (14 ounces) firm tofu (*tauhu*), cubed (½-inch to ¾-inch pieces)
- 1 to 2 tablespoons cooking oil
- 1 teaspoon chopped garlic cloves
- ¼ cup diced red onions (½-inch pieces)
- 1½ teaspoons tomato paste, or 3 teaspoons tomato puree, or 4½ teaspoons tomato sauce, or 2 tablespoons to ¼ cup (1½ ounces) chopped tomatoes
- 1 teaspoon regular soy sauce
- ¼ teaspoon sugar
- ¼ teaspoon salt
- ¼ teaspoon lemon juice

Spice Blend

- 1 teaspoon ground cumin
- ½ teaspoon chile powder
- ½ teaspoon ground coriander
- ½ teaspoon ground fennel seeds
- ¼ teaspoon turmeric powder
- ⅛ teaspoon finely ground black pepper

Garnish

- 2 tablespoons chopped coriander leaves (cilantro)

Ma enjoyed eating tofu and used simple preparations to cook it. Her favorite preparation was seasoning sliced tofu with a paste of turmeric, chile powder, and some other spices, and then pan-frying or deep-frying it. Today, Americans are consuming more tofu, especially the younger generation, and they want it well-seasoned. My daughter, Geeta, was a vegetarian during her middle school years, and I had to be creative with tofu. Unlike most Americans, I grew up eating tofu seasoned and prepared in different ways so cooking with tofu did not intimidate me. I made tofu omelets, stir-fries, curries, and tofu burgers. Even now whenever Geeta comes home, I am still learning new ways to flavor tofu. Below is a recipe Geeta and I enjoy and want to share with you. I slice the tofu and pan-fry the pieces till they are light brown and then season them. This way, the tofu pieces have a firmer texture and an overall better flavor and bite.

DIRECTIONS:

1. Heat skillet (no oil added if non-stick, otherwise a little oil) and pan-fry tofu pieces, stirring gently and turning pieces over, till firm and light brown, about 5 to 6 minutes. Set aside.
2. Combine Spice Blend ingredients and set aside.
3. Heat 1 tablespoon oil in a wok or skillet and sauté garlic for ½ to 1 minute. Add onions and sauté for 1 to 2 minutes.
4. Add Spice Blend and stir for about ½ minute till fragrant, then add tomato paste, puree, or sauce or tomatoes, soy sauce, sugar, and salt, and stir for about 1 minute, adding more oil or water if needed.
5. Add pan-fried tofu, blend with sauce, and stir for about 2 minutes. Add lemon juice, stir to mix, and garnish with coriander leaves.

Serve with cooked white or brown rice, yellow rice (page 118), or herb rice (page 125); and spicy dry curried okra (page 221), stir-fried cabbage (page 226), or spicy water spinach (page 228); and vegetable dhal curry (page 231) or spicy lentil vegetable stew (page 88).

Spicy Sweet Fruit Salad

Makes 6 to 8 servings

Growing up with the spicy fruit salads and many pickled salads (acars) of Malaysia prompted me to make a salad, Malaysian-style, that would appeal to Americans. Many years back, for a New York Women's Culinary Alliance potluck, I made a fruit salad using slices of melon, pineapple, mango, and tangerines tossed with a spicy sweet dressing, the way Malaysians eat their salads. Everyone enjoyed it and the plate was cleaned, so I decided to include the recipe here. The dressing is added and mixed with the fruits just before serving so the fruits do not get mushy.

INGREDIENTS

1 cup (about 5 ounces) cubed ripe mango (¾-inch pieces)

1 cup (5½ ounces) cubed fresh or canned pineapple (¾-inch pieces)

1 cup (about 5 ounces) cubed green melon (¾-inch pieces)

1 cup (4½ ounces) tangerine slices

Dressing

4 to 6 tablespoons light brown sugar

2 teaspoons salt

¼ cup distilled white, rice, or cider vinegar

2 tablespoons freshly squeezed or bottled lime juice

½ teaspoon bottled *sambal oelek*

1 tablespoon thinly sliced fresh ginger (1-inch-long by ⅛-inch-thick)

2 tablespoons finely chopped shallots or red onions

Garnish

¼ cup coarsely ground peanuts or slivered almonds

2 tablespoons finely chopped mint leaves

½ cup pomegranate seeds

Optional: 1 fresh red chile, deseeded, thinly sliced into 1-inch pieces

DIRECTIONS:

1. Place fruits in a non-reactive bowl. Combine all ingredients for dressing.
2. Just before serving, pour dressing over the fruits and toss gently to coat, keeping fruits intact. Top with garnishes.

Serve with cooked white or brown rice or yellow rice (page 118); and spicy fried chicken (page 165), chile chicken (page 163), spicy fish cutlets (page 63), or hot and spicy chicken wings (page 64).

Fruits of Malaysia

Cheesecake with Tropical Fruits

Makes 6 to 8 servings

INGREDIENTS

Crust

1½ cups finely ground graham cracker crumbs
2 tablespoons unsalted butter, melted
2 tablespoons sugar
½ teaspoon ground cardamom

Filling

1 pound cream cheese, at room temperature
1 cup very fine sugar
3 eggs
1 pint sour cream
2 teaspoons vanilla extract
¼ teaspoon pandan extract or pandan-flavored paste

Topping

Sliced mango, pineapple, tangerines, and/or lychees

I have had several types of cheesecakes in the U.S. and abroad. But none can compare to my sister-in-law Diane's. It is a special treat for us to go to Sree (my younger brother) and Diane's home and have her cheesecake for dessert. I had requested that Diane make a Malaysian-flavored cheesecake. To do this she added ground cardamom and pandan flavor. And she topped it with Malaysia's favorite fruits—mango, lychee, and pineapple. The resulting flavor was really creamy and floral and truly addictive.

DIRECTIONS:

1. Heat the oven to 375°F. Combine all ingredients for the crust, using a fork to mix in the butter, resulting in a granular mixture. Coat the sides and bottom of a 6-inch springform pan with some unsalted butter and press crumb mixture evenly onto the bottom of the pan.
2. Beat cream cheese with an electric mixer on low till soft and smooth. Slowly add sugar and beat till smooth.
3. Add eggs one at a time and beat with mixer after each addition.
4. Add sour cream and vanilla extract and pandan extract and beat at low speed till the mixture becomes smooth. Pour carefully into the springform pan.
5. Bake for 20 minutes at 375° F. Turn off the oven and leave cheesecake in oven for 1 hour. Take out and cool at room temperature. Cover with foil and refrigerate for at least 8 hours.
6. To serve, run knife around the edge of pan and then remove sides. Top with sliced fruits.

Serve with *teh masala* (page 259), *teh tarik* (page 262), or any hot tea or coffee.

GLOSSARY AND GUIDE TO BASIC INGREDIENTS AND TECHNIQUES

Asafetida/Asafoetida

(Ferula asa-foetida L (hing type), Family: Umbelliferae)

The name asafetida is derived from the Persian word *aza*, meaning resin, and the Latin word *foetida*, meaning fetid or bad smelling. Malaysians of South Indian extract add asafetida to vegetarian dishes, especially lentil dishes, to enhance their flavor and to prevent flatulence. Strict vegetarians, who will not eat garlic or onions because they consider them aphrodisiacs, also use asafetida as a substitute flavoring. The more common asafetida is *hing*, the water-soluble variety. It is sold as different grades of resin, dried granules, chunks, or powders. It has a strong acrid odor and bitter taste, but when fried in oil, pleasant shallot and garlic-like notes develop.

Asam gelugor or asam keping

(Garcinia atroviridis)

Native to Malaysia, *asam gelugor* is the size of a large apple with a glossy skin, vertically ribbed, and has a yellow color that darkens slightly with age. It cannot be eaten fresh because of its intense sourness, so it is thinly sliced and dried till it gets shriveled and brownish black in color. It has a smoky, earthy, and sour taste, similar to tamarind but with a more pronounced tart taste. It is generally rinsed before use. It gets plump after cooking and is discarded before the dish is served. *Asam gelugor* is sold as dried slices (in Thai stores as *som mawon* or *som khack*) and sometimes is labeled as tamarind skin, but it is not tamarind. Tamarind, *asam kandis* (a small fruit), and *kokum* (*Garcinia indica*, a closely related fruit) can be used as substitutes.

Asian greens

Sawi-sawi (Malay); *choy* (Cantonese); *kira* (Tamil)

Asian greens are staples in Malaysia, prepared in an array of techniques and flavors that vary with the different ethnic groups. There are many varieties of Asian greens in Malaysia and they are bought fresh from traditional open-air wet markets (*pasar basah*) or supermarkets (*pasar raya*). When picking Asian greens, make sure the leaves are bright green and not pale in color with no blemishes or yellowing and smooth without wrinkling. Also, the stalks should be firm and not mushy or dried out.

Bok choy, Chinese mustard greens (*gai choy*), Chinese flowering cabbage (*choy sam*), and Chinese broccoli (*kailan*) are from the cabbage family (*Brassica*). *Bok choy* (*Brassica rapa*) has many varieties. The *bok choy* eaten in Malaysia is the Chinese variety, called *pak choy* (also popular in Southern China and Southeast Asia). It is a smaller type than the *Pekinensis* variety (popular in northern China and commonly eaten in the U.S.). Both types are called Chinese cabbage in the U.S. *Pak choy* is about 17 to 20 inches long with dark green leaves and white stalks. Another popular variety is a smaller (10 to 12 inch) and stubbier Shanghai *choy* or Shanghai *bok choy*, with light green or lime green leaves. Also, there are baby versions (about 4 inches long) of both varieties, which have a delicate flavor and crunchy texture. Chinese flowering cabbage (Brassica sinensis), called *choy sam* or *sawi manis* or *sawi bunga* in Malay, is a variety of *bok choy* with long thin stems (6 to 8 inches), green leaves, and bright yellow flowers. It has a sweeter and mellower flavor than *bok choy* or *pak choy.*

Kailan or Chinese broccoli (*B. oleracea)* is from the same family as broccoli and kale. The mature *kailan* has slightly bitter intense green leaves and small heads of white flowers with thick stout stems. There is also a baby version of *kailan* that has thinner stems and a sweet taste. Spinach, called *bayam* in Malay, is another favorite. Water spinach, also known as *kangkung* or *ong choy* (*Ipomoea aquatica*), is a very popular vegetable with Malaysians. It is also known as water convolvulus or morning glory by Westerners and has high amounts of iron, calcium, and vitamins C and A. *Kangkung* has hollow stems and pointed or oblong leaves that have a green to a dark green color with a reddish center. Leaves are soft textured and tend to go limp after being picked due to high-moisture content. So it is generally cooked immediately after purchase. In Malaysia, one type thrives in swampy waters or even ditches where there is water. Another type is cultivated on land and has pale green and wide leaves. I enjoy the latter type, which has narrow, slender, dark green leaves and short stalks.

When using Asian greens, always snip off or trim the bottom heavier stems. Then separate the stalks or stems from the leaves and swirl in water a few times to remove and dislodge the sand and dirt. Pat dry before using.

Bean sprouts

(Vigna radiata)
taugeh (Malay); *nga choy* (Cantonese)

Bean sprouts have a sweet taste and crunchy texture. They are from the seedlings of mung beans and are tender, bright, creamy-white sprouts, with two yellowish "horns" at one end and a scraggly tail on the other. Chinese immigrants consider it a yin or "cooling" food. They brought them to Malaysia and bean sprouts have since become a favorite in local cooking. They are used as a topping for noodles, soups, and *rojak* (salad) or as a filling for *popiah* (fresh spring rolls). They are also added to stir-fries, and cooked for only a minute or so to maintain their crispiness.

Buy plump bean sprouts, and not limp or discolored ones. It is best to use them immediately or within a few days to retain their crispiness. They can be sealed tightly in a plastic bag and kept in the refrigerator. To keep them longer, cover them with cold water and store in a sealed container, similar to storing tofu. If the water is changed every two days, they can last for up to a week.

Candlenuts

(Aleurites moluccana)
Kemiri or *buah keras* (Malay, Indonesian)

Candlenuts, indigenous to Indonesia, are distantly related to macadamia nuts. *Buah keras*, translated as hard nuts and also called Indian nuts, are oily fruits with a waxy exterior and a walnut-like flavor. They are finely ground to thicken curries and sauces, especially in Nonya and Kristang dishes. Kristangs even make a spicy *sambal* with candlenuts called *bokra sambal*.

Candlenuts must be cooked before use, as they are mildly toxic when raw, similar to raw almonds. Grinding and cooking dissipates its toxicity. Generally, sauces and curries are cooked, so this prevents any issues. Storing candlenuts in the refrigerator or freezer will assure a longer shelf life, about one to two years. If kept at room temperature, they will turn rancid because of their high oil content. If candlenuts are unavailable, substitute macadamia nuts, or even almonds, although the flavor and thickening properties may not be the same, the nutty taste can be achieved.

Cardamom

(Elettaria cardamomum, Family: Zingiberaceae)

buah pelaga (Malay); *yelakai* (Tamil); *bak dan kou* (Cantonese)

Known as the "queen of spices," green cardamom was introduced from South India to Malaysian cooking by Arab traders. A member of the ginger family, there are many different varieties of green cardamom. Cardamom is a dried, firm, un-ripened, green fruit or pod packed with many seeds. The color of the pods varies from dark green to light green or white, depending on how the pods have been processed. They are dark green when the pods are oven-dried, light green when the pods are air dried, and white or buff colored when they are bleached. The seeds in all of these pods are reddish brown to black and are highly aromatic. The green pods have a delicate clean, sweet, and spicy floral flavor with a lemony scent, while the white pods have very little flavor, so when we refer to cardamom pods we mean the green pods. The seeds have an intense flavor when ground after just removing from the pods.

Malaysians flavor their Indian and Arab inspired curries and sauces with the pods (whole or crushed) or the ground seeds. It gives a distinct flavor to Indian, Nonya, and Malay coconut-based chicken, meat, and vegetable *kurmas* and *biryanis* and to puddings and sweets. Whole green cardamom is an important ingredient in *chai*, a spiced hot tea beverage. Cardamom is also used to help relieve nausea and vomiting and to ease stomachaches.

Chile Peppers: Cayennes

(Capsicum annum, Family: Solanaceae)

Chile, chili, or **chilli**: *lada, cili, cabai* (Malay); *milaghai* (Tamil); *lat jiu* (Cantonese)

Fresh red chile: *lada* or *cabai merah* (Malay); *sivapu milaghai* (Tamil); *hoong lat jiu* (Cantonese)

Fresh green chile: *lada* or *cabai hijau* (Malay); *pachai milaghai* (Tamil); *cheng lat jiu* (Cantonese)

Dried whole chile: *lada* or *cabai kering* (Malay); *patta milaghai* (Tamil); *kon lat jiu* (Cantonese); *phrik kaeng* (Thai)

Ground chile pepper, **chile powder**, or **cayenne**: *serbuk cili* (Malay); *thule milaghai* (Tamil); *phrik pon* (Thai)

Bird pepper: *lada burong, cili padi* (Malay); *usi mulaghai* (Tamil); *chai lat jiu* (Cantonese); *phrik khee nu* (Thai)

Malaysians use chilies liberally, and the chilies used are generally the cayenne peppers. They have become an indispensable component of spice pastes (*rempahs*) and curry powders. Within each variety there are several bred cultivars with different pungencies, flavors, textures, and colors. The degree of heat of chile peppers varies depending on the varieties, origins, growing conditions, and drying conditions.

In Malaysia, the terms *cili, chili,* or *chilli* pepper are used. In the U.S., it is *chile* pepper (plural, *chiles* or *chilies*) and in South America it is *aji. Capsicum* is the term used by Malaysians for the sweet bell peppers. Paprika is ground red powder that provides mostly color with some flavor. In the U.S., ground chile powder is also called cayenne powder and is usually ground New Mexican cayenne or ancho chile peppers. The term "chili powder" in the U.S. is a blend of ground cayenne, cumin, oregano, paprika, and garlic powder and is usually used when making chili con carne (a ground meat and/or bean dish).

Cayenne peppers come in different sizes and some are hotter than others. The long, slender, pointed cayennes about 4 inches long are typical of Malaysia. They are shiny bright red or deep green, similar to the Thai *phrik chee* or *khee fa*. If Malaysian cayennes are not available, substitute Holland chilies (*Capsicum annum var. longum*) from Indonesia, also known as finger chilies (which are hybrids of Malaysian and Indonesian cayennes). Red Hollands are long, deep-red chilies with a pointed tip that resemble cayenne peppers in flavor and heat. Or use Fresnos, cherry bell peppers, Thai *phrik chee fa* (also referred to as Thai chilies), *chile de arbol*, or Indian cayennes. If more heat is required, jalapenos, Serranos, and even hotter bird peppers (*cili padi*) can be substituted.

Fresnos (a New Mexican variety) are medium-hot bright red chilies with a sweet taste. They are about 2 to 3 inches long with a conical shape tapering to a sharp point. They are sold in the mainstream supermarkets where they're often labeled as 'red jalapenos.' Jalapenos are dark green or bright red, plump chilies that are good substitutes. Serranos, meaning "from the mountains," are now grown in Thailand (called *phrik khee nu kaset*). They have a deep green color, sometimes ripening to red, and are slender with a rounded point. They are hotter than a jalapeno but closer in heat to the Thai green chilies. If you want milder flavors, you can use milder sweeter chilies, such as Anaheim (also called California Green, long green chile, or New Mexican).

The smaller-size chilies (*Capsicum annum aviculare*) are tiny, 1½-inch-long tapered fiery chilies, better known in Malaysia as *cili padi*. They are a favorite for chile-based dips and condiments. They are also called *phrik khee nu* in Thai or *cabai rawit* in Indonesian, and are available in the U.S. in Asian stores, and are generally green or reddish green, but not fully red.

The dried whole chilies in Malaysia are long and crinkly. There are also imported ones from India that are short and stubby. In the U.S., dried whole chilies are available in plastic bags from Indian (generally *Sanam* chilies), Thai, or other Asian stores. They give a caramelized

HOW TO PREPARE BASICS: CILI BOH

Makes ¾ cup

Dried whole red chilies are pureed with water and made into a paste or puree called cili boh *which forms the basis of many Malay and Nonya dishes in Malaysia, including* sambals, *dips (for noodle dishes and fried rice),* rendangs, *dressings for salads (*rojak*), and is used to perk up many other dishes. Ma, like many, used her own freshly prepared* cili boh. *Today fresh or frozen* cili boh *is available. Commercially prepared* cili boh *has added salt and vegetable oil.*

In most of my recipes, the dried whole chilies are deseeded before blending, so the cili boh *is not just heat but also adds flavor. In many recipes where only one or two chilies are needed, I generally pound the chilies in a mortar and pestle or add the rehydrated dried whole chile into the food processor and blend with other ingredients. You can also substitute bottled* sambal oelek, *although its flavor is not quite the same because it is made from fresh chilies, vinegar, and salt and the chilies used are different. With regards to heat, they are quite comparable.*

1. Place 50 dried whole chilies in a bowl and steep in hot water to cover till they soften, about 10 to 15 minutes. (Using gloves, break up dried chilies before steeping in water to deseed, or slit chilies and deseed after they soften.)
2. Plunge the chilies in cold water (the seeds will separate from pods and go to bottom of bowl).
3. Remove the chile pods and discard the seeds. Place chile pods in food processor or blender with ½ cup water and pulse till a smooth paste.

Note: You can substitute fresh red chilies (type depending on heat desired) for the dried chilies, as many busy cooks do today. Though the flavor is best when cooked the traditional method with dried chilies, you can still achieve good flavor. Use as whole or deseed them before use to cut down the heat. In some recipes I have added deseeded red chilies, such as Fresno, along with the dried whole chilies to give a brighter red color.

taste to dishes and are commonly used by Malaysian cooks for making *cili boh* (chile paste) and *sambals*. In my recipes, you can substitute dried chilies (*Sanaam*) from India. They are thin, flat, 3-inch to 5-inch deep red chilies with heat similar to Malaysian cayennes. Or use dried *chile de arbol*, a dark red chile with a long curved tapered shape. It is close to cayenne in heat and flavor. Or use japones, sold at Mexican stores, which come in different sizes.

Chile peppers have long been recognized by many cultures around the world for their medicinal qualities. When chile peppers are eaten, capsaicin stimulates the release of endorphins which give a pleasurable feeling (like chocolates). Chile peppers are believed to increase circulation, relieve rheumatic pain, treat mouth sores and infected wounds, reduce blood clots, and aid digestion by stimulating saliva and gastric juice flow.

Choose firm, plump, crisp fresh chilies with a shiny skin and fresh smell. For the most flesh, get the heaviest ones for their size. Avoid wrinkled and/or soft fresh chilies with any mushiness toward the stem end or soft brown spoiled spots. Look for dried chile peppers that are whole and flexible rather than brittle and cracked.

With regard to chile powder, use bagged chile powder sold at Indian stores. Use the regular chile powder and not the hot ones. Spice companies sell chile powders, generally mild or with 20,000 and 40, 000 Scoville Heat Units (SHU). The regular chile powder from the Indian stores has a 20,000 to 25,000 SHU. Deeper-colored chile powders are generally ground from the flesh of the chile only, but avoid the lighter-colored powders which may have been ground with their seeds, making for a hotter product. And be careful not to buy chile powders that are colored with red dyes to make them look bright red.

Place fresh chilies in a plastic bag and refrigerate up to 1 to 2 weeks. Store dried chilies in a sealed container or plastic bag, away from light and air, as they will decolorize them and accelerate decay. You can store ground chile powder in the freezer for a longer shelf life.

Chinese celery greens

(Apium graveolens; Family: Apiaceae)
daun sup (Malay); *kun choy* (Cantonese)

Chinese celery is smaller and its flavor stronger than Western celery. It is used as a flavoring and not as a vegetable. The crispy, thin, hollow stems are light green, dark green, or white. The leaves typically have jagged edges. The leaves are added to Chinese-style soups, stews, and stir-fries. But Malays, Nonyas, and Indian Muslims have also become accustomed to its flavor and add it to their soups and stews and hence its Malay name, *daun sup* or soup leaf. It is chopped and added to meat-based soups to enhance flavor. Chinese celery is sold at Asian stores and supermarkets. You can store it in the refrigerator for about 7 to 10 days. Its leaves will start yellowing if stored too long. Western celery can be substituted, but its flavor is milder.

Chinese chives

(Allium tuberosum, Family: Alliaceae)
Kuchai (Malay); *gow choy* (Cantonese)

Chinese chives, unlike regular chives, have a strong flavor. Also known as garlic chives or Chinese leeks, they are members of the garlic and onion family. They have long thick flat green stems with white edible flowers. They have a blunt end and wider stems than regular chives. They are slightly garlicky but stronger in flavor than onion chives. Chinese chives are chopped or sliced and used as a common garnish for many stir-fries, soups, *char kway teow* (stir-fried rice noodles), *mee Siam*, fried rice, grilled meats, fish dishes, and as fillings for dumplings. The Chinese and Nonyas enjoy their bulbs when pickled.

Chinese greens, Chinese mustard greens. *See* Asian greens

Cinnamon

(Cinnamomum cassia, Family: Lauraceae)
kayu manis (Malay); *gun kwai* (Cantonese); *patta* or *lavangum* (Tamil)

The cinnamon used in Malaysia and in the rest of Southeast Asia is cassia or Chinese cinnamon, known as *kayu manis* (sweet wood) in Malaysian. The dried scented bark, sold as whole sticks, are called "quills." Cassia has darker, coarser, and thicker quills than Ceylon cinnamon or canela. The highest quality cinnamon comes from the trunk, and lower quality cinnamon comes from the side branches. Finely ground cinnamon is smooth, not gritty, and this is indicative of good quality cinnamon. Cassia has a sweet, spicy aroma, a bitter taste, and more pungency than the more delicately flavored Ceylon cinnamon. Sweeter and more delicate varieties of cassia are emerging today from Southeast Asia. In Malaysia, cassia is used in sauces, curries, *rendangs*, soups, and desserts. For curries, a cinnamon stick is sautéed in hot oil where it unfolds to release its aroma. It is then added to the curry or rice being cooked. It is a popular spice with Malays, who add it to their meat curries. The Chinese used cinnamon as a medicine as early as 2500 BC to treat blood circulation.

Clove

(Syzyium aromaticum, Family: Myrtaceae)
bunga cinkeh (Malay); *ding heung* (Cantonese); *karampoo* (Tamil)

The clove plant is native to Moluccas (or Spice Islands) in Indonesia. Cloves are the dried, unopened flower buds. The rose-colored buds are picked just before opening and then dried in the sun when the color of the cloves changes to a dark reddish brown. Cloves have a spicy, woody, and burning sweet and musty aroma and they taste sharp, bitter, and pungent. Malaysians add cloves to Indian-inspired *masalas*, *biryanis*, meat dishes, and pickles, as well as Chinese-style barbecued meats or pork. Being indigenous to Indonesia, it isn't surprising that many Malay-inspired savory and sweet dishes, including *rendangs*, *gulais,* spicy condiments, *kuehs*, and teas, have a touch of clove. Locals also use cloves as a pain reliever and as a mild anesthetic for toothaches.

Coconut

(Cocos nucifera, Family: Arecaceae)
Kelapa (Malay); *thenga* (Tamil)

Coconut is a holy fruit for Hindus. Referred to as *shripal* in Sanskrit ('fruit of the gods'), it is broken as an offering to the Gods in religious ceremonies and weddings. Its three eyes represent the Hindu trinity of Lord Shiva, Vishnu, and Brahma. Coconuts are indigenous to Malaysia and South Asia, and their milk, juice, and white fleshy meat have become staples in the Malaysian diet. The liquid from young tender coconuts is called coconut water. The milk extracted from the meat enhances rice dishes, *rendangs*, fiery fish curries, and *kuehs* (sweet cakes). The meat of the mature coconut is grated and used fresh or dried (dessicated) or toasted (*kerisik*) to add a rich and sweet flavor to curries and sauces.

Coconut milk

Coconut milk (*santan* in Malay) is the extraction from the grated meat of a mature coconut mixed with warm water to give a thick creamy white liquid. When made at home a cook cracks open the coconut, then manually grates the flesh using a sit-down grater. Then warm water is added to the grated coconut and blended by hand, after which the mixture is squeezed or strained. This is then repeated two or three times, adding water each time, and getting a first, second, and third extraction of coconut milk. Each extraction becomes more watery and thinner in consistency. The first thick concentrated extraction is added initially to recipes to provide flavor for the sauce being cooked. Subsequently, the second and/or third extractions are added.

Today, many in Malaysia and elsewhere use canned coconut milk. Make sure to buy the unsweetened coconut milk and not the sweetened. After opening the can, stir the contents well to get an even consistency and to break up any lumps. Sometimes, a thick coagulated layer of milk is at the top with a liquid portion underneath. Coconut milk also comes in frozen blocks, and you can cut or grate the amount you need. It is also sold as dessicated (or dried) coconut. To use it, add equal amounts of the shredded coconut and warm water (for thick milk) and puree in blender. Then squeeze out the milk or strain.

During cooking, don't boil coconut milk, rather let it slow simmer. Store leftover coconut milk in a plastic container in the refrigerator for up to a week, and in the freezer for a much longer period.

Cooking Oils

Traditionally, coconut oil and peanut oil are used as cooking oils in Malaysia (oil is called *minyak* in Malay). Chinese dishes were generally cooked with lard or pork fat, while Malay and Indian foods were prepared with coconut oil. But slowly, coconut oil and lard have been replaced with palm, canola, and corn oil. Ma used corn oil from early times for health reasons. Coconut oil has a high saturated fat content so most people have stopped using it. Since palm oil is produced locally, its use has been encouraged in Malaysia. Choosing a cooking oil often depends on the individual, and generally is based on nutrition and flavor preferences. I

HOW TO PREPARE BASICS: KERISIK (TOASTED GRATED COCONUT)

When coconut becomes mature or ripe, the meat is grated and used fresh or dried (called copra *or* kopra*). Commercially, dried grated coconut comes as fine, medium, or coarse. It is toasted or pan roasted (called* kerisik*) and used to flavor and thicken curries and sauces or to add wonderful caramelized notes to fresh salads and desserts. Use freshly grated coconut or packaged dried or dessicated coconut to make* kerisik*. If you purchase dried grated coconut, first rehydrate in water and then dry in toaster oven for a few minutes before toasting it.*

1. Heat a wok or skillet (preferably non-stick) over medium heat. Add the grated coconut and toast while stirring continuously, till the grated coconut has a light brown color. Be careful not to over heat and burn the coconut. It will take about 4 minutes for toasting.
2. Place the toasted coconut in a shallow plate or container to cool for a few minutes.
3. Place in tightly sealed plastic wrap, ziplock bag, or air-tight container and place in freezer. This will have a 3 to 4 month shelf life.

use lightly flavored olive oil in my cooking and I find it works well with any Malaysian dish. For deep-frying I use canola oil as it has a high smoke point. Store oils in a cool dark place because light and heat oxidizes the oil and accelerates its rancidity. When recipes call for ghee (clarified butter), especially for festive dishes, you can use cooking oil as I do.

Coriander Seeds and Coriander Leaves (Cilantro)

(Coriandrum sativum. Family: Umbelliferae)
Seed: *ketumbar* (Malay); *heung* (Cantonese); *kothamalli* (Tamil)
Leaf: *daun ketumbar* (Malay); *heung choy* (Cantonese); *kothamalli elay* (Tamil)

Coriander was brought to Malaysia by Indian and Arab spice traders and became an essential spice for meat, chicken, and fish dishes. Coriander includes the fruit (seed), leaf, stem, and root, each having its own distinct flavor. In the Americas, the leaves are called cilantro, while in Asia they are identified as coriander leaves. The seed has a spicy and nutty flavor with a hint of bitter orange and cedar floral-like undertones. Its color varies from a brownish yellow to a tan brown. Its flavor, color, and size varies depending on its origins.

Coriander seeds flavor *satay* and many Malay festive rice dishes, like *nasi bukhari* and *nasi kemuli*. Coriander leaf (cilantro) has a refreshing piney flavor with notes of anise, lemon, mint, and pepper. Cilantro is pureed with mint, green chilies, and other spices to make the famous local *kurmas* while the seeds form the basis of flavor for *ayam sioh*, a sweet, tangy, and spicy tamarind and coriander-based stew enjoyed by the Nonyas of Malacca.

Coriander seeds help reduce fever and promote a feeling of coolness. Coriander leaves strengthen the stomach and remove phlegm from the bronchial tubes.

Cumin

(Cuminium cyminum, Family: Umbelliferae)
jintan putih (Malay); *siew wui heung* (Cantonese); *jeeragam* (Tamil)

A popular spice in Indian and Malay cooking, cumin got its name from the Sanskrit word *sughandan* meaning "good smelling." Cumin seeds have a nutty, earthy, spicy, and bitter taste with a penetrating, warm, and slightly lemony aroma. When dry roasted, whole cumin seeds develop a more intense aroma and darker color, and are added to South Indian-style and Sri Lankan-style chicken and meat curries. South Indian vegetarians roast whole cumin seeds in oil or ghee with lentils and other spices and then grind them to make a spice blend called *sambar podi* for *sambhars*, curries, and dips. Cumin seeds can be steeped in warm water and the liquid drunk to clean the digestive system and to dispel gas.

Curry or Kari leaf

(Murraya koenigii, Family: Rutaceae [citrus family])
kariveppilai (Tamil); *daun kari* (Malay); *bai karee* (Thai)

South Indian traders introduced curry or *kari* leaf into Malaysia. The leaf is named *kari* or curry after the seasoned sauce (called *kari* in Tamil) to which it was added. The curry leaf is very fragrant when used fresh, but loses its flavor intensity when dried. The fresh leaf is used whole, crushed, and chopped. It has a deep green color with a spicy, strong piney-lemony aroma and a slightly tangerine peel-like taste.

It is an indispensable spice in South Indian and Sri Lankan-style Malaysian cooking. Tamil cooks fry the leaves in hot oil or ghee till they show some translucent spots and become crispy (sometimes adding mustard seeds and crushed garlic cloves), and then drizzle this fragrant oil mixture over *sambhars*, dhals, and even cucumber yogurt salad. Curry leaf gives a wonderful aroma and crunchiness to many other dishes, including *varuvals* and *peratils*.

Buy curry leaves fresh. They can be kept refrigerated in a plastic bag for about two to three weeks or in a freezer for up to six months. Freezing retains their flavor, but they change to a black color. Longer storage dries them up and they lose their intoxicating aroma, but their flavor comes back during cooking. To retain their fresh flavor, it is best not to remove the leaves from the branches till ready to use.

Indians believe curry leaves help blood circulation and an infusion made of roasted leaves stops vomiting. It is also recommended for relieving kidney pains. Recent studies have shown that they have a hypoglycemic action, thereby becoming a possible treatment for diabetes. Curry leaves have also been found to prevent formation of free radicals.

Fennel seed

(Foeniculum vulgare var. dulce, Family: Apiaceae)
jintan manis (Malay); *wuih heung* (Cantonese); *perun jeerakam* (Tamil)

There are many varieties of fennel, but the two main types are sweet fennel and bitter fennel. The sweet fennel is called *Foeniculum vulgare var. dulce* and bitter fennel, *Foeniculum vulgare Mill* (or *Foeniculum officinalle*). Malaysians and Indonesians think of fennel seeds as a variety of cumin and call them *jintan manis*, which means "sweet cumin." The Arab and Indian traders brought fennel seeds to Malaysia, where with coriander and cumin they are added to spicy hot curries. Fennel seeds have a fresh, anise-like aroma with a sweet taste.

Fennel seeds are added to oily fish, such as mackerel and salmon. Malaysian Indians roast the seeds in oil before adding to egg, meat, and fish curries. The Chinese include ground fennel seeds in their five-spice blend to balance the smoked flavors of roast pork, roast duck, and other braised meat dishes. Fennel is also eaten to ease gastrointestinal pains and other stomach discomforts.

Fenugreek seed

(Trigonella foenum-graecum, Family: Leguminosae)
halba (Malay); *wuih lu bah* (Cantonese); *venthiam* (Tamil)

Arab traders introduced fenugreek to Malaysia and Indonesia. The seeds are light to yellow brown and are bitter tasting, but when they are lightly dry roasted their flavor mellows out and some of the bitterness is removed. Fenugreek leaves, called *saag methi*, are used in Punjabi and other North Indian dishes in Malaysia.

Fenugreek seed is an important spice in South Indian, Arab, and many Malay-inspired local dishes, especially fish curries, *sambhars*, and dhals. Tamils ferment rice and lentil flour with fenugreek to make their noted fermented flatbread, *thosai*. In the Northeast states of Terengganu and Kelantan, a Malay favorite is *nasi dagang*, steamed red glutinous rice with coconut milk, ginger, fenugreek, and garlic, served with a rich spicy fish curry.

Today fenugreek is found to prevent sharp rises in blood sugar and to lower cholesterol.

Fish

Ikan

Fish in Malaysia is generally sold whole or as steaks, but not usually as fillets as in the U.S. When choosing fish for recipes, choose a whole fish and cut it up, or buy steaks that have firm flesh, like tuna, trout, halibut swordfish, sardine, or even salmon. Fillets are too tender and will break apart easily with pan-frying, currying, or simmering.

The common mackerel (*ikan kembong*) is a stubby silvery fish with a patch of colors—gray, green and/or blue—along its length. It is a dark oily fish with a strong fishy taste that goes well salted, seasoned, and deep-fried or cooked in coconut milk and chile-based curries. Another mackerel, the Spanish mackerel (*ikan tenggiri*), also referred to as kingfish, has a silver color, some with a yellow horizontal stripe on both sides. It is a commonly loved fish with a delicate, sweet taste that is enjoyed in curries. Red snapper (*ikan merah*) is my favorite, as it has a sweet delicate taste. It is generally seasoned with Malay or Nonya-style spices (*rempah*) and pan-fried, baked, or grilled, and sometimes wrapped with banana leaf before grilling.

A Malay favorite is tuna (*ikan tongkol*). It is simmered in a rich coconut and tamarind-based curry and served for breakfast. There are many hot and/or tangy seafood curries that are popular with Malays, including *udang assam pedas*, *ikan assam rebus*, or *sambal sotong* (squid in chile paste). *Cili* crab is a unique preparation, blending Chinese and Malay flavorings, chilies, *taucheo*, tomatoes, and ginger. Like their Portuguese ancestors, Kristangs live by the water and enjoy fish at most meals, usually snapper, white pomfret, bream, or sea perch, which are seasoned and grilled, baked, or fried. A Kristang favorite is *pesce assa* or spicy baked snapper.

Ikan bilis (*kong yee chye* in Cantonese; *nethilipudi* in Tamil), from the anchovy family and often called sprats, are tiny white fish with a strong flavor. Anchovies are a family of small, common salt-water fish (*Engraulidae*). *Ikan bilis* are the baby versions of the anchovies which live on plankton found in estuaries and bays with muddy bottoms, where the water is shallow and brackish. (Romans fermented them to make a fish sauce called *garum*.) These dried baby anchovies are commonly used in Malaysia to make a fish sauce called *budu*, fish stock, or *sambals*. In Malaysia, *ikan bilis* are dried in the sun and used as the main ingredient in many dishes. They are seasoned, deep-fried to a golden brown color, mixed with roasted peanuts, dusted with chile powder, and served as a delicious cocktail snack. They are also used as a crunchy topping for the all-Malaysian favorite coconut-infused rice called *nasi lemak*. Baby anchovies are also cooked with shallots, chilies, and lime juice and served as a dip, called *sambal ikan bilis*. *Ikan bilis* are also boiled in water to make a sweet fish stock used as a base for soups or noodle broths, or ground to flavor dishes.

Dried *ikan bilis* are sold in plastic bags, which can be refrigerated. They are also sold as granules, paste, or powder that can be added to enhance many seafood dishes and soups, similar to fish sauce or soy sauce.

Galangal

(Alpinia galangal, Family: Zingiberaceae)

lengkuas (Malay); *leung keung* (Cantonese); *arratai* (Tamil); *khaa* (Thai); also called *galingale*, Java *galangal*, *galanga*, Siamese ginger, Thai ginger, or mild ginger.

There are three types of galangal but the most popular type is the greater galangal, a rhizome, which comes fresh or frozen (as whole) and dried (as whole, ground, sliced, or pickled). It is a knobby rhizome with a thin yellowish-brown to pale brown skin with reddish-brown rings. The interior is creamy yellow and is hard and woody in texture. The fresh form has different flavor profile from the dried form. Fresh galangal has an earthy, pungent, and ginger-like taste. Dried galangal has hardly any flavor, and if any, more of a cinnamon-like taste. Dried galan-

HOW TO PREPARE BASICS: FRIED IKAN BILIS

1. Rinse dried *ikan bilis* to clean and remove any debris or impurities. Pat dry.
2. Add oil to deep saucepan and heat. When oil is hot (sprinkle a few drops of water in and it will sizzle), add *ikan bilis.*
3. Deep-fry till golden brown.

As a snack or side dish, you can also season *ikan bilis* and then deep-fry or sauté in oil. There are many ways to season it, but basically use turmeric, chile powder, lime juice, and salt. Marinate for about 15 minutes before frying it. Then squeeze lime juice over.

You can also prepare it the way the Chinese do: Sauté onions, add seasoned fried *ikan bilis*, sweet or thick soy sauce or double black soy sauce with a little sugar, and stir-fry for a few minutes.

gal needs to be soaked in boiling water for 20 to 30 minutes before use. Young rhizomes are pink in color and are more tender and flavorful. By itself, galangal's texture is woody and its flavor is undesirable, but when it is cooked with other ingredients, it enhances their overall flavor profiles.

In Malaysia galangal is a favorite with Nonya cooks who pound it with other spices to make their *rempah* (wet spice pastes) for *laksas*, soups, and curries, while Malays add it to fiery *sambals* and rice dishes, such as *nasi goreng*, *nasi ulam*, and *nasi Padang*. Kristangs add it to their fish curries.

Galangal should not be added in large amounts, as it will give a bitter taste. Use fresh or frozen galangal in recipes and not the dried form as it has very little flavor. Keep in the refrigerator (it should last for about two to three weeks), or freeze, in which case it should keep for six months. Avoid galangal with slimy skin which indicates spoilage. If buying frozen galangal, choose the whole chunks instead of slices and thaw before use. If you don't have galangal, you can substitute fresh ginger (in the same family as galangal).

Garlic

(Allium sativum [softneck variety]; Alliaceae [onion family])
bawang putih (Malay); *suen tauh* (Cantonese); *velai pundoo* (Tamil)

Called white onion (*bawang putih*) by Malaysians, garlic, like shallots or onions, is an indispensable flavoring in Malaysian cooking. Each garlic bulb contains plump and succulent egg-shaped bulblets called cloves. Malaysians crush, slice, pound, chop, or roast the firm clove to give flavor. The flavor of freshly cut garlic ranges from mild and sweet to strongly pungent, depending on the variety.

Whole garlic is odorless when intact but when cut or bruised, releases an enzyme reaction that gives a strong pungent aroma. The sharp bite and pungency generally subsides after cooking or roasting. Cooking softens the flavor, while roasting gives garlic a delicately sweet and nutty flavor.

In Malaysian recipes, garlic (generally added with ginger or galangal) is sautéed in oil before onions or other spices are added to create a wonderful flavor base for stir-fries, curries, soups, or sauces. Chinese and Nonyas pickle garlic in vinegar to flavor noodle dishes, roast pork, and chicken. Indians and Chinese fry whole or crushed garlic in oil and add this flavored oil to enhance many curries, sauces, and dips. The strict Buddhists and Hindus eliminate garlic from their diets because they believe it to be stimulating.

Garlic is eaten to prevent heart disease, decrease cholesterol and blood pressure, enhance the immune system, prevent cancer, and enhance memory.

Ginger

(Zingiber officinale, Family: Zingiberaceae)
halia (Malay); *sang geung* for fresh and *geung* for dried (Cantonese); *inji* for fresh and *suku* for dried (Tamil)

Fresh and dried gingers are called by different names in Asia, as they possess different properties with regards to flavor and medicinal function. Ginger is indigenous to Southeast Asia and its name is derived from the Sanskrit word *shringavera*, meaning, "shaped like a deer's antlers." Ginger is a rhizome that is available fresh, dried, or as a paste. Fresh ginger is sold as young or immature ginger. The mature or older ginger (which is generally sold in U.S. supermarkets) is knobby and branched and firm, with a tough, shriveled, tan-colored skin. Young fresh ginger has a juicy and crispy texture, is less pungent, and has a more delicate flavor. It has pink sheaths at the base of new shoots and a thin light yellow skin. Fresh ginger has a juicy, spicy, refreshing, and slightly sweet lemon-like aroma, along with a strong bite. It is more aromatic than dried ginger.

Fresh ginger is finely chopped or crushed for flavoring curries, condiments, and marinades, as well as for tenderizing and preserving meats. The local Chinese use fresh, pickled, and preserved gingers to create spicy, sweet flavors for rice porridges (*congee*), soups, and stir-fried meats and vegetables. They use dried ground ginger in five-spice to flavor sauces and soups that require long simmering times. Indians and Malays add chopped ginger or its juice to beverages such as tea and lime juice as well as sweets and confections. In most of my recipes, I slice or chop fresh ginger and then crush or pound it in a mortar and pestle. I find that this method adds a more enhanced flavor to many dishes.

Ginger is one of the oldest and more popular medicinal spices for Asians. It has a warming effect on stomachs, soothes digestion, and is traditionally used to neutralize toxins, decrease acidity, and increase blood circulation in the gastrointestinal tract. It is effective against motion sickness and nausea, discharges phlegm, and cleanses the kidneys and bowels. Ma always used ginger juice in warm water as a common home remedy for colds and an upset stomach. Recent studies have shown ginger to be a strong antioxidant to prevent cancers and gastrointestinal disorders and to decrease cholesterol.

Ginger flower or bud

(Etlingera elatior or Phaeomeria speciies, Gingiberaceae)
Bunga kantan (Malay); *bunga kecombrang* or *honje* (Indonesian); *kaalaa* (Thai); *mioga bud* (Japanese)

Bunga kantan is the unopened bud from the wild ginger plant (torch ginger). The bud is reddish pink and gives a pungent, citrusy, and musky taste to Nonya and Malay-style *laksas*, noodles in spicy fish and tamarind-based broths. It is very popular in northern Malaysia, where Malays add it to their curries, *sambals*, and salads (*kerabus*). It goes well with sour-based curries and soups with tamarind juice or lime juice. Malays in rural areas grow the *kantan* tree in their backyards and add it to their fish curries, including *ikan assam pedas* (hot sour fish curry) and stews.

The bud is about 3 inches long and its petals are chopped or thinly sliced before adding to dishes. It has a strong and prolonged taste; therefore, for fresh salads only a small amount is added. It keeps in the refrigerator for about a week, and in the freezer for a much longer period.

Kaffir lime leaves

(Citrus hystrix, Family: Rutaceae [citrus family])
daun limau perut (Malay); *daun jeruk purut* (Indonesian); *bai makrut* (Thai)

Also called Indonesian lime or wild lime, Kaffir lime is indigenous to Southeast Asia. Its leaves and the rind of the limes are both used in cooking. Kaffir lime fruit is a dark green, knobby, pear-shaped, wrinkled fruit, and unlike the lemon or lime, has virtually no juice. Kaffir lime leaves are oval shaped with a glossy green surface with two lobes or leaves attached together. They are sold fresh, frozen, or dried. They add a wonderful aroma to Malay and Kristang seafood stews, fish curries, baked or grilled fish, and *rendangs*. Kristangs and Nonyas chop them and add them to give a kick to many of their *sambals*. The leaves are finely shredded or chopped and added to northern Malaysia's Malay-style salads (*kerabus*) and rice dishes, including the popular herb rice called *nasi ulam*.

Buy the fresh or frozen Kaffir lime leaves that are deep green and glossy, and not the dried leaf, as it has little flavor. Avoid ones that have blemishes or yellow spots or have ice crystals, as these will have less flavor, having been in and out of the freezer. When a recipe calls for 1 Kaffir lime leaf, use 2 lobes. For storage, seal in plastic containers or bags and store in the freezer, where they will keep for at least six to nine months. Their color will change to a duller green but flavor will stay intact. Thaw for two or three minutes before using them.

Laksa leaf

(Polygonum odoratum, Family: Polygonaceae)

daun laksa or *daun kesum* (Malay); *laksah yip* (Cantonese); *rau rum* (Vietnamese); *pak pai* (Thai)

Laksa leaf is also called Vietnamese mint or Vietnamese coriander and is indigenous to Southeast Asia. Although sometimes called mint, it does not belong to the mint family but to the coriander family. In Malaysia, it is called *daun laksa* (*laksa* leaf) because it is an essential flavoring ingredient in *laksas*, a specialty of the Nonyas. The leaf has a pointed apex with a clean, coriander-like lemony taste. It is also part of the herbs used in *ulam* (herb salad) or *nasi ulam* (herb rice) or *nasi kerabu* that the Malays enjoy in Northeast Malaysia. *Laksa* leaves are sold fresh or dried. When fresh, the leaves are dark green. Malays use it to relieve indigestion.

Lemon basil

(Ocimum basilicum citriodorum, Family: Lamiaceae)

daun kemangi or *selasih* (Malaysian, Indonesian); *bai maenglak* (Thai)

Indigenous to Southeast Asia, lemon basil has a slightly spicy, intense lemony taste with a distinct citrusy aroma. It has pale green leaves and soft fuzzy stems. It is used whole, chopped, or minced in Malay-style herb salads, fish curries, and as toppings for rice and noodle dishes, especially in Northern states bordering Thailand. The fresh leaves last in the refrigerator for a few days, after which they shrivel up. It has a unique taste unlike other basils, but if it is not available, you can substitute other basils, sweet basil, pungent Thai basil (anise basil, also called *bai horapha*) and/or mix with lemon balm or lemon verbena.

Lemongrass

(Cymbopogon citratus, Family: Poaceae)

serai (Malay); *ta khrai* (Thai); *sereh* (Indonesian)

Lemongrass has a long stalk (or stem), about two feet, with pale green blade-like leaves at the top and a bulbous base that is woody and fibrous. The hard, fibrous outer sheaths of the lemongrass stalk are peeled and discarded (a couple of layers), and the delicate inner stalk is used. When used whole, it is bruised or macerated with the back of a knife or a pestle to release its flavor. It is discarded before serving. It is also sliced into small rings and pureed with chilies, onions, garlic, and ginger or galangal for *rendangs*, *sambals*, and curries. Malays and Indian Muslims enjoy its fragrance in their soups, curries, and stews. And when used as a brush to baste the chicken, it infuses a wonderful flavor to the *satay*.

Lemongrass comes fresh, frozen, or ground. It has a delicate citral flavor with a fresh, floral-like (rose) aroma. The ground form has very little aroma or taste. Buy firm, thick stalks with-

HOW TO PREPARE BASICS: LEMONGRASS

Lemongrass stalks are cut about 1 to 2 inches from the root end and about four inches from the top. Before use, cut off the top and bottom part, then peel a couple of sheaths and discard.

Depending on the recipe, you can use whole or sliced lemongrass stalks.

To use it whole, using the base of a knife handle or cleaver, or pestle, smash the stalk its entire length till it is pliant and bruised. Then tie into a knot, without breaking it, and add to the pot or saucepan. (The stalk should be removed before serving the dish.)

In some recipes it is sliced (¼-inch to ½-inch pieces) and blended with other ingredients in a food processor for a smooth paste.

out wrinkling or any sign of drying or rotting. Trim the top and bottom portions, place in plastic bag and store in refrigerator for up to a month. Or freeze it for up to four months.

Limes

(Family: Rutaceae)
limau (Malay)

Limes, whose name is derived from the Arabic word *limun*, are an integral flavoring in Malaysia. Their juices are used as a marinade for chicken, mutton, and fish dishes, squirted over spicy dips (such as *sambal belacan*) and noodle dishes or made into thirst-quenching drinks. Limes are indigenous to Indonesia and Malaysia.

Limau nipis, referred to as 'thin lime' in Malay (*Citrus aurantifolia*), is also called Key lime, Mexican lime, or West Indian lime. It is smaller (about 1 to 2 inches) than the regular large green 'Persian' lime (*Citrus latifolia*) (4 to 5 inches) found in American supermarkets. The peel is thin, smooth, and greenish-yellow when ripe. The flesh has a higher acidity than Persian limes and a distinctive lemony aroma. It is popular as drinks and juices. Malays on the East Coast enjoy a lime juice (called *bandrek*), made with *limau nipis*, spices, and sugar.

The most commonly used limes in Malaysia are the kalamansi (calamansi; also called calamondin or musk lime) called *limau kasturi* (*Citrus microcarpa*) or *jeruk Cina*. It is a small lime with an orange pulp which is less acidic but more fragrant than regular limes (a cross between an orange or tangerine and a lime). Noodle dishes are topped with half a *kasturi* lime that you squirt over the noodles or squeeze for dips. Many Malay, Nonya, and Indian Muslim vendors squeeze *kasturi* lime juice over fried or grilled fish or chicken before serving. Kristangs in Melaka salt and dry them for pickles (calling them *bling-bling*) and use them as a substitute for tamarind juice to flavor their pork or chicken *vindaloo*, meat soups, and *sambals*. In my recipes, you can use juice from *kasturi* limes, Key limes, regular limes, or even bottled lime juice. One regular or Persian lime gives 2 tablespoons freshly squeezed juice, 1 *kasturi* lime gives 1 tablespoon juice, and 1 *limau nipis* or Key lime gives 1½ tablespoons juice. The juice from one Persian lime is equivalent to 2 tablespoons bottled lime juice. Buy fresh looking bright green limes that have no brown blemishes or wrinkled skin. They should last for about 2 weeks when stored in the refrigerator.

Lime leaves. *See* Kaffir lime leaves

Long beans or string beans

(Vigna unguiculata, Family: Fabacea)

Kacang panjang (Malay); *dau gok* (Cantonese)

Long beans, also called string beans by Malaysians, are native to Southeast Asia and they are different from the green beans that are sold in American supermarkets. Also known as yardlong beans, long-pod cowpeas, asparagus beans, snake beans, or Chinese long beans, they are 18 inches long and dark or pale green. We grew up with the thicker, pale-green bean, but the thinner variety is sold in the Asian stores in America. I find the thin types a bit too firm and not as flavorful as the thicker types sold in Malaysia, which are tender and juicy with a slightly sweet taste.

Ma used to cut the beans in small pieces and stir-fry them with spices, chilies, eggs, or shrimp, but I particularly enjoy the Malay-style when they are stir-fried with *belacan*. Nonyas and Chinese stir-fry them with dried shrimp, *taucheo* or black bean paste. Malays also add them to their herb salads called *ulam-ulam*. Another popular preparation by Malays is called *sayur lodeh* or *sayur lemak* (long beans simmered with coconut milk). Melaka Nonyas have a well-known long bean and vegetable dish called *ambilar kacang*, simmered with lemongrass, galangal, and chilies in a claypot.

Buy firm, plump long beans and not soggy, wrinkly beans with brown or yellow blemishes. Use them as soon as possible because they lose their texture if kept too long. They are sold in bunches and have a snake-like appearance. Snip off the tips before use, and cut them into 1-inch to 1½-inch by ¼-inch-thick pieces. They keep in the refrigerator for about a week.

Mint leaf

(Mentha arvensis, Family: Lamiacea)

daun pudina (Malay); *bai saranae* (Thai); *rau thom* (Vietnamese)

Malaysian mint, also called corn mint, wild mint, or field mint, has a refreshing aroma of menthol. It is a different variety from peppermint or spearmint. Mint is used as a topping for spicy Nonya noodle dishes called *laksas*, pureed for curries and sauces, or added to teas. Many homes in Malaysia grow mint in their gardens. Chicken, mutton, or vegetable *kurma* is a festive dish for South Indians and Indian Muslims in Malaysia that uses pureed mint leaves with green chilies, cilantro, and spices simmered in coconut milk.

Malays use fresh mint as a garnish in their herb salad called *ulam* (along with basil, cilantro, and other herbs) for its medicinal effect. It is known to stimulate appetite and alleviate colds. Mint is also an excellent refresher in teas and other beverages.

Mustard Seeds and Ground Mustard

(Brassica nigra, Family: Brassicaceae)
biji sawi (Malay); *kadugu* (Tamil); *gaai joi* (Cantonese)

The silvery black or dark brown (almost purplish) mustard (*Brassica nigra*) includes two varieties: one called Oriental used mostly by Chinese, and the other a darker, stronger mustard used by Indians. There are many cultivars of these different brown types, which are hybrids of the black mustard, also called true mustard.

South Indians in Malaysia sauté whole black or dark brown mustard seeds in a little heated ghee or oil till the seeds "pop" and slightly crack open, then add them to sauces, chutneys, pickles, curries, *sambars*, dhal, and fish curries to create a sweet, nutty, wonderful mix of flavors. Cool the 'popped' mustard seeds a little before adding to any cold dish. But you can also add the heated mixture to dhal just before serving to give an aromatic finish. Indians believe that mustard seeds stimulate the flow of salivary and gastric juices to promote appetite. When buying mustard seeds avoid seeds that are shriveled, because they are aged.

Ground mustard is a popular ingredient in many Eurasian and Kristang recipes, reflecting their Portuguese and other European ancestry. Ground mustard, also referred to as mustard flour or powdered mustard (bran removed), is usually a blend of different mustard seeds, with their proportions varying depending on the region. Ground mustard has no aroma, but when it is "rehydrated" with the addition of water or vinegar, an enzymatic reaction is triggered that releases the spice's pungency.

Nutmeg

(Myristica fragrans, Family: Myristicaceae)
buah pala (Malay); *jatikkai* (Tamil)

Nutmeg is indigenous to the Banda Islands (Moluccas) of eastern Indonesia. It is ground, grated, or crushed for use. It has a clove-like, spicy, sweet, bitter taste, and camphor-like aroma. It is sweeter in flavor than mace (the outer lacy covering of the nutmeg). The Indonesians add it to everything, and those who migrated to Malaysia continue to add it to fragrant spice pastes (*rempahs*) to create delicious meat and mutton curries, and to cakes and cookies. Generally the local cooks grate or grind the nutmeg pieces (using a cheese grater or a nutmeg mill) before adding it to dishes. Sometimes a Malay or Kristang cook adds cracked or crushed pieces of nutmeg to simmering curries and sauces or soups. Eurasians add it to desserts and drinks served during Christmas and Easter. For Kristangs (like their ancestors, the Portuguese), nutmeg is an essential spice in their meat stews, soups, curries, and sweets. Nonyas in Malacca also add it to their soups and stews.

Buy firm light brown seeds and grate as needed, but generally, ground nutmeg is used.

Oils. *See* Cooking oils

Palm Sugar

(Palmyra palm; Borassus flabellifer L, Family: Arecaceae)
gula Melaka (Malay); *gula Jawa* (Javanese sugar); *gula merah* or red sugar (Indonesia)

More than one kind of palm yields sugar in South Asia. Sugar is obtained by tapping the inflorescences of some of the fan palms including the sugar palm (*Arenga pinnata, Arenga saccharifera* or *Gomuti* palm) and the palmyra palm (*Borassus flabellifer*). Thus many times, coconut sugar and other palm sugars or even jaggery and *gur* are mixed and sold off as palm sugar. Good quality palm sugar is from palmyra palm but sugar from the Arenga palm (called *gula Jawa*) is a close substitution. Otherwise jaggery or *piloncillo*, a Mexican sugar, can be substitutes. The palm sugars range from a pale honey-gold to deep, dark brown in color with a variable consistency.

Gula Melaka (*B. flabellifer*) is made by first extracting the sap from the flower bud of the palm. Then the sap is boiled till it thickens, after which, traditionally, it is poured into bamboo tubes about 4 inches in length or coconut shells and left to solidify into cylindrical blocks or disks that are flat on one side and round on the other side. Or it is poured into glass jars or plastic bags.

Gula Melaka is an indispensable ingredient in Malay and Nonya puddings, sweets, and *kuehs*. It is sold as round disks, cylinders, or blocks (about 2 to 3 inches in diameter) wrapped in paper or plastic, or in plastic or glass jars. Though it is a solid, it is moist and has a delicious caramel-like flavor with a subtle smoky taste. If *gula Melaka* is unavailable, substitute with *gula Jawa*, or use dark brown sugar or a mix of maple syrup or molasses and brown sugar. Slice the palm sugar into very thin pieces or finely chop it before adding to a dish. Store in a cool dark place or in refrigerator.

Palm vinegar

Palm vinegar or *cuka*, made from the same palm as the sugars, is used by Nonyas of Malacca to add tartness to their savory dishes. It can take the place of tamarind or lime juice for salads or seafood dishes. It also gives a slight sweetness to dishes. Cooks add it towards the end of cooking or even marinate fish and pork with it. Palm vinegar is sold in bottles and comes milky white. Rice vinegar, cider vinegar, or distilled white vinegar can be good substitutes.

Pandan or Pandanus leaf

(Pandanus amaryllifolius, Family: Pandanaceae)
daun pandan (Malay); *chan heung lahn* (Cantonese); *bai toey hom* (Thai)

Pandan leaf (also called screwpine leaf) is indigenous to Southeast Asia and Sri Lanka. It is a long (about two to three feet) dark green leaf that has a combined flavor of rose, almond, and vanilla. Pandan leaf is sold fresh or frozen or as a bright green extract. The dried leaves have no flavor.

Pandan leaf is commonly used as a flavoring and coloring for Malay and Nonya-style dishes.

The leaf is bruised or raked with the tines of a fork to release its aroma, then tied into a knot and added to simmering soups, stews, curries, or puddings. Cooks also wrap it around chicken, pork, glutinous rice, fish, and desserts before they are grilled, roasted, or steamed. Pandan leaves also enhance the flavor of many seasoned rice dishes and beverages. *Nasi lemak* (coconut-infused rice), *nasi kuning* (yellow rice), and *nasi minyak* (ghee rice) and are some of the fragrant pandan-flavored rice dishes.

It is also pulverized and strained and its juice is added to give color and flavor to Malay and Nonya-style desserts, puddings, and coconut drinks. If you buy frozen leaves, keep them frozen and take out only the amount you need just before use, as it takes only a couple of minutes for them to thaw. Clean or rinse before using. If you buy fresh leaves, wrap them in plastic wrap tightly before freezing.

Pandan extracts, essences, and pastes are commercially available as substitutes to provide flavor and a bright green color to cakes and sweets. They are a concentrated form of pandan juice with added colors and stabilizers and come as a greenish thick liquid. They have a nutty and floral flavor with citrusy overtones. They are sold in tiny bottles at Asian grocery stores and vary in quality depending on their source and/or manufacturer.

Pepper: black and white

(Piper nigrum, Family: Piperaceae)

Black pepper: *lada hitam* (Malay); *wuh jiu* (Cantonese); *karu mulaggu* (Tamil)

White pepper: *lada putih* (Malay); *bhak wuh jui* (Cantonese); *vella mulaggu* (Tamil)

Black pepper was introduced to Malaysia through Arab traders, and today Sarawak is one of the world's major producers of black and white pepper. Sarawak pepper has a milder flavor compared to the aromatic Tellicherry pepper or Malabar pepper from India.

The immature green or greenish yellow berry is fermented for a few days and then dried in kilns. During drying, it shrivels and becomes black. This is black peppercorn. White peppercorns are berries that have been stripped of the outer hull and picked when near ripe, when they are yellowish red or red in color. The berries are then soaked in water or steamed to soften and loosen their skin. The outer hulls or skins are removed by rubbing, leaving a smooth, light-colored berry. They are then bleached, rinsed, and sun dried. White peppercorns can also be prepared from black peppercorns by mechanically removing the outer hulls, a process called decortication. This latter type of white pepper tastes more like black pepper. Sarawak produces one of the more popular varieties of white pepper. Black pepper has a wonderful bouquet—a penetrating pungent and woody aroma when freshly ground. It has slight lemony and clove tones. White pepper has a sharp, winey, and biting taste with less harsh notes. It has little aroma and lacks the bouquet of black pepper.

Malaysians use white and black pepper, coarse or finely ground, in many stir-fry dishes, grilled meats, soups, and curries. Cracked peppercorns are made into a sauce with soy sauce and preserved soybean paste for lamb chops or beef steaks by Chinese and Indian Muslims. In Sarawak where pepper is grown, many recipes are created using white pepper, especially pork and chicken dishes. Malays and Nonyas also add white peppercorns to festive rice dishes like *nasi kuning* or *nasi kemuli*. *Sup kambing*, a mutton soup sold by Malay and Indian Muslim vendors, has crushed peppercorns. I use a mortar and pestle to crush the whole black or white peppercorns to a coarse grind if needed in some of my recipes. You can also use cracked peppercorns as a substitute.

Peppers. *See* Chile peppers

Salam leaf

(Eugenia polyantha, Family: Myrtaceae)
daun salam (Malay, Indonesian)

Salam leaf, also called Indonesian bay leaf, is indigenous to Malaysia, Indonesia, and other parts of Southeast Asia. Called *daun salam* in Indonesian, meaning "peace leaf," it is a popular flavoring in Malay beef and mutton curries and soups. Even though it is closely related to the cassia family and has a similar or close enough flavor, it is not a true bay leaf.

The leaves are small, thin, and dark green when fresh but turn brown and brittle and dusty green on drying. It has a woodsy and spicy taste, with slightly lemony and clove undertones. Salam leaf is commonly used with meat dishes. It is initially sautéed or stir-fried to release its flavor into the dish. It combines well with chilies, galangal, lemongrass, and turmeric.

You can buy them fresh or dried. It is sometimes labeled incorrectly as Indian bay leaf, although you can use Indian bay leaf as a substitute because it is closely related. If you cannot get salam or Indian bay leaf, then substitute with regular bay leaf, laurel leaf, or West Indian bay leaf.

Shallots

(Allium ascalonicum. Family: Alliaceae)
bawang merah (Malay)

Shallots are essential ingredients in a Malaysian kitchen, and for Malaysians, onions are not a good substitute. Shallots are not only prized for their flavor but also for the consistency or body they provide to curries, dips, and sauces. They are chopped or sliced and generally sautéed in oil or ghee till golden brown before spices are added. Shallots develop a sweet flavor during cooking.

I remember Ma spending hours peeling shallots—a labor of love for her. Ma would not take the easy way using onions as a substitute, as I do sometimes (much to her chagrin), because she said they have a harsher taste. As I entered into the kitchen each morning, I would see shallots piled up high and ready to be sliced, chopped, or pounded. Or they would be ground on the stone grinder at the back of the kitchen for preparing fresh cooked *sambals*. These ubiquitous *sambals* of Malaysia contain pureed shallots as an essential ingredient with chilies, garlic, ginger, and tamarind or lime juice. They are pureed and added to *rempah* (spice pastes) and condiments, and tumised with ginger and garlic or cooked in sauces, curries, or *rendangs*.

In Malaysia, shallots are an oval shaped cluster of small to medium-size bulbs with a reddish brown to orange brown skin. Their flesh is pinkish white. Asian shallots are smaller, with

HOW TO PREPARE BASICS: FRIED SHALLOTS OR ONIONS

In Malaysia, fried shallots are a common garnish, added as toppings to enhance the flavor of many dishes including rice and noodle dishes, soups, and meat dishes. Festive Malay and Nonya rice dishes such as nasi goreng *(fried rice),* nasi kuning *(yellow rice),* nasi biryani *(spiced rice), and* nasi minyak *(ghee rice) usually are topped with a sprinkling of fried shallots. It adds a sweet caramelized note to these dishes and complements the chilies and spices. Fried shallots also balance the flavor of many spicy as well as pungent noodle dishes.*

1. Thinly slice (⅛-inch thick) enough shallots or red onions to give you 1 cup.
2. Pour ¼ cup oil into small skillet or saucepan and heat. When oil is hot (but not burning), add shallots or onions and stir constantly using a slotted spoon to get even heating. (The oil will initially froth slightly when shallots are added due to the moisture in shallots but the froth will disappear as the shallots cook.)
3. After about 3 to 4 minutes, depending on the temperature of the oil, the shallots or red onions will become a golden color.
4. Remove the shallots or red onions with the slotted spoon and drain on paper towels. They will appear soggy and limp but after a few minutes will become crispy. Pack in airtight container.

a sweeter and milder flavor than the European ones. Shallots do not give any flavor till they are cut or bruised, which causes an enzymatic action to take place, giving rise to a mixture of sulfides.

Buy shallots that have no sprouting or soft spots, but are firm and bright. Store them in the refrigerator. I sometimes substitute shallots with red onions when I run out of shallots or don't have time, especially when preparing fried or sautéed onions. If you do not prefer the fried shallots or onions you can use the sautéed versions.

Scallions or Spring Onions

(Allium fistulosum, Family: Alliaceae)
daun bawang (Malay); *chung tao* (Cantonese)

Also called salad onions or green onions, scallions have long slender flat green stems with immature bulbs. Scallion is a variety of onion that is harvested before the bulb has formed.

Both the leaves and bulbs are consumed. They have a slightly sweet and mild flavor. They are sliced or chopped and commonly added as garnish for Chinese-style soups, stir-fries, rice and noodle dishes, and many chile-based dips. They are also added to *oh chien* (oyster omelet) and other Chinese-style pancakes.

When buying scallions, look for crisp, firm leaves that have a uniform rich green color and that are not discolored, slimy, or wilted. Also bulbs should be crisp and hard. You can keep scallions in the refrigerator for about a week. Wash them before use to dislodge sand and dirt. Peel the outer layer of the stems to get the tender, crunchy interior.

Shrimp-like crustaceans or Krill

geragau/gerago

In Malaysia, krill or tiny shrimp-like crustaceans (called *udang kering*) are made into a dried paste called *belacan*, or *cinchalok*, or *petis udang.*

Belacan (dried shrimp paste)

trassi (Indonesian); *ngapi* (Burmese); *kapi* (Thai); *mam tom* (Vietnamese); *bagoong alamang* (Filipino)

Belacan is prepared from tiny shrimp or shrimp-like crustaceans called krill (*geragau*) and salt, fermented in earthenware pots. This fermented mush is then ground to a paste and sun dried. The dried paste is then shaped into small rectangular blocks or cylinders and dried again. *Belacan* is widely used in Malaysian cooking to flavor many dishes, dips, and curries. It ranges from a soft to a firm paste and its color varies from a pale pinkish brown to a dark brown. *Belacan* has a strong pungent aroma and fishy taste, but after cooking it creates wonderful background notes and enhances the flavor of dishes. Generally, a ½ to 1 teaspoon of *belacan* is sufficient for most dishes, except *sambals* or dips which require more. Toasted *belacan* is mixed with chile paste, shallots, and lime juice to create a pungent, delicious dip for cooked white rice and noodle dishes.

Belacan comes in small blocks wrapped in plastic and paper. After use, keep the remainder in its wrapping and place it in another air-tight plastic bag to prevent its aroma from seeping into any other items in refrigerator. If *belacan* or *trassi* is unavailable, you can use Thai *kapi* (which comes in small plastic containers), Vietnamese *mam tom,* or Filipino *bagoong alamang.* In Malaysia, *belacan* also comes in a powder form, a more convenient form to handle. Bottled *sambal belacan*, made with *belacan* and pureed chilies, is also available but Malaysians prefer to make their own *sambal belacan.*

Cincalok or cinchaluk

Cincalok or *cinchaluk* is a condiment made with krill (*geragau*), that is fermented with boiled rice and salt. It is enjoyed by the Kristangs and Baba-Nonyas of Malacca as a relish with cooked white rice and coconut-based curries. It is also used as a meat marinade and stir-fried with pork. It is sold in jars and bottles and has a strong aroma and a pungent taste like *belacan.* This pinkish relish is mixed with lime juice, shallots, sugar, and *cili padi* and/or ginger and is served as a dip or a condiment (called *sambal cincalok*) to perk up fried fish and many other dishes.

HOW TO PREPARE BASICS: TOASTED BELACAN

Generally, before being added to sambals, belacan *is toasted or sautéed. Malay cooks place it on bamboo skewers and roast over an open charcoal flame till it is charred. For my recipes, you can follow this method.*

1. Place a piece of *belacan* on a small piece of aluminum foil, wrap and press with hand till flattened.
2. Place the packet directly over a gas flame or burner as my family in Malaysia do; or as I do, place it in a toaster oven at 400°F for about 15 minutes, till you get a whiff of its aroma.
3. Unwrap and add to the dish you are cooking. The toasted *belacan* will dissolve into the paste or sauce with stirring. If it is added to an onion-garlic-ginger mix in a skillet, keep mashing the *belacan* with a wooden spoon as you stir, breaking any granules, and blending well.

Note: Belacan's pungent aroma will penetrate the kitchen and other rooms, so keep the blower fan on, or open the windows.

Hae ko (*petis udang*)
Hae ko (*petis udang*) is a sweet and pungent paste that is thick, gooey, and black. It is made from fermented paste of krill with salt and soybeans. The Chinese and Nonyas add it to many of their noodle dishes. It has an intense flavor, and is essential as a topping with chile sauce and toasted sesame seeds for *chee cheong fan* (steamed noodle rolls), a favorite breakfast dish. It is also mixed with chile sauce as a dressing for *rojak* (a spicy vegetable-based salad sold by vendors). The Nonyas in Penang are also fond of *hae koh* to perk up *assam laksa*, a tamarind and fish-based spicy noodle dish, *popiah* (fresh spring rolls), and many other dishes.

Shrimp, Dried Whole
udang kering (Malay); *ha mai* (Cantonese)

These are sun-dried krill, called *udang kering* by locals. They are about ½-inch to ¾-inch long. They come headless or with heads intact and possess a pungent sweet taste. They are pale pink to orange pink and are sold in plastic bags. They also come in ground form. Wash and soak the whole dried shrimp in hot or warm water for about 10 minutes to soften before use. Recipes call for them to be pounded and added to vegetables or processed with other ingredients to a paste and stir-fried in oil. They can be stored in a sealed plastic bag in the freezer for about a year.

They add a wonderful flavor to Nonya, Kristang, and Chinese vegetable stir-fries, salads, and sauces. Ma sometimes added them to her stir-fried vegetables. I pound them and add with onion, garlic, ginger, and lemongrass flavoring pastes to perk up vegetables, noodles, and fried rice.

Buy the ones that are not bright or intensely colored, as those tend to have excessive preservatives.

Soy or soya sauce

kicap, si yeow

Soy sauce or *soya* sauce is a fermented sauce made from roasted soybeans and/or wheat, water, and salt. It was bought to Malaysia by Chinese immigrants. Soy sauce is an important condiment in Chinese, Nonya, Malay, Kristang, and Indian Muslim dishes. Even Indian-style dishes in Malaysia, especially meat, chicken, and seafood dishes, are flavored with soy sauce. Kristang *semur daging* (beef stew with Worcestershire sauce), Indian Muslim *daging kicap* (soy sauce beef), and lamb chops with peppercorn and soy sauce are some popular dishes. Soy sauce is a must for fried rice and many stir-fried vegetable and noodle dishes. There are many types of soy sauce that vary depending on their origins, and these differ greatly in taste, consistency, and aroma.

Depending on the recipes, I substitute sweet or thick soy sauce for the double black soy sauce and adjust the sugar level. If there is no sugar in a recipe, and I substitute thick or sweet soy sauce with double black soy sauce, I also sometimes add about ¼ teaspoon sugar, depending on the recipe. For color I add double black soy sauce but if a recipe requires sweeter flavor, I use thick or sweet soy sauce. Refrigerate soy sauces after use. This should extend their shelf life for a year or longer.

Soy sauce (called regular soy sauce in this book) is the regular, salty, thin, light brown soy sauce (sometimes referred to as light soy sauce in Malaysia) made by Kikkoman, Superior, Tamari, or other brands. "Lite" soy sauce is a reduced salt soy sauce and not the same as the light soy sauce. *Kecap asin* (salty soy sauce) from Indonesia and *kicap cair* from Malaysia are similar to regular soy sauce.

Double black soy sauce is a darker (blackish brown) and slightly thicker soy sauce. It is aged longer and contains added molasses. Its flavor develops during cooking. It has a richer, slightly sweeter, and less salty flavor than regular soy sauce. Malaysians use it to add a light brown color and caramelizing flavor, especially to Chinese and Nonya-style noodles and meat dishes.

Dark or black soy sauce is a lighter grade than double black soy sauce.

Thick soy sauce (*kicap pekat*) is dark soy sauce that has been thickened with starch and sugar and is usually added for color. It has slightly less sugar than sweet soy sauce.

Sweet soy sauce (*kecap manis*) is a thick and sweet soy sauce made with palm sugar. It is similar to molasses.

Kicap inggris (English sauce) is Worcestershire sauce.

Do not use soy sauces with MSG or non-brewed soy sauces prepared with hydrolyzed plant protein (HPP) or hydrolyzed vegetable protein (HVP) and caramel coloring, which are flavor enhancers containing MSG.

Soybean paste, preserved (fermented)

tauco, taucheo or *taucheong*

Taucheo is a miso-like sweet soybean paste or chunky sauce made from fermented soybeans, glutinous rice flour, sugar, and salt. It comes as a thick smooth light brown or dark brown paste with chunks of soybeans or semi-ground soybeans. It adds an earthy sweetness to sauces, soups, and stir-fries. There are two types in Southeast Asia, one has palm sugar and is sweeter and lighter brown in color. The other is black or dark reddish brown with a strong pungent and saltier flavor. It comes in many forms—as a sauce with particles of soybeans, as whole salted black beans, or as pieces or halves of black soybean immersed in a paste or sauce.

The different *taucheos* vary in flavor and salt content, so sometimes you may need to adjust the salt level in a recipe depending on which type you use. You can also use the Chinese fermented soybean paste labeled as brown bean sauce, yellow soybeans, soybean paste, whole soybean sauce, salted soybeans, or bean sauce, adjusting salt and sugar levels as necessary in recipes.

For Chinese and Nonyas, *taucheo* is a must in many dishes, as it gives them a zesty pungent uplift. Pork *pong teh* (pork simmered in a sweet savory cinnamon *taucheo* sauce) and *ayam Sioh* (chicken cooked in a coriander, *taucheo*, and tamarind-based sauce) are Nonya specialties. Chinese *kedai kopi* (coffee shops) and pubs serve delicious lamb chops or beef steaks in a *taucheo*-based black peppercorn sauce. Many fish dishes are prepared with *taucheo*, including *kicap ikan*, a soy sauce, turmeric, and *taucheo*-based fish, prepared by Indian Muslim vendors. *Ikan chuan-chuan* is a Kristang and Nonya dish prepared with tomatoes and *taucheo*.

Star anise

(Illicium verum, Family: Illiaceae)

bunga lawang (Malay); *Baht gokh* (Cantonese); *lavangai poo* or *anasi poo* (Tamil)

Star anise, indigenous to China, is a dominant ingredient in Chinese five-spice and other braised dishes in Malaysia. *Baht gokh* in Cantonese means eight corners and star anise is called the eight-horned fennel, since the Chinese perceived its taste to be similar to fennel.

Also referred to as Chinese anise, star anise is an irregular star-shaped fruit with eight carpels joined around a central core, each carpel containing a seed. It is used whole or ground. The fruits are picked before they ripen and then are sun dried. The carpels are hard and reddish brown in color. Star anise has a licorice-like, sweet, and pungent flavor, similar to fennel and anise but stronger. It can leave a bitter aftertaste if used at high levels and becomes more intense as it is cooked. Typically, it is discarded before the dish is served.

Star anise is characteristic of Malaysian cooking, and is added to barbecues, roast duck, pork, stews, braised meats, steamed chicken, and soups that require long cooking or simmering. Indians and Nonyas add it to curries, soups, and sauces to give them unique tastes and aromas. My Grandma, who was a Chettiar, added it to her meat and shrimp dishes. It lends wonderful taste sensation to many meat and chicken dishes.

Since it is my favorite spice, I have also added it to my *masala* tea to make the tea truly Malaysian. Star anise is also brewed in teas to cure sore throats and coughs.

Tamarind

(Tamarindus indica, Family: Caesalpiniaceae)

Assam Jawa (Malay); *loh tong jee* (Cantonese); *puli* (Tamil)

Tamarind was brought to Malaysia by Arab traders. With the early influence of Indians in Malaysia, tamarind use has crossed over to Malay and Nonya cooking. Tamarind juice provides sweet-sour notes to many Malaysian dishes. It neutralizes fishy tastes, so is used especially in fish dishes. It is also one of the essential flavorings in Worcestershire sauce, which is added to many Kristang and other Eurasian dishes.

Tamarind has a dark brown, curved, brittle pod or outer shell encasing the edible sticky and fibrous dark brown pulp with black seeds. The pods are dried, peeled, deseeded, and packed into blocks. Tamarind is sold as fresh whole pods, dried pulp slices, concentrate, or paste, or as a solid block. The concentrate has no seeds or fiber. Tamarind juice or extract is the strained liquid obtained when the paste is combined with warm or hot water. The pulp has a sweet, sour, fruity taste with a brown sugar-like aroma.

On the East Coast, Malays serve *singgang ikan*, a tangy spicy fish soup with coconut milk and tamarind juice, to celebrate the end of Ramadan, the fasting month. *Sothi* (a coconut milk and tamarind-based soup) and *rasam* (a spicy tomato tamarind-based soup) are favorites with South Indian and Sri Lankan communities. The Sabahans add tamarind juice to *satay goreng*, a stir-fried version of *satay*.

According to Ayurveda, tamarind heals wounds and joint pains, sore throats, and bronchial disorders.

Tamarind comes in blocks or containers and contains some seeds and pieces of pod. Use this to extract tamarind juice (see next page). The already strained tamarind extract or juice is sold as canned or bottled extracts or concentrates, which are convenient to use and also good substitutes. But make sure you mix the contents well before use to obtain an even flavor. Store paste or block in refrigerator tightly wrapped for up to a year. The bottled concentrates or extracts when opened can keep 3 or 4 weeks in the refrigerator.

HOW TO PREPARE BASICS: TAMARIND JUICE OR EXTRACT

1. Cut out or slice about 1 tablespoon tamarind pulp from a block and let soak in about ¼ cup hot or warm water for about 10 minutes.
2. Squeeze the tamarind pulp by hand or strain to obtain its juice. Discard the seeds and pulpy material. This should give you about 3 to 4 tablespoons tamarind juice.

Turmeric

(Curcuma [C] longa or C. domestica, Family: Zingibearaceae)
kunyit (dried), *kunyit basah* (Malay); *wong yeung* (Cantonese); *manjal* (Tamil)

Called *haridra* in the Vedas, the sacred scriptures of the Hindus, turmeric is a must in South Indian curries (especially vegetarian curries), pickles, soups, lentils, vegetables (especially potatoes and cauliflower), fried fish, or *pullaos* of Malaysia. It is used in Hindu religious ceremonies and is a traditional Ayurvedic medicine for treating digestive complaints, colds, and wounds. Its leaves, called *daun kunyit*, are popular in traditional Malay cooking, chopped for *nasi ulam* (salad rice) and curries, and used for wrapping meats and fish before they are cooked.

Turmeric is a rhizome (underground stem) with a brownish yellow, thin skin with concentric rings and a bright yellowish-orange flesh. It is cured (boiled or steamed) to intensify its aroma and color, then dried and sold whole, or ground into powder. The fresh form looks like ginger except it is thinner and its inner flesh is orange yellow. It has a fragrant musky and earthy aroma with gingery, slightly bitter, and peppery notes. The dried turmeric has lost its ginger notes. It loses its aromatic flavor during storage and when exposed to light.

Turmeric is an essential ingredient in all curry powders and is used in most Indian dishes to give a golden yellow color and to help digest the complex carbohydrates. Malays and Nonyas grate fresh turmeric and add it to their festive rice and meat dishes, while Indians generally use the dried powder form in almost all of their savory curried dishes. Malay and Indian cooks generally add turmeric to fish to remove its fishy and other off flavors. I also add turmeric to the Sarawakan specialty *umai,* to add a bit of color and festivity.

Chinese herbalists and Indian Ayurvedics use turmeric, as it has strong anti-inflammatory properties. It is used to treat many health issues, such as liver problems, high cholesterol, and digestive and skin problems. Today turmeric is hailed as the new natural healer, as an anticancer agent, and for lowering cholesterol and preventing Alzheimers.

Like ginger, peel fresh turmeric before use. It is grated or chopped for use. Buy firm, earthy smelling rhizomes, not moldy, slimy, or wrinkled ones. Place in plastic and store in refrigerator and, like ginger, it will last for about one month. If stored in the freezer, it will keep for up to one year. Take out what you need and thaw for about five to eight minutes till it becomes soft. When buying ground turmeric, look for golden yellow or deep yellow powders. Don't buy dried whole turmeric as it is difficult to cut or grind and has hardly any flavor.

Yam Bean

(Pachyrhizus angulatus, Family: Leguminosae
Bengkuang or *sengkuang* (Malay)

Yam bean is a tuberous root vegetable also called *ubi bengkuang* or *ubi sengkuang* that was introduced to Malaysia by the Portuguese. Also called jicama, sweet turnip, Mexican yam bean, *ahipa*, or Mexican water chestnuts, it is a high-protein, low-fat dietary staple for many locals.

It has a crispy texture, like water chestnuts, when peeled and sliced. The variety grown in Asia has a pale brown skin and its flesh is white, crisp, and slightly sweet. It can be eaten raw, seasoned with chile pepper and lemon juice, added to salads (*rojak*), used as filling for *popiah*, or stir-fried. Jicama, which tastes like a cross between an apple and a water chestnut with a delightful crunchy texture, can be substituted for yam bean.

Buy a moderate-size yam bean with a smooth skin, as this will be fresh. If the tuber is extra large and skin is thick, the texture will most likely be fibrous and starchy instead of sweet, moist, and crunchy. Keep it dry as any moisture will get it moldy. Wrap cut tubers tightly with cling wrap to prevent drying out, and store in refrigerator.

MAINTAINING THE QUALITY OF SPICES

Spices should be stored in cool dry conditions to avoid rancidity and help preserve volatile oils and freshness. Refrigeration also slows microbial growth in ground or whole spices. Depending on storage conditions, discard spices after one or two years. Store in a cool dry dark place, away from heat (oven, stove), light (near window or in transparent packaging), or moisture (steam from cooking or use of a wet spoon in container) as these will hasten the loss of spice aroma and flavor and cause caking.

Store spices in tightly closed or airtight containers to maintain freshness. After each use, close container tightly. Exposure to air accelerates flavor loss. Store spices at cool temperatures (in refrigerator at 32°F to 45°F) to help retain flavor and preserve their aromas. Do not store spices in freezer as repeated removal for use results in condensation in the containers, resulting in loss of flavor and aroma.

For further detail on spices, refer to *Handbook for Spices, Seasonings & Flavorings*, 2000, Susheela Raghavan, CRC Press or www.tasteofmalacca.com.

Note on preparing and cooking spices: Traditionally, Malaysians use a mortar and pestle to grind the dry and wet spices and other ingredients. For my recipes, you can grind the dry spices using a spice or coffee grinder, and process the wet spices using a blender or, as I do, a small food processor and pulse them with water to a smooth or coarse paste as required. Addition of water generally is about ¼ cup, but sometimes may be slightly more. When a recipe requires *tumising* (stirring the spice paste till you get an aromatic flavor), you can add more oil in recipe and increase the stirring time to 15 or 20 minutes the way Malaysians usually do. I decreased the amount of oil in my recipes and thereby the cooking time, and still achieve a delicious flavor.

MEASUREMENT EQUIVALENCY CHART

Liquid measurements

1 teaspoon = ⅙ ounce = 5 milliliters
1 tablespoon = ½ ounce = 15 milliliters
2 tablespoons = ⅛ cup = 1 fluid ounce = 29.56 milliliters
4 tablespoons = ¼ cup = 2 fluid ounces = 59.1 milliliters
8 tablespoons = ½ cup = 4 fluid ounces = 120 milliliters
1 cup = 8 fluid ounces = ½ pint = 236 milliliters
2 cups = 16 fluid ounces = 1 pint = 473 milliliters
4 cups = 32 fluid ounces = 2 pints = 1 quart = .95 liter
4 quarts = 128 ounces = 1 gallon = 3.8 liters

Dry measurements

3 teaspoons = 1 tablespoon = ½ ounce = 14.3 grams
2 tablespoons = ⅛ cup = 1 ounce = 28.35 grams
4 tablespoons = ¼ cup = 2 ounces = 56.7 grams
5⅓ tablespoons = ⅓ cup = 2.6 ounces = 75.6 grams
8 tablespoons = ½ cup = 4 ounces = 113.4 grams
12 tablespoons = ¾ cup = 6 ounces = .375 pound
32 tablespoons = 2 cups = 16 ounces = 1 pound

Dry Weight

1 gram = .035 ounce
1 ounce = 28.35 grams
4 ounces = ¼ pound = 113 grams
8 ounces = ½ pound = 226 grams
12 ounces = ¾ pound = 340 grams
16 ounces = 1 pound = 454 grams
32 ounces = 2 pounds = 908 grams

RESOURCES

Most ingredients for Malaysian recipes can be found in your local supermarket or in Asian, Indian, Thai, Indonesian, or Vietnamese groceries.

Stores in the New York metropolitan area:

Whole Foods Market
New York City (Union Square, Tribeca, Columbus Circle, Bowery)
Westchester (White Plains, Greenwich)
Jericho (Long Island)
www.wholefoodsmarket.com

Asia Market Corporation
71-½ Mulberry Street
New York, NY 10013
(212) 962-2028

Bangkok Center Grocery
104 Mosco Street
New York, NY 10013
(212) 732-8916
www.thai-grocery.com

Udom's Corp
81a Bayard Street
New York, NY 10013

Kalustyan's
123 Lexington Avenue
New York, NY 10016
(212) 685-3451
www.kalustyans.com

Kamsen Foods LLC (Asian market)
22 Barker Avenue
White Plains, NY 10601
(914) 428-4500
www.kamsenfoods.com

Bengal Grocery
140 East Post Road
White Plains, NY 10601
(914) 686 5720

Top Line Supermarket
81-37 Broadway
Elmhurst NY 11373
(718) 458–5505

Internet Resource:

Susheela Raghavan's spice blends are available at:
www.tasteofmalacca.com

Other Resources:

Malaysia Tourism Promotion Board
120 East 56th Street, Suite 810
New York, NY 10022
(212) 754-1113
www.tourismmalaysiany.com

Malaysia Kitchen for the World
[a campaign of the Malaysian External Trade Commission (MATRADE)]
313 East 43rd Street, 3rd Floor
New York, NY 10017
www.malaysiakitchennyc.com

INDEX

More Cookbooks from Hippocrene Books . . .

FINE FILIPINO FOOD

Karen Hulene Bartell

Created from recipes collected during the author's travels around this archipelago at the crossroads of ancient trade routes, *Fine Filipino Food* is a testament to a rich mix of cultures. The influence of Chinese and Malaysian traders can be tasted, as well as the mark of Spanish and American colonization. Try your hand at delicious staples like *Pancit* (sautéed rice noodles), *Lumpia* (the Filipino version of egg rolls), *Adobo* (a tangy stewing method used for all kinds of meats), and *Leche Flan* (creamy custard with a caramelized top). Then explore deeper with *Pirurutong Paella* (Black Rice Paella), *Kari-Kare* (Oxtail in Peanut Sauce), and *Bistek Sinigang* (Sour Beef Stew). Complete with helpful substitution and cooking method guides, a glossary of Filipino foods and terms, and a list of sources for Filipino ingredients by state.

ISBN: 978-0-7818-1211-5 · $14.95 pb

FLAVORFUL INDIA

Priti Chitnis Gress

Located in northwestern India, Gujarat is known as the country's "Garden State," and is renowned for its vegetarian specialties. *Flavorful India* showcases the cuisine of Gujarat—from street foods like crunchy snack mix and vegetable fritters, to traditional home-cooked dishes that feature an abundance of locally available vegetables like okra, eggplant, bottle gourd, and many varieties of beans. Spicy dals, delicate flatbreads, and traditional sweets and beverages bring the Gujarati dining experience full circle. A chapter on the meat, poultry, and fish specialties that are enjoyed in the region is also included. This collection of authentic family recipes will introduce you to some of India's most delicious, yet often overlooked, culinary offerings. An introduction to Gujarati culture, sections on spices, ingredients, and utensils, and charming line drawings by the author's father bring the flavors of India to life.

ISBN: 0-7818-1207-0 · $14.95pb

HEALTHY SOUTH INDIAN COOKING
Expanded Edition

Alamelu Vairavan and Dr. Patricia Marquardt

With the addition of fifty new easy-to-prepare dishes, *Healthy South Indian Cooking* is back, now totaling 250 recipes. In the famous Chettinad cooking tradition of southern India, these mostly vegetarian recipes allow home cooks to create dishes such as Potato-filled Dosas with Coconut Chutney; Pearl Onion and Tomato Sambhar; Chickpea and Bell Pepper Poriyal; and Eggplant Masala Curry. *Rasams*, breads, legumes and *payasams* are all featured here, as is the exceptional Chettinad Chicken Kolambu, South India's version of the popular *vindaloo*. Each of these low-fat, low-calorie recipes come with a complete nutritional analysis. Also included are sample menus and

innovative suggestions for integrating South Indian dishes into traditional Western meals. A section on the varieties and methods of preparation for *dals* (a lentil dish that is a staple of this cuisine), a multilingual glossary of spices and ingredients, and 16 pages of color photographs make this book a clear and concise introduction to the healthy, delicious cooking of South India.
ISBN: 0-7818-1189-9 · $32.00hc

THE KERALA KITCHEN
Lathika George

Since ancient times, seafarers and traders have been drawn by the lure of spices to Kerala, a verdant, tropical state on the Malabar Coast of South India. It is this legacy that *The Kerala Kitchen* brings us, through 150 delectable recipes and the unforgettable stories that accompany them. Featured here are such savory delights as *Meen Vevichathu* (fish curry cooked in a clay pot), *Parippu* (lentils with coconut milk), and *Thiyal* (shallots with tamarind and roasted coconut). Equally mouthwatering are an array of rice preparations and tempting desserts. Authentic and easy to prepare, these recipes are adapted for the western kitchen, and accompanied by a guide to spices, herbs, and equipment, as well as a glossary of food terms. Interwoven between these recipes, in the best tradition of the cookbook memoir, are tales of talking doves, toddy shops, traveling chefs, and killer coconuts. Full of beautiful photographs, charming illustrations, and lyrical memories of food and family.
ISBN: 978-0-7818-1184-2 · $32.00hc

MENUS AND MEMORIES FROM PUNJAB
Meals to Nourish Body and Soul
Veronica "Rani" Sidhu

"Sidhu has dipped into—and helped preserve—a rich culinary tradition that extends back hundreds of years."

—Andrew F. Smith, food historian and editor-in-chief of *The Oxford Encyclopedia of Food and Drink in America*

Arranged in a unique format of 22 full menus, this cookbook takes readers on a nostalgic culinary journey through Punjab. Featured are 146 recipes from signature village fare like Buttermilk Stew with Vegetable Pakoras to a stunning Roast Leg of Lamb that has graced the tables of Maharajahs. A colorful historical vignette or family anecdote introduces each menu, bringing the culture and cuisine of Punjab alive for readers. Also included are 16 pages of beautiful color photographs, glossaries of food and religious terms, and a resource guide for finding Indian ingredients.
ISBN: 978-0-7818-1220-7 · $29.95hc

TASTE OF NEPAL

Jyoti Pandey Pathak

Winner of "Best Foreign Cuisine Book" at the 2008 Gourmand World Cookbook Awards, *Taste of Nepal* is a thorough and comprehensive guide to this cuisine. One of very few Nepali cookbooks available, this book features more than 350 authentic recipes, plus sections on Nepali herbs and spices, menu planning, Nepalese kitchen equipment, and delightful illustrations. There is something for everyone in this book—for the most timid cook Fried Rice (*Baasi-Bhaat Bhutuwa*) or Stir-Fried Chicken (*Kukhura Taareko*) are easily achievable, but the adventurous will be tempted to try Goat Curry (*Khasi-Boka ko Maasu*) and Sun-Dried Fish with Tomato Chutney (*Golbheda ra Sidra Maacha*).

ISBN: 0-7818-1121-X · $27.50 hc

CUISINES OF PORTUGUESE ENCOUNTERS
Expanded Edition

Cherie Hamilton

"What a joy to have access to the marvelous foods generated by Portugal's fifteenth and sixteenth century explosion into the worlds of Asia, Africa, the Americas, and the Southern oceans . . . a great story!"

—Nahum Waxman, owner of Kitchen Arts and Letters, NYC

Now expanded to over 300 authentic recipes, this cookbook encompass the entire Portuguese-speaking world. Menus for religious holidays and festive occasions, a glossary, a section on mail-order sources, a brief history of the cuisines, a section of color photographs, and a bilingual index assist the home chef in creating meals that celebrate the rich, diverse, and delicious culinary legacy of this old empire.

ISBN: 978-0-7818-1181-1 • $29.95hc